Marriages of

ROWAN COUNTY, NORTH CAROLINA

1753–1868

State of North Carolina, }

Rowan County.

KNOW ALL MEN BY THESE PRESENTS, THAT WE, George

W. Cox & Othe Gaskle

Of the State aforesaid, are held and firmly bound unto the State of North Carolina, in the just and full sum of Five Hundred Pounds, current money of said State; to the which payment, well and truly to be made and done, we bind Ourselves, our Heirs, Executors, and Administrators. Sealed with our seals, and dated this the 11th day of _June_ Anno Domini 18 57

THE CONDITION OF THE ABOVE OBLIGATION IS SUCH, THAT

WHEREAS, the above bounden Geo. W Cox hath made application for **a License for a Marriage,** to be celebrated between him and _Caroline Swink_ of the County aforesaid: Now, in case it shall appear hereafter that there is no lawful cause to obstruct the said Marriage, then the above Obligation to be void—Otherwise to remain in full force and virtue.

Signed, Sealed, and Delivered, }
In the Presence of,

George W Cox [SEAL.]

The Gaskle [SEAL.]

J. S. Myers

Copy of a marriage bond between George W. Cox and Caroline Swink

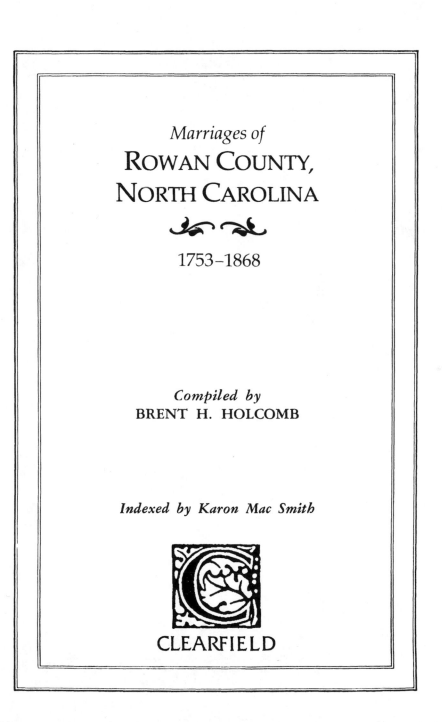

Marriages of
ROWAN COUNTY, NORTH CAROLINA

1753–1868

Compiled by
BRENT H. HOLCOMB

Indexed by Karon Mac Smith

CLEARFIELD

Reprinted for
Clearfield Company, Inc. by
Genealogical Publishing Co., Inc.
Baltimore, Maryland
1996, 1998

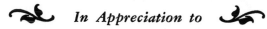 *In Appreciation to*

MURIEL SMITH TURNER

INTRODUCTION

ROWAN COUNTY is one of the most important counties for North Carolina research. At its formation in 1753 (from Anson County) it extended north to the Virginia border and had an indeterminate western boundary. Rowan County was part of the great migration route to the South and West. The various origins of the settlers (German, Scotch-Irish, and English) add to the interest of this county, and to these records in particular.

This volume contains abstracts of all extant marriage bonds for Rowan County. The original bonds are in the North Carolina Archives in Raleigh, and these abstracts were made from microfilm copies of the bonds. Marriage bonds are the only public records of marriage prior to 1851. The marriage bond law was enacted in 1741 and remained in force until 1868. In 1851 the clerk of the county court was required to keep a register of marriages performed by license (issued with the bond). The bonds alone are not proof that a marriage took place, only that a marriage was intended. Marriages could also be performed after publication of banns, and therefore no bond, license, or other public record of the marriage was kept.

As a matter of interest the reader should note that some marriage references may be found in the several volumes of abstracts of wills, deeds, and court minutes of Rowan County compiled by Mrs. Stahle Linn, Jr., of Salisbury, North Carolina. Supplemental information on some of the marriage bonds in this volume may be found in *Marriage and Death Notices from the Carolina Watchman (1832-1890),* published by A Press, Inc., Greenville, South Carolina.

BRENT H. HOLCOMB, C. A. L. S.
Columbia, South Carolina

ROWAN MARRIAGES 1753-1868

Abbot, Benjamin & Mary Hudgens, daughter of William Hudgens, 16 March 1781.

Abbot, Sterling & Nancy Merril, 7 Sept 1816; William Merrel, bondsman; Henry Giles, wit.

Abbot, William, planter & Lydia Grist, spinster, 28 Feb 1780; Benjamin Grist, bondsman; B. Booth Boote, wit.

Abbot, Joseph & Lucy Myres, 13 Feb 1813; Abraham Jacobs, bondsman; Jno. Giles, C. C., wit.

Abbott, William & Hannah Myres, 23 Dec 1812; Abraham Jacobs, bondsman; Jno. Giles, C. C., wit.

Abernethy, J. M. & M. V. Luckey, 16 Dec 1862; F. M. Y. McNeely, bondsman; Obediah Woodson, wit.

Aberton, Abraham & Winny Daniel, 1 Jan 1812; John Roe, bondsman; J. Willson, J. P., wit.

Adair, Elisha & Elizabeth Rees, 21 Jan 1795; Thomas Farmer Reese, bondsman; John Pinchback, Peter Glasscock, wit.

Adams, Abner & Jane McNeely, 3 March 1834; James McNeely, bondsman; Wm. Locke, wit.

Adams, Abraham Jr. & --- Howard, 25 Aug 1791; John Ball, bondsman; Basil Gaither, wit.

Adams, Daniel & Sarah Irvin, 7 Nov 1780; Walter Adams, bondsman; H. Giffard, wit.

Adams, Elim L. & Jane C. McNeely, 29 Aug 1825; John N. Adams, bondsman; Jno. Giles, wit.

Adams, Ephrame & Eleanor Brian, 25 Sept 1789; Daniel Adams, bondsman.

1

Adams, Henry & Betsy Bateman, 8 Feb 1815; James Walling, bondsman; Geo. Dunn, wit.

Adams, Isaac & Hannah Fillips, 25 June 1791; Edmond Adams, bondsman; Basil Gaither, wit.

Adams, Isaac & Margret Winford, 22 May 1792; Daniel Adams, bondsman; G: Enochs, wit.

Adams, J. E. & E. W. Hall, 19 March 1849; J. R. B. Adams, bondsman.

Adams, Jacob & Mary Touson, 7 Jan 1777; Spencer Adams, bondsman.

Adams, Jese & Mary Noland, 6 Aug 1804; William Whitaker, bondsman.

Adams, John & Esther Hawkins, 3 Oct 1795; Isaac Jones, bondsman.

Adams, John & Winne Bussell, daughter of Farssed and Elizebeth Bussell, 15 Aug 1768; Edward Turner, bondsman; Thomas Frohock, wit.

Adams, John & Betsy Reed, 30 Jan 1797; Wm. Adams, bondsman.

Adams, John N. & Martha A. Andrews, 6 May 1829; John Andrews, bondsman; J. H. Hardie, wit.

Adams, Joseph & Jensy Tussey, 22 May 1811; James Walling, bondsman; Geo. Dunn, wit.

Adams, Mathew & Anne Howsley, 20 Feb 1780; Robert Howsley, bondsman; B. Booth Boote, wit.

Adams, Peter & Ann Smith, 29 Dec 1794; Leonard Kreiter (Grider), bondsman; Mat. Troy, wit.

Adams, Peter & Sally Walton, 17 Oct 1816; Ezra Allemong, bondsman.

Adams, Robert & Elisabeth Fleming, 19 Feb 1773; Alexr Endsley, bondsman; Max. Chambers, wit.

Adams, Silvester & Hannah Stinson, 8 July 1790; Ephram Adams, bondsman; Basil Gaither, wit.

Adams, Silvester & Sally Maxwell, 26 Oct 1826; John Adams, bondsman; C. Harbin, J. P., wit.

Adams, Thomas & Mary Lynn, 22 Feb 1787; William Scudder, bondsman; Edm. Gamble, C., wit.

Adams, Thomas & Polley Michel, 19 April 1803; William Harwood, bondsman; Jn. March, J. P., wit.

Adams, William & Elizabeth Edmond, 25 Jan 1766; David Black, Joseph Erwin, bondsmen; Thomas Frohock, wit.

Adams, William & Mary Baker, 6 Dec 1775; Charles Baker, bondsman; Max. Chambers, wit.

Adams, William & Elenor Simpson, 18 March 1795; Ross Simson, bondsman; J. Troyd, D. C., wit.

Adams, William & Elizabeth Hall, 2 Sept 1819; John Tomlinson, bondsman; R. Powell, wit.

Adderton, James & Martha Parker, 15 Aug 1820' Barham Parker,
bondsman; Jno. Giles, wit.

Ader, Peter & Betsy Rickett, 28 April 1816; Samuel Bird, bondsman;
I. Willson, J. P., wit.

Aderton, William & Charity Daniel, 9 Feb 1804; Jas. Daniel,
bondsman; A. L. Osborn, D. C., wit.

Adkins, Atkinson & Anne Johnston, 2 April 1787; Obadiah Smith,
bondsman; Jno. Macay, wit. (not on microfilm)

Adkinson, James & Polly Hartley, 13 Dec 1809; Peter Winkler,
bondsman; Jno. Giles, C. C., wit.

Admire, George Jr. & Ruth Jones, --- 1781; James Jones, bondsman.

Aery, Milas & Sophia Harman, 19 Aug 1843; Saml. Rothrock,
bondsman; John H. Hardie, wit.

Aery, Milas & Anne Smith, 7 June 1847; J. B. Anthony, bondsman;
J. H. Hardie, wit.

Aesan, Christian & Margaret Smith, 4 Sept 1775; Daniel Smith,
John Lowrance, bondsmen; Dd. Flowers, wit.

Agener, Daniel & Rosina Basinger, 12 July 1802; Jacob Ribelen,
bondsman; Jno. Brem, D. C., wit.

Agenger, Henry & Maria Mottellina Kercher, 15 June 1774; Phillip
Vervill, bondsman; Ad. Osborn, wit.

Agenor, Benjamin & Caty Bullon, 17 Dec 1811; John Trexler, bondsman; Geo. Dunn, wit.

Agenor, Peter & Catherine Rough, 21 Oct 1809; John Smather,
bondsman.

Agenor, Samuel & Polly Grubb, 15 April 1816; Saml Lemly, bondsman;
Geo. Dunn, wit.

Agle, George & Susanah Huldemar, 18 Oct 1802; John Agle, bondsman;
A. L. Osborn, D. C., wit.

Agle (Eagle), Peter & Polly Blackwell, 16 Feb 1824; Christian
Rinehart, bondsman.

Agner, Alexander & Luretta Caubble, 4 Jan 1842; D. Woodson,
bondsman; Jno. H. Hardie, wit.

Agner, Henry & Caty Wise, 27 April 1824; John Wise, bondsman;
Hy. Giles, wit.

Agner, Henry & Sarah Arey, 27 Dec 1843; Henry Moyer, bondsman;
John H. Hardie, wit.

Agner, Henry Junr. & Elizabeth Erry, 30 Sept 1775; Anthony Sott,
bondsman; Dd. Flowers, wit.

Agner, Isaac & Christena Mull, 18 July 1827; Lowrence Bringle,
bondsman; J. Hardie, wit.

Agner, Jacob & Betsey Waller, 28 Jan 1818; George Waller, bondsman; Jno. Giles, wit.

Agner, John F. & Crissy Cauble, 10 Dec 1857; D. A. Goodman, bondsman; James E. Kerr, wit.

Agner, Lewis & Laura M. Holshouser, 24 Sept 1849; Alexander Agner, bondsman; J. S. Myers, wit.

Agner, Lewis & Aley C. Julian, 21 Aug 1860; William H. Trexler, bondsman; John Wilkinson, wit.

Agner, Lewis or Ketchey, Lewis, & Aley C. Julian, 21 Aug 1860; J. Wilkinson, D., wit. married 22 Aug 1860 by Levi Trexler, J. P.

Agner, Milas A. & Lucy Ann Winders, 2 May 1844; John G. Elliott, bondsman; Obediah Woodson, wit.

Agner, Milas A. & Martha Jane Owen, 9 March 1859; Benjamin Wise, bondsman; John Wilkinson, wit. married 9 March 1859 by W. R. Fraley, J. P.

Agner, Moses & Margaret Kincaid, 9 July 1859; Nathan Harrison, bondsman; John Wilkinson, wit. married 10 July 1859 by Peter Williamson, J. P.

Airy, Daniel & Rebecca Pittman, 29 Aug 1816; Adam Kauble, bondsman; Jno. Giles, C. C. wit.

Airy, Jeremiah & Christena Eller, 25 March 1819; Abraham Airy, bondsman; Jno Giles, wit.

Akel, Michael & Polly Flemmon, 12 Dec 1813; George Lowry, bondsman; John Hanes, wit.

Albea, B. C. & Elizabeth McCubbin, 21 July 1864; J. W. Albea, bondsman; Obediah Woodson, wit.

Albea, Zachariah & Elizabeth Roberts, 2 Jan 1823; John Cooper, bondsman; Hy. Giles, wit.

Alberson, Jesse & Ann Baily, 22 Aug 1810; Joseph Alberson, bondsman; Jno. Giles, C. C., wit.

Albertson, Joseph & Alie Ruddack, 7 July 1805; James Cannaday, bondsman; William Piggott, J. P., wit.

Albertson, William & Margaret Elliott, 16 Jan 1820; Shaderack M. Goranden, bondsman; Z. Hunt, wit.

Albenny, Benjamin & Sarah Gracey, 4 Jan 1782; John Greacey, bondsman.

Albright, George & Sarah Cress, 4 Aug 1856; Michael Albright, bondsman; J. S. Myers, wit.

Albright, Henry & Christena Kesler, 24 April 1820; John Albright, bondsman; Hy. Giles, wit.

Albright, James A. & --------, (no date); Ira E. Overcash, bondsman.

Albright, Jesse H. & Lydia H. Shuping, 5 Sept 1853; Benjamin Sachler, bondsman; J. S. Myers, wit. married 8 Sept 1853 by C. L. Partee, J. P.

4

Albright, John & Peggy Lamb,26 April 1811; Peter Albright, bondsman.

Albright, John & Mary Sachler, 21 Aug 1821; Petter Albright, bondsman.

Albright, John J. & Hetty S. Sloop, 2 Sept 1851; Noah A. Freeze, bondsman; J. S. Myers, wit.

Albright, Michael & Leah Lipe, 30 Nov 1847; Petter Albright, bondsman; J. H. Hardie, wit.

Albright, Michael & Betsey Leatho,18 Aug 1828; John Carrigan, bondsman; Jno. H. Hardie, wit.

Albright, Peter & Nancy Dillon, 5 Feb 1785; Michael Albright, bondsman.

Albright, Peter & Mary Correll, 9 March 1812; Phillip Correll, bondsman; Geo. Dun, wit.

Albright, Peter & Betsey Fink, 12 Dec 1817; John Albright, bondsman; Milo A. Giles, wit.

Albright, Peter & Catharine A. Cress, 12 Nov 1855; Thomas Cress, bondsman; J. S. Myers, wit. married 15 Nov 1855 by S. C. Alexander.

Albright, Peter & Catharine C. Bostian, 27 April 1857; Jesse Sechler, bondsman; J. S. Myers, wit. married 30 April 1857 by Mr. S. McKenzie, J. P.

Albright, Peter & Catherine S. Overcash, 15 Dec 1860; J. A. McConnaughey, bondsman; John Wilkinson,wit.

Albright, Peter Jr. & Catherine Albright, 17 Jan 1810; Peter Albright Sr., bondsman; Geo. Dunn, wit.

Albright, Simon & Margaret Keaver, 5 March 1822; Peter Albright, bondsman.

Aldredge, Nicholas & Sarah Knock, 9 Aug 1793; Fredrick Allemong, bondsman; Jas. Chambers, wit.

Aldrich, L. S. & Mary E. Chunn, 17 Nov 1858; A. Myers, bondsman; John Wilkinson, wit. married 17 Nov 1858 by J. G. Haughton.

Aldrige, Jon. & ----, 26 Feb 1793; Charles Wood, bondsman; Jos. Chambers, wit.

Alesesser, Fredrick & Betsey Garver, 1 Jan 1822; Leonard Garver, bondsman; Jno. Giles, wit.

Alexander, Allen & Adelaid Graham, 2 May 1836; Thos. A. Hague, bondsman; Hy. Giles, wit.

Alexander, David & Margret Davison, 1 April 1762; Henry Levely, bondsman; John Johnston, bondsman; Wills. Morrison, Will Reed, wit.

Alexander, Gabriel & Jane Black, 19 Jan 1770; David Black, Max: Chambers, bondsmen; Thomas Frohock, wit.

Alexander, James & Margaret Ireland, 7 May 1773; James Ireland, bondsman; Ad. Osborn, wit.

Alexander, John & Jane Luckey, 2 Feb 1786; George Lukey, bondsman.

Alexander, John & Susanna Alexander, 7 Nov 1778; Samel Hogsed, bondsman; Ad. Osborn, wit.

Alexander, Julius & Emma Hall (colored), 27 July 1865; Obadiah Woodson, Clrk; married 27 July 1865 by Geo. B. Wetmore, minister.

Alexander, Marcus & Catherin Rumph, 23 June 1848; Jno. G. Shaver, bondsman.

Alexander, Peter & Elizabeth Bradshaw, 9 Nov 1841; E. W. Elliott, bondsman.

Alexander, William & Mary Brandon, 21 Jan 1769; John Dunn, bondsman; Tho. Frohock,

Aley, Isaac & Sally Setlef, 4 May 1815; Samuel Nedding, bondsman; Jno. Giles, C. C., wit.

Alford, John & Polley Markland, 28 Sept 1811; John Markland, bondsman; W. Ellis, wit.

Algood, Arthur & Margaret L. Coon, 2 Aug 1859; A. A. Cowan, bondsman; John Wilkinson, wit. married 3 Aug 1859 by W. R. Fraley, J. P.

Alldridge, William & Hannah Bell, 18 Dec 1772; John Littel, bondsman; Ad. Osborn, wit.

Allemong, Daniel & Elizabeth Bartlett, 7 Feb 1788; Nicholas Bringle, bondsman; J. McEwin, wit.

Allemong, Henry & Nancy Todd, 25 April 1811; George Betz, bondsman; Jno. Giles, C. C., wit.

Allen, Abraham & Mary Allender Nailer, 13 Dec 1811; Jacob Allen, bondsman; Jn. March Sr., wit.

Allen, Alexander S. & Christena Sossaman, 31 Jan 1852; John H. Allen, bondsman; J. S. Myers, wit.

Allen, Edmond & Nancy Saunders, 30 Jan 1833; Daniel Etcheson, bondsman.

Allen, Gamaliel L. & Nancy M. Beyan, 22 Dec 1836; M. G. Richards, bondsman; C. Harbin, wit.

Allen, Hugh & Martha Swan, 10 Nov 1792; Ed. Trotter, bondsman; Jos. Chambers, wit.

Allen, Isaac & Sally Hawkins, 31 Aug 1813; Ebenezer Frost, bondsman; R. Powell, wit.

Allen, Jacob & Barbary Balance, 31 Oct 1818; Robart McClamroch, bondsman; R. Powell, wit.

Allen, Jacob & Caroline Hill, 13 Feb 1853; William Kester, bondsman.

Allen, Stephen & Sally Deever, 26 Dec 1819; Samuel Smith, bondsman; R. Powell, wit.

Allen, Thomas & Marjera Brion, 26 May 1789; William Huey, bondsman; Will Alexander, wit.

Allen, William & Milly Brent, 22 Oct 1823; William Allen, William Acheson, Jr., bondsmen; La. R. Rose, J. P., wit.

Allgood, James & Letty Etchison, 18 Aug 1821; Elijah Etchison, bondsman; Geo. Coker, wit.

Allimong, Frederick & Hughley Sheroate, 19 Dec 1786; Daniel Allemong, bondsman; Jno. Macay, wit.

Allin, Jeremiah & Susanah Spoon, 2 Oct 1794; Evan Davis, bondsman; John Eccles, wit.

Allison, Adam & Mary Barr (daughter of Ceathrin Barr), 6 Jan 1770; Andrew Allison, bondsman; Thomas Frohock, wit.

Allison, Andrew & Jane Knox, 4 Feb 1820; Richard Gillispie, bondsman; Jno. Giles, wit.

Allison, James & Mollie Kilpatrick, 24 April 1865; R. W. Johnston, bondsman; Obediah Woodson, wit.

Allison, John & Margaret Allison, 8 Feb 1779; Theophilus Allison, bondsman; William R. Davies, wit.

Allison, John & Mary Kerr, 11 Nov 1842; Pleasant Henderson, bondsman.

Allison, Richard & Lettice Neill, 26 July 1785; William Neill, bondsman; E. Magoune, wit.

Allison, Theophilus & Elizabeth Hiel, 10 Jan 1786; Andrew Snoddey, bondsman; Wm. W. Erwin, wit.

Allison, Theo. A. & S. E. Luckey, 14 Dec 1857; J. D. Cowan, bondsman; J. S. Myers, wit. married 15 Dec 1857 by Saml. B. O. Wilson, V. D. M.

Allison, Theophilus J. & Mary Evelina Graham, 27 March 1823; Julius J. Reaves, bondsman; E. Allamong, wit.

Allison, Thomas & Martha Gillispy, 20 Jan 1770; Benja Milner, Thomas Frohock, bondsmen; John Frohock, wit.

Allison, William M. & Elizabeth B. Johnson, 7 Feb 1843; James Clarke, bondsman; Jno. H. Hardie Jr., wit.

Allman, Calvin & Martha Linker, 27 Sept 1864; Nelson Allman, bondsman; Obadiah Woodson, wit.

Allman, Nathan & Mary Lucinda Rogers, 12 Feb 1864; John H. Overcash, bondsman; Obadiah Woodson, wit.

Allman, William & Mary Mann, 4 May 1855; Isaac Burleyson, bondsman; married by D. W. Honeycutte, J. P., 6 May 1855.

Allman, William & Polly Haskey, 1 Aug 1848; Charles Rough, bondsman; J. H. Hardie, wit.

Allridge, William & Hannah Bell, 18 Dec 1772; John Littel, bondsman; Ad. Osborn, wit. (not on microfilm)

Alman, Charles & Barbara Michaley, 30 April 1844; George Hartman, bondsman; Obadiah Woodson, wit.

Almon, Archibald & Jane Loutwick, 28 June 1856; Henry R. Starnes, bondsman; H. W. Hill, Esq., wit. married 29 June 1856 by H. W. Hill, J. P.

Alsobrook, Alexander P. & Malinda C. Craige, 29 Oct 1843; Jno. J. Shaver, bondsman.

Amerson, Richard & ----, --- 180-; George Amers, bondsman.

Anderson, Charles & Eleander Smoot, 5 Dec 1808; James Smott, bondsman; Jno. March Sr., wit.

Anderson, Garland & Salley Frost, 15 July 1813; R. Powell, bondsman; R. Powell, wit.

Anderson, Isaac & Elizabeth Hunter, 14 March 1801; John Howard, bondsman; Jno. Brem, D. C., wit.

Anderson, James & Margaret E. Swink, 8 May 1855; C. S. Brown bondsman; J. S. Myers, wit. married 8 May 1855 by Obaaiah Woodson, J. P.

Anderson, James & Mary Graham, 27 May 1795; Andrew Irwine, bondsman; J. Troy, D. C., wit.

Anderson, James & Nelly Miller, 3 Oct 1801; William Woods, bondsman; Jno Brem, wit.

Anderson, John & Emely Cowan, 28 Dec 1836; Tobias Lemly, bondsman; Jno. Giles, wit.

Anderson, John & Nancy Allemong, 16 Jan 1830; Jno. H. Hardie, bondsman.

Anderson, Michael & Jensy Hartley, 29 Oct 1814; Henry Allemong, bondsman; Geo. Dunn, wit.

Anderson, Nelson & Margaret Smoot, 24 May 1806; Fredrick Thompson, bondsman; John March Sr., wit.

Anderson, Samuel & Anna Knox, 24 Jan 1800; Robert Johnston, bondsman; Edwin J. Osborn, wit.

Anderson, Spotwood, & Patience Piearce, 1 May 1824; Thos. Neal, bondsman; La. R. Rose, wit.

Anderson, Thomas & Martha Dickey, 8 Oct 1792; Michael Troy, bondsman; Jo: Chambers, wit.

Anderson, Timothy & Bettey Sloan, daughter of Henry Sloan, 20 March 1770; William Moore, bondsman; Thomas Frohock, wit.

Anderson, William & Elizabeth Homes, 6 Aug 1779; Francis Homes, bondsman; Jo. Brevard, wit.

Anderson, William & Peggy Moore, 24 Dec 1822; Alfred Moore, bondsman; Jno. Giles, wit.

Andrews, George & Catharine Barr, 8 Dec 1798; John Barr, bondsman; Edwin J. Osborn, D. C., wit.

Andrews, James & Martha Niblock, 14 May 1762; Richard King, Henry Horah, bondsmen; Will Reed, Robeart Johnston, wit.

Andrews, James & Mary Scott, 22 Feb 1782; Robert Scott, bondsman; Ad. Osborn, wit.

Andrews, John & Catharine Bell, 23 May 1807; William Bell, bondsman; Ad. Osborne, wit.

Andrews, John & Jean McCuan, 28 Mar 1776; John Andrews, James McKean, bondsmen; Ad. Osborn, wit.

Andrews, John & Margaret Andrews, 4 March 1783; John Andrews, bondsman; Willm Crawford, wit.

Andrews, John & Ruth Delow, 13 Oct 1805; Bat. Williams, bondsman; Jno Monroe, wit.

Andrews, John N. & Sarah H. Graham, 31 Jan 1826; William P. Graham, bondsman.

Andrews, Joseph & Zephiah Barns, 5 May 1786; W. Moore, bondsman; John Macay, wit.

Anthony, Jack & Bethenia Fergerson, 28 Feb 1843; Richd Walton, bondsman.

Aplen, Lewis & Mary Banerfeet, 28 Sept 1813; Peter Younts, bondsman; J. Willson, J. P., wit.

Apling, Lazarus & Susana Hill, 8 May 1820; Reuben Johnson, bondsman; J. Willson, J. P., wit.

Archbald, Thomas & Martha Edmond, 23 March 1765; John Edmond, bondsman; Thomas Frohock, wit.

Archbald, William & Martha McCorkell, 8 Jan 1765; Alexr. McCorkle, Jno. Archbald, bondsmen; John Frohock, wit.

Archibald, Thomas & Sarah F. Luckey, 30 Jan 1816; William Potts, bondsman; Jno Giles, C. C., wit.

Area, John & Mary Redwine, 23 March 1820; Peter Arey, bondsman.

Arey, Abraham & Catharine Clingerman, 23 Nov 1811; John Airy, bondsman; Jno Giles, C. C., wit.

Arey, Gabriel & Prissy Parker, 23 Oct 1816; Daniel Arey, bondsman; Milo A. Giles, wit.

Arey, Gabriel W. & Mary Miller, 18 Dec 1851; Levi Trexler, wit.

Arey, Peter & Feby Thomas, _____ 1800; Fr. Marshall, bondsman.

Armsfield, Jonathan & Sarah J. Brown, 3 June 1842; Henry Brown, bondsman; Jno. H. Hardie, wit.

Armstrong, Abel & Margret Cowan, 16 Sept 1768; James Dobbin, Jas. Brandon, bondsmen; Thomas Frohock, wit.

Armstrong, James & Deborah Willkie (daughter of Wm. Wilkie, by his consent), 4 Feb 1786; Wm. Wilkie, bondsman; Chs. Caldwell, wit.

Armstrong, Richard & Elizabeth Gibson, 8 Aug 1792; Henry Hughey, bondsman; Chs. Caldwell, wit.

Armstrong, Richard & Margaret Osborn, 27 Dec 1774; Ad. Osborn, bondsman.

Armstrong, William & Margret Woods, 23 Aug 1768; Wm. Temple Cole, John Brandon, bondsmen; Tho. Frohock, wit.

Armsworthey, Daniel & Elizabeth Crumpton, 9 Jan 1828; Thos. D. Gibbs, bondsman; L. R. Rose, J. P., wit.

Armsworthey, Joseph & Rebecka Sheets, 8 Feb 1818; Benjimin Hinkle, bondsman.

Armsworthy, Henry & Elizabeth Smoote, 26 Nov 1824; Richd. Williams, bondsman; L. R. Rose, J. P., wit.

Armsworthy, Henry & Elizabeth Smoot, 15 Jan 1828; James Owens, bondsman.

Armsworthy, John C. & Susannah Bates, 15 Dec 1818; Aquillar Cheshier, bondsman; Jn. March Senr., wit.

Arnhard, David & Claryann Coriker, 14 June 1853; Rufus A. Corriker, bondsman; J. S. Myers, wit.

Arnhard, Henry & Susanna Hartlin, 27 Oct 1808; George Hartline, bondsman; A. L. Osborne, wit.

Arnhart, Charles & Cathrine Mowyer, 22 Oct 1839; George Wise, bondsman; Hy. Giles, wit.

Arnhart, George & Rosanna Airey, 8 Feb 1812; Henry Airey, bondsman; Jno. Giles, C. C., wit.

Arnheart, Eli & Lena Brown, 27 March 1826; Conrad File, bondsman; Jno. H. Hardie, wit.

Arnold, George & Polly Freeze, 27 Nov 1817; John Freeze, bondsman; Jno Giles, wit.

Aronheart, George & Hannah Culp, 6 Aug 1793; John Lentz, bondsman; Jas. Chambers, wit.

Aronhart, John & Nancy Smith, 16 July 1822; Samuel Wilhelm, bondsman.

Arthur, Joseph & Sarah Duncan, 17 June 1783; Thos Duncan, bondsman; As: Osborn, wit.

Arthur, Robert & Sarah Allen, widow, 1 March 1773; Adam Torrence, Moses Winsley, bondsmen; Ad: Osborn, wit.

Arwin, James & Catharine Huston, 13 Nov 1778; James Porter, bondsman; Max: Chambers, wit.

Ary, Barhm C. & Mary Morgan, 1 Sept 1859; D. W. Basinger, bondsman; Levi Trexler, wit; married 1 Sept 1859 by Levi Trexler, J. P.

Ary, Daniel Willson & Eliza Hodge, 31 Dec 1844; David C. Reed, bondsman; J. H. Hardie, wit.

Ashurst, John & Judith Johnson (daughter of Gideon Johnson), 22 Oct 1767; William Frohock, bondsman; Thos Frohock, wit.

Askew, William & Nancy Macdaniel, 8 May 1803; Buckner Caudell, bondsman; Jno. March, J. P., wit.

Aston, Alexander & Anna Braly, 23 March 1793; John Braly, bondsman; Max: Chambers, wit.

Atchason, William Sr. & July Taylor, 11 Dec 1821; William Atchason Jr., bondsman; Geo. Coker, wit.

Atchison, James & Francis Harbin, 1 Nov 1824; Andrew Sain, bondsman; L.R. Rose, J. P, wit.

Athon, Benjamin & Rachal Horn, 11 March 1827; Christopher Smith, bondsman; E. Brake, J. P., wit.

Athon, Fairfax & Joanah Lee, 13 April 1822; John Jones, bondsman; Geo. Coker, wit.

Atkinson, James & Mary Berry, 1 May 1816; William Adams, bondsman; Henry Giles, wit.

Atkinson, James & Anne Johnston, 2 April 1787; Obadiah Smith, bondsman; Jno. Macay, wit.

Atwell, Charles F. & Harriet J. Atwell, 31 July 1865; C.F. Atwell, Horatio N. Woodson, bondsmen; Obadiah Woodson, wit.; married 1 Aug 1865 by Stephen Frontis, M. G.

Atwell, James A. & Jane M. Masters, 24 July 1839; Obediah Woodson, bondsman.

Atwell, James A. & Rose Ann E. Fesperman, 5 Dec 1859; Levi Fesperman, bondsman; James E. Kerr, wit. married 7 Dec 1859 by D. R. Bradshaw, J. P.

Atwell, John H. & Harriet J. Woods, 22 March 1844; John F. Moore, bondsman; Obadiah Woodson, wit.

Atwell, John W. & Ellen Clotfelter, 9 Feb 1830; Wm. F. Cotfelter, bondsman; Jno. H. Hardie, wit.

Atwell, Obadiah W. & Margaret Deal, 18 Feb 1858; James A. Atwell, bondsman; John Wilkinson, wit. married 2 March 1858 by John S. Heilig.

Atwell, Thomas S. & Elizabeth Shuping, 31 Jan 1846; Jacob Sloop, bondsman; John H. Hardie Jr., wit.

Atwell, Thomas S. & Anne E. Woodson, 13 Sept 1832; Jno H. Hardie, bondsman.

Atwell, William L. & Rachel C. Williford, 15 March 1853; Saml W. Frazier, bondsman; J.S. Myers, wit. married 24 March 1853 by Jno. E. McPherson, M. G.

Austen--see also Aston

Austin, Bennet & Margaret Carson, 9 Feb 1817; Basil G. Jones, bondsman; R. Powell, wit.

Austin, David N. & Wilkey Ballance, 16 May 1824; E.D. Austin, bondsman; E. Brock, J. P., wit.

Austin, E.D. & Margaret Hall, 22 Jan 1834; Daniel Seffort, bondsman; Wm. Hawkins, wit.

Austin, Henry R. & Elvira Gaither, 16 Nov 1830; H. R. Austin, bondsman; Wilson Rose, bondsman; L. R. Rose, J. P., wit.

Austin, James & Margaret S. Gambol, 27 May 1816; Bennet Austin, bondsman; R. Powell, wit.

Austin, Ransom & Sarah Smith, 18 Nov 1835; Henry Hellard, bondsman; Jno Giles, wit.

Austin, Samuel & Lyda Railsback, 24 Jan 1803; Wilson Russum, bondsman; J. Hunt, wit.

Austin, Samuel & Tammey Luckey, 15 Sept 1826; Wilson Rose, bondsman; L. R. Rose, J. P., wit.

Austin, Samuel & Margaret Ellis, 30 Dec 1829; Saml Baker, bondsman; Wm. Hawkins, J. P., wit.

Austin, Samuel & Sarah Burgess, 12 Nov 1832; Scarlet Latham, bondsman; Thomas McNeely, J. P., wit.

Auten, James W. & Margaret R. Watts, 13 Feb 1854; G. G. McKnight, bondsman; J. S. Myers, wit. married 16 Feb 1854 by Hugh Parks, J. P.

Avery, Thos & Peggy Buck, 12 May 1797; Jno Avery, bondsman; Jno Rogers, wit.

Avitts, John & Sarah Rimmonton, 18 Oct 1779; John Huntsman, bondsman; Jo. Brevard, wit.

Ayer, Henry W. & E. A. Carlton, 9 April 1859; P. C. Carlton, bondsman; married 9 April 1859 by A. Baker.

Ayers, Solomon & Jane E. Swink, 6 Oct 1858; J. H. Brown, bondsman; married 6 Oct 1858 by J. H. Brown, J. P.

Aytcherson, James Jr. & Christina Miller, 25 Feb 1791; Stephen Noland Senr., bondsman; Basil Gaither, wit.

Aytcheson, Jesse & Charity Deever, 27 Oct 1818; Eli Watkins, bondsman; R. Powell, wit.

Aytcheson, Riley & Mary Black, 22 Jan 1818; Seylas Aytcheson, bondsman; Jno B. Palmer, Saml. Jones, wit.

Aytcheson, Shadrach & Lydia Orrel, 6 Jan 1818; William Aytcheson, bondsman; R. Powell, wit.

Aytchison, Henery & Nicy Addams, 19 Sept 1824; Joseph Miller, bondsman; E. Brock, J. P., wit.

Backster, John & Hannah Owen, 13 April 1792; James Wood, bondsman; Chs. Caldwell, wit.

Baddy, Benjamin & Lavina Beaver, 10 June 1840; Samuel Ribelin, bondsman.

Badgett, James & Eluthabeth Swink, 27 Jan 1837; Tobias L. Lemly, bondsman.

Badgett, Samuel & Jenny Skene, 21 Oct 1790; Jacob Skean, bondsman; C. Caldwell, D. C., wit.

Baddy, Nathan & Anne Brice, 9 Sept 1779; John Baddy, bondsman; Ad. Osborn, wit.

Bagge, Charles F. & Christina Holder, 20 Aug 1801; Lazarus Hege, bondsman; Jno Monroe, wit.

Bagget, Silus & Hannah Brookshire, 5 Oct 1803; Timothy Merrell, bondsman

Baggett, Parker, & Nancy Doty, 13 June 1797; John Doty, bondsman; Jno Rogers, wit.

Baggit, Silas L. & Catharine Rickart, 27 Nov 1800; Gasper R. Rickerd, bondsman; J. Brim, D. C., wit.

Bahel, Jacob & Polly Pence, 1 May 1820; Moses A. Morgan, bondsman; Hy Giles, wit.

Bailey, B. & Jane M. Johnston, 12 Oct 1840; J. L. Beard, bondsman.

Bailey, Daniel & Elizabeth Felps, 24 Aug 1809; John Hampton, bondsman; Joseph Clarke, wit.

Bailey, Daniel & Sally Utzman, 4 May 1811; Jacob J. Grider, bondsman; Ezra Allemong, wit.

Bailey, Hubbard & Polley Welmon, 28 June 1818; William Nelson, bondsman; Jno March Sr., wit.

Bailey, Karr & Patey Degernet, 9 Aug 1808; Charles Caton, bondsman; Jno March, J. P., wit.

Bailey, Radford & Nancy C. Howard, 12 Jan 1848; Richmond Foster, bondsman; J. H. Hardie, wit.

Bailey, Richmond & Elizabeth March, 23 July 1806; Jno March Jr., bondsman; Jno March Sr., wit.

Bailey, Robert & Airey Thompson, 3 Jan 1822; Isaac Parker, bondsman.

Bailey, Saml & Sucky Chaffin, 15 March 1797; William Glasscock, bondsman; Jno Rogers, wit.

Bailey, Samuel & Nancy Daniel, 2 April 1833; Braxton Bailey, bondsman; Thomas McNeely, J. P., wit.

Bailey, T. B. & Mary Walton, 14 April 1845; William Walton, bondsman; Jno. H. Hardie, Jr., wit.

Bailey, Thomas & Jenny Owings, 27 Aug 1816; Aquillar Cheshier, bondsman; Jno March Sr., wit.

Bailey, Thomas & Jean Bailey, 29 Aug 1786; Jno Bailey, bondsman; Jno Macay, wit.

Bailey, Tillson & Maria Walton, 14 April 1845; Wm Walton, bondsman; Jno. H. Hardie Jr., wit.

Bailey, William & Mary Jones, 3 March 1764; Wm Vassery, Matt. Lang, bondsmen; Thomas Frohock, wit.

Bailey, William & Isbell Benson, 10 Aug 1774; Andrew Reed, bondsman; Ad. Osborn, wit.

Bailey, William & Margaret Hendrix, 25 Aug 1816; William Tomlinson, bondsman; R. Powell, wit.

Bailey, William & Margaret Valentine, 10 April 1860; William H. Tunstall, bondsman; John Wilkinson, wit. married -10 April 1860 ,by L. C. Groseclose, Pastor of St. John's Ev. Luth. Church, Salisbury, N.C.

Baily, Karr & Tempey Powell, 16 Jan 1802; Ransom Powell, bondsman; Jno. Brim, wit.

Baily, William & Lucy Foster, 11 June 1792; Robert Dial, bondsman; Basil Gaither, wit.

Baily, William Junr & Jane Patteson, 26 July 1790; William Baily Sear, bondsman; Jona. Harris, D. C., for Charles Caldwell, wit.

Baim, Edward & Margaret L. Brown, 9 June 1846; John Camp, bondsman; J. H. Hardie Junr., wit.

Baim, George & Lovinia Earnhart, 16 Dec 1837; Solomon Caster, bondsman; Hy Giles, wit.

Bain, John & Nancy Trexler, 29 March 1855; Daniel Miller, bondsman; James E. Kerr, wit. married 29 March 1855 by S. J. Peeler, J. P.

Baim, Thomas F. & Easther Ogle, 14 March 1829; Nathan Morgan, bondsman; Jno. H. Hardie, wit.

Baird (Beard) Andw. & Anne Locke, 1 Feb 1790; Jno. Beard, bondsman; C. Caldwell, D. C., wit.

Baity, David & Sarah Hendrix, 20 June 1798; William Cranfill, bondsman; Ma Troy, wit.

Baity, George & Mary Beaman, 19 Dec 1828; William D. Moss, bondsman; L. R. Rose, J. P., wit.

Baity, Richmond & Prudence Brown, 22 March 1833; John Cunningham, bondsman; J. Tomlinson, J. P., wit.

Baity, William Senr & Mary Binkly, 13 June 1829; John Garner, bondsman; J. Inglis, wit.

Baker, Benjamin & Hannah Hunter, 19 Dec 1833; Benjamin Eaton, bondsman; J. Tomlinson, J. P., wit.

Baker, Benjamin & Comfort Sewel, 8 Oct 1779; Samuel Sewel, bondsman; Jo. Brevard, wit.

Baker, Christopher & Agness Forrster, 13 May 1783; Conrad Brem, bondsman.

Baker, David & Rebecker Jones, 14 Feb 1831; Charles Hunter, bondsman; Wm. Hawkins, wit.

Baker, David & Mary McCannon, 6 Dec 1812; John Powell, bondsman; R. Powell, wit.

Baker, Elias & Sarah Holbrook, spinster, 20 May 1780; Beal Baker, bondsman.

Baker, George & Elizabeth Tennison, 19 Sept 1825; John Johnston, bondsman (German signature: Johann Johnston?).

Baker, George H. & Lydia Freeze, 8 Dec 1835; Noah Freeze, bondsman; J. H. Hardie, wit.

Baker, Henrey (Johann Heinrich Baker) & Cathrenah Rosenah Sinque, 28 Aug 1804; Lewis Peck, bondsman; Jno March Senr., William Glasscock, wit.

Baker, Henry & Amelia Walker, 22 Feb 1825; George Baker, bondsman; Hy Allemong, wit.

Baker, Henry & Martha E. Miller, 27 Dec 1847; Joshua Miller, bondsman.

Baker, Henry F. & Mary A. Baker, 22 Aug 1859; James M. Turner, bondsman; John Wilkinson, wit. married 23 Aug 1859 by Jos. Wheeler.

Baker, Horatio & Rachael B. Castor, 29 Dec 1791; Philip Coleman, bondsman; Ad: Osborn, wit.

Baker, Jacob & Susanna Oolmer, spinster, no date; John Hunter, bondsman; Jno Kerr, wit.

Baker, John & Jean Mitchel, 20 May 1790; Sion Smith, bondsman; C. Caldwell, D. C., wit.

Baker, John & Susan Houwk, 29 July 1814; Honry Sechler, bondsman; Jno Giles, C. C., wit.

Baker, John & Nancy A. Gillespie, 26 Nov 1861; Joseph K. Burke, bondsman; Obadiah Woodson, wit.

Baker, John M. & Sarah E. Corriher, 20 Feb 1866; John M. Bostian, bondsman; Obadiah Woodson, wit.

Baker, Joseph & Jane McCulloch, 7 Jan 1796; Nathaniel Johnston, bondsman; J. Troy, wit.

Baker, Joseph & Margaret E. Bostian, 4 July 1865; J. D. Rankin, bondsman; Obadiah Woodson, wit. married 13 July 1865 by Rev. John D. Rankin.

Baker, L. S. & Elizabeth E. J. Henderson, 13 March 1855; Francis M. Henderson, bondsman; James E. Kerr, wit. married 13 March 1855 by John H. Parker, Minister of Prot. Epis. Church

Baker, Moses & Sophia Coon, 29 May 1837; Milus T. McCulloch, bondsman.

Baker, Obediah & Patrina Roberts, 20 Dec 1782; David Woodson, bondsman.

Baker, Philip & Polly Gales, 4 Jan 1820; John Pierce, bondsman; B. Powell, wit.

Baker, Rezin & Elenor Roberts, no date; Obed Baker, bondsman.

Baker, Samuel & Jinsey Ellis, 25 March 1830; Isaac James, bondsman; E. D. Austin, J. P., wit.

Baker, William & Lucinda Holobugh, 22 Oct 1849; Wm. F. Hall, bondsman; James E. Kerr, wit.

Baldridge, John & Margaret Poston, 29 July 1782; Dowinton Poston, bondsman; T. H. McCaule, wit.

Baldrige, John & Isabella Luckey, no date; Jas Luckey, bondsman; Ad: Osborn, wit.

Baldwin, John & Charlotte Pain, 18 Sept 1803; John Hight, bondsman; William Welbon, wit.

Baldwin, Joshua & Elizabeth Wells, 28 Jan 1775; William Wells, bondsman; James Robinson, wit.

Baldwin, Saml & Maryann Whitaker, 10 Jan 1804; Stephan Neal, bondsman; Ad: Osborn, wit.

Baley, Samuel & Tomith Pearson, 11 Aug 1789; Robert Foster, bondsman; Basil Gaither, wit.

Ball, George & Rhoda Kenneday, 15 June 1817; Samuel Cecill, bondsman; Z. Hunt Jr., wit.

Ball, Henderson & Betsey Lethgo, 20 Oct 1834; Wm. Locke, bondsman.

Ball, Jarred & Lydda Trotter, 23 Feb 1818; Jeremiah Thomas, bondsman; Zebulon Hunt, J. P., wit.

Ball, Jaret & Thankful Trotter, 14 March 1819; Philip Cecill, bondsman; E. Brown, wit.

Ball, Jno & Agness Adams, 5 Jan 1788; Abraham Adams, bondsman; J. McEwen, wit.

Ball, John & Deborough Murphy, 28 Feb 1815; William Cecill, bondsman; Silas Peace, wit.

Ball, Joseph & Sophiah Shuler, 18 Nov 1813; William Cecill, bondsman; So. Davis, J. P., wit.

Ball, William & Mary Gordon, 17 April 1813; William Cisel, bondsman; Sol. Davis, J. P., wit.

Ballance, Jesse & Salley Gails, 29 Oct 1816; Thomas Gails, bondsman; R. Powell, wit.

Ballard, John & Catherine Stinticom, 8 Nov 1824; Josiah Houser, bondsman; M. Hanes, wit.

Ballard, Reubin & Barbary Snider, 5 Sept 1825; Wilie Jones, bondsman; L. R. Rose, J. P., wit.

Ballard, Ruben & Polly Gullit, 19 July 1828; Talifaor Chaffin, bondsman; M. Hanes, wit.

Ballentine, James (carpenter), & Ann Burke, 4 Dec 1779; James Townsley (silversmith), bondsman; B. Booth Boote, wit.

Baly, Green & Polly Foster, 13 Dec 1824; Thomas Baly, bondsman; M. Hanes, J. P., wit.

Bame, George & Rosannah Trexler, 1 April 1853; Jesse Rebelin, bondsman; J. S. Myers, wit.

Bame, George & Elizabeth Miller, 21 Sept 1854; J. W. Trexler, bondsman; married 21 Sept 1854 by H. W. Hill, J. P.

Bame, Green & Eliza Hettinger, 2 July 1862; Samuel Bame, bondsman; Obadiah Woodson, wit.

Bame, John & Mary Ketchey, 11 April 1850; Milfed Green Miller,
bondsman; J. S. Myers, wit.

Bame, Levi & Lindy Elizabeth Earnhart, 10 July 1858; Tobias
Hartman, bondsman; James E. Kerr, wit. married 11 July 1858
by J. Barringer, J. P.

Bame, Mathias & Elizabeth Stoner, 30 June 1828; Peter Stoner,
bondsman; Hy. Giles, wit.

Bame, Saml & Anna Hoffman, 5 Nov 1832; George Vogler, bondsman.

Bankherdt, George & Julia A. Wade, 10 May 1861; James E. Kerr,
clerk; J. Wilkinson, deputy; married by S. C. Groseclose,
Pastor of St. John's Ev. Lutheran Church, Salisbury, N. C.

Banks, Elijah & Effy Gordon, 15 March 1780; William McKay,
bondsman; B. Booth Boote, wit.

Banks, Joel & Rachael Hendrix, 12 Feb 1805; Solomon Banks, bondsman; A. L. Osborn, D. C., wit.

Banks, John & Elizabeth Garawood, 31 Jan 1829; Isaac Parker,
bondsman; Thomas McNeely, J. P., wit.

Barber, David & Margaret Cowan (both colored), 17 Feb 1866;
Henry Cowan, bondsman; Obadiah Woodson, wit.

Barber, James & E. J. Marlin, 25 April 1859; John H. Wilson,
bondsman; James E. Kerr, wit. married 26 April 1859 by Geo.
B. Wetmore, minister.

Barber, John Edward & Catherine Young, 30 Nov 1814; Richard
Barber, bondsman; Geo. Dunn, wit.

Barber, Jonathan & Jane Barber, 2 Jan 1839; Hezekiah Turner,
bondsman; Hy. Giles, wit.

Barber, Joseph & M. M. Lyerly, 1 March 1865; M. L. Dixon, bondsman; Obadiah Woodson, wit.

Barber, Luke & Catharine Steele, (not dated), William Young,
bondsman; Jno Giles, C. C., wit.

Barber, Matthew & Margaret C. Knox, 16 Aug 1845; Andrew Graham,
bondsman; J. H. Hardie Junr., wit.

Barber, Richard W. & Polly K. Foster, 28 Feb 1816; William Chunn,
bondsman; Geo. Dunn, wit.

Barber, Robert J. M. & Mary A. Harrison, 16 Sept 1852; Theo. A.
Allison, bondsman; J. S. Myers, wit. married 18 Sept 1852
by Rev. James G. Jacocks, Minister of the Protestant Episcopal
Church.

Barber, Thos & Sarah C. Harrison, 14 Feb 1853; Saml R. Harrison,
bondsman; J. S. Myers, wit. married 15th February 1852 by
James G. Jacocks, Minister of the P. E. Church Rector of
Christ Church, Rowan County, N. C.

Barber, William & Margret Hughey, 8 April 1816; Luke Barber,
bondsman; Geo. Dunn, wit.

Barber, William & Jane E. Marlin, 12 July 1859; Richard Harrison, bondsman; James E. Kerr, wit. married by Geo. B. Wetmore, 12 July 1859.

Barber, William E. & Margaret Lively, 5 May 1840; George M. Lyerly, bondsman; Susan T. Giles, wit.

Barber, William L. & Margaret A. Harrison, 24 May 1858; Benjamin A. Knox, bondsman; James E. Kerr, wit. married 26 May 1858 by Geo. B. Wetmore, Minister of the Protestant Episcopal Church.

Barclay, Jonathan & Mary A. Miller, 31 May 1813; Jeremy Beard, bondsman; Jno. Giles, C. C., wit.

Barcley, John & Geiley Kern, 21 Aug 1790; John Kern, bondsman; C. Caldwell, D. C., wit.

Barcum, Henry & Mary Ann Agner, 26 Sept 1865; George McLellan, bondsman; Obadiah Woodson, wit. married 28 Sept 1865 by Revd. Wm. Lambeth.

Bareshizer, Philip & Dolly Clover, 25 Jan 1789; Will Alexander, wit.

Bar(e)field, James & Rebecca Parker, 29 March 1818; Henry S. Parker, bondsman; R. Powell, wit.

Barger, Andrew & Sally K. Lingle, 11 June 1850; Henry Brown, bondsman; J. S. Myers, wit.

Barger, Andrew & Elizabeth Brown, 4 Aug 1862; Henry Peeler, bondsman; Obadiah Woodson, wit.

Barger, Caleb & Margaret A. Walton, 2 Feb 1853; Albert T. Walton, bondsman; James E. Kerr, wit.

Barger, Jacob & Mary A. L. Fisher, 21 April 1859; John A Clampet, bondsman; married 25 April 1859 by Saml Rothrock, Minister of the Gospel in the Ev. Luth. Church.

Barger, John & Margaret Briggs, 27 Sept 1855; Jacob Lyerly, bondsman; J. S. Myers, wit. married 27 Sept 1855 by J. Thomason, J. P.

Barger, John & Margaret Plummer, 15 Dec 1859; John A. Clampet, bondsman; married 15 Dec 1859 by Moses Powlass, J. P.

Barger, John & Polly Fheen, 14 Dec 1865; Matthew Plumer, bondsman; Obadiah Woodson, wit.

Barger, Peter & Margaret Shuping, 1 Oct 1822; Volentine Pence, bondsman; Jno Giles, wit.

Barger, Samuel & Mealy Beaver, 6 March 1837; Joseph Moury, bondsman; Jno Giles, wit.

Baringer, Jno & Elizabeth Smith, 22 Sept 1796; George Barringer, bondsman; Jno Rogers, wit.

Barkley, James & Sarah Knox, 14 April 1787; Henry Barkley, William Knox, bondsmen; Max: Chambers, wit.

Barkley, Samuel & Mary Davis, 5 July 1784; Henry Davis, bondsman; Hugh Magoune, wit.

Barncastle, John & Caty Little, 17 Aug 1807; Charles Poston, bondsman; John Hanes, J. P., wit.

Barnes--see also Barns

Barnes, Alexander & Dorathy Hill, 20 Dec 1817; Richard Barnes, bondsman; Jno Giles, wit.

Barnes, George T. & Catharine C. Wilson, 25 Oct 1864; F. E. Shober, bondsman; Obadiah Woodson, wit.

Barns, James & Elizabeth Smith, 12 Sept 1800; Lewis Roblin or Robley, bondsman.

Barnes, John & Pheby Miller, 23 April 1825; John Smith, bondsman.

Barnes, Samuel & Rachel Turner, 20 March 1779; James Turner, bondsman; Wm. R. Davie, wit.

Barnes, Samuel & Rebecka Nunly, 26 April 1808; James Barnes, bondsman; Andrew Kerr, wit.

Barnet, Robert & Elenour Mahon, 19 May 1805; Peter Mahon, bondsman; A. L. Osborn, D. C., wit.

Barnhardt, George M. & Mary Ann Hielick, 9 Aug 1841; Mathias Boger, bondsman; Susan T. Giles, wit.

Barnhardt, John C. & Mary Emeline Lipe, 10 May 1865; E. J. Lipe, bondsman Obadiah Woodson, wit.

Barnheart, John & Delia Duke, 27 Feb 1833; George Barnhart, bondsman.

Barns, Abraham & Caty Rider, 21 Nov 1814; Shadrick Hill, bondsman; Jno Giles, wit.

Barns--see also Barnes

Barns, Aquilla & Hanna Lee, 20 Sept 1779; Shadrack Barns, bondsman; Ad. Osborn, wit.

Barns, David & Caty Traylor, 27 Dec 1819; James Barns, bondsman; Jno Giles, wit.

Barns, Richard & Fanny Johnson, 21 Nov 1808; Jonathan Merrell, bondsman; A. L. Osborn, wit.

Barr, Jacob & Catherine Howard, 13 Dec 1824; Alexander Smoot Jr., bondsman.

Barr, James & Elizabeth McCaule, 24 Jan 1785; T. Harris, bondsman.

Barr, James & Elizabeth McCorkle, 18 Dec 1774; Matt: Troy, bondsman; Ad: Osborn, wit.

Barr, John & Mary King, 21 March 1776; Thos: King, bondsman; Ad: Osborn, wit.

Barr, John & Ann H. Cowan, 24 Jan 1817; Joseph Cowan, bondsman; Jno Giles, C. C., wit.

Barr, Patrick & Agness Kilpatrick, 17 Nov 1779; John Kilpatrick, bondsman; Ad. Osborn, wit.

Barr, Richard R. & Martha A. Atwell, 17 Sept 1861; Jno D. Brown, bondsman; Obadiah Woodson, wit. married 19 Sept 1861 by Stephen Frontis, Minister of the Gospel.

Barr, Samuel & Matilda Graham, 20 Aug 1824; Wm. P. Graham, bondsman; Hy. Giles, wit.

Barr, William & Rebecca Patterson, 8 Jan 1839; Hy. Giles, bondsman.

Barret, Anderson & Surancy Pattrack, 17 Aug 1816; John H. Barret, bondsman; Jn March Sr., wit.

Barret, Isaac & Sally Bryant, 14 June 1820; Jonathan Williams, bondsman; Jno Giles, wit.

Barret, John & Polly Park, 18 Dec 1811; Jno Phillips, bondsman; Jno March Sr., wit.

Barrett, Henderson & Amanda Calcott, 19 June 1856; Wilbon Williams, bondsman; J. S. Myers, wit.

Barrett, Henderson & Caroline Calicut, 17 Oct 1860; Martin Richwine, bondsman; Wm. Locke, wit. married 17 Oct 1860 by L. C. Groseclos, Pastor of St. John's Ev. Luthn. Ch., Salisbury, N. C.

Barrier, Daniel M. & Sarah A. Barringer, 10 Oct 1857; Wm. L. Barrier, bondsman; J. S. Myers, wit. married 14 Oct 1857 by Saml. Rothrock, Minister of the Gospel in the Ev. Luth. Church.

Barrier, Edmund & Margaret C. Overcash, 2 Jan 1851; Cornelius Overcash, bondsman; James E. Kerr, wit.

Barrier, Henry & Betsy Ribely, 15 Aug 1812; Peter Eddleman, bondsman; Jno Giles, wit.

Barrier, Jacob W. & Laura N. Brown, 28 April 1864; Henry M. Goodman, bondsman; Obadiah Woodson, wit.

Barrier, John A. & Sophia L. Lentz, 14 Jan 1859; George H. Eagle, bondsman; married 24 Jan 1859 by Saml Rothrock, Minister of the Gospel in the Ev. Luth. Church.

Barringer, Charles & Polly Redwine, 3 Feb 1824; George Hileigh (Heilig), bondsman.

Barringer, Charles & Elizabeth Arey, 26 May 1835; David Goodman, bondsman; Jno H. Hardie, wit.

Barringer, Christopher & Mackalena Messimer, 30 May 1798; Peter Barringer, bondsman; Matt. Troy, wit.

Barringer, David & Mary Airy, 4 Feb 1834; Edward Earnheart, bondsman; Wm. Locke, wit.

Barringer, Henry & Maria Brown, 12 Feb 1844; Thos Dickson, bondsman; J. H. Hardie, wit.

Barringer, Jeremiah & Clarisy Correll, 17 Sept 1850; B. B. Roberts, bondsman; J. S. Myers, wit.

Barringer, Joseph A. & Selena Cranford, 8 Feb 1858; A. M. Sullivan, bondsman.

Barringer, Matthias & Mary Boger, 13 Sept 1794; Daniel Boger, bondsman; J. Troy, D. C., wit.

Barringer, Matthias & Barbara Rentleman, 4 Sept 1801; Jacob Brim, bondsman; Jno Brim, D. C., wit.

Barringer, Moses & Catharine Brown, 4 Oct 1842; John Barringer, bondsman; John H. Hardie, wit.

Barringer, Nicholas R. & Ellen C. Holshouser, 30 Nov 1857; A. M. Kluttz, bondsman; J. S. Myers, wit. married 3 Dec 1857 by C. A. Heilig, J. P.

Barringer, Paul & Luvina Miller, 29 Jan 1830; Charles Barringer, bondsman; Jno H. Hardie, wit.

Barringer, Peter L. & Rosana Miller, 13 April 1842; G. H. Johnson, bondsman; Jno H. Hardie, wit.

Barringer, Peter L. & Olly C. Miller, 17 Jan 1860; Wm. A. Walton, bondsman; Wm. Locke, wit.

Barrott, Robert & Marget Weyatt, 31 Jan 1811; Jno Phillips (Fillips), bondsman; Jno March Sr., wit.

Barry, John & Susanna Patterson, 5 Feb 1779; Caleb Bedwel, bondsman; William R. Davie, wit.

Bartly, John & Jean Knox, 3 Nov 1785; Samuel Knox, bondsman; Margret Chambers, wit.

Basenger, Charles & Mary Shufford (Lufford?), 24 March 1840; Conrad Festerman, bondsman; Susan T. Giles, wit.

Basinger, Jno & Eve Smither, 24 Oct 1803; Michael Cobel, bondsman; A. L. Osborn, wit.

Basinger, John & Susanna Lentz, 10 Nov 1820; John Beard Senr, bondsman; Jno Giles, wit.

Basinger, John & Betsy Trease, 9 May 1815; Henry Weaver, bondsman; Geo. Dunn, wit.

Basinger, Caleb A. & Catharine Ann Eagle, 27 March 1860; Daniel M. Basinger, bondsman; John Wilkinson, wit. married 28 March 1860 by Saml Rothrock, Minister of the Gospel in the Ev. Luth. Church.

Basinger, D. W. & Rhody Morgan, 4 Feb 1862; Atlas Kirk, bondsman; Obadiah Woodson, wit. married 5 Feb 1862 by Levi Trexler, J. P.

Basinger, Eli & Margaret M. Freeze, 15 March 1850; Jacob Lipe, bondsman; J. S. Myers, wit.

Basinger, G. H. & Sarah C. Overcash, 9 Feb 1866; John N. Hess, bondsman; Obadiah Woodson, wit.

Basinger, George & Ann Ghents, 16 Jan 1844; George Fespermann, bondsman; J. H. Hardie, wit.

Basinger, George & Eve Ann Mourey, 17 July 1844; J. D. Glover, bondsman.

Basinger, Henry & Betsey McCrarey, 7 Feb 1809; Lewis Utzman, bondsman; A. L. Osborne, wit.

Basinger, Henry & Maria Hess, 14 Dec 1842; Tobias. Hess, bondsman; David Kerns, wit.

Basinger, James & Louisa Eller, 24 June 1857; William C. Brandon, bondsman; James E. Kerr, wit. married 25 June 1857 by M. A. McKenzie, J. P.

Basinger, James & Elizabeth Owen, 10 Jan 1859; W. C. Brandon, bondsman; John Wilkinson, wit. married 12 Jan 1859 by M. Plumer, J. P.

Basinger, James J. & Catherine C. Earnheart, 31 Oct 1862; Isaac M. Shaver, bondsman; Obadiah Woodson, wit.

Basinger, John & Rosanna Kesler, 19 Jan 1835; James Basinger, bondsman; Jno H. Hardie, wit.

Basinger, John A. & Leah Eagle, 29 May 1865; John N. Hess, bondsman; Obadiah Woodson, wit.

Basinger, Joseph & Chrisey F. Josey, 26 March 1857; John F. Moose, bondsman; J. S. Myers, wit. married 26 March 1857 by Saml Rothrock, Minister of the Gospel in the Ev. Luth. Church.

Basinger, Joseph Jeremiah & Margaret L. Troutman, 31 July 1856; Edward Fesperman, bondsman; J. S. Myers, wit. married 31 July 1856 by Saml. Rothrock, Minister of the Gospel in the Ev. Luth. Church.

Basinger, J. C. & Susan J. Shaver, 31 Aug 1865; William L. Parker, bondsman; Horatio N. Woodson, wit. married 31 Aug 1865 by Revd. Wm. Lambeth.

Basinger, J. M. & Crissy F. Basinger, 9 Aug 1865; John A. Basinger, bondsman; Obadiah Woodson, wit. married 9 Aug 1865 by J. Rumple, V. D. M.

Basinger, J. W. & Julia Ann Victoria Fisher, 11 Feb 1863; D. C. Basinger, bondsman; Obadiah Woodson, wit.

Basinger, Martin & Mary Bruner, 11 June 1785; Martin Beffle, bondsman; Hu. Magoune, wit.

Basinger, Mathias & Margret Payn, 28 April 1818; David Lewis, bondsman; Sol. Davis, J. P., wit.

Basinger, Richard T. & Mary C. Shaver, 19 Oct 1850; Edmon D. Lents, bondsman; James E. Kerr, wit.

Basinger, Thomas & Catharine Stoner, 1 Jan 1851; Jesse Wilhelm, bondsman; James E. Kerr, wit.

Basinger, Thomas & Crisey Rickherd, 9 March 1846; Archible Misenhimer, bondsman; J. S. Myers, wit.

Basinger, William A. & Paulina C. Holshouser, 24 March 1866; John N. Hess, bondsman; Obadiah Woodson, wit.

Bass, Alexander & Nancy Brown, 18 Aug 1815; Saml Wallis, bondsman; Geo. Dunn, wit.

Bass, Drewry & Nancey Parch, 25 June 1818; Benjamin Ellis, bondsman; Saml Jones, J. P., wit.

Bateman, Christopher & Ann Hunter, 5 Dec 1797; David Montgomery, bondsman; Jno Rogers, wit.

Bateman, Christopher & Nancy Ford, 20 Feb 1816; Andrew Kincaid, bondsman; Geo Dunn, wit.

Bateman, William & Ruth Pinxton, 23 Nov 1789; George Lowman, bondsman; Ed. Harris, wit.

Bateman, William & Tildy Coats, 31 Dec 1816; Archibald Craig, bondsman; Jno Giles, Clk., wit.

Bateman, William & Elizabeth Smith, 4 March 1793; Meshack Pinkston, bondsman; Js. Chambers, wit.

Bates, Tearman & Polley Glascock, 25 March 1812; Benjamin Dewlin, bondsman; Jno Marsh Sr., wit.

Baty, William & Nancy Hattox, 20 March 1798; Wm. Haddock, bondsman; Edwin J. Osborn, D. C., wit.

Baughl, E. C. & Sarah E. Boston, 6 Feb 1855; Abraham Keller, bondsman; J. S. Myers, wit. married 6 Feb 1855 E. C. Baughl of Davie County and Sarah E. Bostian of Rowan Co., by Obadiah Woodson, J. P.

Baxter, Caleb E. & Mary Dever, 16 Dec 1833; William J. Ellis, bondsman; Thomas McNeely, J. P., wit.

Baxter, David & _____, not filled out or dated; Joshua Lowrance, bondsman.

Bayless, Thos & Pricilla Andrews, 13 Feb 1797; James Ellis, bondsman; Jno Rogers, wit.

Baze, William M. & Martha J. Rumple, 18 Jan 1856; Daniel Rumple, bondsman; John L. Hedrick, J. P., wit. married 22 Jan 1856 by John L. Hedrick, J. P.

Beacham, Stephen & Nancy Call, 30 Sept 1805; John Call, bondsman; Jn Marsh Sr., wit.

Beadon, Samuel & Lidy Edcherson, 27 May 1815; Thomas Beadon, bondsman; Jn March Sr., wit.

Beal, Joseph & Elizabeth Speaks, 31 March 1818; Thomas Holmes, bondsman; R. Powell, wit.

Beall, Zadock & Nancy Begerly, 16 Sept 1786; Evan Bealle, bondsman; Jno Macay, wit.

Beals, Joseph H. & Margaret Pinkston, 14 April 1827; Richard Steele, bondsman; John H. Hardie, wit.

Beam--see also Bean

Beam, Muadias (Mathias Böhm, German), & Polly Wise, 21 Sept 1790; Jacob Böhm, bondsman; C. Caldwell, D. C., wit.

Beaman, James & Issabel Hendricks, 12 March 1828; Thomas Beaman, bondsman; L. R. Rose, J. P., wit.

Beaman, William & _____, 7 Feb 1823; Thomas Furches, bondsman; L. R. Rose, J. P., wit.

Bean--see also Beam

Bean (Beam?), Alexander & Angeline Briggs, 10 Dec 1853; Thomas Pinkston, bondsman; J. S. Myers, wit.

Bean, Alexander & Caroline Waggoner, 19 Feb 1848; Robt L. McCormaughy, bondsman; J. H. Hardie Jr., wit.

Bean, James W. & Hetty Beaver, 16 Feb 1850; John Hartman, bondsman; James E. Kerr, wit.

Bean, Mumford & Temperance Leach, 3 March 1829; Arthur Morrow, bondsman; Thomas McNeely, J. P., wit.

Bean, William H. & Eve Ann Frick, 17 Aug 1865; Willie Bean, bondsman; Obadiah Woodson, wit. married 20 Aug 1865 by Rev. J. M. Shaver.

Bean, Willie & Rebeca Skeen, 2 Jan 1856; M. G. Morgan, bondsman; Aron Mc_ ___, J. P., wit.

Beanblossom, Frederick & Polly Lane, 24 Jan 1812; Jesse Lane, bondsman; Geo Dunn, wit.

Beard, Andrew & Margaret Smith, 8 Jan 1803; James Macay, bondsman; Hudson Hughes, wit.

Beard, Alexander & Elizabeth Whitaker, 3 Feb 1820; Peter Hinkle, bondsman; Jno Giles, wit.

Beard, Edwd G. or J. & Elizth. Trexler, 18 Jan 1845; Hiram H. Beard, bondsman.

Beard, John & Ellen B. Bryce, 21 April 1856; Jos. Henderson, bondsman; J. S. Myers, wit.

Beard, Jno & Margret Wood, 4 Dec 1780; James McEwen, bondsman; Ad: Osborn, wit.

Beard, John & _____ (not dated), Jno Brem, bondsman and wit.

Beard, John & Ann Maria Kelly, 30 Dec 1820; George Locke, bondsman.

Beard, John L. & Eliza Ford, 29 March 1842; A. C. McLelland, bondsman.

Beard, L. H. & Sallie Pool, 19 May 1862; Thos. E. Brown, bondsman; Obadiah Woodson, wit.

Beard, Lewis & Susan Dunn, 27 Jan 1785.

Beard, Michael & Margaret Zevelly, 9 Jan 1787; Ls. Beard, bondsman.

Beard (Baird), Robert & Rachel Thompson, 22 Jan 1812; William Steel, bondsman; Geo Dunn, wit.

Beard, Valentine & Obedeance Giles, 14 Feb 1775; John Lewis Beard(?), bondsman; Ad: Osborn, wit.

Beard, William & Sally Mulliner, 21 April 1811; William Johnson, bondsman; E. Morgan, J. P., wit.

Beard, William & Elizabeth Brevard, 17 Nov 1783; Zebulon Bravard, bondsman; Ad: Osborn, wit.

Beard, William & Jenny Hunt, 30 Sept 1797; David Hunt, bondsman; Jno Rogers, wit.

Beatty, William C. & Nancy Yarbrough, 1 Nov 1825; William T. Nuckolls, bondsman.

Beaty, Charles & Mary Gibson, 26 May 1787; John Albright, bondsman; Jno Macay, wit.

Beaty, Thos & Margaret Harden, 30 Sept 1786; William Harden, bondsman; Jno Macay, wit.

Beaucham, James & Nancy Enoch, 27 March 1800; Jas. Parks, bondsman; N. Chaffin, wit.

Beaver--see also Beever, Bever

Beaver, Adam M. & Margaret L. Pahel, 19 Oct 1865; W. A. Beaver, bondsman; Obadiah Woodson, wit. married 19 Oct 1865 by Revd. Wm. Lambeth.

Beaver, Alexander & Malinda Glover, 20 Nov 1856; Crawford Beaver, bondsman; J. S. Myers, wit.

Beaver, Alexander & Sally Ketchy(?), 5 June 1835, David Beaver, bondsman; Jno H. Hardie, wit.

Beaver, Allen & Betsy Porter, 16 Sept 1818; Adam Snider, bondsman; Geo Dunn, wit.

Beaver, Allen A. & Dovy E. Corhier, 30 Nov 1859; Jacob R. Coriher, bondsman.

Beaver, Benjm. & Mary Ann Camel; Elias Link, bondsman; Archd Honeycutt, J. P., wit.

Beaver, Benja. & Mary Croner, 7 Aug 1828; Wm Thompson, bondsman.

Beaver, Charles W. & Sarah M. Sifferd, 18 Jan 1858; Reuben W. Bost, bondsman; John Wilkinson, wit. married 1 Feb 1858 by Saml. Rothrock, Minister of the Gospel in the Ev. Luth. Church.

Beaver, Christian & Sally Short, 6 March 1798; Peter Frieze, bondsman; Edwin J. Osborn, D. C., wit.

Beaver, Crawford & Lunda Louisa Bean, 10 May 1858; Alexander Beaver, bondsman; John Wilkinson, wit. married 11 May 1858 by Jno M. McConnaughy, J. P.

Beaver, Daniel & Anna Katharine Beaver, 26 Oct 1852; Samuel Deal, bondsman; Obadiah Woodson, wit.

Beaver, Daniel & Catherine Beaver, 30 Jan 1851; Daniel Sides, bondsman; J. S. Myers, wit.

Beaver, Daniel & Margaret C. Overcash, 16 Nov 1865; Solomon Beaver, bondsman; Obadiah Woodson, wit.

Beaver, Daniel & Anna C. Rimer, married 3 Nov 1852 by Saml Rothrock, Minister of the Gospel in the Ev. Luth. Church. (no bond, only minister's return).

Beaver, David & Catherine C. Cauble, 24 June 1852; Obadiah Woodson, bondsman; J. S. Myers, wit.

Beaver, David & Susannah Garver, 27 Dec 1827; Paul Beaver, bondsman; Jno H. Hardie, wit.

Beaver, David & Polly Luter(?) or Inter(?), 7 Oct 1847; Eli Beaver, bondsman; J. H. Hardie, wit.

Beaver, Devault & Betsey Beaver, 24 April 1798; Peter Beaver (Bieber?, German signature), bondsman; Ed. J. Osborn, D.C., wit.

Beaver, Eli & Lavina Beaver, 17 Feb 1848; David Beaver, bondsman; John H. Hardie Jr., wit.

Beaver, Eli M. & Eve E. Beaver, 23 March 1853; David Beavar, bondsman; J. S. Myers, wit.

Beaver, George & Pena Beaver, 7 Nov 1826; Jacob Pachel, bondsman.

Beaver, George F. & B. E. Corriher, 28 Dec 1865; J. C. Stirewalt, bondsman; Obadiah Woodson, wit.

Beaver, George M. & Sarah A. Fry, 1 May 1851; Noah W. Fry, bondsman; J. S. Myers, wit.

Beaver, Henry & Sally Beaver, 21 Jan 1854; Moses Beaver, bondsman; J. S. Myers, wit.

Beaver (Bieber, German signature), Henry or Heinrich & Margret Clutz, 21 Oct 1801; Paulus Bieber (German signature), bondsman; J. M. Ervin, wit.

Beaver, Henry & Mary Beaver, 30 March 1824; Jacob Correll, bondsman; Hy Giles, wit.

Beaver, Henry & Sophia Lipe, 20 Feb 1833; Daniel Lipe, bondsman; Jno H. Hardie, wit.

Beaver, Henry & Elizth Beaver, 2 Feb 1846; David Link, bondsman; J. H. Hardie, wit.

Beaver, Henry W. & Leah S. Barrier, 3 June 1850; Tobias Barrier, bondsman; James E. Kerr, wit.

Beaver, Jacob & Tena Shulabarrier, 14 Dec 1827; David Beaver, bondsman; J. H. Hardie, wit.

Beaver, Jacob & Catharine M. Hartman, 5 Aug 1828; Alexr. Z. Smith, bondsman; Jno H. Hardie, wit.

Beaver, Jacob & Anna Kelshey, 13 Feb 1843; Alexr. Beaver, bondsman; J. H. Hardie, wit.

Beaver, Jacob M. & Margaret L. Ketner, 15 Dec 1865; M. N. Beaver, bondsman; Obadiah Woodson, wit.

Beaver, Jeremiah & Mary Ann C. Overcash, 1 Jan 1856; Elam A. Patterson, bondsman; J. S. Myers, wit. married 3 Jan 1856 by Saml Rothrock, Minister of the Gospel in the Ev. Luth. Church.

Beaver, Jesse & Catharine L. Bost, 4 Dec 1852; David A. Bost,
bondsman; James E. Kerr, wit.

Beaver, John & Lydia Lipe, 17 Jan 1855; Jacob Lipe, bondsman;
J. S. Myers, wit. married 23 Jan 1855 by J. Ingold, minister.

Beaver, John & Amelia Ann Safrit, 25 Jan 1858; William Safrit,
bondsman; James E. Kerr, wit. married 26 Jan 1858 by John
Yost, J. P.

Beaver, John & Elizabeth Rimmson, 8 Aug 1801; Jacob Smith,
bondsman; Jno Brem, wit.

Beaver, John & Elizabeth Beaver, 28 May 1821; Paul Youst, bondsman.

Beaver, John & Elizabeth Lipe, 4 Feb 1828; Francis Overcash,
bondsman; J. H. Hardie, wit.

Beaver, Jno (Johannes Bieber) & Betsey Hartman, 22 Dec 1829;
Dewalt Miller, bondsman; Jno H. Hardie, wit.

Beaver, Levi A. & Susan E. Albright, 6 April 1857; Peter R.
Albright, bondsman; J. S. Myers, wit. married 9 April 1857
by S. C. Alexander.

Beaver, Levi A. & Sarah E. Bostian, 9 Oct 1860, Henry M. Beaver,
bondsman; John Wilkinson, wit.

Beaver, Michael & Sarah A. Mowory, 24 Nov 1857; John L. Rusher,
bondsman; J. S. Myers, wit. married by L. J. Keck, Justice
of the Peace, 25 Nov 1857.

Beaver, Montford & Sarah L. Linn, 18 Oct 1847; James Scott,
bondsman; John H. Hardie Jr., wit.

Beaver, Moses & Polly A. Beaver, 24 March 1855; Henry Beaver,
bondsman; J. S. Myers, wit. married 29 March 1855 by J.
Ingold, Minister of the Gospel.

Beaver, Moses & Maria Overcash, 2 Oct 1852; Moses Beaver Sr.,
bondsman; J. S. Myers, wit. married 8 Oct 1852 by C. S.
Partee (Porter?), J. P.

Beaver, Peter & Nancy Emery, 12 July 1817; Michael Baker (German
signature), bondsman; Roberts Nanny, wit.

Beaver, Rineholt E. & Delilah Beaver, 10 Feb 1859; Monroe Beaver,
bondsman; John Wilkinson, wit. married 10 Feb 1859 by M.
Plumer, J. P.

Beaver, Rufus & Margaret M. Holshouse, 1 Aug 1861; David Earnhart,
bondsman; M. L. Holmes, J. P., wit.

Beaver, Samuel & Lidia Lints, 1 May 1830; William D. Crawford,
bondsman; M. A. Giles, wit.

Beaver, Simeon & Ann M. C. Beaver, 26 Oct 1858; Jacob Beaver,
bondsman; married 26 Oct 1858 by Jas H. Enniss, J. Police.

Beaver, Solomon & Mary E. Leazer, 19 March 1846; John M. Leazer,
bondsman; J. M. Turner, wit.

Beaver, Tobias & Jane Beaver, 24 March 1862; Crawford Beaver,
bondsman; Obadiah Woodson, wit. married 25 March 1862 by
W. Kimball, Min. of the Gospel.

Beaver, Tobius & Jamima P. Smith, 25 Sept 1849; Michael Philhour
(*Filhour), bondsman; J. S. Myers, wit.

Beaver, Wiley & Anna Yost, 27 Jan 1851; David Beaver, bondsman;
James E. Kerr, wit.

Beaver, William A. & Catharine Beaver, 19 Jan 1858; Henry Beaver,
bondsman; John Wilkinson, wit. married 19 Jan 1858 by M.
Plumer, J. P.

Beavers, George & Lavina Sellivan, 8 June 1813; Daniel Sellivan,
bondsman; E. Morgan, J. P., wit.

Bechtel, John & Susan Bastian, 29 Sept 1818; Andrew Bechtel,
bondsman; George Locke, wit.

Beck, Amos & Rhodah Summers, 20 June 1824; Hamilton Summers,
bondsman; John Cook, J. P., wit.

Beck, George & Sophia Barns, 10 Nov 1803; Richard Barns, James
Barnes, bondsmen; Ad: Osborn, wit.

Beck, Henry & Catharine Young, 12 Jan 1799; John Blessing,
bondsman; Edwin J. Osborn, D. C., wit.

Beck, James & Polly Cashdollar, 1 Dec 1823; Thomas Griffin,
bondsman; L. R. Rose, J. P., wit.

Beck, L. W. & Anna M. Miller, 3 Jan 1866; Milas Miller, bondsman;
Obadiah Woodson, wit.

Beck, Peter & Catharine Hileigh, 18 Aug 1834; Jacob Fisher,
bondsman; Henry Betton, wit.

Beck, Richmond & Sally Hendricks, 16 Sept 1827; John W. Turantine,
bondsman; Thomas McNeely, J. P., wit.

Beck, Sentleger & Elizabeth Madden, 23 Dec 1801; Richard W.
Madden, bondsman; Jno Brem, wit.

Becker, Johan Friederich & Caty Shelhorn, 25 Sept 1818; Jacob
Mickle, bondsman; Thos Hampton, wit.

Becker, Philip S. & Jane E. Owens, 3 Nov 1855; William M. Kincaid,
bondsman; J. S. Myers, wit. married by Obadiah Woodson, J.
P., 8 Nov 1855. Philip Becker of Davie County.

Beding, Thomas & Nancy Piner, 17 Jan 1824; William Orrell,
bondsman; M. Hanes, J. P., wit.

Beeding(?), William & Nancy Markland, 2 April 1823; Fielding
Slater, bondsman; M. Hanes, J. P., wit.

Beeman, John & Mary Neely, (not dated, abstract shows Oct 1784);
Elijah Renshaw, bondsman; H. Magoune, wit.

Beeman, John & Margret Hunter, 19 May 1767; George Smiley,
Oliver Wallis, Junis Quick, bondsmen; Thos Frohock, wit.

Beeman, Joseph & Lucy Holman, 4 June 1815; John Holman, bondsman;
R. Powell, wit.

Beeman, Joshua & Lydia Mooran, 13 May 1828; Thomas Beaman, bondsman; L. R. Rose, J. P., wit.

Beeman, Samuel & Rutha Jones, 10 March 1809; Peter Glascock, bondsman; Jn Marsh, Sr., wit.

Beeman, Thomas & Elizabeth Morean, 21 April 1827; Samuel Beeman, bondsman; Thomas McNeely, J. P., wit.

Beeman, William & Nancy Coker, 27 Jan 1807; Brumbley Coker, bondsman; Jno Marsh Sr., wit.

Beeson, William & Dinah Clamplet, 10 June 1805; James Evens, bondsman.

Been, Benjamin & Nancy DeJarnatt, 19 Feb 1806; Ford DeJarnett, bondsman; John March Sr., wit.

Beenblossom, Christian & Sally Lane, 27 Nov 1809; Martin Birely, bondsman; Jno Giles, wit.

Beeson, Nathaniel & Jane Shurgeer, 6 June 1806; Wm. Manlove Jr., bondsman; William Piggatt, J. P., wit.

Beeson, Richard & Mary Robertson, 1 April 1819; Hugh Robertson, bondsman; Sol. Davis, J. P., wit.

Beevar, Lewis & Nancy McFarland, 23 Nov 1810; David Pryor, bondsman; Jno Giles, C. C., wit.

Beffel, James & Drucilla Dickson, 3 Oct 1829; Benjamin Fraley, bondsman; J. H. Hardie, wit.

Beffil (Beafle), Adam & Jene Canady, 2 Aug 1802; Jno Brem, bondsman.

Beggaly, Martin C. & Elvira Loveless, 20 Dec 1831; William Love-lace, bondsman; Thomas McNeely, J. P., wit.

Behooks, William & Peggy Smith, 9 June 1798; David Cross, bondsman; Ma: Troy, wit.

Bell, James & Margit Denny, 25 March 1764; Willm. Denny, John McKnight, bondsman; Thos Donnell, wit.

Bell, James & _____, 20 June 1769, (no bond, consent form only), consent signed by William White; Samuel Hughey, Margret McKnight, wit.

Bell, James & Ellenor McNeely, 15 Nov 1787; Alexander McNeely, bondsman; J. McEwin, wit.

Bell, James & _____, _____ 1795; Richard Gillespie, bondsman.

Bell, James F. & Mary C. McNeely, 26 May 1837; Thomas Cowan, bondsman; R. Jones, wit.

Bell, James & Isabell Storry, 22 June 1769; Thomas Hill, bondsman (bond not on film, only a portion is shown).

Bell, John & Betsey Reed, 19 March 1812; Hugh Reed, bondsman; John Giles, C. C., wit.

Bell, John J. & Mary C. Coughenour, 16 May 1850; W. J. Palmer, bondsman; James E. Kerr, wit.

Bell, Robert & Jane Miller, 30 Nov 1782; John Miller, bondsman;
William Crawford, wit.

Bell, Walter & Margret Duncan, 3 Jan 1767; Thomas Hill, bondsman;
John Frohock, C., wit.

Bell, William & Margaret McNeely, 1 April 1776; James Brandon,
bondsman; Ad: Osborn, wit.

Bell, William & Jane Campbell, 19 Jan 1818; James Bell, bondsman;
Roberts Nanny, wit.

Bell, William & Elizabeth Jinkins, 13 Oct 1814; Lewis Jinkins,
bondsman; R. Powell, wit.

Bell, W. M. & Sarah E. Parks, 21 July 1865; D. M. Parks, bondsman; Obadiah Woodson, wit.

Bellah, Moses & Elizabeth Anderson, 21 Feb 1792; Wm. Anderson,
bondsman; Chs. Caldwell, wit.

Bellah, Samuel & Jean Morgan, 15 July 1786; Mos. Bellah, bondsman; Jno Macay, wit.

Belt, Abraham & Sally Gardner, 20 Jan 1857; John N. Hess, bondsman; J. S. Myers, wit.

Belt, Gray & Martha Baxter, 6 Feb 1843; John Gillon, bondsman;
J. H. Hardie, wit.

Bencini, Anthony & Elizabeth Miller, 27 Dec 1862; William A.
Walton, bondsman; Obadiah Woodson, wit.

Bencini, Lorenzo D. & Harriet C. Brown, 4 May 1844; J. P.
Krider, bondsman; Obadiah Woodson, wit.

Bennett, Daniel & Sarah Tatt (Talt?), (no date, during admn. of
Gov. Alexander Martin); William Crowel, bondsman; Man: Chambers, wit.

Bennet, Josias & Sarah Howard, 18 Aug 1800; William Howard,
bondsman; John Brem, wit.

Bennitt, Manfield & Elizabeth James, 19 Nov 1817; James Bennett,
bondsman; R. Powell, wit.

Benson, Bruffet & Nancy Grimes, 3 March 1810; John Spry, bondsman; Jno March Sr., wit.

Benson, Daniel & Mary Ham, 25 Aug 1794; John Periman, bondsman;
Fridreck Miller, wit.

Benson, Henderson & Betsey Willson, 1 Oct 1827; R. N. Fleming,
bondsman; J. Hardie, wit.

Benson, Henry & Jane Cathey, 18 Oct 1793; Jno McRavey, bondsman;
Jos: Chambers, wit.

Benson, Hugh S. & Margaret Clary, 13 Feb 1821; Andrew Rickard,
bondsman.

Benson, James & Margret Kerr, 1 Dec 1777; Joseph Kerr, bondsman;
Ad: Osborn, wit.

Benson, John & Sarah C. Rice, 11 Aug 1845; Hiram H. Jenkins, bondsman; J. H. Hardie, wit.

Benson, John B. & Elizabeth A. C. Wright, 17 April 1850; James J. Wright, bondsman; J. S. Myers, wit.

Benson, John M. & Fannie E. Bernard, 18 April 1865; B. F. Crosland, bondsman; Obadiah Woodson, wit.

Benson, Robert & Nancy Lewis, 4 Aug 1827; Thomas Walton, bondsman; Hy. Giles, wit.

Benson, Spencer & Nancy Rice, 26 March 1828; Ro. Benson, bondsman; J. H. Hardie, wit.

Benson, Thomas & Katharine Brown, 10 Nov 1829; William R. Hughes, bondsman.

Benson, William A. & Catharine Barrot, 8 Sept 1820; Jon. Penney, bondsman.

Benston, Robert & Lucy Hutchins, 24 Sept 1796; Jonathan Smith, bondsman.

Benthal, William H. & Maggie E. Shaver, 17 May 1865; L. A. Slater, bondsman; Obadiah Woodson, wit.

Bentley, Daniel & Nancey Lewis, 8 Feb 1782; Peter Lewis, bondsman; Ad: Osborn, wit.

Berger, George H. & Catharine Casper, 23 March 1785; Ad: Osborn, bondsman.

Berger, John & Margret Cruse, 1 Sept 1790; Adam Stigerwalt, bondsman; C. Caldwell, D. C., wit.

Berger, John H. & Susanna Miller, 15 Feb 1790; Peter Berringer, bondsman.

Berkerdite, John & Elizabeth Yockley, 29 Oct 1801; Jacob Mock, bondsman.

Bernhardt, C. T. & Laura C. Linn, 5 June 1865; J. C. Bernhardt, bondsman; Obadiah Woodson, wit.

Bernhardt, J. C. & Laura E. Davis, 15 Sept 1865; R. W. Lents, bondsman; Obadiah Woodson, wit.

Beroth, Henry & Christian Hollibo, 29 May 1775; Jacob Uzman, bondsman; David Flowers, wit.

Berringer, Peter & Catharine Trexler, 10 Dec 1799; John Trexler, bondsman; E. J. Osborn, D. C., wit.

Berry, Richard & Rebina Hawkins, 22 Sept 1767; William Simpson, bondsman; Thom. Frohock, wit. (consent of John Hawkins, father of Rebina Hawkins).

Berryer, Charles & Elizabeth Hagey, 5 Aug 1796; Henry Hagey, bondsman; Jno Rogers, wit.

Berryman, Newlon & Ellnor Kelly, 27 Aug 1827; Joseph J. Sparks, bondsman; M. Hanes, wit.

Berryman, Tollifearo & Julia Cheshur, 7 Aug 1828; Zepheneah
Harris, bondsman; L. R. Rose, J. P., wit.

Beryear, Henry & Sarah Grims, 11 Feb 1813; Phillip Beryear,
bondsman; J. Willson, J. P., wit.

Bescherer, John & Sophia Trexler, 19 May 1853; Thos E. Brown,
bondsman; J. S. Myers, wit. married 19 May 1853 by W. H.
Walton, J. P.

Bessent, William P. & Elizabeth Repults, 25 Aug 1845; Geo. A.
Smith, bondsman; John H. Hardie, Jun., wit.

Bevans, Elias & Margaret Oaks, 1 Feb 1815; John Bevans, bondsman;
Jno Giles, C. C., wit.

Bevans, John & Caty Swisher, 27 Jan 1816; Phillip Whitman,
bondsman; Jno Giles, C. C., wit.

Bever, Paul (Paulus Beiber, German) & Mary Shoeman, 3 Sept 1801;
Jas. Brem, wit.; John Shuman, bondsman.

Bevill, David & Sally Rimer, 6 Aug 1825; Jacob Correll, bondsman; M. A. Giles, wit.

Bevin, Fielding & Polly Moore, 24 Dec 1798; William West, bondsman; Ma: Troy, wit.

Bevin, Randel & Rachael Wood, 15 Feb 1790; Benjamin Story,
bondsman; Ed. Harris, wit.

Bevins, Corbin & Katerine West, 12 Feb 1787; William West,
bondsman; Wm. Cupples, wit.

Bevins, Leonard & Sarah Moore, 16 Oct 1792; Valentine Beard,
bondsman; Jos. Chambers, wit.

Bibby, John & Jane Ruth, 28 July 1762; Mark Whitaker, Joshua
Whiteaker, bondsman; John Frohock, Thos Frohock, wit.

Biffell, Martin & Barbary Roadcap, 28 June 1769; Paul Biffell,
Danl Little, bondsmen.

Biggers, John M. W. & Sarah E. Reese, 1 May 1847; Thos. E. Reese,
bondsman; J. H. Hardie, Jr., wit.

Biggers, Major & Mary Grimes, 1 Sept 1859; Robert F. Freeman,
bondsman; married 1 Sept 1859 by Peter Williamson, J. P.

Bigham, John C. & Margaret A. Litaker, 13 Dec 1855; George E.
Litaker, bondsman; James E. Kerr, wit.

Bigham, Joseph H. & Anna L. Linn, 27 Dec 1858; Samuel Linn,
bondsman; married 29 Dec 1858 by Rev. B. C. Nall of the
Ev. Luth. Synod of N. C.

Bigham, Saml & Sally McClain, 13 Aug 1810; Alexr McLean, bondsman; Jno Giles, C. C., wit.

Bigham, William & Sarah Braly, 7 Nov 1797; Hugh Braly, bondsman;
Ad: Osborn, wit.

Bigs, Benjamin & Abigail Frazer, 15 May 1780; Daniel Clary,
bondsman; B. Booth Boote, wit.

Bile, William, request for license, 2 April 1764; John Rany, David Bale, wit.

Biles, Charles & Catherine Lemly, 15 Feb 1816; Benjamin P. Pearson, bondsman; Geo Dunn, wit.

Biles, Daniel & Jean Conger, 30 Dec 1775; Jonathan Conger, bondsman. Ad: Osborn, wit.

Biles, Daniel & C. E. Kirk, 4 Sept 1865; Alexander Shaver, bondsman; Obadiah Woodson, wit. married 4 Sept 1865 by Rev. Isaac M. Shaver.

Biles, Daniel R. & Elizabeth Corzort, 22 March 1823; John Cooper, bondsman; Jno Giles, wit.

Biles, George S. & Lucinda Fourd, 9 May 1844; Moses Brown, bondsman; J. H. Hardie, wit.

Biles, James & Martha E. Steele, 29 April 1841; Joel H. Jenkins, bondsman.

Biles, John & Margaret Whiteker, 2 July 1790; John Whiteker, bondsman; Basil Gaither, wit.

Biles, John & Caty Walton, 28 Dec 1814; Isaac Walton, bondsman; Jno Giles, C. C., wit.

Biles, John & Betsey Smith, 12 March 1792; Conrad Bream, bondsman; Chs. Caldwell, wit.

Biles, Joseph & Ann Johnson, (not dated, abstract has 16 Nov 1769); William Frohock, Moses Peans, bondsmen; Thomas Frohock, wit.

Biles, Thomas & Tabithah Marbury, 8 March 1783; Charles Biles, bondsman.

Biles, Thomas & Jane Davis, 18 Feb 1800; Christian Kenny, bondsman.

Bile, William & Julietta Pitchey, 27 Aug 1818; Samuel L. Caldwell, bondsman; Milo A. Giles, wit.

Billing, David & Anne Blair, 4 May 1802; Hudson Hughs, bondsman; A. L. Osborn, D. C., wit.

Billings, Henry & Elizabeth Merrill, 6 April 1802; David Billing, bondsman; Jno. Brim, wit.

Billings, John & Jinny Yarborough, 13 Aug 1812; William McCrarey, bondsman; Joseph Clarke, wit.

Billings, John & Sally Davis, 22 Aug 1820; John Burkhart, bondsman.

Bills, John & Susannah Powell, 7 June 1813; Nelson Anderson, bondsman; R. Powell, wit.

Bingham, Lemuel & Jane M. Miller, 5 Dec 1821; Philo White, bondsman; E. Allemong, wit.

Binning, Jacob & Nancy Rowan, 7 Nov 1792; John Braly, bondsman; Jos. Chambers, wit.

Birckhead, Eleazer R. & Margaret Allemong, 13 March 1834; C. B. Wheeler, bondsman; Wm. Locke, wit.

Birckhead, James C. H. & Margaret Coughenour, 18 May 1853; married 20 May 1853 by A. Baker, Pastor of the 1st Presbyterian Church, Salisbury.

Bird, Anthony & Polly Chavis, 2 Aug 1828; Jno Kennedy, bondsman; J. H. Hardie, wit.

Bird, Ervine & Elizabeth Brown, 25 Dec 1844; Thomas Rymer, bondsman; John H. Hardie, Jr., wit.

Bird, Jacob & Caroline Butner, 6 Sept 1838; Adam Brown, bondsman; S. Lemly Jr., wit.

Bird, John & Nancy Allen, 11 Feb 1850; Miles Rusher, bondsman.

Bird, Michael & Caty Foster, 16 March 1812; Henry Allemong, bondsman; Jno Giles, C. C., wit.

Bird, Peter & Diday Valentine, 1 Feb 1819; Miles Washam, bondsman.

Bird, Peter & Suckey Steel, 24 March 1827; J. H. Hardie, bondsman.

Bird, Valentine & Caty Caisey, 14 Aug 1815; David Woodson, bondsman; Geo Dunn, wit.

Bird, William & Jenny Lewis, 2 April 1797; Simon Lewis, bondsman; Jno Rogers, wit.

Bishop, Robert & Mary Chadwick, 29 Oct 1799; Wheeler Chadwick, bondsman; Wm. Melborn, wit.

Bistow, Thomas & Elizabeth Murphy, 7 June 1769; Jas. Craige, bondsman.

Blace (Blaze), David & Elizabeth Wenkler, 31 May 1788; Heinrich Winkler, bondsman; William Alexander, wit.

Black, Adam (Adam Schwartz) & Barberry Biesher, 18 May 1814; Johann Fus, bondsman; Silas Peace, wit.

Black, Calvin M. & Mary Rebecca Kerr, 13 July 1862; A. J. Phillips, bondsman; Obadiah Woodson, wit. married 14 July 1862 by William M. Kincaid, J. P.

Black, Daniel & Unicy James, 7 Sept 1823; Peter Rectton, bondsman; Joseph Hanes, J. P., wit.

Black, David & Maria Wise, 13 July 1850; Charles Klutts, bondsman.

Black, George & Rachel Withrow, 24 Sept 1766 (from abstract); Samuel Withrow, John Carson, bondsman; Thomas Frohock, wit.

Black, Hazel & Bitsey Daniel, 2 July 1803; John Wilcox, bondsman; A. L. Osborn, D. C., wit.

Black, Henry & Sylva Daniel, 21 Aug 1802; John Boon, bondsman; A. L. Osborn, D. C., wit.

Black, Jacob Junr & Euley Copple, 21 March 1822; Jacob Fouts, bondsman; David Mock, wit.

Black, John & Sarah Humphryes, 13 Oct 1832; Wm Baity Jr.,
bondsman; J. Tomlinson, J. P., wit.

Black, Robert & Eleanor Russell, 5 March 1762; Henry Horah,
John Cussens, bondsmen; Will Reed, wit.

Black, William & Sally Emerson, 15 Jan 1811; William H. Ker,
bondsman; Reuben Emerson, wit.

Black, Wm & Susana Bollen, 31 Jan 1811; John Ross, bondsman;
Jas Morgan, J. P., wit.

Blackburn, Harbert & Martha Norton(?), 4 March 1779; John
Brandon, bondsman; William R. Davie, wit.

Blackwelder, Charles & Elizabeth Yost, 12 April 1841; Leonard
Overcash, bondsman; Susan T. Giles, wit.

Blackwelder, Charles & Catherine Teele, 3 Oct 1842; Alexander
Bost, bondsman; David Kerns, wit.

Blackwelder, Christian & Elizabeth Hough, 17 Apr 1810; Leonard
Overcash, bondsman; Jno Giles, C. C., wit.

Blackwelder, Christian & Mary Willeford, 28 Oct 1844; John
Overcash Jr., bondsman; J. H. Hardie, wit.

Blackwelder, Ely & Nancy Brown, 18 Dec 1846; Burton Brown,
bondsman; John H. Hardie Jr., wit.

Blackwelder, E. R. & Jane C. Lowrance, 4 June 1864; George E.
Bostian, bondsman; Obadiah Woodson, wit.

Blackwelder, Henry C. & Mary E. Stirewalt, 19 Feb 1866; J. C.
Rodgers, bondsman; H. N. Woodson, wit.

Blackwelder, John & Sarah Krider, 23 Dec 1835; Joseph Cook,
bondsman; J. H. Hardie, wit.

Blackwelder, Samson T. & Mary A. Stirewalt, 6 Sept 1865; Samuel
Deal, bondsman; Horatio N. Woodson, wit.

Blackwelder, William A. & Lydia Bostain, 5 Feb 1855; Julius M.
Heilig, bondsman; James E. Kerr, wit. married 13 Feb 1855
by D. B. Bradshaw, J. P.

Blackwell, Benjamin & Sophia Shuman, 12 Oct 1816; Jacob Riblin,
bondsman; Jno Giles, C. C., wit.

Blackwell, Benjamin & Elizabeth H. Thomason, 23 Feb 1843;
Hezekiah Turner, bondsman.

Blackwell, Benjamin & Amanda Trexler, 16 Jan 1847; Jno H. Hardie,
bondsman; John H. Hardie Jr., wit.

Blackwell, James & Elizabeth M. Johnston, 27 Feb 1839, N. F.
Hall, bondsman; John Giles, wit.

Blackwell, John & Nelly Sanders, 1 Feb 1809; Robert Wood,
bondsman; A. L. Osborne, wit.

Blackwell, John & Jemima Ann Dobbin, 26 Feb 1857; Jos. E. Dobbin,
bondsman; James E. Kerr, wit. married 26 Feb 1857 by J. J.
Summerell, J. P.

Blackwell, John & Pauline C. Wise, 16 Dec 1857; William A. Wise, bondsman; J. S. Myers, wit. married 16 Dec 1857 by S. J. Peeler, J. P.

Blackwell, Joseph & Sarah A. Howard, 8 Dec 1831; Robert Newton Craige, bondsman; Hy Giles, wit.

Blackwell, William & Sarah M. Thomason, 29 Aug 1837; Burgess Thomason, bondsman; R. Jones, wit.

Blackwood, John & Mahetable Latham, 18 Jan 1832; Ephram Gaither, bondsman; Thomas McNeely, J. P., wit.

Blads, Isaac & Polly Gatreen, 11 Nov 1808; Green Gatberry, bondsman; A. L. Osborne, wit.

Blaids, Edward & Sally Nichols, 31 July 1815; Jonathan Merrell, bondsman; Jno Giles C. C., wit.

Blair, James & _____; Hy Giles, bondsman; Matt: Troy, wit.

Blaiz, Jacob & Peggy Billings, 10 March 1813; Alfred Harris, bondsman; Geo Dunn, wit.

Blake, Joseph & Sarah Elrod, 2 April 1816; John Markland, bondsman; Thos Hampton, wit.

Blake, Thomas & Susanna Elrod, 7 Oct 1809; Jno Alford, bondsman; W. Ellis, wit.

Blakemore, Thomas & Anne Corneleson, 6 Sept 1774; Garrett Corneleson, bondsman; Ad: Osborn, wit.

Blaze--see also Blaiz, Blace

Blaze, George & Hannah Flemmong, 20 Nov 1821; John N. Smoot, bondsman; Milo A. Giles, wit.

Blaze, John & Winney Lovelace, 31 July 1816; Isaac Simpson, bondsman; Jno Giles, C. C., wit.

Bloomfield, David & Rachael Barkley, 21 Oct 1791; Wilson Macay, bondsman; Chn. Harris, wit.

Blue, Archbald & Martha Forest, 18 July 1791; Moses Bellah, bondsman; C. Caldwell, D. C., wit.

Blue, Douglass & Charity Hill, 18 May 1791; Moses Bellah, bondsman; Charles Caldwell, D. C., wit.

Blue, James & Polly Bullen, 18 Feb 1824; Daniel Clary, bondsman.

Blue, James & Christena Correll, 22 Sept 1846; John Glover, bondsman; J. H. Hardie, wit.

Bluster, Harvey & Susannah E. Waggoner, 4 March 1862; Jacob B. Wilhelm, bondsman; Obadiah Woodson, wit. married 6 March 1862 by Jno Carrigan, J. P.

Bluster, Hervy & Sally Uenis, 9 April 1839; Peter Peninger, bondsman; John Giles, wit.

Bodenhamer, Christian & Temperance Danniel, 19 Sept 1810; George Bodenhamer, bondsman; S. Davis, J. P., wit.

Bodenhamer, Jacob & Elizabeth Spurgins, 1 Jan 1792; Peter
Bodenhamer, bondsman; Jno Monro, wit.

Bodenhamer, Jacob & Nancy Crouch 25 Dec 1811; John Bodenhamer,
bondsman; Sol. Davis, J. P., wit.

Bodenhamer, Peter & Elizabeth Goss, 1 March 1813; Joseph Goss,
bondsman; E. Morgan, wit.

Bodenhemer, William & Mary Welch, 7 Aug 1808; John Odell,
bondsman.

Boger, Daniel & Eda Coble, 2 Jan 1838; Mathias Boger, bondsman;
E. R. Birckhead, wit.

Boger, David & Polly Josey, 14 Dec 1833; William Murphy, bondsman; Jno Giles, wit.

Boger, George & Sophia Stirewalt, 18 Feb 1834; Adam Roseman,
bondsman; Wm. Locke, wit.

Boger, Jacob & Caty Corl, 12 Sept 1800; Thomas Goodman, bondsman; J. Brem, wit.

Boger, Jacob & Barbara Hartline, 25 Aug 1821; Frederick Holshouser,
bondsman; George Locke, wit.

Boger, John & Leah Holshouser, 8 March 1852; J. M. Goodman,
bondsman; J. S. Myers, wit.

Boger, John & Mary Ann Smith, 22 Jan 1831; Frederick Stirewalt,
bondsman; Jno H. Hardie, wit.

Boger, Moses & Margaret E. Klutts, 17 Jan 1866; Horatio N.
Woodson, bondsman.

Boggs, Andrew & Sally Daniel, 27 Jan 1835; Otho Hartman, bondsman; Jno H. Hardie, wit.

Boggs, Jesse & Terisa Hartman, 11 Feb 1835; West H. Hartman,
bondsman; Jno H. Hardie, wit.

Bogle, Peter & Caty Trutman, 10 Dec 1812; Philip Cruse, bondsman; Jno Giles, C. C., wit.

Bolch, Jacob & Sollomy Grime, 21 March 1775; George Louman,
bondsman; Ad: Osborn, wit.

Bolen, William L. & Eliza Russell, 19 Sept 1846; Geo M. Weant,
bondsman; Jno H. Hardie, wit.

Boler--see Boulwar

Boles, E. L. & Eliza Casper, 1 Aug 1842; Jno H. Hardie, bondsman.

Bolin, Charles & Sophia Eller, 16 Jan 1826; Abraham Lentz, bondsman.

Bolin, James & Sarah McKnight, 24 April 1797; Jno Rogers,
bondsman; Jno Rogers, wit.

Bollinger, Heinrich & Mary Savits, 20 Dec 1778; Georg Savitz,
bondsman; Willm. R. David, wit.

Bollinger, Jacob & Caty Savits, 15 June 1784; George Savits, bondsman; Hugh Magoune, wit.

Bone, John & Rebeca Potts, 24 Oct 1787; Henry Potts, bondsman; ~Dd. Caldwell, wit.

Bone, William & Elizabeth Potts, 10 March 1781; James Potts, bondsman; Ad: Osborn, wit.

Bone, William & Margret Lansden, 25 Feb 1783; Robert Lansden, bondsman; Ad: Osborn, wit.

Booe, Benjamin & Sally Arrowood, 14 April 1800; Philip Harwood, bondsman; E. J. Osborn, D. C., wit.

Booe, Daniel & Polley Dowlin, 14 April 1806; Richmond Bailey, bondsman; Jn March Sr., wit.

Booe, Daniel & Fanar March, 5 Dec 1812; John Nail Jr., bondsman; Jno March Sr., wit.

Booe, George & Elizabeth Cline, 24 Aug 1830; Thomas Hicks, bondsman; Hy Giles, wit.

Booe, Greenberry & Elizabeth Casey, 11 Aug 1832; Richmond Casey, bondsman; J. Tomlinson, wit.

Booe, Jacob & Fanny Glascock, 25 Dec 1799(?); Phillip Baker, bondsman; Edwin J. Osborn, wit.

Booe, John & Elizabeth Chesher, 15 Jan 1814; James Austin, bondsman; Jn March Sr., wit.

Booe, Philip & Ellendar Sain, 29 Dec 1819; Wiley Sain, bondsman; R. Powell, wit.

Booe, Ruliff & Mary Bushellson, 9 March 1776; John Hunter, bondsman; Ad: Osborn, wit.

Booe, William & Sarah Wellman, 21 Oct 1833; Wilson Rose, bondsman; L. R. Rose, J. P., wit.

Boolph, Thomas & Mary Harison, 20 Jan 1783; Abner Scutor, bondsman; William Crawford, wit.

Boon, John & Polly Wells, 6 Sept 1803; Samuel Little, bondsman; A. L. Osborn, D. C., wit.

Boone, Benjamin & Mary Wilson, 25 Feb 1783; Ebenezer Pratt, bondsman.

Boone, John & Martha Quin, (abstract has 19 Oct 1768); Jas Cooper, bondsman; Thos Frohock, wit.

Booth, Zachariah & _____, 22 Aug 1795; Matt: Troy, bondsman; Matt: Troy, wit.

Boshart, Jacob & Ann Fullenwider, 22 Dec 1798; Henry Follenwider, bondsman; J. Troy, wit.

Bosock, C. & Patsy Griffin, 29 Dec 1865; James H. Collins, bondsman; Obadiah Woodson, wit.

Bosock, Christian & Patsy Griffin, 30 Dec 1865; Noah Peeler, bondsman; Obadiah Woodson, wit.

Boss, Andrew & Jeroma Miller, 15 Sept 1845; Henry F. Miller, bondsman; Jno H. Hardie, wit.

Boss, David & Patsey Brown, 25 Nov 1821; Michael Hughs, bondsman; Ams. Wright, wit.

Bost, Abraham & Catharine Quillman, 19 Oct 1847; J. L. Beard, bondsman; John H. Hardie Jr., wit.

Bost, Alexander & Martha Walker, 20 March 1843; Matthias Sydes, bondsman; J. H. Hardie, wit.

Bost, Alexander & Catharine R. Leazar, 13 Sept 1847; John Yost, bondsman; J. H. Hardie, wit.

Bost, Anderson & Eliza Parkes, 25 Feb 1846; Lawrence A. Bringle, bondsman.

Bost, Conrod & Maria Ann Fisher, 31 July 1798; Henry Sossaman, bondsman; Edwin J. Osborn, D. C., wit.

Bost, Daniel & Nancy Barger, 28 May 1833; William Bost, bondsman; Jno H. Hardie, wit.

Bost, David A. & Leah Klutts, 10 March 1855; Philip P. Meroney, bondsman; James E. Kerr, wit.

Bost, George E. & Caroline Klutts, 3 April 1848; Samuel Sifford, bondsman; J. L. Beard, wit.

Bost, Henry & Margret Blackwelder, 14 Dec 1838; Charles Blackwelder, bondsman; John Giles, wit.

Bost, Henry C. & Dorcas E. Fraley, 12 Jan 1865; J. C. Bernhardt, bondsman; Obadiah Woodson, wit.

Bost, Jacob W. & Catherine Miller, 9 April 1860; Tobias Miller, bondsman; John Wilkinson, wit. married 12 April 1860 by Saml Rothrock, Minister of the Gospel in the Ev. Luth. Church.

Bost, John & Sophia Brown, 23 May 1839; Henry W. Brown, bondsman; John Giles, wit.

Bost, John & Elizabeth Overcast, 14 June 1840; Caleb Overcast, bondsman; Susan T. Giles, wit.

Bost, John & Elizth. C. Miller, 13 June 1843; Daniel D. Ridenhour, bondsman; J. H. Hardie, wit.

Bost, Levi & Caty Remer, 26 Nov 1827; Moses Remer, bondsman; J. H. Hardie, wit.

Bost, Moses A. & Caroline Beaver, 3 June 1850; Esrom Weaver, bondsman; James E. Kerr, wit.

Bost, Reuben W. & Catharine E. Brown, 9 Oct 1854; Joseph Beaver, bondsman; James E. Kerr, wit. married 12 Oct 1854 by Saml. Rothrock, Minister of the Gospel in the Ev. Luth. Church.

Bost, William & Catharine Goodhart of Anson County, 19 Jan 1762; William Williams, John Johnston, bondsmen; Will Reed, Willm. Carson, wit.

Bostain, Jacob & Patsy Salmons, 7 June 1808; Jno Mohan, bondsman; D. M. Nesbit, wit.

Bostain, James & Elizabeth Fink, 26 Nov 1808; Jacob Bostain, bondsman; A. L. Osborn, D. C., wit.

Bostan, Michael & Nancy Graham, 10 April 1839; William E. Barber, bondsman; Abel Cowan, J. P., wit.

Bostian, Aaron & Mina Lovy Ann Strup, 22 Feb 1858; Enos Sechler, bondsman; James E. Kerr, wit. married 25 Feb 1858 by Rev. B. C. Nall.

Bostian, Alexander & Mary E. Smith, 18 May 1852; Michael Bostian, bondsman; J. S. Myers, wit. married 20 May 1852 by Saml. Rothrock, Minister of the Gospel in the Ev. Luth. Church.

Bostian, Alpheus J. & Margaret C. Lyerly, 17 Feb 1858; Geo. E. Bostian, bondsman; John Wilkinson, wit. married 25 Feb 1858 by Jas. M. Wagner.

Bostian, Andreas & Sarah Hunchparier, 25 May 1775; Gorg Savitz, bondsman.

Bostian, Andrew & Christiana Krisster, 6 Feb 1807; Hen: Rattz, bondsman.

Bostian, Andrew & Elizabeth Bostian, 26 Oct 1839; Henry Smith, bondsman.

Bostian, Andrew & Eliza E. Upright, 22 March 1862; James Leazar, bondsman; Obadiah Woodson, wit. married 22 March 1862 by D. A. Davis, J. P.

Bostian, Andrew & Esther Voils, 11 Sept 1858; E. R. Blackwelder, bondsman; James E. Kerr, wit. married 16 Sept 1858 by W. A. Houck, J. P.

Bostian, Andrew Jr. & Sophia Shuping, 4 Jan 1831; Philip Litacan, bondsman; Hy Giles, wit.

Bostian, Andrew A. & Louisa Beaver, 26 Feb 1857; married by Saml Rothrock, Minister of the Gospel in the Ev. Luth. Church. (no bond, minister's return only).

Bostian, Andrew A. & Rose Ann Klutts, 3 Jan 1861; Alexander Klutts, bondsman; Wm. Locke, wit.

Bostian, Andrew L. & Elizabeth Maria Freeze, 21 Jan 1861; W. A. Walton, bondsman married 29 Jan 1861 by D. R. Bradshaw, J. P.

Bostian, Charles & Cena Eagle, 10 Feb 1846; John Eagle, bondsman.

Bostian, D. M. & Charlotte E. Heilig, 17 March 1866; J. A. Bostian, bondsman; Obadiah Woodson, wit.

Bostian, Daniel & Catharine Litiker, 29 April 1844; John Litaker, bondsman; J. H. Hardie, wit.

Bostian, David & Elizabeth Smith, 19 April 1831; Michael Bostian, bondsman; Jno H. Hardie, wit.

Bostian, Eli & Margaret Yost, 17 July 1851; Henry C. Goodman, bondsman; James E. Kerr, wit.

Bostian, Jacob & Caty Shuping, 20 Feb 1818; Peter Ketner, bondsman; Jno Giles, wit.

Bostian, Jacob & Solomy Stirewalt, 21 Feb 1815; Jacob Shuping, bondsman; Geo Dunn, wit.

Bostian, Jacob & Mary Shaver, 29 Dec 1857; N. N. Fleming, bondsman; J. S. Myers, wit. married 31 Dec 1857 by James M. Wagner, Past.

Bostian, Jacob & Mary Kifeneck, 8 April 1859; J. C. Roseman, bondsman; John Wilkinson, wit. married 14 April 1859 by Milo A. J. Roseman, J. P.

Bostian, Jacob & Polly Weaver, 28 Feb 1829; Solomon Weaver, bondsman.

Bostian, Jacob & Mary L. Lynn, 22 April 1848; Thomas T. Maxwell, bondsman.

Bostian, Jacob & Sarah Ramer, 13 June 1839; Mathew Pinkston, bondsman; Jno Giles, wit.

Bostian, James A. & Margaret E. Shuping, 7 Feb 1859; George N. Sloop, bondsman.

Bostian, John & Mary Duke, 17 July 1820; Phillp Cruse, bondsman.

Bostian, John & Elizabeth Correkin, 7 Nov 1844; John Robinson, bondsman; Jno Giles, wit.

Bostian, John & Polly Eliza Yost, 23 Dec 1844; Michael Bostian, bondsman; John H. Hardie, Jr., wit.

Bostian, Jno W. & Margt. E. Goodman, 5 May 1845; Moses A. Goodman, bondsman; Jno H. Hardie, wit.

Bostian, Michael & Sally Duke, 29 April 1828; Jacob Bostian, bondsman; Jno H. Hardie, wit.

Bostian, Michael & Catharine Roseman, 16 May 1842; Charles Bostian, bondsman; Wm(?) Sneed, wit.

Bostian, Michael & Teany Casper, 2 Feb 1822; Johannes Smith, bondsman; Hy Giles, wit.

Bostian, Philip & _____, 12 Dec 1796; Adam Casper, bondsman; Humphry Marshall, wit.

Boston, Andrew L. & Malissa Holbrook, 20 March 1848; Andrew L. Boston, bondsman; J. H. Hardie, wit.

Boston, Andrew L. & Eliza J. Smith, 18 Dec 1849; Andre(w) Bostian, bondsman; J. S. Myers, wit.

Boston, Andy & Sally Sefford, 3 March 1832; John Sefferd, bondsman; J. H. Hardie, wit.

Boston, David & Barbarra Lydekker, 3 Nov 1789; Peter Faust, bondsman; Evan Alexander, wit.

Boston, David & Polly Litaker, 16 Sept 1834; Daniel Willhelm, bondsman; H. Bitton, wit.

Boston, George & Mary Korreher, 22 May 1805; George Raimer, bondsman; A. L. Osborn, wit.

Boston, George & Judah Cope, 4 Jan 1820; John Shive, bondsman; Hy Giles, wit.

Bostian, Jesse & Lydia Shulzbarger, 28 Feb 1820; James Correll, bondsman.

Boston, John & S. A. Repult(?), _____; Ge. Gillespie , bondsman.

Boston, John W. & Sophia Sechler, 24 March 1851; Jesse Sechler, bondsman; J. S. Myers, wit.

Boston, Peter & Betsey Casper, 29 Nov 1825; Peter Ketner, bondsman; Jno Giles, wit.

Boswell, Gustavus & Polly Bozwell, 25 Oct 1820; Daniel J. Smoot, bondsman; R. Powell, wit.

Boswell, William & Mary Cole, 18 Nov 1818; Martin May, bondsman; Roberts Nanny, wit.

Bouchell, Robt M. & Jane G. Polk, 1 May 1838; Wm. Locke, bondsman; W. Chambers, wit.

Boucher, Charles & Barbara E. Sloop, 7 Aug 1865; Rudolph S. W. Sechler, bondsman; Obadiah Woodson, wit.

Boulware, John & Elizabeth Sparks, 5 Nov 1801; Hardy Jones, bondsman; Jno Brem, D. C., wit.

Boushell, Thomas F. & Goodwin Torrence, 16 April 1822; John B. Tate, bondsman.

Bowden, John & Elizabeth James, 2 Dec 1802; James James, bondsman; Osborn, D. C., wit.

Bowen, John & Mary Moore, 23 Dec 1785; Val. Beard, bondsman.

Bowers, Barnabas & Judah Yarbrough, 25 ___ 1802; Henry Smith, bondsman; J. McEwen, wit.

Bowers, David & Catherin Grimes, 29 July 1821; John Miller, bondsman; Silas Peace, wit.

Bowers, Henry & Susannah Frees, 17 Dec 1808; George Hartman, bondsman; A. L. Osborn, wit.

Bowers, James & Barbara Bowers, 10 May 1758; Thos Forster, bondsman.

Bowers, Malachi & Sarah Gheen, 28 Dec 1813; James Rex, bondsman; Jno Giles, C. C., wit.

Bowie, John K. & Carrie Calloway, 15 Jan 1861; John L. Peden, James F. Johnston, bondsmen.

Bowles, William W. & Rachel R. Brown, 10 Nov 1841; Jas. D. Smith, bondsman; J. S. Johnston, wit.

Bowlwin, Thomas & Mary Cooke, 22 Feb 1790; William Aldredge, bondsman.

Bowman, Daniel & Polly Simmons, 14 Jan 1799; Henry Giles, bondsman; Edwin J. Osborn, wit.

Bowman, James H. & Elizabeth S. McCorkle, 9 Aug 1825; Thomas L. Cowan, bondsman; Hy Giles, wit.

Bowman, William & Elizabeth McFarson, 14 May 1785; John McPherson, bondsman; Ad: Osborn, wit.

Boyd, Alexander & Jane Biles, 2 Nov 1820; Charles L. Bowers, bondsman; Milo A. Giles, wit.

Boyd, Hugh & Jean Boyd, 13 Dec 1782; Thos Anderson, bondsman; William Crawford, wit.

Boyd, John & Hannah Boyd, 16 Feb 1788; Thos Thompson, bondsman; Ad: Osborn, wit.

Boyden, Abram (colored) & Alice Spindle (colored), 21 Aug 1865; Obadiah Woodson, clerk; married 23 Aug 1865 by J. B. Laurens, Min.

Boyden, Nathaniel & Jane C. Mitchell, 2 Dec 1845; Jere Clarke, bondsman.

Boyer, John & Ann Holder, 2 Nov 1834; Apton Slater, bondsman; Thomas McNeely, J. P., wit.

Bozsworth, Isaiah W. & Lane Ann Griffin, 17 May 1855; Tillman Austin, bondsman; James E. Kerr, clerk.

Bozworth, David & Polly Verble, 9 March 1813; Ezekiel East, bondsman; Geo Dunn, wit.

Brace, Samuel & Dorothy Davis, 4 Feb 1778; William Brandon, bondsman.

Bracken, Thomas & Mary Bunonger, 21 March 1788; William Butler, bondsman; J. McEwen, wit.

Bracket, William & Mary Boo, 12 March 1796; James Brackin, bondsman; J. Troy, wit.

Brackin, John & Polley Martin, 6 April 1816; Joshua Briniger, bondsman; Jn March Sr., wit.

Brackin, James & Sally Jefferys, 30 Sept 1795; Samuel Brackin, bondsman; J. Troy, D. C., wit.

Bracking, Saml & Ann Breneger, 20 Dec 1789; William Butler, bondsman; Basil Gaither, wit.

Braddock, Isaac & Nancey Lacy, 11 April 1820; John Wood, bondsman; Hy Giles, wit.

Braddy, David & Rebecca Earnhart, 5 Oct 1857; Allen Trexler, bondsman; Levi Trexler, wit. married 8 Oct 1857 by Saml Rothrock, Minister of the Gospel in the Ev. Luth. Church.

Braddy, Stephen & Christena Hoffner, 28 June 1830; John Braddy, bondsman, J. H. Hardie, wit.

Bradford, John & E. A. Atwell, 27 Oct 1837; Obadiah Woodson, bondsman.

Bradley, David & Ellinor Clark, 12 March 1804; Henry Helford, bondsman; Jn March Sr., wit.

Bradley, John W. & Nancy Long, 3 Feb 1813; Alexander Frohock, bondsman; Geo Dunn, wit.

Bradshaw, David B. & Margaret Miller, 4 May 1839; Jacob Shuliberinger, bondsman; Jno Giles, wit.

Bradshaw, Latan F. & Julia Ann V. Correll, 5 April 1858; William Overman, bondsman; John Wilkinson, wit. married 6 April 1858 by S. C. Alexander.

Bradshaw, Orston (Austin) & Harriet Elers, 26 Feb 1823; Fredrick Foard, bondsman; John P. Hodgens, J. P., wit.

Bradshaw, Robert & Betsy Harden(?), 3 April 1790; Dugless Haden, bondsman; C. Caldwell, D. C., wit.

Bradshaw, Robert & Elizabeth Burris, 14 June 1813; Frederick Foard, bondsman; Jno Giles, C. C., wit.

Bradshaw, Robert & Betsey Foard, 8 Jan 1817; John March Sr., bondsman; Roberts Nanny, wit.

Bradshaw, Robert & Sarah McCreary, 16 Sept 1829; John Foard, bondsman.

Bradshaw, Robert & Jane Leppard, 23 April 1846; Robert Ellis, bondsman; J. H. Hardie, Jr., wit.

Bradshaw, William H. & Elizabeth Humphries, 25 March 1819; Ezra Allemong, bondsman; Jno Giles, wit.

Brady, Calvin M. & Clemintine C. Miller, 13 July 1861; married 14 July 1861 by Levi Trexler, J. P. (return only, no bond).

Brady, John & Sarah Hoffner, 16 Feb 1829; Andrew Earnhart, bondsman.

Brady, John A. & Leah Stoner, 6 Jan 1866.

Braley, Walter & Honour Carson, 21 Feb 1788; Hugh Carson, bondsman; J. McEwin, wit.

Braly, John & Mary Beatie, 5 May 1783.

Braly, Jno & Mary Carson, 22 May 1790; William St. Carson, bondsman; C. Caldwell, D. C., wit.

Braly, Rowan C. & Elizabeth B. Erwin, 24 Feb 1823; Danl. W. Coleman, bondsman.

Braly, William & Margaret Woods, 8 ___ 1793; Jno Braly, bondsman.

Brandon, Benjn & Mary Knox, 4 Feb 1788; James Wilson, bondsman; Davd Crawford, wit.

Brandon, Christopher & Sarah Newman, 15 Oct 1789; John Brandon, bondsman.

Brandon, George & Rebecca Neely, 22 March 1779; Wm. Temple Coles, bondsman; Ad: Osborn, wit.

Brandon, George & Sidney McGuire, 24 Jan 1797; George McGuire, bondsman; Jno Rogers, wit.

Brandon, John & Jane Knox, 10 March 1789; Absalom Knox, bondsman; R. Martin for Ad: Osborn, C. C., wit.

Brandon, John & Mary Cowan, 20 Dec 1814; Stephen Cowen, bondsman; Geo Dunn, wit.

Brandon, John & Elizabeth Gibson, 9 May 1821; Joshua Gay, bondsman; Jno Giles, wit.

Brandon, John H. of Cabarrus County & Jane Hagin, 16 Jan 1812; George Miller, bondsman; Matt. Brandon, wit.

Brandon, Richard of Cabarras County & Margaret L. Brandon, 16 March 1808; Col. John Brandon, bondsman; Matt. Brandon, wit.

Brandon, Rufus A. & Elizabeth Plummer, 19 Feb 1851; James M. Owen, bondsman; J. S. Myers, wit.

Brandon, Samuel & Polly Morning, 5 April 1824; Jesse Hellard, bondsman; Hy Giles, wit.

Brandon, William & Elizabeth Elrod, 27 Jan 1818; Solomon Elrod, bondsman; Thos Hampton, wit.

Brandon, William & Jane Brandon, 9 Feb 1818; Joseph A. Brandon, bondsman; Jno Giles, wit.

Brandon, William & Hannah Erwin, 6 Sept 1775; David Woodson, bondsman; Dd. Flowers, wit.

Brandon, Wm. C. & Susanna Torrence, 22 Sept 1841; Jacob Willhelm, bondsman; J. S. Myers, wit.

Branick, James & Sarah Sylvia, 9 April 1830; Wilie Jones, bondsman; L. R. Rose, J. P., wit.

Brantley, William W. & Mary Ann Davis, 31 Dec 1858(sic); Charles A. Rose, bondsman; married 31 Dec 1859 (sic), by H. S. Robard, J. P.

Brauley, Samuel R. & Malinda C. Barr, 12 March 1860; Daniel M. Lefler, bondsman; D. R. Bradshaw, wit. married 14 March 1860 by D. R. Bradshaw, J. P.

Brawley, Samuel M. & Mary E. Hager, 8 April 1857; R. B. Gray, bondsman; J. S. Myers, wit. married 9 April 1857 by J. F. McCorkle, J. P.

Brawley, Samuel M. & Nancy E. Rumple, 9 Nov 1855; John S. E. Hart, bondsman; J. S. Myers, wit. married 4 Dec 1855 by John L. Hedrick, J. P.

Brazier, Laban & Deborah Dial, 29 Aug 1804; William Hunt, bondsman; J. Hunt, wit.

Brazil, William & Mary Hall, 6 Oct 1802; Abram Trott, bondsman.

Bready, Archabil & Margret Erwin, 28 May 1779; Samuel Irwin, bondsman; Ad: Osborn, wit. consent from George Irwin, father of Margret, 27 May 1779.

Bready, R. A. & Martha Hart, 21 June 1856; J. S. E. Hart, bondsman; J. S. Myers, wit.

Bready, R. M. & Margaret E. J. Hart, 18 Aug 1852; Wm. McHaynes, bondsman; J. S. Myers, wit.

Brem, John M. & Nancy Barber, 28 Nov 1844; Wm. Pierce, bondsman; John H. Hardie Jr., wit.

Brenninger, John & Lucretia Linville, 9 Feb 1779; Samuel Bryan, bondsman; William R. David, wit.

Brennly, John Henry & Catharine Easter, 4 Aug 1793; Peter Easton, bondsman; Jno Monro, wit.

Brevard, John & Mary Dusenberry, 9 Jan 1815; James Huie, bondsman; Geo Dunn, wit.

Brevard, John Junr & Hannah Thompson, 22 Dec 1783; Ad: Brevard, bondsman; T. H. McCaule, wit.

Brewer, Benjamin & Lidia Nolen, 30 July 1800; Stephen Nolen, bondsman; John Brem, wit.

Brewer, William & Mary Shumaker, 10 June 1790; Richard Speakes, bondsman; Basil Gaither, wit.

Briggs, Edmund & Ruthy Dobins, 13 Jan 1823; Alexander McBroom, bondsman.

Briggs, Edmund & Commilla Rary, 23 July 1857; H. H. Grindstaff, bondsman; J. S. Myers, wit. married 29 July 1857 by Moses Powlass, J. P.

Briggs, Edmund & Prucilla Dobbins, 27 Feb 1827; Richard Graham, bondsman; J. H. Hardie, wit.

Briggs, John & Julia M. Burkhead, 10 May 1855; Jacob Lyerly, bondsman; J. S. Myers, wit.

Briggs, John & Catharine Swan, 25 Oct 1826; Alexander Dobbins, bondsman; Hy Giles, wit.

Briggs, Nathan & Mary Scriviner, 29 Sept 1779; Thomas Briggs, bondsman; Jo. Bravard, wit.

Briggs, Thomas & Esther Parks, 19 Oct 1792; Simon Watson, bondsman; Jos. Chambers, D. C., wit.

Brigs, William & Elizabeth Henley, 21 Oct 1801; Jacob Redwine, bondsman; Jno Brem, wit.

Briles, George & Barbra Coonrod, 25 Nov 1793; David Coonrod, bondsman; Jno Monro, wit.

Briles, Joseph D. & Mary Bolen, 13 July 1858; Wm. A. Lyerly, bondsman; John Wilkinson, wit. married 15 July 1858 by J. H. Brown, J. P.

Brindel, John & Sary Mullekin, 30 Jan 1820; James Johnson, bondsman; Saml Jones, J. P., wit.

Brindle, Abraham & Alice Brown, 5 Nov 1811; John Hanes, bondsman; H. Ellis, J. P., wit.

Brinegar, Jno A. & Ann Brown, 13 Oct 1832; Ephraim Gaither, bondsman; Thomas McNeely, J. P., wit.

Bringer, Jacob & Mary Pock (or Prock), 5 Dec 1768; Mathias M. Prock, William Brown, bondsmen; John Frohock, wit. consent from Margert Pock, mother of Mary, 5 Dec 1768.

Bringle, Christian & Catharin Agner, 23 Jan 1805; John Weaver, bondsman; A. L. Osborn, D. C., wit.

Bringle, Christopher & Elizabeth Lukey, 22 April 1858; J. S. Myers, D. C., wit. married 24 April 1858 by E. Mauney, J. P.

Bringle, David L. & Harriet E. Verble, 19 June 1862; P. P. Maroney, bondsman; Obadiah Woodson, wit.

Bringle, John & Crissy Cauble, 25 June 1831; John Shuman Jr., bondsman; Jno H. Hardie, wit.

Bringle, John C. & Mollie J. Boggs, 3 Feb 1866; William A. Walton, bondsman; Obadiah Woodson, wit.

Bringle, Lawrence A. & Elizabeth Shepherd, 25 Feb 1846; Jacob S. Myers, bondsman; J. M. Turner, wit.

Bringle, Michael A. & Carrie H. Cox, 28 March 1860; David L. Bringle, bondsman; James E. Kerr, clerk. married 28 March 1860 by Thomas W. Guthrie, Minister of the Gospel, M. E. Church, South.

Bringle, Nicholas & Dorothy Kesler, 28 Dec 1854; J. N. File, bondsman; H. W. Hill, J. P., wit.

Bringle, Nicholes & Rosa Agner, 15 May 1843; Green Miller, bondsman; J. H. Hardie, wit.

Bringle, Peter & Peggy Hess, 14 Dec 1812; Hu. Horah, bondsman; Jno Giles, C. C., wit.

Bringle, Peter & Nancy Verble, 31 Jan 1834; Jacob Fisher, bondsman.

Bringle, Thomas & Caty Limbough, 20 Dec 1820; Daniel Limbough, bondsman; Milo A. Giles, wit.

Brinkle, Nicholes & Nancy Ketchey, 4 Sept 1841; Miles Miller, bondsman; Susan T. Giles, wit.

Brinkley, Michael & Sarah Wood, 28 April 1814; John Brinkley, bondsman; Joseph Clarke, wit.

Brinkley, Richard & Suzanah Davis, 22 Feb 1816; Michael Craver Junr., bondsman; Joseph Clarke, J. P., wit.

Brinkley, William D. & Leitia Stewart, 29 Dec 1853; Jesse H. Howard, bondsman; J. S. Myers, wit.

Broadnax, E. T. & A. J. Jones, 18 Dec 1858; H. C. Jones Jr. bondsman; James E. Kerr, wit. married 22 Dec 1858 by T. G. Haughton, Rector of St. Luke's.

Broadway, William & Mary E. Lookabill, 15 July 1813; David
Lookabill, bondsman; Ezra Allemong, wit.

Brock, Thomas & Katharine Hendricks, 8 Nov 1825; Noah Brock,
bondsman; E. Brock, J. P., wit.

Brock, William & Franky Chaffin, 12 July 1822; Wiley Ward,
bondsman; Geo Cotten, wit.

Brockway, William W. & Mary A. McDaniel, 7 Nov 1854; A. H.
Caldwell, bondsman; J. S. Myers, wit.

Brodway, John & Pheby Dancy, 4 Aug 1819; Michael Doaty, bondsman; Jno Giles, wit.

Brogden, Henry & Sarah Cresoon, 22 Aug 1827; Jonah Moore, bondsman; Wm. Hawkins, J. P., wit.

Brogdon, Wm. & Rebekah Wells, 28 Sept 1819; William Wells,
bondsman; R. Powell, wit.

Brooks, Hawkins & Susan Gheen, 30 March 1853; Michael Swicegood,
bondsman; J. S. Myers, wit.

Brooks, Humphrey & Lettice Boleware, 24 Feb 1788; William Wommock,
bondsman; J. McEwin, wit.

Brooks, Samuel & Betsy Rider, 1 Sept 1812; Davould Beck, bondsman; Jno Giles, C. C., wit.

Brookshire, Benjamin & Milly Bingham, 18 July 1796; Boyd Wilson,
bondsman; J. Troy, wit.

Brookshire, Manring & Elizabeth Sludder, 14 Dec 1790, Jesse
Brookshire, bondsman.

Broomhead, James & Sally Gaskey, 4 Sept 1814; Valentine Weaver,
bondsman; Geo Dunn, wit.

Brotherton, Thomas & Mary McLeland, 17 March 1783; John Bowe,
bondsman; T. H. McCaule, wit.

Brougher, Frederick & Mary A. Stork, 25 Dec 1821; Saml. Lemly,
bondsman; Ezra Allemong, wit.

Brown (Braun), Abraham & Mary Hardmon, 27 Jan 1769; Joseph
Hardmon, Michel Waller, bondsmen; Thos Frohock, wit.

Brown (Braun), Abraham & Catherine Hess, 11 March 1811; Henry
Brown, bondsman; Ezra Allemon, wit.

Brown, Abraham & Catherine Bonother, 18 Oct 1784; Charles Dunn,
bondsman; Hu Magoune, wit.

Brown, Adam & Eve Ann Eller, 18 Jan 1853; Tobias Eller, bondsman; J. S. Myers, wit. married 18 Jan 1853 by Obadiah Woodson, J. P.

Brown, Adam & Susan Bird, 17 Jan 1857; Moses Brown, bondsman;
J. S. Myers, wit.

Brown (Braun), Adam & Fanny Thomas, 1 Feb 1820; Jesse West,
bondsman; Jno Giles, wit.

Brown, Adam M. & Mary A. Fesperman, 25 Sept 1857; Saml Reeves Sr., bondsman; J. S. Myers, wit. married 29 Sept 1857 by J. H. Brown, J. P.

Brown, Alexander & Sophia C. Miller, 2 July 1850; James R. McDonald, bondsman; J. S. Myers, wit.

Brown, Alexander & Mary Kistler, 29 Sept 1835; Benjamin Fraley, bondsman; John Giles, wit.

Brown, Alexander & Elizabeth Walton, 15 Dec 1838; Jeremiah M. Brown, bondsman; John Giles, wit.

Brown, Allen & Mary Smitheal (Smithdeal?), 6 April 1841; Jeremiah M. Brown, bondsman; Mary Harrison, wit.

Brown, Andrew & Rosena Willims, 1 April 1837; Solomon Brown, bondsman; Tobias L. Lemly, wit.

Brown, Andrew J. & Catherine T. McCorkle, 9 July 1850; J. D. Ramsey, bondsman; J. S. Myers, wit.

Brown, Andrew J. & Jane A. Potts, 23 Oct 1851; Samuel R. Harrison, bondsman. (bride and groom of Iredell County), married 23 Oct 1851 by H. L. Robards, J. P.

Brown, Archibald M. & Elen Smith, 31 Dec 1833; George W. Smith, bondsman.

Drown, Denjamin & Polly Miller, 31 Oct 1815; William McLean, bondsman; Jno Giles, C. C., wit.

Brown, Benjamin J. & Louisa Parks, 21 May 1846; Wm. R. Allen, bondsman; J. H. Hardie Junr., wit.

Brown, Burton & Hetty Bivins, 25 March 1848; Ely Blackwelder, bondsman; Jno H. Hardie, wit.

Brown, Calvin L. & Letitia Ribelin, 27 Jan 1866; Nathan Brown, bondsman; Obadiah Woodson, wit.

Brown, Calvin S. & Anne E. McConnaughey, 25 May 1847; Jos. F. Chambers, bondsman.

Brown, Charles & Sethey Thomas, 16 July 1814; John Ellis, bondsman; Geo Dunn, wit.

Brown (Braun), Christian & Barbara Troutman, 7 Oct 1794; Adam Troutman, bondsman; J. Troy, D. C., wit.

Brown, Conrod & Patience Penny, (abstract has Oct 1792); David Brown, bondsman; Jo Chambers, wit.

Brown, Daniel & Mary Miller, _____ 1768; William Patton, bondsman; H; McGound, wit.

Brown, Daniel & Ann Rablin, 26 Aug 179_; Martin Rablin, bondsman; Jas Chambers, wit.

Brown, Daniel & Sally Agner, 22 Feb 1820; Jacob Agner, bondsman; Hy Giles, wit.

Brown, Daniel & Sally Eller, 2 Sept 1823; Jacob Brown, bondsman.

Brown, Daniel & Polly Lyerly, 29 Nov 1843; Jacob Brown, bondsman; J. H. Hardie Jr., wit.

Brown, David & Sarah Miller, 16 April 1803; Michel Brown, bondsman; Adlai L. Osborn, D. C., wit.

Brown, David & Peggy Eddleman, 24 Sept 1833; Paul Miller, bondsman; Wm. Locke, wit.

Brown, David & Margt. Lippard, 10 June 1848; Wilson A. Lentz, bondsman; J. H. Hardie, wit.

Brown, Edward W. & Jane G. McConnaughey, 16 Dec 1850; Hand James, bondsman; James E. Kerr, wit.

Brown, G. Henry & M. A. Houston, 29 Jan 1866; Obadiah Woodson, bondsman; H. N. Woodson, wit.

Brown, George & Barbara Wassboug, 2 Jan 1779; Jacob Brown, bondsman; William R. Davie, wit.

Brown, George A. & Maria S. Brown, 14 Aug 1849; Michael L. Brown, bondsman; James W. Kerr, wit.

Brown, George W. & Cornelia R. Long, 27 May 1843; Joseph F. Chambers, bondsman.

Brown, Henry & Mary Egner, 6 Oct 1802; Henry Egner, bondsman; J. McEwen, wit.

Brown, Henry & Patience Anderson, 18 April 1827; Josiah Inglis, bondsman; Wm. Hawkins, J. P., wit.

Brown, Henry & Magdelena Barrier, 28 Jan 1845; Michael L. Brown, bondsman; John H. Hardie Jr., wit.

Brown, Henry L. & Rachael Ann Hampton, 21 Feb 1842; Michael L. Brown, bondsman; J. H. Hardie, wit.

Brown, Henry M. & Mary L. Yost, 25 Jan 1866; Samuel Linn, bondsman; Obadiah Woodson, wit.

Brown, Henry T. & Isabella E. Sloan, 3 June 1854; D. Witt C. Parks, bondsman; J. S. Myers, wit.

Brown, Hugh L. & Mary E. Pinkston, 3 Sept 1858; M. L.McFntire, bondsman; James E. Kerr, wit. married 15 Sept 1858 by L. C. Groseclose.

Brown, Isaiah & Jean McKee, 22 July 1783; Alexr. McKee, bondsman; Ad: Osborn, wit.

Brown, Jacob & Elizabeth Artmire, 29 Aug 1774; Daniel Little, bondsman; Ad. Osborn, wit.

Brown, Jacob & Caty Roseman, 7 May 1802; Daniel Brown, bondsman; Jno Brem, wit.

Brown, Jacob & Anna L. Eddleman, 28 July 1830; David Klutts, bondsman; Jno H. Hardie, wit.

Brown, Jacob & Lewisy Arey, 7 June 1845; Otha Van Pool, bondsman.

Brown, James & Mary A. Shuford, 20 Oct 1851; J. D. Ramsey, bondsman.

Brown, James & Sarah Julian (both colored), 22 Sept 1865; married 22 Sept 1865 by Revd. Wm. Lambeth.

Brown, James & Alice Whitehead (both colored), 12 Oct 1865; married 12 Oct 1865 by J. Rumple, V. D. M.

Brown, James & Sarah Smith, 23 July 1794; Tobias Farror, bondsman; J. Troy, D. C., wit.

Brown, James & Ritter Hampton, 25 March 1812; Benjamin March, bondsman; Jn March Sr., wit.

Brown, Jas. & Fanney Johnston, 19 Aug 1785; Moses Linster, bondsman.

Brown, James H. & Malinda Swink, 14 Sept 1858; W. H. Irby, bondsman; James E. Kerr, wit. married 14 Sept 1858 by J. H. Brown, J. P.

Brown, James L. & Selah S. Ridenour, 9 Jan 1861; John Wilkinson, bondsman; married 10 Jan 1861 by L. C. Groseclose.

Brown, James L. & Catharine Rendleman, 7 July 1835; Jno H. Hardie, bondsman.

Brown, James M. & Elizabeth B. Master, 11 Oct 1826; Edwin McGahey, bondsman; Hy. Giles, wit.

Brown, Jeremiah & Mary Marian, 29 June 1792; Thomas Davis, bondsman; Chs. Caldwell, wit.

Brown, Jeremiah & Elizabeth Holdhouser, 1 April 1825; Andrew Eller, bondsman.

Brown, Jeremiah & Mary Brown, 23 Nov 1825; Andrew Holshouser, bondsman; Hy Giles, wit.

Brown, Jeremiah & Margaret Fraley, 18 Jan 1834; Henry Giles, bondsman.

Brown, Jeremiah M. & Mary E. Lucus, 3 June 1843; Richd. W. Long, bondsman; J. H. Hardie, wit.

Brown, Jeremiah M. & Charlotte Brown, 18 June 1846; John H. Hardie, bondsman.

Brown, John & Elisabeth Brown, 21 July 1788; Hugh Gray, bondsman; Ad: Osborn, wit.

Brown, John & Elizabeth Sanderson, 15 Feb 1802; Philip Brown, bondsman; Jno Brem, wit.

Brown, John & Margaret Josie, 9 April 1796; John Josie, bondsman; Tibby T--Y, wit.

Brown, John & Mary McCulloch, 26 Nov 1788; John Bowman, bondsman; Edmd Yarbrough, wit.

Brown, John & Sarah Beryman, 29 July 1800; Lewis Bryan, bondsman; John Brem wit.

Brown, John & Catharine Wilds, 23 Sept 1823; Adam Brown, bondsman; Hy Giles, wit.

Brown, John & Polly Troutman, 17 March 1827; Adam Brown, bondsman; J. H. Hardie, wit.

Brown, John & Nancy Baits, 3 Feb 1831; James M. Isams(?), bondsman; Wm. Hawkins, wit.

Brown, John C. & Lucretia M. Bringle, 1 Aug 1853; John Y. Rice, bondsman.

Brown, John D. & Louisa Pool, 5 Aug 1841; Wm. Overman, bondsman; D. A. Davis, wit.

Brown, John D. A. & Sarah C. Fisher, 5 Feb 1859; Michael L. Brown, bondsman; married 10 Feb 1859 by John L. Smithdeal.

Brown, John F. & Catharine Smith, 30 Aug 1837; Wm. J. Edwards, bondsman; R. Jones, wit.

Brown, Joseph & Susannah Whitaker, 23 Feb 1785; George Davidson, bondsman.

Brown, Joseph & Fa-ny Roberts, 23 Nov 1823; Thomas Griffin, bondsman; L. R. Rose, J. P., wit.

Brown, Jos. & Chrisy Cauble, 23 Dec 1847; Wm. R. Burge, bondsman; John H. Hardie, Jr., wit.

Brown, Jutsan & Susanna Albright, 17 Feb 1818; Lock Atwell, bondsman; Roberts Nanny, wit.

Brown, Levi & Susanna Kerns, 26 May 1831; Henry Giles, bondsman.

Brown, Levi & Emily Williamson, 31 Dec 1846; Thomas H. Pierce, bondsman; John H. Hardie, Junr., wit.

Brown, Littleton & Luenda Leopard, _____ March 1838; Levi Butner, bondsman; E. R. Birckhead, wit.

Brown, Michael & Mariah Long, 3 April 1817; Tho. L. Cowan, bondsman; Roberts Nanny, wit.

Brown, Michael & Ann Chambers, 15 Nov 1852; Hand James, bondsman; James E. Kerr, wit.

Brown, Michael & Barbary Mowrey, 30 July 1798; Fredrick Miller, bondsman; Edwin J. Osborn, wit.

Brown, Michael & Jane Phillips, 6 Sept 1848; Lewis Jacobs, bondsman; Jno H. Hardie, J. P., wit.

Brown, Michael & Jeane M. Phillips, 27 June 1805; William T. Brown, bondsman; Andrew Kerr, wit.

Brown, Michl. & Crissa Shuping, 23 Jan 1849; Matthias Boger, bondsman.

Brown, Michael L. & Susan Ann Shuping, 31 Oct 1864; Henry Brown, bondsman; Obadiah Woodson, wit.

Brown, Michael L. & Elizabeth Miller, 12 April 1831; Peter Miller, bondsman; Jno A. Giles, wit.

Brown, Michael S. & Susanna Smith, 11 July 1822; David Holdhouser, bondsman.

Brown, Michael S. & Margaret Duke, 21 Aug 1849; J. S. Myers,
bondsman.

Brown, Moses & Margaret Brown, 14 Dec 1854; Meshack Pinkston,
bondsman; J. S. Myers, wit.

Brown, Moses & Jane Lyerly, 5 June 1859; Allison Fink, bondsman;
James E. Kerr, wit. married by _____ Robards, J. P. 5 June
1859.

Brown, Moses & Cathy Swink, 10 June 1797; John Hampton, bondsman; Jno Rogers, wit.

Brown, Moses & Phoebe Biles, 14 Oct 1830; Allen Brown, bondsman.

Brown, Moses A. & Melisa C. Misenheimer, 1 Sept 1852; John W.
Fisher, bondsman; J. S. Myers, wit.

Brown, Moses L. & Latitia Hartman, 3 Aug 1826; Charles L. Bowers,
bondsman; John H. Hardie, wit.

Brown, Nathan & Sally Jones, 26 June 1827; Silas Templeton, wit.

Brown, Peter A. & Eliza S. Lippard, 20 Nov 1856; Eli S. P.
Lippard, bondsman; J. S. Myers, wit. married 26 Nov 1856 by
Saml Rothrock, Minister of the Gospel in the Ev. Luth. Church.

Brown, Peter M. & Christeana E. Crawford, 30 May 1853; Moses L.
Brown, bondsman; J. S. Myers, wit.

Brown, Peter M. & Elizabeth Pool, 2 Jan 1828; Charles L. Bowers,
bondsman.

Brown, Peter M. & Martha Gay, 17 Feb 1835; Alfred Brown, bondsman; Jno H. Hardie, wit.

Brown, Philip & Mary Fraley, 21 Sept 1819; Charles L. Bowers,
bondsman.

Brown, Phillip & Catharine Lintz, 29 Nov 1802; Henry Giles,
bondsman; A. L. Osborn, D. C., wit.

Brown, Phillip & Betsy Hager, 9 June 1813; Joseph Brown, bondsman; Jno Giles, C. C., wit.

Brown, Philip & Rebekah Baker, 1 March 1790; Charles Dunn,
bondsman.

Brown, R. S. & Malvina E. Willeford, 27 May 1865; W. S. Rogers,
bondsman; Obadiah Woodson, wit.

Brown, Richard C. & Mary C. Miller, 22 Jan 1856; Moses Brown,
bondsman; J. S. Myers, wit.

Brown, Richard L. & Nancy E. Agner, 27 Jan 1866; Nathan Brown,
bondsman; Obadiah Woodson, wit.

Brown, Robert & Sophia Barns, 3 June 1820; Thomas Miller,
bondsman; Jno Giles, wit.

Brown, Robert & Sarah Hosler, 6 May 1843; Jacob Lefler, bondsman; J. H. Hardie, wit.

Brown, Robert M. & Eliza J. Bunn, 31 July 1856; John S. Nichols, bondsman; D. W. Honeycutt, wit.

Brown, Robert O. & Elizabeth Griffin, 25 Sept 1841; James Clark, bondsman; Susan T. Giles, wit.

Brown, Samuel C. & Elizabeth Miller, 30 April 1838; Edward Rufty, bondsman.

Brown, Samuel W. & Mary L. Gheen, 20 Feb 1857; Horace H. Beard, bondsman; James E. Kerr, wit. married 20 Feb 1857 by J. E. Brown, J. P.

Brown, Solomon & Amey Miller, 19 Dec 1836; Henry Brown, bondsman; J. H. Hardie, wit.

Brown, Thomas & Margaret Brinegar, 22 Dec 1829; Ishmael Brinegar, bondsman; J. H. Hardie, wit.

Brown, Thomas E. & Eleanora Verble, 25 Feb 1841; Dolphin A. Davis, bondsman.

Brown, Timothy & Polly Beaty, 11 Jan 1797; Henry Pohl, bondsman; Jno Rogers, wit.

Brown, Tobias & Phebe Airey, 4 Nov 1840; Benjamin F. Fraley, bondsman; Jno Giles, wit.

Brown, Wilie & Phebe Deaton, 27 Sept 1849; James D. Glover, bondsman; J. S. Myers, wit.

Brown, William & Elizabeth Huff, 4 Jan 1768; Jonathan Huff, Andrew Endsworth, bondsmen; Thomas Frohock, wit.

Brown, William & Dianna Davis, 6 May 1772; Jno Blalocky, Henry Strante, bondsmen; John Frohock, wit.

Brown, William & Eliz. Hughey, 15 Oct 1783; Jams. Houston, bondsman.

Brown, Willm. & Phoebe Gillom, 12 Jan 1786; Philip Fishburn, bondsman; Wm. Erwin, wit.

Brown, William & Betsy Pryor, 5 Jan 1814; Philip Brown, bondsman; Geo Dunn, wit.

Brown, William & Lucy Chaffin, 3 Sept 1793; Valentine Holderfield, bondsman; Jos. Chambers, wit.

Brown, Wm & Margaret Haden, 14 Aug 1804; Danl Cress, bondsman; A. L. Osborn, D. C., wit.

Brown, William & Peggy Phillips, 12 Jan 1805; Peter Mahan, bondsman; Moses A. Locke, wit.

Brown, William & Minty West, 14 Feb 1820; George Waller, bondsman; Jno Giles, wit.

Brown, William & Catharine Day, 26 Oct 1820; Joseph Idol, bondsman; Zebulon Hunt, wit.

Brown, William & Caroline Fisher, 21 Sept 1841; James Biles, bondsman.

Bruer, Rheubin & Polly Lane, 24 Sept 1817; John Swilivant,
bondsman; Mack Crump, wit.

Bruff, John & Zebely Livingood, 7 June 1818; William Warner,
bondsman; Thos Hampton, Charles Hoover, wit.

Brumley, Peter & Susan Becket, 19 Nov 1849; Demsy Page, bondsman.

Bruner, Henry & Edy Harris, 21 Sept 1814; Adam Cauble, bondsman;
Jno Giles, C. C., wit.

Bruner, Jacob & Phebe Creson, 12 May 1804; Samuel Roberts,
bondsman; Ad: Osborn, wit.

Bruner, Jacob & Elizabeth Hofner, 19 Dec 1837; Phillip Lemley,
bondsman; John Giles, wit.

Bruner, John & Easter Murr, 21 May 1812; John Smith, bondsman;
Geo Dunn, wit.

Bruner, Jno Jos. & Mary Ann Kencaid, 26 Jan 1843; Albert T.
Powe, bondsman.

Bruner, Michael & Mary McDearmen, 1 Sept 1816; Frs. Gardner,
bondsman; Milo A. Giles, wit.

Bruner, Michael & Eliza Tarr, 10 July 1821; Jno Utzman, bondsman.

Bryan, Braxter & Lydia Harbin, 30 March 1811; Benjamin Dullen,
bondsman; Jn March Sr., wit.

Bryan, Henry & Elizabeth Sparks, 11 Feb 1786; Thos Enochs,
bondsman; Wm. W. Erwin, wit.

Bryan, James & Margaret Johnson, 8 Dec 1790; John Johnston,
bondsman; C. Caldwell, C. C., wit.

Bryan, John & Rebeccah Orten 26 Aug 1774; John Orten, bondsman;
Ad: Osborn, wit.

Bryan, Joseph & Easther Hampton, 30 Nov 1772; John Bryan,
bondsman; Ad: Osborn, wit.

Bryan, Lewis & _____, 7 Dec 1796; Henry McGuyre, bondsman;
Humphry Marshall, wit.

Bryan, Lewis H. & Jane C. Andrew, 22 Oct 1817; Wm. Chaffin,
bondsman.

Bryan, Samuel & Rachael Jacks, 10 March 1779; Rudolf March,
bondsman; Ad: Osborn, wit.

Bryan, Samuel & Elizabeth Johnson, 10 April 1805; Daniel Hinkle,
bondsman; Jn March Sr., wit.

Bryan, Thos & Jane Horn, 30 Oct 1802; Erasmus Canter, bondsman;
Ad: Osborn, wit.

Bryant, John & Susanah Howard, 17 March 1818; Aquillar Cheshier,
bondsman; John March Sr., wit.

Bryson, Andrew & Agnes Naill, 17 Dec 1783; James Naill, bondsman; Major Wylie, wit.

Bryson, Samuel & Martha Bogle, 14 June 1776; Samuel Bogel, bondsman, Ad: Osborn, wit.

Bucey, Samuel & Katharine Seigler, 10 Feb 1794; Laurence Sigler, bondsman, John Pinchback, Ly Pinchback, wit.

Buchanan, James & Peany Shaver, 30 Jan 1826, Jacob File, bondsman; Hy Giles, wit.

Buchanan, John & Delinda Wyatt, 26 Aug 1848, Wiley Morgan Senr., bondsman; J. H. Hardie, wit.

Buck, Abraham & Elizabeth Waggoner, 24 Feb 1789, Will Alexander, wit.

Buck, Martin & Mary Jenkins, 22 July 1820, Henry Buck, bondsman.

Buckner, Benjamin & Becky Arrawood, 30 Nov 1813; John Buckner, bondsman; Jno Giles, C. C., wit.

Buckner, Edward & Rachal Hendricks, 16 Dec 1801, John Bucner, bondsman; Jno Brem, wit.

Buckner, Edward & Nancy Thompson, 30 Sept 1807; John Stincehcomb, bondsman; Jn March Sr., wit.

Buckner, James & Mary Robards, 12 March 1817; Elijah Owings, bondsman; Jn March Sr., wit.

Buckner, James & Catharine Simon, 17 Sept 1822; John Eagle, bondsman.

Buckner, Jesse & Lydia Claybrook, 13 Sept 1824; Jesse Tatum, bondsman; Hy Giles, wit.

Buckner, John & Lucy Daniel, 24 June 1807; Daniel Buckner, bondsman; Jn March Sr., wit.

Buckner, John & Lucretia Tatom, 22 July 1786; Henry Whiteaker, bondsman.

Buckner, Levi & Sarah Booth, 16 Dec 1812; John Buckner, bondsman; Jno March Sr., wit.

Buckwell, Henry & Sarah Deal, 29 Dec 1864; William Smith, bondsman; Obadiah Woodson, wit.

Buis, Alexr. W. & Marenda Fraly, 12 July 1831; Benjamin Fraley, bondsman; Jno H. Hardie, wit.

Buis, John & Sarah Wyatt, 8 Nov 1791; J. Geo. Laumann, bondsman; Chs. Caldwell, wit.

Buis, John Junr & Martha Wyatt, 12 Jan 1793; Laurence Clinart, bondsman; Jno Monro, wit.

Bullen, Conrad & Molly Tracksler, 18 Sept 1796; John Weant, bondsman; Jno Rogers, wit.

Bullen, George & Chlora Castor, 9 Oct 1792; Jacob Castor, bondsman; Jo Chambers, wit.

Bullen James R. & Eve An K. Erwine, 17 Feb 1851; Clark Redwine, bondsman; J. S. Myers, wit.

Bullen, John & Catharine Shireman, 24 Nov 1794; Conrad Bullen; bondsman.

Bullen, John & Susannah Harkey, 3 Oct 1829; Henry Harkey, bondsman; J. H. Hardie, wit.

Bullen, John & Tena Hofner, 11 May 1844; John Hartman, bondsman.

Bullen, George & Hester Stroser, 18 Jan 1772; Jacob Brown, Conrad Bullen, bondsmen.

Bullin, Leonard & Betsey Jackson, 19 Feb 1818; John Leach, bondsman; Jno Giles, wit.

Bun, Odom & Ezbell Myers, 14 March 1822; John Williams, bondsman; J. Willson, wit.

Bunch, James & Hanna Walks, 7 Feb 1782; Samuel Van Etten, bondsman.

Bunch, Samuel & Catherine Howard, 11 Sept 1813; John Jacobs, bondsman.

Bunden, Abner & Phebee Beison, 7 Aug 1810; Peter Janson(?), bondsman; S. Davis, J. P., wit.

Bunn--see also Bun

Bunn, Jost Westly & Mary E. Lyerly, 3 Nov 1855; Wm. Marbry, bondsman; Jac. C. Barnhardt, wit. married by Jac. C. Barnhardt, J. P., 4 Nov 1855.

Bunn, William F. & Betsey Vanderburg, 6 Sept 1865; Obadiah Woodson, bondsman, H. N. Woodson, wit. married 7 Sept 1865 by Robt M. Brown.

Buntain, Abraham & Nancy Renshaw, 8 Dec 1814; John Kennedy, bondsman; Jno Giles, C. C., wit.

Buntain, Robert & Sarah Renshaw, 18 Jan 1775; Elijah Renshaw, bondsman; James Robinson, wit.

Buntin, James & _____, 23 June 1763; Jos Ervin, John Buntin, bondsman; John Frohock, wit.

Buntin, John Jr. & Mary McClure, 16 June 1767; John Bunten Sr., George Smiley, bondsmen; Thos Frohock, wit.

Buntin, John & Delia Allison, 21 Dec 1819; Thos L. Cowan, bondsman.

Bunting, Baswell C. & Margaret Kennedy (both free persons of color), 19 June 1852; Evander Calvin, bondsman; J. S. Myers, wit. married 20 June 1852 by Obadiah Woodson, J. P.

Bunton, William & Mary Cowan, 31 Jan 1793; Thomas Barkley, bondsman; Jos. Chambers, wit.

Burch, William W. & Mary Jane Austin, 27 Dec 1838; Jno W. Lewis, bondsman; Abel Cowan, J. P., wit.

Burgess, Moses & Rachel Graves, 17 Aug 1833; Wilson Rose, bondsman; C. Harbin, wit.

Burgies, Edward & Nelley Welmon, 31 May 1817; John Buries, bondsman; Jno Marsh Sr., wit.

Burgin, Benjamin & Lear Man, 18 Nov 1772; Daniel Little, bondsman; Ad: Osborn, wit.

Burk, Edward & Mary Lush, 26 Sept 1813; Samuel Shuyen, bondsman; J. Willson, J. P., wit.

Burke, Edmund & Rebecca C. Cowan, 21 Oct 1854; Wm. L. Barber, bondsman; James E. Kerr, wit.

Burke, Henry & Mary Young, 20 Dec 1809; William Burke, bondsman; Jno Giles, C. C., wit.

Burke, John B. & Jane Cowan, 12 Dec 1816; Robert Cowan, bondsman.

Burke, John P. & Elizabeth W. Barber, 5 May 1843; Thomas C. Hyde, bondsman; A. H. Caldwell, wit.

Burke, Joseph & Margret Grant, 29 Dec 1766; John England, James Burk, bondsmen; Gidon Wright, wit.

Burke, Joseph K. & _____, 8 Jan 1857; Saml. R. Harrison, bondsman; James E. Kerr, wit.

Burke, William & Polly Cowan, 20 Oct 1812; Jno Niblack, bondsman; Geo Dunn, wit.

Burke, William P. & Sarah E. Brown, 1 Jan 1855; John Rice, bondsman; J. S. Myers, wit.

Burkhard, George & Mary Kipley, 24 June 1783; Henry Winkler, bondsman.

Burkhart, Henry & Barbara Lookabill, 17 Feb 1814; Philip Garner, bondsman; Geo Dunn, wit.

Burkhead, James C. H. & Margaret Coughernour, 18 May 1853; Julius D. Ramsey, bondsman; James E. Kerr, wit.

Burkheart, John & Nelly Carne, 23 Jan 1820; John Younce, bondsman; Amos Wright Jr., wit.

Burnes, Alfred & Mary A. Valentine, 17 June 1854; J. S. Myers, wit.

Burnes, Ransom & Jane Grimes, 22 July 1854; Alferd Burns, bondsman; J. S. Myers, wit. Ransom Burns & Jane Grimes, both free persons of color, of the Town of Salisbury, married 23 July 1854 by Obadiah Woodson, J. P.

Burns, John & Mary Lopp, 8 April 1794; Charles Burns, bondsman; Jo: Chambers, wit.

Burrage, William & Hulda Parks, 26 Sept 1803; Jacob Redwine, bondsman; Ad: Osborn, D. C., wit.

Burrege, Geo. P. & Mariah Pierce, 15 Sept 1853; Thomas Wiatt, bondsman; Levi Trexler, wit.

Burris, Joseph T. & Elizabeth Dobbins, 22 Dec 1824; Bennet A. Reeves, bondsman; Milo A. Giles, wit.

Burris, Joshua & Elis. Duffy, 24 March 1810; William Howard, bondsman; Jno Giles, C. C., wit.

Burrys, Richard & Nancy C. Pool, 16 July 1839; William E. Barber, bondsman; Abel Cowan, J. P., wit.

Burroughs, Caleb & Sally Basler, 20 June 1800; Joseph Young, bondsman; N. Chaffin, wit.

Burroughs, Charles & Nancy Renshaw, 18 Oct 1793; James Heathman, bondsman; Jos: Chambers, wit.

Burroughs, Charles & Elizabeth Haden, 13 Jan 1804; Max. Chambers, bondsman; A. L. Osborn, D. C., wit.

Burroughs, Richard & Savanna Lyerly, 1 Feb 1854; A. E. Cress, bondsman; James E. Kerr, wit.

Burton, Emsley & Sarah Stuart, 24 Oct 1816; Asa Wayman, bondsman; Zebulon Hunt, J. P., wit.

Burton, Thomas & Patience Caneday, 31 Dec 1808; Jesse Burton, bondsman; William Piggatt, J. P., wit.

Burton, Thomas & Sarah Epps, 18 Feb 1809; John Burton, bondsman; S. Davis, J. P., wit.

Burton, Thomas & Milly Perry, 18 Nov 1823; Thomas Lanier, bondsman; J. H. Harrison, wit.

Bussell, Beedom & Charity Smith, 4 Sept 1767; John Turner, Cornelwull Smith, bondsmen; John Frohock, wit.

Bussell, John & Mary Bella, 16 Aug 1791; Daniel Brown, bondsman; Cunm. Harris for C. Caldwell, D. C., wit.

Bussey, Charles & _____, 28 March 1765; James Whitaker, Francis Taylor, bondsmen; John Frohock, wit.

Bussh, Heinrich Bessand & Sophia Sayle, 10 June 1767; Christopher Rindelman, bondsman; Thos Frohock, wit.

Butler, David & Judeth Williams, 18 March 1818; Alfred McCulloh, bondsman; Jno March Sr., wit.

Butler, David & Elizabeth Reed, 19 Nov 1821; Noah Reed, bondsman; Hy Giles, wit.

Butler, Elisha & Sarah Click, 2 April 1814; William Butler, bondsman; Jno March Sr., wit.

Butler, Henry & _____, _____ 180_; Wm. Pennington, bondsman.

Butler, John & Sally Peneton, 5 April 1804; Joel Banks, bondsman; Hudson Hughes, wit.

Butler, Thos & Polly Smith, 21 Oct 1802; Harrod B. Pruitt, bondsman; A. L. Osborn, D. C., wit.

Butler, Wm & Elizabeth Bean, 14 April 1804; Edmond Butler, bondsman; A. L. Osborn, D. C., wit.

Butner, David & Mary Crane, 9 April 1768; Wm. Vassary, bondsman; Tho Frohock, wit.

Butner, David & Betsy Rose, _____; Charles Butner, bondsman; Jno Rogers, wit.

Butner, David & Sally Swink, 5 June 1819; John Butner, bondsman; Jno Giles, wit.

Butler, David & Susannah Thomas, 28 July 1804; Audlin Moore, bondsman; A. L. Osborn, D. C., wit.

Butner, Edward & Polly Parks, 17 Nov 1802; Joel Banks, bondsman; A. L. Osborn, D. C., wit.

Butner, Hermon & Jemima Merrill, 28 Feb 1775; Jonathan Conyer, bondsman.

Butner, John & Margaret Smith, 15 April 1806; David Butner, bondsman.

Butner, Levi & Pamelia Cauble, 10 Nov 1835; Jno H. Hardie, bondsman.

Butner, Peter & Betty Bussell, 3 Aug 1775; Pressley Bussell, bondsman; Ad: Osborn, wit.

Butner, Thomas & Sarah Elrode, 11 July 1764; Adam Butner, bondsman; Thomas Frohock, wit.

Butner, Thomas & Betsey Bufle, 15 Jan 1800; John Brown, bondsman.

Butner, William & Esther Kern, 5 Feb 1795; Daniel Kern, bondsman; J. Troy, wit.

Butram, William & Sarah Patterson, 29 Jan 1780; William Patterson, bondsman; B. Booth Boote, wit.

Button, Joseph B. & Caroline Keisler, 27 April 1853; Willis Elkins, bondsman; J. S. Myers, wit.

Buttrum, Levi & Elizabeth Kedwell, 4 Nov 1800; John Canada, bondsman; John Brem, wit.

Buxton, Thomas & Milly Perry, 18 Nov 1823; Thomas Lanier, bondsman; J. W. Harrison, wit.

Byal, Phillip & Christian Lukenbell, 10 Jan 1800; John Lukenbell, bondsman; Edwin J. Osborn, wit.

Byer, Phillip & Mary Someson, 9 Feb 1767; Frederick Someson, Casber Smidt, bondsmen; Thos Frohock, wit.

Byerly, Andrew & Sally Grimes, 25 April 1819; Mathis Brimes, bondsman; Jno Giles, wit.

Byers, Hamilton & Nancy Downsley, 2 March 1848; A. W. Owen, bondsman; Jno H. Hardie, wit.

Byers, Joseph Jr. & Martha Locke, 10 June 1816; Henry Will Cannon, bondsman; Moses A. Locke, wit.

Byers, Theophilus & Eliza Crawford, 13 June 1852; John Lyerly, bondsman; James E. Kerr, wit. married 13 June 1852 by Moses Powlass, J. P.

Byers, Washington & Ann C. Locke, 10 April 1824; Rufus Reid, bondsman; Geo Locke, wit.

Byrd, Jno & Elizth. Weaver, 7 Aug 1834; Adam Brown, bondsman;
J. H. Hardie, wit.

Byrd, Jno Jr. & Anna Casper, 10 Oct 1834; Adam Brown, bondsman.

Byrd, Michael & Lydia A. Phifer, 18 Nov 1850; Wm. A. Luckey,
bondsman; James E. Kerr, wit.

Cabel, Johannes & Katherine Fisher, 9 June 1788; Tobias Farrar,
bondsman; William Alexander, wit.

Cain, James & Mary Kipley, 14 Aug 1834; Silas Huie, bondsman.

Cain, Samuel & Elizabeth Cain, 14 Dec 1821; Thomas Cain, bondsman; Jno Giles, wit.

Cain, Thomas H. & Nancy Beemer, 28 July 1828; Wm. Cain, bondsman; Wm. Hawkins, J. P., wit.

Calahan, James & Mary Wason, 14 Aug 1783; John Wasson, bondsman;
Jno McNairy, wit.

Calahan, John & Jane Templeton, 19 Aug 1775; George Tempelton,
bondsman; David Flowers, wit.

Calahan, Valintin & Elizabeth McCrudy, 28 May 1776; Jams. Banes,
bondsman; Ad: Osborn, wit. (consent from Andrew McCreedy)

Calahan, William & Eliza. Sheppard, 29 Jan 1768; Michael Anderson, bondsman; John Frohock, wit.

Caldwell, John & Elizabeth Wright, 2 Oct 1803; Moses Welborn,
bondsman; William Welborn, wit.

Caldwell, Max. C. & Fanny Kern, 25 April 1857; Benjamin Julian,
bondsman; J. S. Myers, wit. married 26 April 1857 by J. H.
Brown, J. P.

Cales, James & Letty Brooks, 24 Dec 1790; Peter Faust, bondsman;
C. Caldwell, C. C., wit.

Call, Daniel & Nancey Hinkle, 1 April 1816; David Call, bondsman;
Jno March Sr., wit.

Call, Daniel & Margaret Smith, 16 Feb 1791; William Deadman,
bondsman; Basil Gaither, wit.

Call, David & Edy Walker, 26 April 1817; Howard Walker, bondsman;
R. Powell, wit.

Call, Henry & Salley Chasser, 17 April 1807; Jonathan Cheshere,
bondsman; Jno March Sr., wit.

Call, Henry & Polley Jones, 27 April 1814; Jesse Walker, bondsman; Jn March Sr., wit.

Call, Henry & Polly Stalman, 21 Dec 1818; William Howard, bondsman; Jn March Sr., wit.

Call, Jacob & Elethia Chesher, 27 Oct 1809; George Sheek,
bondsman; Jn March Sr., wit.

Call, Jacob & Sarah Etcheson, 4 Jan 1825; Wiley Jones, bondsman;
Jn March Sr., wit.

Call, John & Elizabeth Edon, 3 March 1810; James Brown, bondsman; Jno March Sr., wit.

Call, John & Mary Chaplin, 29 Aug 1835; Anderson Beauchamp, bondsman; C. Harbin, wit.

Call, Joseph & Emeley Deever, 6 March 1809; William Howard, bondsman; Jn March Sr., wit.

Call, Joseph & Rebecah Glasscock, 25 Dec 1823; William Glasscock, bondsman; L. R. Rose, J. P., wit.

Call, Philip & Sarah Jones, 25 Oct 1823; Drury Jones, bondsman; L. R. Rose, J. P., wit.

Callahan, Edward & Mary Nickles, 23 Oct 1768; John Callahan, George Folsom, bondsmen; Thoms. Frohock, wit. consent from Joshua Nickels, father of Mary Nickles, dated 25 Oct 1768.

Callicut, Paschal & Margaret Pool, 29 March 1860; Henderson Barrett, bondsman; James E. Kerr, wit. married 29 March 1860 by L. C. Groseclose, Pastor of St. John's Ev. Luth. Ch., Salisbury, N. C.

Calvin, Evanda M. & Maria Burns, 10 April 1845; William Taylor, bondsman; Jno H. Hardie Jr., wit.

Campbell, Abel & Susy Fernoy, 18 June 1813; Alex. Stephens, bondsman; Wm. Stephens, wit.

Camaeron, Abel & Susey Fernoy, 18 June 1813; Alex Stephens, bondsman; Wm. Stephens, wit.

Camel, David & Anna Canup, 21 April 1837; John Canup, bondsman; Tobias L. Lemly, wit.

Camel, Henry & Mary Ann Earnheart, 1 Jan 1856; Edward Earnhart, bondsman; J. S. Myers, wit. married 3 Jan 1856 by W. H. Walton, J. P.

Camel, William & Mary Neely, 3 Sept 1816; Micajah Cannon, bondsman; Henry Giles, wit.

Cameron, Absalom & Charity Grice, 10 Jan 1822; Henry Sleighter (Heinrich Slichter), bondsman.

Cameron, Absalom & Mary Cole, 20 Feb 1786; John Lewis Beard, bondsman; John Macay, wit.

Cameron, James & Clementine C. Hilick, 26 March 1840; Simeon Hilick, bondsman; Susan T. Giles, wit.

Cameron, James & Mary Hartman, 4 Feb 1850; Jas. M. Reid, bondsman; M. L. Holmes, wit.

Cameron, John & Rebeckr Shipard, 6 May 1815; Fredrick Law (Low), bondsman; Wm. Bean, wit.

Cameron, William & Nancy Huffman, 2 Aug 1832; Wm. G. Shaw, bondsman; L. R. Rose, J. P., wit.

Cameron, William & Patsey Barnes, 9 Sept 1799; Jesse Ballard, bondsman; Ew. Jay Osborn, wit.

Campbell--see also Camel

Campbell, Archd. & Elizabeth Hill, 4 Jan 1786; Abram Hill, bondsman; W. W. Erwin, wit.

Campbell, Cabel & Mary Baskett, 12 Jan 1786; Chas. Wood, bondsman; Wm. W. Erwin, wit.

Campbell, Cyrus & Sarah Holamon, 16 Feb 1824; Jno Utzman, bondsman; Hy Giles, wit.

Campbell, Duncan & Polly Smith, 29 Sept 1818; George Lock, bondsman.

Campbell, Ely & Martha Renshaw, 23 Jan 1822; William Smith, bondsman.

Campbell, Ely & Molly (Matty?) Smith, 8 April 1811; Thos Renshaw, bondsman.

Campbell, Elisha & Rachael Cowan, 17 Jan 1803; John Fulton, bondsman; Adlai L. Osborn, D. C., wit.

Campbell, George & Jane Buntin, 17 Nov 1818; Henry Hughey, bondsman; Roberts Nanny, wit.

Campbell, George Stueart & Margaret Steele, 3 March 1834; Michael Bulyer, bondsman; Thomas McNeely, J. P., wit.

Campbell, Hugh & Elizabeth Greer, 15 Oct 1772; Robt Rogers, Robert Linn, bondsman; Ad: Osborn, C. C., wit. consent from Robert Greer, Father of Elisabeth Greer, 15 Oct 1722, wit: James White, Samuel Irwin.

Campbell, James & Margret Bane, (not dated); Richard Holmes, bondsman.

Campbell, James & Isabela Cleary, 31 Jan 1832; Frelard Beck, bondsman; Thomas McNeely, J. P., wit.

Campbell, John & Juda Peterson, 14 Feb 1775; William Brandon, John Lock, bondsmen.

Campbell, John & Hannah Forcum, 29 April 1809; Benjamin Gatton, bondsman; Jn March Sr., wit.

Campbell, John & Mary Haden, 23 Sept 1823; Citizen S. Woods, bondsman; Hy Giles, wit.

Campbell, John & Mary A. Miller, 5 March 1838; Martin Josey, bondsman; William Howard, wit.

Campbell, John & Sena Felker, 30 Dec 1861; Wiley Felker, bondsman; Obadiah Woodson, wit. married 2 Jan 1862 by W. A. Luckey, J. P.

Campbell, Jno & Jane McFetters, 28 Nov 1792; Charles McFaiters, bondsman; Jos. Chambers, wit.

Campbell, Jonathan Alston & Lavina Elston, 29 Oct 1792; Robert Bracly, bondsman; Jos. Chambers, D. C., wit.

Campbell, Joseph R. & Eleanor M. Young, 14 Nov 1850; D. Burton Wood, bondsman.

Campbell, Middleton & Elizabeth Rutledge, 23 Jan 1812; Joseph Depoister, bondsman; John March, wit.

Campbell, Samuel A. & Margaret Cowan, 28 July 1817; John J. Gracy, bondsman; Roberts Nanny, wit.

Campbell, Samuel & Polly Lindsey, 7 Aug 1816; Robert Moore, bondsman; Jno Giles, Clk, wit.

Campbell, Stewart & Elleanor R. Steele, 21 July 1853; Jesse Hall, bondsman; J. S. Myers, wit.

Campbell, Thomas & Hannah Brandon, 14 Nov 1817; John S. Nichols, bondsman; R. Powell, wit.

Campbell, Thos S. & Elizabeth J. Allen, 11 Sept 1839; Thos T. Maxwell, bondsman.

Campbell, Wm & Elizath. Lyerly, 5 Feb 1848; Isaac Lyerly, bondsman; J. H. Hardie, wit.

Campbell, William & Ann Hendren, 3 April 1792; John Hendren, Bondsman; Brice W. James, wit.

Campbell, William A. & Mary M. Goodman, 12 March 1861; Noah Canup, bondsman.

Camppell, Robert & Rachael Neely, 26 Oct 1816; William Camppell, bondsman; Milo A. Giles, wit.

Canaday, Christopher & Rebecca Bateman, 8 Oct 1798; Christopher Bateman, bondsman; Ma. Troy, wit.

Canatzer, Nathaniel of Davie County, & Eliza S. Fraley of the town of Salisbury, Rowan County, married 28 April 1853 by Obadiah Woodson, J. P. (no bond)

Cannon, Cornelius & Ratchel Hutchens, 8 Nov 1801; Horatio Jones, bondsman; J. Hunt, wit.

Canter, Edward & Mary Wood, 10 Nov 1798; Daniel Eaton, bondsman; E. Jay Osborn, D. C., wit.

Canter, Erasmus & Rebecka Horn, 26 Dec 1801; Thomas Horn, bondsman; Jno Brem, wit.

Canter, James & Polly Davis, 6 March 1805; Elijah Adams, bondsman; J. Hunt, wit.

Canter, James & Elizabeth Duncan, 24 June 1819; Erasmus Canter, bondsman; R. Powell, wit.

Canter, James M. & Christena Kesler, 16 March 1849; Tobias Kesler, bondsman; John H. Hardie, Jr., wit.

Canup, Benjamin F. & Margaret M. Ketchey, 28 Feb 1856; David Ketchey, bondsman; J. S. Myers, wit. married 28 Feb 1856 by W. H. Walton, J. P.

Canup, David & Philpena Miller, 13 Feb 1845; John Miller, bondsman; Jno H. Hardie Jr., wit.

Canup, Henry & Eve Earnheart, 17 June 1826; Jno Earnheart, bondsman; J. H. Hardie, wit.

Canup, Henry A. & Crissy A. Gheen, 18 Feb 1865; W. H. Crawford, bondsman; Obadiah Woodson, wit.

Canup, Henry Thomas & Rosa Agner, 27 Jan 1857; J. S. Myers, bondsman; married 27 Jan 1857 by W. H. Walton, J. P.

Canup, Milas & Elizabeth Agner, 27 Aug 1851; Adam Earnhart, bondsman; J. S. Myers, wit.

Canup, Noah & Jane C. Keply, 20 Dec 1851; Jacob Keply, bondsman; J. S. Myers, wit.

Canup, Samuel & Mary Ann Keply, 8 March 1850; Lafayette Green, bondsman; J. S. Myers, wit.

Caply, Peter & Rachael Simison, 9 April 1821; Daniel Agner, bondsman; Hy Giles, wit.

Capp, Christophel & Prusilla Landers, 17 May 1779; Johannes Cochnour, bondsman; Ad. Osborn, wit.

Caradens, Thomas & Elizabeth Bell, 7 Jan 1773; John Cathey, bondsman; Ad: Osborn, wit. consent from Thomas Bell, father of Elizabeth, 6 Jan 1773; David Sloan, wit.

Cardwell, Perrin & Sarah Cearley, 11 March 1767; Oliver Wallis, Peter Johnson, bondsmen; Thos Frohock, wit. consent from Henry Cearly, father of Sarah, 8 March 1767.

Carico, Wm & Martha Stephenson, 2 Jan 1813; Abel Carrico, bondsman; R. Powell, wit.

Carlile, Robert & Elizabeth Cash, 3 Feb 1779; John Cochran, bondsman; Ad: Osborn, wit.

Carlock, Fredrick & Isabel Corothers, 2 Aug 1784; Enoch Morgan, bondsman; H. Magoune, wit.

Carmon, Samuel & Mary Kerr, 7 April 1789; Saml Kerr, bondsman; Will Alexander, wit.

Carnel, Edward & Elizebeth Deaver, 5 May 1809; Samuel Deaver, bondsman; Jn March Sr., wit.

Carney, David L. & Sarah Abbot, 5 July 1783; Walter Bell, bondsman; T. H. McCaule, wit.

Carns, William & Lelly Baxter, 6 March 1789; Nicholas Veilhawer, bondsman; Will Alexander, wit.

Carrel, Eli & Catharine Murrige, 11 Aug 1809; Edward Murrige, bondsman; Jno Giles, wit.

Carrel, Luke & Elizabeth Murphy, 25 Jan 1792; Joseph Sawyers, bondsman; Chs Caldwell, wit.

Carrick, James & Ruth Skeene, 26 Feb 1847; William Burrage, bondsman; Jno H. Hardie, wit.

Carrick, John & Sally Beane, 19 March 1805; John Howzer, bondsman; Ad: Osborn, wit.

Carrick, Joseph & Sally Burridge, 5 Dec 1823; William H. Houser, bondsman; Jno Giles, wit.

Carrick, Joseph & Anne Frick, 28 Nov 1848; Joseph Bean, bondsman; J. H. Hardie Jr., wit.

Carrico, Abel & Ibby Stephenson, 1 Feb 1813; Wm. Carrico, bondsman; R. Powell, wit.

Carrigan, James F. & Clarrissa A. Miller, 7 Jan 1859; Joshua Miller, bondsman.

Carrigan, John & Sarah Caruthers, 18 Sept 1822; James Carrigan, bondsman.

Carrigan, Lemuel C. & Mary M. Upright, 15 Jan 1855; John Upright, bondsman; James E. Kerr, wit.

Carriker, Jacob L. & Sally M. Fesperman, 20 April 1853; Solomon W. Gense, bondsman; J. S. Myers, wit. married 20 April 1853 by J. M. Brown, J. P.

Carrol, Wm & Molly Bird, 28 July 1800; Thomas Bird, bondsman; Edwin J. Osborn, wit.

Carson, James & Patsy Cathey, 26 Feb 1804; Jno Dusenbury, bondsman; A. L. Osborn, wit.

Carson, John & Mary McBroom, 8 Feb 1767; James Marlin, bondsman; Thomas Frohock, wit.

Carson, John & Sarah Slaven, 31 Aug 1775; Robt Nevins, bondsman; David Flowers, wit.

Carson, John & Elizabeth Bostian, 25 Sept 1809; Abel Carson, bondsman; Jno Giles, wit.

Carson, John & Anny Stirewalt, 21 Dec 1835; Andrew Bostian Jr., bondsman; Jno Giles, wit.

Carson, John & Mary Thompson, 29 May 1838; James H. McBroom, bondsman; S. Lemly Jr., wit.

Carson, John S. & Jane L. Graham, 25 Nov 1856; J. W. Steele, bondsman; J. S. Myers, wit. married 2 Dec 1856 by Saml B. O. Wilson, V. D. M.

Carson, Robert & Elisabeth Paterson, 25 Nov 1785; Robert Tempelton, bondsman.

Carson, Robert & Ellis Patterson, 20 Dec 1782; James Patterson, bondsman; T. H. McCaule, wit.

Carson, William L. & Sarah J. Carson, 25 Jan 1862; B. S. Thompson, bondsman; Obadiah Woodson, wit.

Carson, William Stewart & Rachel Blair, 12 Jan 1792; Jno Braly Junr., bondsman; Chs Caldwell, wit.

Carter, Edward F. M. & Sarah E. Dent, 10 Aug 1859; Wilson Penninger, bondsman; James E. Kerr, wit.

Carter, H. G. & Elizth. J. Morphis, 20 Dec 1847; H. H. Beard, bondsman; John H. Hardie, wit.

Carter, James & Margarett Slagle, 19 Sept 1793; Michael Creaver, bondsman; Jno Monro, wit.

Carter, James M. & Mary B. Robeson, 10 Feb 1853; W. A. Nash, bondsman; married 10 Feb 1853 by Walter W. Pharr.

Carter, James M. & Mary A. Deal, 14 Nov 1865; Samuel Deal, bondsman; Obadiah Woodson, wit.

Carter, John E. & Nancy Ribelin, 27 Aug 1852; John Stokes, bondsman; J. S. Myers, wit. married 2 Sept 1852 by Levi Trexler, J. P.

Carter, R. H. & Eunies Cowan, 19 Oct 1837; Preston Harry, bondsman.

Cartner, Frederick & Margaret Felker, 12 Feb 1846; Levi Niblock, bondsman; J. M. Turner, wit.

Cartner, Fredrick & Caty Felkir, 2 Jan 1815; John Boston, bondsman; Geo Dunn, wit.

Cartner, George W. & Ellener Bostian, 16 March 1844; George W. McLean, bondsman; Obadiah Woodson, wit.

Cartner, James & Sarah Keller, 24 Nov 1827; Henry Guffey, bondsman; L. R. Rose, J. P., wit.

Cartner, William & Sophia Ann Felkner, 20 March 1860; B. K. Kerr, bondsman; Wm. Locke, wit. married 29 March 1860 by W. A. Luckey, J. P.

Cartwright, Joseph & Eve Miller, 24 March 1770; Michael Miller, bondsman; Thos Frohock, wit.

Carvender, James & Elizebeth Prewitt, 11 May 1815; Benjamin March, bondsman; Jn March Sr., wit.

Casey, Archibald & Ketharine Ovenshine, 16 July 1793; John Lince, bondsman; Jos Chambers, wit.

Casey, Daniel & Arina M. James, 9 May 1829; John Blackwood, bondsman; L. R. Rose, J. P., wit.

Casey, Daniel & Elizabeth Marlor, 30 May 1830; Richmon Casey, bondsman; Wm. Hawkins, wit.

Casey, David & Caty Whitiler, 12 March 1808; John March Jr., bondsman; Jn March Sr., wit.

Casey, Henry & Betsey Ellis, 30 April 1813; John Ellis, bondsman; Jno Giles, C. C., wit.

Casey, Samuel & Isabel Adams, 28 Sept 1787; George Willcoke, bondsman; Spruce Macay, wit.

Casey, Samuel & Sarah Hatley, 7 June 1807; Josiah Hatley, bondsman; John March Senr., wit.

Casey, William & Sarah Taylor, 18 Nov 1787; Daniel Allemong, bondsman; Jno Macay, wit.

Casey, William & Elizabeth Trout, 7 Sept 1817; Jonathan Madden, bondsman; R. Powell, wit.

Casey, William & Katharine Berger, 15 May 1793; Saml Dayton, bondsman; Jos Chambers, wit.

Cash, John & Nancy Riley, 26 Oct 1832; Wm. Jones, bondsman; Jas. Frost, J. P., wit.

Cashdollar, Alexander & Polly Speers, 23 June 1816; Frederic May, bondsman; R. Powell, wit.

Casper, Adam & Catharine Cauble, 9 April 1827; John Smithdeel, bondsman; John H. Hardie, wit.

Casper, Adam M. & Mary C. Allen, 18 Oct 1858; John L. Rusher, bondsman; John Wilkinson, wit. married 19 Oct 1858 by Milo A. J. Roseman, J. P.

Casper, Alexander & Elisabeth Hartmon, 8 Sept 1856; Monrow Casper, bondsman; H. W. Hill, J. P., wit. married 9 Sept 1856 by H. W. Hill, Esqr.

Casper, Andw. & Betsey Waller, 26 March 1831; Conrod Casper, bondsman; J. H. Hardie, wit.

Casper, Conrad & Barbara Klotz, 28 Jan 1809; Grunewald(?) Lintz, bondsman; A. L. Osborne, wit.

Casper, Conrod & Rachel Morgan, 12 Sept 1821; Nathan Morgan, bondsman; Hy Giles, wit.

Casper, Conrod & Sophia Eddleman, 5 Nov 1824; Adam Etleman, bondsman; Henry Allemong, wit.

Casper, David & Rachael Shuping, 3 April 1843; Squire Peeler, bondsman, J. H. Hardie, wit.

Casper, David & Lavina Casper, 19 Feb 1844; Jesse Kesler, bondsman.

Casper, David & Milby Troutman, 19 May 1851; Simeon Klutts, bondsman; J. S. Myers, wit.

Casper, David & Rebecca Jane Link, 30 Aug 1860; Franklin W. Thomason, bondsman; James E. Kerr, wit. married 30 Aug 1860 by L. C. Groseclose, Pastor of St. John's E. Luth. Church, Salisbury, N. C.

Casper, Ezra & Caroline Lunbergh, 10 Sept 1843; Houell Parker, bondsman; J. H. Hardie, wit.

Casper, George & Nancy Leonard, 5 March 1819; Jacob Klotz (Cluts), bondsman; Jno Giles, wit.

Casper, Henry & Elizabeth Hartline, 17 June 1786; Jacob Smith, bondsman; Jno Macay, wit.

Casper, Henry & Rachael Ross(?), 23 March 1830; Peter Stoner, bondsman; Jno H. Hardie, wit.

Casper, Henry & Elizabeth Bostian, 15 March 1842; George W. Carter, bondsman; Jno H. Hardie, wit.

Casper, Jacob & Teeny Bird, 28 May 1811; John Fennel, bondsman; Ezra Allemong, wit.

Casper, Jacob & Catharine Rymer, 2 July 1842; Jno H. Hardie, bondsman; Adam A. Smithdeal, wit.

Casper, Peter & Nancy Cauble, 17 Sept 1829; Jno Byrd, bondsman; Jno H. Hardie, wit.

Casper, Jacob & Christena Warner, 7 Jan 1863; W. A. Walton, bondsman; Thomas McNeely, wit.

Casper, John & Caty Eddleman, 20 Aug 1812; George Heilig, bondsman; Jno Giles, C. C., wit.

Casper, John & Catharine Saford, 28 May 1836; Carl Sefrind (German signature), bondsman; Jno Giles, wit.

Casper, J. C. & Margaret Josey, 21 Oct 1865; J. F. Casper, bondsman; Obadiah Woodson, wit.

Casper, Levi & Naomi Trexler, 27 March 1841; Henry W. Casper, bondsman; J. L. Beard, wit.

Casper, Levi & Catharine Morgan, 18 Sept 1847; Daniel Klutts, bondsman.

Casper, Monroe & Turly Hill, 26 Jan 1854; J. W. Clemmons, bondsman; J. S. Myers, wit. married 26 Jan 1854 by Jacob File, J. P.

Casper, Peter & Catharine Frick, 11 Jan 1823; Jacob Klotz, bondsman; Hy Giles, wit.

Casper, Solomon & Rachael Trexler, 5 Oct 1835; Hy Giles, bondsman.

Caster, Henry & Milly Caber, 1 Aug 1811; Mathias Frick, bondsman; Ezra Allemong, wit.

Caster, Daniel & Peggy Bostian, 20 Nov 1827; Peter Boston, bondsman; J. H. Hardie, wit.

Caster, Henry (Heinrich Gerster?) & Mary Hess, 1 Dec 1797; Elias Maier, bondsman; Jno Rogers, wit.

Caster, Jacob F. & Caroline Casper, 20 March 1860; Adam M. Casper, bondsman; Wm. Locke, wit. married 21 March 1860 by Milo A. J. Roseman, J. P.

Caster, John & Polly Ghents, 11 Dec 1829; Philip Caster, bondsman; Jno H. Hardie, wit.

Caster, John A. & Mary Elizabeth House, 7 Nov 1847; Wiley Gense, bondsman; James E. Kerr, wit.

Castor, Henry A. & Lidia Sechler, 7 Feb 1853; William W. Caster, bondsman; J. S. Myers, wit.

Castor, John & Polly Rose, 8 April 1824; William Rose, bondsman; H. Allemong, wit.

Cates, Phillip & Betsy Bullon, 11 July 1803; Michael Cates, bondsman; A. L. Osborn, D. C., wit.

Cathey, Hugh & Jane Bailey, 4 Aug 1774; James Brandon, bondsman; Ad. Osborn, wit. consent from Charles Bailey, father of Jane, 3 Aug 1774.

Cathey, James & Isabell Sloan, 14 Feb 1770; Archd. Sloan, Robert Gorden, bondsmen; John Frohock, wit.

Cathey, Richard & Elizabeth Giles, 6 Sept 1774; Willian Giles, bondsman; Ad: Osborn, wit.

Cathey, William & Else Hagan, 24 Oct 1772; John Hagin, bondsman.

Caton, Charles & Rebecah Weyatt, 27 Feb 1810; John Stinchcomb, bondsman; Jn March Sr., wit.

Caton, George Dent & Nancy Hurley, 19 Dec 1789; John Caton, bondsman; Will Alexander, wit.

Caton, Jesse & Esther Sparks, 20 Jan 1787; Charles Caton, bondsman; Jno Macay, wit.

Caton, Jesse & Elizebeth Orrel, 26 Jan 1813; Edger Orrel, bondsman; Jn March Sr., wit.

Caton, Stephen & Susannah Tatom, __ Dec 1817; John Hill, bondsman; Roberts Nanny, wit.

Caton, Stephen & Catherine Hendricks, 2 Feb 1826; John Foard, bondsman; L. R. Rose, J. P., wit.

Caton, William & Cynthya Smith, 7 Nov 1803; Thomas Smith, bondsman; A. L. Osborn, D. C., wit.

Cauble, Alexander & Margaret Hornbarrier, 18 Mar 1838; David Cauble, bondsman; Hy Giles, wit.

Cauble, Daniel & Jane Hartmon, 29 March 1826; Jacob Fulenwider, bondsman.

Cauble, Daniel & Katharine Shuping, 18 Aug 1841; David Cauble, bondsman; J. S. Johnston, wit.

Cauble, David & Sophia Miller, 29 Jan 1834; Jacob Fulenwider, bondsman; Wm. Locke, wit.

Cauble, David A. & Louisa E. Winders, 9 Feb 1848; Wm. B. Caughenour, bondsman.

Cauble, Frederick & Anny Basinger, 25 Jan 1812; Jacob Cauble, bondsman; Jno Giles, C. C., wit.

Cauble, George & Rosey Cobble, 3 Jan 1817; Fredrick Miller, bondsman; Roberts Nanny, wit.

Cauble, George & Polly Freeze, 23 Nov 1818; Henry Misamer, bondsman; Jno Giles, wit.

Cauble, Geo A. & Susan Mowery, 24 March 1855; Joseph Smithdeal, bondsman; J. S. Myers, wit. married 25 March 1855 by Obadiah Woodson, J. P.

Cauble, Green & Maria Hess, 4 Sept 1852; Peter Rough, bondsman; J. S. Myers, wit.

Cauble, Henry & Francis Cauble, 10 March 1831; Wm. D. Crawford, bondsman; Jno H. Hardie, wit.

Cauble, Henry & Celia Hill, 28 Dec 1854; Jacob Correll, bondsman; J. S. Myers, wit.

Cauble, Henry & Catherine Miner, 21 June 1859; Philip P. Meroney, bondsman; married 29 June 1859 by J. L. Smithdeal.

Cauble, Isaac & Selena Cauble, 17 April 1844; Alexander Agner, bondsman; Obadiah Woodson, wit.

Cauble, Jacob & Barbary Moury, 11 Jan 1791; Nathan Morgan, bondsman; C. Caldwell, D. C., wit.

Cauble, Jacob & Susannah Houldsouser, 25 March 1811; Frederick Miller, bondsman; Jno Giles, C. C., wit.

Cauble, Jacob & Catharine Trexler, 5 March 1845; Jno H. Hardie, bondsman.

Cauble, Jacob & Maria Brown, 9 Jan 1856; Wm. F. Julian, bondsman; married 9 Jan 1856 by Obadiah Woodson, J. P.

Cauble, Jacob & Sally Lyerly, 22 April 1829; Jacob Fulenwider, bondsman; Jno H. Hardie, wit.

Cauble, John & Elizabeth Pool, 14 Feb 1817; Jacob Cauble, bondsman; Jno Giles, wit.

Cauble, John & Eleonore Williams, 5 Dec 1842; Danl Boger, bondsman; Jno H. Hardie, wit.

Cauble, John & Charlotte Walton, 24 July 1844; John Ketchey, bondsman; John H. Hardie, wit.

Cauble, John & Sallie C. Fesperman, 3 Jan 1866; Henry W. Klutts, bondsman; Obadiah Woodson, wit.

Cauble, John M. & Maria Cauble, 18 Oct 1851; Mal C. Caldwell, bondsman; J. S. Myers, wit.

Cauble, Joseph G. & Camilla C. Earnheart, 18 March 1866; John Cauble, bondsman; Obadiah Woodson, wit.

Cauble, Michael & Catharine Gheen, 27 Dec 1853; Asberry Sprig, bondsman; J. S. Myers, wit. married 29 Dec 1853 by Obadiah Woodson, J. P.

Cauble, Michael & Lucretia Hartman, 11 March 1854; Whitson Kimball, bondsman; J. S. Myers, wit. married 12 March 1854 by W. A. Walton, J. P.

Cauble, Miles & Elenora Swink, 13 March 1851; William B. Coughenour, bondsman; James E. Kerr, wit.

Cauble, Moses & Rachael Earnheart, 27 Jan 1834; Daniel Cauble, bondsman; Wm. Locke, wit.

Cauble, Moses & Mary L. Klutts, 6 June 1848; Fredrick Waller, bondsman; J. H. Hardie, Jr., wit.

Cauble, Otho & Sarah A. Elliott, 1 Sept 1855; George W. Jacobs, bondsman; J. S. Myers, wit. married 2 Sept 1855 by Obadiah Woodson, J. P.

Cauble, Peter & Polly Brown, 19 Dec 1816; Frederick Miller, bondsman; Roberts Nanny, wit.

Cauble, Peter & Margaret Miller, 1 April 1829; Jacob Fulenwider, bondsman; Jno H. Hardie, wit.

Cauble, Peter & Polly Miller, 1 Sept 1835; Benjamin Blackwell, bondsman; John Giles, wit.

Cauble, Peter & Catharine Peeler, 27 Sept 1855; Benjamin Earnhart, bondsman; J. S. Myers, wit. married 27 Sept 1855 by
W. H. Walton, J. P.

Cauble, Samuel & Elizabeth Godfrey, 18 Jan 1825; Henry Robins,
bondsman; Hy Giles, wit.

Cauble, William A. & Mary C. Trexler, 14 Dec 1859; Jacob Klutts,
bondsman; married 15 Dec by D. Barringer, J. P.

Caudell, Ishmel & Catharine Owens, 25 Aug 1810; Andrew Merrel,
bondsman; Jno Giles, C. C., wit.

Caudle, Wesley & Elizabeth Sain, 21 Sept 1812; John Booe, bondsman; Jn March Sr., wit.

Caughenour, William B. & Elizabeth Cauble, 17 Feb 1847; Isaac
Lyerly, bondsman; J. H. Hardie, wit.

Causey, William & Sarah Tisinger, 8 June 1822; Geo. W. Tisinger,
bondsman; Andrew Swicegood, wit.

Caven, John & Jean Young, _____ 1785; William Young, bondsman.

Cavender, James & Mary Smith, 8 July 1794; Elijah Cornwell,
bondsman; J. Troy, D. C., wit.

Cecill, Allen & Elizabeth Stout, 29 Dec 1807; Philip Cecill,
bondsman; Wm. Welbon, wit.

Cecill, Benjamin & Osee Kenneday, 9 Feb 1817; George Bell,
bondsman; Z. Hunt, J. P., wit.

Cecill, Benjamin & Elizabeth Cecill, 12 March 1822; Jarred
Cecill, bondsman; Z. Hunt, wit.

Cecill, Jarred & Sarah Cecill, 22 April 1822; John Cecill,
bondsman; Z. Hunt, wit.

Cecill, Philip & Rachel Cecill, 7 Oct 1821; Levi S. Amburn,
bondsman; Z. Hunt, wit.

Cecill, Reason & Margaret Haworth, 1 Oct 1818; Jarred Ball,
bondsman; Zebulon Hunt, wit.

Cecill, Samuel & Henneretta Jiams, 3 Aug 1817; Wm. Cecill,
bondsman; Jac(?) Brummell, wit.

Cegelo, Leonard & Jane Carson, 28 Jan 1817; William Jordan,
bondsman; Jno Giles, Clk., wit.

Cetchey, John & Catharine Hildrebranch, 30 July 1800; John
Blake, Christian Shewman, bondsmen.

Chadwick, Joseph & _____; Wheeler Chadwick, bondsman; Wm.
Welbon, wit.

Chaffin, John Garland & Marey Bryan, 11 June 1805; William
Howard, bondsman; Jn March Sr., wit.

Chaffin, Braxton & Arana Pelly, 10 Nov 1829; John Brannock,
bondsman; L. R. Rose, J. P., wit.

Chaffin, Christopher & Elizabeth March, 15 Jan 1825; Nathan
Pack, bondsman; Hy Giles, wit.

Chaffin, John A. & Emily Gaither, 11 Jan 1825; William O.
Chaffin, bondsman; E. Brock, J. P., wit.

Chaffin, Joshua & Susanah Bradley, 26 April 1810; James Pack,
bondsman; Jno March Sr., wit.

Chaffin, N. S. A. & Julia Wheeler, 6 Nov 1844; Alexander N.
Chaffin, bondsman; John H. Hardie, Jr., wit.

Chaffin, Standley & Sarey Owings, 21 Oct 1805; John March,
bondsman; Jn March Sr., wit.

Chaffin, Stanley & Ellender Bryan, 3 May 1805; John March,
bondsman; Jn March, wit.

Chaffin, William O. & Temperance Hendricks, 7 Feb 1829; Robt
L. Hargrave, bondsman; C. Harbin, J. P., wit.

Chambers, Arthur & Ruth Woods, 9 May 1776; Samuel Woods, bondsman; Ad: Osborn, wit.

Chambers, Elijah Patton & Margret Rutherford, 4 Jan 1791; Alexr.
Graham, bondsman.

Chambers, Galbreath & Nancy Glasscock, 27 Jan 1829; William
Sheek, bondsman; C. Harbin, J. P., wit.

Chambers, Henery & Agness McHenry, 11 May 1775; John McHenry,
bondsman; David Flowers, wit.

Chambers, Henry & Jane Cowan, 2 Nov 1815; Robert Cowan, bondsman; Jno Giles, wit.

Chambers, Henry & Polly Cowan, 11 Jan 1823; John Rainey, bondsman; Hy Giles, wit.

Chambers, James & Margaret Ervin, 10 Oct 1782; Abraham Erwin,
bondsman; Ad: Osborn, wit.

Chambers, James & Margaret Knox, 27 Dec 1784; Alex McKee, bondsman.

Chambers, John & Parthea Troy, 27 May 1812; Henry Chambers,
bondsman; Geo Dunn, wit.

Chambers, Jno & Rebecah Graham, 13 June 1774; Jas. Cathey, bondsman; Ad: Osborn, wit. consent from James Graham, father of
Rebecah, 13 June 1774.

Chambers, Joseph & Mary Campbell, 14 Sept 1778; George Reid,
bondsman; Ad: Osborn, wit.

Chambers, Jos. F. & Laura Brown, 26 Aug 1843; Jno H. Hardie,
bondsman.

Chambers, Joseph Jr. & Margaret Brown, 8 Jan 1818; Thomas
Allison, bondsman; Milo A. Giles, wit.

Chambers, Martin & Mary Paine (wid), 21 Nov 1819; Samuel Stout,
bondsman.

Chambers, Maxwell & Katharine B. Troy, 14 Jan 1830; Jno H.
Hardie, bondsman.

Chambers, Patterson & Sarah Griffin, 27 Dec 1821; Bryan Ellis, bondsman; A. R. Jones, wit.

Chambers, Patterson & Phebe Adams, 19 March 1835; William Coll, bondsman; C. Harbin, wit.

Chambers, Robert & Janes Batey, 15 Jan 1768; John Mitchell, John Beaty, bondsmen; Thos Frohock, wit.

Chambers, Robert & Lettice Boyd, 10 May 1776; Robert Boyd, bondsman; Ad: Osborn, wit.

Chambers, Thomas S. & Mary M. Graham, 30 Dec 1847; Thos Cowan, bondsman.

Chambers, William & Cassandra W. Robison, 6 Nov 1785; Edmd McFee, bondsman; Max Chambers, wit.

Chambers, William & Ann C. McConnaughey, 13 April 1825; Ezra Allemong, bondsman.

Chambers, William Hamilton & Eleanor Johnston, 4 Feb 1785; Adam Lawrence, bondsman; Ad: Osborn, wit.

Chambers, Wm. & Mary Chambers, 7 Nov 1800; Max Chambers, bondsman; Jn Brem, wit.

Chambers, Wm S. & Susannah Cowan, 20 Jan 1843; David Cowan, bondsman.

Chamlin, John & Eby May, 1 March 1819; Alexr May, bondsman; R. Powell, wit.

Chamness, Micajath & Martha White, 2 June 1803; Jeremiah Haworth, bondsman; William Piggatt, J. P., wit.

Chance, T. F. & Laura Lewis, 31 May 1864; H. A. Wise, bondsman; Obadiah Woodson, wit.

Chandler, Alexander & Rebecca Demby, 26 June 1860; Jas. W. Clark, bondsman; Wm. Locke, wit. married 26 June 1860 by T. W. Guthrie, Minister of the Gospel M. E. Church, South.

Chaplain, James & Polly Stephenson, 14 Dec 1819; Benjamin Taylor, bondsman.

Chaplin, Henery & Christiney Call, 11 Feb 1819; Benjn Taylor, bondsman; John March Sr., wit.

Chaplin, John & Mary Pope, 4 March 1813; Charles Pope, bondsman; Isaac Ople, John Burton, wit.

Chapman, John A. & Rachel Cunningham, 29 March 1806; William Andrews, bondsman; Jn March Sr., wit.

Chapman, Sterling & Nancy Smith, 26 Nov 1813; David Smith, bondsman; Jno Giles, C. C., wit.

Charles, Elisha & Mary Pain, _____ 180_; Smith Charles, bondsman.

Charles, George & Christian Michael, 3 Jan 1787; Fredk. Michal, bondsman; Jno Macay, wit.

Charles, John & Tabitha Teague, 29 March 1821; Solomon Charles, bondsman; So Davis, J. P., wit.

Charles, Jonathan & Margaret Garrison, 4 March 1819; John Charles, bondsman; Sol. Davis, wit.

Chavis, Joel & Oliph Lee, 18 Dec 1828; Jacob Jones, bondsman; Jno H. Hardie, wit.

Chavis, John & Eliza Dunson (free persons of color), 13 Oct 1852; E. Calvin, bondsman; James E. Kerr, wit. married by J. M. Brown, J. P., 14 Oct 1852.

Cheek, Robert & Isabella K. Chapman, 5 Sept 1818; A. T. Robinson, bondsman. Robt. Nanny, wit.

Cherry, Robert & Sarah McCuiston, 31 July 1769; John McCuiston, John Anderson, bondsmen; Charles McAnally, wit.

Cheshire, Tennison & Barbara Mock, 11 June 1818; John Locke, bondsman; Roberts Nanny, wit.

Chesher, Jonathan & Elizabeth Willman, 3 Jan 1828; William Cook, bondsman; L. R. Rose, J. P., wit.

Cheshier, Aquillar & Polley Henline, 20 June 1815; Arthur Smith, bondsman; Jn March Sr., wit.

Cheshier, John Sr. & Susannah Cole, 28 Nov 1815; John Chesheir Jr., bondsman; R. Powell, wit.

Cheshier, Tenneson & Evy Sain, 21 Aug 1821; William Sain, bondsman; Geo Collen, wit.

Cheshier, Thomas & Sarah Richardson, 7 Jan 1832; Scarlet Latham, bondsman; Thomas McNeely, J. P., wit.

Cheshire, Jonathan Jr. & Nancy Sainer, 25 Sept 1826; Tenneson Cheshier, bondsman; C. Harbin, J. P., wit.

Cheshur, Jonathan & Elizabeth Sain, 13 Jan 1824; Willey Sain, bondsman; L. R. Rose, J. P., wit.

Chesire, Zachariah & Susanah Flemons, 16 Sept 1820; John Mathews, bondsman; Sol. Davis, wit.

Chesler (Kessler), George & Christiana Eller, 10 Oct 1814; John Plowman, bondsman; Geo Dunn, wit.

Chesser, John & Rebecca Click, 13 March 1820; Burch Chesheir, bondsman; R. Powell, wit.

Chesser, John & Temperance Beaman, 8 Dec 1829; Wilson Rose, bondsman; L. R. Rose, J. P., wit.

Children, John & Mary Leech, 12 Nov 1791; Hugh Cunningham, bondsman.

Chessur, George & Christina Bruner, 27 Dec 1821; Zachariah Chessur, Philip Miars, bondsmen; James Love, J. P., wit.

Chipman, Obidah & Keziah Davis, 3 Jan 1816; Paris Chipman, bondsman.

Chipman, Paris & Elizabeth Sanders, 6 June 1790; John Chipman, bondsman; Jno Monro, wit.

Chivers, Andrew & Molly Pharoah, 15 Dec 1798; William Knop, bondsman.

Chrall, John & Mary Ann Troutman, 5 Jan 1802; Adam Troutman, bondsman.

Christy, James & Letitia McLaughlin, 9 Jan 1839; James Gray, bondsman; John Houston, wit.

Christy, John & Abigal Fraser, 23 Feb 1816; William Steel, bondsman; Geo Dunn, wit.

Christy, John A. & Albertine E. McLaughlin, 30 March 1847; George M. Shuford, bondsman; John H. Hardie, Jr., wit.

Christy, Joseph & Geddy Suffin, 3 Aug 1784; James Frazer, bondsman; Hugh Magoune, wit.

Christy, Richard & Nancy Downs, 1 March 1823; Wm. Downs, bondsman.

Chriver, John & Catherin Strep, 1 Nov 1783; Peter Brown, bondsman.

Chumney (Chumley), John & Elizabeth Andrews, 13 Dec 1767; Joseph Andrews, bondsman; L. S. McEwen, wit.

Chunn, Robert & Maria Hide, 27 May 1835; John Dobbins, bondsman.

Chunn, William & Mary Locke, 10 Dec 1821; Ezra Allemong, bondsman.

Church, Amos & Elisabeth Swink, 25 Feb 1783; Henry Giles, bondsman; William Crawford, wit.

Cicell, John & Nancy Jaims (Iaims?), 18 Dec 1812; John Ball, bondsman; J. Wilson, J. P., wit.

Cifford, Philip & Elizabeth Fisher, 27 Dec 1819; Philip Yost, bondsman; Hy Giles, wit.

Claiborgne, H. F. & Rosanah Earnhart, 31 Dec 1864; John Rabb, bondsman; Thomas McNeely, wit.

Clampert, Maskle & Edith Cowan, 1 Aug 1816; Jno Dicky, bondsman; Henry Giles, wit.

Clampet, John A. & Nancy A. Wilhelm, 20 Feb 1866; Joseph K. Burke, bondsman; Obadiah Woodson, wit.

Clampet, Thomas & Elizabeth Pinkston, 30 April 1840; John Pinkston, bondsman; Susan T. Giles, wit.

Clampit, Jonathan & Elizabeth Davis, 3 Nov 1786; Joseph Horten, bondsman; Jno Macay, wit.

Clark, Eli S. & Elizabeth Swan, 23 Aug 1827; Wesley Clark, bondsman; Wm. Hawkins, J. P., wit.

Clark, George & Elizabeth Allen, 14 March 1781; John Smith, bondsman; Ad. Osborn, wit.

Clark, Henry H. & Camilla Fesperman, 22 March 1866; A. W. Howerton, bondsman; Obadiah Woodson, wit.

Clark, James W. & Eliza Pinkston, 19 Dec 1849; Richard Lowry, bondsman; J. S. Myers, wit.

Clark, John & Charlotte Arey, 17 April 1850; William P. Watts, bondsman; J. S. Myers, wit.

Clark, John & Amanda Williamson, 8 Feb 1849; Abram Weaver, bondsman.

Clark, John M. & Susanna Hutchenson, 12 March 1820; Joel Kinyon, bondsman; R. Powell, wit.

Clark, Joseph & _____, 11 Oct 1797; Elijah _____, bondsman; Jno Rogers, wit.

Clark, Morris & Jane Henshaw, 15 Feb 1769; James Townsend, Francis Hartley, bondsmen; Thos Frohock, wit.

Clark, Robert & Tempey Etiheson, 11 April 1815; Arthur Smith, bondsman; Jn March Sr., wit.

Clark, Thomas & Nancy Fitzpatrick, 22 Sept 1788; John Davis, bondsman; William Alexander, wit.

Clark, Warner & Eliza Williamson, 6 June 1842; Rd. W. Long, bondsman.

Clark, Wesley & Mary Swann, 3 June 1820; Jesse Swann, bondsman; R. Powell, wit.

Clark, William & Anny Denard, 12 Nov 1768; William Sherrill, bondsman; Thomas Frohock, wit.

Clark, William & Sarah Jones, 17 Aug 1775; George Gonder, bondsman; David Flowers, wit.

Clarke, John & Eliza Clarke, 9 June 1845; Benj Julian, bondsman; Jno H. Hardie, wit.

Clary, Daniel & Sarah Nesbit, 6 Nov 1786; H. Young, bondsman; Jno Macay, wit.

Clary, Daniel & Elizabeth Hora, 13 Feb 180_; F. Marshal, bondsman; A: Osborn, wit.

Clary, David & Cathrine Pinkstone, 21 May 1804; Daniel Clary, bondsman.

Clary, Evin & Polly Little, 10 Sept 1823; Daniel Casey, bondsman; L. R. Rose, J. P., wit.

Clary, John & Kelly Tinnecks, 3 May 1798; Saml Moore, bondsman; Edwin J. Osborn, wit.

Claunch, Richard & Sally Drake, 11 July 1814; William Howard, bondsman; John Hains, wit.

Claver, Fredrich & Mary Cooke, 23 Feb 1789; John _____, bondsman; Wm. Alexander, wit.

Clavons, John & Polly Ringh(?), 28 July 1813; Thomas Reevs, bondsman; Jno Giles, wit.

Clay, James & Mary Carruthers, 23 July 1789; Frederick Carlock, bondsman; Will Alexander, wit.

Claybrook, George & Judith Dedman, 14 Nov 1814; Moses Claybrook, bondsman; Jno Giles, wit.

Clayton, Frederick & Patsy Stewart, 28 Aug 1814; Charles Hinkle, bondsman; Jno Giles, wit.

Clayton, George & Margaret Thompson, 3 Jan 1784; John Thomson, bondsman; T. H. McCaule, wit.

Clayton, Lambert & Sarah Davidson, 14 Dec 1782; Jas. Ker, bondsman; T. H. McCaule, wit.

Cleaver, John & Susan Cope, 17 Jan 1826; Jacob Cope, bondsman; Hy Giles, wit.

Clefford, William & Barbara Thomson, 24 July 1824; Tillmon Roberts, bondsman; E. Brock, J. P., wit.

Clement, Jesse & Malindey Nail, 1 Jan 1828; Wiely Sain, bondsman; L. R. Rose, J. P., wit.

Clement, Jno & Nancy Bailey, 20 Jan 1821; G. Y. Clement, bondsman; A. R. Jone, wit.

Clements, Henry & Rosanna Sain, 4 Feb 1820; Jacob Allen, bondsman; R. Powell, wit.

Clemens, Ezekiel & Phoebe Reed, 10 June 1803; George Reed, bondsman; Ad: Osborn, wit.

Clemmons, John & Rebecka Johnston, 5 Sept 1801; John Eacles, bondsman; Jno Brem, wit.

Clever, Andrew & Elizabeth Rainer(?), 16 Sept 1847; Noah A. Freeze, bondsman; J. H. Hardie, Jr., wit.

Clever, John (Johannes) & Margaret Miser, (no date, during term of Gov. Alexr. Martin); Frederick Alleman, bondsman; Max: Chambers, wit.

Cleve, Jacob & Christena Billing, 11 Aug 1788; Leonard Cash(?), bondsman; Willm Crawford, wit.

Click, Henry H. & Sarah Owings, 26 March 1835; Hy Giles, bondsman.

Click, Jacob & Margret Ralls, 5 Jan 1814; Nicholas Click, bondsman; Jno March Senr., wit.

Click, John G. & Margaret A. Graham, 15 Dec 1854; E. W. Tatum, bondsman; James E. Kerr, wit.

Click, Michael & Sarah Butler, 27 April 1809; Nicholas Click, bondsman.

Click, Nic. & Catherine Cope, 14 Oct 1802; Barnet Kreiter, bondsman; A. L. Osborn, wit.

Clifford, Abirah & Rosana Hall, 2 Feb 1835; John Jones, bondsman; Thomas McNeely, J. P., wit.

Clifford, Joseph & Susanah Wells, 15 April 1809; Peter Eaton, bondsman; Jn March Sr., wit.

Clifford, Michael & Nelly Leach, 1 Oct 1815; Elisha Leach, bondsman; R. Powell, wit.

Clifton, Elijah & Bethena Terrill, 22 Dec 1801; Andrew Chivers, bondsman; Jno Brem, wit.

Clenard, Danl & Mary Hinkle, 8 Nov 178_; Geo Hoover, bondsman;
Jno Macay, wit.

Clenart, Andrew & Catharine Evens, 13 Jan 1820; John Haines,
bondsman; Jno Monroe, wit.

Cline, Abraham & Lea Barger, 16 April 1822; John Barger, bondsman.

Cline, Adam & Eve Catharine Stirewalt, 9 Nov 1858; F. A. Stirewalt, bondsman; James E. Kerr, wit. married 19 Nov 1858 by
Saml Rothrock, Minister of the Gospel in the Ev. Luth. Church.

Cline, Charles & Sarah Jaol, 6 Feb 1819; William Davis, bondsman; Sol. Davis, J. P., wit.

Cline, Henry & Catharine Barns, 18 Dec 1810; Cornelius Smith,
bondsman; Jno Giles, wit.

Cline, Henry & Susanna Beck, 23 April 1812; Jacob Helsley,
bondsman; Jno Giles, wit.

Cline, Jacob & Nancy Doty, 25 April 1804; Philip Harmon, bondsman; Ph. Beck, wit.

Cline, Jacob & Catharine Gobble, 18 March 1794; Bastian Lentz,
bondsman; Max: Chambers, wit.

Cline, James & Mary Smith, 25 March 1830; Adam Smith, bondsman;
Hy Giles, wit.

Cline, James & Margaret A. Swisher, 27 July 1854; J. S. Johnston,
bondsman; J. S. Myers, wit.

Cline, John & Polly Rumley, 28 April 1830; George Booe, bondsman.

Cline, Peter & Rachell Lee, _____ 1785; Edmond McAtee, bondsman.

Cline, Phillip & Polly Rial, 17 Sept 1812; Peter Cline, bondsman; Ezra Allemong, wit.

Clodfeller, Joseph & Charity Yokeley, 29 July 1821; Daniel
Clodfeller, bondsman; So. Farrington, J. P., wit.

Clodfelter, J. L. & F. C. Montgomery, 13 May 1865; L. P.
Earnheart, bondsman; Obadiah Woodson, wit. married 28 May
1865 by W. A. Wood, Minister of the Gospel.

Clodfelter, Moses & Jane E. Frieze, 1 Jan 1845; William Cooper,
bondsman; Jno Giles, wit.

Clodfelter, Philip & Jemima Foster, 3 Dec 1822; John Lawrence,
bondsman; Jno Giles, wit.

Clodfelter, Joel & Elizabeth Corrin(?), 26 Feb 1834; John B.
Todd, bondsman; Abel Cowan, wit.

Close, Eligah & Sarah Jonson, 2 Jan 1820; Isaac Gordy, bondsman;
Sol. Davis, wit.

Clotfelter, Andrew & Mary Link(?), _____ April 1812; Adam
Nifory, bondsman; J. Willson, J. P., wit.

Clotfelter, David & Nancy Short, 24 Feb 1807; Joel McCorkle,
bondsman; A. L. Osborne, wit.

Clotfelder, Jacob & Elizabeth Hinkle, 29 Sept 1804; Peter Hinkle, bondsman; Jno Monroe, wit.

Clotfelter, Jacob & Margrat Hagge, 28 June 1790; Felix Clotfelder, bondsman; J. Monro, wit.

Cloud, Henry & Emily B. Lindsay, 26 Oct 1853; John P. Gowan, bondsman; James E. Kerr, wit.

Club, Samuel & Esther Willis, 26 Feb 1784; Charles Lowry, bondsman; T. H. McCaule, wit.

Cluts, David & Salmy Peeler, 6 July 1824; Jacob Cluts, bondsman; Chs Witherow, wit.

Cluts, Jacob & Catey Earnhart, 11 July 1799; Martin Hofner, bondsman; Edwd Yarbrough, wit.

Clutz, Jacob & Molly Clutz, 30 Nov 1814; John Clutz, bondsman; Geo Dunn, wit.

Clutz, John & Elizabeth Beaver, 4 Aug 1815; Henry Clutz, bondsman; Jno Giles, wit.

Cluts, William & Teny Clutz, 19 March 1821; Leonard Clutz, bondsman; Milo A. Giles, wit.

Clynerd, Peter & Sophe Saraman, 18 Sept 1783; Peter Faust, bondsman; Jno Macay, wit.

Coatner, Josiah & Eliza Brown, 5 March 1822; George Cauble, bondsman.

Coats, Allen & Elizabeth Harman, 10 Jan 1801; Archd Patterson, bondsman; J. Brem, D. C., wit.

Coats, James & Edy Addams, 6 Dec 1818; John Coats, bondsman; Jno Giles, wit.

Coats, Orrin & Elizabeth Coats, 13 April 1826; William Elliot, bondsman.

Coats, Thomas & Gilly(?) Coats, 24 Nov 1804; Elijah Nannelly, bondsman; Moses Locke, wit.

Coats, William & Malinda Barrett, 20 Feb 1819; Abraham Sharp, bondsman; Jno Giles, wit.

Coats, Wiley & Sarah Adams, 2 Jan 1795; Cornelius Smith, bondsman; J. Troy, D. C., wit.

Cobb, Reuben & Hannah Elizabeth Williams 31 Oct 1864; James C. Newby, bondsman; Obadiah Woodson, wit.

Cobble, Adam & Betsey Corl, 25 Feb 1803; Peter Trexler, bondsman; Adlai L. Osborn, D. C., wit.

Coble, Eli W. & Elizabeth Burgess, 31 Jan 1828; Moses Burgess, bondsman; L. R. Rose, J. P., wit.

Coburn, James & Nancy Rimer, 4 Feb 1841; Tobias File, bondsman; Jno Giles, wit.

Cochran, Andrew & Ann Woods, 17 Sept 1785; Samuel Cochran, bondsman; Ad: Osborn, wit.

Cochran, John & Elizabeth Patten, 7 Feb 1773; Robert Patten
Andrew Cochran, bondsmen; Ad Osborn, wit.

Cochran, Robert & Jane Jamison, 1 April 1796; William Jamison,
bondsman; J. Troy, D. C., wit.

Cochran, William & Sarah Fleming, 29 March 1824; Cyrus Fleming,
bondsman; Hy Giles, wit.

Cochrill, James & _____, _____ 179_; Charles F. Mabius,
bondsman.

Codler, Stephen & Elizabeth Poor, 25 June 1795; Moses Poor,
bondsman; John Eccles, Esqr., wit.

Coffey, Patrick & Maria Burns, 14 Oct 1823; Felix McLean,
bondsman; Hy Giles, wit.

Coffen, John & Nancy Hall, 30 July 1798; William Dobson(?),
bondsman; Geo Fisher, wit.

Coffin, John M. & Laura Henderson, 17 Dec 1851; Jos. F. Chambers,
bondsman; J. S. Myers, wit.

Coffman, John H. & Elizabeth A. Locke, 23 Oct 1850; J. E. Moose,
bondsman; J. S. Myers, wit.

Coffman, John H. & Margaret C. Anderson, 23 Dec 1851; J. S.
Myers, bondsman; James E. Kerr, wit.

Coggins, Jarratt & Rebecca Redwine, 1 Jan 1827; Edwd Burrage,
bondsman; J. H. Hardie, wit.

Coggins, Jonathan & Polly Cox, 12 Oct 1813; Jesse Kinney, bondsman; Geo Dunn, wit.

Coghlan, Jno & Margaret Huston, 9 Sept 1779; Jno Bailey, bondsman; Ad Osborn, Jo: Brevard, wit.

Coile, James & Jean Harrington, 12 Sept 1778; William Harrington,
bondsman; Ad: Osborn, wit.

Coker, George & Frances Rogers, 6 Dec 1812; William Coker,
bondsman; R. Powell, wit.

Coker, Isaac & Jane T. Furches, 14 Aug 1833; Benjamin Eaton,
bondsman; J. Tomlinson, wit.

Coker, Marmaduke G. & Jane W. Daily, 1 Nov 1833; Benjamin Eaton,
bondsman; J. Tomlinson, wit.

Coker, William & Sarah Mills(?), 5 May 1807; Walter Mills,
bondsman; Jn March Sr., wit.

Coker, William & Salley James, 25 Dec 1815; Isaac James,
bondsman; R. Powell, wit.

Coker, William & Amelis Eaton, 3 Oct 1834; Stephen L. Howell,
bondsman; Hy Giles, wit.

Coldiron, George & Elizabeth Crowel, 3 Nov 1795; Johannes Kobl(?),
(John Cobble), bondsman; J. Troy, wit.

Coldiron, Jacob & Nancy B. Ervin, 11 Jan 1820; Jesse Howard,
bondsman; Milo A. Giles, wit.

Cole, James & Elizabeth Daniel, 30 Sept 1803; Jno McClelland, bondsman; A. L. Osborn, D. C., wit.

Cole, John & Nancy Purlee, 26 Aug 1769; Adam Harmon, bondsman; Thomas Frohock, wit.

Cole, Mark & Sarah Cameron, 24 June 1794; Joseph Parks, bondsman; J. Troy, D. C., wit.

Cole, Shepherd & Betsey Blackwelder, 3 Dec 1827; Martin Rodgers, bondsman; J. H. Hardie, wit.

Cole, Sheppard & Peve Cope, 13 Jan 1847; Jacob Gouger, bondsman; Jno H. Hardie, wit.

Cole, Stephen & Elizabeth Conger, 27 Oct 1789; Mark Cole, bondsman.

Cole, William & Elizabeth Smith, 7 Nov 1830; Jno Blackwood, bondsman; L. R. Rose, J. P., wit.

Cole, Wm & Mary Hulame(?), 17 June 1834; William Huland, bondsman; Jno H. Hardie, wit.

Cole, William & Elizabeth Gibbons, 17 Aug 1865; Horatio N. Woodson, bondsman; Obadiah Woodson, wit. married 17 Aug 1865 by A. J. Mock, J. P.

Cole, Wm. Hunter & Rebecca Porter, 28 March 1812; Thomas Porter, bondsman; Jno Giles, C. C., wit.

Coleman, George P. & Mary Deal, 10 Nov 1849; Charles Blackwelder, bondsman; James E. Kerr, wit.

Coleman, Jacob & Polly Parks, 18 Feb 1828; Jacob Gouger, bondsman.

Coleman, John & Peggy Coleman, 30 May 1804; Jno Leazer, bondsman; A. L. Osborn, wit.

Coleman, Julius A. & Elizabeth A. Nichols, married 24 May 1860 by Saml Rothrock, Minister of the Gospel in the Ev. Luth. Church. (no bond, minister's return only)

Coley, G. D. & Harriet Heilig, 3 Jan 1857; Samuel A. Creson, bondsman; J. S. Myers, wit.

Collins, David & Thompson Fosting, 1 Oct 1772; Henry Zeody, Alex Brown, bondsmen.

Colly, J. T. & Selena Cook, 9 April 1862; James M. Colley, bondsman; Obadiah Woodson, wit. married April 1862 by W. M. Kincaid, J. P.

Colvert, John A. & Nancy Cole, 3 Nov 1812; Joseph N. Colvert, bondsman; Geo Dunn, wit.

Conatzer, Nathaniel & Eliza S. Fraly, 28 April 1853; Asberry Sprig, bondsman; J. S. Myers, wit.

Conger, John Jr. & Mary Ross, 5 June 1769; Jonathan Conger, bondsman; Thomas Frohock, wit. consent of John Conger, 6th June.

Conger, John & Judea Owen, __ Feb 1795; Mich. Troy, bondsman.

Conger, Joshua & Lucy Owen, 12 Nov 1794; William Moore, bondsman; J. Troy, D. C., wit.

Connelly, Bernard & Susan J. Minor, 17 April 1856; John W.
Jenkins, bondsman; J. S. Myers, wit.

Conner, James & Anna Thomason, 10 March 1846; Fred. Mourey,
bondsman; J. H. Hardie, wit.

Conner, Mikel & Preshes Boswell, 23 March 1808; Isaac Ward,
bondsman; Jno March Sr., wit.

Conrad, Peter & Elizabeth Sitten, 10 Feb 1791; John Grove,
bondsman; C. Caldwell, D. C., wit.

Conrod, David & Eve Hedrick, 22 Dec 1810; Peter Hedrick, bondsman; Joseph Clarke, wit.

Conrod, Jacob & Susanna Brinkle, 21 Nov 1818; David Conrod,
bondsman; Zebulon Hunt, wit.

Cook, Alexander B. & Nancy T. Freeland, 19 May 1845; Andrew W.
Cook bondsman; J. H. Hardie, wit.

Cook, Alfred & Sarah Torrentine, 23 Feb 1826; Jno Clement,
bondsman; Hy Giles, wit.

Cook, George W. & Eliza Ann _____, 14 April 1822; Scarlet Glascock,
bondsman; John Cook, J. P., wit.

Cook, Jacob & Judith Harris, _____ 180_; Othl. Peirce, bondsman;
Wm. Wilson, wit.

Cook, Jacob & Caty Gobble, 13 July 1802; Jacob Gobble, bondsman;
Jno Brem, D. C., wit.

Cook, James & Ann McConnell, 15 Aug 1774; Joseph Dickson, bondsman; Ad. Osborn, wit.

Cook, John & Mary McCuiston, 18 July 1769; Hugh Forster, Walter
McCuiston, Francis Mcnary, bondsmen; Thomas Frohock, William
Mebane, wit.

Cook, John & Mary Willcockson, 22 Jan 1793; Saml Casey, bondsman; Basil Gaither, wit.

Cook, John & Sarah Mock, 12 June 1818; Charles Downes, bondsman;
Jn March Sr., wit.

Cook, John W. & Elizabeth C. Bufh, 30 Jan 1855; Wm. W. Morgan,
bondsman; J. S. Myers, wit.

Cook, Joseph & Sarah Phillips, 27 Dec 1841; McGuin Phillips,
bondsman; Susan T. Giles, wit.

Cook, Martin & Polly Ratey, 5 Oct 1808; Thomas Todd, bondsman;
A. L. Osborn, wit.

Cook, Mathias & Elizabeth Keller, 2 Nov 1829; William Nash,
bondsman; L. R. Rose, J. P., wit.

Cook, Robert S. & Mary Ann Owen, 9 Dec 1856; W. B. Trott,
bondsman.

Cook, Thomas M. & Polly S. Thompson, 22 March 1819; Moses
Thompson, bondsman; Jno Giles, wit.

Cook, William & Hester Aytcherson, 1 May 1791; Walter Aytcheson,
bondsman; Nichos. W. Gaither, wit.

Cooke, James & Morgant Thompson, 22 June 1789; John Hide,
bondsman.

Cooke, John & Rebeckah Lauson, 7 May 1788; Benj. McConnell,
bondsman; M. Osborne, wit.

Cooke, Thos & Ann Clayton, 20 Jan 1781; Lambert Clayton, bondsman.

Coon, Geo & Julia Ann Pence, 28 Dec 1844; R. W. Gardner, bondsman.

Coon, George & Mary Swisher, 20 Dec 1849; James Caldwell, bondsman.

Coon, Jacob & Elizebeth Rice, 15 Oct 1808; Spencer Stephens
(Stevens), bondsman; Jno March Senr., wit.

Coon, Jacob & Sarah Pence, 17 May 1842; Jno Giles, wit.

Coon, James & Lucinda Gaskey, 12 Aug 1857; Fergus M. Graham,
bondsman; J. S. Myers, wit. married 13 Aug 1857 by W. R.
Fraley, J. P.

Coon, John & Susan Casper, 19 Nov 1835; John Scott, bondsman;
Jno H. Hardie, wit.

Coon, Paul & Martha Kincaid, 5 Aug 1830; Elias Lee, bondsman;
Jno H. Hardie, wit.

Coon, Paul & Piety Hulin, 10 March 1835; Peter Kesler, bondsman;
Jno H. Hardie, wit.

Coon, Richard M. & Sophia M. Misenheimer, 7 Sept 1865; William
Safrit, bondsman; Horatio N. Woodson, bondsman; married
7 Sept 1865 by Whitson Kimball, minister.

Coone, Valentine & Margret Booe, 23 Dec 1762; Johann Michael
Baker, John Mithel(?), bondsmen; John Frohock, wit.

Coons, Anthony & Rosianna Simmons, 16 June 1769; Peter Snowden,
Benja. Milner, bondsmen; John Frohock, wit.

Cooper, David & Ann Miller, 23 April 1798; David Stewart, bondsman; E. J. Osborn, D. C., wit.

Cooper, David M. & Delilah C. Caneker, 10 Sept 1853; John W.
Leazar, bondsman; James E. Kerr, wit.

Cooper, Geo. W. & Nancy Henly, 15 Aug 1844; Peter Vankanon,
bondsman; J. H. Hardie, wit.

Cooper, Harvey & Jensey Davis, 15 Aug 1820; Benjamin Cooper,
bondsman.

Cooper, Henry & Rebecca Hollis, 19 Jan 1794; John Blaze, bondsman; Jo. Chambers, wit.

Cooper, John & Lidia Johnston, 22 July 1762; Conrad Michel,
Jacob _____, bondsmen; John Frohock, wit.

Cooper, John & Sarah Riddle, 11 Feb 1789; James Jurdon, bondsman; Will Alexander, wit.

Cooper, John & Priscilla Cowan, 9 Jan 1811; Joseph Cowan, bondsman; Geo Dunn, wit.

Cooper, John & Peggy Kimball, 9 Oct 1823; Harbert Wallace,
bondsman.

Cooper, John & Rachael Smith, 16 Dec 1824; Edward Yarbrough,
16 Dec 1824; Hy Giles, wit.

Cooper, John & Clarrissa S. Sloop, 10 April 1860; James S.
Graham, bondsman; John Wilkinson, wit.

Cooper, Nebimiah & Susannah Michael, 1 Nov 1802; A. L. Osborn,
D. C., wit.

Cooper, Samuel & Margat McBride, 16 Aug 1786; John Ferguson,
bondsman; Jno Macay, wit.

Cooper, Samuel & Agness W. Hunt, 18 Feb 1813; Michael Harris,
bondsman; John Hanes, wit.

Cooper, Samuel & Nancy Womac, 6 July 1819; John Merrill, bondsman; Hy Giles, wit.

Cooper, Thomas & Elizabeth Smith, 27 Feb 1798; Samuel Miller,
bondsman; Edwin J. Osborn, wit.

Cooper, William & Sarah Clodfelter, 10 June 1841; James Cowan,
bondsman; J. S. Beard, wit.

Cooper, Wm & Elizabeth Graham, (no date, probably 1782-85);
Fergus Graham, bondsman; H. Magoune, wit.

Cooper, Wm. & Sally Coupee, 12 April 1827; William Hughes,
bondsman; M. A. Giles, wit.

Cooper, Wilson & Luny(?) Davis, 13 Oct 1819; Joseph Harrison,
bondsman; Hy Giles, wit.

Cope, Daniel & Sarah Correll, 9 April 1842; John N. Hess,
bondsman; J. H. Hardie, wit.

Cope, Frederick & Sally Wiatt, 7 March 1822; William Wyett,
bondsman; An. Swicegood, wit.

Cope, Henry & Nancy Wyatt, 18 Dec 1833; Samuel Garwood, bondsman; Thomas McNeely, J. P., wit.

Cope, Jacob & Lear Duke, 27 Dec 1825; Andrew Cope, bondsman;
Jno Giles, wit.

Cope, Jacob & Barbara Peck, 16 Nov 1794; Peter Peck, bondsman.

Cope, John & Margaret Bostion, 8 May 1804; Henry Pence, bondsman; Hudson Hughes, wit.

Cope, John & Nancy Gullet, 15 Nov 1822; Wm. Coker, bondsman;
Geo Coker, J. P., wit.

Cope, John & Emeley Tucker, 28 Feb 1807; William Griffin,
gondsman; Jn March Sr., wit.

Cope, Philip & Polly Bostain, 14 July 1831; Horatio Woodson, bondsman; Jno H. Hardie, wit.

Copple, Jacob & Delila Plummer, 5 Jan 1822; Ezekiel Powers, bondsman; Ams. Wright, wit.

Coreker, Jacob & Lizy Freesen, 19 Feb 1811; Rudolph Sechler, bondsman; Geo Dunn, wit.

Corel, Jacob A. W. & Barbary Mowry, 10 May 1855; Miles Rusher, bondsman; James E. Kerr, wit.

Corel, John & Susannah Albright, 17 Dec 1808; Peter Albright, bondsman; A. L. Osborne, D. C., wit.

Coriher, George & Sarah L. Coleman, 22 Oct 1833; Daniel Leazar, bondsman; Hy Giles, wit.

Coriker, John & Mary E. Hudson, 4 Feb 1833; William Leazer, bondsman.

Corl, Adam A. & Letitia Smith, 24 Dec 1864; Ransom Jacobs, bondsman; Obadiah Woodson, wit.

Corl, Alexander & Mary Klutts, 7 June 1844; Joseph Miller, bondsman; J. H. Hardie, wit.

Corl, Daniel & Marie Perry, 26 Nov 1830; Wm. D. Callicott, bondsman; J. H. Hardie, wit.

Corl, Jacob & Margaret Bird, 6 Nov 1830; John Shaver, bondsman; Hy Giles, wit.

Corl, Jacob & Mary Sedwell, 2 Nov 1857; Joseph Corl, bondsman; James E. Kerr, wit. married 5 Nov 1857 by D. W. Honeycutt, J. P.

Corl, Michael & Sally Swink, 18 June 1834; Thomas M. Ford, bondsman; Jno H. Hardie, wit.

Corl, Michael & Jane Hulin, 27 Jan 1848; Leonard L. Krider, bondsman; J. H. Hardie, Jr., wit.

Corl, Michael & Sarah Hulen, 4 Sept 1849; W. David Weant, bondsman; J. S. Myers, wit.

Corl, Michael & Eliza Koontz, 18 June 1856; Woodson Mills, bondsman; J. S. Myers, wit.

Corl, Rufus & Charlotte S. Eagle, 2 Jan 1861; J. W. Littan, bondsman; John Wilkinson, wit. married 3 Feb 1861 by L. C. Groseclose, Pastor of St. John's Ev. Luth. Church, Salisbury, N. C.

Cornatzer, Daniel & Elizabeth Chambers, 31 Dec 1822; George Sanar, bondsman; L. R. Rose, wit.

Cornatzer, John & Nancy Mullicon, 13 May 1824; William Hanand, bondsman; Joseph Hanes, wit.

Cornelison, Conrod & Susanna Strange, 5 Feb 1785; Peter Todd, bondsman.

Cornell, Benjamin & Polly Ellis, _____ Aug 1828; John Giles, wit.

Cornell, Benjamin & Polly Ellis, 15 Oct 1828; David Harbin, bondsman; C. Harbin, J. P., wit.

Cornish, James & Polly Helemstetter, 17 Feb 1818; William Cornish, bondsman; Jno Giles, wit.

Corothers, James & Agness Woods, (no date, durning admn. of Gov. Martin); James Woods, bondsman; Hugh Magoune, wit. (date probably 1782-1785).

Correl, John & Polly Kern(?), 30 Sept 1815; Gerhart Sollenberger, bondsman; Jno Giles, wit.

Correll, Christian & Sallie Freeze, 21 July 1818; John Litaker, bondsman; Roberts Nanny, wit.

Correll, Daniel & Nelly Pence, 28 Oct 1822; John Correll, bondsman.

Correll, Daniel & Mary Ann Freeze, 19 May 1852; John Sloop, bondsman; James E. Kerr, wit.

Correll, David & Frany Freeze, 21 Nov 1838; Jacob Shulibaringer, bondsman; S. Lemly Jr., wit.

Correll, David & Mary D. Misenhamer, 12 Nov 1847; B. F. Fraley, bondsman.

Correll, David J. & Sarah Sechler, 9 May 1853; Jesse Sechler, bondsman; J. S. Myers, wit.

Correll, Hezekiah & Ellen Parks, 4 Nov 1851; Abner Pace, bondsman; J. S. Myers, wit.

Correll, Jacob & Betsey Freeze, 22 Feb 1819; John Litaker, bondsman; Jno Giles, wit.

Correll, Jacob & Christena Falk, 23 March 1834; Adam Stirewalt, bondsman; Hy Giles, wit.

Correll, James & Betsey Shuldeberger, 25 Dec 1818; Jesse Bostian, bondsman; Jno Giles, wit.

Correll, John & Betsey Custer, 19 July 1810; Henry Custer, bondsman; Jno Giles, C. C., wit.

Correll, John & Mary Catherine James, 16 July 1844; James W. Daes, bondsman.

Correll, John L. & Selma Cauble, 6 Oct 1856; Jerrey Marsh, bondsman; J. S. Myers, wit. married 28 Oct 1856 by John Rice, J. P.

Correll, Phillip & Franny Freeze, 23 July 1817; John Liteaker, bondsman; Milo A. Giles, wit.

Correll, William & Matholine Paulus, 15 Nov 1790; John Correl, bondsman; C. Caldwell, D. C., wit.

Correll, William W. & Margaret A. Marlin, 18 April 1857; William Barber, bondsman; J. S. Myers, D. C., wit. married 21 April 1857 by Saml. B. O. Wilson, V. D. M.

Corricar, David & Ritty Stuart, 12 March 1805; John Stuart, bondsman; Moses A. Locke, wit.

Corrier, William & Sally Pechal, 5 March 1836; John Boston, bondsman; Abel Cowan, wit.

Corriker, George & Jane E. Corriker, 26 Feb 1859; David Earnhardt, bondsman.

Corriker, George & Margaret Sackler, 27 May 1839; C. A. Rose, bondsman; Jno Giles, wit.

Corriker, Henry & Christena Seckler, 23 March 1835; Moses Seckler, bondsman; Jno H. Hardie, wit.

Corriker, Henry & Catherine Coleman, 17 Nov 1823; John Graham, bondsman; Hy Giles, wit.

Corriker, John & Ruth Cannon, 2 Feb 1831; William Otrich, bondsman; Hy Giles, wit.

Corriker, Richard A. & Priscilla Seckler, 20 Feb 1860; Gen. A. J. Seckler, bondsman; John Wilkinson, wit.

Corriker, Rufus A. & Susan A. Deal, 24 Sept 1855; Richard A. Corriker, bondsman; J. S. Myers, wit. married 27 Sept 1855 by J. S. Heilig.

Corsine, R. F. & Catharine Phifer, 19 Jan 1866; J. C. Phifer, bondsman; Obadiah Woodson, wit.

Corwcil, Peter & Fedney Mowry, 3 April 1797; Jacob Cobble, bondsman; Jno Rogers, wit.

Corzine, Richard & Ruth Emberson, 9 Aug 1832; Henry Baker, bondsman.

Coston, Jacob & Margaret Powless, 14 April 1789; Peter Faust, bondsman; Will Alexander, wit.

Cotes, James & Robena Ryle, 13 March 1759; Joshua Ryle, John Johnson, bondsmen.

Cotes, Sion & Lucy Simpson, 3 Sept 1802; John Adams, bondsman.

Cottiser, Henry & Caty Criss, 20 Dec 1784; Fredrick Gelshaw, bondsman; H. Magoune, wit.

Cotton, Elijah & Margaret Penny, 3 Sept 1807; Daniel Shuford, bondsman.

Cotton, Isaac & Polly Stephens 2 April 1792; Cyrus Cotton, bondsman; Chs. Caldwell, wit.

Couch, Samuel & _____, 22 Nov 1803; James Martin, bondsman; William Welborn, wit.

Coughenhour, Jacob & Caroline Monroe, 19 May 1838; Drew Smith, bondsman; Jno Giles, wit.

Coughenhoven, John & Mary Freese, 8 July 1794; William Smether, bondsman; J. Troy, D. C., wit.

Coughenour, Jacob & Christena R. Brandon, 23 Dec 1834; Mathew Brandon, bondsman; Jno H. Hardie, wit.

Coughenour, John & Sarah D. Brown, 28 June 1821; Michael S. Brown Jr., bondsman.

Coughonour, Christian & Polly Shaver, 26 March 1798; David Miller, bondsman; Edwin J. Osborn, D. C., wit.

Courtney, John & Catharine Pool, 10 March 1825; Allen Burroughs, bondsman; W. Harris, wit.

Cowan, A. Varner & Rebecca Cowan, 31 July 1827; John Huie, bondsman; Jno Giles, wit.

Cowan, Abel & Lucretia Brandon, 6 May 1816; Tho. L. Cowan, bondsman; Geo Dunn, wit.

Cowan, Abel & Maria McKenzie, 28 Jan 1826; George McConnaughey, bondsman.

Cowan, Abel Armstrong & Margaret M. McConnehey, 20 June 1818; Henry Hughey, bondsman; Jno Giles, wit.

Cowan, Able A. & Mary A. Locke, 16 July 1854; R. B. Patterson, bondsman; J. S. Myers, wit.

Cowan, Benjamin & Jean Steele, 5 June 1805; Thomas Todd, bondsman; Tho. L. Cowan, wit.

Cowan, Benjamin F. & Elizabeth Cowan, 16 July 1822; Abner B. Cowan, bondsman; Hy Giles, wit.

Cowan, Christopher J. & Eliza C. McNeely, 4 Dec 1824; James Alexander Jr., bondsman; Hy Allemong, wit.

Cowan, D. L. & Sallie J. Sloan, 4 Sept 1865; Robt H. Smith, bondsman; Obadiah Woodson, wit.

Cowan, D. P. & Sarah McNight, 31 Aug 1841; John M. Cowan, bondsman; J. S. Johnston, wit.

Cowan, David & _____, _____; Alexander Dobbin, bondsman; James Robinson, wit.

Cowan, David & Rebekah Dobbins, 23 Aug 1790; John Dobbin, bondsman; C. C. Caldwell, wit.

Cowan, David & Nancy Bowman, 11 March 1793; James Bowman, bondsman; Jos. Chambers, wit.

Cowan, Henry & Elizabeth Rex, 8 Jan 1824; Thomas Bailey, bondaman.

Cowan, Isaac & Jinsy Swann, 9 Sept 1812; Saml. Young, bondsman; Geo Du_n, wit.

Cowan, James & Ester Lewis, 22 Aug 1775; Henry Dobbin, bondsman; David Flowers, wit.

Cowan, James & Nancy L. Gillispie, 22 Dec 1828; George Gillispie, bondsman; Jno H. Hardie, wit.

Cowan, John & Lucinda Kilpatrick, 18 June 1819; George J. Niblack, bondsman; John Giles, wit.

Cowan, John & Sally Robinson, 7 June 1820; Jos. E. Todd, bondsman; Jno Giles, wit.

Cowan, John & Mary G. Roberson, 30 Dec 1835; Levi Cowan, bondsman; J. H. Hardie, wit.

Cowan, John F. & Elizabeth C. Smith, 27 Oct 1828; Hy. Giles, bondsman.

Cowan, John M. & Rebecca Cowan, 6 Sept 1851; Julius F. Ramsey, bondsman; J. S. Myers, wit. married 9 Sept 1851 by J. M. H. Adams, Minister of the Presbyterian Church.

Cowan, Joseph & Elizabeth Swann, 20 Jan 1818; Abel A. Cowan, bondsman; Milo A. Giles, wit.

Cowan, Joseph & Rebecca Howison, 22 Oct 1823; Hezekiah T. Harrison, bondsman.

Cowan, Joseph & Sarah Young, 4 Sept 1826; Saml Young, bondsman; Jno Giles, wit.

Cowan, Nathan & Ruhamah Briggs, 20 Feb 1833; John Dobbins, bondsman; Jno H. Hardie, wit.

Cowan, Nenian & J. E. Erwin, _____; T. C. Graham, bondsman.

Cowan, R. T. & M. C. Knox, 7 Nov 1859; James B. Parker, bondsman; James E. Kerr, wit. married 8 Nov 1859 by Saml. B. O. Wilson.

Cowan, Richard H. & Margaret Locke, 11 Nov 1851; Thos C. McNeely, bondsman; James E. Kerr, wit.

Cowan, Richard O. & Elizabeth L. Irvine, 7 Jan 1845; Robert W. Hughey, bondsman.

Cowan, Robert & Matilda McHenry, 1 _____ 1820; James Cowan, bondsman; Jno Giles, wit.

Cowan, Robert & Elizabeth Camell, 24 July 1792; Benjamin Cowan, bondsman; S. Mitchell, wit.

Cowan, Robert F. & Theresa Overcash, married 10 March 1858 by J. E. Pressly, (no bond, minister's return only).

Cowan, Robert V. & Nancy Capels, 16 May 1832; Robt Airey, bondsman; Jno H. Hardie, wit.

Cowan, Samuel & Phebe Lewis, 14 June 1783; Samuel Lewis, bondsman; Wm. Crawford, wit.

Cowan, Stephen & Patsy Caldwell, 21 Oct 1782; David Cowan, bondsman; Evan Alexander, wit.

Cowan, Stephen & Unice Holland 19 Sept 1820; Duncan McGill, bondsman; Jno Giles, wit.

Cowan, Stephen F. & Ann M. Graham, 21 March 1842; Henry C. Burke, bondsman; Jno. H. Hardie, wit.

Cowan, t homas & Catharine Foster, 22 May 1803; David Foster, bondsman; Adlai L. Osborn, D. C., wit.

Cowan, Thomas & Margaret Young, 4 Aug 1841; Thos. C. Graham Sr., bondsman; J. S. Johnston, wit.

Cowan, Thomas L. & Elizabeth Brown, 26 April 1810; Joseph Chambers, Peter Brown, bondsmen; James Cowan, wit.

Cowan, William & Mary Hinds, 7 July 1784; Ralph Hinds, bondsman; Hugh Magoune, wit.

Cowan, William & Jane Steel, 11 April 1786; Ninain Stell, bondsman; John Macay, wit.

Cowan, William & Sarah Stewart, 23 Dec 1759; James Stewart,
bondsman; John Howard, wit.

Cowan, William & Catharine Armstrong, 5 April 1791; John Tate,
bondsman; C. Caldwell, D. C., wit.

Cowan, William & Anne Foster, 19 Feb 1805; Isaac Cowan, bondsman.

Cowan, William & Ruannah Cowan, 31 Oct 1826; Abel A. Luckie,
bondsman; J. H. Hardie, wit.

Cowan, William S. & Polly Anderson, 7 Sept 1808; John S. Todd,
bondsman; A. L. Osborne, D. C., wit.

Coward, Alexander & Mary Irvine, 22 Oct 1795; John Dickey,
bondsman; J. Troy, wit.

Cowen, Henry & Susannah Cowan, 26 Feb 1798; Isaac Hughey,
bondsman; Edwin J. Osborn, D. C., wit.

Cowden, John & Jane Brown, 25 March 1768; Griffeth Rutherford,
Francis Lock, bondsmen; John Frohock, wit.

Cowin, George & Jean Cowan, 19 Feb 1803; Richd Steele, bondsman;
A. L. Osborn, D. C., wit.

Cowin, Isaac & Mary Pelton, 8 Nov 1780; Nicholas Aldridge,
bondsman; H. Gifford, wit.

Cowin, Isack & Sarah Steward, 17 Dec 1783; David Steward, bondsman; Jno McNairy, wit.

Cox, Caleb & Nancey Seals, 28 May 1787; Joseph Cox, bondsman;
Jno Macay, wit.

Cox, David & Martha Cole, 5 April 1788; Wm. Hamton, bondsman;
J. McEwin, wit.

Cox, Ephraim & Susannah Person, 9 July 1768; Alexd. Thompson,
bondsman; Thom. Frohock, wit. consent of Denny Person,
father of Susannah.

Cox, George W. & Caroline Swink, 11 June 1852; Atha Cauble,
bondsman; J. S. Myers, wit. married 12 June 1852 by Wm.
Heathman, J. P.

Cox, James & Sarah Macewell, 7 July 1792; James Harp, bondsman.

Cox, Jesse McJ. & Judith Watkins, 20 Nov 1819; Solomon Sanders,
bondsman; R. Powell, wit.

Cox, John & Susanna Beaver, 23 March 1802; Bostian Lentz, bondsman.

Cox, Jonathan & Mary Kousce, 8 May 1779; Joseph Cox, bondsman;
Jos. Brevard, wit.

Cox, Joshua & Mary Neal, 17 May 1769; Adam Mitchell, Thomas
Niel, Richard Cox, bondsmen; William Bostick, Samuel Shaw, wit.

Cox, Mark & Polly Curkhead, 5 Dec 1820; Wm. Redwine, bondsman; Henry Allemong, wit.

Cox, Moses & Hannah Beard, 13 July 1799; Abel Hunt, bondsman.

Cox, Thos & Deborah Diggins, 4 Dec 1804; Jno Frost, bondsman; A. L. Osborn, D. C., wit.

Cox, William & Mary Loften, 4 March 1811; David Cox, bondsman.

Cox, William & Barbary Miller, 20 March 1836; James Aderton, bondsman; H. Bringle, wit.

Coxx, William & Rachael Ribly, 26 June 1815; David McMahon, bondsman; Jno Giles, wit.

Coy, Thomas & Hanniah Davis, 3 May 1785; Henry Winkler, bondsman; Hugh Magoune, wit.

Coyt, Thomas & _____, _____; William Wray, bondsman; Tibby Troy, wit.

Cozart, Anthony & Mary Ann Thomason, 24 March 1831; David Pinkston, bondsman; Jno H. Hardie, wit.

Cozart, Hiram W. & Rachel Philips, 8 June 1837; Littleton Brown, bondsman; Tobias L. Lemly, wit.

Cozort, David F. & Londy M. Lowder, married 7 April 1867 by J. Thomason, J. P. (no bond, minister's return only).

Craford, H. C. & F. L. Rainey, 19 Dec 1863; A. L. Hall, bondsman; Obadiah Woodson, wit.

Crafts, Joseph & Sarah Wells, 16 Dec 1782; Thos Willis, bondsman; William Crawford, wit.

Craig, Hugh & Mary Billingsby, 8 Dec 1799; John Cragg, bondsman; Wm. Welborn, wit.

Craig, James & Mary Kerr, 20 Feb 1786; Richard Wright, bondsman; Ad. Osborn, wit.

Craig, John & Elizabeth Andrews, 17 Oct 1795; George Andrews, bondsman; J. Troy, D. C., wit.

Craig, Thomas H. & Susan Jones, 15 March 1838; James Owens, bondsman; E. R. Birckhead, wit.

Craig, William & Ann McPherson, 7 Oct 1772; William Steel, bondsman; Max Chambers, wit. consent from Joseph McPherson, brother of Ann, 2 Oct 1772; Susanna Linn, wit.

Craige, David & Mary Foster, 10 July 1776; Alexr Brown, bondsman; Ad. Osborn, wit.

Craige, David & Polly Foster, 24 Dec 1803; John Weant, bondsman; A. L. Osborn, D. C., wit.

Craige, James & Peggy Shroat, 23 Feb 1813; John Weant, bondsman; Jno Giles, wit.

Craige, Richard & Oney Pinkston (colored), 16 Sept 1865; Obadiah Woodson, wit. married 16 Sept 1865 by Zuck Houghton.

ROWAN MARRIAGES 1753-1868

Craige, Samuel & Mariah L. Howard, 16 March 1842; Wm. Locke, bondsman; J. H. Hardie, wit.

Craige, William & Deborah Orman, _____ 1783; Joseph Chambers, bondsman; Wm. Crawford, wit.

Craigg, Crozier & Sarah Billingsly, 26 May 1803; John Craigg, bondsman; William Piggatt, J. P., wit.

Craiglo--see Cegelo

Cralie, Julius & Lydia Milton, 24 June 1860; J. A. Galemore, bondsman; John Wilkinson, wit. married 24 June 1860 by Peter Williamson, J. P.

Cranch, John & Mary Reed, 7 Nov 1825; Noah Reed, bondsman.

Crane, John & Susanah Scott, 16 March 1767; John Lewis Beard, Robt Pearis, bondsmen; Thos Frohock, wit.

Cranfiel, Jabin & Sarah Mellar, 2 May 1823; Pleasant Mellar, bondsman; John Cook, J. P., wit.

Cranfill, David & Polly Brogden, 14 May 1820; David Batey, bondsman; R. Powell, wit.

Cranfill, Joshua & Elizabeth May, 13 Nov 1817; William Steelman, bondsman; R. Powell, wit.

Cranfill, Levi & Lucinda Hudson, 7 Sept 1829; David Trivitt, bondsman; J. Inglis, wit.

Cranfill, Lewis & Catharine Reavis, 27 Aug 1832; Thos. H. Cain, bondsman; Jas. Frost, J. P., wit.

Cranfill, Nathan & Oner Trivitt, 28 Nov 1826; Morgan Baity, bondsman; J. Inglis, wit.

Cranfill, William & Mary Beaty, 11 Dec 1798; Abram Hall, bondsman; Edwin J. Osborn, D. C., wit.

Cranfill, William M. & Margaret Beeman, 24 Dec 1832; Joshua Cranfill, bondsman; Jas Frost, J. P., wit.

Cranford, Burgess & _____, 14 March 1825; David Holobaugh, bondsman; Jno H. Hardie, wit.

Cranford, Tilman & Fanny Miller, 22 Feb 1837; Warren Gheen, bondsman; Tobias L. Lemly, wit.

Cranford, Tilman & Martha E. Green, 4 March 1846; Abner W. Owen, bondsman; J. M. Turner, wit.

Cranford, W. H. & Londa Porter, 19 Sept 1865; Horatio N. Woodson, bondsman; Obadiah Woodson, wit. married 21 Sept 1865 by Henry Barringer, J. P.

Cranford, Wilburn & Elizabeth A. Todd, 7 June 1851; Jacob S. Myers, bondsman; James E. Kerr, wit.

Craven, Lewis & _____, _____ 1813; Joseph Hagee, bondsman; J. Wilson, J. P., wit.

Craver, J. W. & Francis J. Shoaf, 12 July 1862; J. C. Shoaf, bondsman; m 12 July 1862 by David Lentz, J. P.

92

Craver, Michael & Susanna Sowers, 19 Feb 1813; Henry Sowers, bondsman; Geo Dunn, wit.

Crawford--see also Craford

Crawford, Abel & Elinor Bell, 23 Feb 1785; Hugh Robison, bondsman; H. Magoune, wit.

Crawford, Joseph & Polly Cauble, 11 May 1816; James Eagle, bondsman; Jno Giles, C. C., wit.

Crawford, Thomas M. & Mary Price, 16 Dec 1856; A. N. Flemming, bondsman; James E. Kerr, wit.

Crawford, Thomas M. & Mary A. L. Klutts, 22 Dec 1864; C. A. Henderson, bondsman; Obadiah Woodson, wit.

Crawford, William D. & Lucretia E. Mull, 20 Jan 1829; Hy Giles, bondsman.

Creason, Abraham & Polly Horn, 7 April 1816; Joseph Horn, bondsman; R. Powell, wit.

Creason, Charles & Shapa Emery, 12 March 1827; Henry Lutewick, bondsman; J. H. Hardie, wit.

Creason, Samuel & Elizabeth N. Huie, 11 July 1851; T. A. Hatley, bondsman; J. S. Myers, wit.

Creason, Samuel Jr. & Betsy Hartman, 4 Sept 1822; Christian Goodman, bondsman.

Creson, Samuel & Sophia Brown, 9 Sept 1794; James Brown, bondsman; J. Troy, D. C., wit.

Cresort, Charles & Sarah Lyerly, 28 Nov 1839; Richmond Wyatt, bondsman; J. L. Beard, wit.

Cress, Absalom & Anna Louisa Propst, 9 May 1865; John Coon, bondsman; Obadiah Woodson, wit.

Cress, Calvin & Adeline L. Bean, 24 Feb 1855; William L. Jenkins, bondsman; J. S. Myers, wit. married 25 Feb 1855 by M. A. Agner, J. P.

Cress, Edward & Margaret E. Moore, 30 Nov 1824; Hy. Giles, bondsman.

Cress, Eli & Sally Holshouser, 22 May 1848; Joseph Miller, bondsman.

Cress, Henry & Darcus Kimbrel, 25 Oct 1832; Dewalt Lentz, bondsman.

Cress, John & Leah Bost, 6 May 1842; John Bost, bondsman.

Cress, John & Nancy Bost, 28 Nov 1858; W. F. Owen, bondsman; James E. Kerr, wit. married 28 Nov 1858 by Rev. B. C. Nall.

Cresson, Michael & Barbara Parks, 1 Jan 1819; Lawrence Porter, bondsman; Jno Giles, wit.

Cresson, Samuel & Catharine Elliott, 23 Nov 1836; John Basinger, bondsman; Jno Giles, wit.

Crews, Thomas & Sarah Baxter, 20 June 1816; Daniel Dwiggins,
bondsman; R. Powell, wit.

Crider, Benjamin & Sally Miller, 8 March 1813; George Miller,
bondsman; Geo Dunn, wit.

Crider, George H. & Loretta Verblc, 28 March 1844; David West,
bondsman; Obadiah Woodson, wit.

Crider, Jacob & _____, 22 May 1797; Jacob Caster, bondsman;
Ls. Beard, wit.

Crider, Jacob & Betsey Swink, 16 Feb 1818; Epps Robinson, bondsman; Roberts Nanny, wit.

Crider, John & Sally Baker, 17 March 1820; George Krider,
bondsman; Milo A. Giles, wit.

Crider, Leonard & Margaret Vervill, 14 Feb 1775; George Gonter,
bondsman; Ad. Osborn, wit.

Crider, Peter & Catharine Shroat, 7 Nov 1809; Daniel Vervel,
bondsman; Jno Giles, D. C., wit.

Cristy, Thomas & Elizabeth McLaughlin, 11 Jan 1852; David
Earnhart, bondsman; James E. Kerr, wit. married 19 Jan 1853
by John McConnaughey, J. P.

Criswell, Andrew & Jenny Hartley, 7 Jan 1802; John Garrett,
bondsman; Jno Brem, wit.

Criswell, John Alexander & Sophie Freeze, 9 Jan 1824; William
Otrich, bondsman; Hy Giles, wit.

Critenton, Jeremiah & Charity Mason, 8 May 1820; Edward Mason,
bondsman; R. Powell, wit.

Crittenden, John & Sarah M. Stanley, 14 June 1813; Alex. Long,
bondsman; Jno Giles, C. C., wit.

Crittendon, William & Jean Evans, 26 Feb 1824; William Gabard,
bondsman; L. R. Rose, J. P., wit.

Crook, Henry J. & Mary M. Skean, 13 Feb 1866; Willie Bean,
bondsman; Obadiah Woodson, wit.

Crook, John & Elizabeth Park, 8 Feb 1847; Wiley Beam, bondsman;
J. H. Hardie Jr., wit.

Crosbey, William G. & Margret Erwin, 4 March 1805; Isaac Swann,
bondsman.

Croser, Leonard & Rosena Bruner, 22 May 1787; John Lewis Beard,
bondsman; Jno Macay, wit.

Cross, David Jr. & Welthy Gilstrap, 7 Aug 1800; David Cross, Sr.,
bondsman; John Brem, wit.

Cross, George & Susannah Smith, 10 April 1806; A. L. Osborn,
D. C., wit.

Cross, Joel & Susannah Moore, 17 Aug 1794; John Moore Jr.,
bondsman; J. Troy, D. C., wit.

Cross, Joshua & Catharine Philips, 6 Dec 1790; Zachariah Cross, bondsman; C. Caldwell, D. C., wit.

Cross, Silas & Margaret Miller, 9 Aug 1864; James R. Cross, bondsman; Obadiah Woodson, wit.

Crotser, Daniel & Nancy Owens, 26 April 1825; William Walton, bondsman; Hy Giles, wit.

Crotser, David & Harriet Julia Ann Myers, 28 June 1862; John Eagle, bondsman; Obadiah Woodson, wit.

Crotser, George & Syntha H. Kirk, married 13 Nov 1853 by Levi Trexler, J. P. (bond missing, minister's return only)

Crotser, Jacob & Elizabeth Harrison, 5 Nov 1811; Henry Fite, bondsman; Jno Giles, wit.

Crottser, John & Cintha Jordan, 22 June 1830; John Canup, bondsman; Saml Reeves, wit.

Crotzer, George & Sally Pame, 16 Sept 1828; Nathan Morgan, bondsman; J. H. Hardie, wit.

Crotzer, Philip & Catharine Moyr, 13 Oct 1785; Jno Melcher Eller, bondsman; Max Chambers, wit.

Crouch, Charles & Katharin Glasscock, 17 Dec 1820; Jonathan Bodenhamer, bondsman; Joe Brummel, W. Bodenhamer, wit.

Crouder, Joshua & Rebecca Smith, 19 Jan 1776; Archd. Kerr, bondsman.

Crouse, Daniel & Seraney Crouse, 5 March 1803; John Crouse, bondsman; John March, wit.

Crouse, Samuel & Sarah Smith, 23 Dec 1811; Jesse A. Walker, bondsman; Jn March Sr., wit.

Crouse, William & Beckey Cross, 13 July 1789; Chris Hawley, bondsman; Will Alexander, wit.

Crow, Adam & Ellender Peck, 14 Aug 1786; Will Peck, bondsman; Jno Macay, wit.

Crowel, David & Elizabeth Hodge, 19 Sept 1835; Newton Horne, bondsman; Jno Shaver, J. P., wit.

Crowel, John & Jennet McMahan, 9 Aug 1792; James McMackin, bondsman; Chs Caldwell, wit.

Crowel, Peter & Mary Fraileigh, 28 Nov 1789; William Crowel, bondsman.

Crowell, Cyrus & Margaret Valentine (colored), 22 Aug 1865; Obadiah Woodson, wit. married 22 Aug 1865 by J. Rumple, V. D. M.

Crowell, David & Betsey Lentz, 12 Jan 1811; George Lentz, bondsman; Jno Giles, wit.

Crowell, David & Tener Hager, 24 Aug 1812; John Thomas, bondsman; Saml. S. Savage, wit.

Crowell, W. H. & Margaret E. Noe, 28 Feb 1866; Horatio N.
Woodson, bondsman; Obadiah Woodson, wit.

Crowl, Peter & F. Fight, 28 Nov 1808; John Thomas, bondsman;
A. L. Osborne, D. C., wit.

Cruise, Adam & Rosena Cress, 18 Oct 1784; George Goodman,
bondsman; H. Magoune, wit.

Crump, Rowland & Sarah Campbell, 3 Oct 1820; William Harris,
bondsman; Jno Giles, wit.

Cruse, Allen & Lydia V. Mourie, 20 June 1839; A. W. Buis,
bondsman; Jno Giles, wit.

Cruse, Daniel & Maria Mowrey, 16 April 1849; Moses Lyerly,
bondsman.

Cruse, Henry & Elizabeth Leopard, 22 April 1819; John Barger,
bondsman; Jno Giles, wit.

Cruse, Joseph & Rachel Beaver, 29 May 1856; Jesse Beaver,
bondsman; J. S. Myers, wit. married 1 June 1856 by Saml
Rothrock, Minister of the Gospel in the Ev. Luth. Church.

Cruse, Peter & Caty Boger, 27 Aug 1796; Jacob Lingle, bondsman;
Jno Rogers, wit.

Cruse, Philip & Mary Kincaid, 27 Aug 1817; Henry Stirewalt,
bondsman; Jno Giles, wit.

Cruse, Tobias & Catharine L. Rimer, 25 April 1854; Moses Klutts,
bondsman; J. S. Myers, wit.

Cryder, Philip & Betsy Grinder, 23 Nov 1796; Jacob Rusher,
bondsman; Jno Rogers, wit.

Culbertson, Daniel & Lydia S. Repult, 4 Feb 1851; Richard
Culbertson, bondsman; James E. Kerr, wit. married 6 Feb 1851
by Wm. A. Hall.

Culbertson, Gillaspie & Susanna S. Gray, 20 Nov 1823; Jesse
Marlin, bondsman.

Culbertson, John & Elizabeth McConnell, 7 Feb 1767; John Hagin,
bondsman; Thos Frohock, wit.

Culbertson, Richard & Fanny Knox, 6 March 1854; James J.
McConnaughey, bondsman; J. S. Myers, wit. married 8 March
1854 by Jesse Rankin, Minister Pres. Church.

Culbertson, Samuel & Lydia Gillespie, 28 Jan 1797; John Martin,
bondsman; Jno Rogers, wit.

Culbertson, Samuel S. & Barbara C. Fraly, 22 Feb 1853; Mumfort
S. Fraly, bondsman; J. S. Myers, wit. married 24 Feb 1853
by A. Baker, Pastor of the Presbyterian Church, Salisbury.

Culp, Edmund & Catherine E. Beaver, 24 June 1845; Edmond Zell,
bondsman; Jno H. Hardie, Jr., wit.

Culp, Henry & Catharine Lipe, 10 Aug 1802; Henry Dowland,
bondsman; A. L. Osborn, D. C., wit.

Culp, Peter & Susan Cox, 9 Dec 1804; Wm. Rogers, bondsman;
A. L. Osborn, D. C., wit.

Culver, John & Elizabeth Kennedy (colored), 27 Sept 1865;
Obadiah Woodson, wit. married 27 Sept 1865 by Zuck Houghton.

Culverhouse, Hugh & Rebecca Wood, 22 Dec 1835; William Murphy,
bondsman; J. H. Hardie, wit.

Cumens, Eliazar & Isabel Caswell, 19 Dec 1778; James Fraser,
bondsman; William R. Davie, wit.

Cummings, William & Mary Clary, 25 July 1829; Cyrus Albey,
bondsman; L. R. Rose, J. P., wit.

Cummins, Robert & Mary Creswell, 4 Jan 1780; Elizar Cummins,
bondsman; B. Booth Boote, wit.

Cummins, Samuel & Elizabeth Nevins, 28 Jan 1783; John Edgar,
bondsman; William Crawford, wit.

Cummins, Samuel & Mary Ann Philips, 6 March 1790; Evan
Alexander, bondsman.

Cuningham, John & Hannah Davis, 28 Jan 1794; John Davis, bondsman; Jo Chambers, wit.

Cunningham, Griffith K. & Nancy Sloan, 13 Dec 1808; Casper
Fredle, bondsman; A. L. Osborne, D. C., wit.

Cunningham, Hugh & Elizabeth Smith, 15 Sept 1774; John Johnston,
bondsman; Ad. Osborn, wit.

Cunningham, Hugh & Mary Kent, 10 Feb 1780; Jonathan Conger,
bondsman; B. Booth Boote, wit.

Cunningham, Hugh & Margaret Upton, 12 Nov 1819; Zachariah Alben,
bondsman; Hy Giles, wit.

Cunningham, John & Betty Cooper, 13 Aug 1819; Hugh Cunningham,
bondsman; Jno Giles, wit.

Cunningham, Josiah & Sarah Heasley, 18 Aug 1811; Hugh Cunningham,
bondsman; Joseph Clark, wit.

Cunningham, Robert & Mary Simmison, 9 May 1804; William Simeson,
bondsman; Ad. Osborn, wit.

Cunningham, Thomas & Matty Hulin, 30 Dec 1815; Adam Srote,
bondsman; Jno Giles, wit.

Cunningham, William & Ann Hendrix, 12 Oct 1789; Henry Hendrix,
bondsman; Basil Gaither, wit.

Cunningham, William & Nancy Cunningham, 25 Dec 1816; John H.
Swink, bondsman; Henry Giles, wit.

Cunningham, William & Editha Parker, 18 Sept 1832; Marmaduke G.
Coker, bondsman; J. Tomlinson, J. P., wit.

Curfis, Caleb & Catharine Freize, 13 Nov 1810; John Litaker,
bondsman; Jno Giles, wit.

Curif, Henry & Elizabeth Beaver, 14 Jan 1837; Caleb Stirewalt,
bondsman.

Curray, John & Elizabeth Glasscock, 7 Oct 1822; Wm. Beaman, Jr., bondsman; John Cook, J. P., wit.

Curre, John & Margaret C. McKnight, 12 Nov 1821; William Martin, bondsman.

Current, Andrew J. & June S. Renshaw, 14 Sept 1858; Sanford Henley, bondsman; James E. Kerr, wit. married 16 Sept 1858 by Jas. A. Hawkins, J. P.

Current, John & Susanna Remington, 18 Dec 1782; William Clark, bondsman; William Crawford, wit.

Curt, Victor & Lydia E. Swink, 12 Dec 1864; James Murphy, bondsman; Obadiah Woodson, wit.

Curzine, George & Susanna Ruteleg, 7 Feb 1809; Susanna Ruteleg, bondsman; A. L. Osborne, wit.

Cuteral, Charles & Sopha Bell, 12 Oct 1815; Cornell James, bondsman.

Cutherell, Guidian & Polly Smith, 24 Sept 1827; Smith McLannon, bondsman; E. Brock, J. P., wit.

Cuthrell, Thomas & Anna McLanna, 3 Oct 1826; John McLanna, bondsman; E. Brock, J. P., wit.

Cutrel, Nathaniel & Sally Fulford, 7 Oct 1824; David Taylor, bondsman; E. Brock, J. P., wit.

Cutting, R. L. & Elizabeth Weant, 2 May 1853; John A. Stockton, bondsman; J. S. Myers, wit.

Daily, Charles & Anna Skiles, 16 Oct 1797; John B. Palmer, bondsman; Jno Rogers, wit.

Dagenheart, Henry & Chrisn. Ketchy, 22 Feb 1797; John Hildebrand, bondsman; Jno Rogers, wit.

Dancey, Edward & Susanna Phenoy, 1 April 1794; John Dancey, bondsman; Jo. Chambers, wit.

Dancey, John & Abigail Davis, 27 Aug 1783; Myseck Davis, bondsman.

Dancey, N. L. & Sallie E. Bradshaw, 26 Dec 1860; Carmi J. Wagoner, bondsman; John Wilkinson, wit.

Dancey, William & Hannah Willson, 5 Jan 1788; John Whittaker, bondsman; J. McEwen, wit.

Dancey, William & Hannah Byerly, 17 Jan 1822; Andrew McBride, bondsman; Hy Giles, wit.

Dancy, John & Jean Fritz, 26 Nov 1798; Isam Wood, bondsman; Edwin J. Osborn, D. C., wit.

Dancy, John & Abigal Loyd, 16 Dec 1810; Green Gadbery, bondsman.

Dancy, John & Peggy Wingler, 28 Oct 1801; James Bingleton, bondsman; Jas. McEwen, wit.

Daniel, Elisha & Mary Miller, 10 Feb 1796; Sion Daniel, bondsman; Fredrick Miller, wit.

98

Daniel, Elleck & Sarah Martin, 11 Nov 1807; John Martin, bondsman; Jn March Sr., wit.

Daniel, Ephraim & Evy Smith, 25 Sept 1810; David Miller, bondsman; Jno Giles, C. C., wit.

Daniel, James & Rebecca Atherton, 5 April 1779; David Woodson, bondsman; Ad Osborn, wit.

Daniel, James W. & Nancy Henly, 6 July 1814; Abraham Redwine, bondsman; Geo Dunn, wit.

Daniel, John & Nancy Hudson, 15 Nov 1793; Kennon Brown, bondsman; Jos. Chambers, wit.

Daniel, John & Polley Morgin, 21 Sept 1813; Ellick Daniel, bondsman; Jn March Sr., wit.

Daniel, Josiah & Hannah Foster, 30 Dec 1831; Joel H. Jinkins, bondsman; Thomas McNeely, J. P., wit.

Daniel, Peter & Sally Lofton, 28 March 1803; Stephen Linch, bondsman; A. L. Osborn, D. C., wit.

Daniel, Peter & Nancy Wilson, 19 March 1820; Andrew Clinart, bondsman; Jno Monroe, wit.

Daniel, Randall & Christena Grimes, 3 June 1819; Gasper Todd, bondsman; Sol Davis, wit.

Daniel, Wilie & Mary Veach, 22 May 1824; Alfred McCulloh, bondsman; Hy. Giles, wit.

Daniel, William & Polly Williams 15 Aug 1815; William Butler, bondsman; Jno Giles, wit.

Daniel, Woodson & Nancy Harris, 16 Dec 1804; William Stokes, bondsman; A. L. Osborn, D. C., wit.

Daniel, Zadock & Crecy Curties, 12 Oct 1807; John Buckner, bondsman; Jn March Sr., wit.

Daniels, Paul & Elizabeth Smith, 19 Aug 1790; Moses Pirkins, bondsman; Jon. Monro, wit.

Darden, John & Rosanna Goodman, 15 Feb 1812; Geo. Goodman, bondsman; Geo Dunn, wit.

Darr, Andrew & Molly Barrier, 15 June 1817; Valentine Sowers, bondsman; Silas Pearce, wit.

Darr, David & Mary Sappinfield, 19 Sept 1815; Michael Sowers, bondsman; Silas Pearce, wit.

Darr, John & Elizabeth Conrad, 23 Jan 1809; George Shoeman, bondsman; A. L. Osborn, wit.

Dauson, James & Jane Citchen, 15 Aug 1786; Hugh Gray, bondsman.

Davenport, Aquila & Ann Higdon, 6 May 1813; Walter Higdon, bondsman; Jno Giles, C. C., wit.

Daves, Evan & Fanny Bolar, 3 March 1800; Thomas Boulin, bondsman; Matt Troy, wit.

Daves, Joseph & Susannah McCrary, 28 Dec 1779; William Selvers, bondsman; B. Booth Boote, wit.

Davice, Benjamin & _____, _____ 179_; John Elliss, bondsman.

Davidson, George & Rosanna Falls, 13 Jan 1784; William Falls, bondsman; T. H. McCaule, wit.

Davidson, John & Nancy Brevard, 27 Nov 1799; Joseph Byars, bondsman; B. Booth Boote, wit.

Davidson, John R. & Eugenia O. McConnaughey, 8 March 1843; Jno M. McConnaughey, bondsman; _____ Sneed, wit.

Davidson, Joshua & Sally Harville, 24 June 1813; John Patterson, bondsman; Jno Giles, C. C., wit.

Davidson, Samuel A. & Nancy C. Lowery, 16 May 1826; Richard Loury, bondsman; Jno Giles, wit.

Davidson, Thomas F. & Margaret A. Trexler, 29 Dec 1858; W. F. Owen, bondsman; James E. Kerr, wit. married 30 Dec 1858 by W. R. Fraley, J. P.

Davidson, William & Mary Brevard, 10 Dec 1767; Hugh Brevard, James Holmes, bondsmen.

Davies, Morgan & _____, 19 Jan 1763; Benjamin Evans, Madad Reed, bondsmen; John Frohock, wit.

Davis--see also Daves, Davice

Davis, Alfred & Elizabeth Williams 29 Nov 1852; L. M. Williams, bondsman; James E. Kerr, wit. married 29 Nov 1852 by J. M. Brown, J. P.

Davis, Benjamin & Isbell Holland, 6 Feb 1776; John Conger, bondsman; Ad. Osborn, wit.

Davis, Benjamin & Susana Shamell, 1 Nov 1797; Isaac Shemwell, bondsman; Jno Rogers, wit.

Davis, Benjamin & Mary Johnston, 24 Oct 1800; Randolph Johnston, bondsman; J. Brem, wit.

Davis, Benjamin & Anna Stafford, 15 March 1801; John Davis, bondsman.

Davis, Brisco & Polly Parker, 5 March 1804; Nathaniel Parker, bondsman.

Davis, D. A. & Mary E. Horah, 12 Nov 1844; Jno. D. Brown, bondsman.

Davis, Daniel & Rebecca Beal, 20 Dec 1814; James Davis, bondsman; Geo. Dunn, wit.

Davis, Edward & Kizzy Serratt, 9 Jan 1795; Henry Davis, bondsman; J. Troy, D. C., wit.

Davis, Edward & Rachel Williams, 18 Jan 1797; Geo Cole Iron, bondsman; Jno Rogers, wit.

Davis, Edward & Anna Knup, 15 Dec 1801; Jesse Davis, bondsman; Jno Brem. wit.

Davis, Evan & Mary Wilson, 21 Feb 1795; David Enochs, bondsman; John Eccles, Esq., wit.

Davis, Gabriel & Nancy McCreary, 29 Nov 1791; Thomas Coyl, bondsman; Chs. Caldwell, wit.

Davis, George & Catharine Trexler, 23 Jan 1804; George Quilman, bondsman; A. L. Osborn, D. C., wit.

Davis, Henry & Nancy Gerrat, 7 Oct 1791; George Kinder, bondsman; Chas. Caldwell, wit.

Davis, Isaac Ross & Caty Readwine, 15 June 1798; Benjamin Davis, bondsman; Ma. Troy, wit.

Davis, Jacob A. & Delia Allen, 8 Feb 1855; George Lyerly, bondsman; J. S. Myers, wit.

Davis, James & Mary Winnford, 26 Nov 1793; Gabriel Enochs, bondsman; G. Enochs, wit.

Davis, James & Jean Morrow, 21 July 1803; James Webb, bondsman; A. L. Osborn, D. C., wit.

Davis, James & Elizabeth Morrow, 23 Nov 1814; Wm. Madden, bondsman; Geo Dunn, wit.

Davis, James, son of James, & Elizabeth Morrow, 17 March 1829; Allen M. Davis, bondsman; Thomas McNeely, J. P., wit.

Davis, James & Rebecca Smith, 10 March 1855; Noah Griffin, bondsman; J. S. Myers, wit. married 11 March 1855 by Obadiah Woodson, J. P.

Davis, James M. & Scyntha E. Rose, 23 Jan 1856; Alex. Readling, bondsman; J. S. Myers, wit. married 23 Jan 1856 by Jas. H. Enniss, J. P.

Davis, Jesse & Charity Hunt, 16 March 1799; Hugh Davis, bondsman; Jno L. Henderson, wit.

Davis, Jesse & Polly Ferabee, 8 Feb 1814; Henry Davis, bondsman; Sol. Davis, J. P., wit.

Davis, John & Elizabeth Bryant, 22 Feb 1787; Andrew Olga, bondsman; John Macay, wit.

Davis, John & Rachael Serat, 16 Dec 1789; James Elliss, bondsman.

Davis, John & Sally Patton, 24 Oct 1797; John Cunningham, bondsman; Jno Rogers, wit.

Davis, John & Polly Redwine, 12 Oct 1808; John Loftin, bondsman; A. L. Osborn, wit.

Davis, John & Margaret Maddox, 16 Dec 1815; George Seaner, bondsman; Thos Hampton, wit.

Davis, John & Jean Luckey, 14 July 1817; James Davis, bondsman; R. Powell, wit.

Davis, John B. & Martha A. Curlee, 24 Dec 1859; William M. Barker, bondsman; James E. Kerr, wit. married 25 Dec 1859 by L. C. Groseclose, Pastor of St. John's Ev. Lutheran Church, Salisbury, N. C.

Davis, Jonathan & Ann Cunningham, 4 Jan 1817; John Burkhart, bondsman; Jno Giles, Clk., wit.

Davis, Joseph & Rebecca Little, 28 Dec 1824; James Davis, bondsman.

Davis, Michael & Sally Trexler, 31 Aug 1826; Hy. Giles, bondsman.

Davis, Peter & Elizabeth Sutley, 9 April 1811; William Davis, bondsman; S. Davis, J. P., wit.

Davis, Richard & Margaret Wood, 4 Feb 1797; Jno Howard, bondsman; Jno Rogers, wit.

Davis, Richard & Elizabeth D. Woods, 5 Dec 1838; Oliver C. Woods, bondsman; John Giles, wit.

Davis, Robert Clark & Betsey Redwine, 19 Aug 1798; Isaac Ross Davis, bondsman; Ma. Troy, wit.

Davis, Samuel & Judiah Childress, 9 June 1798; Thomas Harper, bondsman; Ma. Troy, wit.

Davis, Samuel & Mary Cliffor, 21 July 1823; James Davis, bondsman; Hy. Giles, wit.

Davis, Thomas & Henrietta Hays, 13 Dec 1793; James Parks, bondsman; Jo Chambers, wit.

Davis, Thomas & Elizabeth Harris, 10 April 1828; Jolson Berryman, bondsman; M. Hanes, wit.

Davis, William & Anny Linn, 16 May 1800; William Thomas, bondsman; Matt. Troy, wit.

Davis, William & Anna Thomas, 9 Dec 1804; Soloman Davis, bondsman; Jno Monroe, wit.

Davis, William & Rosannah Kellers, 28 Aug 1816; Wm. B. Willson, bondsman; Jn. March Sr., wit.

Davis, William & Catharine Steelman, 13 Sept 1818; John Carter, bondsman; R. Powell, wit.

Davis, Wilson & Zilpha Powe (colored), 5 Sept 1865; married 5 Oct 1865 by Zuck Howerton; J. W. Raddick, wit.

Day, Michael & Abigal Hoose, 6 Dec 1815; Mathew Sappenfield, bondsman; Silas Peace, wit.

Day, Valentine & Eve Reigher, 4 Aug 1767; Christopher Sprayhir, bondsman; Thomas Frohock, wit.

Deadman, Eligah & Edney Balance, 30 Sept 1820; William Etcheson, bondsman; Jno Giles, wit.

Deal, Adam & Anna Readling, 8 Sept 1841; John O. Baker, bondsman; J. S. Myers, wit.

Deal, Alexander & Mary Lingle, 12 Nov 1849; Charles Blackwelder, bondsman; J. S. Myers, wit.

Deal, Franklin W. & Martha J. Atwell, 23 May 1859; Obadiah W. Atwell, bondsman.

Deal, George H. & Julia Ann C. C. Sloop, 15 March 1866; Adam M. Correll, bondsman; Obadiah Woodson, wit.

Deal, Henry & Mary Upright, 13 March 1818; Samuel Upright, bondsman.

Deal, Henry (Henrich Diel) & Mary Upright, 18 March 1818; Samuel Albrecht (Samuel Mirigh), bondsman.

Deal, Henry & Elizabeth Lingle, 10 Aug 1850; Charles Black-welder, bondsman; James E. Kerr, wit.

Deal, Jacob & Polly Casper, 28 March 1844; Henry Deal, bondsman; Obadiah Woodson, wit.

Deal, Jacob & Mary M. Seckler, 9 April 1844; John Deal (Johannes Diehl, Germ.), bondsman; J. H. Hardie, wit.

Deal, John & Mary Lingle, 29 Jan 1816; Jacob Deal (Jacob Diehl, German), bondsman; Geo. Dunn, wit.

Deal, John & Anna Deal, 27 March 1849; Henry Deal, bondsman; J. H. Hardie, wit.

Deal, John Jr. & Mary Ann Shuping, 31 May 1842; Andrew Shuping, bondsman; Jno. H. Hardie, wit.

Deal, John L. & Nancy L. Barnheardt, 9 Jan 1856; Charles Blackwelder, bondsman; J. S. Myers, wit. married 10 Jan 1856 by C. S. Partee, J. P.

Deal, Peter & Mary Ann Correll, 11 Dec 1848; Jacob Correll, bondsman.

Deal, Samuel & Polly Beaver, 27 Sept 1845; Daniel Beaver, bondsman; J. H. Hardie, Jur., wit.

Deal, Samuel & Amanda C. Stirewalt, 4 Dec 1865; Daniel Deal, bondsman; Obadiah Woodson, wit.

Deal, Solomon & Susannah Overcash, 18 April 1853; John Deal, bondsman; J. S. Myers, wit.

Deal, William A. & Saloma Lingle, 24 Sept 1855; Wilson A. Lingle, bondsman; J. S. Myers, wit. married 25 Sept 1855 by J. Ingold.

Deal, William E. & Jane E. Leazar, 12 Feb 1855; Rufus A. Corriher, bondsman; James E. Kerr, wit. married 14 Feb 1855 by C. L. Partee, J. P.

Dealy, Charles & Sally Etchison, 12 March 1805; Archibald Kincade, bondsman; Moses A. Locke, wit.

Dean, Y. S. & Martha A. Howard, 2 April 1849; H. L. Robard, bondsman; Jno H. Hardie Jr., wit.

Deaton, Hirum & Clarissa A. Overcash, 13 Nov 1857; R. G. McLean, bondsman; J. S. Myers, wit. married 14 Nov 1857 by John E. Pressly, minister.

Deaton, James & Catharine Bostian, 20 June 1829; Thos. Deaton, bondsman.

Deaton, John G. & Susan Butner, 20 March 1858; Daniel Verble, bondsman; John Wilkinson, wit. married 21 March 1858 by Peter Williamson, J. P.

Deaton, Laymon & Celia Cope, 25 Nov 1837; Pinckny S. Deaton, bondsman; Hy. Giles, wit.

Deaton, Samuel S. & Sarah E. Conger, 26 Feb 1855; Jos. Henderson, bondsman; James E. Kerr, wit. married 28 Feb 1855 by J. Ingold, minister of the gospel.

Deaver, Joshua & Rebecca Houze, 4 Feb 1818; Pleasant Pruit, bondsman; Saml Jones, W. Phillips, wit.

Deaver, Richard & Henrittor Ring, 22 Dec 1810; Joseph Call, bondsman; Jn. March Sr., wit.

Deaver, Samuel & Elizabeth Farmer, 23 Feb 1787; Rd. Henderson, wit.

Deaver, Samuel & Susanah Hausen, 4 Feb 1814; Lemuel Hilton, bondsman; John Hames, wit.

Deaver, Samuel & Cloha Harvis, 16 May 1821; Jesse Etchison, bondsman; Geo Coker, wit.

Decamp, Zacariah & Elizabeth Kinder, 28 Sept 1791; Christian Schrode, bondsman; Chs. Caldwell, D. C., wit.

Deckar, Claud & Mary Cotton, 14 Nov 1701; George Hoover, bondsman.

Decker, Clark & Agness Brown, 22 July 1795; Philip Brown, bondsman; J. Troy, wit.

Dedman, John & Susanah Hunt, 9 Oct 1805; Ebanezer Moore, bondsman; Saml Williamson, wit.

Dedmon, Jesse & Anna Daniel, 16 March 1820; Ishmael Caudle, bondsman; Jno. H. Hardie, wit.

Dedmon, Mark & Hanna Baily, 7 Nov 1785; Wm. Baily, bondsman; Max. Chambers, wit.

Degle, Thomas & Rebecca Nealy, 24 July 1779; Thomas Renshaw, bondsman; Jo. Brevard, wit.

Delap, Daniel & Debrah Salisbury, 7 March 1803; William Monroe, bondsman; Jno Monroe, wit.

Delap, William & Nancy Salisbury, 5 Nov 1801; Agner Monroe, bondsman; Jno Monroe, wit.

Delliner, Soloman & Catharine Rendleman, 19 May 1828; Mathias Penninger, bondsman; J. H. Hardie, wit.

Denham, William & Nancy Simpson, 29 March 1798; Henry McGuire, bondsman; Edwin J. Osborn, D. C., wit.

Dent, Thomas H. & Ann Trott, 21 Nov 1796; Saml. Trott, bondsman; Jno Rogers, wit.

Dent, Thomas H. & Sarah W. Linster, 26 Jan 1839; Jacob Fraley, bondsman; John Giles, wit.

ROWAN MARRIAGES 1753-1868

Dent, Townsend & Mary Hightower, 12 May 1797; Turner Pinkston, bondsman; Jno Rogers, wit.

Dent, Wilford & Rachael Smith, 11 May 1837; Pharley Ellis, bondsman; H. Belton, wit.

Depoyster, Abraham & Sally Tillet, 25 Feb 1813; John Hendly, bondsman; Jno March Sr., wit.

DeRosset, Dr. M. J. & Addie Meares, 14 Oct 1863; J. G. Wright, bondsman; Obadiah Woodson, wit.

Dever, William & Phebee Adams, 10 Feb 1820; Ely B. Etcheson, bondsman; R. Powell, wit.

Devold, Jacob & Elizabeth Goodman, 5 June 1779; John Misenhimer, bondsman; Jo Brevard, wit.

Dew, John & Sally Swann, 4 Aug 1813; Joseph Hall, bondsman; Geo Dunn, wit.

Dial, Joseph & Margaret Hinkle, 13 March 1786; Jesse Hinkle, bondsman; W. Cupples, wit.

Dial, Joshua & Susanah March, 10 Jan 1814; Benjamin March, bondsman; Jn March Sr., wit.

Dial, Robert & Elizabeth Cunningham, 24 Aug 1788; William Cunningham, bondsman; W. Alexander, wit.

Dial, Samuel & Sarah Etcheson, 20 April 1813; John Forst, bondsman; R. Powell, wit.

Dick, John & Mary Tanner, 17 Nov 1799; Peter Hendricks, bondsman; Edwin J. Osborn, wit.

Dickerson, Ezekiel & Susan Shipton, 30 June 1815; John Simmons, bondsman; Jno Giles, C. C., wit.

Dickey, David & Rosanna Morrison, (no date, during Gov Caswell's admn.); Joseph Mahafey, bondsman; Ad. Osborn, wit.

Dickey, David & Nancy Hamon, 16 July 1801; James Dickey, bondsman; Jno Brem, wit.

Dickey, James & Ruthey Evans, 22 Nov 1804; Danl. Clary, bondsman; Moses A. Locke, wit.

Dickey, James Jr. & Betsy Smith, 4 Feb 1823; James Dickey Sr., bondsman; Hy. Giles, wit.

Dickey, Moses & Nancy Johnston, 1 March 1796; John Johnston, bondsman; J. Troy, D. C., wit.

Dickey, William (no date, bride, or wit.)

Dickson, Charles B. & Sarah Ann Graham, 20 Sept 1855; Jesse Thomason, bondsman; James E. Kerr, wit. married 20 Sept 1855 by Jno Thomason, J. P.

Dickson, Charles B. & Mary Ann E. Smith, 14 Feb 1861; Julian C. Klutts, bondsman; John Wilkinson, wit. married 17 Feb 1861 by Wm. T. Marlin.

Dickson, Clemoth B. & Shaby Cresson, 26 Aug 1833; Wm. Locke, bondsman; Wm. Locke, wit.

Dickson, Ebem & Elizabeth Wilkerson, 28 Feb 1818; Hugh Wilkerson, bondsman; Jno Giles, wit.

Dickson, Joseph T. & Margaret Lyerly, 27 Sept 1827; James Beffel, bondsman; J. H. Hardie, wit.

Dickson, Michael B. & Jane C. Rex, 13 July 1854; George W. Lyerly, bondsman; J. S. Myers, wit. married 13 July 1854 by J. M. Brown, J. P.

Dickson, Richard & Nancy Taylor, 13 Sept 1788; Wm. Casey, bondsman; W. Alexander, wit.

Dickson, Richard & Elizabeth Beven, 27 Nov 1803; John Pierson, bondsman; J. H. Pitchey, Robert Gay, wit.

Dickson, Solomon Beach & Hannah Allen, 27 July 1804; Nathaniel Barron, bondsman.

Dickson, Thomas & Margaret Brown, 15 Jan 1818; George Locke, bondsman.

Dickson, William & Polly Todd, 20 April 1815; Jno Utzman, bondsman; Geo Dunn, wit.

Dicky, Hayes & Margaret Morrow, 8 April 1797; Joseph Hall, bondsman; Jno Rogers, wit.

Dillard, Fealding & Patsey Beadles, 6 Jan 1801; Joseph Beadles, bondsman; J. Brem, D. C., wit.

Dillon, Jacob & Susanna Shewman, 14 April 1792; Adam Powles, bondsman; Chs. Caldwell, wit.

Dillon, John & Susey Dillon, 8 Nov 1817; Peter Earnheart, bondsman; Jno Giles, wit.

Dillon, Jonathan P. & Minerva A. Beddox, 13 Jan 1846; Hezekiah Turner, bondsman; J. M. Turner, wit.

Dillon, Peter & Lidia Clemmons, 22 Aug 1811; John Clemmons, bondsman; John Hanes, wit.

Dillow, Michael & Rachael Shuman, 18 Sept 1815; John Lentz, bondsman; Jno Giles, C. C., wit.

Dimmit, William & Stacy Walker, 13 Jan 1802; John Dimmit, bondsman; A. L. Osborn, D. C., wit.

Dinkins, Frederick & Sarah Locke, 28 Jan 1819; Abel Cowan, bondsman; Jno Giles, wit.

Dison, Greenbury & Edith Ward, 19 Dec 1831; Joseph Horn, bondsman; Thomas McNeely, J. P., wit.

Dobbin, Alexander & Jenet Miller, 4 Nov 1788; Benjamin Hide, bondsman; W. Alexander, wit.

Dobbin, Hugh A. & Laura M. Verble, 9 Feb 1843; Thos C. Wall, bondsman; _____ Sneed, wit.

Dobbin, Hugh A. & Margaret M. Lippard, 31 Jan 1849; F. D. Locke, bondsman.

Dobbin, James & Margaret McNight, 24 Jan 1770; James McNight, James McKoun, bondsmen; Thomas Frohock, wit.

Dobbin, Nimrod M. & Margaret E. Graham, 17 April 1850; Richard F. Graham, bondsman; J. S. Myers, wit.

Dobbins, Alexander & Mary L. Graham, 20 Dec 1837; Hugh A. Dobbin, bondsman; John Giles, wit.

Dobbins, Hugh & Agnes Stutt, 23 Oct 1795; John Thomson, bondsman.

Dobbins, Samuel & Susanah Cowon, 10 Jan 178_; Nicholas W. Gaither, bondsman; Basil Gaither, wit.

Dobbins, Will & Elizabeth Erwin, 8 Sept 1768; Alexander Erwin, Joseph Luckie, bondsmen; Thos Frohock, wit.

Dobson, William & Martha Neily, 10 May 1793; James Arnett, bondsman; Jno Monro, wit.

Doby, John & Bina Johnson, 21 Aug 1805; Wm. Fox, William Teal, bondsmen; A. L. Osborn, wit.

Doland, Henry & Susannah Smith, 9 May 1803; Fredrick Miller, bondsman; A. L. Osborn, D. C., wit.

Doland, Timothy & Mary Barringer, 27 Oct 1800; George Barringer, bondsman; John Brem, wit.

Donaldson, Alexander & Nancy McGloughlin, 19 April 1804; Jno. Donaldson, bondsman; A. L. Osborn, D. C., wit.

Donaldson, Alexander B. & Ann L. Penny, 20 March 1827; Thos. Smith, bondsman; John H. Hardie, wit.

Donnahoe, Thomas & Ann Lykins, 9 July 1767; Hugh Montgomery, bondsman; John Frohock, wit.

Donnel, Thomas & Margret King, 26 Aug 1786; John Allison, bondsman; A. D. Osborn, wit.

Donnell, Andrew & Agnes Braly, 29 Sept 1779; John Braly, bondsman; Jo. Brevard, wit.

Donnell, Sulah P. & Serena Miller, 28 Nov 1854; A. D. Hix, bondsman; James E. Kerr, wit. return shows Serena Miller of Stanly County; married 28 Nov 1854 by Obadiah Woodson, J. P.

Donoho, Hiram & Margaret Beek, 13 March 1832; John Brian Jr., bondsman; L. R. Rose, wit.

Donovan, Matthew & Anne Brandon, 19 March 1792; Joseph Robinson, Robert Gay, bondsmen; Chs. Caldwell, wit.

Doolin, George & Lydia Bryan, 8 Jan 1827; David Harbin, bondsman.

Doolin, William & Charlotte Ellis, 19 Dec 1827; William Sheek, bondsman; C. Harbin, J. P., wit.

Dooling, George W. & Nancy Bailey, 21 Oct 1828; Prestly D. Glasscock, bondsman; Thomas McNeely, J. P., wit.

Dooty, Conrad & Lovis Hoover, 27 Aug 1779; Conrod Shaver, bondsman; Ad. Osborn, wit.

Dornall, William & Margaret King, 14 Feb 1769; Wm. Alexander, Wm. Millikan, bondsmen; Thos Frohock, wit. consent of Thomas King, 13 Feb 1769.

Dorton, John & Minny Foster, 15 Dec 1808; Daniel Sain, bondsman; Jno March Sr., wit.

Dotson, Joseph & Sadacy Rogers, 22 July 1817; Andrew Cope, bondsman; Roberts Nanny, wit.

Dotson, Thomas J. & E. N. Gouger, 18 Sept 1839; John O. Baker, bondsman; J. L. Beard, D. C., wit.

Doty, Michael & Caty Lookinbill, 9 March 1814; Philip Swicegood, bondsman; Geo Dunn, wit.

Doty, Moses & Barbara Goss, 14 Feb 1787; Daniel Wood, bondsman; Jno Macay, wit.

Dougherty, Patrick & Ann Horah (no date, Gov. Ashe's admn., 1795-1798); John Troy, bondsman.

Doughty, John & Nancy Goss, 30 April 1789; Moses Doty, bondsman; Will Alexander, wit.

Douthet, Abram & Nancy Jarvis, 6 Aug 1818; Abram Douthit Jr., bondsman.

Douthet, James & Elizabeth Ellis, __ Aug 1828; Jno Giles, wit.

Douthet, John Jr. & Elinor Davis, 9 March 1764; Philip Howard Jr., James Davis Jr., bondsmen; Thomas Frohock, C. C., wit.

Douthit, Abram Jr. & Valinder Jervis, 29 Dec 1816; Abram Douthet Sr., bondsman; T. Hampton, wit.

Douthit, Jacob & Sarah Flemmons, 9 Oct 1813; William Brindle, bondsman; Jn March Sr., wit.

Douthit, James & Elizabeth Ellis, 9 Sept 1828; Joel Ellis, bondsman; C. Harbin, J. P., wit.

Douthit, James & Priscilla Peebles, 23 Sept 1809; John Davis, bondsman; John Hanes, wit.

Douthit, Jesse & Levy Cummons, 8 May 1811; Abram Douthit, bondsman; John Hanes, wit.

Douthit, John D. & Elmina Buis, 22 Feb 1834; Branton Bailey, bondsman; Thomas Mc_____, wit.

Douthit, Joseph & Seiner Clemmons, 19 Dec 1808; John Clemmons, bondsman; John Hanes, wit.

Douthit, Philip & Margaret Cooper, 1 Dec 1810; Thomas Douthit, bondsman; W. Ellis, J. P., wit.

Douthit, Stephen & Caty Peebels, 25 April 1818; John Jones, bondsman; Saml Jones, wit.

Douthit, William & Sarah Job, 31 Jan 1772; George McNight, John Douthit Jr., bondsmen; Thomas Frohock, wit. consent of Thos Job, father of Sarah Job, 28 Jan 1772.

Douthit, William Jr. & Dilley Bevel, 21 Dec 1815; Wm. Douthit Sr., bondsman; Thos Hampton, wit.

Dowel, Peter & Elizabeth Pack, 16 April 1810; John Pack, bondsman; Jn March Sr., wit.

Dowell, John & Sally Dowell, 2 Jan 1797; John Hawkins, bondsman; Jno Rogers, wit.

Dowell, Peter & Elizabeth Collier, 7 Sept 1785; Richard Dowell, bondsman.

Dowell, Richard & Mary McDaniel, 10 Dec 1787; John Dowell, bondsman; J. McEwen, wit.

Dowland, David & Pinkey Woods, 29 March 1824; Hy. Giles, bondsman; Hy. Giles, wit.

Downs, Charles & Catharine Voris, 24 Oct 1786; Aaron Voorehis, bondsman; Spruce Macay, wit.

Downs, James & Rebecca Benson, 21 Nov 1825; Marcus D. Benson, bondsman.

Downs, Ruel & Julian Lipe, 31 Dec 1825; Abraham Lipe, bondsman; Jno Giles, wit.

Downum, Richard A. & Clarisa Rose, 29 Aug 1846; Henderson Misenheimer, bondsman; Jno H. Hardie, wit.

Doyl, Samuel & Haley Lovelace, 5 March 1794; Gregory Doiel, bondsman; John Pinchback, Isabella Kinkade, wit.

Doyl, Thomas & Huldy Baxter, 21 Feb 1797; Gregory Doyl, bondsman; Jno Rogers, wit.

Drake, William & Sarah Bailey, 6 Dec 1817; James Spy, bondsman; Saml. Jones, wit.

Drawhorn, Michael & Ruth Smith, 21 Sept 1806; Jesse Draughorn, bondsman; Wm. Welbo__, wit.

Dreher, Daniel J. & Martha A. C. Heilig, 3 Jan 1866; Caleb T. Bernhardt, bondsman.

Driver, Warner & Jez. A. Ward, 8 Dec 1836; P. H. Cain, bondsman; Thos. Cheshir, wit.

Driver, Wilson & Sarah Godbey, 28 May 1833; George Godbey, bondsman; Thomas McNeely, J. P., wit.

Drown, Thomas & Ann Perkines, 26 July 1812; Michael Drown, bondsman; Sol. Davis, J. P., wit.

Druley, Nicholas & Sally Standley, 24 April 1804; Joseph Stanley, bondsman; J. Hunt, wit.

Druly, John & Elizabeth Bedwell, 26 Nov 1804; Erasmus Canter, bondsman.

Dry, Charles W. & Cressey Hartman, 5 Feb 1857; Moses Dry, bondsman; H. W. Hill, Esq., wit. married 5 Feb 1857 by H. W. Hill, Esqr.

Dry, D. M. & Lydia L. Eagle, 12 April 1859; M. W. Baker, bondsman; married 12 April 1859 by Peter Williamson, J. P.

Dry, Jacob M. & Martha E. Rendleman, 25 May 1864; Jacob M. Rendleman, bondsman; Obadiah Woodson, wit.

Duey, John & Betsey Mabett, 23 Aug 1805; Anthony Mabett, bondsman; J. Hunt, wit.

Duff, George & Jane Kerr, 11 March 1796; William Kerr, bondsman.

Duffy, William & Prudence Carson, 1 Aug 1780; John Carson, bondsman; H. Gifford, wit.

Drugger, Sampson, & _____, _____ 180_; J. McConnelly, bondsman; Jno Barns, wit.

Duke, Clevers & Lucy Smith 13 June 1768; John Wyld, bondsman; Tho Frohock, Geo. Magoune, wit.

Duke, Daniel M. & Mary W. Gibson, 8 Feb 1831; John Gibson, bondsman; John H. Hardie, wit.

Duke, Thomas & Sophia Hilack, 9 June 1810; Jacob Duke, bondsman; Jno Giles, C. C., wit.

Dulin, Benjamin & Elizabeth Sparks, 9 Dec 1815; David Call, bondsman; John March Sr., wit.

Dulin, Richard & _____, 29 Feb 1840; John A. Hartman, bondsman; Jno Giles, wit.

Duncan, Benjamin & Rachael Kesler, 7 March 1842; A. C. McLelland, bondsman; J. H. Hardie, wit.

Duncan, David & Cathrinah McCulloh, 6 Jan 1766; James Carson, bondsman; Thomas Frohock, wit.

Duncan, Marshall Jr. & Bety Densten Rogers, 2 Apr 1765; Maxwell Duncan Sr., Thomas Denston Rogers, bondsmen; John Duncan, John Callahan, Darby Callahan, wit. Bety Densten Rogers, daughter of the widow Catharine Densten Rogers.

Dunn, George & Elizabeth Canup, 3 Sept 1851; Abner S. Elliott, bondsman; J. S. Myers, wit.

Dunn, James & Nelly Gheen, 2 Feb 1818; Jonathan Hulan, bondsman; Jno. Giles, wit.

Dunn, John & Sarah Cross, 26 May 1758; Andrew Cathey, James Dorthey, bondsmen.

Dunn, John & Serah Grier, 8 March 1782; John Johnson, bondsman; T. H. McCaule, wit.

Dunn, Silas & Mary Gheen, 10 May 2788; Thomas Gheen, bondsman; Js. McEwen, wit.

Dunn, William & Salomie Knup, 6 Feb 1861; John Lucas, bondsman; Wm. Locke, wit. married 10 Feb 1861 by Wm. H. Trott, J. P.

Durham, Jephthah & Polley Butner, 29 Dec 1798; Will, Cupples, bondsman; Ma. Troy, wit.

Durham, John & Martha Hamilton, 21 July 1810; Jacob Parks, bondsman; Geo. Dunn, wit.

Durham, Thomas & Miley White, 28 Jan 1802; Benjamin Merrill, bondsman; A. L. Osborn, D. C., wit.

Durham, Thomas & Sally Haiden, 2 Nov 1802; Robt. McKee, bondsman; A. L. Osborn, D. C., wit.

Durkee, Benjamin & Margaret Edmons, 30 April 1866; John L. Bogle, bondsman; H. N. Woodson, wit.

Dusenberg, Samuel & Dossey Raunsval, __ March 1790; Jonathan Miles, bondsman.

Dusenbery, H. B. & Mary Cameron, 9 Jan 1866; Samuel Reeves Jr., bondsman; Obadiah Woodson, wit.

Dusenbery, Henry R. & Lydia Davis, 1 Oct 1819; Alexander Beard, bondsman.

Dusenbery, John & Susana Wassic, 14 Oct 1810; Tho. Todd, bondsman; Jno Giles, C. C., wit.

Dwiggens, Ashley & Mary Holeman, 18 Oct 1827; Alex. Smoot, bondsman; L. R. Rose, J. P., wit.

Eagle, David & Charlotte C. Phillips, 6 March 1839; Daniel Eddelman, bondsman; John Giles, wit.

Eagle, George & Sally Ghentz, 7 Feb 1824; Nathan Morgan, bondsman; Hy. Giles, wit.

Eagle, Georg A. & Ann Chambers, 13 Nov 1852; Wm. W. Morgan, bondsman.

Eagle, John & Letitia M. Huffman, 3 Dec 1857; Tobias Hartman, bondsman; J. S. Myers, wit. married 3 Dec 1857 by Jos. A. Linn, minister of Luth. Church.

Eagle, John P. & Leah Klutts, 18 March 1856; Caleb Basinger, bondsman; James E. Kerr, wit. married 20 March 1856 by Saml. Rothrock, Minister of the Gospel in the Ev. Luth. Church.

Eagle, Joseph & Mary Ann Wyatt, 1 Dec 1859; John Eagle, bondsman.

Eagle, Peter & Peggy Stirewalt, 30 April 1814; Joseph Basinger, bondsman; Jno Giles, wit.

Eagle, Samuel & Elizabeth C. Paterson, 26 July 1856; Samuel W. Frazier, bondsman; John L. Hedrick, J. P., wit.

Eagle, Solomon & Agness N. Hodge, 18 Dec 1834; Isaac Ribelin, bondsman; Jno. H. Hardie, wit.

Eakels, Jeremiah & Elizabeth Johnson, 3 Aug 1820; James Johnson, bondsman.

Earnest, David & Rebecah Helfer, 8 June 1830; Henry Keller, bondsman; L. R. Rose, J. P., wit.

Earnest, George & Delily Busy, 8 Feb 1793; John Daniel, bondsman; Jos. Chambers, wit.

Earnhardt, Clarkson & Margaret Hager, 30 Sept 1857; Thomas Fry, bondsman; J. S. Myers, wit. married 30 Sept 1857 by D. W. Honeycutt, J. P.

Earnhardt, Jacob & Sarah Hill, 5 Aug 1861; J. B. Harris, bondsman; F. W. Scott, J. P., wit.

Earnhart--see also Arnhard, Ernhart

Earnhart, Abram & Amy Braddy, 7 Oct 1857; David Braddy, bondsman; Levi Trexler, wit. married 8 Oct 1857 by Levi Trexler, J. P.

Earnhart, Adam & Mary C. Holshouser, 15 Nov 1851; Milas Canup, bondsman; James E. Kerr, wit. married 16 Nov 1851 by W. A. Walton, J. P.

Earnhart, Alexander & Maria Earnhart, 26 Aug 1835; Jacob Fulenwider, bondsman; Hy Giles, wit.

Earnhart, Alexander & Elizabeth C. Stoner, 7 June 1858; Daniel Miller, bondsman; H. W. Hill, J. P., wit. married 7 June 1858 by H. W. Hill, J. P.

Earnhart. Alexander & Eve Miller (colored), 24 Jan 1866; Stephen Shad, bondsman; Obadiah Woodson, wit.

Earnhart, Andrew & Susanna Hoffner, 18 July 1820; Henry Hoffner, bondsman; Hy. Giles, wit.

Earnhart, Benjamin & Camilla C. Cauble, 2 Feb 1853; Asa Ribelin, bondsman; J. S. Myers, wit.

Earnhart, Caleb & Adelaide Eller, 6 Aug 1859; Daniel Hoffman, bondsman; James E. Kerr, wit.

Earnhart, Charles & Levina Thomas, 26 June 1833; Jacob Fulenwider, bondsman; J. H. Hardie, wit.

Earnhart, Charles & Lea Ernhart, 27 April 1841; Jacob Fulenwider, bondsman; J. L. Beard, wit.

Earnhart, Crusoe & Rosannah Hartman, 21 May 1859; William H. Trexler, bondsman; James E. Kerr, wit. married 22 May 1859 by S. J. Peeler, J. P.

Earnhart, David & Elizabeth Powlus, 15 May 1837; Isaac Earnhart, bondsman; R. Jones, wit.

Earnhart, Edward & Christena L. Casper, 15 Oct 1856; James Elam, bondsman; James E. Kerr, wit. married 15 Oct 1856 by W. A. Walton, J. P.

Earnhart, George & Lucay Parker, 2 May 1811; George Earnhart, bondsman; Jno Giles, C. C., wit.

Earnhart, George & Elizabeth Porter, 28 Jan 1833; Moses Cauble, bondsman.

Earnhart, George & Eve A. Waller, 3 Oct 1850; James Earnheart, bondsman; J. S. Myers, wit.

Earnhart, Harmon & Mary Shaver, 26 Jan 1826; Isaac Earnhart, bondsman; Hy. Giles, wit.

Earnhart, Henry & Eve Verball, 24 June 1791; J. G. Laumann, bondsman; Chs. Caldwell, D. C., wit.

Earnhart, Isaac & Margaret Smith, 23 Nov 1822; Saml. Lemly, bondsman.

Earnhart, Isaac & Sarah Troutman, 9 April 1832; John Troutman, bondsman; J. H. Hardie, wit.

Earnhart, Isaac N. & Letia Jacobs, 13 April 1848; Hatfield Ogden, bondsman; J. H. Hardie, wit.

Earnhart, Jacob & Susan Troutman, 10 July 1805; Adam Kabul, bondsman; A. L. Osborn, D. C., wit.

Earnhart, James & Malinda Lowrance, 17 April 1844; John H. McLaughlin, bondsman; Obadiah Woodson, wit.

Earnhart, John & Elizabeth Eller, 29 Dec 1795; Jacob Earnhart, bondsman; J. Troy, wit.

Earnhart, John & Catherine Cobble, 23 May 1796; Peter Faust, bondsman; J. Troy, wit.

Earnhart, John & Catey Hoffman, 29 Jan 1821; Andrew Earnhart, bondsman; Hy. Giles, wit.

Earnhart, John & Sally Pool, 31 Aug 1833; Abraham Peeler, bondsman; Jno Giles, wit.

Earnhart, L. S. & Amanda C. Shuping, 4 Jan 1866; W. C. Fesperman, bondsman; Obadiah Woodson, wit.

Earnhart, Moses G. & Eve Earnhart, 16 July 1857; Allen Trexler, bondsman; Levi Trexler, wit. married 16 July 1857 by Levi Trexler, J. P.

Earnhart, Peter & Barbara Shuman, 2 May 1804; Jacob Troutman, bondsman; A. L. Osborn, D. C., wit.

Earnhart, Philip & Elizabeth Pool, 4 Jan 1820; Abraham Arnhart, bondsman; Hy. Giles, wit.

Earnhart, Philip & Evy Correl, 12 Feb 1821; Adam Troutman, bondsman; Hy. Giles, wit.

Earnhart, Robard & Youncey Fisher, 3 Aug 1861; Joseph A. Brady, bondsman; Levi Trexler, wit.

Earnhart, Solomon & Elizabeth Wise, 24 May 1855; Cornelius Kesler, bondsman; married 24 May 1855 by S. J. Peeler, J. P.

Earnhart, Tobias & Sarah Ann Heltinger, 5 June 1851; John Smith-deal, bondsman; James E. Kerr, wit. married 8 June 1851 by W. A. Walton, J. P.

Earnhart, William C. & Leah Braddy, 9 Dec 1863; Moses Trexler, bondsman; Obadiah Woodson, wit.

Earnheart, A. C. & Elizabeth Gallemon, 6 Feb 1856; Morgan Mesenheimer, bondsman; James E. Kerr, wit.

Earnheart, Albert S. & Josey C. Arey, 5 Dec 1857; G. H. Peeler, bondsman; J. S. Myers, wit. married by H. W. Hill, J. P., 5 Dec 1857.

Earnheart, Alexander & Sarah Fulk, 29 March 1842; L. A. Bringle, bondsman.

Earnheart, Alexander & Mary Edwards, 10 May 1848; Leonard S. Krider, bondsman; J. H. Hardie, Jr., wit.

Earnheart, Caleb & Polly Hotchins, 29 Feb 1848; George Earnhart, bondsman; J. H. Hardie, wit.

Earnheart, Calvin M. & Mary C. Trexler, 13 Nov 1858; Joseph Beaver, bondsman; married 18 Nov 1858 by Saml. Rothrock, Minister of the Gospel in the Ev. Luth. Church.

Earnheart, Charles & Milly Agner, 24 Oct 1829; Daniel Rough, bondsman; J. H. Hardie, wit.

Earnheart, David & Eve L. Beaver, 6 Feb 1862; Eli Earnheart, bondsman; Saml Rothrock, wit. married 6 Feb 1862 by Saml. Rothrock, Minister of the Gospel in the Ev. Luth. Church.

Earnheart, Edward & Sarah Mull, 5 May 1838; Silas Earnheart, bondsman; S. Lemy Jr., wit.

Earnheart, Henry & Betsey Swin, 23 Nov 1818; Abraham Earnheart, bondsman; Jno Giles, wit.

Earnheart, Henry & Anna L. Klutts, 4 June 1862; John Earnheart, bondsman; J. H. Hardie, wit.

Earnheart, Jacob & Anna Troutman, 10 July 1843; Stephen Kirk, bondsman; J. H. Hardie, wit.

Earnheart, James & Sophia Klutts, 14 Aug 1837; John Peacock, bondsman; Tobias L. Lemly, wit.

Earnheart, James P. & Sophia C. Trexler, 28 Aug 1865; Calvin May, bondsman; Obadiah Woodson, wit.

Earnheart, John & Catherine S. Goodman, 16 Jan 1850; Henry A. Miller, bondsman; J. S. Myers, wit.

Earnheart, Killian & Betsy Kiker, 26 July 1816; Michael Dillom, bondsman; Jno Giles, wit.

Earnheart, Michael & Caroline Eller, 27 Sept 1842; J. H. Hardie, bondsman; Martha Hardie, wit.

Earnheart, Moses & Polly Eller, 19 Oct 1852; George Eller, bondsman; J. S. Myers, wit. married 19 Oct 1852 by Jacob File, J. P.

Earnheart, Nathaniel & Margaret Earnheart, 7 Sept 1861; H. S. Swink, bondsman; Obadiah Woodson, wit.

Earnheart, Peter & Rachael Earnheart, 12 Jan 1828; Henry Wilhelm, bondsman; J. Hardie, wit.

Earnheart, Philip & Polly Brown, 30 March 1813; Jacob Sossaman, bondsman; Jno Giles, C. C., wit.

Earnheart, Silas & Carline Goodman, 5 April 1837; Edward Earnheart, bondsman; Tobias L. Lemly, wit.

Earnheart, Silas & Sarah Cauble, 4 Nov 1856; Michael Peeler,
bondsman; James E. Kerr, wit. married 4 Dec 1856 by L. C.
Groseclose.

Earnheart, Silas & Caroline Ritchey, 29 Dec 1860; Edward Pool,
bondsman; Wm. Locke, wit.

Earnheart, Thomas & Mary Cauble, 28 Oct 1842; Benjamin F. Fraley,
bondsman; Jno. H. Hardie, wit.

Earnheart, Thomas & Mary A. Wise, 2 June 1863; David Mahaley,
bondsman; Obadiah Woodson, wit.

Eary, Abraham & Mary Fatchy, 10 Feb 1803; John Gatchy, bondsman;
Ad. Osborn, D. C., wit.

Eary, Henry & Sophia Frailey, 14 Aug 1812; John Thomas, bondsman;
Geo Dunn, wit.

Easter, John & Polly Livengood, 6 Jan 1819; George Livengood,
bondsman; Roberts Nanny, wit.

Easther, Michael & Catharine Bolebauch, 29 Aug 1815; Michael
Leonard, bondsman; David Mock, wit.

Eaton, Daniel & Elizabeth Canter, 17 March 1798; Ebed Jones,
bondsman; Edwin J. Osborn, D. C., wit.

Eaton, George & Elizabeth Hughey, 11 June 1779; Joseph Eaton,
bondsman; Ad. Osborn, wit.

Eaton, Isaac & Pheeby Hall, 27 Nov 1768; Wm. McConnell, George
Gray, bondsmen; John Frohock, wit.

Eaton, John & Joannah Clifford, 28 Oct 1829; Joseph Clifford,
bondsman; L. R. Rose, J. P., wit.

Eaton, Peter & Susanah Brunt, 11 April 1812; Samuel Jones,
bondsman; Jn March Sr., wit.

Eaton, Samuel & Elizabeth West, 31 Aug 1801; George Hall,
bondsman; Jno Brem, wit.

Eccles, John & Mary Johnston, 1 March 1788; Isaac Jones, bondsman; Mas McEwen, wit.

Echeson, Edmund & Ediph Richardson, 14 Oct 1779; Richard William,
bondsman; Jo. Brevard, wit.

Eckhcls, Peter & Nancy Markland, 5 Dec 1817; Jeremiah Eakels,
bondsman; Thos Hampton, wit.

Eckle, Jacob & Anne Mary Little, 5 Jan 1779; John Lewis Beard,
bondsman; Wm. R. Davie, wit.

Ector, Samuel & Susannah Porter, 30 Aug 1774; Wm. Porter, bondsman; Ad. Osborn, wit. consent from James Porter, father of
Susannah, 30 Aug 1774, wit by Saml Ector, William Porter.

Eddelman, Ambrose & Elizabeth Barringer, 14 Jan 1835; David
Roseman, bondsman; Jno H. Hardie, wit.

Eddinger, William M. & Maria Schuler, 4 Sept 1855; James M.
Patton, bondsman; J. S. Myers, wit.

Eddleman, Jeremiah A. & Mary L. Sifferd, 23 April 1866; H. M.
Goodman, bondsman; Obadiah Woodson, wit.

Eddleman, Peter & Polly Linn, 17 Dec 1812; Henry Barrier, bondsman; Jno Giles, C., wit.

Eddleman, S. P. & Eliza M. Klutts, 13 Feb 1866; C. H. Eagle,
bondsman; Obadiah Woodson, wit.

Eddleman, W. C. & Rose C. Goodman, 21 Aug 1865; W. W. Miller,
bondsman; Obadiah Woodson, wit. married 24 Aug 1865 by
Simeon Scherer.

Eddlemon, Adam & Elizabeth Shuping, 6 Feb 1821; Peter Eddlemon,
bondsman; Hy. Giles, wit.

Edgar, John & Elizabeth Cummins, 8 March 1780; William Wells,
bondsman; Jno Kerr, wit.

Edleman, Peter & Cathrine Earey, 31 Jan 1787; Jno Macay, wit.

Edmiston, John F. & Eady Elis, 5 Dec 1842; Robert H. Crawford,
bondsman; J. Sneed, wit.

Edmiston, Samuel & Sirena Fluman, 30 Oct 1812; Michael Fluming,
bondsman; Jno Giles, wit.

Edmiston, Samuel R. & Sarah Ann Smith, 8 April 1851; John C.
Hargrave, bondsman; James E. Kerr, wit.

Edmund, George & Anna L. Eller, 16 July 1844; Tobias Hess,
bondsman; J. H. Hardie, wit.

Eds, Ezekiel & Polly Barrot, 12 Jan 1799; John Phillips, bondsman; Edwin J. Osborn, D. C., wit.

Edward, Amos & Peggy Freely, 14 Nov 1808; Adam Coll, bondsman;
A. L. Osborne, wit.

Edwards, Charles M. & Martha Poarch, 13 Aug 1822; Andrew Miller,
bondsman; Jno. Giles, wit.

Edwards, David & Elizabeth King, 12 Jan 1861; G. W. Swink, bondsman; John Wilkinson, wit. married 13 Jan 1861 by W. R.
Fraley, J. P.

Edwards, Griffith & Mary Barrott, 19 Oct 1774; Isaiah Parker,
bondsman; Ad. Osborn, wit. consent from Jonathan Berot,
father of Pole (Polly, Mary) Berot, 17 Oct.

Edwards, James M. & Martha E. Brown, 29 Aug 1855; Hiram Lawson,
bondsman; James E. Kerr, wit. married 29 Aug 1855 by C. M.
Pepper.

Edwards, John & Frances Patterson, __ Aug 1796; John Jacobs,
bondsman; J. Troy, wit.

Edwards, John M. & Susanna Brown, 3 April 1821; Benjamin Brown,
bondsman; Hy. Giles, wit.

Edwards, Joseph & Mary Wolfscale, 3 May 1785; Joseph Bevens,
bondsman; H. Magoune, wit.

Edwards, Logan L. & Elizabeth Hulin, 29 March 1849; Alexander
Earnheart, bondsman.

Edwards, Mathew & Ellen Strange, 15 Dec 1829; Willson McCreery,
bondsman; Jno. H. Hardie, wit.

Edwards, Theodrick & Catharine E. Smith, 1 Dec 1842; Michael
Davis, bondsman; T. Sneed, wit.

Edwards, Thomas & Nelly Brown, 12 Oct 1816; Benjamin Brown,
bondsman; Jno Giles, C. C., wit.

Edwin, George & Nancy Natherey, 12 Dec 1833; Tobias Hess, bondsman; Elizabeth Giles, wit.

Efird, Adam & Catharine L. Miller, 7 Aug 1851; Jesse W. Miller,
bondsman; James E. Kerr; wit.

Eggers, Landrin & Joanna Silvers, 16 April 1779; John Green,
bondsman; Jno Kerr, wit.

Egner, David & Margaret Wise, 18 June 1785; Peter Riblen,
bondsman; H. Magoune, wit.

Eithholtz, George & Anne Rotecap, 13 June 1774; George Lauman,
bondsman; Ad. Osborn, wit.

Elam, James & Elizabeth Casper, 4 Nov 1854; Edward Earnhart,
bondsman; J. S. Myers, wit.

Elder, Andrew & Margaret Cohort, 19 Feb 1787; Andw. McClenachan,
bondsman; R. Henderson, wit.

Elder, James & Sarah Stevenson, 3 March 1767; Wm. Steel, James
Stevenson, bondsmen; Thos Frohock, wit.

Elison, Andrew & Jean Todd, 4 Sept 1786; John Alison, bondsman;
Jno Macay, wit.

Elledge, James & Sally Willcox, 14 Dec 1801; Jacob Keller, bondsman; Jno Brem, wit.

Ellenberger, John Frederick & Catharine Motz, 28 Jan 1794; Simon
Motz, bondsman; Jo. Chambers, wit.

Eller--see also Ellor

Eller, Adam & Mary J. Earnheart, 11 April 1857; Conrad Eller,
bondsman; J. S. Myers, wit. married 12 April 1857 by S. J.
Peeler, J. P.

Eller, Alexander & Sarah M. Misenhammer, 3 July 1839; John M.
Johnson, bondsman; Abel Cowan, J. P., wit.

Eller, Alexander & Nancy Cox, 16 March 1846; Henry Miller, bondsman; J. H. Hardie, wit.

Eller, Alexander & Quilly Casper, 2 Jan 1855; Philip Lemly,
bondsman; H. W. Hill, J. P., wit. married 2 Jan 1855 by
H. W. Hill, J. P., license has Aquilla Casper.

Eller, Amos & Betsey Eller, 17 July 1821; Coonrod Eller, bondsman; Hy. Giles, wit.

Eller, Andrew & Caty Brown, 19 Sept 1821; John Hembree, bondsman; Jno Giles, wit.

Eller, Andrew & Polly Eller, daughter of Fredk. Eller, 26 April 1826; Saml. Eller, bondsman; J. H. Hardie, wit.

Eller, Benjamin & _____, 14 March 1837; Jacob Fulenwider, bondsman.

Eller, Charles & Catharine Eller, 4 Jan 1825; Jacob Eller, bondsman; Hy. Giles, wit.

Eller, Charles & Sophia Brown, 29 Oct 1826; Andrew Eller, bondsman; J. H. Hardie, wit.

Eller, Charles A. & Margaret Ruan Phillips, 28 April 1863; W. H. Walton, bondsman; Obadiah Woodson, wit.

Eller, Christian & Catharine Lemly, 18 April 1810; John Lineberger, bondsman; Jno Giles, C. C., wit.

Eller, Conrad & Mary Eller, 8 Aug 1820; Paul Eller, bondsman; Jno Giles, wit.

Eller, Conrad & Anna B. Johnson, 28 Feb 1865; John Bringle, bondsman; Obadiah Woodson, wit.

Eller, David & Polly Hampton, 6 Dec 1817; John Eller, bondsman; Robs. Nanny, wit.

Eller, David & Nancy Cauble, 27 May 1841; J. L. Beard, bondsman.

Eller, Davie & Sarah Leonard, 31 Jan 1815; Daniel Waggoner, bondsman; Jno. L. Henderson, wit.

Eller, Edward & Eliza Eller, 19 July 1845; Tobias Eller, bondsman; Jno H. Hardie Jr., wit.

Eller, Farley & Julia Ann May, 18 Jan 1860; Alexander May, bondsman; James E. Kerr, wit. married 19 Jan 1860 by S. J. Peeler, J. P.

Eller, George & Mary Yokely, 21 Nov 1814; David Eller, bondsman; Jno Giles, wit.

Eller, George & Teny McCann, 23 June 1821; John Basenger, bondsman; Henry Allemong, wit.

Eller, George & Sally Hartman, 28 Sept 1836; David Beaver, bondsman; J. H. Hardie, wit.

Eller, George & Ceny Goodman, 18 June 1842; George Hartman, bondsman; Jno H. Hardie, wit.

Eller, George & Rosena Goodman, 29 Dec 1842; Jacob File, bondsman.

Eller, Green & Sophia C. Lowde, 10 Feb 1855; Edward Eller, bondsman; J. S. Myers, wit. married 15 Feb 1855 by M. S. McKenzie, J. P.

Eller, Hamilton & Salena Safrit, married 1 Oct 1845 by W. Kimball, Pastor of St. _____ Church, Rowan Co.

Eller, Henry & Hannah Beane, 22 Jan 1800; Peter Crowell, bondsman; Edwin J. Osborn, wit.

Eller, Henry & Hessy Poole, 20 Oct 1818.

Eller, Henry & _____, _____ 182_; George Kesler, bondsman;
Wms. Harris, wit.

Eller, Henry & Salena Safrit, 29 Sept 1865; Michael Beaver,
bondsman; Obadiah Woodson, wit.

Eller, Isaac & Mary Eller, 14 Nov 1820; Jacob Eller, bondsman;
Hy. Giles, wit.

Eller, Isaac & Milly Eller, 5 Oct 1826; Charles Eller, bondsman;
J. H. Hardie, wit.

Eller, Jacob & Mary Eller, 25 July 1814; George Eller, bondsman;
Jno Giles, C. C., wit.

Eller, Jacob & Christena Ketchy, 16 Sept 1819; Jacob Egner,
bondsman; Hy. Giles, wit.

Eller, Jacob & Rosena Eller, 9 May 1820; Christian Eller,
bondsman; Jno Giles, wit.

Eller, Jacob & Mary C. Havener, 25 Jan 1864; Lewis P. Earnheart,
bondsman; Obadiah Woodson, wit.

Eller, James & Leah Earnheart, 13 Aug 1857; Cornelius Eller,
bondsman; J. S. Myers, wit. married 16 Aug 1857 by S. J.
Peeler, J. P.

Eller, James J. & Crissy L. Keply, 5 Feb 1866; Farley Eller,
bondsman; H. N. Woodson, wit.

Eller, Jesse & Frances Brown, 18 Aug 1851; G. H. Peeler, bondsman; J. S. Myers, wit.

Eller, Jesse Benjamin & Adelia Linebarrier, 4 Apr 1860; David
Weil, bondsman; John Wilkinson, wit. married 8 April 1860 by
R. J. Linn, J. P.

Eller, John & Susanna Eller, 9 Oct 1782; John Eller, bondsman;
Wm. Crawford, wit.

Eller, John & Catherine Foit, 10 Aug 1785; Conrod Foit, bondsman.

Eller, John & Suzana Kerns, 5 Nov 1792; Gabriel Kerns, bondsman;
Jos. Chambers, wit.

Eller, John & March Aronhart, 14 Dec 1793; John Melcher Eller,
bondsman; Jos. Chambers, wit.

Eller, John & Mary Loposser, 10 Dec 1816; Jacob Eller, bondsman;
Roberts Nanny, wit.

Eller, John & Caty Fennel, 4 Nov 1825; David Eller, bondsman;
Hy. Giles, wit.

Eller, John & Anna L. Frick, 24 Dec 1841; James Biles, bondsman;
G. S. Johnston, wit.

Eller, John & Eve Eller, 2 June 1846; Jno H. Hardie, bondsman.

Eller, John & Barbara J. Stoner, 20 July 1852; Adam Heddinger,
bondsman; J. S. Myers, wit.

Eller, John & Susan D. Mahaley, 26 Nov 1859; Daniel Verble, bondsman; Wm. Locke, wit. married 27 Nov 1859 by J. K. Burke, J. P.

Eller, John & Mary Belford, 20 Feb 1827; George Frick, bondsman.

Eller, John Sr. & Margarett Lemly, 26 April 1808; John Eller Jr., bondsman; Andrew Kerr, wit.

Eller, John M. & Mary Kepley of Davidson County, 27 Oct 1855; Geo B. Swink, bondsman; J. S. Myers, wit. married 30 Oct 1855 by Obadiah Woodson, J. P.

Eller, Joseph & Malinda Airey, 20 Feb 1837; John Bringle, bondsman; Jno. H. Hardie, wit.

Eller, Joseph & Sally Kepler, 25 June 1821; John Eller, bondsman; Hy. Giles, wit.

Eller, Joseph & Evaline Miller, 17 Jan 1839; Tobias Myers, bondsman; Hy. Giles, wit.

Eller, Joseph & Julia Ann Redwin, 8 March 1862; Conrad Eller, bondsman; Obadiah Woodson, wit. married 23 March 1862 by Peter Williamson, J. P.

Eller, Joshua & Catharine Linebarger, 7 Nov 1857; Miles J. Walton, bondsman; J. S. Myers, wit. married 9 Nov 1857 by S. J. Peeler, J. P.

Eller, Michael & Nancy Harkey, 21 Nov 1839; John M. Eller, bondsman; John Giles, wit.

Eller, Michael & Anny Harkey, 25 Nov 1841; James Biles, bondsman; J. S. Johnston, wit.

Eller, Michael & Linda Miller, 21 Sept 1863; W. A. Walton, bondsman; Obadiah Woodson, wit.

Eller, Milas & Anna Bird, 5 June 1851; George Basinger, bondsman; James F. Kerr, wit.

Eller, Milas & Angeline Vestal, 19 April 1866; Elam F. Miller, bondsman; Obadiah Woodson, wit.

Eller, Moses & Luticia M. Lentz, 9 March 1852; married 9 March 1852 by W. A. Walton, J. P.

Eller, Neporus & Leah D. Wilhelm, 11 May 1852; William L. Wilhelm, bondsman; J. S. Myers, wit.

Eller, Obadiah & Caroline Barger, 4 Jan 1866; Green Eller, bondsman; Obadiah Woodson, wit.

Eller, Peter & Susanna Lemley, 17 April 1809; George Lemley, bondsman; Ad. Osborn, wit.

Eller, Peter & Lucyndy Ross, 31 March 1835; Henry Mosamor, bondsman; D. H. Bringle, wit.

Eller, Phillip & Betsey Eller, 17 July 1804; Conrad Eller, bondsman; A. L. Osborn, D. C., wit.

Eller, Samuel & Nancy Peirce, 21 March 1825; Michael Rymer, bondsman; W. Harris, wit.

Eller, Samuel & Polly Earnheart, 25 Nov 1861; James Eller, bondsman; Obadiah Woodson, wit. married 28 Nov 1861 by H. W. Hill.

Eller, Solomon & Catharine Eller, 7 March 1825; Andrew Eller, bondsman; W. Harris, wit.

Eller, Tobias & Margaret Brown, 9 Jan 1850; George Peeler, bondsman; J. S. Myers, wit.

Eller, Tobias & Polly Arey, 14 June 1855; Adam Eller, bondsman; J. S. Myers, wit. married 14 June 1855 by S. J. Peeler, J. P.

Eller, Zachariah & Christena Eller, 1 Jan 1839; Tobias Myers, bondsman; Hy. Giles, wit.

Ellexson, Jeremiah & Wineford Gilstrap, 24 March 1804; John Connelson, bondsman; A. L. Osborn, D. C., wit.

Elliot, Elisha & Sarah Tilmon, 17 March 1819; Isaac Pope, bondsman.

Elliot, James & Elizabeth McKee, 21 Nov 1808; William McGuire, bondsman; A. L. Osborn, wit.

Elliot, Samuel & Susan A. Beaver, married 18 July 1861 by Moses Powless, J. P. (no bond, return only).

Elliott, Abner S. & Mary E. Gheen, 28 Sept 1853; T. T. Gheen, bondsman; J. S. Myers, wit.

Elliott, Hillary & Mary Phillips, 11 Dec 1834; E. E. Philips, bondsman; Jno. Giles, wit.

Elliott, Isaac & Charaty Howard, 25 Aug 1798; Fredk. Martch, bondsman; M. A. Troy, wit.

Elliott, John & Susanna Claver, 18 Sept 1787; Jno Macay, wit.

Elliott, Joseph & Hannah Brown, 4 June 1767; Peter Johnson, Robert Pearis, bondsmèn; Thos Frohock, wit.

Elliott, Josiah & Mary Dent, 2 May 1822; Richard Plumer, bondsman.

Elliott, Julius A. & Naomi M. Dobbin, 19 July 1860; Joseph E. Dobbin, bondsman; John Wilkinson, wit.

Elliott, Kinchen & Ellen G. Williamson, 31 March 1828; Richard Loury, bondsman; Hy. Giles, wit.

Elliott, Kinchen & Ellen Trott, 17 July 1844; J. H. Hardie, bondsman.

Elliott, Lemuel & Polly Cline, 21 Feb 1822; Richard Plummer, bondsman; George Locke, wit.

Elliott, Lemuel & Catharine Smith, 27 Feb 1822; Jonathan Hulan, bondsman.

Elliott, S. L. & Margaret S. Menius, 29 Sept 1865; J. A. Hall, bondsman; Obadiah Woodson, wit. married 1 Oct 1865 by Jas. T. Cuthrell, minister.

Elliott, Samuel & Sarah Menius, 7 Jan 1858; Matthew D. Waggoner, bondsman; James E. Kerr, wit.

Elliott, Upshaw & Reuhanah Cowan, 3 Oct 1850; Willis Trott, bondsman; J. S. Myers, wit.

Elliott, U. D. & Millie Jane Elliott, 27 April 1854; Thomas L. Thompson, bondsman; James E. Kerr, wit. married 27 April 1854 by A. Henderson, J. P.

Elliott, William & Nancy Bierly, 22 Feb 1814; William Coats, bondsman; Jno. Giles, C. C., wit.

Elliott, William & Nancy Hall, 6 Aug 1844; H. W. Watson, bondsman; J. H. Hardie, wit.

Ellis, Alexander & Delinda Mark, 21 Dec 1833; Farley Ellis, bondsman; Hy. Giles, wit.

Ellis, Anderson & Judy Bayley, _____ 180_; (no bondsman, wit.)

Ellis, David & Elizabeth Davis, 2 Dec 1799; James Park, bondsman; Edwin J. Osborn, D. C., wit.

Ellis, Etheldred & Elizabeth NcNight, 14 July 1795; Stephen Ellis, bondsman; John Eccles, Esq., wit.

Ellis, Evan & Tempey Smith, 31 March 1824; Caswoll Harbin, bondsman; L. R. Rose, J. P., wit.

Ellis, Evan Jr. & Catharine Beechem, 17 Dec 1791; William Ellis, bondsman; Chs. Caldwell, wit.

Ellis, Farly & Eliza Courtney, 7 Jan 1830; Saml. Reeves, bondsman; Jno. H. Hardie, wit.

Ellis, Farly & Margaret Besherer, 12 May 1853; Saml. Reeves, Sr., bondsman; J. S. Myers, wit.

Ellis, Francis & Polly Abbott, 9 Nov 1814; John B. Todd, bondsman; Geo. Dunn, wit.

Ellis, Ira & Frances Starr, 2 Feb 1830; Evan Ellis, bondsman; C. Harbin, J. P., wit.

Ellis, Isaac & Elizabeth Railsback, 26 April 1791; David Railsback, bondsman; Basil Gaither, wit.

Ellis, Isham P. & Elizabeth Miller, 11 Sept 1827; Davie Harbin, bondsman; C. Harbin, J. P., wit.

Ellis, James & Lucy Davis, 20 June 1788; David Barclay, bondsman.

Ellis, James & Peggy Philips, 2 April 1803; Joshua Jones, bondsman; Jn March, wit.

Ellis, James & Rebecca Welman, 4 _____ 1820; William Athason, bondsman; R. Powell, wit.

Ellis, Jesse & Nancy Mederies, 6 Oct 1807; James Wilson, bondsman; Jn March Sr., wit.

Ellis, Joel & Mary D. Pelly, 5 Jan 1824; William S. Jones, bondsman; L. R. Rose, J. P., wit.

Ellis, John & Margret Bryan, 11 March 1779; Jeremiah Power, bondsman; Ad. Osborn, wit.

Ellis, John & Rebecca Loftin, 14 June 1796; James Morgan, bondsman; J. Troy, wit.

Ellis, John & Elizabeth Loften, 16 Jan 1804; Stephen Treadwell, bondsman; A. L. Osborn, D. C., wit.

Ellis, John & Sarah James, 18 Aug 1807; Alan Forcoum, bondsman; Jn. March Sr., wit.

Ellis, John & Polly Bradshaw, 14 Nov 1809; William Haden, bondsman; Geo Dunn, wit.

Ellis, John & Marietta E. Graham (colored), 19 April 1866; George Little, bondsman; Obadiah Woodson, wit.

Ellis, Quinten & Susanna Davis, 26 July 1820; Silas Dunn, bondsman; Hy. Giles, wit.

Ellis, Quinten & Polly Wilhelm, 22 April 1822; George Hufty, bondsman.

Ellis, Radford & Elizabeth Macay, 6 May 1778; Spruce Macay, bondsman.

Ellis, Radford & Elizabeth Glover, 4 Jan 1821; David Miller, bondsman; Hy. Giles, wit.

Ellis, Richard & Thamor Brown, 26 Oct 1820; Charles Hoover, bondsman; Thos Hampton, J. E. Brown, wit.

Ellis, Samuel & Martha Howard, 15 July 1788; Bazel Summers, bondsman; Wm. Alexander, wit.

Ellis, William Jr. & Ann Riddle, 27 March 1792; Jno Johnston, bondsman; Basil Gaither, wit.

Ellis, Willis & _____, _____ 179_; Mich. Troy, bondsman.

Ellis, Willis & Mary A. White, 2 May 1840; William A. McCree, bondsman; Susan T. Giles, wit.

Ellor, George & Caty Ellor, 9 Sept 1814; Henry Ellor, bondsman; Geo Dunn, wit.

Ellor, Henry & Polly Ellor, 10 Oct 1815; John Basinger, bondsman; Geo Dunn, wit.

Ellott, Elkena & Gincey Gheen, 17 Aug 1819; Henry Allemong, bondsman; Jno Giles, wit.

Elrod, William & Pheby Philips, 8 Jan 1811; Jno Elrod, bondsman; W. Ellis, J. P., wit.

Elsser, Frederick & Sarah Bowers, 13 Dec 1827; Adam Trexler, bondsman; Jno H. Hardie, wit.

Elston, Elias & Jemh. McCartney, 12 Nov 1796; Robt. Bartley, bondsman; Jno Rogers, wit.

Elston, Jonathan & Barbara Smith 18 April 1791; Alston Campbell, bondsman; Chs. Caldwell, D. C., wit.

Elston, Jonathan & Mary Wiatt, 9 Aug 1793; Robert Barckley, bondsman; Jos. Chambers, wit.

Elston, Jonathan & Mary Floyd, 26 March 1800; Ruben Homes, bondsman; Edwin J. Osborn, wit.

Elston, Josiah & Rebecca Lewis, 30 Sept 1789; Daniel Mcguicr, bondsman; Evan Alexander, wit.

Elston, William & Hay Doty, 5 May 1797; William Grist, bondsman; Jno Rogers, wit.

Elvison, James & Rosanna J. Pettigroe, 30 Dec 1809; Jno Myris, bondsman; Jno Giles, C. C., wit.

Embler, William & Franky Seers, 15 May 1794; Peter Helms, bondsman; Jo Chambers, wit.

Emerson, William & Jane Adams, 2 Sept 1847; James H. McNeely, bondsman; J. H. Hardie, Jr., wit.

Emery, Joel & Eve Fite, 17 March 1828; Jacob Beaver, bondsman; Jno H. Hardie, wit.

Emery, William W. & Mary Ann Allen, 1 June 1852; Joseph Smithdeal, bondsman; J. S. Myers, wit. married 2 June 1852 by Azariah Williams, a Regular Minister of the Missionary Bapt. order.

Emison, George & Beckey Furniter, 3 Dec 1806; Richard Emison, bondsman; A. Osborn, C. C., wit.

Emory, William W. & Maryann Allen, married 2 June 1852 by Azariah Williams, a Regular Minister of the Missionary Bapt. order.

Engert, Abram & Rachall Swinson, 15 Feb 1769; Abraham Creson, Jonathan Robins, bondsmen; Thos Frohock, wit.

Englebert, R. W. & Anna A. Hartman, 23 Dec 1864; William A. Shelley, bondsman; Obadiah Woodson, wit.

Englebert, Y. G. & Catharine Wilkinson, 27 Dec 1863; S. T. Brown, bondsman; Obadiah Woodson, wit.

Enlow, M. L. & Mary Jane Weaver, 5 May 1860; H. J. Pendleton, bondsman; John Wilkinson, wit.

Ennis, John & Jane Black, 30 Jan 1767; James Black, bondsman; John Frohock, wit.

Enochs, David & Elizabeth Wilson, 29 Jan 1794; Enoch Enochs, bondsman; G. Enochs, wit.

Enochs, Enoch & Alidia Rumley, 30 Sept 1789; Michael Smith, bondsman; Basil Gaither, wit.

Enocks, Thomas & Nancy Bryan, 16 Oct 1786; Michael Smith, bondsman; Spruce Macay, wit.

Ensley, David & Mary Cannady, 29 April 1811; James Payne, bondsman; Sol. Davis, J. P., wit.

Ernhart, Peter & Susana Ernhart, 28 Nov 1840; Moses Cauble, bondsman; J. L. Beard, wit.

Ervin, Christopher & Mary Lyall, 26 Feb 1782; John Oliphant, bondsman.

Ervin, John & Jane Brown, 19 Oct 1772; David Brown, bondsman;
Ad. Osborn, wit.

Ervin, Joseph & Sarah B. Young, 9 Feb 1846; Jos. F. Chambers,
bondsman; J. H. Hardie Jr., wit.

Ervin, Samuel L. & Elizabeth Patterson, 23 Nov 1857; J. D. Erwin,
bondsman; James Kerr, wit. married 26 Nov 1857 by B. C. Hall.

Ervin, William & Mary Addams, 13 Oct 1788; John Adams, bondsman;
Mag. Osborn, wit.

Erwin, Alexander & Mrs. Margret Patton, 21 Jan 1786; William
Sharpe, bondsman; Ad. Osborn, wit.

Erwin, Campbell & Sally Bateman, 1 May 1818; George J. Niblock,
bondsman; Jno Giles, wit.

Erwin, Eli & Mary Cook, 13 Jan 1821; Thos. M. Cook, bondsman;
Henry Allemong, wit.

Erwin, George & Mary Lourance, 7 Feb 1800; Joseph Young, bondsman; Hu. Braly, wit.

Erwin, James & Jennet Andrews, 10 Oct 1766; Germa Baxter, George
Niblack, bondsmen; Thomas Frohock, wit.

Erwin, John & Alice Brandon, 28 July 1779; Matt Brandon, bondsman; Jo Brevard, wit.

Erwin, John & Margret Young, 25 April 1786; Samuel Young,
bondsman; Jno Macay, wit.

Erwin, John & Jane Webb, 1 Jan 1821; Caleb Webb, bondsman;
Hy. Giles, wit.

Erwin, John & Becca Sanders, 24 Feb 1824; Robert Erwin, bondsman;
Jno Giles, wit.

Erwin, John & Elizabeth Keisler, 17 Feb 1830; John Brodway,
bondsman.

Erwin, Joseph & Catharine Cowan, 17 May 1792; Thomas Cowan,
bondsman; Chas. Caldwell, wit.

Erwin, Robert & Jenney Tenneson, 28 Feb 1825; John Erwin,
bondsman.

Erwin, William & Elizabeth Ord, 3 March 1762; James Erwin Jr.,
Wm. McConnely, bondsmen; Tho Frohock, wit.

Erwin, William & Isabella Brown, 10 Feb 1775; John Oliphant,
bondsman; James Robinson, wit.

Erwin, William & Rachael Woods, 21 Nov 1795; William Crosbey,
bondsman; J. Troy, wit.

Erwin, William & Matilda Sharpe, __ May 1788; William Sharpe,
bondsman; Ad. Osborn, wit.

Espey, Samuel & Elizabeth Sloane, 5 April 1785; John Sloan,
bondsman.

Esteb, Thomas & Hannah M. Cannon, 17 Jan 1803; Will Hunt,
bondsman.

Estep, Jacob & Nancy Moore, 3 Jan 1816; Starling Moore, bondsman; Jn. March Sr., wit.

Estep, Moses & Elizabeth Jones, 1 Sept 1803; Abraham Estep, bondsman; J. Hunt, wit.

Estes, Edmond & Charlotty Golding, 7 Dec 1820; Alexander Nesbitt, bondsman; A. R. Jones, wit.

Estip, Samuel & Susannah Adams, 3 Nov 1789; Henry Walker, bondsman; Evan Alexander, wit.

Etcherson, Daniel & Nancy Weab, 26 Dec 1815; Shadrick Etcheson, bondsman; Jn March Sr., wit.

Etcherson, Jesse & Nancey Felton, 13 Nov 1810; Arthur Smith, bondsman; Jn March Sr., wit.

Etcherson, John & Dianer Adams, 6 Feb 1816; Elijah Adams, bondsman; Jn March Sr., wit.

Etcherson, John & Nancy Jobe, 18 March 1817; Andrew Griffin, bondsman; Jn March Sr., wit.

Etcheson, Edmond & Susanna Hunter, 18 Oct 1812; Waters Harbin, bondsman; R. Powell, wit.

Etcheson, Elijah & Margaret Williams, 18 Jan 1823; William Jobe, bondsman; L. R. Rose, J. P., wit.

Etcheson, Henry & Mary Chaffer, 22 Nov 1794; Jacob Boo, bondsman.

Etcheson, James & Elizabeth Becton, 26 Feb 1817; Thomas Becton, bondsman; Jn March Sr., wit.

Etcheson, James & Francis Harbin, 1 Nov 1824; Andrew Sain, bondsman; L. R. Rose, J. P., wit.

Etcheson, Luckie & Nancy Shaw, 15 Feb 1826; Elijah Gibbs, bondsman; J. C. Weddington, wit.

Etcheson, Walter & Catharine Miller, 5 Feb 1819; Daniel Etcheson, bondsman; R. Powell, wit.

Etcheson, William & Polly Kinnick, 27 Jan 1828; Henry Etchison, bondsman; E. Brock, J. P., wit.

Etcheson, Willie & Mary Crumpton, 11 Dec 1817; Shadrach Etcheson, bondsman; R. Powell, wit.

Etchoson, Jesse & Rebecca Stinson, 10 March 1803; Robert Swan, bondsman.

Etheridge, Thomas & Elizabeth Camp, 8 May 1824; Joseph M. Hauser, bondsman; E. Brock, J. P., wit.

Etleman, Adam & Caty Lippard, 8 May 1815; John Berger, bondsman; Geo. Dunn, wit.

Eton, Benjamin & Emilie Fox, 26 Nov 1808; Vester Eton, bondsman; A. L. Osborne, D. C., wit.

Ettleman, John & Kitty Bliss, 6 Jan 1789; Watt Alexander, wit.

Eudey, William & Julia Lilly, 13 May 1858; George H. Fesperman, bondsman; John Wilkinson, wit. married 13 May 1858 by L. J. Kirk, J. P.

Evans, Eli & Elizabeth Ellit, 3 May 1804; Henrey Snow, bondsman; Jn March, J. P., wit.

Evans, Marcus & Winnefred Granger, 12 June 1820; Moses Granger, bondsman; R. Powell, wit.

Evans, Sergeant & Susannah Duffey, 20 March 1827; Hethspod Webb, bondsman; Jno H. Hardie, wit.

Evans, Solomon & Honaur Hutzon, 5 Feb 1828; John Guffey, bondsman; C. Harbin, J. P., wit.

Evans, Thomas & Sarah C. Green, 11 Dec 1845; Thos W. Foster, bondsman; J. H. Hardie, wit.

Evans, Waine & Polly Crider, 18 Jan 1813; Jas. Gillaspie, bondsman; Geo Dunn, wit.

Evans, William & Nicey Graham, 28 June 1804; William Graham, bondsman; J. Hunt, wit.

Evans, William & Elizabeth B. Granger, 12 June 1819; William Mason, bondsman; R. Powell, wit.

Evatt, James & Susan Jones, 21 June 1785; Wm. Evatt, bondsman; Hu. Magoune, wit.

Evens, John & Betty Laurance, 21 Jan 1782; Walter Bell, bondsman; Ad. Osborn, wit.

Everhart, Michael & Mary Livengood, 12 Feb 1822; John Everhart, bondsman; An. Swicegood, wit.

Everheart, John & Mary Sophia, 24 Aug 1788; Henry Giles, bondsman; Wall. Alexander, wit.

Everitt, Alexander & Harriet A. Carrigan, 4 June 1844; Henry Hauck, bondsman; Obadiah Woodson, wit.

Evns, Hendrick & Mary _____, 10 Sept 1813; Elijah Northerns, bondsman; W. N. Bean, J. P., wit.

Erum, David & Eliza A. Rary, 31 Jan 1832; James Hall, bondsman; Thomas McNeely, J. P., wit.

Eytcheson, Ely & Polly Deaver, 2 Dec 1815; Samuel Deaver, bondsman.

Ezell, Frederick & Mary Cox, 28 March 1780; Benjamin Rounsavell, bondsman; B. Booth Boote, wit.

Fagenwinter, Christopher & Barba Few, 1 Oct 1785; John Fischer, bondsman; Max. Chambers, wit.

Fagg, Joel & Amey Peoples, 4 June 1817; Albert Peebles, bondsman.

Faggenwenter, Henry & Catharine Rany, 15 April 1813; James Briggs, bondsman; Jno. L. Henderson, wit.

Falcker, Samuel & Betsey Kern, 14 Aug 1817; Thomas Mock, bondsman; Jno Giles, wit.

Falkerson, Frederick & Sarah Gibson, 2 July 1766; Abraham
Fulkerson, Geo Gibson, Wilam Robeson, bondsmen; Jacob Leasch,
Christ. Gotte Reuter, wit.

Falls, John & Rachal Clayton, 2 June 1772; George Houston,
bondsman; Thomas Frohock, wit.

Falls, William & Mary Simonton, 13 March 1786; Theophilus
Simonton, bondsman.

Fane, Melcher & Susanna Coonrod, 15 Feb 1815; William Coonrod,
bondsman; En. Morgan, J. P., wit.

Farabe, Jesse & Ruth Jackson, 10 Sept 1818; B. D. Jones,
bondsman; Sol. Davis, J. P., wit.

Farabee, Joseph & Mary Harvey, 9 May 1813; John Farabee, bondsman; Sol. Davis, J. P., wit.

Farmer, Michal & Jane Stephenson, 14 Jan 1820; Alexander
Nesbitt, bondsman; R. Powell, wit.

Farr, John & Elisabeth Woodside, 14 Jan 1773; William Ross,
bondsman; Max. Chambers, wit.

Farrell, John & Catharine Goodman, 17 Jan 1791; Sam Graham,
bondsman; Cs. Caldwell, D. C., wit.

Faulkner, Benjamin & Christene Shoaf, 16 April 1815; Daniel
Wagner, Jno Michall, Henry Shoff, bondsmen; Jno Goss, J. P.,
wit.

Fausler, George & Anna Manship, 19 Feb 1819; Moses Smith, bondsman; Sol. Davis, J. P., wit.

Faw, Henry & Anne Hier, 27 May 1816; John Hire, bondsman;
Joseph Clarke, wit.

Feagin, Daniel & Polly Reed, 23 Feb 1821; James Reed, bondsman.

Fee, John & Parthena Kellon, 23 Oct 1779; Mark Whiteaker, bondsman; Jo Brevard, wit.

Feemster, William & Mary Sharpe, 29 May 1783; John Wallace,
bondsman; T. H. McCaule, wit.

Feezer, George & Christena Smith, 18 Aug 1787; Frederick Smith,
bondsman; Jno Macay, wit.

Feezer, Jacob & Anne Hendricks, 21 Oct 1813; John Feezer, bondsman; Geo. Dunn, wit.

Felker, A. W. & Catherine N. E. Garver, 5 Aug 1861; J. Wilkinson,
D; married 11 Dec 1861 by D. A. Davis, J. P.

Felker, George & Sarah Elizabeth Ketchie, 15 Feb 1864; John J.
Towel, bondsman; Obadiah Woodson, wit.

Felker, Jacob & Elizabeth Frize, 18 Sept 1823; George Miller,
bondsman; Hy. Giles, wit.

Felker, Jacob & Leah Klutts, 1 Sept 1853; Caleb Klutts, bondsman; James E. Kerr, wit.

Felker, John & Polly Cartner, 20 March 1815; Frederic Cartner, bondsman; Jno Giles, C., wit.

Felker, William & Elizabeth Rex, 14 May 1853; William A. Luckey, bondsman; J. S. Myers, wit. married 19 May 1853 by Jos. A. Hawkins, J. P.

Felps, Aventon & Sarah Harris, 21 April 1786; John Arwood, bondsman; John Macay, wit.

Felps, Avinton & Mary Hage, 2 April 1817; Ezekiel Felps, bondsman; Thos. Hampton, wit.

Felps, John & Mary Williams 12 Feb 1766; Saml. Williams, Ambross Hudgens, bondsmen; Thomas Frohock, wit.

Felps, John & Mary Caton, _____ Jan 1786; Archd. Kerr, bondsman; W. Cupples, wit.

Felps, Samuel & Polly Harper, 14 Oct 1791; George Laumann, bondsman; C. Caldwell, wit.

Felps, Thomas & Hanna Auldridges, 20 April 1792; Norman Owens, bondsman; Chs. Caldwell, wit.

Felps, Thomas & Mary Worry, 19 April 1812; Peter Hufman, bondsman; W. Ellis, J. P., wit.

Felps, Willi & Elizabeth Jones, 20 April 1768; Mark Whiteaker, bondsman; Thomas Frohock, wit. consent from Samuel Jones for his daughter to marry Wm. Felps.

Fennel, John & Polly Agle, 25 Jan 1802; Robert Anderson, bondsman; Jno Brem, wit.

Ferebee, Thomas Jr. & Catharine Howell, 22 Feb 1836; Joshua Howell, bondsman.

Fergerson, Moses & Eliza Bass, 28 Dec 1835; Richard Walton, bondsman; J. H. Hardie, wit.

Ferguson, Andrew & Elizabeth McFarland, 11 May 1791; Thomas Foley, bondsman; Chs. Caldwell, D. C., wit.

Ferguson, Hugh & Honor Duffy, 27 Nov 1816; Jas. Gillaspie, bondsman; Jno Giles, C. C., wit.

Ferguson, John & Elizabeth Hamelton, 25 Aug 1789; William Nevens, bondsman; Will Alexander, wit.

Ferguson, Paul & Catharine Graham, 21 Nov 1791; John Graham, bondsman; Chs. Caldwell, wit.

Ferguson, Thomas & Sarah McDowel, 30 March 1776; Robert McBride, bondsman; Ad. Osborn, wit. consent from William McDowl for his daughter Sarah, 30 March 1776.

Ferguson, William M. & Sarah Corzine, 8 Sept 1827; Andrew Corzine, bondsman; Jno Giles, wit.

Ferrand, Stephen L. & Margaret G. Steele, 27 Feb 1819; John Beard Jr., bondsman; Jno Giles, wit.

Ferrel, Micaga & Fronhy Carter, 29 Feb 1812; John Brinkly, bondsman; J. Willson, J. P., wit.

Ferrell, John & Phebe Barker, 9 Feb 1814; John Barker, bondsman;
Jno Giles, wit.

Ferrington, Solomon & Barbre Harman, 8 June 1801; Samuel
Ferington, bondsman.

Fesperman, Edmund & Margaret D. Miller, 18 Jan 1848; Harvey B.
Reese, bondsman; J. H. Hardie, wit.

Fesperman, Henry & Sally Hampton, 30 July 1842; Obeddiah
Hampton, bondsman.

Fesperman, Jacob & Barbara Ritchie, 21 March 1825; John
Fesperman, bondsman.

Fesperman, Jacob & Margaret J. Gibbons, 15 Jan 1849; Moses Brown,
bondsman; J. H. Hardie, wit.

Fesperman, John & Sophia Ritchie, 1 May 1824; Jacob Fesperman,
bondsman; Hy. Giles, wit.

Fesperman, McCamy O. & Sophronia C. Overcash, 27 July 1853; P.
P. Meroney, bondsman married 27 July 1853 by J. M. Brown,
J. P.

Fesperman, Michael & Cynthea Gardner, 25 Dec 1833; Benjamin
Fraley, bondsman; Jno Giles, wit.

Fesperman, Moses A. & Mary Klutts, 4 March 1856; Moses Brown,
bondsman; J. S. Myers, wit. married 5 March 1856 by Saml.
Rothrock.

Fesperman, Simeon G. & Mary E. Albright, 16 March 1859; Caleb
Hampton, bondsman.

Fesperman, Wiley M. & Nancy Christena Harriss, 23 Oct 1861;
David A. Bost, bondsman; Obadiah Woodson, wit.

Fesperman, William F. & Adaline Glover, 30 Oct 1858; Moses Brown,
bondsman; John Wilkinson, wit. married 4 Nov 1858 by L. J.
Kirk, J. P.

Festerman, Daniel M. & Mary B. Mock, 17 Aug 1837; Henry Baker,
bondsman; Tobias L. Lemly, wit.

Fezer, Peter & Mary Fry, 6 Oct 1769; Vallentine Fry, John Frohock,
bondsmen; Thos Frohock, wit.

Fichpatrick, John & Mable Guston, 3 April 1787; Thos Hannon,
bondsman; Jno Macay, wit.

Fight--see also Fite

Fight, Conrad & Elizabeth Brown, 14 Feb 1788; Peter Fight, bondsman; Samuel Carter, wit.

Fight, Henry T. & Susan E. Walton, 12 June 1865; Jacob S.
Myers, bondsman; Obadiah Woodson, wit.

Fight, Peter & Barbara Hellinger, 11 July 1791; Martin Bassinger,
bondsman; C. Caldwell, D. C., wit.

File--see also Foil

File, Daniel & Ann Parks, 24 March 1828; Jacob File, bondsman; Hy. Giles, wit.

File, Eli & Rhoda Morgan, 7 Aug 1843; Archibald Misenhimer, bondsman; Jn. H. Hardie, wit.

File, Ivey & Elizabeth Peeler, 21 Aug 1856; John F. Agner, bondsman; James E. Kerr, wit.

File, Ivey W. & Amanda Earnhart, 3 Sept 1859; Noah File, bondsman; James E. Kerr, wit. married 5 Sept 1859 by S. J. Peeler, J. P.

File, Jacob & Betsey Eddleman, 15 March 1817; Jacob Kistler, bondsman; Milo A. Giles, wit.

File, Jacob & Malinda Wise, 11 July 1855; James J. McConnaughey, bondsman; J. S. Myers, wit. married 19 July 1855 by Levi Trexler, J. P.

File, Martin & Mary Stanly, 13 March 1838; Howel Parker, bondsman; E. R. Backhedd, wit.

File, Michael & Elizabeth Hartman, 17 Sept 1849; Caleb Klutts, bondsman; J. S. Myers, wit.

File, Michael & Mary Park, 9 Aug 1821; Jacob File, bondsman.

File, Michael & Basha Parks, 3 June 1843; Amos Rough, bondsman; J. H. Hardie, wit.

File, Moses & Sophia Starns, 2 April 1827; Henry Lutewick, bondsman; Hy. Giles, wit.

File, Noah & Camilla Lyerly, 22 Feb 1855; Alexander Lyerly, bondsman; J. S. Myers, wit. married 22 Feb 1855 by Obadiah Woodson, J. P.

File, Richard & Eliza Saunders (both colored), 28 Oct 1865; Obadiah Woodson, Clk. married 28 Oct 1865 by D. L. Bringle, J. P.

File, Tobias & Sarah Eddleman, 27 Nov 1843; Peter Eddleman, bondsman.

Filhauer, Nicholas & Catharine Goodman, 6 Feb 1790; John Goodman, bondsman.

Finch, James B. & Mary Brown, 26 Nov 1804; Wm. T. Brown, bondsman; Moses A. Locke, wit.

Fincher, Jonathan & Betsy Pitman, 4 Jan 1797; Jesse Pitman, bondsman; Jno Rogers, wit.

Fink, Allison & Euphemia E. Pinkston, 20 April 1857; Moses A. Smith, bondsman; J. S. Myers, wit. married 21 April 1857 by J. M. Brown, J. P.

Fink, Jacob C. & Mary Jane Crosby, 17 Aug 1861; Joseph F. McLean, bondsman; Obadiah Woodson, wit. married 20 Aug 1861 by Stephen Frontis, Minister of the Gospel.

Fink, J. H. & Wilhelmina Martin, 29 Dec 1865; J. S. Martin, bondsman; Obadiah Woodson, wit.

Fink, John & Mary Goodman, 4 May 1790; Michael Goodman of Mecklenburg Co., bondsman; C. Caldwell, D. C., wit.

Fink, John M. & Sarah Lingle, 30 Jan 1858; Jas. Slater, bondsman; James E. Kerr, wit. married 11 Feb 1858 by B. C. Hall.

Fink, Peter & Betsey Frieze, 5 June 1819; Henry Sechler, bondsman; Jno Giles, wit.

Finney, John & Rachel Ashley, 6 Oct 1772; Andrew Presler, bondsmar.; Max. Chambers, wit.

Finny, James & Mary McCuone, 25 March 1776; John Buntin, bondsman; Ad. Osborn, wit.

Finton, John & Elizabeth Coon, 4 Nov 1789; Peter Wood, bondsman; Ed. Harris, wit.

Fips, John & Caty Dry, 28 July 1801; Henry Bower, bondsman; Jno Brem, wit.

Fisher, Charles & Elizabeth R. Caldwell, 17 July 1845; Jno H. Hardie, bondsman.

Fisher, Charles H. & M. S. Ketchie, 22 Oct 1865; D. M. Cress, bondsman; Obadiah Woodson, wit. married 23 Oct 1865 by W. Kimball, Pastor of the Ev. Luth. Chapel, Rowan Co.

Fisher, Daniel & Rose Ann Cruse, 17 March 1852; Peter A. Fisher, bondsman; James E. Kerr, wit. married 18 March 1852 by Saml. Rothrock, Minister of the Gospel in the Ev. Luth. Church.

Fisher, David & Mary A. L. Brown, 4 Sept 1855; Daniel Fisher, bondsman; J. S. Myers, wit. married 6 Sept 1855 by Saml Rothrock, Minister of the Gospel in the Ev. Luth. Church.

Fisher, Friederick & Barbara Tarr, 30 Jan 1793; Barnabas Krider, bondsman; Jos. Chambers, wit.

Fisher, George & Catharine Fisher, 16 March 1790; Osmis Penninger, bondsman; Ed. Harris, wit.

Fisher, George & Cartrout Laumon, 23 Oct 1790; Jacob Fisher, bondsman; Cs. Caldwell, wit.

Fisher, George & Suckey Taplin, 8 Feb 1812; Daniel Tenpenny, bondsman; Jno Giles, wit.

Fisher, George M. & Amy Klutts, 30 May 1853; A. M. Klutts, bondsman; J. S. Myers, wit. married 2 June 1853 by Saml. Rothrock, Minister of the Gospel in the Ev. Luth. Church.

Fisher, Harmon & Elizabeth Peninger, 16 July 1800; George Fisher, bondsman; Nl. Chaffin, J. P., wit.

Fisher, Jacob & Jane Sloane, 25 Feb 1793; Jas. Hill, bondsman.

Fisher, Jacob & Tenny Miller, 15 Aug 1821; Andrew Rickard, bondsman; Hy. Giles, wit.

Fisher, Jacob Jr. & Nelly Brown, 6 June 1820; John Shuman, bondsman; Milo A. Giles, wit.

Fisher, Jacob R. & Laura C. Holshouser, 18 Jan 1858; John W.
Fisher, bondsman; John Wilkinson, wit. married 20 Jan 1858
by Thornton Butler, V. D. M.

Fisher, John & Lissey Seafard, 13 June 1798; Harman Fisher,
bondsman; Ma. Troy, wit.

Fisher, John & Tabiathe Baxter, 17 Dec 1812; Abram Brindle,
bondsman; John Hanes, wit.

Fisher, John & Sally Rosemon, 18 Oct 1820; Martin Rendlman,
bondsman; Hy Giles, wit.

Fisher, John & Polly Gentle, 6 Feb 1821; Peter Potts, bondsman;
Ja. Hanes, J. P., wit.

Fisher, John & Sarah Hardridge, 17 July 1822; Micajah Haworth
Jr., bondsman; L. Hunt, wit.

Fisher, John & Anna Smith, 23 Dec 1852; Leonard S. Krider,
bondsman; James E. Kerr, wit. married 23 Dec 1852 by J. M.
Brown, J. P.

Fisher, John & Leah Cruse, 25 Oct 1865; Martin Richwine, bondsman; Horatio N. Woodson, wit.

Fisher, John A. & Tonney Bunn, 29 Sept 1852; John Stoker, bondsman; J. S. Myers, wit.

Fisher, John C. & Mary Ann Livingood, 5 Oct 1863; Daniel Harkey,
bondsman; Obadiah Woodson, wit.

Fisher, John V. & Sarah N. Brown, 21 March 1848; William Brown,
bondsman; J. H. Hardie, wit.

Fisher, John V. & Catharine L. Holshouser, 10 Feb 1866; George
M. Fisher, bondsman; Obadiah Woodson, wit.

Fisher, John W. & Christena L. Hartman, 30 July 1856; James L.
Brown, bondsman; J. S. Myers, wit. married 5 Aug 1856 by
Saml. Rothrock, Minister of the Gospel in the Ev. Luth. Church.

Fisher, Joseph & Rachel Tucker, married 14 July 1861 by A. W.
Mangum.

Fisher, Lawson & Jane Brown, 9 April 1855; John W. Fisher, bondsman; J. S. Myers, wit. married 12 April _____ by Thornton
Butler, V. D. M.

Fisher, Michael & Christian Aronhart, 20 Nov 178_ ; John Aronhart,
bondsman; Jno Macay, wit.

Fisher, Peter & Elizabeth Eller, 2 Dec 1865; Abner Brewer,
bondsman; Obadiah Woodson, wit.

Fisher, Peter A. & Elizabeth C. Brown, 26 July 1852; David Fisher,
bondsman; James E. Kerr, wit. married 27 July 1852 by Saml
Rothrock, Minister of the Gospel in the Ev. Luth. Church.

Fisher, Risdon & Presylla Buckner, 29 June 1798; Dilly Wallams,
bondsman; Ma. Troy, D. C., wit.

Fisher, William & Rhoda Rudduck, 31 July 1822; Micajah Haworth
Jr., bondsman.

Fishur, Jacob & Christian Crossman, 8 Sept 1768; Adam Walcker, Jacob Berry, bondsmen; Thomas Frohock, wit.

Fite, Amos & Sarah Earnhart, 13 April 1825; Danl. H. Criss, bondsman; Hy. Giles, wit.

Flanagan, Edwqrd & Mary Costillo, 12 Dec 1825; Wm. T. Bradfield, bondsman; Jno Giles, wit.

Fleming, Andrew J. & Margaret E. Graham, 27 April 1849; Jno H. Hardie, bondsman.

Fleming, Cyrus & Rosinda McNeely, 24 Nov 1825; Geo. Fleming, bondsman; Hy. Giles, wit.

Fleming, Henry & Margaret Ray, 17 Aug 1784; Andrew Kennedy, bondsman.

Fleming, James & Elisabeth Mitchell, 24 Jan 1785; Elijah Mitchel, bondsman; T. H. McCaule, wit.

Fleming, James S. & Margaret T. Leazer, 19 Feb 1840; Joseph M. Wallace, bondsman; Susan T. Giles, wit.

Fleming, John & Elizabeth Fleming, 13 Oct 1767; John Oliphant, James Petterson, bondsmen; Thos Frohock, wit. consent from Elisabeth Fleming, 13 Oct 1767 for her daughter Elizabeth.

Fleming, John & Ann Barckley, 7 Oct 1784; Andw. Kennedy, bondsman.

Fleming, John G. & Margaret C. Krider, 17 March 1845; W. P. Luckey, bondsman; Jno H. Hardie, Jr., wit.

Fleming, Mitchel & Agness Kennedy, 27 Jan 1784; Andw Kennedy, bondsman; T. H. McCaule, wit.

Fleming, Richard F. & Mary W. Wallace(?), 7 Jan 1843; James S. Fleming, bondsman.

Fleming, Robert N. & Elizabeth Neely, 11 Feb 1822; Alexander Neely, bondsman; Jno Giles, wit.

Fleming, Sam & Polly Foster, 28 March 1809; David Foster, bondsman; A. D. Osborne, wit.

Fletcher, William & Betsey Noah, 9 July 1849; Zedekiah Anderson, bondsman; J. H. Hardie, wit.

Floid, James & Elizabeth Regan, 5 Jan 1819; Obediah Twedwell, bondsman; Z. Hunt, wit.

Floyd, G. W. & Susan Henderson, 4 Sept 1850; Franklin Horah, bondsman; J. S. Myers, wit.

Floyd, Jeremiah & Caty Shevler, 8 Oct 1811; Abraham Shevler, bondsman; J. Wilson, J. P.

Foard--see also Ford

Foard, John & Tabitha Baily, 2 Aug 1849; Jno S. Shaver, bondsman.

Foard, John & Martha Ross, 1 July 1856; Wm. M. Barker, bondsman; J. S. Myers, wit.

Foard, John C. & Sarah W. Young, 19 Dec 1843; Daniel Wood, bondsman; J. H. Hardie, wit.

Foard, Osborn G. & Elizabeth A. Allison, 11 Oct 1854; married 11 Oct 1854 by Jas. P. Simpson, Pastor Methodist Church Rowan Co., N. C.

Foard, John C. & Margaret Y. Irwin, 2 April 1857; Wm. M. Kincaid, bondsman; J. S. Myers, wit. married 2 April 1857 by Saml. B. O. Wilson, V. D. M.

Foard, John C. & N. C. Johnston, 14 July 1862; M. L. Chunn, bondsman; Obadiah Woodson, wit.

Foard, John F. & Laura C. McConnoughey, 19 March 1847; Jessee H. Hodgons, bondsman; R. W. Foard, wit.

Foard, Osborn G. & Elizabeth A. Allison, 11 Oct 1854; Tho. C. Graham, bondsman.

Foard, Osborne G. & Ann F. Cowan, 6 Jan 1846; Matthew Boger, bondsman; J. H. Hardie Jr., wit.

Foard, Robt W. & Maria Emeline Partee, 4 Feb 1837; Jno. H. Hardie, wit.

Foard, Wyatt & Betsy Person, 2 June 1783; John Barby, bondsman.

Foil, Henry & Peggy Roap, 6 Dec 1797; Thomas Goodman, bondsman; Jno Rogers, wit.

Foil, Jacob & Betsey Boger, 24 Oct 1797; Daniel Boger, bondsman; Jno Rogers, wit.

Foil, Philip & Elisabeth Benson, 20 April 1792; John Fisher, bondsman; Chs. Caldwell, wit.

Folich, John & Hannah Colp, 1 Dec 1794; John Goodman, bondsman; J. Troy, D. C., wit.

Folk, Jacob & Catherine Rymer, 22 April 1847; Mathias Rimer, bondsman; J. H. Hardie, Jr., wit.

Folk, Samuel E. & Margaret Giles, 17 Jan 1852; Alexander Earnhart, bondsman; James E. Kerr, wit. married 17 Jan 1852 by W. A. Walton, J. P.

Folts, Henry & Elizabeth Smith, 17 Aug 1790; Adam Shrode, bondsman; C. Caldwell, D. C., wit.

Forbis, James & Phebe Bryan, 10 March 1779; Charles Dunn, Archd. Kerr, bondsmen; Wm. R. Davie, wit.

Ford--see also Foard

Ford, Daniel & Polly McCrary, 7 May 1819; Timothy Ford, bondsman; Jno Giles, wit.

Ford, Frederick & Unity Bradshaw, 14 Nov 1810; Humphry Linster, bondsman; Jno Giles, wit.

Ford, John & Dotia Winkler, 16 Aug 1815; Daniel Ford, bondsman; Jno Giles, C. C., wit.

Ford, John & Polly Ellis, 12 July 1817, Ezra Allemong, bondsman; Roberts Nanny, wit.

Ford, Mathew & Tabitha Swink, 8 May 1830; Philip Jacobs, bondsman; H. Giles, wit.

Ford, Peter & Sarah Baldwin, 1 Nov 1774; John Baldwin, bondsman; Ad. Osborn, wit. consent from Jno Baldwin, 29 Oct 1774, for his daughter Sarah.

Ford, Thomas & Elizabeth Krider, 9 Dec 1829; Jacob G. Smith, bondsman; Jno. H. Hardie, wit.

Ford, William & Emma Hunt, 4 June 1791; Arthur Hunt, bondsman; Charles Caldwell, D. C., wit.

Ford, William M. & Eliza Johnson, 11 Dec 1840; J. L. Beard, bondsman.

Foreman, John & Willy Kendricks, 17 Jan 1794; John Hendricks, bondsman.

Forgus, Samuel & Martha Campbell, 22 July 1778; John Campbell, bondsman; Spruce Nanny, wit.

Ferguson, William & Nancy Harris, 27 Oct 1802; Eli Petiford, bondsman; A. L. Osborn, D. C., wit.

Forrest, James & Nancy Stokes, 9 Dec 1834; John E. Hearn, bondsman; Jno. H. Hardie, wit.

Forror, Tobias & Barbara Smith, 12 Aug 1790; Henry Sleighter, bondsman; Cs. Caldwell, D. C., wit.

Forster, Samuel & Dinah Short, 28 Aug 1795; John Todd, bondsman.

Forster, Thomas & Isabel Smith, 23 Dec 1862; Wm. R. Wilson, bondsman; Obadiah Woodson, wit.

Forsyth, Henderson & Mary F. Foster, 22 Nov 1836; Robert W. Foard, bondsman.

Foster, Benjamin & Elizabeth Stinchcomb, 26 Sept 1817; George Foster, bondsman; Roberts Nanny, wit.

Foster, Daniel & Polly Daniel, 9 Nov 1818; John Martin, bondsman; R. Powell, wit.

Foster, David & Mary Cowan, 27 Feb 1773; John Cowan, bondsman; Max Chambers, wit.

Foster, David & Elizabeth Roseborough, widow, 4 March 1780; Jno Luckie, bondsman.

Foster, David & Ann Kelpatrick, 27 Jan 1795; Wm. Kilpatrick, bondsman.

Foster, David & Mary Posten, 15 Jan 1805; Joel McCorkle, bondsman; Moses A. Locke, wit.

Foster, David C. & Abigail Graham, 3 May 1840; John M. Tabor, bondsman.

Foster, Edeson & Barbara Wasson, 6 June 1798; Wm. Wasson, bondsman; M. A. Troy, wit.

Foster, Elijah & Lovey Brickhouse, 2 July 1826; John Brunt, bondsman; C. Harbin, J. P., wit.

Foster, George & Sarah Tabor, 7 Jan 1824; Thomas Haneline, bondsman; Joseph Hans, J. P., wit.

Foster, Giles & Sarah Bailey, 30 Nov 1824; Kerr B. Foster, bondsman.

Foster, Hesekiah Jr. & Rebecah Doyle, 24 Jan 1829; Joseph G. Doyle, bondsman; L. R. Rose, J. P., wit.

Foster, Hilery & Hariet Beviel, 21 Sept 1822; Elijah Ward, bondsman; Enoch Brock, J. P., wit.

Foster, James & Elsy Smith, 28 Dec 1785; Oeter Coleman, bondsman; Wm. W. Erwin, wit.

Foster, James & Anne Torrentine, 29 Jan 1825; William Gabard, bondsman; L. R. Rose, wit.

Foster, Jehu & Jane Higdon, 14 Dec 1833; Stephen F. Cowan, bondsman.

Foster, Jesse & Nancy Weaver, 28 Dec 1811; John Dordon, bondsman; Jn March Sr., wit.

Foster, Jesse & Polly Galord, 23 Oct 1822; James Foster Jr., bondsman.

Foster, John & Martha Morrison, 20 March 1768; John Mitchell, Patrick Morrison, bondsmen.

Foster, John & Hannah Hughett, 4 Nov 1782; Jno Baker, bondsman; Ad. Osborn, wit.

Foster, John & Joanna Baily, 3 March 1797; William Garwood, bondsman; Jno Rogers, wit.

Foster, John M. & Martha A. Rice, 27 June 1853; John Rice, bondsman; J. S. Myers, wit.

Foster, Joseph & Martha McConnehill, 29 May 177_ (before 1777); Joseph McConochie, bondsman; Davd Flowers, wit.

Foster, Samuel & Elizabeth Henline, 16 March 1805; Richmond Bailey, bondsman; Jno March Sr., wit.

Foster, Samuel & Neomi Booe, 19 Sept 1821; Alexd. Nesbett, bondsman.

Foster, Samuel C. & Laura A. Foster, 12 Nov 1860; J. J. Summerell, bondsman; James E. Kerr, wit. married 14 Nov 1860 by J. J. Summerell, J. P.

Foster, Thomas & Bashabah Beatch, 12 Oct 1811; George March, bondsman; Jn. March Sr., wit.

Foster, Thomas & Betsy Baily, 25 Oct 1804; William Garwood, bondsman; A. L. Osborn, D. C., wit.

Foster, Thomas E. & Nancy Dougthet, 16 Oct 1824; Henry S. Parker, bondsman; Geo. Locke, wit.

Foster, Thomas J. & Catherine C. Luckey, 21 May 1860; Julius
S. Caldwell, bondsman; John Wilkinson, wit. married 21 May
1860 by T. W. Guthrie, Minister of the Gospel, M. E. Church,
South.

Foster, William & Agness Allen, 2 Aug 1779; Hugh Allen, bondsman;
Jo. Brevard, wit.

Foust, John & Julia Ann Earnhart, 26 Aug 1852; George Craton,
bondsman; James E. Kerr, wit.

Fouts, David & Elender Sullivan, 16 Nov 1821; Pleasant J.
Campbell, bondsman; Silas Peace, wit.

Fouts, Jacob & Molly Long, 13 Dec 1819; Philip Hepler, bondsman;
Silas Peace, William Kenneday, wit.

Fouts, John & Mary Younce, 21 Aug 1769; Danl. Little, bondsman;
Thomas Frohock, wit.

Fouts, John & Caty Lentz, 7 Sept 1819; Andrew Rickart, bondsman;
Milo A. Giles, wit.

Fouts, W. H. & Mary E. Richey, 30 Aug 1865; Noah Ritchy, bondsman; Obadiah Woodson, wit.

Fowler, Allen & Polly Conner, 28 June 1816; Henry Shammell,
bondsman; Jno Giles, C. C., wit.

Fowler, Williams & Elizabeth Davis, 13 Sept 1804; Jno Ross,
bondsman; A. L. Osborn, D. C., wit.

Fowlkes, S. J. & Mary Goodman, 6 May 1861; James E. Kerr, bondsman; married 7 May 1861 by D. Barringer, J. P.

Fox, Charles & Patsey Whiteaker, 27 Oct 1819; Jonathan Canter,
bondsman; R. Powell, wit.

Frailey, Jacob & Elizabeth Brown, 22 July 1793; Phillip Brown,
bondsman; Jos. Chambers, wit.

Fraley--see also Frölich

Fraley, Alexander & Mary Watson, 18 May 1833; Jno. H. Hardie,
bondsman.

Fraley, Anthony & Amy Howell, 23 Aug 1816; Jacob Ribelin,
bondsman; Robts, Nanny, wit.

Fraley, Charles & Eliza Earnhart, 13 Aug 1840; Henry Cauble,
bondsman; Susan T. Giles, wit.

Fraley, Daniel & Caroline Fraley, 30 Sept 1865 (both colored);
Obadiah Woodson, wit. married 30 Sept 1865 by Suck Haughton.

Fraley, David & Elenor Robinson, 1 April 1818; Thos. Todd,
bondsman; Jno Giles, wit.

Fraley, Frank & Josephine Colburn (both colored); 20 Feb 1866;
Silas McCubbins, bondsman; Obadiah Woodson, wit.

Fraley, Jacob & Isabella Heathman, 12 April 1843; Wm. Turner,
bondsman; Jno H. Hardie, wit.

Fraley, Jacob & Polly Hodge, 17 March 1849; Samuel Fraley, bondsman; J. H. Hardie, wit.

Fraley, Jesse & Nancy Turner, 24 Oct 1839; Newberry F. Hall, bondsman; John Giles, wit.

Fraley, John & Polly Lyerly, 9 Sept 1818; Christopher Lyerly, bondsman.

Fraley, John & Barbary Lyerly, 22 Dec 1815; George H. Weatheron, bondsman; Jno Giles, C. C., wit.

Fraley, John B. & Margaret Monroe, 28 April 1849; Nathaniel Inniss, bondsman; John H. Hardie, Jr., wit.

Fraley, John H. & Jane Correll, 15 May 1861; married 16 May 1861 by S. C. Groseclose, Pastor of St. John's Ev. Luth Church, Salisbury, N. C.

Fraley, Samuel & Loretta Gheen, 24 April 1828; Cyrus W. West, bondsman; Jno. H. Hardie, wit.

Fraley, Thomas D. & Margaret A. Lyster, 27 Aug 1857; M. S. Fraley, bondsman; J. S. Myers, wit.

Fraley, William R. & Jane E. Kincaid, 15 Feb 1845; Moses A. Goodman, bondsman; Jno H. Hardie, wit.

Fraly, Charles & Sally May, 26 Jan 1824; John Arey, bondsman.

Fraly, David & Betsy Lierly, 19 Jan 1811; George Fraley, bondsman; Geo. Dunn, wit.

Fraly, Jacob & Mary Eller, 10 Nov 1836; John M. Eller, bondsman.

Frank, Christian & Mahetable Bailey, 14 Jan 1828; Robert Bradshaw, bondsman; J. H. Hardie, wit.

Frank, Jacob & Susanna Roan, 4 June 1768; Adam Roan, bondsman; John Frohock, wit.

Frank, John & Barbara Lopp, (no date, during Gov. Martin's Admn); Martin Frank, bondsman; Max. Chambers, wit.

Frank, John & Elizabeth Headrick, 10 Jan 1819; George Hedrick, bondsman; R. Harriss, J. P.

Frank, Joseph A. & Barbara Upright, 24 Sept 1835; Moses Bost, bondsman; Hy. Giles, wit.

Frank, William & Barbara Byerly, 12 Nov 1796; Jonathan Walk, bondsman; Jno Rogers, wit.

Franklin, Benjamin & Ruthe Mott, 11 Feb 1819; Isaac Parke, bondsman; John March Sr., wit.

Franklin, John Thomas & Mary Ann Manuel (colored); 11 Aug 1865; Obadiah Woodson, wit. married 12 Aug 1865 by Zuck Haughton.

Fraser, James & Honnour Seratt, 6 June 1785; Darby Henley, bondsman; Hu. Magoune, wit.

Fraser, John & Jane Devenport, 4 Sept 1816; Charles Swan, bondsman; Milo A. Giles, wit.

Frazer, John Campbell & Elizabeth Sutfin, 15 May 1780; Daniel
Clary, bondsman.

Frazer, Peter & Sarah Cowan, 11 June 1794; Henry Giles, bondsman;
J. Troy, D. C., wit.

Frazey, Aaron & Hannah Hobbles, 24 July 1775; John Conger, John
Davis, bondsmen; David Flowers, wit.

Fredle, John & Catharine Fisinger, 28 Jan 1813; Frederick
Fisinger, bondsman; Jno Giles, wit.

Freedel, John & Easther Basinger, 30 June 1803; John Trexler,
bondsman; Adlai L. Osborn, D. C., wit.

Freedle, Willis & Betsey Yarborough, 6 Feb 1819; Green McGee,
bondsman; Jno Giles, wit.

Freeland, James & Nancy Coleman, 23 Sept 1840; Thos. A. Freeland,
bondsman; Susan T. Giles, wit.

Freeland, Thomas A. & Mary A. Hodge, 9 Aug 1860; married 10 Aug
1860 by Wm. T. Martin, J. P.

Freelee, Thomas A. Jr. & Mary A. Hodge, 9 Aug 1860; William Dunn,
bondsman; James H. Kerr, wit.

Freeman, Aaron & Mary Bently, 17 Dec 1769; Benjamin Bently,
bondsman; Thomas Frohock, wit   consent from Thos. Bently,
for his daughter Mary, 17 Dec 1769, Benjamin Bentley, James
Freeman, wit.

Freeman, Isaac & Agness Faggott, 19 Jan 1762; John Johnston,
Henry Horah, bondsmen; Will Reed, John Frohock, wit.

Freeman, J. W. & Letitia Koontz, 23 Nov 1865; Horatio N. Woodson,
bondsman; Obadiah Woodson, wit.

Freeman, James C. & Ann Eliza Wetmore (colored), 16 Oct 1865;
Foard Heathman, bondsman; Obadiah Woodson, wit. married 19
Oct 1865 by Geo. B. Wetmore, minister.

Freeman, John & Betsey Myres, 7 Aug 1817; George Miers, bondsman;
Jno Giles, wit.

Freeman, John S. & Maria Moss, 21 Jan 1836; Chas. N. Price,
bondsman; Hy. Giles, wit.

Freeman, Julius & Rebecca McMoulin, 11 Jan 1821; Thomas Hall,
bondsman; Milo A. Giles, wit.

Freeman, Linard & Love Birth, 17 Aug 1808; John Freeman, bondsman; A. L. Osborn, wit.

Freeman, Richamond & Sarah Cotton, 23 Feb 1841; Thomas M. Ford,
bondsman; J. L. Beard, wit.

Freeman, Robert F. & Elizabeth E. Agner, 16 March 1859; Peter
Williamson, bondsman; married 16 March 1859 by Peter Williamson, J. P.

Freeman, Russel & Celia Good, 1 Sept 1796; Moses Reed, bondsman;
Jno Rogers, wit.

Frees, Daniel & Margret Graham, 29 Jan 1808; Jacob Troutman, bondsman; A. L. Osborn, C. C., wit.

Freese, Daniel & Betsey Freeze, 26 Jan 1819; Andrew Cope, bondsman; Jno Giles, wit.

Freez, Caleb C. & Maryann Beaver, 11 Aug 1856; John Pet Freeze, bondsman; John L. Hedrick, J. P., wit.

Freeze--see also Freze, Frieze

Freeze, Adam & Cashiah Laurance, 24 Feb 1814; Daniel Lourance, bondsman; Jno Giles, wit.

Freeze, Andrew & Catharine Shulibarrier, 1 Feb 1826; John Litacar, bondsman; Hy Giles, wit.

Freeze, Calab & Isabella M. Brown, 27 Aug 1847; Michael Allbright, bondsman; J. H. Hardie Jr., wit.

Freeze, Caleb & Polly Wilhelm, 15 Jan 1828; George Freeze, bondsman; J. H. Hardie, wit.

Freeze, George & Sophia Bost, 16 July 1827; Levi Bost, bondsman; J. H. Hardie, wit.

Freeze, George & Mary S. Lipe, 17 March 1856; James Basinger, bondsman; J. S. Myers, wit.

Freeze, Henry & Peggy Cavan, 2 April 1800; George Reve, bondsman; N. Chaffir, wit.

Freeze, Henry E. & Synthia C. Sloop, 6 Nov 1848; Chas A. Rose, bondsman; J. H. Hardie, Jr., wit.

Freeze, Jacob & Catharine Seighler, 8 May 1792; Elizabeth Freeze, bondsman; Chs. Caldwell, wit.

Freeze, Jacob & Ann E. Woodside, 11 March 1850; Thomas A. Fleming, bondsman; James E. Kerr, wit.

Freeze, Jacob & Mary C. Thompson, 14 Dec 1859; William L. Carson, bondsman; John Wilkinson, wit.

Freeze, James S. & Eliza L. Lingle, 10 Nov 1849; Noah Ritchey, bondsman; James E. Kerr, wit.

Freeze, John & Hannah Lowrance, 9 Aug 1814; John Freeze, bondsman; Geo. Dunn, wit.

Freeze, John & Elizabeth Arnold, 27 Nov 1817; George Arnold, bondsman; Jno Giles, wit.

Freeze, John & Anny Rose, 2 Feb 1824; Abraham Sachlar, bondsman; Hy. Giles, wit.

Freeze, John & Susan Sechler, 4 March 1824; John Litacar, bondsman; Hy. Giles, wit.

Freeze, John & Elizabeth Lipe, 8 Feb 1848; Jacob Lipe, bondsman.

Freeze, John Jr. & Barbara Seichler, 13 May 1796; John Freeze Sr., bondsman; J. Troy, wit.

Freeze, John F. & Maria K. Sloop, 12 July 1849; C. A. Rose, bondsman.

Freeze, John F. & Cynthia E. Boston, 21 Jan 1861; Geo. E. Bostian, bondsman; Wm. Locke, wit. married 22 Jan 1861 by D. R. Bradshaw, J. P.

Freeze, John L. & Margret M. Poston, 12 May 1849; Hill S. Poston, bondsman; J. H. Hardie, wit.

Freeze, Michael & Dovey A. C. Seckler, 19 March 1860; Jacob Shuliberinger, bondsman; James E. Kerr, wit.

Freeze, Michael & Catharine Carell, 8 Aug 1818; Johannes Crider(?), bondsman; Jno Giles, wit.

Freeze, Noah A. & Martha Ann Sechler, 10 Aug 1848; Chs. A. Rose, bondsman; J. H. Hardie, Jr., wit.

Freeze, Peter & Betsy Bostian, 17 Aug 1812; Caleb Curfees, bondsman; Jno Giles, wit.

Freeze, Thomas & Alvina Locke, 28 Feb 1837; Michael Shuping, bondsman; Jno Giles, wit.

Freeze, William F. & Mary M. Miller, 17 Nov 1855; Leonard F. Rodgers, bondsman; J. S. Myers, wit.

Freighley, John & Elizabeth Basinger, 21 Oct 1800; Geo. Basinger, bondsman.

Frew, William & Sarah Ann Kesler, 11 June 1844; Alexander Boyd, bondsman; Obadiah Woodson, wit.

Freze, John & Mary Freze, 9 May 1785; Hu. Magoune, wit.

Frick, Andrew & Anna File, 4 Jan 1844; Daniel Miller, bondsman; Obadiah Woodson, wit.

Frick, George & Elizabeth Earnhart, 28 Sept 1837; Hy. Giles, bondsman.

Frick, Jacob & Evaline Ludwick, 7 July 1852; Philip Lemley, bondsman; J. S. Myers, wit.

Frick, John & Eve Ann Bullen, 14 Feb 1860; John Trexler, bondsman; Levi Trexler, wit. married 14 Feb 1860 by Levi Trexler, J. P.

Frick, Joseph & Joanna Parks, 17 July 1844; Morgan Misenhamer, bondsman; J. H. Hardie, wit.

Frick, Levi & Crissy Stoner, 15 May 1858; Philip Lemly, bondsman; James E. Kerr, wit. married 19 May 1858 by H. W. Hill, J. P.

Frick, Leviy & Julia Ann Frick, 25 Jan 1864; Alfred M. Peeler, bondsman; Obadiah Woodson, wit.

Frick, Matthias & Rachael Caler, 16 Aug 1794; Leonard Kaler, bondsman; J. Troy, D. C., wit.

Frierson, John & Aeley Dickey, 11 Sept 1810; Saml. Rosebrough, bondsman; Geo Dunn, wit.

Frieze, David & Mary E. Correll, 23 April 1855; E. M. Correll, bondsman; J. S. Myers, wit. married 2 May 1855 by J. Ingold.

Frieze, Jacob & Christina Buck, 23 May 1805; Daniel Buck, bondsman; A. L. Osborn, C. C., wit.

Frieze, Samuel & Barbara Boston, 15 May 1810; Jacob Lipe, bondsman; Geo. Dunn, wit.

Frik, Andrew & Teany Eller, 7 Jan 1819; John Eller, bondsman; Henry Giles, wit.

Frisbey, Josiah & Elizabeth Imbler, 2 Nov 1794; Peter Arthur Givons, bondsman.

Frits, Adam & Sally Linnard, 21 June 1812; Jacob Linnard, bondsman; E. Morgan, J. P., wit.

Fritz, Felix & Mary Agner, 31 Dec 1845; Oliver Glover, bondsman; J. H. Hardie, wit.

Fritz, Felix & Catharine Gallimore, 18 Aug 1856; Henry A. Walton, bondsman; J. S. Myers, wit.

Fritz, Felix & Christena J. Lefler, 19 Aug 1857; Nicholas Bringle, bondsman; J. S. Myers, wit. married 20 Aug 1857 by W. A. Walton, J. P.

Fritz, George & Mary Wilson, 3 Jan 1780; Rowland Jenkins, bondsman; Jno. Kerr, wit.

Fritz, Reubin & Polly Billing, 18 May 1822; Joseph Fritts, bondsman; Jno. Giles, wit.

Frock, Conrod & Franny Lemely, 14 March 1772; Killiam Ross, bondsman; John Frohock, wit.

Frölich, Georg & Margaret Agenor, 15 June 1796; Heinrich Eigender, bondsman; J. Troy, wit.

Frölich, Jacob & Kathrine Charles, 2 May 1768; Heinrich Frölich, Danl Little, bondsmen.

Frontis, Stephen & Julia C. Leazer, 26 Sept 1859; G. W. McLean, bondsman; married 24 Sept 1859 by John E. Pressly, minister.

Frost, Boon & Nancey McClamroch, 2 Feb 1823; Wiley Gaither, bondsman; L. R. Rose, J. P., wit.

Frost, Ebenezer & Sarahy Fairchild, 5 Dec 1769; Jonathan Boone, Danl Little, bondsmen; Thomas Frohock, wit consent 3 Dec 1769 from Ebenezer Fairchild for his daughter Sarah.

Frost, Ebenezer & Elizabeth Willson, 2 Nov 1775; William Vancleave, bondsman; Ad. Osborn, wit.

Frost, Ebenezer & Rebecka Bailey, 12 April 1796; Brit. Bayliss, bondsman; Tibby Troy, wit.

Frost, Ebenezer & Elizabeth Gaither, 11 June 1816; James Frost, bondsman; R. Powell, wit.

Frost, Enoch & Susannah Brinon, 4 Dec 1826; Tillmon Roberts, bondsman.

Frost, John & Rebecca Boon, 21 Aug 1793; John Wilson, bondsman; Jos. Chambers, wit.

Frost, John & Elizabeth Hunt, 22 March 1817; R. Powell, bondsman; R. Powell, wit.

Frost, Samuel & Sally Andrews, 22 June 1814; Thomas F. Hunt, bondsman; Jno Giles, wit.

Frost, Samuel & Jane Roberson, 24 March 1832; Jno. H. Hardie, bondsman.

Frost, Wilson & Polly Wilson, 21 March 1809; James Wilson, bondsman; A. D. Osborne, wit.

Fry, Henry & Polly Smith, 13 June 1804; David Smith, bondsman; A. L. Osborn, D. C., wit.

Fry, James & Margaret Nothern, 2 March 1802; John Sims, bondsman.

Fry, James T. & Sarah Hagler, 24 April 1857; Jesse Waller, bondsman; James E. Kerr, wit. married 26 April 1857 by H. W. Scott, J. P.

Fry, John & Christina Waller, 23 Nov 1779; Michael Waller, Christopher Sibery, bondsmen.

Fry, Levy & Nelly Manor, 22 April 1815; John Peck, bondsman; Jno Giles, wit.

Fry, Noah W. & Mary E. Brandon, 31 Oct 1859; Moses Brown, bondsman.

Fry, Peter & Marillisey Cottner, 2 June 1775; Jacob Cutner, bondsman; Ad. Osborn, wit. consent from Jacob Cutner (Gootner), 30 May 1775, for his daughter Merilisey.

Fulenwider, Jacob & Anne Cauble, 1 March 1821; John Hartline, bondsman; Jno Giles, wit.

Fulenwider, John & Jane Redwine, 16 Sept 1851; Caleb Hartman, bondsman; James E. Kerr, wit.

Fulford, Matthew & Edney Simmons, 12 June 1827; Daniel Brock, bondsman; Ed. Broc, J. P., wit.

Fulk, Jacob & Margaret Waller, 13 Sept 1824; Mark Waller, bondsman; Hy. Giles, wit.

Fulk, James & Mary Hare, 6 Aug 1844; Jno Rymer, bondsman; J. H. Hardie, wit.

Fulk, William & Betsy Underwood, 13 Sept 1809; Nathan Morgan, bondsman; Geo Dunn, wit.

Fullenwider, Henry & Ellenor Leonard, 20 Aug 1783; John Fulenwider, bondsman; William Crawford, wit.

Fullenwider, John & Mary Fullinwider, 9 May 1796; Jacob Miller, bondsman; J. Troy, D. C., wit.

Fulton, John & _____, _____ 180_.

Fults, Daniel & Jamima Sparks, 2 Sept 1816; James Orrell, bondsman; Thos Hampton, wit.

Fults, Peter & Cathrine Wichmon, 10 Aug 1785; Geo Hartman, bondsman; Peter Fry, wit.

Fultz, Henry & Caty Smith, 9 Nov 1814; Jacob G. Smith, bondsman; Geo. Dunn, wit.

Fultz, Peter F. & Emily Chaffin, 11 Oct 1853; John G. McLellan, bondsman; J. S. Myers, wit.

Fultz, William & Elizabeth Dunn, 13 March 1821; Jacob G. Smith, bondsman; Hy Giles, wit.

Fur, Henry & Catharine Wysell, (no date, during admn. of Gov. Alex. Martin); Conrod Brem, bondsman; Max. Chambers, wit.

Furches, John & Rachel Hunter, 5 March 1815; Edmond Aytcheson, bondsman; R. Powell, wit.

Furr, John & Catherin Liviley, 4 Aug 1783; Daniel Little, bondsman; John McNairy, wit.

Furr, John A. & Mary Ann Long, 23 Feb 1846; Mathias Mayer, bondsman; J. H. Hardie, wit.

Furr, Samuel M. & Lucille M. McNeely, 2 Nov 1853; Jas. C. Caldwell, bondsman; J. S. Myers, wit.

Fuser, John & Elizabeth Cole, 15 Aug 1800; James Smith, bondsman.

Gabard, John M. & Nelly Veatch, 8 Nov 1823; Jos. Snider, bondsman; L. R. Rose, J. P., wit.

Gabard, William & Susannah Foster, 30 Dec 1824; James Foster, bondsman.

Gadberry, Green & Joanna Loyd, 21 Oct 1809; Thomas Pinkerton, bondsman.

Gadberry, Nathaniel & Betsy Slagle, 20 Feb 1810; Jonathan Merrill, bondsman; Jno Giles, C. C., wit.

Gadberry, James & Elizabeth Elliott, 27 Aug 1807; Henry Coats, bondsman; A. L. Osborn, D. C., wit.

Gadbury, Thomas & Sally Smith, 4 May 1805; Theodore McKee, bondsman; A. L. Osborn, D. C., wit.

Gailes, Josiah & Catherin McClarrin, 10 Jan 1764; John Sharp, John Watson, bondsmen; John Frohock, wit.

Gaither, Basil & Elender Sain, 7 Jan 1833; Wilson Rose, bondsman.

Gaither, Basil Jr. & Tabitha Smart, 8 March 1803; Nathaniel Pearson, bondsman; A. L. Osborn, D. C., wit.

Gaither, Beal & Polly Roggers, 24 Aug 1811; Thos. C. Jones, bondsman; Jn March Sr., wit.

Gaither, Benjamin & Ellenor Prather, 30 July 1818; Thomas Prather, bondsman; R. Powell, wit.

Gaither, Ephram & Sarah M. Johnson, 14 Jan 1835; James K. Nisbet, bondsman.

Gaither, Greenberry & Luranah Veatch, 15 Jan 1814; Thomas Foster, bondsman; Jn March Sr., wit.

Gaither, Isam & Sarah Leach, 1 Jan 1828; James Leach, bondsman; L. R. Rose, J. P., wit.

Gaither, John & Susannah Johnson, 17 Feb 1795; Basil Gaither, bondsman; B. John Pinchback, Mary Pinchback, wit.

Gaither, Johnsey & Sarah Coon, 19 March 1810; Thos. C. Jones, bondsman; Jn March Sr., wit.

Gaither, Leander & Mary Marlin, 20 Feb 1850; Henry C. Lippard, bondsman; J. S. Myers, wit.

Gaither, Nicholas W. & Tabitha Baley, 18 Sept 1792; Brice W. Ijames, bondsman; Basil Gaither, wit.

Gaither, Nicholas W. & Caty Hampton, 10 Jan 1819; Basel Gaither, bondsman.

Gaither, Thomas & Edy Busey, 8 ___ 1800; Matthew Busey, bondsman; John Brem, wit.

Gaither, Walter & Elizabeth Smoot, 5 May 1807; Nicholas W. Gaither, bondsman; A. L. Osborn, wit.

Galaway, James B. & A. C. Tanner, 22 April 1858; R. B. Pendleton, bondsman; John Wilkinson, wit. married 22 April 1858 by J. M. Brown, J. P.

Galbreath, Thomas & Mary Moore, 13 Feb 1797; William Woods, bondsman; Jno Rogers, wit.

Gales, John & Sarah Baxtor, 6 Nov 1823; Benjamin Harden, bondsman; L. R. Rose, J. P.

Gales, P. Scott & Mary Jane Donoho, 5 March 1863; William F. Gales, bondsman; Obadiah Woodson, wit.

Gales, William & Margaret Hinkle, 21 Nov 1821; Wesley C. Brown, bondsman; Jno Giles, wit.

Gales, William & Isbal Burton, 3 Feb 1820; Ransom Powell, bondsman; R. Powell, wit.

Gales, William F. & Barbara A. Dickson, 16 Dec 1857; F. A. Meroney, bondsman; J. S. Myers, wit.

Galagher, Hugh & Elizabeth Martin, 26 Aug 1775; Joseph McPherson, bondsman; David Flowers, wit.

Gallagher, Hugh & Sarah Campbell, 4 May 1778; Andrew Hays, bondsman; Ad. Osborn, wit.

Gallamore, Noah & Mary Boss, 29 June 1817; Joseph Goss, bondsman; R. Harris, J. P., wit.

Galley, James & Mary McClane, 6 Aug 1766; Wm. Steel, bondsman; Peter Fryley, Sec., Thomas Frohock, C. C., wit.

Gallimore, Boswell & Eve Earnheart, 5 Feb 1845; Moses Earnhart, bondsman.

Gallimore, Bozwell & Rachel Mesimer, 7 Nov 1846; Green Redwine, bondsman; J. H. Hardie, Jr., wit.

Gallimore, James & Esther Lane, 5 Dec 1815; Frederick Beanblossom, bondsman; Jno Giles, C. C., wit.

Gallimore, Samuel & Mary Mahaley, 4 July 1825; Henry Mahaley, bondsman; M. A. Giles, wit.

Ganor, John & Sarah Bryan, 16 April 1793; Andrew Hunt, bondsman; Charles Hunt, wit.

Gant, William & Catharine M. Shuping, 20 April 1859; Alexander Shuping, bondsman; James E. Kerr, wit. married 21 April 1859 by L. J. Kirk.

Gardiner, J. W. & Jane E. Fesperman, 12 Nov 1861; Peter A. Ritchie, bondsman; Obadiah Woodson, wit. married 13 Nov 1861 by Whitson Kimball, Minister.

Gardiner, James & Jennet Brumhead, 1 Nov 1797; Hugh Horah, bondsman; Jno Rogers, wit.

Gardiner, Samuel & Margaret R. Phillips, 4 Jan 1828; Jacob Beaver, bondsman; Jno H. Hardie, wit.

Gardner, C. H. & Elizabeth Blue, 29 Jan 1855; James Anderson, bondsman; James E. Kerr, wit.

Gardner, Francis & Jennet Kerr, 19 May 1778; Joseph Kerr, bondsman; Ad. Osborn, wit.

Gardner, Francis & Sophia Clarke, 16 Feb 1803; A. L. Osborn, D. C., wit.

Gardner, John & Margaret Moore, 23 July 1786; Henry Horah, bondsman; Jno Macay, wit.

Gardner, John & Polly McDaniel, 1 Oct 1811; Lewis Beard, bondsman; Jno Giles, C. C., wit.

Gardner, John & Nancy Coon, 25 Sept 1845; Richard M. Gardner, bondsman; J. H. Hardie, Jr., wit.

Gardner, John & Margaret Newman, 30 Aug 1843; Michael L. Brown, bondsman; J. H. Hardie, wit.

Gardner, Richard W. & Mary Ann Coon, 30 July 1846; William Gardner, bondsman; J. H. Hardie Jr., wit.

Gardner, Richard W. & Susannah Acocks, 30 March 1852; Richard Harrison, bondsman; J. S. Myers, wit. married 30 March 1852 by Obadiah Woodson, J. P.

Gardner, William & Angeline Wyatt, 2 Jan 1860; J. J. Summerell, bondsman; John Wilkinson, wit. married 3 Jan 1861 by J. J. Summerell, J. P.

Garland, Guterage & Bridget Hampton, 26 Sept 1778; Ezekiel Hampton, bondsman; Spurce Macay, wit.

Garner, Benjamin & _____, 23 July 1798; Ebenezer Eaton, bondsman; Edwin J. Osborn, D. C., wit.

Garner, Burgess & Marey Hicks, 16 Aug 1806; John Garner, bondsman; John March, wit.

Garner, Edward & Catharine Cowan, 18 Nov 1829; Alexander Dobbins,
bondsman; J. H. Hardie, wit.

Garner, Henry & Elizabeth Lopp, 10 Aug 1792; Peter Lopp, bondsman; Chs. Caldwell, wit.

Garner, Henry Atchison & Elizabeth Reves, 26 May 1810; Jesse
Reves, bondsman; Jno March Sr., wit.

Garner, John & Charity Little, 27 July 179_; Spenser Stevens,
bondsman.

Garner, John & Catharine Hartman, 2 Nov 1807; Michael Hartman,
bondsman; A. L. Osborn, D. C., wit.

Garner, John Sr. & Margaret Sigler, 15 July 1818; George Wilkins,
bondsman; R. Powell, wit.

Garner, John W. & Sarah Howerton, 10 May 1863; Wm. Loftin,
bondsman; Obadiah Woodson, wit.

Garner, Lewis H. & Sarah Maroney, 9 May 1833; William F. Kelly,
bondsman; Thomas McNeely, J. P., wit.

Garner, William & Sarah Lee, 17 Oct 1830; Zadock G. Tomlinson,
bondsman; L. R. Rose, J. P., wit.

Garrawood, Jacob & Winny Glascock, 15 Sept 1795; Henry Glascock,
bondsman; J. Troy, wit.

Garren, Mathias & Catharean Varner of Randolph County, 13 Jan
1819; Andrew Varner, bondsman; P. Copple, J. P., wit.

Garret, John & Caty Miller, 22 June 1803; Peter Miller, bondsman; John March, wit.

Garrett, Daniel & Nancey Merrill, 27 Feb 1802; Abner Merrill,
bondsman.

Garrett, John & Easter Hadly, 27 Jan 1803; Danl. Garrett, bondsman; A. L. Osborn, D. C., wit.

Garrison, John & Lucretia Vaune, 12 Feb 1772; Thos Garrison,
bondsman; Ad. Osborn, wit.

Garrot, John & Elizabeth Fisher, 14 April 1789; John Hildebrand,
bondsman; Wall Alexander, wit.

Garver, Lenard Benjamin & Mary Ann Falker, 31 Dec 1860; Daniel
M. Bostian, bondsman; Wm. Locke, wit. married 3 Jan 1861 by
Henry Miller, J. P.

Garver, Valentine & Lucinda Tennison, 8 Dec 1835; John Garver,
bondsman; J. H. Hardie, wit.

Garver, Volentine & Charlotte Perish, 9 July 1845; Michael P.
Walker, bondsman; John H. Hardie, Jr., wit.

Garvey, John & Phibly Scrivener, 2 Oct 1810; Jas. Gillaspie, bondsman; Jno Giles, C. C., wit.

Garwood, Ebenezer & Anna Foster, 24 Jan 1835; Jno H. Hardie, bondsman.

Garwood, Jacob & Nancy Rice, 11 Feb 1804; James Garwood, bondsman.

Garwood, James & Sarah Frost, 9 Nov 1802; Peter H. Swink, bondsman; A. L. Osborn, D. C., wit.

Garwood, Samuel & Rebecca Cope, 24 April 1830; Ebenezer Garwood, bondsman; Hy. Giles, wit.

Garwood, Thomas & Margaret Glascock, 7 Jan 1805; Isaac Garwood, bondsman; A. L. Osborn, D. C., wit.

Garwood, William & Elizabeth Foster, 14 Jan 1794; Jacob Garwood, bondsman; Jo Chambers, wit.

Garwood, William & Sally Bailey, 6 May 1814; David Craige, bondsman; Geo Dunn, wit.

Gasky, Joshua & Laura Hartman, 12 March 1860; J. J. Stewart, bondsman; James E. Kerr, wit. married 13 March 1860 by J. J. Summerell, J. P.

Gatton, Benjamin & Matilda Rutledge, 27 Feb 1802; Greenberry Gaither, bondsman; Jno Brem, wit.

Gatton, John Hambleton & Elizabeth Johnson, 22 Aug 1811; John Scot Price, bondsman; Jn March Sr., wit.

Gay, Robert & Anne Elder, 2 Dec 1779; Henry Beroth, bondsman; B. Booth Boote, wit.

Gay, William & Mary Willson, 7 March 1800; Andrew Irving, bondsman; Matt. Troy, wit.

Gayler, William & Esther Caruthers, 5 March 1823; Jno L. Henderson, bondsman.

Gears, John & Priscilla Gullet, 4 Dec 1822; John Cope, bondsman; L. R. Rose, J. P., wit.

Gee, Pat Stuart & Mary Speer, 12 Dec 1786; Robert Cochran, bondsman; Ad. Osborn, wit.

Gens, Somon Wily & Maria Fesperman, 22 March 1848; George H. Fesperman, bondsman; J. H. Hardie Jr., wit.

Gense, Solomon Wiley & Nancy M. Deal, 28 March 1860; Caleb Hampton, bondsman; James E. Kerr, wit. married 29 March 1860 by J. S. Heilig.

Gents, William & Polly Fesperman, 29 July 1822; John Lippard, bondsman.

Gerrison, James & Sarah Cradlebough, 16 Aug 1805; Eleazer Smith, bondsman.

Getchey, Frederick & Esther Cline, 11 April 1787; John Hildabrand, bondsman.

Getchy, John & Barbary Coons, 28 July 1803; Peter Simmons, bondsman; A. L. Osborn, D. C., wit.

Getz, Michael & Catharine Groves, 31 Aug 1802; Solomon Groves, bondsman; J. McEwin, wit.

Gecaudan, Shadrack M. & Elizabeth Gilpin, 21 Aug 1816; Edward Burge, bondsman; Jno Giles, C. C., wit.

Gheen, David & Nancy N. Cranford, 25 Jan 1861; Wm. Dunn, bondsman; John Wilkinson, wit. married 27 Jan 1861 by Wm. H. Trott, J. P.

Gheen, David B. & Fanny L. Winders, 22 Dec 1858; Wm. H. Sloan, bondsman.

Gheen, James & Mary Pinxton, 16 April 1788; Thomas Gheen, bondsman; Js. McEwin, wit.

Gheen, James & Elizabeth Roberts, 13 Jan 1812; Aaron Pinkston, bondsman; Geo Dunn, wit.

Gheen, James & Sally Bowers, 11 Nov 1823; David Gheen, bondsman; Jno Giles, wit.

Gheen, Joseph & Elizabeth Rutherford, 7 March 1822; Jonathan Hulin, bondsman.

Gheen, Joseph & Ann Todd, 4 April 1797; Thomas Gheen, bondsman; Jno Rogers, wit.

Gheen, Joseph & Mary Steward, 26 Jan 1804; Thomas Gheen, bondsman.

Gheen, Joshua & Jane Cranford, 2 April 1841; Howell Parker, bondsman; Jno Giles, wit.

Gheen, Levi & Margaret Hulen, 9 Feb 1825; Eleaney Elliott, bondsman; W. Harris, wit.

Gheen, Milas & Polly Brown, 20 Dec 1845; John G. Elliott, bondsman; J. M. Turner, wit.

Gheen, Milas A. & Rachael McCrary, 7 Aug 1848; Michael A. Brown, bondsman; J. H. Hardie, wit.

Gheen, Thomas & Mary McBride, 17 May 1788; Hugh McBride, bondsman; W. Alexander, wit.

Gheen, Thomas & Peggey Trexler, 31 Oct 1822; Jonathan Hulan, bondsman.

Gheen, Thomas T. & Margaret A. Sloan, 15 Nov 1855; Wm. H. Sloan, bondsman; J. S. Myers, wit. married 15 Nov 1855 by Js. Thomason, J. P.

Gheen, Warren & Sarah Winders, 17 Feb 1836; Chas. N. Price, bondsman.

Gheen, Warren & Sarah Wallens, 10 April 1845; John Cook, bondsman.

Gheen, William H. & Mary Lyerly, 6 March 1858; David B. Gheen, bondsman; John Wilkinson, wit. married 7 March 1858 by W. R. Fraley, J. P.

Ghent, Jacob & Jane Benson, 29 Aug 1809; Jno Beard, bondsman; Jno Giles, C. C., wit.

Gibbing, Patrick & Loviah Jones, 16 Jan 1811; Abraham Johson, bondsman; S. Davis, J. P., wit.

Gibbins, Alex & Martha Cox, 20 July 1850; George Dunn, bondsman.

Gibbins, James & Phelby Mosier, 19 Dec 1792; Peter Ar. Gibbons, bondsman; Jos. Chambers, wit.

Gibbons, Alexander & Frances Eller, 19 Dec 1857; Geo. B. Swink, bondsman; J. S. Myers, wit. married 23 Dec 1857 by Peter Williams, J. P.

Gibbons, Julius & Sarah Robling, 7 June 1824; James Robling, bondsman; Jno Giles, wit.

Gibbons, Peter & Susanna Strange, 7 March 1818; Jacob Rickard, bondsman; Robs Nanny, wit.

Gibbs, Elisha & Amanda Mason, 2 March 1863; J. W. Jones, bondsman; Thomas McNeely, wit.

Gibbs, Thomas & Anna Saner, 4 Jan 1823; Francis Barny Castles, bondsman; Tho Hampton, wit.

Gibbs, Thomas D. & Margarett Smith, 4 Dec 1826; Daniel Armsworthy, bondsman; L. R. Rose, J. P., wit.

Gibson, Archibald & Jane Agle, 7 Oct 1828; Jno Rogers, bondsman; Jno H. Hardie, wit.

Gibson, George & Margaret Lock, 17 May 1780; Francis Lock, bondsman; Jno Kerr, wit.

Gibson, Hugh & Lucinda Admiston, 15 April 1826; James Downs, bondsman; J. H. Hardie, wit.

Gibson, James & Mary Woods, 14 Oct 1779; James Gibson, bondsman; Jo Brevard, wit. (confusion about groom, may be James Hacket).

Gibson, James & Martha Edmiston, 26 Aug 1822; Alexander C. Scott, bondsman; Jno Giles, wit.

Gibson, John & Elizabeth Lock, 13 Jan 1775; Francis Lock, bondsman; Ad. Osborn, wit.

Gibson, John A. & Ruth E. Braly, 26 Dec 1848; G. G. McKnight, bondsman.

Gibson, Joseph & Mary McCree, 16 Dec 1789; James Gibson, bondsman; Ed. Harris, wit.

Gibson, William & Pricilla Brandon, 29 Jan 1805; William Hampton, bondsman; A. L. Osborn, D. C., wit.

Gibson, William & Polly Buck, 12 Feb 1819; Martin Buck, bondsman; Jno Giles, wit.

Gilbert, William & Susannah Robertson, 15 April 1775; William Snow, bondsman; Ad. Osborn, wit consent from John Robertson, 15 April 1775.

Giles, Absalom & Nancey Singer, 21 Aug 1778; Dennis Dickson, James Rutherford, bondsmen; Ad. Osborn, wit.

Giles, Antoney & Lovey Freeman, 14 June 1814; Elijah Veatch, bondsman; Jn March Sr., wit.

Giles, Henry & Elizabeth Dunn, 19 June 1786; Alexander Long, bondsman; Jno Macay, wit.

Giles, John & Rachel Williams, 10 Jan 1782; William Hamton, bondsman; William Crawford, wit.

Giles, John & Mary Snapp, 3 Oct 1788; Henry Giles, bondsman; W. Alexander, wit.

Giles, Major & Mary Dehart, 2 Nov 1779; Elias Dehart, bondsman; Jo Brevard, wit.

Gillam, William & Therissa Matthew, 3 July 1823; Edward F. Randolph, bondsman.

Gillaspie, Thomas & Catherin Beard, 24 Aug 1796; Henry Giles, bondsman.

Gillean, Jesse & Ann Thompson, 21 Jan 1824; Julius J. Reeves, bondsman.

Gillehan, Abraham & Mary Enslow, 12 April 1779; Jas. McBroome, bondsman; Jno Kerr, wit.

Gillem, Andrew & Elizabeth Helser, 16 June 1821; Jacob Helser, bondsman; Hy. Giles, wit.

Gillespie, David & Mary Luckey, 18 April 1785; Robert Luckey, bondsman; H. Magoune, wit.

Gillespie, David & Mary Marlin, 16 Feb 1814; Wm. Kilpatrick, bondsman; Geo. Dunn, wit.

Gillespie, George & Ann S. Cowan, 17 Nov 1830; Jno. Foster, bondsman; Hy. Giles, wit.

Gillespie, Isaac & Mary Anne McGuire, 12 April 1791; John McGuire, bondsman; C. Caldwell, D. C., wit.

Gillespie, John & Polly Brandon, 14 March 179_; Robert Gillespie, bondsman; Edwin J. Osborn, D. C., wit.

Gillespie, John & Margaret Kerr, 31 Jan 1786; David Fleming(?), bondsman; W. Cupples, wit.

Gillespie, John C. & Jane S. Graham, 11 Oct 1843; Andrew Graham, bondsman; Jno. H. Hardie, Jr., wit.

Gillespie, John C. & Harriet Marlin, 17 Jan 1849; Thos. J. Gillespie, bondsman; J. H. Hardie, wit.

Gillespie, Joseph F. & Terisa Sloan, 1 March 1842; Theophilus A. Gillespie, bondsman; J. H. Hardie, wit.

Gillespie, Joseph G. & Obedience G. Smith, 24 Jan 1814; James H. McNeely, bondsman; John Giles, wit.

Gillespie, McCoy & Aley Graham, 3 March 1812; Alex. Graham, bondsman.

Gillespie, Richard & Agnes Graham, 11 April 1804; James Knox, bondsman; A. L. Osborn, D. C., wit.

Gillespie, Thomas & M. Luckey, 5 Sept 1785; Robert Luckey, bondsman.

Gillespie, Thomas C. & Caroline E. Austin, 2 Aug 1847; William F. Hall, bondsman; Robert Murphy, wit.

Gillespie, Thomas J. & Mary J. Gillespie, 27 Sept 1852; John R. Knox, bondsman; James E. Kerr, wit. married 28 Sept 1852 by P. M. Dalton.

Gillespy, James & Jane Graham, 9 Jan 1765; Jno Graham, James Graham, bondsmen; John Frohock, C. C., wit.

Gillian, Hezekiah C. & Elizabeth Lyerly, 4 March 1846; M. S. Fraley, bondsman; J. M. Turner, wit.

Gillian, Hezekiah C. & Martha J. Ressult, 12 June 1850; Thos. C. McNeely, bondsman; J. S. Myers, wit.

Gillie, James & Isebel Marshall, 5 July 1783; Wm. McDaniel, bondsman; Robt Hall, wit.

Gillispie, Thomas & Cathrine Beard, 24 Aug 1796; Henry Giles, bondsman; Jno Rogers, wit.

Gillom, John & Jerushe Morris, 2 April 1816; Amos Regan, bondsman; Geo. Dunn, wit.

Gilpin, Benjamin & Rebecca Potts, 29 April 1789; John Stokes, bondsman.

Gingles, Samuel & Eleonar Beatty, 14 Dec 1782; Thos. Beaty, bondsman; T. H. McCaule, wit.

Gipson, James & Rebecca Robson, 10 March 1787; Barton Dyson, bondsman; Jno. Macay, wit.

Givens, James & Martha Bourlin, 16 Oct 1794; James Borland, bondsman.

Glandon, Isaac & Elizabeth Cridlebough, 26 Nov 1818; Elijah Elliott, bondsman; Z. Hunt, wit.

Glascock, Gregory & Catharine Sain, 27 Jan 1818; John Sain, bondsman; R. Powell, wit.

Glascock, Harmon & Nancy Garrowood, __ Oct 1792; William Garwood, bondsman; Jo Chambers, wit.

Glascock, Henry & Peggy Glascock, 16 March 1793; Spencer Glascock, bondsman; Jos. Chambers, wit.

Glascock, Spencer & Polly Enochs, 12 Sept 1791; John Bailey, bondsman; Cunn. Harris, wit.

Glass, Jacob & Elizabeth Biggers, 19 Nov 1851; Andrew Freeze, bondsman.

Glasscock, Charnal & Mary Luckey, 25 Oct 1794; Peter Glasscock, bondsman; B. John Pinchback, Lydia Pinchback, wit.

ROWAN MARRIAGES 1753-1868

Glasscock, James & Sally Boo, 28 April 1804; Jacob Booe,
bondsman.

Glasscock, Presley D. & Elizabeth Garwood, 7 Sept 1825; George
Duling, bondsman; L. R. Rose, J. P., wit.

Glasscock, Presley D. & Elizabeth Dooling, 19 Mar 1829; Joseph
Garwood, bondsman; C. Harbin, J. P., wit.

Glasscock, William & Mary Hales, 4 Sept 1795; Robt. Foster,
bondsman; Mich. Troy, wit.

Glasscock, William & Marryann Taylar, 5 April 1817; Daniel Call,
bondsman; R. Powell, wit.

Glasscock, William & Margaret Hicks, 15 Feb 1825; Nathan Stanley,
bondsman; L. R. Rose, J. P., wit.

Glasscock, William S. & Elizabeth H. Chapman, 23 Jan 1822;
Radford Foster, bondsman; A. R. Jones, wit.

Gleason, James & Ruth Palmer, 5 Dec 1865; Horation N. Woodson,
bondsman; Obadiah Woodson, wit.

Glidewell, John & Elizabeth Linn, 24 Oct 1822; Alexander Clarke,
bondsman; Jno Giles, wit.

Glover, Andrew & Sophia Lemly, 30 Nov 1820; George Goodman,
bondsman; Hy. Giles, wit.

Glover, A. M. & Mary A. Miller, 6 Jan 1862; A. M. Brown, bondsman; Obadiah Woodson, wit. married 7 Jan 1862 by E. E.
Phillips, J. P.

Glover, Charles & Matila Earnhart, 13 June 1857; Allen Trexler,
bondsman; Levi Trexler, wit. married 16 June 1857 by Levi
Trexler, J. P.

Glover, James D. & Nancy Morris, 16 Sept 1845; H. A. Jacobs,
bondsman.

Glover, John & Betsey Hill, 12 March 1827; Charles Verble, bondsman; J. H. Hardie, wit.

Glover, Oliver & Rebecca Poole, 7 July 1818; Jacob Fulenwider,
bondsman; Roberts Nanny, wit.

Glover, William & Jean McBride, 4 June 1796; Thomas Gheen, bondsman; J. Troy, D. C., wit.

Glover, William N. & Levina Beaver, 3 April 1856; Alexander
Beaver, bondsman; J. S. Myers, wit.

Gobbl, John & Hamy Maner, 23 Sept 1816; John Peak, bondsman;
Jno Giles, C. C., wit.

Gobel, John & Mary Cold Iron, 20 May 1793; Petter Coble, bondsman; Jos. Chambers, wit.

Goff, George E. & Mary Frost, 1 Feb 1792; Ebenezer Frost, bondsman; Basil Gaither, wit.

Going, Britton & Mary Chambers, 13 April 1791; Martin Miller,
bondsman; Basil Gaither, wit.

Goins, Ezekil & Sarah Gunter, 14 July 1779; William Butler, bondsman; Jo Brevard, wit.

Golden, A. J. & Lucinda A. Thompson, 11 July 1865; W. H. Bailey, bondsman; Obadiah Woodson, wit. married 11 July 1865 by J. Rumple, V. D. M.

Golding, William G. & Loretta Tarr, 24 Oct 1829; Ezra Allemong, bondsman; J. H. Hardie, wit.

Goldmen, Henry & Nelly Conckwright, 9 Sept 1780; Charles Hart, bondsman; Henry Giffarde, wit.

Gonger, F. M. & E. M. Bostian, 12 Feb 1856; Jas. H. Gonger, bondsman; J. S. Myers, wit. married 14 Feb 1856 by James Wagner, Pastor E. Luth. Church.

Gonter, George & Aby Atkins, 3 Aug 1774; George Lauman, bondsman; Ad. Osborn, wit.

Goodman, Abram & Margret Crotser, 30 July 1854; John Eagle, bondsman; H. W. Hill, J. P., wit. married 30 July 1854 by H. W. Hill, J. P.

Goodman, Adam & Sally Eddleman, 20 Sept 1816; Philip Eagle, bondsman; Jno Giles, wit.

Goodman, Alfred M. & Elizabeth Clodfelter, 19 Sept 1845; Alfred N. Goodman, bondsman; J. H. Hardie Jr., wit.

Goodman, Alfred M. & Maria F. McCrary, 27 Dec 1852; Jesse Thomason, bondsman; James E. Kerr, wit. married 29 Dec 1852 by J. Thomason, J. P.

Goodman, Caleb & Selana Hoffman, 16 Dec 1841; Miles Rusher, bondsman; J. H. Hardie, wit.

Goodman, Caleb & Anna Kesler, 14 Aug 1850; Moses Eller, bondsman; Obadiah Woodson, wit.

Goodman, Christian & Polly Creeson, 17 Jan 1817; George Goodman, bondsman; Roberts Nanny, wit.

Goodman, Christian & Rosanna Cresson, 5 March 1824; Joseph E. Todd, bondsman.

Goodman, Christopher & Milly Knup, 5 May 1851; Noah Canup, bondsman; J. S. Myers, wit.

Goodman, Daniel & Sophia Goodman, 21 June 1841; Paul Goodman, bondsman; Jno Giles, wit.

Goodman, George & Elizabeth Hill, 25 June 1812; John Darden, bondsman; Geo. Dunn, wit.

Goodman, George & Katherine Hornbarger, 3 Oct 1850; John Earnheart, bondsman; J. S. Myers, wit.

Goodman, George & Provide Gheen, 23 Oct 1858; Jacob A. Klutts, bondsman; John Wilkinson, wit. married 24 Oct 1858 by Moses Powless, J. P.

Goodman, Henry & Nelly Bostian, 6 March 1840; John Fink, bondsman; J. L. Beard, wit.

Goodman, Henry & Sophia Hartman, 13 April 1849; John W. Trexler, bondsman; J. H. Hardie Jr., wit.

Goodman, Jacob F. & Mary B. Knox, 14 Oct 1843; James C. Caldwell, bondsman; Jno H. Hardie Jr., wit.

Goodman, John & Polly Litaker, 14 Sept 1814; Phillip Litaker, bondsman; Henry Allemong, wit.

Goodman, John & Susanna Summers, 4 Nov 1824; Joseph Cowan, Jr., bondsman.

Goodman, John & Susannah Camp, 3 Feb 1846; Tobias Goodman, bondsman; J. H. Hardie Jr., wit.

Goodman, Michael & Rosannah Speck, 9 Nov 1785; Jacob Utzman, bondsman; Wm. Latham, wit.

Goodman, Michael & Sarah A. Graeber, 14 Oct 1856; Joseph Henderson, bondsman; J. S. Myers, wit.

Goodman, Michael W. & Mary Ann Graham, 23 April 1842; Jos. F. Chambers, wit. Jno H. Hardie, wit.

Goodman, Moses & Elizabeth Josey, 28 March 1829; Andrew Setzer, bondsman; Jno H. Hardie, wit.

Goodman, Moses & Mary L. Peeler, married 20 March 1859 by David Barringer, J. P.

Goodman, Moses A. & Clarissa C. Hilick, 5 Sept 1846; Henry A. Miller, bondsman.

Goodman, Paul & Edy Williams, 28 May 1835; Leonard Klutts, bondsman; Hy. Giles, wit.

Goodman, Thomas & Mary Coddle, 1 Sept 1797; Michl. Goodman, bondsman; Jno Rogers, wit.

Goodman, Tobias & Hannah Ridling, 28 Feb 1805; John Setzer, bondsman.

Goodman, Tobias & Rebecca Tally, 11 Sept 1814; Peter Heldebrand, bondsman; Geo Dunn, wit.

Goodman, Tobias & Anna Kepley, 14 March 1842; George Harkey, bondsman; J. H. Hardie, wit.

Goodman, Tobias & Ellin Turner, 27 May 1844; James Caldwell, bondsman; J. H. Hardie, wit.

Goodman, Tobias & Rosey Crotzer, 22 Nov 1852; B. F. Walton, bondsman; J. S. Myers, wit.

Goodman, William H. & Cornella L. Fulenwider, 25 Sept 1856; John Earnhart, bondsman; J. S. Myers, wit.

Goodnight, Jacob & Betsy Cauble, 19 May 1812; Michael Goodnight, bondsman; Jno Giles, C. C., wit.

Goodnight, John S. & Clarasa E. Baker, 25 March 1851; Fergus M. Graham, bondsman; J. S. Myers, wit.

Goolsby, Wade & Jane Crook, 9 Oct 1787; Mark Cole, bondsman; Jno Macay, wit.

Gorden, James & Mary Riddle, 12 Feb 1779; John Riddle, bondsman; Wm. Crosby, wit.

Gordin, William & _____, 2 Dec 1813; Joseph Farabee, bondsman; Sol. Davis, J. P., wit.

Gordnall, Fredrick & Cristina Hill, 1 Aug 1775; Peter Sites, bondsman; Ad. Osborn, wit.

Gordon, George & Catharine Stokes (colored), 2 April 1866; Horatio N. Woodson, bondsman; Obadiah Woodson, wit.

Gordon, Robert & Mary Carson, 11 March 1773; John Purviance, bondsman; Ad. Osborn, wit.

Goslin, John & Judith Davis, 10 March 1780; Thomas Smith, bondsman; Jno Kerr, wit.

Goss, David & Elizabeth Boss, 29 March 1794; Geo. Dunn, bondsman; Jo. Chambers, wit.

Goss, David & Elizabeth McBride, 19 March 1817; William McBride, bondsman; Roberts Nanny, wit.

Goss, Ephraim & Anne Workman, 23 March 1795; Jesse Harris, bondsman; Ad. Osborn, wit.

Goss, Frederick & Sarah Elston, 1 Jan 1787; Leond. Rickard, bondsman; Jno Macay, wit.

Goss, Jacob & Rebeka Billing, 24 Sept 1791; John Billing, bondsman; C. Caldwell, D. C., wit.

Goss, John & Sally Merrell, 21 Jan 1804; Azariah Merrell, bondsman; A. L. Osborn, D. C., wit.

Goss, Kinchen & Catharine Severs, 25 June 1827; Ezra Allemong, bondsman.

Goss, Leonard & Mary Smith, 2 Aug 1802; Jno Smith, bondsman; Jno Brem, D. C., wit.

Götche, Johann & Catharine Hildebrand, 30 July 1800; John Blake, Christian Shewman, bondsmen.

Gott, Sutten & Amealia Cotton, 24 May 1787; Gregory Doyel, bondsman; Fanny Macay, wit.

Gowan, John P. & Mary L. Luckey, 13 Dec 1848; Thos. Chambers McNeely, bondsman; John H. Hardie Jr., wit.

Graber, Jeremiah L. & Elizabeth Eddleman, 17 May 1849; Edmond H. Rosemann, bondsman.

Graeber, Augustus F. & Margaret A. Mesenheimer, 7 Oct 1850; Elisha Smith, bondsman; J. S. Myers, wit.

Graeber, Augustus F. & Maria C. Rendleman, 20 Aug 1864; Thomas McNeely, bondsman; Obadiah Woodson, wit.

Graham, Abel & Polly Knox, 14 Oct 1817; Samuel Graham, bondsman.

Graham, Alexander & Catharine Skyles, 5 Feb 1840; William E. Barber, bondsman; Susan T. Giles, wit.

Graham, Alexander & Elvira Linster, 7 July 1856; Thos. S.
Chambers, bondsman; J. S. Myers, wit.

Graham, Alexander D. & Ann L. Barclay, 15 Dec 1819; John W.
Graham, bondsman; Jno Giles, wit.

Graham, Andrew & Jane L. Young, 13 Oct 1845; John D. Young,
bondsman; Jno. H. Hardie, Jr., wit.

Graham, Benjamin & Faithful Hall, 19 Nov 1782; William Hall,
bondsman; Ad. Osborn, wit.

Graham, Christopher & Jane Gillespie, 18 Feb 1812; Jas. Gilespie,
bondsman; Jno Giles, C. C., wit.

Graham, Cowan & Elizabeth M. Thompson, 17 June 1844; Joseph C.
Graham, bondsman; J. H. Hardie, wit.

Graham, David & Margaret Parks, 8 Nov 1799; James Kerr,
bondsman.

Graham, Edward & Mary Noland, 24 Feb 1794; Peter Little, bondsman; G. Enochs, wit.

Graham, Fargus & _____, 3 March 1804; Samuel Miller, bondsman; A. L. Osborn, D. C., wit.

Graham, Fergus & Sally Baker, 22 April 1828; David C. Locke,
bondsman; Hy. Giles, wit.

Graham, Fergus M. & Crisey Miller, 27 March 1854; J. W. Miller,
bondsman; J. S. Myers, wit. married 28 March 1854 by John
S. Heilig.

Graham, Hezekiah C. & Caroline Chambers, 19 March 1846; Wm.
Campbell, bondsman; J. M. Turner, wit.

Graham, J. A. & Sophia Miller, 6 Aug 1860; Thomas Rimer, bondsman; James E. Kerr, wit. married 6 Aug 1860 by George
Rendleman, J. P.

Graham, Jacob S. & Catharine S. Barclay, 18 Dec 1833; Robert
Chunn, bondsman; Wm. Locke, wit.

Graham, Jacob S. & Eliza A. Peninger, 9 Jan 1839; Hugh A. Dobbins,
bondsman; Hy. Giles, wit.

Graham, James & Jean Cowan, 22 June 1803; William Robison, bondsman; Adlai L. Osborn, D. C., wit.

Graham, James & Margaret Penny, 24 Aug 1814; John Penny, bondsman; Jno Giles, C. C., wit.

Graham, James & Anna G. McBroom, 5 June 1833; Robert Chunn,
bondsman; Jno H. Hardie, wit.

Graham, James & Margaret Porter, 6 May 1786; William Young,
bondsman; John Macay, wit.

Graham, James & Mary E. McBroom, 17 Feb 1846; Hugh A. Dobbin,
bondsman; J. M. Turner, wit.

Graham, James Jr. & Agness Kerr, 27 Nov 1771; David Kerr,
bondsman.

Graham, James G. & Nancy S. Burke, 5 Jan 1849; M. A. Locke, bondsman; J. H. Hardie, wit.

Graham, James S. & Jane E. Young, 2 Jan 1858; Joseph A. Graham, bondsman; John Wilkinson, wit. married 7 Jan 1858 by S. C. Alexander.

Graham, John & Sarah Bunten, 27 Jan 1785; John Bunten, bondsman.

Graham, John & Jeane Donaldson, 21 Dec 1786; William Donaldson, bondsman; Jno Macay, wit.

Graham, John & Margaret Hall, 6 Sept 1791; Peter Faust, bondsman; C. Caldwell, D. C., wit.

Graham, John & Martha Anderson, 14 Jan 1804; John Hall, bondsman; A. L. Osborn, D. C., wit.

Graham, John S. & Sally Smith, 20 Jan 1819; Thomas Todd, bondsman; Roberts Nanny, wit.

Graham, John W. & Peggy Barclay, 21 Dec 1825; Samuel A. Barkley, bondsman; Jno Giles, wit.

Graham, Joseph & Jane Skiles, 24 Feb 1796; Richard Gillespie, bondsman.

Graham, Joseph C. & Grizzy E. Dobbins, 19 Sept 1849; N. M. Dobbin, bondsman; James E. Kerr, wit.

Graham, Moses & Ann Cowan, 31 May 1804; Richard Graham, bondsman; A. L. Osborn, D. C., wit.

Graham, R. F. & Mary C. Barringer, 16 Sept 1865; J. C. O. Graham, bondsman; Obadiah Woodson, wit.

Graham, Ricard & Jane Erwin, 20 Oct 1779; Joseph Graham, bondsman; Jo Brevard, wit.

Graham, Richard & Priscilla A. Graham, 11 Dec 1837; Archibald Gillespie, bondsman; Jno Giles, wit.

Graham, Richard & Sophia Lyerly, 28 April 1841; John C. Gillespie, bondsman; Susan T. Giles, wit.

Graham, Richard F. & Nancy E. Dobbin, 27 Oct 1852; Thomas K. Turner, bondsman; J. S. Myers, wit.

Graham, Richard Steel & Elizabeth A. Harrison, 5 Feb 1856; Thos. Barber, bondsman; J. S. Myers, wit. married 7 Feb 1856 by Geo. B. Wetmore, Minister of Protestant Episcopal Church.

Graham, Thomas C. & Elizabeth C. Young, 3 Feb 1840; Joseph Chambers, wit.

Graham, Thomas C. & Mary Cowan, 21 Nov 1832; Doctor R. Graham, bondsman; Jno H. Hardie, wit.

Graham, W. T. & Margaret E. Gheen, 16 Sept 1856; Wm. L. Barber, bondsman; James E. Kerr, wit. married 17 Sept 1856 by Jesse Rankin, Minister Presby. Church.

Graham, William & Margret Graham, 2 June 1767; Charles Purviance, bondsman; Thos. Frohock, wit.

Graham, William & Peggy Anderson, 27 Dec 1811; William Anderson, bondsman; Jno Giles, C. C., wit.

Graham, William & Elizabeth Rex, 10 April 1844; Matthew L. Pinkston, bondsman; J. H. Hardie, wit.

Graham, William P. & Mary K. Barr, 9 July 1825; Absalom K. Barr, bondsman; M. A. Giles, wit.

Graves, Conrod & Mary Fraser, 9 Jan 1767; Phillip Jacob Fraser, bondsman; Thoms. Frohock, wit.

Graves, George & Elizabeth Booe, 18 Dec 1792; John Nail, bondsman; Jos. Chambers, wit.

Graves, George & Sarah Foster, 22 April 1818; John Foster, bondsman; Jn March Sr., wit.

Graves, John & Amilley Adams, 2 April 1806; Henson Philips, bondsman; Jn March Sr., wit.

Graves, John & Nancy Potts, 18 Aug 1814; William Daniel, bondsman; Jno Giles, C. C., wit.

Graves, John & Nancy Foster, 21 July 1832; James Foster, bondsman; L. R. Rose, J. P., wit.

Gray, A. H. & Mary E. Hampton, 5 March 1857; Jas. Tansey, bondsman; J. S. Myers, wit. married 5 March 1857 by Jno H. Parker, Minister of Pro. Epis. Church.

Gray, David & Ann Gray, 3 Dec 1793; William Brassel, bondsman; Jo. Chambers, wit.

Gray, Edwin L. & Elizabeth Shuford, 18 Dec 1838; John A. Brown, bondsman; Hy. Giles, wit.

Gray, George & Mary Stuart, 1 July 1769; Daniel Lewis, bondsman; J. Frohock, wit.

Gray, George A. & Laura M. Lock, 30 March 1866; William G. Watson, bondsman; Horation N. Woodson, wit.

Gray, Hugh & Isabella Moore, 31 March 1789; James Milho-land, bondsman.

Gray, Hugh M. & Levina S. Graham, 30 Nov 1836; D. C. Foster, bondsman; R. Jones, wit.

Gray, J. A. & Ella Jane McNeely, 17 April 1865; B. H. Luker, bondsman; Obadiah Woodson, wit. married 18 April 1865 by W. B. Watts, Minister of the Gospel.

Gray, Robert B. & Maria L. Graham, 23 Aug 1854; Jas. G. Ramsay, bondsman; J. S. Myers, wit.

Greacey, John & Jenny Laurance, 11 Feb 1784; Abraham Laurance, bondsman; T. H. McCaule, wit.

Green, Benjamin & Sarah Kenaday, 16 Dec 1817; James Daniel, bondsman; E. Brown, And. Brown, wit.

Green, Charles D. & Patsey Markland, 28 Aug 1823; Fielding Slater, bondsman; M. Hanes, J. P., wit.

Green, Enoch & Elizabeth Booth, 9 Sept 1794; Zachariah Booth, bondsman; David Cowan, wit.

Green, Enoch & Lewsey Harwood, 5 Jan 1811; Henry Harwood, bondsman; Jn March Sr., wit.

Green, Fortune & Sarah Dent, 2 Oct 1855; Thomas Pinkston, bondsman; Obadiah Woodson, wit. married 2 Oct 1855 by Obadiah Woodson, J. P.

Green, F. S. & S. C. McLelland, 11 Jan 1859; F. D. Carlton, bondsman.

Green, Henry & Sarah Boyden (both colored), 25 Aug 1865; married 26 Aug 1865 by James T. Cuthrell, Minister.

Green, Isaac & Mary Booth, 22 Dec 1793; Zachriah Booth, bondsman; Jo. Chambers, wit.

Green, James & Mary Sexton, 7 March 1788; Hugh Horah, bondsman; J. McEwin, wit.

Green, Jeremiah & Mary Wiseman, 31 Oct 1775; John Ford, bondsman; Ad. Osborn, wit.

Green, Jeremiah & Catharine Correll, 30 Dec 1856; P. R. Minor, bondsman; J. S. Myers, wit. married 1 Jan 1857 by M. S. McKenzie, J. P.

Green, Jeremiah Jr. & Anne Hartley, 2 April 1790; Jeremiah Green Sr., bondsman; C. Caldwell, D. C., wit.

Green, John & Hannah Hunt, 16 Jan 1779; Owen Hunt, bondsman; Wm. R. Davie, wit.

Green, Lafayette & Sarah Knup, 1 Jan 1848; Joseph Kirkpatrick, bondsman; J. H. Hardie, wit.

Green, Thomas & Betsey Clotfelter, 27 Feb 1819; Malachi G. Bowen, bondsman; Jno Giles, wit.

Greer, J. H. & Ellen Reeves, 7 July 1858; Ransom Williams, bondsman; John Wilkinson, wit. married 7 July 1858 by L. C. Groseclose.

Gregeson, George & Rachel Holmes, 20 May 1820; Alex. Boyd, bondsman.

Gregory, George & Catharine Hagler, 19 Dec 1803; Jacob Hegler, bondsman; A. L. Osborn, D. C., wit.

Gregory, John & Betsy Lyerly, 22 Jan 1813; Christian Tarr, bondsman; Geo. Dunn, wit.

Gregory, Landsley & Mary Hooker, 13 Nov 1826; Samuel Simpson, bondsman; Thomas McNeely, J. P., wit.

Grey, Thomas & Jane McGahee, 1 Feb 1786; Ann Erwin, bondsman; Wm. W. Erwin, wit.

Gribble, Richard & Eliza Richards, 26 May 1856; John Waters, bondsman; Jac. C. Barnhardt, wit. married 26 May 1856 by Jac. C. Barnhardt, J. P.

Grier, Isaac H. & Margaret S. Parks, 20 Oct 1858; G. G. Smith, bondsman; James E. Kerr, wit. married 21 Oct 1858 by John E. Pressly, Minister.

Griffin, Andrew & Mary Sanders, 5 June 1825; Nathen Cornell, bondsman; Ja. C. Beddington, wit.

Griffin, Ezekiel & Cathrine Thomas, 27 Sept 1786; Samuel Bailey, bondsman; Jno Mackay, wit.

Griffin, Jesse & Ann Clarey, 18 Feb 1772; Daniel Clary, Benjamin Griffin, Timothy Ford, bondsmen; Thos Frohock, wit.

Griffin, John C. & Amanda J. McGhee, 11 April 1857; Micajah Griffin, bondsman; M. S. Myers, wit. married 12 April 1857 by R. G. Barrett, Pastor M. E. Church, Salisbury, N. C.

Griffin, John H. & Elizabeth Lemly, 6 Jan 1845; Geo. M. Weant, bondsman; Jno H. Hardie, wit.

Griffin, Josiah G. & Amanda McDonnell, 7 March 1857; John C. Griffin, bondsman; J. S. Myers, wit. married 8 March 1857 by R. G. Barrett, Pastor M. E. Church in Salisbury, N. C.

Griffin, M. P. & Anna M. Shipton, 12 Sept 1865; Daniel Miller, bondsman; Horatio N. Woodson, wit. married 14 Sept 1865 by Rev. Isaac M. Shaver.

Griffin, Noah J. & Margaret Smith, 15 Feb 1858; James E. Kerr, wit. married 15 Feb 1858 by R. S. Moran.

Griffin, Noah J. & Sarah A. Smith, 18 July 1855; G. Griffin, bondsman; J. S. Myers, wit. married 18 July 1855 by Obadiah Woodson, J. P.

Griffin, Ollover & Sarah Ralsback, 9 Feb 1810; David Baker, bondsman; Jn March, Sr., wit.

Griffin, Samuel & Mary Sossaman, 14 Nov 1848; James Deaton, bondsman; Jno H. Hardie Jr., wit.

Griffin, Thomas & Naney Lash, 21 Sept 1826; Abraham R. Jones, bondsman; Thomas McNeely, J. P., wit.

Griffin, Wesly & Eliza Austin, 22 May 1855; C. A. Morphis, bondsman; D. W. Honeycutt, wit. married 23 May 1855 by Jos. A. Linn, Pastor.

Griffin, Youkley & Salley Mullicar, 21 Jan 1796; Benjamin Mullican, bondsman; Fredrick Miller, wit.

Griffith, Charles & Cecelia Chunn, 3 Nov 1817; Wm. B. Wood, bondsman; Jno Giles, wit.

Griffith, Edward & Elizabeth Sharpe, 4 April 1783; James Sharpe, bondsman.

Griffith, John & Ann McKewrath, 3 Oct 1764; Ro. King, John Kilpatrick, bondsmen; Thomas Frohock, wit.

Griffith, John & Jane Harden, 2 Nov 1785; William Hardin, bondsman; Max Chambers, wit.

Griffith, R. W. & Julia E. Krider, married 16 Dec 1857 by Saml. B. O. Wilson, V. D. M.

Griffith, Richard W. & Mary E. Fleming, 23 Sept 1853; C. C. Krider, bondsman; J. S. Myers, wit.

Griggs, Henry & Anne Jowe, 26 Feb 1791; Joseph Parke, bondsman.

Grimes, Benjamin & Fanny Anderson, 6 Sept 1826; John Kinder, bondsman; J. H. Hardie, wit.

Grimes, Derry & Scena Parks, 13 Sept 1826; Alfred Kerr, bondsman; J. H. Hardie, wit.

Grimes, George W. & Peany Brinkle, 4 Feb 1819; Moses A. Locke, bondsman; Milo A. Giles, wit.

Grimes, Jabers & Nancy Barlow, 7 Nov 1821; John Black, bondsman; Geo. Cotten, wit.

Grimes, Jonas & Polly Sink, 29 March 1819; Matthias Grimes, bondsman; Jno Giles, wit.

Grimes, Matthias & Eve Day, 6 Jan 1818; Michael Day, bondsman; Silas Peace, wit.

Grimsley, George & Sally Camel, 10 July 1821; David Miller, bondsman; Hy. Giles, wit.

Grist, William & Celia Brady, 2 April 1780; John Brady, bondsman; B. Booth Boote, wit.

Groeaf, Abraham & Mary Adam, 23 Nov 1779; John Adam, bondsman; B. Booth Boote, wit.

Groessel, John Henri & Elizabeth Kaler, 17 June 1793; Ludwick Kaler, bondsman; Jos. Chambers, wit.

Groff, George Davidson & Easter Figgins, 10 Mar 1821; Archibald Fegin, bondsman; Hy. Giles, wit.

Gross, Fredrick & Elizabeth Hallis, 21 Oct 1791; Rudolph Neat, bondsman; Chs. Caldwell, wit.

Gross, Simon & Mary Shermer, 13 Feb 1770; Simon Gross Sr., Adam Lash, bondsmen; Thos Frohock Peter Shirmer, wit. consent from Petter Shermer and wife, 10 Feb 1770, wit William Davies, Simon Gross Seinier.

Groves, Joseph & Margaret Eller, 4 Sept 1796; Jacob Utzman, bondsman; Jno Rogers, wit.

Grub, Conrod & Elizabeth Hartman, 26 March 1795; Christian Cryder (Christian Kreider), bondsman; Ad. Osborn, wit.

Grub, Daniel & Alen Nuncasser, 23 Nov 1821; J. Jacob Shoaf, bondsman.

Grub, Daniel & Margrate Grub, 9 May 1822; Samuel Farrington, bondsman; J. Willson, wit.

Grub, Jacob & Susannah Hedrick, 15 Feb 1817; George Grub, bondsman; Jno Giles, Clk, wit.

Grubb, Conroad & Caty Headrick, 2 Dec 1820; John Grubb, bondsman; Andrew Swicegood, wit.

Grubb, David & Caty Young, 11 March 1822; Conroad Grubb, bondsman; An. Swicegood, wit.

Grubb, Henry & Hannah Reed, 15 March 1815; Levy Reed, bondsman; Geo. Dunn, wit.

Grubb, John & Mary Koons, 30 Nov 1809; Michael Koons, bondsman; Joseph Clarke, Jacob Michael, wit.

Grubb, John & Elizabeth Fraly, 20 Dec 1828; Green Redwine, bondsman; Jno H. Hardie, wit.

Grucklen, William & Elizabeth Smothers, 9 Jan 1789; Walt. Alexander, wit.

Guffy, Henry & Rachel Bean, 30 Jan 1807; Saml. Lucky, bondsman; A. L. Osborn, D. C., wit.

Guffy, Henry & Elizabeth Walker, 27 Sept 1828; William Luckey, bondsman; L. R. Rose, J. P., wit.

Guffy, John & Patty Hughes, 26 March 1801; Saml. Hughes, bondsman; Jno Brem, D. C., wit.

Gullet, John & Margaret L. Webb, 29 Oct 1852; Michael B. Dickson, bondsman; J. S. Myers, wit. married 4 Nov 1852 by A. J. Fleming, J. P.

Gullet, John & Charlotte Thompson, 23 Jan 1855; D. J. Webb, bondsman; J. S. Myers, wit. married 23 Jan 1855 by H. L. Robards, J. P.

Guffy, John F. & Lemira Henley, 14 July 1860; M. D. Van Eaton, bondsman; John Wilkinson, wit. married 24 July 1860 by M. C. Thomas, M. M. E. Church.

Gullet, Richmond & Nancey Butlar, 5 Jan 1831; Jno Giles, Cl., wit.

Gullet, Richmond & Lucinda Dent, 3 Nov 1857; McAfee Linster, bondsman; J. S. Myers, wit. married 3 Nov 1857 by S. P. Robard.

Gullet, Richmond & Mary Ann Thorn, 3 June 1859; Samuel Elliott, bondsman; James E. Kerr, wit.

Gullet, William & Jinney Davison, 27 Nov 1808; Andrew Tucker, bondsman; John March Sr., wit.

Gullett, Andrew & Sarah Purviance, 20 Feb 1866; James A. Holt, bondsman; Obadiah Woodson, wit.

Gunther, August & Polly Eller, 19 Oct 1854; Eli Seaford, bondsman.

Guy, William & Keziah Wellman, 23 Oct 1817; James Ellis, bondsman; Roberts Nanny, wit.

Gwinn, Peter & Sarah Taylor, 27 Nov 1769; David Baley, Oliver Wallis, bondsmen; Thomas Frohock, wit.

Hacket, James & Mary Woods, 14 Oct 1779; James Gibson, bondsman; Jo Brevard, wit.

Hackett, A. L. & Mary L. Powe, 26 Oct 1858; N. N. Fleming, bondsman; John Wilkinson, wit. married 27 Oct 1858 by A. Baker, Pastor of the Pres. Church in Salisbury.

Hackett, James & Fanny C. Johnston, 14 Dec 1813; Andrew Kerr, bondsman; Geo. Dunn, wit.

Haden, Alexander & Rebecca Frost, 23 Jan 1826; Henry Ellis, bondsman; M. A. Giles, wit.

Haden, D. F. & Susan Shuman, 10 April 1841; Danl. Shaver, bondsman.

Haden, Franklin W. & Aureney Miller, 9 June 1835; Willis Coats, bondsman; Hy. Giles, wit.

Haden, James W. & Elizabeth J. Bradshaw, 16 Sept 1851; Thos. C. McNeely, bondsman; James E. Kerr, wit. married 17 Sept 1851 by T. Page Ricaud, Pastor M. E. Church, Salisbury, Station, N. C. Conference.

Haden, Jesse & Rosana Sloan, 29 Aug 1797; John Sloan, bondsman; Jno Rogers, wit.

Haden, William D. & Elizabeth Linster, 3 May 1796; Moses Linster, bondsman; A. Balfour, wit.

Haden, William D. & Elizabeth Ham, _____ 1802; Isaac Linser, bondsman; Jno Brem, wit.

Hadlock, Robert & Elizabeth Coleman, 6 Sept 1793; Owen Manley, bondsman; Jos. Chambers, wit.

Hadon, Joseph & Jenny Headon, 8 Jan 1783; Richd. Pearson, bondsman; William Crawford, wit.

Hafley, Adam & Mary Ridennour, 5 May 1803; Peter Coyle, bondsman; Ad. Osborn, wit.

Hagar, Thomas & Nancy E. MaKey, 10 May 1857; Leander C. McCauly, bondsman; J. S. Myers, wit. married 19 March 1857 by J. F. McCorkle, J. P.

Hage, Jacob Jr. & Catharine Weasner, 19 June 1818; Valuntine Hage, bondsman; Thos. Hampton, wit.

Hage, Jonathan & Polley Silliven, 2 July 1822; Andrew Craver, bondsman; An. Swicegood, wit.

Hage, Joseph & Pheobe Leonard, 16 Nov 1814; Lewis Craver, bondsman; Geo. Dunn, wit.

Hager, George & Elizabeth Fyte, 17 Jan 1791; Jacob Utzman, bondsman; C. Caldwell, D. C., wit.

Hager, Jacob & Christina Roberts, 31 March 1820; Tobias Airey, bondsman; Jno. Giles, wit.

Hagey, Jacob & Betsey Brookshire, 28 Dec 1799; Henry Hagey, bondsman; Edwin J. Osborn, wit.

Hagey, John & _____, 16 Aug 1796; Chrisr. Levingood, bondsman; Jno Rogers, wit.

Hagin, George Jr. & Rusanah Long, 10 June 1765; John Long Sr., Danl. Little, bondsmen.

Haglar, Peter & Elizabeth Reynolds, 14 Feb 1790; Thomas Reynolds, bondsman; Jno Kerr, wit.

Hagler, John & Polly Love, 21 April 1795; Thomas Love, bondsman; J. Troy, wit.

Hague, James & Anne Foster, 16 May 1812; Wm. Haden, bondsman;
Geo. Dunn, wit.

Hague, Thomas A. & Sarah Waddle, 12 Nov 1827; James M. Slaughter,
bondsman; J. H. Hardie, wit.

Haines, George & Sally Crouch, 28 July 1820; Isaac L. Ward,
bondsman; Jno Monroe, wit.

Haines, John & Saly Eller, 24 July 1820; George Haines, bondsman; J. Willson, wit.

Haines, Moses & Mary Deatherage, 6 March 1816; Leonard Smith,
bondsman; John March Sr., wit.

Hainline, Christopher & Elizabeth Cross, 29 Aug 1786; Joshua
Cross, bondsman; Jno Macay, wit.

Hainline, Nathan & Polley Sheats, 24 Aug 1807; John March,
bondsman; Jn March Sr., wit.

Hains, James & Sarah Andrews, 15 Feb 1804; James Andrews, bondsman; Hudson Hughes, wit.

Hains, William & Rachel Griffin, 8 Feb 1818; John Cash, bondsman; R. Powell, wit.

Hair, Jacob F. & Cecelia Campbell, 23 Dec 1847; Perry Haire,
bondsman; J. H. Hardie Jr., wit.

Haire, James & Milly Hair, 18 Oct 1853; Levi Wilhelm, bondsman;
J. S. Myers, wit.

Hairston, Peter W. & Fanny M. Caldwell, 21 June 1859; L. Blackmer,
bondsman; James E. Kerr, wit. married 22 June 1859 by T. G.
Haughton, Rector &c.

Haithcock, James D. & Mary Ann Lentz, 7 June 1841, A. M. Miller,
bondsman.

Haldaman, Jacob & Margaret Kiesler, 24 May 1839; Jas. L. Cowan,
bondsman; Abel Cowan, J. P., wit.

Halde, Joseph & Mary Bailey, 30 Nov 1789; Peter Faust, bondsman.

Hale, John H. & Margaret Hunt, 12 Sept 1822; Charles Hoover,
bondsman; Z. Hunt, wit.

Hale, Samuel & Elizabeth Myers, 9 Aug 1820; John H. Hale, bondsman; Silas Peace, wit.

Hall, A. L. & Sue P. Miller, 1 June 1865; James T. Sloan, bondsman; Obadiah Woodson, wit. married 1 June 1865 by Simeon
Scherer.

Hall, A. N. & Nancy C. Gillespie, 4 Jan 1841; Thomas C. Gillespie,
bondsman.

Hall, Abner & Nancy Howard, 31 Oct 1825; Henry C. Owens, bondsman.

Hall, Abraham & Elizabeth Humphreys, 24 March 1816; Thos. West,
bondsman; R. Powell, wit.

Hall, Adam & Sarah Freeman, 26 March 1778; William Frohock, bondsman; Ad. Osborn, wit.

Hall, Allmand & Margaret Pennington, 4 May 1818; Tho. L. Cowan, bondsman; Milo A. Giles, wit.

Hall, Alvah & Polly Moore, 9 Oct 1827; George Moore, Jr., bondsman; C. Harbin, J. P., wit.

Hall, Andrew & Jean Linster, 12 March 1793; John Hall, bondsman; Jos. Chambers, wit.

Hall, Calvin & Margaret Cruse, 6 Sept 1854; Owen N. Browne, bondsman; J. S. Myers, wit.

Hall, David & Sarah Busey, 20 Feb 1765; Adam Hall, Saml. Busey, bondsmen; John Frohock, wit.

Hall, David & Susanna Speaks, 23 April 1824; Nicholas Rimer, bondsman; Hy. Giles, wit.

Hall, David & Nancey Renshaw, 24 March 1830; Elhanon Jinkins, bondsman; L. R. Rose, J. P., wit.

Hall, Doctor J. & Elizabeth Welch, 15 Oct 1824; Joseph Welch, bondsman; L. R. Rose, J. P., wit.

Hall, Edward P. & Amanda H. Neely, widow, 15 Oct 1860; Abner L. Hall, bondsman; John Wilkinson, wit. married 16 Oct 1860 by Geo. B. Wetmore, Minister.

Hall, Fergus & _____, 13 Dec 1796; Joel McCorkle, bondsman; Humphry Marshall, wit.

Hall, George & Clementine Turner (colored), 21 April 1866; George Turner, bondsman; Obadiah Woodson, wit.

Hall, Hugh & Lavina Hall, 23 July 1814; Richmond Hall, bondsman; Jno Giles, C. C., wit.

Hall, Isaac & Sarah Furches, 13 April 1815; Moses Hall, bondsman; R. Powell, wit.

Hall, Isaac A. & Polly Elliott, 23 April 1828; Richd. Loury, bondsman.

Hall, James & Rachel Johnston, 9 Jan 1792; James Bowman, bondsman; Chs. Caldwell, wit.

Hall, James & Nelly Speake, 22 Aug 1818; James Speake, bondsman; Milo A. Giles, wit.

Hall, James & Julia Ann Lyerly, 28 Feb 1843; Jas. Alexander Jr., bondsman.

Hall, James & Elizabeth _____, 2 Jan 1780; Robert Johnston, bondsman; Jno Kerr, wit.

Hall, James D. & Alma Brandon, 11 Dec 1839; Michael Broun, bondsman; Jno Giles, wit.

Hall, James O. & Marcris Miller, 19 Sept 1861; William A. Lentz, bondsman; Obadiah Woodson, wit. married 19 Sept 1861 by J. Crim, Pastor of Salem Ch.

Hall, John & Mary Hare, 10 May 1781; Robt Hare, bondsman; Ad. Osborn, wit.

Hall, John & Sarah Anderson, 2 March 1796; Robert Luckie, bondsman, J. Troy, wit.

Hall, John & Ann Luckey, 19 March 1816; David Lucky, bondsman; Geo. Dunn, wit.

Hall, John & Peggy Lourie, 30 April 1817; Thomas Wilson, bondsman; Jno. Giles, Clk., wit.

Hall, John & Mary Johnson, 1 July 1819; Stewert Hall, bondsman; Hy. Giles, wit.

Hall, John & Elizabeth Parker, 24 Jan 1825; Wesley Clark, bondsman; L. R. Rose, J. P., wit.

Hall, John & Nancy Robby, 9 July 1825; Henry Allemong, bondsman; Ralph Kepler, wit.

Hall, Joseph & Katharine Wilson, 7 Aug 1788; Andrew Hall, bondsman; Wm. Alexander, wit.

Hall, Joseph & Margaret Linster, 27 Aug 1793; John Tate, bondsman; Joseph Chambers, wit.

Hall, Joseph & Hannah Campbell, 16 March 1796; John Hall, bondsman; J. Troy, wit.

Hall, Josephus W. & Mary Cowan, 1 Dec 1803; Newberry F. Hall, bondsman.

Hall, Joshua & Jane McClallen, 13 April 1765; Moses White, John Miller, Alex McCulloch, bondsmen; Thomas Frohock, wit.

Hall, Moses & Lydia Hunter, 25 June 1815; Isaac Hall, bondsman; R. Powell, wit.

Hall, N. F. & E. A. Lowery, 13 March 1850; Mexl. C. Caldwell, bondsman; J. S. Myers, wit.

Hall, Newberry F. & Martha E. Shuford, 22 March 1854; Thomas D. Graham, bondsman; J. S. Myers, wit. married 23 March 1854 by A. Baker, Pastor of the Presbyterian Church.

Hall, P. J. & Sofiah Casper, 26 March 1865; Daniel Wagoner, bondsman; A. M. Sullivan, J. P., wit.

Hall, Pleasant & Ebbe Fortner, 5 Sept 1811; Jesse Langley, bondsman; Joseph Clarke, John Buie Jr., wit.

Hall, Pleasant & Sarah Plyer, 14 Oct 1819; Thomas Hall, bondsman; Hy. Giles, wit.

Hall, Pleasant & Polly Wood, 20 Feb 1821; Jarratt Wood, bondsman; Milo A. Giles, wit.

Hall, R. F. & Mary E. Hall, 25 April 1855; Thos D. Graham, bondsman; J. S. Myers, wit. married 25 April 1855 by Saml. B. O. Wilson, V. D. M.

Hall, Ric & _____, 180_; (no wit. or bondsman).

Hall, Robert & Mary Wason, _____ (during Gov. Martin's Admn.); Andw Reid, bondsman.

Hall, Stewart & Rebecca Speaks, 9 Oct 1822; David Hall, bondsman; Hy. Giles, wit.

Hall, T. F. & S. E. Bradshaw, 13 April 1861; S. J. Swicegood, bondsman; John Wilkinson, wit. married 16 April 1861 by Stephen Frontis, Minister of the Gospel.

Hall, Thomas & Nancy Wood, 6 Nov 1801; Jacob Walser, bondsman; Jno Brem, wit.

Hall, Thomas & Margaret Graham, 3 Sept 1822; Abner Hall, bondsman; Henry Allemong, wit.

Hall, W. F. & Marietta L. Graham, 20 Dec 1856; T. A. Allison, bondsman; James E. Kerr, wit. married 23 Dec 1856 by Saml. B. O. Wilson, V. D. M.

Hall, William & Elizabeth Wilson, 7 Jan 1783; James Wilson, bondsman; Willm. Crawford, wit.

Hall, William & Susanna Parker, 10 Oct 1825; Freland Beck, bondsman; L. R. Rose, J. P., wit.

Hallman, Anthony & Elizabeth Gingery, 11 July 1774; John Lewis Beard, bondsman; Ad. Osborn, wit.

Hallman, George C. & Sarah Gallimore, 10 Dec 1857; Wm. Mowery, bondsman; J. S. Myers, wit.

Hallum, John Jr. & Elizabeth Morris, 9 Jan 1765; William Patrick, John Tedwell, bondsmen; John Frohock, C. C., wit. consent from George Morris, 7 Jan 1765.

Hambree (Emery), Joel & Eve Fite, 17 March 1828; Jacob Beavers, bondsman; Jno H. Hardie, wit.

Hamelton, Samuel & Mary Hege, 26 Dec 1810; George Fisher, bondsman; W. Ellis, J. P., wit.

Hamilton, A. G. & Susan Beck, 15 Oct 1857; John Pennington, bondsman; J. S. Myers, wit. married 15 Oct 1857 by Peter Williamson.

Hamilton, Francis & Betsy Newsom, 24 April 1804; Davenport Newsom, bondsman; A. L. Osborn, D. C., wit.

Hamilton, James & Mary Baley, 19 Nov 1771; William Bailiey, bondsman; Thomas Frohock, wit.

Hamilton, Josiah & Lidia Parks, 12 March 1833; Jesse Parks, bondsman; Hy. Giles, wit.

Hamilton, Luke & Elizabeth Nicholds, 18 April 1781; John Nichols, bondsman; James Houston, wit. consent 18 April 1781 from Jno Nichols, father of Elizabeth.

Hamlet, R. W. & Virginia F. Mitchell, 28 Dec 1858; John Hutcheson, bondsman; James E. Kerr, wit. married 28 Dec 1859 by Jos. Robards, J. P.

Hamley, Rufus C. or Handy & N. S. Swink, 1 Oct 1856; married 1 Oct 1856 by J. W. Naylor, Mst.

Hammer, William H. & Susannah Pickler, 17 Jan 1831; Philip F. Meroney, bondsman; Jno H. Hardie, wit.

Hammond, Anthony & Susanna Horner, 23 Feb 1779; Jas. Robinson, bondsman.

Hampton--see also Hamton

Hampton, Caleb & Sarah Ritchie, 17 March 1838; John Fesperman, bondsman; Hy. Giles, wit.

Hampton, Ephraim & Elizabeth Enochs, 28 March 1794; Isaac Smith, bondsman; G. Enochs, wit.

Hampton, James & Elizabeth Richey, 10 _____ 1840; John Fesperman, bondsman.

Hampton, James B. & Susan A. Locke, 2 Feb 1831; Ashbel Smith, bondsman; Jno H. Hardie, wit.

Hampton, John & Leonora Faust, 23 Oct 1800; John Pool, bondsman.

Hampton, Obediah & Sally Monroe, 13 Dec 1820; Danl. Clary, bondsman; Jno Giles, wit.

Hampton, Obediah & Elizabeth Goodman; 14 March 1840; Jacob Bruner, bondsman; Susan T. Giles, wit.

Hampton, Robert & Polley March, 18 July 1808; John March Jr., bondsman; Jn March Sr., wit.

Hampton, Thomas & Sarah Hussey, 16 April 1818; George Saner, bondsman; Richd. Ellis, wit.

Hampton, William & Nancy Vanpoole, 24 Feb 1803; David Gardner, bondsman; Adlai L. Osborn, D. C., wit.

Hampton, William & Catharine Daugherty, 12 Dec 1822; James Dougherty, bondsman.

Hamstatler, Christian & Margaret Wiseman, 26 March 1795; William Ford, bondsman; Ad. Osborn, wit.

Hamton, David & Mary Bryan, 18 Aug 1786; Wm. Hamton, bondsman; Jno Macay, wit.

Hamton, John & Judith Woodson, 9 June 1795; Wm. Hamton, bondsman; J. Troy, wit.

Hamton, Obediah & Sarah Ross, 23 July 1805; Joseph Brown, bondsman; A. L. Osborn, D. C., wit.

Hamton, William & Rachel Westcote, 12 Jan 1770; William Nisbet, James Morgan, bondsmen; Thomas Frohock, wit.

Hanah, Joseph & Mary Davis, 5 Jan 1789; Hugh Cunningham, bondsman; W. Alexander, wit.

Hancock, William M. & Margaret Clemmer, 1 March 1792; Balser Dorthono, bondsman; Basil Gaither, wit.

Handy, Rufus A. & N. S. Swink, 1 Oct 1856; A. D. Lewis, bondsman; J. S. Myers, wit.

Hanes, John & Belinda Lambert, 2 Nov 1822; Jesse Reavis, bondsman; John Cook, J. P., wit.

Hanes, Joseph & Sary March, 19 Oct 1819; George Hanes, bondsman; Saml Jones, J. P., wit.

Hanes, Joseph & Catharine Seam (?), 9 June 1808; Michael Akels, bondsman; John Hanes, Jacob Hanes, wit.

Hanes, Joseph & Mary Snow, 13 May 1823; John Dunaway, bondsman; J. Berryman, J. P., wit.

Hanes, Mikel & Sarah Smith, 23 July 1813; Jacob Hanes, bondsman; Jn March, wit.

Hanks, Thomas & Crese Hargroves, 2 March 1789; Thompson Hargrove, bondsman.

Hanly, William & Polly Blackwell, 21 March 1813; William Biles, bondsman; Jno Giles, C. C., wit.

Hanlin, Thomas & Hannah Owings, 11 May 1811; Robt. Hampton, bondsman; Jn. March Sr., wit.

Hanna, James & Elizabeth Lyon, 4 Feb 1813; Patrick Dougherty, bondsman; Geo. Dunn, wit.

Hanna, James & Margaret Maxwell, 7 May 1817; Daniel Lock, bondsman; Moses A. Locke, wit.

Hannan, William & Elizebeth Hendricks, 1 Feb 1817; Antoney Silvers, bondsman; Jn March Sr., wit.

Hannon, John & Catharine Shoemaker, 28 Dec 1811; John Simmons, bondsman; Jno Giles, C. C., wit.

Hannons, William & Betsey Blaze, 27 Nov 1816; John Blaze, bondsman; Roberts Nanny, wit.

Hanseman, William & Mary Blackwilder, 9 Feb 1790; George Savitz, bondsman; Ed. Harris, wit.

Harben, Edward W. W. & Easter Etcherson, 24 Aug 1809; Jacob Allen, bondsman; Jn March Sr., wit.

Harbin, Caswell & Elizabeth Smoote, 26 March 1829; James F. Martin, bondsman; L. R. Rose, J. P., wit.

Harbin, David & Elizabeth Cornell, 10 March 1825; Alexr. Smoot, bondsman; J. C. Weddington, wit.

Harbin, James W. & Nancy Miller, 11 Jan 1832; Jacob Allen, bondsman; Wm. Hawkins, wit.

Harbin, William & Lucy Commons, 11 Nov 1801; Resin Harbin, bondsman; J. Hunt, wit.

Harbison, William & Lydia Bozewell, 9 Aug 1815; John Gray, bondsman; R. Powell, wit.

Hardee, Peter & Ann Fisher (colored), 25 Jan 1866; John A. Harris, bondsman; Obadiah Woodson, wit.

Harden, Benjamin & Marthy Henderson, 6 June 1826; David N. Austin, bondsman; Wm. A. Hawkins, wit.

Harden, Gabriel & Jean Vandavour, 22 Sept 1817; Jonathan Madden, bondsman; R. Powell, wit.

Harden, Samuel M. & Christena Roberts, 17 June 1815; Isham Hains, bondsman; Geo. Dunn, wit.

Hardin, Alexander & Ann Bishop, 16 July 1773; Wm. Steel, bondsman; Max. Chambers, wit.

Hardin, Isaac & Elizabeth Adams, 10 June 1824; John Maxwell, bondsman; L. R. Rose, J. P., wit.

Hardman, Samuel & Nancy Loyd, 8 Nov 1808; John Richardson, bondsman; A. L. Osborne, C. C., wit.

Harford, Abraham & Rebeka _____, _____; Thon Buffle, bondsman.

Hargrave, Frederick & Mary Pagg, 23 Jan 1790; Benajah Nordyke, bondsman; J. Monro, wit.

Hargrave, Frederick & Elonor Beard, 17 Feb 1813; James Zebely, bondsman; Geo. Dunn, wit.

Hargrave, William & Tirzah McKnight, 22 May 1824; Jos. McKnight, bondsman.

Hargraves, Samuel & Milly Lipe, 8 May 1830; John McCain, bondsman.

Hargue, James & Elizabeth Beaty, 8 Aug 1771; John McHargue, bondsman; Ad. Osborn, wit.

Harkey, Christopher & Rachael Miller, 1 Aug 1835; Jacob Miller, bondsman; Hy. Giles, wit.

Harkey, Daniel & Liddy Pearce, 12 Jan 1859; Henry Harkey, bondsman; D. W. Honeycutt, wit.   married 12 Jan 1859 by D. W. Honeycutt, J. P.

Harkey, Daniel & Nancey M. Kepley, 1 Aug 1861; Robbert W. Kepeley, bondsman; M. L. Holmes, J. P., wit.

Harkey, Daniel & Drusilla E. Earnheart, 29 Oct 1863; Ephraim H. Mesemer, bondsman; Jos. A. Linn, wit.

Harkey, David & Sophia Bame, 6 Nov 1822; Henry Harkey, bondsman; Jno. Giles, wit.

Harkey, George & Elizabeth Goodman, 29 Nov 1837; Tobias Goodman, bondsman.

Harkey, Henry & Barbara Miller, 19 Dec 1829; Saml. Jones, bondsman; J. H. Hardie, wit.

Harkey, Henry & Catharine Earnheart, 7 March 1857; Martin Richwine, bondsman; J. S. Myers, wit.   married 10 March _____ by D. Barringer, J. P.

Harkey, John W. & Margaret Corl, 4 Nov 1844; Alexander Corl, bondsman; John H. Hardie, wit.

Harkey, Moses G. & Elizabeth Earnheart, 27 March 1857; Thos. M. Crawford, bondsman; J. S. Myers, wit.

Harkey, Tobias & Sophia Hartline, 15 Jan 1824; Henry Harkey, bondsman; Hy. Giles, wit.

Harky, Henry & Margaret Beaver, 20 March 1817; John Harkey, bondsman; Roberts Nanny, wit.

Harley, Samuel & Sarah Moore, 7 Oct 1803; John Veach, bondsman.

Harman, George & Barbra Lopp, 27 Dec 1791; Gaspher Hinkle, bondsman; Jno Monro, wit.

Harmon, David & Katy Peck, 23 Jan 1808; Daniel Harmon, bondsman.

Harole, John & Sarey Nobody, 25 Oct 1809; Vaulengtine Arnet, bondsman; Jn March Sr., wit.

Harper, Samuel & Mary Ford, 26 Aug 1784; John Ford, bondsman.

Harper, Thomas & Sarah Wilson, 12 Feb 1789; Samuel Harper, bondsman; Will Alexander, wit.

Harris, Charles & Sally Harris, 8 April 1790; James Harris, bondsman; C. Caldwell, D. C., wit.

Harris, David & Ellendor Thomas, 17 Aug 1819; R. Powell, bondsman; R. Powell, wit.

Harris, Eli & Jane Hunt, 25 Dec 1812; Tho. L. Cowan, bondsman.

Harris, George & Peggy Gaddis, 1 Nov 1813; William Stout, bondsman; E. Morgan, wit.

Harris, George M. & Sarah Shaver, 12 May 1830; Jacob Coughenour, bondsman; Jno H. Hardie, wit.

Harris, Isham & Anne Campbell, 5 April 1791; John Erwin, bondsman; C. Caldwell, D. C., wit.

Harris, J. F. & Ivicey Ann Kesler, 25 April 1866; Thomas E. Brown, bondsman; Obadiah Woodson, wit.

Harris, Jesse & Martha Hoafhines, 20 July 1830; David Harris, bondsman.

Harris, John & Ruth Cowan, 30 July 1795; Samuel Luckie, bondsman.

Harris, Joseph & Martha Leadwell, 6 July 1856; Valentine Mauney, bondsman; E. Mauney, wit. married 6 July 1856 by Ephraim Mauney, J. P.

Harris, Joshua & Anna L. Lingle, 14 Feb 1855; Wilson A. Lingle, bondsman; James E. Kerr, wit. married 14 Feb 1855 by A. Baker, Pastor of the Presbyterian Church, Salisbury, N. C.

Harris, N. D. & Antoinette West, 28 Feb 1865; William Smithdeal, bondsman; N. H. Blackwood, wit.

Harris, Nicholas & Janey Hall, 24 July 1810; John Harris, bondsman; Jno Giles, C. C., wit.

Harris, Richard & Catherine Wacaster, 10 June 1814; John Wacaster, bondsman; R. Powell, wit.

Harris, Richard & Mary Johnston, 17 May 1815; Wm. M. Johnston, bondsman; Henry Allemong, wit.

Harris, Robert & Mary E. Cowan, 27 Aug 1849; T. C. McNeely, bondsman; James E. Kerr, wit.

Harris, Samuel & Frankey Bryand, 7 Feb 1809; Hampton Sparks, bondsman; Jn March Sr., wit.

Harris, Samuel & Margret James, 17 Dec 1814; Thos James, bondsman; Jn March Sr., wit.

Harris, William & Margaret Sloane, 20 Sept 1784; Fergus Sloan, bondsman; T. H. McCaule, wit.

Harris, Williamson & Teany Fisher, 11 Aug 1809; Jacob Fisher, bondsman.

Harris, Zephaniah & Tabby Hix, 25 Nov 1790; David Jones, bondsman; C. Caldwell, wit.

Harrison, Benjamin & Mary Huff, 4 Oct 1774; Thomas Huff, bondsman; Ad. Osborn, wit.

Harrison, G. B. & Jane Webb, 25 Nov 183_; John C. Palmer, bondsman.

Harrison, Hardy & Polly Varner, 5 June 1819; Elisha Nichols, bondsman; Jno Giles, wit.

Harrison, Hezekiah T. & Margaret A. Cowan, 16 Nov 1825; Saml. Young, bondsman; M. A. Giles, wit.

Harrison, J. M. & Fannie Owens, 9 April 1861; T. A. Allison, bondsman; James E. Kerr, wit. married 9 April 1861 by W. A. Luckey, J. P.

Harrison, James & Mary M. Belton, 20 June 1827; Hy. Giles, bondsman.

Harrison, Kinchn & Susanna Griffith, 4 April 1809; Henry Hunter, bondsman; A. D. Osborne, wit.

Harrison, Kinchn & Elizabeth Hage, 25 Jan 1814; Thomas Reeves, bondsman; Jno Giles, C. C., wit.

Harrison, Matthew & Rachael Cline, 28 March 1838; Joseph Dobbins, bondsman; Jno. Giles, wit.

Harrison, Matthew & Nelly Davis, 20 Jan 1819; Bennet Nooe, bondsman; Roberts Nanny, wit.

Harrison, Nathan & Eunice Linster, 27 Aug 1850; Saml. Ro. Harrison, bondsman; James E. Kerr, wit.

Harrison, Nathan & Elvira Cox, 12 April 1854; Henry Koon, bondsman; James E. Kerr, wit.

Harrison, Owen & Sarah Reevs, 20 Jan 1813; Samuel Reeves, bondsman; Geo. Dunn, wit.

Harrison, Richard & Ann Young, 13 Nov 1816; John C. Reeves, bondsman; Jno Giles, Clk., wit.

Harrison, Richard & Julia A. E. Woolworth, 25 June 1856; J. S. Myers, bondsman.

Harrison, Samuel & Charlotte Scherlock, 25 June 1813; Martin Owen, bondsman; Jno Giles, C. C., wit.

Harrison, Samuel & Charlotte Rodes, 12 June 1814; John Veach, bondsman; Silas Peace, wit.

Harrison, Samuel R. & Mary Murphey, 31 March 1852; Thos. J. Meroney, wit.

Harrison, William & Esther Savits, 4 June 1786; Samuel Wilkinson, bondsman; Jno Macay, wit.

Harrod, Joseph & Susannah Sill, 23 Feb 1795; John Berringer, bondsman; J. Troy, D. C., wit.

Harrowood, Zacheriah & Eve Garrett, 13 March 1769; John Harrowood, Joseph Goss, bondsmen; Tho. Frohock, wit.

Harry, Jacob & Mary Davis, 7 Dec 1801; Jacob Brummell, bondsman.

Hart, Andrews A. & America Lyerly, 23 Oct 1855; Wm. M. Lourance, bondsman; J. S. Myers, wit. married 24 Oct 1855 by S. C. Alexander.

Hart, David & Peggy Black, 29 May 1789; Charls. Hart, bondsman; Will Alexander, wit.

Hart, James & Ann Lowrance, 19 Jan 1789; Joshua Lowrance, bondsman; W. Alexander, wit.

Hart, John S. E. & Charlotte Lyerly, 17 Dec 1864; A. A. Hart, bondsman; W. G. Watson, wit.

Hart, Mathew & Elizabeth Steele, 24 Dec 1789; Andw. Hart, bondsman; Ed. Harris, wit.

Hart, Samuel & Francis Boocker, 11 Jan 1825; Jonathan Graham, bondsman; Hy. Giles, wit.

Hart, Sydney H. & Esther E. Baker, 20 Dec 1849; A. G. Holder, bondsman; J. S. Myers, wit.

Hart, William & Jane Steel, 11 Feb 1787; Jas. Hart, bondsman; Mar. Osborn, wit.

Harter, William G. & Margaret V. Nutall, 30 Dec 1846; Saml. Rothrock, bondsman; Jno H. Hardie, wit.

Harth, John & Hannah Cain, 20 Feb 1825; Joseph Forcum, bondsman; John Cook, wit.

Hartley, Thomas & Milly Burges, 9 Oct 1787; Arid Len Moore, bondsman; Jno Macay, wit.

Hartley, Thomas A. & Elizabeth Lawson, 11 July 1851; Samuel A. Creason, bondsman; J. S. Myers, wit. married 24 July 1851 by T. Page Ricaud, Minister of the Gospel.

Hartline, George & Mary Earnhardt, 9 Aug 1793; John Aronhart, bondsman; Jos. Chambers, wit.

Hartline, George & Betsy Bostian, 17 Jan 1815; John Lence, bondsman; Geo. Dunn, wit.

Hartline, Henry & Sophia Kesler, 5 Jan 1826; Adam Hofman, bondsman.

Hartline, Jacob & Sally Pool, 5 Aug 1823; Henry Hartman, bondsman; Jno. Giles, wit.

Hartline, Jon & Betsey Cauble, 3 Nov 1817; Philip Earnhart, bondsman; Jno. Giles, wit.

Hartly, Laban & Nancy Brodeway, 23 Jan 1811; Andrew Swisgood, bondsman; Geo. Dunn, wit.

Hartman, Adam & Catharine Harkey, 16 Oct 1839; Miles Rusher, bondsman; John Giles, wit.

Hartman, Charles & Mary Ann Hill, 9 Aug 1850; George L. Wilhelm, bondsman; J. S. Myers, wit.

Hartman, Charles A. & Christina L. Peeler, 26 Jan 1854; George W. Hartman, bondsman; James E. Kerr, wit.

Hartman, Charls A. & Sophia Cress, 12 March 1851; David Beaver, bondsman; J. S. Myers, wit.

Hartman, George & Catharine Freeze, 29 Dec 1804; James Blue, bondsman; A. L. Osborn, D. C., wit.

Hartman, George & Louisa Luterwick, 15 Aug 1846; Miles Rusher, bondsman; John H. Hardie Jr., wit.

Hartman, Georg W. & Catharine Phips, 30 Sept 1843; David Woodson, bondsman; J. H. Hardie, wit.

Hartman, Henry & _____, 30 April 1767; Wm. McCornely, Phill Brown, bondsmen; John Frohock, wit.

Hartman, Henry & Liddy Misoner, 7 April 1817; George Rusher, bondsman; Milo A. Giles, wit.

Hartman, Henry L. & Mary Ann Deaton, 5 Jan 1858; James E. Kerr, bondsman; John Wilkinson, wit. married 6 Jan 1858 by Peter Williamson.

Hartman, Jacob & Judah Owen, 4 June 1796; Henry Giles, bondsman; J. Troy, wit.

Hartman, Jacob & Tempy Baxter, 10 Sept 1810; John Hartman, bondsman; W. Ellis, J. P., wit.

Hartman, Jesse & Margaret Klutts, 22 May 1856; George L. Wilhelm, bondsman; H. R. Helper, wit. married 22 May 1856 by David Barringer, J. P.

Hartman, John & Ev____ Cobble, 3 May 1792; Adam Kauble, bondsman; Chs. Caldwell, wit.

Hartman, John & Eve Earnhart, 2 Oct 1798; Henry Earnhart, bondsman.

Hartman, John & Molly Smitters, 22 Jan 1799; Adam Coble, bondsman; Edwin J. Osborn, D. C., wit.

Hartman, John & Elizabeth Cathey, 28 Nov 1803; Tho. Todd, bondsman; A. L. Osborn, D. C., wit.

Hartman, John & Mary Bullon, 18 Oct 1815; Jacob Rusher, bondsman; Geo. Dunn, wit.

Hartman, John & Betsey Lentz, 1 Aug 1823; Henry Lentz, bondsman;
Jno Giles, wit.

Hartman, John & Margaret Eller, 4 Jan 1836; David Beaver,
bondsman; Hy. Giles, wit.

Hartman, John & Nancy Black, 21 Aug 1858; Henry Goodman, bondsman; James E. Kerr, wit. married 24 Aug 1858 by David
Barringer, J. P.

Hartman, John Sr. & Catharine Reeves, 30 May 1839; J. S. Myers,
bondsman; Jno Giles, wit.

Hartman, John B. & Emeline Gribble, 11 Oct 1861; J. S. Myers,
bondsman; Obadiah Woodson, wit.

Hartman, John Henry & Partha L. Ribelin, 4 Dec 1860; John Hartman, bondsman; Wm. Locke, wit. married 4 Dec 1860 by Wm
Lambeth, Baptist Minister.

Hartman, Othy & Rebeca Wiatt, 2 April 1835; Brantly Wiatt,
bondsman; J. H. Bringle, wit.

Hartman, P. H. & Malinda C. Earnheart, 9 Oct 1865; John Cauble,
bondsman; Obadiah Woodson, wit. married 19 Oct 1865 by W.
Kimball, Pastor of St. Pauls Church, Rowan.

Hartman, Peter & Liza Agner, 7 Nov 1810; George Rattz, bondsman;
Jno Giles, C. C., wit.

Hartman, Peter & Sally Hoffman, 17 April 1827; Abraham Lentz,
bondsman; J. H. Hardie, wit.

Hartman, Peter & Seany Brown, 5 Aug 1828; Benjamin Fraley,
bondsman; Hy. Giles, wit.

Hartman, West H. & Hannah Hill, 14 Nov 1853; Green Redwine,
bondsman; James E. Kerr, wit.

Hartman, William & Lavinia File, 4 Feb 1834; Alexander Hulin,
bondsman; Wm. Locke, wit.

Hartsill, Jonathan & Mary Beaver, 5 March 1792; Philip Dry,
bondsman.

Harwood, Henry & Martha Brian (no date, during Gov. Spaight's
admn.); Charles F. Mabins, bondsman.

Harwood, Jacob & Elizabeth Walser, 20 Dec 1804; David Walser,
bondsman; Moses A. Locke, wit.

Harwood, John & Esther Leine, 14 Dec 1792; William Harwood,
bondsman; Jos. Chambers, wit.

Harwood, Philip & Mary Wood, 3 May 1802; John Harwood, bondsman;
John Brem, wit.

Harwood, William & Sarah Tabor or Talor, 10 Sept 1818; Hezekiah
Smith Jr., bondsman; Jn March Sr., wit.

Harwood, Zacheriah & Rachel Griswell, 10 Sept 1793; Philip
Walser, bondsman; Jos. Chambers, wit.

Hasler, Peter & Lovy Freeman, 21 Feb 1852; married 4 March 1852
by Archd. Honeycutt, J. P.

Hath, Jarman & Betsey McKnight, 4 Nov 1796; John Hancock, bondsman; Jno Rogers, wit.

Hathman, Hezekiah & _____, _____; William Foy, bondsman; Jno Rogers, wit.

Hatley, Simeon & Susan Noah, 1 Oct 1858; John Hatly, bondsman; James E. Kerr, Clk., wit. married 3 Oct 1858 by E. Mauney, J. P.

Hatton, Charles & Jane Chambers, 31 Dec 1779; William Chambers, bondsman; B. Booth Boote, wit.

Haughton, Henderson & Judy Jenkins (colored), 16 Aug 1865; married 16 Aug 1865 by Z. Haughton, Pastor.

Haughton, Thomas G. & Ann Parker, 20 Feb 1860; L. Blackmer, bondsman; James E. Kerr, wit. married 20 Feb 1860 by Geo. B. Wetmore.

Haunberger, Henry & Elizabeth Cobble, 9 June 1803; Adam Cobble, bondsman; Adlai L. Osborn, D. C., wit.

Hawkings, Abraham & Sarah Dowell, 27 Oct 1798; James Dowell, bondsman; Wm. Henderson, wit.

Hawkins, John & Polly Goodman, 27 Dec 1796; John Crumpt, bondsman; Jno Rogers, wit.

Hawkins. John & Mary Pickler, 16 Nov 1824; Aquilla Cheshier, bondsman; Hy. Giles, wit.

Hawkins, Joseph A. & Jane G. Hall, 16 March 1844; Thomas Hall, bondsman; Obadiah Woodson, wit.

Hawkins, Joshua & Dorothy Beam, 8 April 1780; Thos. Beam, bondsman; Jno. Kerr, wit.

Hawkins, Thomas J. & Nancy J. Brown, 5 Feb 1826; Alexander Smoot, bondsman; Wm. Hawkins, J. P., wit.

Hawkins, William & Mary Allen, 19 Jan 1817; Jacob Allen, bondsman; R. Powell, wit.

Haworth, John & Rebecah Craven, 5 Aug 1819; Elijah Haworth, bondsman; Sol. Davis, J. P., wit.

Haworth, Josiah & Rebekah Lowmey, 24 April 1804; Jeremiah Haworth, bondsman; William Piggatt, J. P., wit.

Haworth, Micajah & Mary King, 29 Aug 1820; Joshua Fisher, bondsman; Silas Peace, wit.

Haworth, William & Elizabeth Stanley, 9 Dec 1817; Barnet Idol, bondsman; Sol. Davis, wit.

Hayes, Joseph & _____, _____; David Anderson, bondsman; Jno Rogers, wit.

Haynes, John & Margaret Andrew, 29 April 1783; James Andrews, bondsman.

Haynes, Thomas W. & Laura C. Brown, 14 May 1850; John H. Coffman, bondsman.

Hays, Charles & Catereny Mock, 28 Oct 1808; John Miller, bondsman; Jn March Sr., wit.

Hays, Charles & Martha Ratlidge, 25 Jan 1830; Wilson Rose, bondsman; L. R. Rose, J. P., wit.

Hays, David & Margret Blue, 10 Oct 1788; Douglass Blue, bondsman; Wm. Alexander, wit.

Hays, Jeremiah & Sarah Downs, 16 April 1825; Wm. Downs, bondsman; Hy. Giles, wit.

Headrick, Peter & Barbara Myers, 18 Feb 1797; Peter Smith, bondsman; Jno Rogers, wit.

Headrick, Philip & Molly Konrod, 19 Jan 1818; Jacob Konrod, bondsman; Ezekiel Brown, wit.

Heans, Phillip & Susanah Fray, 20 Oct 1801; Christian Heans, bondsman; Jno Monroe, wit.

Hearn, Moses & Betsey Hearn, 9 March 1803; Hugh Horah, bondsman; A. L. Osborn, D. C., wit.

Hearn, William & Ruth Skeal, 29 Nov 1799; Jacob Skeal, bondsman; Edwin J. Osborn, wit.

Hearn, William & Elizabeth Rily, 2 Sept 1817; Jarrot Harris, bondsman; Jno. Giles, wit.

Hearne, James & Elizabeth Miller, 9 May 1792; John Melker, bondsman; Chs. Caldwell, wit.

Heartley, Dennis & _____, 13 Feb 1813; John Shoaf, bondsman; Jno Giles, C. C., wit.

Heartley, Ruben & Joanna Green, 6 Nov 1798; Alexander Vickers, bondsman; Wm. Henderson, wit.

Heartley, Thomas & Maca Ann Lovelace, 12 Dec 1816; Samuel Dunning, bondsman; Roberts Nanny, wit.

Heathcock--see also Haithcock

Heathcock, James D. & Mary Ann Lentz, 7 June 1841; A. M. Miller, bondsman.

Heathman, James F. & Amanda Allen, 22 March 1853; Thomas D. Fraley, bondsman; J. S. Myers, wit.

Heathman, John N. & Nancy E. Thomason, 11 Sept 1854; John Rice, bondsman; J. S. Myers, wit.

Heathman, William & Dorcas Dent, 27 March 1821; Abner Hall, bondsman.

Hebel, Charles & Mollie Brown, 10 Jan 1866; Jacob DeHart, bondsman; Obadiah Woodson, wit.

Heddinger, Adam & Margaret Stoner, 17 Aug 1850; Nathan Heddings, bondsman; J. S. Myers, wit.

Heddinger, John & Fanny Earnheart, 8 Nov 1851; Adam Earnhart, bondsman; J. S. Myers, wit.

Hedgecok, Thomas & Elisabeth Wood, 10 July 1783; Hugh Davis, bondsman; John McNairy, wit.

Hedrick, Adam & Barbary Hageny, 30 Jan 1769; David Smith, Gasper Smith, bondsmen; Tho. Frohock, wit.

Hedrick, Adam & Susanah Loopp, 23 Jan 1821; Thomas Laning, bondsman; An. Swicegood, wit.

Hedrick, Peter & Maria Zink, 23 Jan 1810; Adam Snider, bondsman; George Snider, wit.

Hege, George & Elizabeth Grub, 13 or 18 March 1807; Friedr. Wm. Hertel, bondsman; Lazarus Hege, J. P., wit.

Hegler, John & Susan McGregory, 13 Dec 1803; Adam Heply, bondsman; A. L. Osborn, D. C., wit.

Heileig, James W. & Rachel L. Holshouser, 25 Dec 1841; Elias Lee, bondsman; J. S. Johnston, wit.

Heileig, John & Margaret Casper, 27 June 1850; Jacob Rusher, bondsman; J. S. Myers, wit.

Heilick, Simeon & Eliza Fraley, 21 July 1841; Jno. Jos. Bruner, bondsman; Susan T. Giles, wit.

Heilig, Allen H. & Mary Jane Julian, 29 April 1858; married by J. J. Summerell, J. P.

Heilig, David & Elizabeth Coleman (colored); married 5 Aug 1865 by A. J. Mocks, J. P.

Heilig, George M. or Green & Mary Ann Gluster, 10 Jan 1860; John F. Moose, bondsman; James E. Kerr, wit. married 10 Jan 1860 by A. S. Partee, J. P.

Heilig, George S. & Julia Ann Holshouser, 27 Aug 1857; James L. Brown, bondsman; James E. Kerr, wit. married 27 Aug 1857 by B. C. Hall.

Heilig, James M. & Margaret Ann Coon, 25 Oct 1860; John Klutts, bondsman; James E. Kerr, wit. married 25 Oct 1860 by Milo A. J. Raseman, J. P.

Heilig, James H. & Nancy C. Julian, 3 Oct 1864; Thomas McNeely, bondsman; Obadiah Woodson, wit.

Heilig, John F. & Amanda J. Heilig, 27 Sept 1865; Richard F. Graham, bondsman; Obadiah Woodson, wit. married 28 Sept 1865 by W. Kimball, Pastor of St. Pauls Ev. Luth. Church.

Heilig, Julius M. & Charlotte E. Moose, 16 July 1859; W. F. Fesperman, bondsman; married 19 July 1859 by B. C. Hall, Pastor.

Heilig, Richard A. & Luretta Miller, 5 Nov 1857; Wm. A. Brown, bondsman; J. S. Myers, wit. married 5 Nov 1857 by Samuel Rothrock, Minister of the Gospel in the Ev. Luth. Church.

Heiligh, Michael & Sally Josey, 4 March 1827; James Linn, bondsman; J. H. Hardie, wit.

Heinrich, George & Lucinda Moose, 12 Feb 1856; J. S. Myers, bondsman; James E. Kerr, wit. married 12 Feb 1856 by A. Baker, Pastor of the P. Church, Salisbury.

Helderbrand, Peter & Sophia Sanonea, 4 Nov 1824; George W. Grimes, bondsman.

Helfer, Daniel & Gartwood Nelson, 23 Aug 1825; Garret Nelson, L. R. Rose, J. P., wit.

Helfer, Hardie H. & Elizabeth Long, 16 May 1848; Jno. H. Hardie, bondsman.

Helfer, Henry & Mary Bradly, 19 July 1804; Jacob Helfer, bondsman; A. L. Osborn, D. C., wit.

Helfer, William & Clisa Mourey, 6 March 1843; T. C. McNeely, bondsman; J. H. Hardie, wit.

Hellard, David & Polly Owens, 10 Nov 1829; Jesse Hellard, bondsman.

Hellard, George & Katharine Shrock, 29 Jan 1793; Henry Shrock, bondsman.

Hellard, Jesse & Mary Swan, 24 Nov 1825; Jno. Fraley, bondsman; Hy. Giles, wit.

Helm, Peter & Leah Shoults, 5 Oct 1792; William Bodenhamer, bondsman; Jno Monro, wit.

Helmstetler, Daniel & Elizabeth Livengood, 11 Aug 1821; George Livangood, bondsman; An. Swicegood, wit.

Helmstler, Peter & Nancy Vannoy, 29 Sept 1787; Jaret Wood, bondsman; Spruce Macay, wit.

Helper, Daniel & Sally Brown, 25 Oct 1817; William Hawkins, bondsman; R. Powell, wit.

Helper, Jacob & Sary Husbands, 15 June 1805; John Helper, bondsman; Andrew Kerr, wit.

Helslay, Jacob & Nicy Brooks, 27 Sept 1814; Peter Winkler, bondsman; Jno Giles, C. C., wit.

Helton, Lifas & Milly Moorefield, 5 Nov 1792; Jacob Huff, bondsman; Jos. Chambers, wit.

Hembree, Joel & Eve Fite, 17 March 1828; Jacob Beaver, bondsman; Jno. H. Hardie, wit.

Hemphill, James Jr. & Elisabeth Patton, 23 Sept 1772; James Hemphill Sr., John Mackie, bondsmen; Max. Chambers, wit.

Hemphill, M. F. & Julia A. S. Thompson, 17 Dec 1856; James Tausay, bondsman; J. S. Myers, wit.

Hemphill, John & Agnes Herrill, 16 July 1783; Alexander Penny, bondsman; Robt. Hall, wit.

Henderson, A. & Mary S. Ferrand, 14 Dec 1840; C. K. Wheeler, bondsman.

Henderson, Agrippa & Leathe Etcheson, 16 May 1818; Sillis Eytcheson, bondsman; Jn March Sr., wit.

Henderson, Cornelius & Polly Hall (colored), 27 Aug 186⁵, married by Zuck Haughton.

Henderson, John & Cathrine Sulgrave, 27 Feb 1804; Silas Peace, bondsman; William Piggatt, wit.

Henderson, John & Elizabeth Whittica, 27 Feb 1830; Alfred Beck, bondsman; Wm. Hawkins, J. P., wit.

Henderson, John L. & Maria McConnaughey, 19 Jan 1855; Jos. F. Chambers, bondsman; married 23 Jan 1855 by John H. Parker, Minister of Prot. Epis. Church.

Henderson, John R. & Jane Foster, 14 May 1853; Chas. F. Baker, bondsman; Obadiah Woodson, wit. married 20 May 1853 by A. Baker, Pastor of the Presbyterian Church, Salisbury.

Henderson, Joseph & Margaret L. Wood, 30 Dec 1856; Owen N. Brown, bondsman; J. S. Myers, wit. married 30 Dec 1856 by R. G. Barrett, Pastor of the M. E. Church, South.

Henderson, Rufus G. & Euphemia S. Knox, 3 Oct 1849; Jos. F. Chambers, bondsman; J. S. Myers, wit.

Henderson, Samuel & Sarah Burnett, 8 Jan 1782; Mesheck Hodges, bondsman; Ad. Osborn, wit.

Henderson, William & Ezebal Ansley, 30 May 1804; Samuel McCurry, bondsman; William Piggatt, J. P., wit.

Henderson, William & Sarah C. Wilkerson, 1 April 1830; Geo. M. Harris, bondsman; Jno H. Hardie, wit.

Hendley, Washington & Sophia Fraley, 21 Dec 1826; William Briggs, bondsman; J. H. Hardie, wit.

Hendly, John & Ade Charmen, 18 Aug 1808; Willm. Ellis, bondsman; A. L. Osborn, wit.

Hendly, John & Nancy Vannetair, 25 Nov 1819; Richard Emerson, bondsman; Hy. Giles, wit.

Hendren, Oliver & Arania Ijams, 16 Aug 178_; Isaac Jones, bondsman.

Hendricks, Benjamin & Caty Crause, 3 Jan 1816; Joshua Hendricks, bondsman; Jn March Sr., wit.

Hendricks, David & Elizabeth Jones, 2 Feb 1815; Elijah Johnson, bondsman; Sol. Davis, J. P., wit.

Hendricks, George & Margaret Lewis, 1 Oct 1857; Adam Trexler, bondsman; James E. Kerr, wit. married 1 Oct 1857 by Moses Powlass, J. P.

Hendricks, George & Mary Doby, 14 Feb 1859; Paul A. Sifferd, bondsman; James E. Kerr, wit. married 4 May 1859 by D. R. Bradshaw, J. P.

Hendricks, Henry & Isabella Luckey, 27 March 1795; Lazarus Whitehead, bondsman; Ad. Osborn, wit.

Hendricks, Jacob & Franey Roland, 21 June 1792; John Hendricks, bondsman; Basil Gaither, wit.

Hendricks, Jesse & Elizebeth Adams, 15 Sept 1812; Philip Nail, bondsman; Jn March Sr., wit.

Hendricks, John & Sarah Lewis, 27 Dec 1780; James Hendricks, bondsman; H. Gifford, wit.

Hendricks, John & Elizabeth Holeman, 23 March 1815; William Humphreys, bondsman; R. Powell, wit.

Hendricks, Joseph & _____, 4 Aug 1779; William Forbes, bondsman; Jo. Brevard, wit.

Hendricks, Joshua & Margret Wolfskill, 8 April 1779; Joseph Wolfskill, bondsman; Ad. Osborn, wit.

Hendricks, Joshua & Franey Crouse, 15 Oct 1810; Daniel Crouse, bondsman; Jn March Sr., wit.

Hendricks, William & Margaret Wilkinson, 7 Jan 1794; John Brandon, bondsman; John Pinchback, Margret Hendricks, wit.

Hendricks, William & Mary Renshaw, 18 July 1830; Henry F. Willson, bondsman; L. R. Rose, J. P., wit.

Hendricks, William & Martha Steuart, 22 Oct 1785; John Hendricks, bondsman; Max. Chambers, wit.

Hendricks, William R. & Betsey Coon, 3 Oct 1810; James Hendricks, bondsman; Jno Giles, C. C., wit.

Hendrickson, John & Elizabeth Berry, 20 Dec 1784; Joseph Todd, Benjamin Todd, bondsmen; Max. Chambers, wit.

Hendrix, Amos & Elizabeth Hendricks, 14 Jan 1779; Tobias Hendrix, bondsman; Wm. R. Davie, wit.

Hendrix, Anderson & Peggey Myers, 21 Jan 1808; Rezin Park, bondsman; Jn March Sr., wit.

Hendrix, Daniel & Isbel Pendry, 23 July 1803; Saml. Pendry, bondsman; A. L. Osborn, D. C., wit.

Hendrix, Henry & Jane Hanely, 11 Feb 1792; Henry Shrock, bondsman; Chs. Caldwell, wit.

Hendrix, John & Elizabeth Howard, 6 May 1835; Gamaliel L. Allen, bondsman; C. Harbin, wit.

Hendrix, John & Eliza Welch, 15 Sept 1788; Thomas Welch, bondsman; W. Alexander, wit.

Hendrix, John & Lennie Hendren, 29 Jan 1803; George James, bondsman; Adlai L. Osborn, D. C., wit.

Hendrix, Thomas & Susannah Davis, 17 _____ 1819; Tho. Craige, bondsman.

Hendron, Beal W. & Nancy Hudson, 9 June 1814; William Hudson, bondsman; Jno. Giles, C. C., wit.

Heney, John & Fanny Bryan, married 9 May 1853 by Obadiah
Woodson, J. P.

Henley, Cubit & Mary Beam, 27 Feb 1807; Samuel Valk, bondsman.

Henley, William & Jenny Parks, 3 May 1791; Jas. Daniel, bondsman; Charles Caldwell, wit.

Henline, John & Elizabeth Owings, 19 Feb 1810; George March,
bondsman; Jn March Sr., wit.

Henly, Darby & Mary Young, 21 Sept 1787; J. G. Lauman, bondsman;
Spruce Macay, wit.

Henly, John D. & Sarah W. Kincaid, 1 June 1848; Thomas T. Locke,
bondsman; J. H. Hardie, Jr., wit.

Hennig, William & Eliza Sears, 3 May 1859; John M. Horah,
bondsman; Henry Horah, wit.

Henry, Elam T. & Amanda S. Belk, 30 Sept 1858; John L. Sloan,
bondsman; John Wilkinson, wit.

Henry, Hugh & Rosanna Robison, 4 Sept 1779; Jas. McBroom,
bondsman; Ad. Osborn, wit.

Henry, John & Fanny Bryan, 9 May 1853; Wm. M. Jacobs, bondsman;
J. S. Myers, wit.

Hepler, Thomas & Susannah Peck, 23 Jan 1821; John Peck, bondsman; Silas Peace, wit.

Hern, Jesse & Mary Fennell, 22 Dec 1801; Fredk. Fennell, bondsman; Jno. Brem, wit.

Herrel, Hugh & Rebeckah Lackin, 19 May 1787; Fanny Macay, wit.

Herris, Aron & Jennet Kennington, 22 April 1783; James Leven-
ford, bondsman.

Hess, Benjamine & Margaret M. Canup, 29 Jan 1866; S. C. Ketchy,
bondsman; Horatio N. Woodson, wit.

Hess, Charles & Nancy E. Eller, 27 Nov 1855; Chas. Almon, bondsman; J. S. Myers, wit. married 28 Nov 1855 by S. J. Peeler,
J. P.

Hess, Daniel & Lena Shuping 23 Feb 1831; Manchester Johnson,
bondsman; Hy. Giles, wit.

Hess, Elijah & Margaret Eller, 17 June 1847; Alexr. Parnell,
bondsman; John H. Hardie, wit.

Hess, George & Peggy Bullong, 19 May 1798; John Lobwader, bondsman; Ma. Troy, wit.

Hess, Henry O. & Elizabeth Taylor, 7 Oct 1865; H. C. Taylor,
bondsman; Obadiah Woodson, wit. married 8 Oct 1865 by Rev.
Wm. Lambeth.

Hess, J. A. & A. E. Stirewalt, 8 July 1859; J. R. Harris, bondsman; James E. Kerr, wit. married 12 July 1859 by Jas. M.
Wagner, Pastor.

Hess, John & Susannah Cryte, 19 April 1790; Martin Basinger, bondsman; C. Caldwell, D. C., wit.

Hess, John & Nancy Agner, 22 July 1823; Hy. Giles, bondsman.

Hess, John & Betsey Eller, 11 July 1829; Tobias Hess, bondsman; Jno. H. Hardie, wit.

Hess, John & Eve Ann Verble, 20 Sept 1854; Samuel W. Brown, bondsman; J. S. Myers, wit. married 21 Sept 1854 by S. J. Peeler, Esq.

Hess, John & Mary A. Eller, 6 Sept 1856; David R. Trexler, bondsman; J. S. Myers, wit. married 7 Sept 1856 by W. A. Walton, J. P.

Hess, John H. & Delia Swink, 26 Nov 1861; Henry Bassinger, bondsman; Obadiah Woodson, wit. married 26 Nov 1861 by Peter Williamson, J. P.

Hess, John N. & Elizabeth Correll, 27 Dec 1841; Caleb Shuping, bondsman; J. S. Hardie, wit.

Hess, Joseph & Molly Fellcer, 12 Nov 1827; Moses Lam, bondsman; J. H. Hardie, wit.

Hess, Joseph & Elizabeth Call, 13 Feb 1836; William Howard, bondsman; C. Harbin, wit.

Hess, Richard & Mary N. C. Wetchstine, 30 March 1864; Henry Basinger, bondsman; Obadiah Woodson, wit.

Hess, Tobias & Tensy Bullon, 12 Nov 1821; John Freedle, bondsman; Hy. Giles, wit.

Hess, Tobias & Nancy Stogdon, 6 May 1847; James Blue, bondsman; J. H. Hardie, Jr., wit.

Hess, Tobias & Clementine Blue, 19 March 1850; Henry Basinger, bondsman; J. S. Myers, wit.

Hess, William & Christena Hess, 19 Aug 1852; James W. Hatley, bondsman; J. S. Myers, wit.

Hetinger, Daniel & Sophia Eller, 2 Sept 1829; Isaac Eller, bondsman; Hy. Giles, wit.

Hetinger, John & Caty Eller, 15 Jan 1823; Jacob Eller, bondsman.

Hettinger, John & Fanny Earnheart, 8 Nov 1851; married 9 Nov 1851 by W. A. Walton, J. P.

Hettinger, Michael & Mary Ellor, 5 Aug 1795; John Eller, bondsman; J. Troy, wit.

Hewston, Joseph & Elizabeth Brandon, 8 June 1814; William Brandon, bondsman; Jno Giles, C. C., wit.

Hiatt, Allen & Rhoda Hunt, 19 Dec 1818; Alexr. Rea, bondsman; Thos. Hampton, wit.

Hibbets, James & Angess Johnson, 1 Dec 1790; Jno. Johnston, bondsman; C. Caldwell, wit.

Hickman, John & Nancy Patten, 31 Oct 1785; Wm. Patton, bondsman; Max. Chambers, wit.

Hickman, Joseph & Sally Steele, 9 March 1861; Hutson Valentine, bondsman; James E. Kerr, wit.

Hicks, Joshua & Diana Adams, 19 Sept 1794; Benjamin Hicks, bondsman; J. Troy, D. C., wit.

Hicks, Thomas & Elizabeth Deadman, 29 Oct 1787; Wm. Hamton, bondsman; Jno. Macay, wit.

Hide, Benjamin & Mary Endsly, 9 Jan 2775; Abel Armstrong, bondsman; Ad. Osborn, wit.

Hide, Benjamin & Margaret Hughs, 3 Aug 1774; Abel Armstrong, bondsman; Max Chambers, wit.

Hide, James & Lydia Cowan, 3 Dec 1808; Isaac Hughey, bondsman; A. L. Osborne, wit.

Hide, Joseph & Jane McBroom, 5 Dec 1832; William Barber, bondsman; John Giles, wit.

Hides, William & Jane Thompson, 1 Aug 1764; Francis Lock, bondsman; Thomas Frohock, wit.

Higdon, Joseph & Margaret Holbrook, 5 April 1786; Enoch Enochs, bondsman; John Macay, wit.

Higdon, Levi & Ann Barber, 10 Aug 1808; John B. Dent, bondsman; Tho. L. Cowan, wit.

Hightower, Leroy & Margarit Jacobs, 16 Aug 1800; Richd. Davis, bondsman.

Hileg, Michael & Sally Brown, 11 Nov 1829; Jeremiah Brown, bondsman.

Hileman, George & _____, 12 Sept 1814; John Hileman, bondsman; Geo. Dunn, wit.

Hileman, John & Peggy Beaver, 8 Aug 1811; George Bever, bondsman; Jno Giles, C. C., wit.

Hilick, John & Sophia Fesperman, 27 May 1834; Philip Litacar, bondsman; Hy. Giles, wit.

Hill, Abram & Lydia Morgan, 26 April 1839; Daniel Weaver, bondsman; John Giles, wit.

Hill, Abram & Catharine R. Lynbarger, 31 May 1859; James Nathan Morgan, bondsman; James E. Kerr, wit. married 31 May 1859 by Levi Trexler, J. P.

Hill, Archibald & Polly Mowrey, 23 April 1828; Alexander Lamb, bondsman; Jno. H. Hardie, wit.

Hill, David & _____, 23 March 1804; John Andrews, bondsman; Ad. Osborn, wit.

Hill, Abram & Elizabeth A. Hill, 25 March 1819; Henry Hill, bondsman; Jno Giles, wit.

Hill, Godfrey & Aley Filhour (colored), 21 April 1866; Hiel
Filhour, bondsman; Obadiah Woodson, wit.

Hill, Guy & Anny Seaford, 6 Jan 1846; Thomas Rimer, bondsman;
J. H. Hardie Jr., wit.

Hill, Henry & Anne Lam, 11 Sept 1815; John Darden, bondsman;
Mary Giles, D. C., wit.

Hill, Henry & Mary Ann Glover, 2 Dec 1865; Cornelius O. Smith,
bondsman; Obadiah Woodson, wit.

Hill, Henry W. & Elizabeth Pool, 13 Jan 1847; Otho Z. Pool,
bondsman; Jno. H. Hardie, wit.

Hill, Henry W. & Christina R. Yost, 6 March 1856; Henry Hill,
bondsman; James E. Kerr, wit. married 6 March 1856 by J. H.
Enniss, J. P.

Hill, Isaac & Mary Barnes, 12 Jan 1768; John Hunter, bondsman;
J. McEwen, wit.

Hill, Isaac & Margaret Pines, 7 Dec 1815; William Dickson,
bondsman; Jno. Giles, C. C., wit.

Hill, Isaac & Elizabeth Roblin, 20 March 1823; David Barns,
bondsman.

Hill, Jacob & Rachel Morgan, 27 Jan 1823; David Barns, bondsman.

Hill, John & Margret Logan, 22 June 1769; James Hill, Jas. Macay,
bondsmen; consent from James Logan, 21 June 1769.

Hill, John & Mary Lynn, widow, 4 Jan 1780; Joseph Childes,
bondsman; B. Booth Boote, wit.

Hill, John & Anna Hicks, 8 Aug 1801; William Hall, bondsman;
Jno Brem, D. C., wit.

Hill, John & Saneth Andrews, 31 Dec 1811; George Andrews, bondsman; Jno Giles, C. C., wit.

Hill, John & Sally Dedman, 30 Dec 1817; Stephen Caton, bondsman;
Roberts Nanny, wit.

Hill, John & Sarah Mecenhimmer, 24 Jan 1846; Henry W. Hill,
bondsman; J. M. Turner, wit.

Hill, Milas & Caroline Montgomery, 18 April 1855; G. W. Weant,
bondsman; J. S. Myers, wit. married 18 April 1855 by Wm.
Lambeth.

Hill, Moses & Sophia Pool, 31 March 1825; Jacob Hill, bondsman;
W. Harris, wit.

Hill, Richard & Lemender Hampton, 28 Feb 1811; Davd Hampton,
bondsman; Jn March Sr., wit.

Hill, Richard B. & Mary McB. Fisher, 5 May 1846; Jno. B. Lord,
bondsman.

Hill, Ruben & Sarah Rice, 23 Dec 1802; Henry Hill, bondsman;
Hudson Hughes, wit.

Hill, Rufus A. & Ally Park, 29 June 1853; Augustus W. Park, bondsman; Levi Trexler, wit.

Hill, Seth & Betsy Lamb, 9 Feb 1822; Henry Hill Jr., bondsman.

Hill, Shadrick & Susey Barns, 5 Oct 1815; William Bateman, bondsman; Jno Giles, C. C., wit.

Hill, Thomas & Rachael Smith, 6 Oct 1779; Benj. Rounsavall, bondsman; Jo Brevard, wit.

Hill, Thomas & Betsy Rudisil, 20 Jan 1807; Lewis Beard, bondsman; A. L. Osborn, D. C., wit.

Hill, Thomas & Mary C. McConnaughey, 1 Dec 1858; B. R. Moore, bondsman; John Wilkinson, wit. married 8 Dec 1858 by T. G. Haughton, Rector.

Hill, William & Polly Pegginger, 11 Dec 1818; Michael McKein, bondsman; Jno Giles, wit.

Hill, William J. & Milly Pool, 23 Nov 1841; Henry Hill Jr., bondsman; Jno H. Hardie, wit.

Hill, William J. & Avaline Black, 30 Aug 1847; Alexander Lamb, bondsman; J. H. Hardie, Jr., wit.

Hill, William J. & Rachel H. Shepherd, 12 July 1851; John L. Hill, bondsman; J. S. Myers, wit. married 17 July 1851 by Levi Trexler, J. P.

Hillard, David & Jane Williams, 7 Feb 1786; R. Pearson, bondsman; W. W. Erwin, wit.

Hillis, Robert & Sarah McDowell, 1 April 1776; Will. McDowell, bondsman; Ad. Osborn, wit.

Hilton, Elifus & Easter Rupart, 24 March 1807; Wm. Coker, bondsman; Jn. March Sr., wit.

Hilton, Joseph & Rebecah Johnson, 10 Feb 1807; William Glascock, bondsman; Jn March Sr., wit.

Hilton, Lemuel & Elizabeth Maddox, 19 March 1817; Saml. Jones, bondsman; T. Hampton, wit.

Hine, John & Phebe Philips, 7 May 1818; Henry Davis, bondsman; Sol. Davis, J. P., wit.

Hines, Cornelius & Sarah Yarberry, 1 Dec 1816; Wm. Jones, bondsman; Sol. Davis, J. P., wit.

Hines, Frederick & Pheby Grimes, 11 Feb 1811; Samuel Barnacasel, bondsman; W. Ellis, J. P., wit.

Hines, John & Chorysas Pate, 10 Dec 1815; Allen Rice, bondsman; Sol. Davis, J. P., wit.

Hinkle, Benjamin & Maryan Harwood, 16 June 1812; Jacob March, bondsman; Jn March Sr., wit.

Hinkle, Charles & Susana March 13 May 1797; Jacob March, bondsman; Jno. Rogers, wit.

Hinkle, David & Polly Sanders, 21 Dec 1820; Francis Sanders, bondsman; R. Powell, wit.

Hinkle, George & Frances Shaffer, 17 Sept 1795; John Mull, bondsman; J. Troy, wit.

Hinkle, Henry & Catharine Glasscock, 13 Jan 1820; Abraham Keller, bondsman; R. Powell, wit.

Hinkle, John & Mary Rosenbum, 26 Feb 1790; Jacob Hinkle, bondsman; Jno Monro, wit.

Hinkle, Mathias & Barbary Shofe, 28 Nov 1813; Jacob Shoaf, bondsman; Joseph Clarke, wit.

Hinkle, Michael & Sarah Beecham, 26 Nov 1787; Cornelius Howard, bondsman; Mat. Troy, wit.

Hinkle, Peter & Elizabeth Wilson, 3 Feb 1829; Alexr. Beard, bondsman; Jno Giles, wit.

Hinkle, William & Elenda Hunter, 11 Dec 1793; Joseph Dial, bondsman; B. John Pinchback, Lydia Pinchback, wit.

Hipler, Philip & Elizabeath Fouts, 19 Dec 1815; Michael Myers, bondsman; Silas Peace, wit.

Hisenhour, Michael & Barbary Agleston, 11 July 1799; Peter Hisenour, bondsman.

Hitchcock, Asell & Hannah Teague, 16 June 1808; Elisha Hitchcock, bondsman; Solomon Davis, J. P., wit.

Hitchcock, Elisha & Elizabeth Idol, 27 July 1802; David Smith, bondsman; Wm. Welborn, wit.

Hitchcock, Isaac & Sarah Hayworth, 17 Nov 1814; Joseph Idol, bondsman; Sol. Davis, wit.

Hitchcock, William & Ruth Mcolline, 28 Sept 1813; Absalom Lowe, bondsman; Sol. Davis, J. P., wit.

Hodge, Abram A. & Nancy Morgan, 13 April 1854; Jacob Morgan, bondsman; Levi Trexler, wit. married 13 April 1854 by Levi Trexler, J. P.

Hodge, George & Elizabeth Parker, 27 March 1805; Joseph Hughes, bondsman; A. L. Osborn, D. C., wit.

Hodge, Jesse & Ruhammah Palmer, 3 Dec 1811; John Park, bondsman; Henry Allemong, wit.

Hodge, John F. & Camilla L. Klutts, 24 July 1858; William Miller, bondsman; James E. Kerr, wit. married 24 July 1858 by Wm. T. Marlin, J. P.

Hodge, William & Patsey Tucker, 14 Nov 1809; Jonathan West, bondsman; A. Hunt, wit.

Hodgens, George & Elizabeth Campbell, 18 July 1825; William Knup, bondsman; Hy. Giles, wit.

Hodgens, John P. & Nancy S. Haden, 1 Aug 1816; Thos. C. Jones, bondsman; Roberts Nanny, wit.

Hodges, Jesse & Philpeny Isahour, 6 Jan 1852; Wiley Morgan, bondsman; Levi Trexler, wit.

Hoffman, Daniel & Margaret L. Peeler, 7 July 1863; William A. Walton, bondsman; Obadiah Woodson, wit.

Hoffman, David A. & Nellie Emma Graham, 9 Oct 1861; William A. Hoffman, bondsman; Obadiah Woodson, wit.

Hoffman, Michael & Christina Holdhouser, 19 Oct 1816; Frederick Holdhouser, bondsman; Ezra Allemong, wit.

Hoffman, Michael C. & Nancy Eagle, 1 March 1866; John Eagle, bondsman; Obadiah Woodson, wit.

Hoffner, Nathan J. & Clementine L. Bringle, 7 July 1860; married 8 July 1860 by Levi Trexler, J. P.

Hofman, Daniel & Jane Williams, 21 Sept 1835; James Porter, bondsman; John Giles, wit.

Hofner, George & Liza Peeler, 21 Feb 1812; John Peeler, bondsman; Jno. Giles, C. C., wit.

Hofner, Martin & Susanna Clutz, 26 Feb 1812; Leonard Kluttz, bondsman; Geo. Dunn, wit.

Hofner, Martin & Lea Hofner, 13 March 1838; Andrew Earnhart, bondsman; Hy. Giles, wit.

Hofner, Leonard & Jarushey Morgan, 14 Nov 1836; Reuben Harkey, bondsman.

Hoggatt, Aaron & Tabitha Hambleton, 25 July 1798; John Cornes, bondsman; Geo. Fisher, wit.

Hoggatt, Warner & Martha Hunt, 27 Sept 1821; William English, bondsman; Z. Hunt, wit.

Hogstan, Arcbald & Anne Stone, 16 Oct 1779; Jas. Hacket, bondsman; Jo. Brevard, wit.

Hoitses, John & Anna Margretta Toll(in), 22 Feb 1770; Jacob Bonn, Nicholas Toll, bondsmen; Jacob Lintz, wit.

Holbrook, Caleb & Priscilla Baker, 1 April 1780; Ab. Baker, bondsman; Jno Kerr, wit.

Holbrook, William & Sarah Baker, 14 May 1785; Caleb Holbrook, bondsman; H. Magoune, wit.

Holbrooks, James F. & Matilda Bostian, 2 Oct 1859; Jacob M. Richey, bondsman; James E. Kerr, wit. married 2 Oct 1859 by C. S. Partee, J. P.

Holder, Alphonso G. & Susan Smith, 4 Nov 1851; Chas. D. Smith, bondsman; married 5 Nov 1851 by Jno H. Coffman.

Holderfield, Val. & Henny Noland, 13 April 1789; John Loury, bondsman; Wall. Alexander, wit.

Holderman, Abraham & Enny Stirewalt, 1 Jan 1825; Samuel Lemly, bondsman.

Holdsouser, John & Sally Coldiron, 17 Feb 1817; Enoch Phillips, bondsman; Roberts Nanny, wit.

Holebough, George & Susannah Savage, 13 June 1787; Henry Beroth, bondsman; Jno Macay, wit.

Holeman, Daniel & Anne Sanders, 28 Dec 1772; James Sanders, bondsman; Ad. Osborn, wit.

Holeman, David & Rachel Frost, 8 Nov 1798; Ebenezar Frost, bondsman; Jno. L. Henderson, wit.

Holeman, Isaac & Lissis Nichols, 25 Aug 1804; David Holeman, bondsman; J. Hunt, wit.

Holeman, Jacob & Liddy Pinchback, 23 Nov 1795; John Thomas Pinchback, bondsman; J. Troy, wit.

Holeman, Thomas & Margret Sutherland, 16 May 1778; Daniel Sutherland, bondsman; Ad. Osborn, wit.

Holeman, William & Martha Pinchback, 28 Dec 1799; Jno. T. Pinchback, bondsman; Edwin J. Osborn, D. C., wit.

Holland, John & Christiana Robison, 26 Aug 1783; Alexr. Gunn, bondsman; T. H. McCaule, wit.

Holland, Richard & Nisian Taylor, 30 Nov 1775; Adlai Osborn, bondsman.

Hollar, John & Margaret Low, 19 Oct 1794; Martin Basinger, bondsman; Mat. Troy, C., wit.

Hollenaugh, John & Elizabeth Barberick, 27 Jan 1780; Lawrence Snapp, bondsman.

Hollis, William & Elizabeth Reed, 15 Feb 1790; Eldad Reid, bondsman; Ed. Harris, wit.

Holloway, D. F. & E. L. Misenheimer, 16 Sept 1857; Wm. F. Fesperman, bondsman; J. S. Myers, wit. married 16 Sept 1857 by B. C. Hall.

Hollsbouser, Wendle & Sophia Clutz, 16 Nov 1801; Jacob Clutz, bondsman; Jno Brem, wit.

Holman, Isaac & Mary Neely, 8 Aug 1825; Richmond Glasscock, bondsman; L. R. Rose, J. P., wit.

Holman, Jeremiah & Sarah Pinchback, 7 Jan 1802; Jno. T. Pinchback, bondsman; Jno Brem, wit.

Holman, Joseph & Elizabeth Wilson, 12 April 1768; Oliver Wallis, bondsman; Tho. Frohock, wit. consent from James Wilson, 11 April 1768.

Holman, Wilson & Elizabeth Turner, 22 Oct 1832; Ephram Gaither, bondsman; Thomas McNeely, J. P., wit.

Holmes, Ezra & Jincy Miller, 10 Dec 1814; Conrad Stoner, bondsman; Jno Giles, C. C., wit.

Holmes, James & Mary Nail, 4 March 1772; William Bell, bondsman; Thomas Frohock, wit. consent from James Nail, 4 March 1772, William Bell, wit.

Holmes, John & Susannah Blackwell, 9 Dec 1793; Isaac Blackwood, bondsman; B. John Pinchback, Lydia Pinchback, wit.

Holmes, John D. & Sally Crider, 5 Jan 1815; Wm. Dickson, bondsman; Henry Allemong, wit.

Holmes, R. J. & Rose S. C. Heilig, 17 Aug 1852; Martin Richwine, bondsman; J. S. Myers, wit.

Holmes, Richard & Elizabeth McGauhey, 1 Jan 1781; James McFeeters, bondsman.

Holmes, Robert & Mary Luckie, 2 Dec 1769; John Mitchel, Wm. Steele, bondsmen; Thomas Frohock, wit. consent from Robert Luckie, father of Mary.

Holmes, Thomas & Barbara Crider, 25 Jan 1803; Danl Cress, bondsman; F. Coupee, A. L. Osborn, D. C., wit.

Holmes, Thomas & Susanna Smith, 4 Feb 1818; Jesse Whitaker, bondsman; R. Powell, wit.

Holms, Jesse & Nancy Owen, 9 Feb 1811; Jas. Smith, bondsman; Geo. Dunn, wit.

Holms, Rubin & Elizabeth Freeling, 10 Oct 1811; Jno H. Freeling, bondsman; Jn March Sr., wit.

Holobaugh, George & Catherine Fraley, 21 Dec 1810; Peter Egan, bondsman; Ezra Allemong, wit.

Holobaugh, John & Peggy Enness, 21 April 1813; Abraham Earnhart, bondsman; Ezra Allemong, wit.

Holshauser, Henry & Barbary Lingle, 14 Dec 1802; Peter Trautman, bondsman; Adlai L. Osborn, D. C., wit.

Holshoser, Andrew & Sophia Klutts, 9 March 1835; Joseph Miller, bondsman; Jno. H. Hardie, wit.

Holshoser, Montford & Peane Paine, 26 Aug 1837; Tobias L. Lemly, bondsman; T. L. Lemly, wit.

Holshoulser, Paul & Eleanor Lentz, 21 April 1851; Mathise M. Lentz, bondsman; J. S. Myers, wit.

Holshoulser, Paul & Margaret Hudgins, 16 June 1856; J. S. Myers, bondsman.

Holshous, Wiley M. & Margaret Holshouser, 18 Dec 1851; Jacob Rusher, bondsman; J. S. Myers, wit.

Holshouser, Alexander & Sophia L. Bost, 9 March 1866; Jacob Klutts, bondsman; Obadiah Woodson, wit.

Holshouser, Alex. L. & Saloma Miller, 25 March 1830; David Linn, bondsman.

Holshouser, Andrew & Leah Klutts, 7 Nov 1859; Henry Peeler, bondsman; James E. Kerr, wit.

Holshouser, Andrew Jr. & Mary Cauble, 21 Dec 1825; John Travis, bondsman.

Holshouser, Casper & Sally Barger, 21 May 1811; Henry Barger, bondsman; Geo. Dunn, wit.

Holshouser, Charles & E. Klutts, 21 Aug 1838; Joseph Miller, bondsman.

Holshouser, Crawford & Elizabeth Harkey, 6 Nov 1865; J. A. W. Corel, bondsman; Horatio N. Woodson, wit.

Holshouser, Eli & Laura C. Miller, 29 Nov 1859; C. M. Holshouser, bondsman; John Wilkinson, wit. married 7 Dec 1859 by Saml Rothrock, Minister of the Gospel in the Ev. Luth. Church.

Holshouser, Elihu & Mary Ann Cameron, 19 Oct 1858; A. M. Sullivan, bondsman; F. W. Scott, J. P., wit. married 21 Oct 1859 by Saml. Rothrock, Minister of the Gospel in the E. Luth. Church.

Holshouser, Frederick & Teany Miller, 12 March 1824; Casper Holshouser, bondsman.

Holshouser, Jacob & Rachel Brown, 10 Jan 1829; Elihu Houlshouser, bondsman; J. H. Hardie, wit.

Holshouser, Jacob & Anny Beaver, 18 April 1850; Paul Haulsholser, bondsman; J. S. Myers, wit.

Holshouser, Jacob & Delila Nowrey, 26 Dec 1837; Daniel Bieler (Peeler), bondsman.

Holshouser, Jacob Jr. & Catharine Holshouser, 6 Sept 1842; Obadiah Hampton, bondsman; John H. Hardie, wit.

Holshouser, Jacob R. & Sarah Lyerly, 13 Feb 1860; Andrew L. Kluttz, bondsman; Wm. Locke, wit. married 23 Feb 1860 by Thornton Butler, V. D. M.

Holshouser, James & Sally Klutts, 20 April 1847; Calvin Cress, bondsman; J. S. Myers, wit.

Holshouser, John & Mary Holshouser, 2 Nov 1829; David Holtshouser, bondsman; Jno H. Hardie, wit.

Holshouser, John & Julia Ann Earnhart, 23 Feb 1858; James E. Kerr, bondsman; John Wilkinson, wit. married 24 Feb 1858 by Saml. Rothrock, Minister of the Gospel in the Ev. Luth. Church.

Holshouser, John & Pauline Cauble, 30 Jan 1837; Andrew Holshouser, bondsman; Jno. Giles, wit.

Holshouser, John Rufus & Trissa Caroline Overcash, 31 Aug 1865; John N. Hess, bondsman; Horatio N. Woodson, wit. married 31 Aug 1865 by Rev. Wm. Lambeth.

Holshouser, Michael & Betsey Miller, 19 March 1803; Elijah Snap, bondsman; Adlai L. Osborn, D. C., wit.

Holshouser, Milas A. & Sophia L. Peeler, 10 Apr 1854; Henrey G. Lentz, bondsman; J. S. Myers, wit. married 13 April 1854 by Saml Rothrock, Minister of the Gospel in the Ev. Luth. Church.

Holshouser, Otho & Laura M. Brown, 8 March 1864; P. A. Heilig, bondsman; Obadiah Woodson, wit.

Holshouser, Paul & Mary L. Peeler, 4 Aug 1851; Henry Peeler Jr., bondsman; J. S. Myers, wit.

Holshouser, Paul & Catharine C. Trexler, 10 Feb 1863; Martin Richwine, bondsman; Obadiah Woodson, wit.

Holshouser, Sampson & Elizabeth Cotton, 7 Feb 1852; Ransom Burnes, bondsman; James E. Kerr, wit.

Holshouser, Wiley & Mary Lukebill, 17 Feb 1849; John Crook, bondsman; Jno H. Hardie Jr., wit.

Holshouser, Wilie M. & Margaret Holshouser, 18 Dec 1851; married 18 Dec 1851 by E. E. Philips, J. P.

Holshouser, William & Barbara Holshouser, 27 April 1847; Henry Fesperman, bondsman; J. H. Hardie, wit.

Holt, A. L. & Miss Sarah L. Petrea, 20 Dec 1865; R. W. Petrea, bondsman; H. N. Woodson, wit.

Holt, John A. & Augusta M. Riter, 10 Arpil 1852; Jas. Slater, bondsman; James E. Kerr, wit. married 13 April 1852 by John H. Parker.

Holtamon, Joseph & Eliza Tate, 10 June 1829; Fredk. Stirewalt, bondsman; J. H. Hardie, wit.

Holton, Thomas & Margaret Coupee, 8 Aug 1817; Benjamin P. Pearson, bondsman; Jno Giles, wit.

Holtshoser, Wiley & Margaret Garner, 11 April 1840; Benjamin Beaver, bondsman.

Holtshouse, Andrew & Poley Pool, 21 Dec 1798; John Pool, bondsman; Edwin J. Osborn, D. C., wit.

Holtshouser, Andrew & Nancy Hampton, 2 Jan 1822; Ezra Allemong, bondsman; Hy. Giles, wit.

Holtshouser, David & Nelly Fisher, 30 Aug 1826; Hy. Giles, bondsman.

Holtsmer, Isaac & Mary Wiles, 3 Jan 1866; Christian Bosock, bondsman; Obadiah Woodson, wit.

Honbagar, Elias & Anny Wilhelm, 24 Jan 1852; Valentine Propst, bondsman; J. S. Myers, wit.

Honbarger, Henry & Catharine Earnhart, 30 Oct 1837; Henry Giles, bondsman.

Honeycut, Rufus R. & Dorcas Permilla Leazar, 17 March 1855; John D. Hobbs, bondsman; James E. Kerr, wit. married 19 March 1855 by D. R. Bradshaw, J. P.

Honeycut, Tobias & Esther C. Weant, 15 March 1848; Wm. W. Jacobs, bondsman; J. H. Hardie, wit.

Honeycutt, David W. & Mary L. Umstead, 8 July 1854; Martin Richwine, bondsman; J. S. Myers, wit. married 9 July 1854 by Jas. Merphy, Pastor of the M. E. C. So.

Hooker, A. H. & Leah Louisa Bostian, 13 Nov 1865; G. M. Beaver, bondsman; Obadiah Woodson, wit.

Hooker, Allen H. & Ann Bostian, 4 April 1853; Jos. Henderson, bondsman; J. S. Myers, wit.

Hooker, Benjamin & Mary Parks, 13 Dec 1862; Burgess G. Cranford, bondsman; Obadiah Woodson, wit.

Hooks, George & Elizabeth Phillips, 5 July 1857; Peter Rough, bondsman; J. S. Myers, wit. married 5 July 1857 by Peter Williamson, J. P.

Hooks, William & Anna Parks, 1 Aug 1864; Jacob O. Miller, bondsman; Obadiah Woodson, wit.

Hooks, Willoby & Anna Kritz, 23 Jan 1793; Thomas Scrivener, bondsman; Jos. Chambers, wit.

Hoose, Henry & Betsey Murry, 30 June 1840; David Woodson, bondsman; Jno. Giles, wit.

Hootsman, Daniel & Mary Kern, 4 Nov 1800; Jacob Lyerly, bondsman; John Brem, wit.

Hoover, Frederick & Esther Wooliver, 19 Nov 1813; Jacob Woollever, bondsman; Henry Allemong, wit.

Hoover, Jacob & Polly Hufman, 24 Oct 1809; Jacob Hufman, bondsman; W. Ellis, J. P.

Hoover, Jacob & Susanna McDaniel, 15 Sept 1821; William Atchason, bondsman; Saml. Jones, wit.

Hopkins, Alsey & Polly Corl, 12 Dec 1840; David Corle, bondsman; J. L. Beard, wit.

Hopkins, Edward & Jenny Ellis, 6 Feb 1819; Radford Ellis, bondsman; Henry Giles, wit.

Hopkins, Edward & Patience Coggins, 11 Oct 1825; James Daniel, bondsman; Hy. Giles, wit.

Hopkins, James & Mary Ellis, 19 Jan 1822; Absalom Wall, bondsman; Hy. Giles, wit.

Hopper, Thomas & Nancy Stewart, 16 Feb 1791; John Moulder, bondsman.

Horah, Franklin & Margaret Reeves, 22 June 1852; Elijah Renshaw, bondsman; J. S. Myers, wit. married 23 June 1852 by Jas. P. Simpson, M. E. C. S.

Horah, George & Sophia Klutts, 29 Feb 1864; Joseph Horah, bondsman; Robt. Murphy, wit.

Horah, Henry & Nancey Hampton, 12 Feb 1784; Jno. McNairy, bondsman; Jno. McNairy, wit.

Horah, Hugh & Mary Moore, 14 Jan 1788; Henry Horah, bondsman; J. McEwin, wit.

Horah, John M. & Margaret S. Ballard, 20 Oct 1847; Benj. Julian, bondsman.

Horah, Robert M. & Emelia B. Ballard, 24 March 1840; James Biles, bondsman; J. L. Beard, D. C., wit.

Horah, William H. & Louisa Furrer, 6 Jan 1814; Saml. Lemly, bondsman; Geo. Dunn, wit.

Horn, John & Elizabeth Woods, 12 Feb 1805; Edward Canter, bondsman; J. Hunt, wit.

Horn, Stephen & Polley Eaton, 26 Dec 1824; Lewis White, bondsman; E. Brock, J. P., wit.

Horn, Thomas & Rebeckah Brandon, 4 Jan 1827; Abel McNeely, bondsman; Thomas McNeely, J. P., wit.

Hornbarrier, William & Elizabeth Coldiron, 22 Oct 1793; George Coldiron, bondsman; Jos. Chambers, wit.

Hornbarringer, George A. & Mary Fullenwider, 18 June 1839; Matthew Jones, bondsman; John Giles, wit.

Hornbeak, John & Martha A. Bracken, 21 Dec 1824; George Rex, bondsman; Hy. Giles, wit.

Hornberger, Daniel & Catharine Lingle, 6 Nov 1804; Henry Hornberger, bondsman; A. L. Osborn, D. C., wit.

Horney, John & Mary Caldwel, 15 Jan 1803; Philip Horney, bondsman.

Horsler, Michael & Polly Cotton, 16 July 1791; Martin Basinger, bondsman; C. Caldwell, D. C., wit.

Hoskins, John & Mary Dowell, 15 Jan 1794; William Howard, bondsman; G. Enochs, wit.

Hoskins, John & Sally Oaks, 9 July 1821; Andrew Griffin, bondsman; Geo. Coker, wit.

Hosler, Peter & Lovy Freeman, 21 Feb 1852; John Lentz, bondsman; James E. Kerr, wit.

Houck, George & Margaret Bell, 24 May 1824; William Houck, bondsman; Hy. Giles, wit.

Houck, George & Elizabeth J. McCorkle, 13 Dec 1830; Henry Houck, bondsman; Hy. Giles, wit.

Houck, Henry & Mary A. McCorkle, 7 Dec 1824; Jno. Utzman, bondsman; Hy. Allemong, wit.

Houck, William & Mary Hartzog, 21 April 1803; Michael Baker, bondsman; Adlai L. Osborn, D. C., wit.

Houck, William A. & Catharine L. Fisher, 10 Nov 1852; Samuel F. Crimminger, bondsman; James E. Kerr, wit.

Houk, David & Rosena Garber, 21 Sept 1801; George Houk, bondsman.

Houk, Felix & Catharine Mock, 13 June 1793; Jno. Monro, bondsman; James Arnett, wit.

Houke, George & Barbara Houke, 27 Aug 1801; Jacob Baker, bondsman; Jno Brem, D. C., wit.

.ldson, James & Susanna Enez, 14 July 1779; Thos. Sherriff, bondsman; Jo. Brevard, wit.

Houlshouser, Andrew & Betsy Barger, 25 Dec 1813; Francis Gardiner, bondsman; Geo. Dunn, wit.

Houlshouser, David & Christena Clutz, 8 June 1818; Andrew Holshouser, bondsman; Roberts Nanny, wit.

Houlshouser, Elihu & Polly Clutz, 10 Oct 1823; David Holshuser, bondsman.

Houlshouser, Frederick & Sally Peeler, 21 Feb 1812; Daniel Boger, bondsman; Jno Giles, C. C., wit.

Houltz, Thomas & Catherina Barbuck, widow, 2 Nov 1771; Paul Red Smith, Adam Biffel, bondsmen; Thomas Frohock, wit.

Houpt, Valentine & Jeane Watts, 29 Nov 1787; Wm. Watts, bondsman; Ad. Osborn, wit.

House, Daniel & Leah Smith, 15 March 1845; Jno. F. Stirewalt, bondsman.

House, Henry & Peggy Walton, 20 Oct 1825; Jacob Dayvault, bondsman; Jno Giles, wit.

House, Henry & Polly Mowery, 30 Aug 1854; David Cauble, bondsman; J. S. Myers, wit. married 31 Aug 1854 by E. E. Philips, J. P.

House, Jacob & Betsy Freeze, 20 Jan 1816; Peter Freese, bondsman; Geo. Dunn, wit.

House, James Henry & Sarah M. Eagle, 31 Jan 1856; George A. Eagle, bondsman; J. S. Myers, wit. married by H. S. Robard, J. P., 31 Jan 1856.

Houser, George & Peggy Agle, 21 July 1810; George Agle, bondsman; Geo. Dunn, wit.

Houser, Jacob & Elizabeth Snider, 27 July 1800; John Snider, bondsman.

Houser, Jacob & Jane Uptegrove, 29 March 1811; John Snyder, bondsman; John Hanes, wit.

Houser, Jacob & Mary Yarrel, 16 April 1814; George Hanes, bondsman; Saml. Jones, wit.

Houser, Jacob & Sarah West, 24 March 1815; Samuel Deane, bondsman; Jno Giles, wit.

Houston, James & Martha A. Lowrance, 17 Feb 1859; O. P. Houston, bondsman; married 22 Feb 1859 by S. C. Alexander.

Houston, James & Asenath Brevard, 24 Sept 1774; Joseph Dickson, bondsman; Ad. Osborn, wit. consent from Robt. Brevard, 24 Sept. 1774.

Houston, John & Margaret Barr, 19 Sept 1823; Hy. Giles, bondsman.

Houston, John C. & Polly Graham, 30 May 1804; John Baker, bondsman; A. L. Osborn, D. C., wit.

Howard, Alpheus & Hannah Kincaid, 20 Oct 1830; Joseph Blackwell, bondsman; Jno H. Hardie, wit.

Howard, Benjamin & Nancy Luckey, 19 Dec 1819; Jacob Krider, bondsman; Jno Giles, wit.

Howard, Benjamin & Sarah Stephens, 7 Nov 1812; Benjamin Dulin, bondsman; Jn March Sr., wit.

Howard, Benjamin W. & Mary C. Cazort, 5 March 1850; Charles F. Waggoner, bondsman; John Wilkinson, wit. married 5 March 1859 by W. R. Fraley, J. P.

Howard, David & Nancy Tomlinson, 30 Nov 1823; George Howard, bondsman; A. R. Jones, wit.

Howard, Eli & Mary Boyd, 25 Oct 1806; Hugh Monro, bondsman; Jno Monroe, wit.

Howard, George & Polley Baits, 28 Aug 1813; Benjamin March, bondsman; John March Sr., wit.

Howard, Jesse H. & Susan Murr, 30 Nov 1844; Jacob Lefler, bondsman; John H. Hardie, Jr., wit.

Howard, John & _____, 22 May 1759; John Long, Benja. Milner, bondsmen.

Howard, John & Dinah Pinkston, 17 Aug 1779; Benjamin Howard, bondsman; Jo Brevard, wit.

Howard, John & Betsey McDannel, 21 Oct 1791; Henry Hardister, bondsman; Cunw. Harris, D. C., wit.

Howard, John & Margaret Gaither, 26 Jan 1795; Eli Gaither, bondsman; B. John Pinchback, Lydia Pinchback, wit.

Howard, John & Martha Gheen, married 15 May 1853 by J. Thomason, J. P.

Howard, Joseph & Sally Enochs, 20 Dec 1796; Humphrey Marshall, bondsman; Jno Rogers, wit.

Howard, Joseph & Margret Crouse, 19 Jan 1809; Daniel Crouse, bondsman; Jn March Sr., wit.

Howard, Joshua & Elsey Brion, 7 March 1789; Cornelius Howard, bondsman; Will Alexander, wit.

Howard, Josua & Nancy Beach, 26 Oct 1801; Norman Owens, bondsman; Jno Brem, wit.

Howard, Matthew & Lissia Jacobs, 31 Dec 1816; Obadiah Hamton, bondsman; Geo. Dunn, wit.

Howard, Morgan & Hannah Smith, 5 March 1828; Isaac Parker, bondsman; J. H. Hardie, wit.

Howard, Philip & Nancey Dosey, 20 Sept 1797; Wm. Howard, bondsman; Jno Rogers, wit.

Howard, Phillip & Susannah Gardner, 19 Oct 1774; John Brandon, John Bone, bondsmen; Ad. Osborn, wit.

Howard, Phillip & Sarah Dowell, 6 May 1824; Aquilla Cheshier, bondsman.

Howard, Thomas & Hariett Gaither, 29 Oct 1799; Eli Gaither, bondsman; Edwin J. Osborn, D. C., wit.

Howard, Thomas A. & Mary J. Sloan, 18 Nov 1851; Robert Sloan, bondsman; J. S. Myers, wit.

Howard, William & Elizabeth Chaffin, 5 Aug 1794; John Stinchcomb, bondsman; J. Troy, wit.

Howard, William & Nelley Walker, 7 Sept 1810; Cornelius Howard, bondsman; Jn March Sr., wit.

Howard, William & Rutha Chaffen, 6 July 1816; Joseph Howard, bondsman; Jn. March Sr., wit.

Howard, William & Elinor Beard, 19 Sept 1816; Saml. Hill Jr., bondsman; Jno Giles, Cl., wit.

Howard, William & Martha A. McCulloch, 11 Sept 1841; James L. Cowan, bondsman; J. S. Johnston, wit.

Howell, John & Martha Gheen, 11 May 1853; James B. Naley, bondsman; J. S. Myers, wit.

Howerton, Reuben & Sharloty Owen, 29 May 1857; Wm. W. Emery, bondsman; J. S. Myers, wit.

Howes, James & Nansey Sims, 11 Dec 1786; John Sims, bondsman; Ad. Osborn, wit.

Huddleston, William & Elizabeth Smart, 13 Aug 1766; William Smart, bondsman; Thomas Frohock, wit.

Hudgens, William & Elizabeth Potts, 23 Jan 1792; William Ryan, bondsman; Chs. Caldwell, wit.

Hudson, Charles & Rebecca Miller, 10 Aug 1805; Peter Walton, bondsman; A. L. Osborn, D. C., wit.

Hudson, Charles A. & Mary Ann Sossoman, 16 Jan 1847; William A. Lyerly, bondsman; John H. Hardie Jr., wit.

Hudson, Davidson & Susan J. Smith, 24 Feb 1853; G. H. Peeler, bondsman; J. S. Myers, wit.

Hudson, Davidson & Mary S. Wilhelm, 26 Nov 1853; William C. Brandon, bondsman.

Hudson, James & Elizabeth Clamp, 17 Sept 1802; Thos. Cook, bondsman; Js. McEwin, wit.

Hudson, James A. & Emily Craige, 22 Jan 1866; William J. Mills, bondsman; Obadiah Woodson, wit.

Hudson, John & Dianah E. Hughes, 23 Jan 1823; Uriah C. Parker, bondsman; L. R. Rose, J. P., wit.

Hudson, John W. & Mary L. Moyer, 10 Dec 1853; Josiah Griffin, bondsman; J. S. Myers, wit. married 22 Dec 1853 by A. Baker, Pastor of the Presbyterian Church, Salisbury.

Hudson, Laurence & Margaret Hendron, 12 Aug 1825; Wm. N. Morgan, bondsman; M. A. Giles, wit.

Hudson, Nathaniel J. & Jane V. Erwin, 25 Oct 1825; Joseph Cowan, bondsman; Hy. Giles, wit.

Hudson, W. H. & Sarah C. Keistler, 27 July 1863; W. L. Stansill, bondsman; Obadiah Woodson, wit.

Hudson, William & Supiah Temples, 3 Nov 1812; Vinson Wood, bondsman; J. Willson, J. P.; Jno Hyatt, wit.

Hudson, William & Susanna Morgan, 15 June 1813; Robs. Nanny, bondsman; Jno Giles, C. C., wit.

Hudson, Wm. G. & Susannah B. Smith, 12 April 1830; William R. Hughes, bondsman; Jno. H. Hardie, wit.

Hudsone, Thomas & Eleonor Johnson, 11 March 1773; James Erwin, John Andrews, bondsmen; Ad. Osborn, wit.

Hudspeth, John & Mary Vaughn, 14 Sept 1771; John Doyle, bondsman; Thomas Frohock, wit.

Huey, Thomas & Mary Bryant, 7 Feb 1787; John Johnston, bondsman; Jno Macay, wit.

Huey, William & Elizabeth Fillips, 3 July 1791; Samuel Casey, bondsman; Basil Gaither, wit.

Huff, Daniel & Rhashel Bodenhimer, 8 Oct 1815; John Bodenhamer, bondsman; Sol. Davis, J. P., wit.

Huff, Jacob & Liddy Macrary, 22 Jan 1791; Elijah Merrell, bondsman; Cunn. Harris, D. C., wit.

Huff, Valentine Jr. & Jemimah Hughes, 14 June 1792; Nichols. W. Gaither, bondsman; Basil Gaither, wit.

Huff, William H. & E. M. Cauble, 7 Feb 1861; John Thompson, bondsman; Wm. Locke, wit. married 7 Feb 1861 by D. W. Honeycutt, J. P.

Huffman, Anthony & Jane Cunningham, 27 May 1813; Jacob Huffman, bondsman; Joseph Clarke, Henry Cooper, wit.

Huffman, Daniel & Rachael Parks, 17 Jan 1781; Henry Giffard, wit.

Huffman, David & Peggy Miller, 7 Jan 1805; Saml. Barkley, bondsman; A. L. Osborn, Cl., wit.

Huffman, Uriah & Delinda Parks, 2 Dec 1833; Spruce M. Park, bondsman; Hy. Giles, wit.

Huffman, William A. & Jane E. Hoffner, 7 March 1861; John Eagle, bondsman; James E. Kerr, wit.

Hufman, George & Nancy Fisher, 19 May 1825; Peter Hartman, bondsman; Jno. H. Hardie, wit.

Hufman, George W. & Elizabeth Klutts, 3 Feb 1855; Alexander Kirk, bondsman; James E. Kerr, J. S. Myers, wit.

Huggisn, John & Margaret Brevard, 12 Dec 1772; James Kerr, bondsman; consent from Robt Brevard, father of Margret, 12 Dec 1772.

Huggins, Robert & Rachael Jetton, 13 Feb 1787; Ad. Brevard, bondsman; Ad. Osborn, wit. consent from John Jetton of Mecklenburg Co., N. C., 13 Feb 1787.

Hughes, Hudson & Mary Balfour, 8 Sept 1796; Robt. Troy, bondsman; Jno Rogers, wit.

Hughes, James & Delany Purlem, 1 Nov 1836; Philip Hughes, bondsman; Hy. Giles, wit.

Hughes, John & Martha Bartie, 25 Jan 1795; Thomas Cooper, bondsman.

Hughes, Richmond & Rachel Smith, 13 July 1811; Richard Worthington, bondsman; Geo. Dunn, wit.

Hughes, Samuel & Elizabeth Guffy, 16 Dec 1792; John Hughes, bondsman; Jos. Chambers, wit.

Hughes, Samuel & Elizabeth Lowman, _____; Thos Dodson, bondsman.

Hughes, Sergent & Judith Hayden, 3 Nov 1788; Hy. Young, bondsman; Wm. Alexander, wit.

Hughes, Timothy R. & Nancy Gainer, 22 Feb 1834; Will F. Kelly, bondsman; Thomas McNeely, J. P., wit.

Hughey, Andrew & Peggy Hughey, 25 Jan 1810; Henry Hunter, bondsman; Geo. Dunn, wit.

Hughey, Andrew & Polly Erwin, 11 June 1816; Samuel Hughy, bondsman; Jno Giles, C. C., wit.

Hughey, Ezekiel & Sally Harrison, 12 Sept 1804; Wm. Thompson, bondsman; A. L. Osborn, D. C., wit.

Hughey, Henry & Mary Cook, 20 March 1773; Hugh McKnight, bondsman.

Hughey, Jacob & Margaret Cook, 5 Sept 1782; Stephan Cowan, bondsman; T. H. McCaule, wit.

Hughey, Jacob & Fanny Niblock, 2 March 1819; James B. Wilson, bondsman.

Hughey, John J. & Zabiah J. Cowan, 11 Feb 1858; married 21 Jan 1858 by Saml. B. O. Wilson, V. D. M.

Hughey, Robert W. & Elizabeth W. Barber, 28 Jan 1845; Andrew Graham, bondsman; J. H. Hardie, wit.

Hughey, Samuel & Jane Orton, 26 June 1769; Benjamin Hide, bondsman; Thos Frohock, wit. consent from James Orten and Henry Hughey, wit by James Withrow, Robert Hughey.

Hughey, Samuel & Nancy Smith, 27 Jan 1818; Jno Patton, bondsman; Jno Giles, wit.

Hughey, Samuel & _____, _____; J. Troy, bondsman; J. Troy, D. C., wit.

Hughlin, William & Matilda Robards, 22 Dec 1828; Robert Lyster, bondsman.

Hughs, Christopher & Polly McLohlin, 24 Jan 1810, Jas. Gillaspie, bondsman; Geo. Dunn, wit.

Hughs, Thomas & Susannah Parker, 11 Nov 1804; Saml. Hughs, bondsman; A. L. Osborn, D. C., wit.

Huie, Benjamin & Levina Cowan, 5 March 1825; Wilson Hall, bondsman; Jno Giles, wit.

Huie, Jacob J. & Mary A. Bodenheimer, 20 April 1850; Samuel A. Creason, bondsman; J. S. Myers, wit.

Huie, Robert & Mary Partee, 26 Sept 1833; Hy. Giles, bondsman; Wm. Locke, wit.

Huie, Samuel & Myra Cowan, 13 Feb 1826; Benjamin Phifer, bondsman; Hy. Giles, wit.

Huie, Silas & Philipena Grimes, 15 Nov 1837; John Shuman Jr., bondsman; Jno. H. Hardie, wit.

Hulan, Jesse & Clarisa Lyerly, 28 Aug 1852; William Julian, bondsman; J. S. Myers, wit.

Hulan, Jesse & Angeline Swink, 16 Feb 1854; George W. Jacobs, bondsman; J. S. Myers, wit.

Hulan, John & Nancy Canady, 18 Sept 1810; William Hulan, bondsman; Jno Giles, C. C., wit.

Hulan, Thomas & Julia Ann Holt, 16 May 1843; Warren Gheen, bondsman.

Hulen, Thomas & Clementine Farr, 21 April 1831; David Watson, bondsman; Jno. H. Hardie, wit.

Hulin, Alex & Sophia Bruner, 4 March 1834; William Hartman, bondsman; J. H. Hardie, wit.

Hulin, Alexander & Elizabeth Goodman, 11 June 1839; Jacob Bruner, bondsman; Jno Giles, wit.

Hulin, Alexander & Anny Hartman, 6 Dec 1841; Levi Trexler, bondsman; Jno Giles, wit.

Hulin, Arthur & Tabitha Hulin, 19 March 1814; John Hulin, bondsman; Geo. Dunn, wit.

Hulin, Jesse & Elizabeth Tarr, 12 July 1860; Alfred Kenley, bondsman; Wm. Locke, wit. married 12 July 1860 by Wm. H. Trott, J. P.

Hulin, Jonathan & Eliza Trexler, 27 Dec 1827; Adam Trexler, bondsman; Jno. H. Hardie, wit.

Hulin, Orran & Liddy Reeves, 11 Oct 1816; Robt. Wood, bondsman; Milo A. Giles, wit.

Hulin, Robert & Catharine Cauble, 1 Feb 1848; Farly Ellis, bondsman; J. H. Hardie, wit.

Hulin, William & Jean Cunigham, 15 Feb 1804; William Hulin, bondsman.

Hull, Joel W. & Nancy Agner, 28 March 1843; Jno W. Bostian, bondsman; J. H. Hardie,. wit.

Hull, Joseph & Sarah Miller, 29 Sept 1779; Moses Hull, bondsman; Jo. Brevard, wit.

Humphress, Nathan & Lilless Smith, 26 July 1824; Nathan Stanely, bondsman; L. R. Rose, J. P., wit.

Humphrey, John & Susanna Bradford, 7 Jan 1793; John Shepperd, bondsman; Jos. Chambers, wit.

Humphreys, William & Deborah Hall, 2 June 1815; Moses Hall, bondsman; R. Powell, wit.

Hunt, Abel & Duanna Beard, 17 Feb 1787; John Green, bondsman; P. Henderson, wit.

Hunt, Andrew & Luse Giles, 27 Sept 1764; Wm. Giles, Jacob Likins, bondsmen; Thoms. Frohock, wit.

Hunt, Arthur & Elizabeth Willson, 10 March 1790; John Green, bondsman.

Hunt, Arthur & Jinney Whitaker, 17 Sept 1791; Peter Whitaker, bondsmen; Cunm. Harris, wit.

Hunt, Daniel & Polly Wiseman, 6 Jan 1797; William Ford, bondsman; Jno Rogers, wit.

Hunt, Daniel & Betsy Cole, 10 May 1798; William Wiseman, bondsman; Edwin J. Osborn, D. C., wit.

Hunt, Elijah & Elizabeth Smith, 30 Dec 1813; Jonathan Tussey, bondsman; Jno Giles, C. C., wit.

Hunt, Enoch & Elizabeth Chaffin, 2 June 1794; John Hamton Jr., bondsman; J. Troy, D. C., wit.

Hunt, Gersham & Lucy Thomas, 30 May 1801; Adam Hederick, bondsman; Jno Brem, wit.

Hunt, Jonathan & Rachal Hampton, 7 Aug 1769; William Hamton, bondsman; Thom. Frohock, wit.

Hunt, Jonathan & Nancy Laurans, 11 Nov 1804; Gersham Hunt, bondsman.

Hunt, Owen & Polly Loyd, 28 Sept 1808; Jonathan Hunt, bondsman; A. L. Osborne, wit.

Hunt, Samuel & Peggy Mabett, 19 July 1804; Anthony Mabet, bondsman; J. Hunt, wit.

Hunt, Stephanus & Elizabeth Coffin, 22 May 1803; Micajah Haworth, bondsman.

Hunt, Wilson & Agnus Burnet, _____; Abraham Lowrance, bondsman.

Hunter, Abner & Mary McKnight, 8 March 1851; David C. McKnight, bondsman; Jno H. Hardie, wit.

Hunter, Charles & Elizabeth Chaffin, 18 Jan 1851; Braxton Hunter, bondsman; Wm. Hawkins, wit.

Hunter, David & Abigal Berry, 14 June 1775; William Brandon, John Cooper, bondsmen; Ad. Osborn, wit. consent from Wm. Berry, father of Abigal, 12 June 1775.

Hunter, John & Dorathy Booe, 11 Aug 1769; Stophle Booe, bondsman; Thos Frohock, wit.

Hunter, John & Rachel Jones, 8 Dec 1828; Tenison Cheshier, bondsman; Thomas McNeely, J. P., wit.

Hunter, John & Clementine Rufty, 14 Oct 1856; J. G. Knox, bondsman; James E. Kerr, wit. married 16 Oct 1856 by Moses Powlass, J. P.

Hunter, Richard & Mary Clerk, 8 June 1786; Andw. Hunter, bondsman.

Hunter, Thomas & Anne Sloane, 27 March 1787; Danl McGoodwin, bondsman; Ad. Osborn, wit.

Hunter, William & Hannah Hunter, 2 Sept 1800; Thomas Burgis, bondsman; J. Brem, wit.

Hurler, Michael & Jemima Warner, 19 Dec 1798; John Hildebrand, bondsman; Edwin J. Osborn, D. C., wit.

Hurley, Cornelius & Betsey Been, 25 June 1818; Stephen Hurley, bondsman; Wm. Daniel, J. P., wit.

Hurley, Jonathan & Rebeckey Hicks, widow, 4 Dec 180_; Andrew Edwards, bondsman; Jean Erwin, wit.

Hurley, William & Mary Hurly, 16 May 1815; Cornelius Hurly, bondsman; Wm. Bean, J. P., wit.

Husbands, Harmon & Sarah Renshaw, 7 Aug 1804; Hugh Jenkins, bondsman; Ad. Osborn, wit.

Husbands, William H. & Betsey Holshouser, 9 Dec 1862; William B. Atwell, bondsman; Obadiah Woodson, wit.

Hussey, Samuel & Sarah Carter, 1 Aug 1864; A. M. Miller, bondsman; Obadiah Woodson, wit.

Hussey, Samuel & Julia Ann Edwards, 7 Nov 1864; Martin Williams, bondsman; Obadiah Woodson, wit.

Hust, James & _____ Hodsen, 3 June 1765; Stephen Baly, bondsman; Thomas Frohock, wit. consent from Valentine von Hodsen, father of the bride, 3 June 1765, John Frohock, wit. Jo Conol, wit.

Huston, Archibald & Rosanna Cunningham, 6 Oct 1784; Andrew Snoddy, bondsman.

Huston, Donald & Margaret Monro, 31 Dec 1779; William McKoy, bondsman; B. Booth Boote, wit.

Huston, Joseph & Martha Lucas, 5 March 1783; Samuel Huston, bondsman.

Hutchens, Anderson & Ede Ellis, 24 Oct 1815; James Huie, bondsman; Geo. Dunn, wit.

Hutcheson, John & Georgia A. Mitchell, 23 Nov 1858; W. G. Clendenin, bondsman; John Wilkinson, wit. married 23 Nov 1858 by A. Baker, Pastor of the P. Church.

Hutchison, E. Nye & Elizabeth C. Jenkins, 26 July 1865; J. Rumple, bondsman; Obadiah Woodson, wit. married 26 July 1865 by J. Rumple, V. D. M.

tchison, James R. & Mary Short, 18 March 1829; Doctor R.
Graham, bondsman; Jno H. Hardie, wit.

Hutson, Gabril & Elizabeth Tutrow, 22 Dec 1813; David Bradley,
bondsman; Jno March Sr., wit.

Hutson, Seth & Polly Kern, 24 Oct 1797; Daniel Kern, bondsman;
Jno Rogers, wit.

Hutson, Thomas & Elizabeth Williams, 20 Dec 1788; Lowrance
Williams, bondsman; W. Alexander, wit.

Hyde, John & Peggy Thompson, 22 June 1803; William Robison,
bondsman; Adlai L. Osborn, D. C., wit.

Hyde, Thomas C. & Jane C. Burke, 15 Jan 1845; James G. Graham,
bondsman; J. H. Hardie, wit.

Idol, Barnit & Ruth Piggott, 4 March 1813; Joseph Idol, bondsman; Wm. Piggott, J. P., wit.

Idol, Mathias & Elizebeth Welch, 17 Dec 1801; John Teague,
bondsman.

Ijams, Beal & Elizebeth Little, 4 April 1791; Nichos. W.
Gaither, bondsman.

Ijams, Brice W. & Betsey Anderson, 31 March 1803; Gassaway
Gaither, bondsman; Edwin J. Osborn, wit.

Ijams, J. William & Caty Hanes, 15 Feb 1812; Thomas Gears,
bondsman; Jn March Sr., wit.

Ijams, Joseph & Elizabeth Baxter, 5 Feb 1820; Jacob Willson,
bondsman; R. Willson, wit.

Ijams, Vachel & Martha Cunningham, 19 Sept 1791; Isaac Jones,
bondsman; C. Caldwell, D. C., wit.

Ijams, Vachel & Lelah Gather, _____ (no date, during Gov. Martin's
admn.); Benjn. Gaither, bondsman; Basil Gaither, wit.

Ingles, Samuel & Mary Stuart, 3 Jan 1787; Peter Cline, bondsman.

Inglish, Samuel & Elisabeth Renshaw, 1 Feb 1812; Elijah Renshaw,
bondsman; Jn March Sr., wit.

Ingram, John Jr. & Jane Stokes, 31 Dec 1841; David Corle, bondsman; J. S. Johnston, wit.

Inness, Nathaniel & Charlotte Marin Cole, 18 Oct 1851; William
Camel, bondsman; James E. Kerr, wit.

Inness, Thomas & Anny Hollabaugh, 13 Nov 1815; George Holobough,
bondsman; Ezra Allemong, wit.

Inness, William & Margret Pennerry, 6 Aug 1787; Mat. Troy,
bondsman; Fanny Macay, wit.

Inness, William C. & Clementina Elliott, 16 April 1857; Geo M.
Lyerly, bondsman; J. S. Myers, wit. married 16 April 1857
by M. A. Agner, J. P.

Inniard, Abraham & Rachel Swaim, 15 Feb 1769; John Swain, Jonathan Robins, Mathias Robins, wit. (consent from John Swain only).

Irvin, John & Ann J. Young, 30 Jan 1837; James Kerr, bondsman; Jno Giles, wit.

Irvin, Joseph & Loretto T. Anderson, 5 June 1833; Ebenezer Dickson, bondsman; Jno H. Hardie, wit.

Irvine, George & Elizabeth Lyall, 2 Feb 1796; James Kerr, bondsman; J. Troy, wit.

Irwin--see also Arwin

Irwin, Abijah & Elizebeth Eaton, 28 Nov 1812; Abraham Depoyster, bondsman; Jn March Sr., wit.

Irwin, Campbell & Sally Bateman, 1 May 1818; George J. Niblock, bondsman; Jno Giles, wit.

Irwin, Enoch & Sarah Clifford, 30 March 1808; Abraham Depoyster, bondsman.

Irwin, Isaac & Rachel Glascock, 24 Sept 1822; Josiah Inglis, bondsman; L. R. Rose, J. P., wit.

Irwin, Jabez & Elizabeth Leach, 21 March 1831; James Leach, bondsman; L. R. Rose, J. P., wit.

Irwin, John & Nansey Berry, 22 Sept 1767; Alexander Erwin, Jacob Crawford, bondsmen; Thoms. Frohock, wit.

Irwin, Robert & Elizabeth Eaton, 22 Feb 1783; Mat. Troy, bondsman; Citty Keen, wit.

Irwin, William & Mary Cathey, 24 March 1796; Alexander Cathey, bondsman; J. Troy, wit.

Isaacs, John & Anny Allen, 15 Nov 1792; Jacob Myers, bondsman; Jno Monro, wit.

Isahour--see also Hisenour

Isahour, John & Rosanna Overcash, 16 Dec 1837; Abraham Goodnight, bondsman; Jno Giles, wit.

Isahower, Jacob & Lea Lentz, 5 Jan 1835; John Lingle, bondsman; Hy. Giles, wit.

Isahower, Jacob & Elizabeth L. Leopard, 30 Nov 1841; Henry M. Isahower, bondsman; Jno H. Hardie, wit.

Ivy, William & Rachel Galloway, 22 Aug 1819; John Clifford, bondsman; R. Powell, wit.

Jackson, Andrew (26 years old, son of Joel Jackson), & Sarah Troutman (24 years old), 11 May 1867; William T. Jackson (26 years old, son of Moses Jackson), bondsman; Saml. Rothrock, wit.

Jackson, Daniel & Sarah Cowan, 17 Feb 1795; John Shew, bondsman; Mich Troy, wit.

Jackson, John & Beshaby Bean, 25 April 1820; John Park, bondsman.

Jacobs, Abraham & Lucey Abbot, 11 Nov 1809; Benjamin P. Pearson, bondsman; Jno Giles, C. C., wit.

Jacobs, Daniel & Evy Shaver, 29 July 1797; Christian Jacobs, bondsman; Jno Rogers, wit.

Jacobs, David & Rhoda Nelson, 23 June 1824; Isaac D. Jones, bondsman; L. R. Rose, J. P., wit.

Jacobs, George W. & Delinda Cauble, 14 Aug 1856; Miles Williams, bondsman; J. S. Myers, wit.

Jacobs, Henry A. & Nancy Creason, 30 Dec 1843; Adam A. Smithdeal, bondsman; Obadiah Woodson, wit.

Jacobs, Henry A. & Elizabeth Williamson, 24 Dec 1845; Stephen G. Murr, bondsman; John H. Hardie Jr., wit.

Jacobs, James & Peggy Walton, 21 Aug 1817; Joseph Walton, bondsman; Jno Giles, wit.

Jacobs, John & Polly Cohenour, 14 Oct 1811; John Reudasil, bondsman; Geo. Dunn, wit.

Jacobs, Lewis & Elizabeth Walton, 14 Sept 1840; Geo. M. Murr, bondsman.

Jacobs, Lewis & Carmilla Gheen, 19 Dec 1848; Hirim Sharp, bondsman; J. H. Hardie Jr., wit.

Jacobs, Philip & Elizabeth Srote, 3 Dec 1822; George Michael Murr, bondsman.

Jacobs, Ransom & Susan Fultz, 28 Dec 1843; Wm. C. Love, bondsman; J. H. Hardie, wit.

Jacobs, William M. & Margaret Swink, 24 July 1850; J. S. Myers, bondsman; James E. Kerr, wit.

Jacobs, William W. & Hannah Julian, 28 Aug 1849; Hirim Sharp, bondsman; James E. Kerr, wit.

James--see also Jeams

James, Annan & Hannah Bowden, 23 Nov 1814; Saml. Harris, bondsman; Jn March Sr., wit.

James, Annan & Elizabeth Bowden, 15 June 1818; John Nail, bondsman; Jn. March Sr., wit.

James, Benjamin & Rebecah Horn, 5 July 1822; Wm. Coker, bondsman; Geo. Coker, wit.

James, Cornell & Nancy Brickhouse, 29 Dec 1812; James Cornell, bondsman; Jn March Sr., wit.

James, Evan & Jane Bowers, 19 June 1788; Hy. Young, bondsman.

James, Francis A. & Mary E. Todd, 24 April 1837; Roland H. Carter, bondsman; Tobias L. Lemly, wit.

James, Isaac & Ellenor Allen, 11 Dec 1815; William Coker, bondsman; R. Powell, wit.

James, Jesse & Sophia Lemly, 9 Feb 1815; James Gillaspie, bondsman; Jno Giles, C. C., wit.

James, Nicholas & Susannah Hinkle, 25 Nov 1806; Jacob Spach, bondsman; Lazarus Hege, J. P., wit.

James, Samuel W. & Mary M. Wall, 21 Dec 1847; J. H. Enniss, bondsman.

James, William & Polley Lowrey, 29 Dec 1812; Samuel Deaver, bondsman; Jn March Sr., wit.

Jamison, Milas S. & Louisa A. Kilpatric, 17 Dec 1850; Obadiah Woodson, bondsman; J. S. Myers, wit.

Jarratt, William & Sally Williams, 6 Sept 1812; John Hogg, bondsman; E. Morgan, J. P., wit.

Jarrel, William & Susannah Parks, 3 Jan 1770; Thomas Bicknell, Wm. Steel, bondsmen; Thomas Frohock, wit. consent from John Parks, father of Susanah, 1 Jan 1770; wit: Joseph White, Thomas Bicknell.

Jarrett, Samuel & Elizabeth Sherimam, 11 Nov 1794; Nicholas Pringle, bondsman; J. Troy, D. C., wit.

Jarvice, Nathan & Salley Peck, 26 Sept 1811; James Jarvice, bondsman; Willie Ellis, J. P., wit.

Jarvis, Elisha & Drusillah Smith, 6 May 1786; Jacob Bodders, bondsman; John Macay, wit.

Jarvis, James & Sally Pagit, 6 Jan 1795; Jonathan Merkland, bondsman; John Eccles, wit.

Jarvis, James Jr. & Delphy Chisher, 5 Aug 1822; Matthew Markland, bondsman; Tho. Hampton, wit.

Jarvis, Jonathan & Susanna Chesher, 2 Jan 1821; Charles D. Green, bondsman; Saml Jones, wit.

Jarvis, Zadock Jr. & Lucy Owens, 13 Feb 1813; James Jarvis Jr., bondsman; John Hanes, wit.

Jarvise, James & Ruthy Stalling, 12 Nov 1804; Humphre Mulliam, bondsman; Jno March, Anderson Rice, wit.

Jeams, Annon & Sary Cornol, 25 July 1824; Andrew Griffin, bondsman; M. Hanes, J. P., wit.

Jenkans, William & Saray Inglar, 11 March 1800; Joseph Jenkans, bondsman; Matt. Troy, wit.

Jenkins, Hugh & Elizabeth Hudgins, 12 July 1797; James McLaughlin, bondsman; Jno Rogers, wit.

Jenkins, James & Sarah Patten, 6 Dec 1779; Eleazar Comens, bondsman; B. Booth Boote, wit.

Jenkins, John W. & Margaret Gheen, 4 April 1855; James M. Patton, bondsman; J. S. Myers, wit. married 4 April 1855 by Obadiah Woodson, J. P.

Jenkins, J. Henry & Julia America (colored), 30 Aug 1865; married 9 Sept 1865 by Reuben J. Holmes, J. P.

Jenkins, Samuel & Mary Graham, 24 March 1778; William Graham, bondsman; Ad. Osborn, wit.

Jenkins, William & _____, _____; Joseph Clarke, bondsman;
Jno Rogers, wit.

Jennings, John M. B. & Sallie E. Chelton, 28 Feb 1865; David L.
Bringle, bondsman; Obadiah Woodson, wit.

Jernigan, Henry B. & Jinna Watkins, 7 Dec 1816; Eli Watkins,
bondsman; Jn March Sr., wit.

Jetton, Abram & Agness Brown, 25 Oct 1782; John Brown, bondsman;
Ad. Osborn, wit.

Jhonson, Jhon & Eliza Webb, 29 Aug 1828; John Krider, bondsman.

Jinkins, Elhanor & Letitia Maxwell, 3 Feb 1827; W. B. Willson,
bondsman; L. R. Rose, J. P., wit.

Jinkins, John & Patience S. Parker, 8 Aug 1797; David Parker,
bondsman.

Job, Samuel & Rachel Call, 21 April 1806; James Gordon, bondsman; Jn March Sr., wit.

Job, William & Mary Folcom, 25 July 1825; John Etcheson, bondsman; J. C. Weddington, wit.

Jobb, Thomas & Hannah Johnston, 10 March 1779; Robert Willson,
bondsman; Ad. Osborn, wit.

Johnnassee, Thomas & Fanney Trivitt, 26 April 1816; Henry Keller,
bondsman; R. Powell, wit.

Johns, Robert & Elizabeth Lukey, 4 June 1853; Martin Richwine,
bondsman; James E. Kerr, wit. married 5 June 1853 by D. W.
Honeycutt, J. P.

Johnson--see also Jhonson

Johnson, Alfred L. & Ann Horah, 6 May 1851; Samuel Reeves, Jr.,
bondsman; license has Alfred L. Johnston, married 6 May 1851
by T. Page Ricaud, Minister of the Gospel.

Johnson, Francis & Barbara Lyerle, 12 March 1822; Henry Blume,
bondsman.

Johnson, G. Wesley & Martha Taylor, 22 Aug 1834; Stephen L.
Howell, bondsman; H. Butlar, wit.

Johnson, Hansel & Sally Earnheart, 10 June 1844; Farly Ellis,
bondsman; Obadiah Woodson, wit.

Johnson, Henry & Cathrine Whiteacker, 14 May 1785; Alexander
Whiteakker, bondsman; Hu. Magoune, wit.

Johnson, James & Nancy Brookshear, 2 May 1811; George Johnson,
bondsman; Joseph Clarke, Mathew Macy, wit.

Johnson, James & Lydia Elrod, 23 Oct 1821; Arthur Smith,
bondsman; Geo. Coker, wit.

Johnson, James Jr. & Anna Akle, 22 Aug 1822; Robt Hampton,
bondsman; Tho Hampton, wit.

Johnson, Joel & Margaret Hughs, 2 Jan 1816; Abraham R. Jones,
bondsman; A. Nesbett, wit.

Johnson, John & Isbell Erwyn, 11 Dec 1771; Joseph Erwin, bonds-man; Thomas Frohock, wit.

Johnson, John & Betsey Burke, 11 Sept 1797; Joseph Pickler, bondsman; Jno Rogers, wit.

Johnson, John & Sarah Elrod, 4 May 1814; Thos Douthit, bondsman; Saml Jones, wit.

Johnson, John & Polly Huie, 8 Feb 1823; Philip D. Hunt, bonds-man; L. R. Rose, J. P., wit.

Johnson, John C. & Susan Shoaf, 24 Oct 1855; John L. Wright, bondsman; J. S. Myers, wit. married 24 Oct 1855 by J. J. Summerell, J. P.

Johnson, John Smith & Celery Tompson, 10 March 1798; William Johnston, bondsman; Edwin J. Osborn, wit.

Johnson, John Smith & Peggy Muree, 7 Feb 1800; Daniel Sharp, bondsman; Nl. Chaffin, wit.

Johnson, John W. & Maggie S. Yost, 13 July 1865; J. C. Johnson, bondsman; Obadiah Woodson, wit. married 13 July 1865 by Rev. Wm. Lambeth.

Johnson, L. E. & L. R. Moffitt, 25 Dec 1863; James E. Kerr, bondsman; Obadiah Woodson, wit.

Johnson, Mathew & Nancy Horn, 13 May 1804; Thomas Horn, bonds-man; J. Hunt, wit.

Johnson, Pascal & Polley Cunningham, 17 Oct 1824; Lewis White, bondsman; E. Brock, J. P., wit.

Johnson, Peter & Sarah Beason, 30 Aug 1802; William Clampitt, bondsman; Wm. Welborn, wit.

Johnson, Reuben & Elizabeth Haymore, 22 June 1820; Michael Brinkley, bondsman; An. Swicegood, wit.

Johnson, Robert & Susanna Jenkins, 24 Aug 1791; Hugh Jenkins, bondsman; C. Caldwell, D. C., wit.

Johnson, Robinson & Elizabeth Biles, 25 May 1796; Jonathan Biles, bondsman; J. Troy, wit.

Johnson, Thomas & Mary Elizabeth Whitacre, 20 Nov 1767; Mark Whitacre, bondsman; John Frohock, wit.

Johnson, Thomas & Margret Patton, 9 June 1788; Robert Patton, bondsman; Ad. Osborn, wit.

Johnson, William & Fany Blear, 10 Dec 1783; Hugh Andrews, bondsman; Moses Wylie, wit.

Johnson, William & Dianna Adams, 31 March 1788; Jacob Poole, bondsman; John McNary, wit.

Johnson, William & Hanner Evans, 25 July 1812; John Berryman, bondsman; Jn March Sr., wit.

Johnson, William & Elizabeth Luckey, 8 Oct 1816; John Davis, bondsman.

Johnson, William & Sophia Lingle, 17 April 1834; Alexander Lamb, bondsman; Jno H. Hardie, wit.

Johnson, William & Sarah Davis, 20 Jan 1813; Daniel Davis, bondsman; Geo Dunn, wit.

Johnson, William & Susanna Phillips, 30 June 1860; Jacob N. Kepley, bondsman; Wm. Locke, wit. married 1 July 1860 by Moses Powlass, J. P.

Johnson, William & Louisa C. Morgan, 8 Jan 1866; C. W. Morgan, bondsman; Obadiah Woodson, wit.

Johnstne, Joseph & Elizabeth Reed, 11 Aug 1767; Robert Tate, bondsman; Thomas Frohock, wit.

Johnstone, Alex & Isabel Lowry, 11 Aug 1784; Saml. Lowry, bondsman.

Johnston, C. W. & Mary Dixon, 4 March 1862; Jno. M. Knox, bondsman; Obadiah Woodson, wit. married 4 March 1862 by Rev. B. S. Krider.

Johnston, Charles L. & Sarah C. Dry, 7 Nov 1865; R. G. Poston, bondsman.

Johnston, David & Mary McMachin, 25 March 1785; Jos. Biles, bondsman; Hugh Magoune, wit.

Johnston, David & Sarah Ball, 3 June 1815; John Robling, bondsman; Geo. Dunn, wit.

Johnston, David & Sarah Thompson, 23 Dec 1824; Cyrus W. West, bondsman; Henry Allemong, wit.

Johnston, Francis & Mary McKinzie, 15 Feb 1813; Saml. McCulloch, bondsman; Jno Giles, wit.

Johnston, Francis & Susanna Brotherton, 20 Dec 1784; Thomas Brothertin, bondsman; Ad. Osborn, wit.

Johnston, George R. & Sarah C. McCulloch, 5 May 1840; Jno. M. McConnaughy, bondsman; Thm. Sneed, wit.

Johnston, James & Mary Chamblin, 22 Aug 1820; Christian Sheek, bondsman; Hy. Giles, wit.

Johnston, James C. & Sarah C. McKnight, 10 Dec 1858; G. G. McKnight, bondsman; John Wilkinson, wit. married 21 Dec 1858 by Stephen Frontis.

Johnston, James M. & Nancy Baker, 23 Aug 1854; Hezekiah Tanner, bondsman; J. S. Myers, wit.

Johnston, Jesse & Mahulda Kerr, 14 May 1836; Nathan Johnston, bondsman; Jno Giles, wit.

Johnston, John & Polly Chaffin, 30 Sept 1797; N. Chaffin, bondsman; Jno Rogers, wit.

Johnston, John & Elizabeth Lock, 17 May 1762; Francis Lock, George Lock, bondsmen; Will Reed, Jacob Nichols, wit.

Johnston, John & Sarah Vandaval, 21 Jan 1794; Owen Maeley, bondsman; Jo Chambers, wit.

Johnston, John & Catharine Peck, 18 July 1811; Lewis Peck, bondsman; Jno Giles, C., wit.

Johnston, John W. & D. C. McKnight, 26 Aug 1865; H. B. Reese, bondsman; Obadiah Woodson, wit.

Johnston, J. Sloan & Sarah Reeves, 5 May 1840; Leander Killian, bondsman; Susan T. Giles, wit.

Johnston, Lamuel D. & Polly Morrison, 6 May 1823; John Kinder, bondsman; Jno Giles, wit.

Johnston, Lee & Ann Renshaw, 19 Aug 1825; Richard Loury, bondsman.

Johnston, Manchester & Magdalane Gardner, 17 June 1810; Jacob Sossaman, bondsman.

Johnston, Reese & Ann Kincaid, 22 Sept 1841; Alphaus Howard, bondsman; J. S. Myers, wit.

Johnston, Robert & Mary Stone, 12 Nov 1766; James Hannah, bondsman; Thomas Frohock, wit.

Johnston, Robert & Ellen Gillespie, 1 Nov 1802; Richard Gillespie, bondsman; A. L. Osborn, D. C., wit.

Johnston, Robert A. & Cynthia C. Reese, 29 Nov 1851; Samuel W. Frazier, bondsman; James E. Kerr, wit. married 3 Dec 1851 by Saml. B. O. Wilson, Minister of the Presbyterian Church.

Johnston, Rufus D. & Aly Graham, 21 July 1832; Mortimer D. Johnston, bondsman; J. H. Hardie, wit.

Johnston, Samuel & Elizabeth Collins, 16 Feb 1802; John Paterson, bondsman; Jno Brem, wit.

Johnston, Strangeman & Mary Whitaker, 6 March 1798; Elijah Marlow, bondsman; Edwin J. Osborn, D. C., wit.

Johnston, T. M. & America Watkins, 1 Dec 1864; Amos Harris, bondsman; Obadiah Woodson, wit.

Johnston, William & Elizabeth Akels, 18 March 1820; Thos Douthit, bondsman; Saml Jones, J. P., wit.

Jonds, Rudolph & Zabarey Reed, 20 March 1809; William Jonds, bondsman; A. L. Osborne, wit.

Jones, Benjamin & Hannah Teague, 1 March 1819; John Spurgin, bondsman; Sol. Davis, wit.

Jones, Basil G. & Mary Brown, 13 Dec 1824; Godfrey Clement, bondsman; L. R. Rose, J. P., wit.

Jones, Ebed & Mary Wells, 22 Dec 1796; James Wells, bondsman; Jno. Rogers, wit.

Jones, Edmon & Nancy Drake, 26 Feb 1814; Saml. Harries, bondsman; Saml Jones, wit.

Jones, Edmun & Anny Low or Lord, 26 Dec 1821; Jacob Cornatz, bondsman; A. R. Jones, wit.

Jones, Exra & Margaret Hunt, 10 March 1796; James Wells, bondsman; J. Troy, wit.

Jones, Harper F. & Amanda C. Jones, 30 Aug 1855; A. W. Owen, bondsman; J. S. Myers, wit.

Jones, Henry & Sarey Kinnion, 12 Oct 1811; John Jones, bondsman; Jn March Sr., wit.

Jones, Henry A. & Ann E. B. Cook, 6 Dec 1844; Andrew W. Cook, bondsman; John H. Hardie Jr., wit.

Jones, Henry B. & Celia Kinder (colored), 12 Aug 1865; married 13 Aug 1865 by T. G. Haughton, rector.

Jones, Isaac & Nelley Gaither, 2 April 1787; Basil Gaither, bondsman; Jno Macay, wit.

Jones, Isaac & Barshaba Helton, 15 March 1803; James Helton, bondsman; William Piggatt, J. P., wit.

Jones, Isaac D. & Mary Booe, 25 May 1826; J. H. Hardie, bondsman.

Jones, J. W. & Bettie C. Harris, 11 Aug 1857; James Horah, bondsman; J. S. Myers, wit. married 11 Aug 1857 by R. G. Bassett, Pastor of M. E. Church, Salisbury.

Jones, Jacob & Jinny Mourltin, 12 Aug 1823; Joel Chevis, bondsman; Hy. Giles, wit.

Jones, James & Susanna Kinkaid, 10 March 1783; James Kinkaid, bondsman.

Jones, James & Elizabeth Ward, 18 Aug 1801; Lewis Jenkins, bondsman; Is. Beard, wit.

Jones, James & Ellender Stout, 16 July 1812; William Jones, bondsman; Sol. Davis, J. P., wit.

Jones, James H. & Lucy Jane Brady, 7 April 1858; Jno. J. Shaver, bondsman; John Wilkinson, wit. married 7 April 1858 by W. R. Fraley, J. P.

Jones, John & Ruth Whitacre, 20 Oct 1774; John Jones, bondsman; Ad. Osborn, wit.

Jones, John & Rebecca Chambers, 15 Dec 1777; Ad. Osborn, wit.

Jones, John & Esther Fisher, 24 June 1797; Risdon Fisher, bondsman; Jno. Rogers, wit.

Jones, John & Marthew Lee, 31 May 1806; William Jones, bondsman; Jn March Sr., wit.

Jones, John & Elizebeth Wells, 14 Dec 1811; Joseph Clifford, bondsman; Jn March Sr., wit.

Jones, John & Eleanor M. Austin, 4 Dec 1827; Abner Bryan, bondsman; E. Brock, J. P., wit.

Jones, John & Amanda Mask, 5 Aug 1850; Caleb Pendergrass, bondsman; H. Kelly, J. P., wit.

Jones, Jonathan & Kaziah Osbon, 11 July 1812; William Ozborn, bondsman; Sol. Davis, J. P., wit.

Jones, John & Martha Wells, 29 Sept 1772; James Jones, John Wells, bondsmen; Max. Chambers, wit. consent from Catrin Jones, mother of Marthew Wells, 28 Sept 1772.

Jones, Joseph & Lucy Foster, 3 Oct 1785; James Foster, bondsman; Max Chambers, wit.

Jones, Joseph & Rebecca Parks, (no date, during Gov. Martin's admn.); John Parks, bondsman; Jo. Chambers, wit.

Jones, Joseph & Nancy Ballard, 30 May 1812; William Berryman, bondsman; Jn March Sr., wit.

Jones, Larkin G. & Martha M. Jones, 31 Jan 1837; William P. Stockton, bondsman.

Jones, Martin & Caroline E. Repult, 9 Jan 1866; R. R. Crawford, bondsman; Obadiah Woodson, wit.

Jones, Mingo & Crissy Overman (colored), 7 Oct 1865; married 7 Oct 1865 by Zuck Haughton.

Jones, Philip & Catherin Richard, 28 Dec 1815; John W. Suthier, bondsman.

Jones, Richard & Elizabeth Parker, 7 Aug 1805; Nathin Gaither, bondsman; Jn March Sr., wit.

Jones, Robert & Polly Douthard, 28 Feb 1803; Jones Enochs, bondsman; A. L. Osborn, D. C., wit.

Jones, Rowland & Nancy Willson, 18 March 1808; Thos. Hilton, bondsman.

Jones, Samuel & Drusilla Brown, 14 Oct 1802; Hudson Hughes, bondsman; A. L. Osborn, wit.

Jones, Samuel & Nancy Skinner, 14 March 1813; John Jones, bondsman; R. Powell, wit.

Jones, Thomas & Polly Lock, 23 Oct 1788; Mathew Lock, bondsman; Wil Alexander, wit.

Jones, Thomas & Liddey King, 22 Nov 1808; Benjamin Edan, bondsman; Jn March Sr., wit.

Jones, Thomas & Sally Killan, 10 Nov 1816; Amos Regan, bondsman; Silas Peace, wit.

Jones, Thomas & Delila Puliam, 20 July 1825; Thomas Robley, bondsman; Hy Giles, wit.

Jones, Thomas & Henrietta Maria Morrison, 26 Sept 1842; David Kerns, bondsman.

Jones, Thomas & Sarah Oneal, 22 May 1827; Abner Oneal, bondsman; L. R. Rose, J. P., wit.

Jones, Thomas C. & Betsey Eliza Hodgens, 30 Oct 1813; John March Jr., bondsman; Jn March Sr., wit.

Jones, Wesly & Margaret Graves, 12 Sept 1822; Jacob March, bondsman; L. R. Rose, J. P., wit.

Jones, Wilie & Polly House, 31 Dec 1826; Josephus Hilton, bondsman; M. Hanes, wit.

Jones, William & Mary Vandevare, 9 Sept 1778; John Vandeveer, bondsman.

Jones, William & Minsy Merrell, 6 March 1805; Charles Hudson, bondsman; Mat. S. Crump, wit.

Jones, William & Elisebeth Hilton, 6 Feb 1827; Josephus Heilton, bondsman; M. Hanes, wit.

Jonnesee, John & Francina Husbands, 26 June 1814; Elijah Lyon, bondsman; R. Powell, wit.

Jons, Rowland & Mary Sheets, 20 Sept 1822; Michael Hanes, bondsman; Tho. Hampton, wit.

Jordan, John & Mary Yeost, 25 Dec 1812; Wm. Hays, bondsman; Geo Dunn, wit.

Jordan, Philip & Christiena Cretelow, 30 Oct 1792; George Bost, bondsman; Jos. Chambers, wit.

Jordon, River & Elizabeth Phips, 5 Sept 1810; George Basinger, bondsman; Jno Giles, C. C., wit.

Jorann, Solomon & Elizabeth Shuping, 13 Aug 1835; William S. Butner, bondsman; Hy. Giles, wit.

Josey, Alexander (Sandy) & Sally Hornbarrier, 16 Feb 1833; John Fesperman, bondsman; J. H. Hardie, wit.

Josey, Alexander & Margaret E. Eagle, 31 Jan 1866; J. H. House, bondsman; H. N. Woodson, wit.

Josey, Caleb & Elizabeth Pinkston, 28 Nov 1854; Alexander Moury, bondsman.

Josey, Daniel & Anny Fesperman, 9 Sept 1839; Nicholas Shuping, bondsman; Hy. Giles, wit.

Josey, Fielding S. & Sarah Sides, 15 Jan 1866; M. C. Josey, bondsman; Obadiah Woodson, wit.

Josey, John & Mary Coble, 3 March 1794; Hanry Rintleman, bondsman; Jo. Chambers, wit.

Josey, John & Elizabeth Josey, 8 May 1838; Matthew Jones, bondsman.

Josey, Martin & Margaret Mourie, 29 Oct 1833; George Saferet, bondsman; Hy. Giles, wit.

Josey, Moses & Anna M. Setzer, 8 Feb 1840; Peter Miller, bondsman; Jno Giles, wit.

Josey, Peter & Polly Klutz, 21 Dec 1818; Andrew Lyerly, bondsman; Henry Allemong, wit.

Josey, Samuel & Sally Hoover, 21 Dec 1821; George Waller, bondsman; Jno Giles, wit.

Josey, Theophilus & Mary C. L. Earnhardt, 16 Aug 1859; E. E. Philips, bondsman.

Josey, William & Mary Lourer, 25 March 1810; John Mourey, bondsman; Geo. Dunn, wit.

Joyner, John A. & Nancy McNight, 19 Aug 1823; Isaac Lee, bondsman; E. Brock, J. P., wit.

Julian, Benjamin & Clarissa E. Gibson, 5 Oct 1846; Jas. H. Enniss, bondsman; J. H. Enniss, wit.

Julian, James & Susan Cooper, 28 June 1861; married 28 June 1861 by Peter Williamson, J. P.

Julian, James & Jane Tarrh, 1 Jan 1866; H. Daniel Verble, bondsman; Obadiah Woodson, wit.

Julian, James F. & Aly Walton, 18 Aug 1853; Wm. A. Julian, bondsman; James E. Kerr, wit.

Julian, William & Fanny Thomason, 29 June 1815; William Owen, bondsman; Geo. Dunn, wit.

Julian, William & Elizabeth Thorn, 17 June 1840; Jas. I. Long, bondsman.

Julian, William A. & Emily C. Reed, 8 Aug 1853; Jno. A. Weisman, bondsman; J. S. Myers, wit. Emily C. Reed, of Alamance County; married 9 Aug 1853 by Obadiah Woodson, J. P.

Julian, William H. & Clarissa Tarrh, 16 Feb 1865; Robert W. Price, bondsman; Obadiah Woodson, wit.

Julin, David & Elizabeth Merril, 14 Feb 1795; Hu. Horah, bondsman.

Kailor--see Kehller

Kaler, Leonard & Mary Parks, 14 March 1795; James Reed, bondsman; J. Troy, D. C., wit.

Kanartzer, Jacob & Polley Drake, 8 Feb 1812; John Cornatzer, bondsman; Jn March Sr., wit.

Karn, Daniel & Susannah Walton, 17 Jan 1803; David Woodson, bondsman; A. L. Osborn, D. C., wit.

Karr, William & Anne Houston, 19 March 1795; Daniel Huston, bondsman; J. Troy, D. C., wit.

Karrker, John & Sarah Beaver, 29 June 1840; David Bostian, bondsman; Susan T. Giles, wit.

Kauble, Adam & Christian Airy, 5 May 1810; Fredrick Mowrie, bondsman; Ezra Allemong, wit.

Kaufman, Samuel & Mary Rowland, 21 Oct 1794; William Willcockson, bondsman; Mat. Troy, wit.

Keerans, I. F. & Susan J. Smith, 15 Sept 1858; S. J. Peeler, bondsman; married 15 Sept 1858 by S. A. Adams.

Keeth, Sihon & Sarah Kanup, 6 Oct 1817; Henry Weaver, bondsman; Milo A. Giles, wit.

Keeth, Sihon & Barbara Stoner, 21 Feb 1846; Jacob S. Myers, bondsman; J. M. Turner, wit.

Kehller, Peter & Mary Hettinger, 25 Aug 1791; Tobias Ferrer, bondsman; Cunm. Harris, wit.

Keisler, Jeremiah M. & Lunda W. Bell, 11 April 1852; married 13 April 1852 by Jas. P. Simpson.

Keisler, John & Mary Berringer, 21 March 1798; Barnhet Krieter, bondsman; Ad. Osborn, wit.

Keisler, John & Sarah Clodfelter, 30 Nov 1824; Jo. E. Todd, bondsman; Hy. Allemong, wit.

Keith, George & Anna Catharine Lentz, 4 Jan 1862; Aaron G. Lents, bondsman; Jos. A. Linn, agt., wit. married 5 Jan 1862 by Jos. A. Linn.

Kell, James & Lettice Kneal, 30 Aug 1783; James Faries, bondsman; Robt. Nall, wit.

Kellar, William & Polly Neil, 9 Sept 1824; Daniel Nail, bondsman; L. R. Rose, J. P., wit.

Keller, Abraham & Sarah Hinkle, 13 April 1809; Henry Keller, bondsman; Jn March Sr., wit.

Keller, Christopher & Joannah Smith, 31 Jan 1827; Henry Hellard, bondsman; J. H. Hardie, wit.

Keller, Henry & Susanah Latham, 13 Jan 1806; John March Jr., bondsman; Jn March Sr., wit.

Keller, Henry & Susannah Smith, 26 Dec 1821; Daniel Earnest, bondsman; A. R. Jones, wit.

Keller, John & Rose Walker, 15 Oct 1798; John Webb, bondsman; Edwin J. Osborn, D. C., wit.

Keller, John & Mary Bare, 30 Sept 1817; Danel Hendricks, bondsman; Jno. H. Freeling, wit.

Keller, John & Catherine Hellard, 13 April 1837; David Hendrix, bondsman.

Keller, Joseph & Anna Maxwell, 2 May 1820; John Maxwell, bondsman; Hy. Giles, wit.

Keller, Samuel & Sophia Beavers, 17 March 1825; Willian White, bondsman; W. Harris, wit.

Kelley, James & Frances Swinny, 27 May 1817; Levi Reed, bondsman; T. Hampton, wit.

Kelley, Joshua & Susannah Kiles, 18 Oct 1791; Andw. McClenachan, bondsman; Cunm. Harris,wit.

Kelly, John & Margret Hess, 20 July 1859; William Hess, bondsman; John Wilkinson, wit. married 21 July 1859 by Peter Williamson, J. P.

Kelly, John & Mary Mitchel, 31 Jan 1844; Obadiah Woodson, bondsman; J. H. Hardie, wit.

Kelly, Will F. & Sarah Ann Gaither, 9 Oct 1827; Abel McNeely, bondsman; Thomas McNeely, J. P., wit.

Kelton, Robert & Elizabeth Wasson, 17 April 1787; Samuel
Wasson, bondsman.

Kendall, Solomon & Elisabeth Chadwick, 1 Sept 1817; John Chadwick,
bondsman; Z. Hunt, J. P., wit.

Kendell, Casper & Elizabeth Redcape, 21 July 1767; John Frohock,
John Lewis Beard, bondsmen.

Keneday, Sherwood & Phebe Wilson, 18 Nov 1821; Thomas Twidwell,
bondsman; Z. Hunt, Alfred M. Peace, wit.

Kenerly, Robert C. & Mary W. Barr, 24 July 1856; S. C. Rodgers,
bondsman; J. S. Myers, wit.

Kenly, George & Sarah Hess, 12 Nov 1836; John Hess, bondsman;
Hy. Giles, wit.

Kenerly, Samuel A. & Sallie C. Rogers, 20 Jan 1859; Robert C.
Kenery, bondsman; married 25 Jan 1859 by David Brown.

Kennaman, George & Mary Danniel, 30 Aug 1815; Jeremiah Smith,
bondsman; J. Manlove, wit.

Kenneday, John & Maray Dannel, 12 Nov 1813; Sherwood Kenneday,
bondsman; George Pope, William Kenneday, wit.

Kenneday, John & Eliza Hancock, 5 April 1854; James Mitchell,
bondsman; J. S. Myers, wit.

Kenneday, William Jr. & Elizabeth Kenneday, 20 Sept 1821; William
Kenneday Sr., bondsman; Silas Peace, wit.

Kennedey, William G. & Hannah Hill, 3 March 1846; John S. Johnston,
bondsman; J. S. Myers, wit.

Kennedy, Alexander & _____, _____ July 1788; (no bondsman).

Kennedy, Andrew & Rachael Penny, 17 Nov 1784; Wm. Wells, bondsman.

Kennedy, James & Elizabeth Cotton, 16 Sept 1852; Wade W. Hampton,
bondsman; James E. Kerr, wit.

Kennerly, Daniel & Mary R. Correll, 22 June 1840; Michael Overcast, bondsman; Susan T. Giles, wit.

Kennerly, Daniel C. & Milly Jane Johnston, 3 Sept 1859; Peter T.
Monroe, bondsman; James E. Kerr, wit. married 4 Sept 1859 by
Peter Williamson, J. P.

Kennerly, John P. & Margaret Corell, 13 March 1843; James Scott,
bondsman; J. H. Hardie, wit.

Kennerly, Pinckney A. & Margaret Hess, 28 Feb 1842; Danel F.
Kennerly, bondsman; Jno. H. Hardie, wit.

Kennerly, Robert C. & Mary W. Barr, married 30 July 1856 by J.
K. Graham, J. P.

Kennerly, Samuel & Elizabeth Isahour, 21 July 1832; Stephen
Cowan, bondsman; J. H. Hardie, wit.

Kennody, John & Elizabeth Owens, 8 Dec 1814; Joseph Gheen,
bondsman; Jno Giles, wit.

Kenny, Leonard & Margaret E. Criswell, 21 April 1856; Solomon Brown, bondsman; J. S. Myers, wit.

Kenny, William & Serena Lookabill, 29 March 1853; Noah W. Fry, bondsman; J. S. Myers, wit.

Kent, John & Elizebeth Berry, 16 Nov 1820; Humphrey Mullikin, bondsman; An. Swicegood, wit.

Kent, William & Eliza Valentine, 16 Jan 1836; Jessy Valentine, bondsman.

Kenup, William & Nancy Campbell, 16 Aug 1825; George Hudgins, bondsman.

Kepley--see also Caply

Kepley, Jacob & Loretta Johnston, 28 Feb 1856; John Lyerly, bondsman; J. S. Myers, wit.

Kepley, John & Charlotte Allen, 27 Dec 1819; Henry Allen, bondsman; Hy. Giles, wit.

Kepley, John & Sophia Hartman, 16 June 1826; Isaac Agner, bondsman.

Kepley, Robert & Sarah L. Holsehouser, 15 March 1859; Noah Canup, bondsman; married 17 March 1859 by Saml. Rothrock, Minister of the Gospel in the Ev. Luth. Church.

Kepley, William & Nancy Freedle, 16 March 1821; Jacob Rickard, bondsman; Hy. Giles, wit.

Keply, Miles & Margaret Lyerly, 20 July 1850; Philip Lemly, bondsman; J. S. Myers, wit.

Kern, Henry & Susanna Traves, 31 March 1812; Rbt. Wood, bondsman; Jno Giles, C. C., wit.

Kern, Obadiah & Aeley Austin, 14 Nov 1857; Fd. Warner, bondsman; J. S. Myers, wit.

Kern, Peter & Marry Moore, 25 Jan 1809; Wm. H. Brandon, bondsman; A. L. Osborne, wit.

Kern, Peter & Elizabeth Owen, 13 Sept 1842; J. M. Brown, bondsman.

Kerns, Daniel & Eliza Thomas, 23 Dec 1830; James Mull, bondsman.

Kerns, G. W. & Ann M. Woodson, 25 Sept 1865; T. J. Harris, bondsman; Horatio N. Woodson, wit. married 26 Sept 1865 by J. Rumple, V. D. M.

Kerns, John & Patsey Smith, 3 Jan 1828; Michael H. Smith, bondsman; J. H. Hardie, wit.

Kerns, Peter & Fanny Cauble, 19 Sept 1851; J. M. Brown, bondsman; James E. Kerr, wit. married 21 Sept 1851 by J. M. Brown, J. P.

Kerr, Andrew & Jean Neal, 3 Nov 1774; Andrew Neill, bondsman; Ad. Osborn, wit.

Kerr, Benjamin & Sylva Johnston (colored), 25 Jan 1866.

Kerr, George S. M. & Catherine Baker, 13 May 1859; Henry F. Baker, bondsman; married 13 May 1859 by M. A. Luckey.

Kerr, Henry M. & Catherine Kilpatrick, 5 Dec 1810; William B. Graham, bondsman; Ezra Allemong, wit.

Kerr, James & Jane Davidson, 3 May 1773; George Davison, bondsman; Ad. Osborn, wit.

Kerr, James & Frances Dunn (no date, during Gov. Caswell's admn). Mat. Troy, bondsman; Max. Chambers, wit.

Kerr, James & Margaret Liles, 2 Feb 1796; George Irvine, bondsman; J. Troy, wit.

Kerr, James Jr. & Matilda Knox, 30 Dec 1839; Alexander Torrence, bondsman; Jno Giles, wit.

Kerr, James E. & Catharine L. Huie, 18 Sept 1833; Wm. Locke, bondsman; Wm. Locke, wit.

Kerr, James McKnight & Mary C. Burk, 26 Jan 1858; married 27 Jan 1858 by Saml. B. O. Wilson.

Kerr, John & Sarah Buntin, 25 Jan 1785; James Buntin, bondsman; Hugh Magoune, wit.

Kerr, Joseph & Mary Allison, 31 Oct 1785; Jno Allison, bondsman; Spruce Macay, wit.

Kerr, Matthew & Margaret C. Moore, 20 Dec 1859; John Moore, bondsman; John Wilkinson, wit. married 29 Dec 1859 by Stephen Frontis.

Kerr, Nathaniel & Sarah Edmondson, 15 Aug 1848; Allison Fleming, bondsman; J. H. Hardie, wit.

Kerr, Nathaniel John & Eleonar Huggins, 26 July 1784; Stephen Cowan, bondsman; T. H. McCaule, wit.

Kerr, Samuel & Polly Todd, 1 April 1812; James Wilson, bondsman; Jno. Giles, C. C., wit.

Kerr, Stephen & Jean Wilson, 21 April 1780; William Wilson, bondsman; Jno Kerr, wit.

Kerr, Robert & Martha Smith, 16 Jan 1866; Henry Moore, bondsman; Obadiah Woodson, wit.

Kerr, William & Rosanna Neal, 28 Oct 1779; Andrew Neill, bondsman; Jo. Brevard, wit.

Kerr, William A. & Sarah J. Jamison, 10 April 1865; J. E. Jamison, bondsman; A. E. Jamison, wit. married 12 April 1865 by W. B. Watts, Minister of the Gospel.

Keslar, Jeremiah M. & Lunda M. Bell, 11 April 1852; Geo. M. Weant, bondsman; J. S. Myers, wit.

Kesler, Alexander & Catharine Lyerly, 10 May 1843; J. H. Hardie, bondsman.

Kesler, Cornelius & Anna Hartman, 29 July 1845; Jacob Rusher, bondsman; Jno H. Hardie Jr., wit.

Kesler, George & Rosey Basinger, 12 April 1826; Henry Allemong, bondsman.

Kesler, George B. & Eda Maria Linebarrier, 25 Aug-1859; William Basinger, bondsman; John Wilkinson, wit. married 25 ____ 1859 by S. J. Peeler, J. P.

Kesler, Green C. & Margaret M. File, 16 July 1852; Henry B. Casper, bondsman; J. S. Myers, wit. married 20 July 1852 by Levi Trexler, J. P.

Kesler, Henry Wilson & Nancy Hoffman; 17 March 1846; Moses Kesler, bondsman; J. H. Hardie, wit.

Kesler, Isaac & Eliza Lynn, 19 July 1848; J. H. Hardie, bondsman.

Kesler, Jesse & Anny Lentz, 30 Nov 1840; Thomas Basingers, bondsman; Jno Giles, wit.

Kesler, Miles & Catharine Huffman, 8 Feb 1841; Michael Eller, bondsman; Jno Giles, wit.

Kesler, Moses & Elizabeth Brown, 16 April 1850; Charles W. Kesler, bondsman; J. S. Myers, wit.

Kesler, Moses L. & Sarah Parks, 12 July 1853; Noah Park, bondsman; J. S. Myers, wit.

Kesler, Moses L. & Charlott Eller, 14 July 1857; Jacob Frick, bondsman; married 14 July 1857 by H. W. Hill, Esqr.

Kesler, Peter & Phreany Corriher, 12 Feb 1839; Mathias Bogen, bondsman; Hy. Giles, wit.

Kesler, Tobias & Nancy Roseman, 13 Sept 1841; George A. Kesler, bondsman; Susan T. Giles, wit.

Kesler, William & Sarah Jane Baker (colored), 21 Sept 1865; married by Wm. Lambeth.

Kesler, William A. & Ellen Jane Arey, 25 March 1864; W. H. Walton, bondsman; Obadiah Woodson, wit.

Ketchey, Adam & Ann M. Beaver, 20 Jan 1843; Peter Ketchey, bondsman; J. H. Hardie, wit.

Ketchey, David & Margaret L. Rix, 25 April 1850; Charles A. Rose, bondsman; James E. Kerr, wit.

Ketchey, Henry & Rosan Ann Fraly, 13 Dec 1834; Jacob Fraley, bondsman; John H. Hardie, wit.

Ketchey, Lewis & Aley C. Julian, 21 Aug 1860; married 22 Aug 1860 by Levi Trexler, J. P.

Ketchey, John & Margaret D. Swink, 30 July 1862; Benjamin F. Weant, bondsman; Obadiah Woodson, wit. married 31 July 1862 by Jno P. Shaver, J. P.

Ketchey, Solomon & Catherine Garner, 27 March 1837; Caleb Setzer, bondsman; Tobias L. Lemly, wit.

Ketchey, Solomon & Catharine Garner, married 27 Sept 1859 by Saml Rothrock, Minister of the Gospel in the Ev. Luth. Church.

Ketchey, Solomon & Susannah Garner, 26 Sept 1859; John F. Moose, bondsman.

Ketchey, Stephen C. & Martha M. Smith, 1 Feb 1866; Henry Canup, bondsman; Obadiah Woodson, wit.

Ketchie, William R. & Sallie J. Patterson, 31 March 1866; C. H. Fisher, bondsman; Obadiah Woodson, wit.

Ketchy, David A. & Elizabeth C. Morgan, 6 Dec 1859; John L. Ketchey, bondsman; James E. Kerr, wit. married 8 Dec 1859 by Levi Trexler, J. P.

Ketchy, Henry & Mary A. Walton, 12 May 1846; Henry Moyer, bondsman; J. H. Hardie Jr., wit.

Ketchy, Rinehold & Jane M. Duke, 20 Jan 1837; Alexander Beever, bondsman.

Ketner, George M. & Susanna Shaver, 9 Sept 1844; Daniel House, bondsman; John H. Hardie Jr., wit.

Ketner, George M. & Margaret Seaford, 20 May 1852; John Ketner, bondsman; J. S. Myers, wit.

Kethear, John & Catharine Crider, 21 Feb 1805; Abraham Ary, bondsman; Moses A. Locke, wit.

Ketner, John & Mary A. Seaford, 18 Feb 1858; married by Saml. Rothrock, Minister of the Gospel in the Ev. Luth. Church.

Ketner, Peter & Sally Roseman, 6 Feb 1843; Andy Boston, bondsman; Jno Giles, wit.

Kidwell, Elijah & Hannah Butner (no date, during Gov. Martin's admn.); John McCulloh, bondsman.

Kidwell, John & Mary Swink, 30 Dec 1782; Thomas Kidwell, bondsman; William Crawford, wit.

Kiestler, John W. & Jane E. McNeely, 29 Dec 1804; W. H. Hudson, bondsman; Obadiah Woodson, wit.

Kiestler, William & Elizabeth Biggers, 9 May 1836; Robert H. W. Biggers, bondsman.

Killan, William & Amry Scott, 8 Oct 1820; Samuel Stout, bondsman; Silas Peace, Jacob _____, wit.

Killion, Daniel & Mary Smith, 29 March 1803; William Monroe, bondsman; Jno Monroe, wit.

Killpatrick, Andrew & Jane Nichols, 12 Nov 1772; Joshua Nichols, bondsman; Ad. Osborn, wit.

Kilpatrick, David & Nancy McNight, 18 July 1829; Thomas McKnight, bondsman.

Kilpatrick, Jabez N. & Lavina McCorkle, 27 Feb 1829; John F. McCorkle, bondsman; Jno H. Hardie, wit.

Kilpatrick, Moses Dickey & Jane Graham, 27 March 1812; Abel Graham, bondsman; Jno Giles, C. C., wit.

Kilpatrick, Rufus H. & Eliza Young, 30 Dec 1828; Lewis G. Slaughter, bondsman.

Kilpatrick, William & Agness McNeely, 9 Feb 1795; James McNeely, bondsman; J. Troy, wit.

Kimball, Calyer & Catharine Cauble, 3 Jan 1825; Williamson Harris, bondsman.

Kimball, Henry J. & Margaret M. Hall, 6 Dec 1854; Thomas B. Leslie, bondsman; James E. Kerr, wit. married 19 Dec 1854 by Saml. B. O. Wilson, V. D. M.

Kimball, J. G. & L. A. Gheen, 26 Dec 1863; D. S. Lentz, bondsman; Obadiah Woodson, wit.

Kimball, Joel & Sarah Lents, 28 Feb 1831; Richamond Reed, bondsman; Jno H. Hardie, wit.

Kimball, Whitson & Patience E. File, 13 March 1854; Michael Cauble, bondsman; J. S. Myers, wit. married 15 March 1854 by W. A. Walton, J. P.

Kimbrough, Aron & Nancy Stewart, 10 Feb 1805; Wm. Gunter, bondsman; Wm. Welborn, wit.

Kimbrough, Jeremiah & Sarah Mendenhall, 19 Sept 1799; David Kimbrough, bondsman; Wm. Welborn, wit.

Kimbrough, Ormon & Sarah Taylor, 30 Jan 1826; Benjamin Brock, bondsman; E. Brock, wit.

Kimmer, Henry H. & Mary C. Stiller, 1 April 1863; William Howard, bondsman; Obadiah Woodson, wit.

Kimnick, John A. & Anney Call, 7 Nov 1803; Henrich Kahll, bondsman; Jn March, J. P., wit.

Kincaid, Andrew & Mary Howard, 3 April 1793; Joseph Kincaid, bondsman; Edwin J. Osborn, D. C., wit.

Kincaid, Andrew & Mary Lefler, 30 Nov 1853; Nathan Harrison, bondsman; J. S. Myers, wit. married 1 Dec 1853 by A. Baker.

Kincaid, Andrew J. & Susan Sanders, 11 March 1839; Andrew Jackson, bondsman; Hy. Giles, wit.

Kincaid, Archibald & Rebecca Thompson, 2 April 1805; John Trott, bondsman; A. L. Osborn, D. C., wit.

Kincaid, James & Hannah Briggs, 14 June 1827; Matthew Howard, bondsman.

Kincaid, James & Nancey Duncan, 2 Sept 1797; Wm. Sanders, bondsman; Jno Rogers, wit.

Kincaid, Jesse & Hannah Kincade, 4 Nov 1823; William Julian, bondsman; Jno Giles, wit.

Kincaid, Samuel & Elizabeth Thomason, 9 Dec 1812; John Biles, bondsman; Jno Giles, wit.

Kincaid, Thomas & Claracy Brandon, 15 July 1824; William Juleon, bondsman; Chs. Withers, wit.

Kincaid, Thomas & Polly Elliott, 26 Oct 1830; Matthew Howard, bondsman; Jno H. Hardie, wit.

Kincaid, Thomas & Mary G. Owens, 7 Sept 1855; Wm. R. Fraley, bondsman; J. S. Myers, wit.

Kincaid, Wiley & Ann Selana F. Swisher, 18 March 1845; James M. Willson, bondsman.

Kincaid, Wiley & Nancy West, 1 April 1847; David Mahaley, bondsman; John H. Hardie Jr., wit.

Kincaid, William H. & Ellen Blackwell, 2 May 1839; Wm. H. Elliott, bondsman; J. S. Myers, wit.

Kinder, James & Lucy Kenney, 3 June 1855; David Manuel, bondsman; James E. Kerr, wit. married 3 June 1855 by J. M. Brown, J. P.

Kindly, Shadrach & Margaret Briles, 16 June 1791; Esau Wright, bondsman; Jno Monro, wit.

Kiney, Daniel S. & Maria Fisher, 20 Jan 1845; Eli Blackwelder, bondsman; Jno H. Hardie Jr., wit.

King, James & Cathrine Ellrod, 12 May 1768; Arthur O'Neal, Richd. Green, bondsmen; John Frohock, wit. consent from Anna Allrod, mother of Cathrine, 11 May.

King, James & Priscilla Gallet, 21 Aug 1834; Jesse Jones, bondsman; J. Tomlinson, J. P., wit.

King, John & Rachell Young, 30 Dec 1768; James Blyth, Griffeth Rutherford, bondsmen.

King, John & Eleanor Kerr, 15 May 1792; David Kerr, bondsman; Ad. Osborn, wit.

King, John & Jean Philips, 15 Aug 1826; Michel Brown, bondsman.

King, John & Elizabeth Tenpenny, _____; Jas. Townsley, bondsman; Max. Chambers, wit.

King, Nicholas & Louisa Groner, 2 Oct 1862; J. S. Johnston, bondsman; married 2 Oct 1862 by T. G. Haughton.

King, Samuel & Martha Andrews, 23 Nov 1804; Jno Andrews, bondsman; A. L. Osborn, D. C., wit.

King, Thomas & Polly Jones, 12 Aug 1829; Daniel Etcheson, bondsman; C. Harbin, J. P., wit.

King, Thomas & Mary Hall, 23 Dec 1774; James Hall, bondsman; Ad. Osborn, wit.

King, Thomas F. & R. A. Goodman, 23 Aug 1850; O. P. Houston, bondsman; Obadiah Woodson, wit.

King, William & Anis Hagins, 30 March 1818; Jno. D. Gracy, bondsman.

Kingsbury, Henry & Nancy Bradley, 20 Dec 1816; William Howard, bondsman; Jno Giles, Clk., wit.

Kingsbury, Henry & Lucy Ann Walls, 2 April 1842; John S. Johnston, bondsman.

Kinney, Christian & Katharine Smith, 31 Oct 1792; Benjamin Smith, bondsman; Jos. Chambers, wit.

Kinney, Isaac & Susannah Workman, 14 July 1813; Jonathan Coggins, bondsman; Ezra Allemong, wit.

Kinney, Jesse & Sarah Cox, 3 Feb 1814; Abraham Johnston, bondsman; Geo. Dunn, wit.

Kinnick, James & Margret Acle, 24 Feb 1817; David Harris, bondsman; John March Sr., wit.

Kinup, John & Caty Miller, 30 June 1819; Washington Hendron, bondsman; Hy. Giles, wit.

Kinyoun, Joel & Margaret Bush, 10 Dec 1817; Cornelus Smith, bondsman; R. Powell, wit.

Kinyoun, Limuel & Zilfy Ballance, 9 Sept 1827; Jacob Allen, bondsman; Wm. Hawkins, J. P., wit.

Kirf, Frederick William & Elizabeth Eagle, 1 May 1858; John A. Barrier, bondsman; John Wilkinson, wit. married 12 May 1858 by Saml. Rothrock, Minister of the Gospel in the Ev. Luth. Church.

Kirf, Jacob R. & Elizabeth Castor, 9 March 1859; Eli S. P. Lippard, bondsman; married 9 March 1859 by A. Henderson, J. P.

Kirk, Alexander & Emeline Earnheart, 18 Aug 1848; Stephen Kirk, bondsman.

Kirk, Daniel C. & Mary Shaver, 21 Dec 1848; Jesse Parker, bondsman; Jno H. Hardie Jr., wit.

Kirk, Kimbrell & Mary Eagle, 17 Aug 1858; Eli Lentz, bondsman; John Wilkinson, wit.

Kirk, Penuel & Crissy Shaver, 4 June 1853; Alexander Kirk, bondsman; James E. Kerr, wit.

Kirk, Stephen & Mary Earnheart, 23 May 1843; Edward Moss, bondsman; J. H. Hardie, wit.

Kirk, Wiley & Susannah Earnheart, 20 Oct 1847; Stephen Kirk, bondsman; John H. Hardie Jr., wit.

Kirkpatrick, Joseph & Sophia Knup, 1 Jan 1847; Lafayette Green, bondsman; J. H. Hardie, wit.

Kistler, Henry & Catharine Barringer, 26 March 1832; J. H. Hardie, bondsman.

Kistler, Jacob & Mary Pool, 24 Aug 1818; Joseph E. Dobbin, bondsman; Jno Giles, wit.

Kistler, John & Susanah Lopp, 24 March 1792; Philip Sizloff, bondsman; Jno Monro, wit.

Kistler, Valentine & Nancy Marshall, 30 March 1822; Hugh J. Willkinson, bondsman; Jno Giles, wit.

Kitner, Peter & Elizabeth Litaker, 5 Nov 1816; Daniel Shuford, bondsman; Milo A. Giles, wit.

Klotz, Jacob & Rachael Miller, 14 Jan 1809; Henry Biber, bondsman; A. L. Osborne, D. C., wit.

Klotz, Jacob & Caty Casper, 26 Feb 1812; Leonard Kluttz, bondsman; Geo. Dunn, wit.

Klountz, Christian & Margret Neal, 6 Aug 1791; George Klountz, bondsman; Charles Caldwell, D. C., wit.

Kluts, David & Tena Brown, 7 Sept 1826; Leonard Clutts, bondsman; J. H. Hardie, wit.

Kluts, John & Hannah Lefford, 7 March 1800; Lunner Klotz, bondsman.

Kluts, Tobias & Barbara Leapard, 14 Oct 1785; David Klutz, bondsman; Max. Chambers, wit.

Klutts, Alexander & Eliza Maria Brown, 14 Sept 1858; Peter A. Brown, bondsman; James E. Kerr, wit. married 16 Sept 1858 by Thornton Butler, V. D. M.

Klutts, Andrew L. & Loretto C. Holshouser, 13 Feb 1860; Jacob R. Holshouser, bondsman; Wm. Locke, wit. married 15 Feb 1860 by Thornton Butler, V. D. M.

Klutts, Caleb & Amelia Holshuser, 14 July 1837; Tobias L. Lemly, bondsman & wit.

Klutts, Caleb & Elizabeth Moose, 20 April 1841; J. L. Beard, bondsman.

Klutts, Caleb & Mary A. L. Owens, 2 Oct 1856; John A. Snider, bondsman; J. S. Myers, wit. married 2 Oct 1856 by B. C. Hall.

Klutts, Charles & Elizabeth Corl, 30 Dec 1833; David Klutts, bondsman; Wm. Locke, wit.

Klutts, Charles & Christena Walton, 25 March 1841; Moses Klutts, bondsman; Susan T. Giles, wit.

Klutts, Daniel & Catharine Cruse, 30 Sept 1846; Alexander Brown, bondsman; Jno H. Hardie, wit.

Klutts, Davault & Margaret L. Peeler, 16 Jan 1856; Moses A. Fesperman, bondsman; James E. Kerr, wit. married 17 Jan 1856 by W. A. Walton, J. P.

Klutts, Davault & Mary Jane Kirk, 16 Sept 1858; Andrew Klutts, bondsman; James E. Kerr, wit. married 23 Sept 1858 by Thornton Butler, V. D. M.

Klutts, David & Harriet Heilig (colored), 5 Aug 1865; married 5 Aug 1865 by A. J. Mock, J. P.

Klutts, David J. & Rachel Bostian, 23 Feb 1856; Julius M. Heilig, bondsman; James E. Kerr, wit. married 27 Feb 1856 by P. A. Sifferd, J. P.

Klutts, Eli & Phreney A. Correll, 21 July 1852; Jesse Thomason, bondsman; J. S. Myers, wit.

Klutts, Eli & Mary E. Linn, 22 March 1859; F. M. Y. McNeely, bondsman.

Klutts, George & Nancy Sifford, 23 Oct 1836; John Seaford, bondsman; Hy. Giles, wit.

Klutts, Henry & Sarah Lents, 19 Aug 1828; Leonard Kluts, bondsman; J. H. Hardie, wit.

Klutts, Henry & Susan Seaford, 9 June 1845; Casper Holshouser, bondsman.

Klutts, Henry & Sophia Sifferd, 15 Jan 1857; Alex. W. Buis, bondsman; J. S. Myers, wit. married 15 Jan 1857 by E. E. Phillips, J. P.

Klutts, Henry & Sarah E. Blackwelder, 14 May 1857; John H. Verble, bondsman; J. S. Myers, wit. married 14 May 1857 by L. C. Groseclose.

Klutts, Jacob & Eliza M. Holshouser, married 21 July 1853 by Saml. Rothrock, Minister of the Gospel in the Ev. Luth. Church.

Klutts, Jacob & Mary Trexler, 16 June 1860; John Cauble, bondsman; John Wilkinson, wit.

Klutts, James & Matty Garner, 18 Dec 1848; William Howard, bondsman; John H. Hardie Jr., wit.

Klutts, Jesse & Sarah E. Smith, 6 Oct 1853; Davault Kluttz, bondsman; J. S. Myers, wit.

Klutts, Jesse & Frances Smith, 24 March 1866; Stephen A. Rowe, bondsman; Obadiah Woodson, wit.

Klutts, John & Elizabeth Klutts, 5 March 1821; Adam Stirewalt, bondsman.

Klutts, Levi & Margaret L. Fraly, 20 May 1850; Elisha Smith, bondsman; J. S. Myers, wit.

Klutts, Michael & Ann E. Klutts, 31 Aug 1850; J. S. Myers, bondsman.

Klutts, Moses & Eve Trexler, 8 Dec 1840; Leonard Klutts, bondsman.

Klutts, Moses & Leah Lyerly, 29 April 1844; Andrew Holshouser, bondsman; J. H. Hardie, wit.

Klutts, Paul & Peggy Barringer, 29 March 1820; Peter Real, bondsman; Jno Giles, wit.

Klutts, R. J. & Eva L. Peeler, 2 Nov 1859; N. R. Windsor, bondsman; John Wilkinson, wit. married 3 Nov 1859 by E. E. Phillips, J. P.

Klutts, Samuel & Polly Cauble, 11 Oct 1848; Isaac Cauble, bondsman; J. H. Hardie Jr., wit.

Klutts, Simeon & Anna Trexler, 7 Feb 1848; Charles Klutts, bondsman.

Klutts, Solomon & Maria Cruse, 27 Feb 1854; Theophilus Josey, bondsman; James E. Kerr, wit. married 28 Feb 1854 by Saml. Rothrock, Minister of the Gospel in the Ev. Luth. Church.

Klutts, Tobias & Elizabeth Klutts, 18 May 1854; Davault Klutts, bondsman; J. S. Myers, wit. married 18 May 1854 by W. A. Walton, J. P.

Kluttz, Adam & Louisa M. Cauble, 4 April 1853; David D. Peeler, bondsman; J. S. Myers, wit.

Klutts, Ausborn M. & Mary C. Barringer, 21 May 1853; Moses Barringer, bondsman; J. S. Myers, wit.

Kluttz, Caleb & Flora V. Walton, 30 Aug 1853; Jesse Klutts, bondsman; J. S. Myers, wit. married 30 Aug 1853 by D. Barringer, J. P.

Kluttz, George & Mary Holdhouser, 4 June 1821; David Holshouser, bondsman; Hy. Giles, wit.

Kluttz, George B. & Martha Propst, 18 Feb 1849; Edward H. Roseman, bondsman; Jno H. Hardie Jr., wit.

Kluttz, Henry & Elizabeth Kluttz, 7 Nov 1826; Heny. Lentz, bondsman; Hy. Giles, wit.

Kluttz, Jacob & Eliza M. Holshouser, 18 July 1853; Roberson J. Kluttz, bondsman; J. S. Myers, wit.

Kluttz, John & Levinia Holtshouzer, 8 Aug 1833; David Holshousr, bondsman; R. Cochran Jr., wit.

Kluttz, Leonard & Sophia Clutz, 8 Feb 1812; Martin Hofner, bondsman; Jno Giles, C. C., wit.

Kluttz, Solomon & Anna B. Moose, 12 Sept 1842; Alfred W. Cauble, bondsman; J. H. Hardie, wit.

Klutz, Conrod & Barbara Miller, 4 March 1797; John Miller, bondsman.

Klutz, Leonard & Eve Sefort, 6 Oct 1791; Tobias Forroe, bonds-man; C. Caldwell, D. C., wit.

Klutz, Martin & Crate Pealor, 1 Jan 1821; Jacob Klotz, bondsman; Hy. Giles, wit.

Knartzar, Jacob & Jeane Bartleson, 25 Sept 1787; Zacharah Bartelson, bondsman; Ad. Osborn, wit.

Knatzer, Nicholas & Cath: Henline, 10 Aug 1769; Johannes Henlein, bondsman; Thomas Frohock, wit.

Knep, Caleb & Margarett Porter, 22 May 1844; Jessee Porter, bondsman; John H. Hardie Jr., wit.

Knop, Daniel & Mary Black, 4 Aug 1792; George Davis, bondsman; Chs. Caldwell, wit.

Knotzer, Geo Christger & Barbury Neate, 15 March 1800; William Steavans, bondsman; Matt. Troy, wit.

Knouse, George & Mary Mock, 5 Sept 1813; Jacob Mock, bondsman; J. Willson, J. P., wit.

Knox, Benjamin & Catharine Wilson, 8 Nov 1791; Alexr. Wilson, bondsman.

Knox, Benjamin & Jane Luckey, 20 Aug 1823; James G. Knox, bondsman; Hy. Giles, wit.

Knox, Benjamin & Jane L. Young, 18 Dec 1860; James Knox, bondsman; married 19 Dec 1860 by W. A. Wood.

Knox, David & Mary M. Goodman, 27 May 1842; Tobias Goodman, bondsman; J. H. Hardie, wit.

Knox, George & Easther Renshaw, 30 Nov 1803; Armstrong Brandon, bondsman; A. L. Osborn, D. C., wit.

Knox, J. G. & Mary A. Rufty, 18 March 1858; Jacob Fesperman, bondsman; James E. Kerr, wit. married 18 March 1858 by J. H. Brown, J. P.

Knox, James & Lidia Gillispie, 4 Nov 1772; Jas. Gillespie, bondsman; Ad. Osborn, wit.

Knox, James & Elenor Graham, 19 Feb 1797; Richard Graham, bondsman; Jno Rogers, wit.

Knox, James & Elizabeth Post, 17 Nov 1804; Robert Foster, bondsman; Moses S. Locke, wit.

Knox, James & F. C. Gillespie, 10 Jan 1853; Samuel F. Young, bondsman; J. S. Myers, wit.

Knox, James G. & Miriam M. Houk, 2 Jan 1843; Samuel E. McCorkle, bondsman.

Knox, James G. & Jane C. Burke, 14 July 1830; Richd. Lowry, bondsman; J. H. Hardie, wit.

Knox, John & Esther Luckey, 15 April 1780; Robert Luckie, bondsman; B. Booth Boote, wit.

Knox, John & Jinne Gillespie, 25 May 1798; Richard Gillispie, bondsman; Ma. Troy, wit.

Knox, John & Mary Chunn, 3 April 1827; David McHenry, bondsman; Hy. Giles, wit.

Knox, John R. & Jane A. Gillespie, 3 Aug 1852; T. J. Gillespie, bondsman; James E. Kerr, wit. married 5 Aug 1852 by James G. Jacocks, Rector of Christ Church, Rowan, N. C.

Knox, Samuel & Elizabeth Burris, 19 March 1821; James Gray, bondsman.

Knox, William & Margaret Armstrong, 10 April 1802; Samuel Armstrong, bondsman; Jno Brem, D. C., wit.

Knox, William & Jane Niblock, 1 Feb 1820; James Gray, bondsman; Jno Giles, wit.

Knox, William & Zillah Foster, 18 April 1821; Benjamin Knox, bondsman; George Locke, wit.

Knox, William & Sarah Webb, 7 Nov 1843; J. S. Johnston, bondsman; A. H. Caldwell, wit.

Knox, William M. & Jane C. Graham, 21 Oct 1842; James H. Smith, bondsman.

Knup, Christian & Mary White, 8 Dec 1779; George Holmes, bondsman; Jno Kerr, wit.

Knup, Daniel & Betsy Powers, _____ 1816; Edward Davis, Jno
Giles, bondsmen; Geo. Dunn, wit.

Knup, David & Milly Powlaw, 26 Feb 1822; Leonard Knup, bondsman.

Knup, David & Caty Bridy, 15 March 1831; Green Morgan, bondsman;
Jno H. Hardie, wit.

Knup, David S. & Mary Elizabeth Gheen, 12 June 1858; George Dunn,
bondsman; John Wilkinson, wit. married 13 June 1858 by W. R.
Fraley, J. P.

Knup, Frederick & Margaret Floyd, 17 June 1801; Francis Floyds,
bondsman.

Knup, John & Polly Stoner, 29 Aug 1812; Abraham Arnhart, bondsman; Geo Dunn, wit.

Knup, John & Polly Stoner, 8 July 1818; John Gardner, bondsman;
Henry Giles, wit.

Knup, Leonard & Mary Klutts, 26 Oct 1820; David Holshouser,
bondsman; Jno. Giles, wit.

Knup, Noah & Betsey Hartline, 17 Sept 1806; George Hartline,
bondsman; A. L. Osborn, wit.

Knup, Wila & Elizabeth Arey, 20 March 1846; David Earnhart,
bondsman; J. H. Hardie Jr., wit.

Koon, Jacob & Nancy Leonard, 18 April 1798; Oliver Townsley,
bondsman.

Koon, Jacob & Caroline Beaver, 3 Dec 1857; John D. Henly, bondsman; J. S. Myers, wit. married 3 Dec 1857 by N. F. Hall, J. P.

Kraus, Charles A. & Mary C. Krimminger, 23 Dec 1864; Wm. A.
Lyerla, bondsman; Obadiah Woodson, wit.

Krider, Barnabas Scott & Maria C. Cowan, 20 June 1854; A. G.
Holden, bondsman; J. S. Myers, wit.

Krider, George & Sally Srote, 23 March 1820; Thos. Holton,
bondsman.

Krider, Jacob & Sally Wood, 29 June 1815; John Albright, bondsman; Geo. Dunn, wit.

Krider, John P. & Mary Cougenour, 30 Nov 1844; Lorenzo D. Bencini,
bondsman; John H. Hardie Jr., wit.

Krider, Leonard S. & Leonoro Bost, 30 Jan 1845; Adam A. Smithdeal, bondsman; J. H. Hardie, wit.

Krite, Michal & Elizabeth Basinger, 29 March 1797; David
Woodson, bondsman; Jno Rogers, wit.

Krotzer, George & Syntha H. Kirk, 7 Nov 1853; Christopher Goodman, bondsman; J. S. Myers, wit.

Kunt(s) (Coons), Jacob & Elizabeth Hoge, 5 Dec 1816; Michael
Coons, bondsman; Joseph Clarke, wit.

Kyle, William & Jenney Huey, 5 Oct 1785; William Cuppls, bondsman.

Lackey, George & Anne Stephenson, 2 Dec 1780; Ad. Osborn, wit.

Lackey, Thomas & Margaret Stevenson, 7 Sept 1775; William Lackey, bondsman; Dd. Flowers, wit.

Lackey, W. F. & Isabella S. Lefler, widow, 13 Sept 1865; Robert C. Kennerly, bondsman; Obadiah Woodson, wit. married 13 Sept 1865 by Rev. Wm. Lambeth.

Lackey, William & Agness Stevenson, 14 Nov 1775; William Stevinson, bondsman; Ad. Osborn, wit.

Lagal, Richard & Susanah Hinkle, 5 Sept 1822; Daniel Cornatzer, bondsman; Geo. Coker, wit.

Lagle, George & Pallaton Daniel, 10 Oct 1822; Joseph Snider, bondsman; L. R. Rose, J. P., wit.

Lagle, Henry & Hannah Dickins, 12 Jan 1814; John Foster, bondsman; Jn March Sr., wit.

Laird, Nathanael & Agnes Scott, 17 Jan 1781; Frances Holmes, bondsman; H. Giffard, wit.

Lam, James & Mary Blue, 31 Dec 1788; John Blue, bondsman; W. Alexander, wit.

Lam, John & Nancy Moore, 2 Oct 1794; Douglas Blue, bondsman; J. Troy, D. C., wit.

Lamb, Alexander & Rachael Tompson, 8 April 1829; Henry Hill, bondsman; Jno. H. Hardie, wit.

Lamb, Alexander & Margaret T. Turner, 22 Jan 1851; Andrew Shuping, bondsman; J. S. Myers, wit.

Lamb, James J. & Elizabeth A. Cranford, 21 Oct 1865; Peter Scramlin, bondsman; Obadiah Woodson, wit. married 22 Oct 1865 by M. S. McKenzie, J. P.

Lamb, William & Lavina Eller, 21 April 1860; Otho Swink, bondsman; Wm. Locke, wit. married 22 April 1860 by Peter Williamson, J. P.

Lamb, William A. & Sarah Jonekin, 12 Feb 1849; Jno. Sullivan, bondsman; J. H. Hardie, wit.

Lame, James & Polly Brown, 21 March 1803; Wm. H. Mahan, bondsman; A. L. Osborn, wit.

Lamm, Moses & Mary Allbright, 21 March 1816; James Lamm, bondsman; Geo. Dunn, wit.

Lancaster, Eli & Elizabeth Korf, 9 April 1850; James C. Roseman, bondsman; James E. Kerr, wit.

Lance--see also Lentz

Lance, Peter & Mary Hartline, 2 July 1786; Henry Casper, bondsman; Jno Macay, wit.

Lance, Peter & Susana Brown, 24 Feb 1795; Phillip Brown, bondsman; Mich Troy, wit.

ROWAN MARRIAGES 1753-1868

Lance, Samuel & Rosey Sault, 3 April 1786; John Williams,
bondsman; John Macay, wit.

Lancherry, Rego & Jane Johnson, 7 April 1860; W. W. Emery, bondsman; John Wilkinson, wit. married 8 April 1860 by Peter
Williamson, J. P.

Landman, John & Celia Bruer, 7 March 1783; Daniel _____, bondsman; Will Crawford, wit.

Lane, Caleb J. & Elizabeth Rex, 3 Sept 1843; Warren Gheen, bondsman; Jno H. Hardie, wit.

Lane, Hiram & Nancy Jones, 1 Jan 1803; Charles Pidgeon, bondsman.

Lane, John A. & Kate L. Howard, 13 June 1865; Claude E. Mills,
bondsman; Obadiah Woodson, wit.

Lane, Joshua & Nancy Bird, 12 May 1818; Peter Adee, bondsman;
J. Willson, wit.

Lane, William P. & Taby Wellman, 27 July 1816; John Stephenson,
bondsman; Jn March Sr., wit.

Laney, George & Marey Welch, 29 Feb 1769; Titus Laney, Adam
Roan, bondsmen; Thos. Frohock, wit.

Langford, John & Martha Whitehead, 7 June 1779; Andrew Freeman,
bondsman; Jo. Brevard, wit.

Langly, Charlo & Elizebeth Hall, 1 Dec 1820; Jonathan Roberson,
bondsman; Andrew Swicegood, wit.

Langly, John & Sally Weaver, 11 March 1832; William Davis, bondsman; C. Harbin, J. P.

Lanier, Clement & _____, _____; David Miller, bondsman;
Jno Brem, wit.

Lanier, Lewis & Tabitha Kittle, 12 Jan 1801; Samuel Roberts,
bondsman; John Brem, D. C., wit.

Lanning, Enos & Sarah Warner, 21 Jan 1793; William Warner, bondsman; Jos. Chambers, wit.

Lanning, Joseph & Roasena Sminth, 28 Dec 1820; Enos Lanning,
bondsman; Andrew Swicegood, wit.

Lanning, Joseph & _____, _____; Isom Woods, bondsman; Tibby
Troy, wit.

Lanning, William & Rachel Wilson, 27 Nov 1822; Tho. Lanning,
bondsman; An. Swicegood, wit.

Lansdon, Robert & Susanah Bone, 20 Sept 1786; Hugh Bone, bondsman; Mar. Osborn, wit.

Lantz, Jacob & Mary Yoose, 12 May 1802; Boston Lants, bondsman;
Jno. McClelland, wit.

Lantz, John & Nancy C. Fraley, 13 April 1845; John E. Boger,
bondsman; Jno H. Hardie Jr., wit.

Lash, George & Ann Weltshire, 2 June 1762; Jacob Lash, James
Van de Merck, bondsmen.

232

Latham, Harmon & Betsy Glascock, 29 March 1804; Barny Bowers, bondsman; A. L. Osborn, D. C., wit.

Latham, Harmon R. & Marion J. James, 20 Dec 1832; Joshua Howell, bondsman; J. Tomlinson, J. P., wit.

Latham, James & Cassey Wellman, 24 Jan 1828; Wilson Rose, bondsman; L. R. Rose, J. P., wit.

Lathgo, Joseph & Anney Elot, 18 July 1805; William Patterson, bondsman; Oh. Beck, wit.

Lathram, Robert & _____, 19 March 1804; Joseph Kincaid, bondsman; M. Stokes, wit.

Lathrum, Benjamin & Caty Trusty, 30 Sept 1812; Shugers King, bondsman; Jno Giles, C., wit.

Laughlin, Robert & Elsey Shelton, 22 Nov 1811; John Brayn, bondsman; Ezra Allemong, wit.

Lauman, George & Sarah Jones, 17 Aug 1775; Jacob Uttzman, bondsman; David Flowers, wit.

Laurance, George & Mary E. Eller, 19 Oct 1865; Lewis H. Wood, bondsman; Obadiah Woodson, wit. married 20 Oct 1865 by Wm. P. Kontz, Chaplain, 128th Ind.

Lawrence, Adam & Rachel McLeland, 26 July 1783; James Ramsay, bondsman; T. H. McCaule, wit.

Lawrence, Addison S. & Margaret E. Graham, 30 Dec 1858; W. F. Watson, bondsman; James E. Kerr, wit. married 4 Jan 1859 by S. C. Alexander.

Lawson, Hiram & Margaret A. C. Overcash, 20 Jan 1855; George Morgan, bondsman; J. S. Myers, wit.

Lawson, Hugh Jr. & Rebekah McConnel, 26 May 1770; David Criswell, Wm. McConnel, bondsmen. consent from John McConnel Senr., 22 May 1770, father of Rebakah.

Lawson, Thomas H. & Elener Brown, 21 Dec 1840; William J. Edwards, bondsman; Jno Giles, wit.

Lawson, Woodey & Elizabeth Goodman, 25 June 1853; Geo. M. Weant, bondsman.

Lawwell, Saml. & Jinny James, 13 Aug 1798; Barnibas Bowers, bondsman.

Lazenby, Robert W. & Seneth Bostian, 2 June 1838; Alfred N. Lazenby, bondsman; S. Lemly Jr., wit.

Lazenby, W. S. & Mary Curry, 21 Feb 1859; James C. Caldwell, bondsman; James E. Kerr, wit. married 21 Feb 1859 by G. D. Bernheim.

Leach, David & Catharine Nail, 26 Oct 1822; Enoch Leach, bondsman; A. R. Jones, wit.

Leach, Elisha & Nancy Glasscock, 27 Dec 1816; Joseph Abbrock, bondsman; R. Powell, wit.

Leach, Enoch & Diannah Rowzee, 7 Aug 1818; John Hindricks, bondsman; John March Sr., wit.

Leach, Hugh & Mary Collett, 14 March 1817; Nicholas Thomas, bondsman; Silas Peace, wit.

Leach, James & Peggy Campbell, 13 March 1805; John Trott, bondsman; Moses A. Locke, wit.

Leach, John & Hannah P. Renshaw, 20 April 1817; Elijah Renshaw, bondsman; R. Powell, wit.

Leach, John & Eve Cathey, 17 Feb 1819; Moses A. Morgan, bondsman; Jno. Giles, wit.

Leach, John H. & Huldah Baxter, 10 Dec 1815; Francis Renshaw, bondsman; R. Powell, wit.

Leach, Richard & Elizabeth Maxwell, 12 March 1825; Henry Willson, bondsman; L. R. Rose, J. P.

Leach, Richard & Barbara Simpson, 27 Aug 1860; Tobias Hess, bondsman; John Wilkinson, wit. married 27 Aug 1860 by J. Thomason, J. P.

Leach, Thomas & _____, 16 Oct 1814; James Renshaw, bondsman; R. Powell, wit.

Leach, Zadok & Nancy Lovelace, 29 March 1794; James Leach, bondsman; B. John Pinchback, Lydia Pinchback, wit.

Leagel, John & Jenney Notson, 21 Sept 1807; James Johnnecy, bondsman; Jn March, wit.

Leatherman, Isaac & Sophiah Heasly, 10 March 1814; Christian Leatherman, bondsman; Joseph Clarke, wit.

Leatherman, Jonas & Martha Reed, 6 Dec 1816; Daniel Leatherman, bondsman; T. Hampton, wit.

Leazar, Augustus & Cornelia F. McCorkle, 22 Dec 1865; Geo. A. Atwell, bondsman; Obadiah Woodson, wit.

Leazar, Daniel & Mary Corriher, 10 June 1834; Jo. Leazar Jr., bondsman; Abel Cowan, wit.

Leazar, Daniel & Elizabeth Woods, 3 Feb 1855; David K. Woods, bondsman; J. S. Myers, wit.

Leazar, Jacob & Catey Sloop, 23 June 1803; John Coleman, bondsman; A. L. Osborn, D. C., wit.

Leazar, James W. & Elizabeth Leazar, 9 Oct 1849; Henry Menas, bondsman; James E. Kerr, wit.

Leazar, John & Elizabeth Coleman, 13 Jan 1801; William Coleman, bondsman; Jno Brem, D. C., wit.

Leazar, John Jr. & Isabella Jamison, 1 June 1835; Hy. Giles, bondsman.

Leazar, Levi A. & Catharine Upright, 16 Aug 1848; Samuel S. Upright, bondsman; J. H. Hardie, wit.

Leazar, Reuben & Catherine R. Yost, 13 April 1845; Matthew Woods, bondsman; Jno. H. Hardie, Jr., wit.

Ledford, Buise & Hannah Jonson, 31 Dec 1815; John Johnson, bondsman; Sol. Davis, J. P., wit.

Ledford, Samuel & Mary Herman, 18 Nov 1794; Laurence Clinard, bondsman; Fredrick Miller, wit.

Ledwell, Daniel & Hannah Pool, 20 Dec 1828; Wm. Black, bondsman; Jno. H. Hardie, wit.

Ledwell, Luke & Elizabeth Sell, 29 May 1855; Jacob Corle, bondsman; D. W. Honeycutt, wit. married 29 March 1855 by D. W. Honeycutt, J. P.

Lee, Edward & Patsy Jones, 29 March 1823; Jac. Miller, bondsman; M. Hanes, J. P., wit.

Lee, Henry C. & Mary C. Creson, 3 March 1849; L. D. Bencini, bondsman.

Lee, Hillary & Aley Garner, 29 Jan 1827; Thos. H. Garner, bondsman; Wm. Hawkins, J. P., wit.

Lee, James & Mary Smith, 17 Aug 1779; Thomas Jones, bondsman; Jo. Brevard, wit.

Lee, James & Ratchel Todd, 16 April 1804; James Todd, bondsman; J. Hunt, wit.

Lee, James J. & Mahala Buie, 16 Aug 1837; Henry Belton, bondsman; Tobias S. Lemly, wit.

Lee, Nathan & Anne Rich, 11 Nov 1809; Hillery Lee, bondsman; A. Hunt, wit.

Lee, Robert C. & Mary Howell, 12 Feb 1825; John T. Campbell, bondsman; L. R. Rose, J. P., wit.

Lee, William & Nancy Cox, 10 May 1815; Ransom Williams, bondsman; Wm. Bean, J. P., wit.

Leech, Richard & Elizabeth Linebarrier, 14 Feb 1850; J. S. Myers, bondsman; James E. Kerr, wit.

Leeper, James & Mary Blar, 4 Nov 1766; Hugh Blayer, Thomas Blear, bondsmen.

Leezer, Daniel & Mary Coleman, 8 Feb 1809; William Coleman, bondsman; Ad. Osborn, wit.

Leezier, Henry & Betsey Baker, 2 Dec 1816; Jacob Goodnight, bondsman; Jno Giles, C. C., wit.

Lefler, Daniel & Issabella Barr, 2 Feb 1857; Robert Kenerly, bondsman; J. S. Myers, wit. married 11 Feb 1857 by D. R. Bradshaw, J. P.

Lefler, Henry & Rebecca Scott, 14 Sept 1841; Richmond Foster, bondsman.

Lefler, Jacob & Sarah Brown, 31 July 1834; William Brown, bondsman; Hy. Giles, wit.

Lefler, John & Mary Daniel, 20 Jan 1842; John McLeod, bondsman; J. S. Johnston, wit.

Lefler, William & Julian Mowry, 25 Dec 1865; Tobias Miller, bondsman; Horatio N. Woodson, wit.

Lefler, William M. & Crissey Stoner, 29 July 1853; Reid Misenhimer, bondsman.

Lefflerr, Henry & Elizabeth Rusher, 27 Aug 1814; John Leffler, bondsman; Jno Giles, C. C., wit.

Leghtell, Thomas & Elizabeth C. Knox, 22 May 1841; James Knox, bondsman; J. H. Hardie, wit.

Leib, Jacob & Mary Qulman, 4 April 1794; John House, bondsman; Jo. Chambers, wit.

Lemley, Jacob & Sarah Hill, 29 Oct 1853; Obadiah Woodson, bondsman; J. S. Myers, wit. married 6 Nov 1853 by H. W. Hill, J. P.

Lemly, Benjamin T. & Susan Bruner, 11 Oct 1860; William W. Hoffner, bondsman; H. W. Hill, wit.

Lemly, David A. & Mary J. Crowell, 20 Aug 1859; John Frick, bondsman; James E. Kerr, wit.

Lemly, George & Catherine Linbarier, 29 Aug 1805; Tho. Todd, bondsman; Andrew Kerr, wit.

Lemly, Moses & Sally Bruner, 19 Oct 1827; Samel Creeson, bondsman; Hy. Giles, wit.

Lemly, Philip & Eliz. Kecher, 2 Aug 1785; Jno. Eller, bondsman.

Lemly, Philip & Elizabeth Casper, 18 Sept 1839; Moses Lamly, bondsman; Hy. Giles, wit.

Lemly, Philip & Margaret Harkey, 24 Feb 1851; Jesse Wilhelm, bondsman; J. S. Myers, wit.

Lemly, Tobias & Maria Pool, 30 July 1840; Henry Belton, bondsman; Elizabeth Giles, wit.

Lemly, Samuel & Betsy Furrer, 20 Jan 1811; Jas. Gillaspie, bondsman; Geo. Dunn, wit.

Lemons, Larkin & Ann Elizabeth Weaver, 21 Oct 1865; J. H. Martin, bondsman; Obadiah Woodson, wit. married 22 Oct 1865 by D. L. Bringle, J. P.

Lenard, Thomas & Ginney Barlow, 30 Aug 1820; Joshua Riley, bondsman; Geo. Coker, wit.

Lence, Boston & Betsey Lance, 20 Feb 1817; John Lence, bondsman; Milo A. Giles, wit.

Lence, Dawalt & Catharine Miller, 18 Jan 1811; Exra Allemong, wit.

Lence, George & Lancy Casper, 30 Jan 1818; Peter Lance, bondsman; Roberts Nanny, wit.

Lence, Henry & Susan Knup, 11 Jan 1823; Peter Lents, bondsman; M. A. Giles, wit.

Lence, John & Elizabeth Lince, 4 Sept 1816; Conrad Stoner, bondsman; Milo A. Giles, wit.

Lenningham, Allen & Catharine Patrick, 24 Aug 1809; Nathan Madden, bondsman; Jno Giles, C. C., wit.

Lents, Aberham & Evy Hartmon, 13 March 1820; George Smithel, bondsman.

Lents, George J. & Margaret Ann Elizabeth Roseman, 1 Sept 1864; J. A. Smith, bondsman; Obadiah Woodson, wit.

Lents, John & Milly Clutz, 29 Sept 1814; Jos. Chambers Jr., bondsman; Jno Giles, C. C., wit.

Lents, John T. & Sarah L. Klutts, 14 April 1852; Jacob Klutts, bondsman; James E. Kerr, wit.

Lents, Mathise & Caroline Klutts, 6 May 1851; Moses Fesperman, bondsman; J. S. Myers, wit.

Lents, Simeon & Catherine Aegle, 1 March 1837; Alfred Brown, bondsman; Tob. S. Lemly, wit.

Lentz--see also Lance, Lantz

Lentz, Abram & Catharine Wilhelm, 25 April 1861; Henry R. Kesler, bondsman; H. W. Hall, wit.

Lentz, Bostian & Catherine Peeler, 29 March 1845; David Clutts, bondsman; Jno H. Hardie Jr., wit.

Lentz, Bostian & Sophie Frietly, 14 March 1797; Frederick Miller, bondsman; Jno Rogers, wit.

Lentz, Bostian & Mary Houldsouser, 20 March 1824; Michael Hoffman, bondsman; Jno Giles, wit.

Lentz, Clark & Hannah Barringer (colored), 27 Oct 1865; married 28 Oct 1865 by H. Barringer, J. P.

Lentz, Dauvelt & Catharine Cluts, 7 _____ 1800; Peter Lentz, bondsman; Nl. Chaffin, J. P., wit.

Lentz, Davalt & _____, _____ 179_; _____ bondsman; Jno Brem, D. C., wit.

Lentz, David & Nelly Bost, 18 June 1834; John Wilds, bondsman; Hy. Giles, wit.

Lentz, Dawald & Christena Helick, 24 June 1841; J. S. Myers, bondsman; Jno Giles, wit.

Lentz, Dawalt & Sally Lipe, 28 Jan 1828; Jno Lentz, bondsman; Jno Giles, wit.

Lentz, Edmund D. & Barbara Shaver, 4 Aug 1851; David C. Parker, bondsman; James E. Kerr, wit. married 11 Sept 1851 by Levi Trexler, J. P.

Lentz, Eli C. & Sarah L. Hall, 15 April 1858; John P. Thomason, bondsman; John Wilkinson, wit. married 15 April 1858 by Wm. T. Martin, J. P.

Lentz, Henry & Betsy Link, 25 March 1814; Abraham Lentz, bondsman; Jno Giles, C. C., wit.

Lentz, Henry & Catharine Brown, 1 Feb 1848; John H. Hardie, bondsman.

Lentz, Henry G. & Elizabeth Hudgens, 10 April 1854; Thos. C. McNeely, bondsman; married 13 April 1854 by Saml Rothrock, Minister of the Gospel in the Ev. Luth. Church.

Lentz, Jacob & Christina Smather, 6 March 1813; John Smather, bondsman; Geo. Dunn, wit.

Lentz, Jacob & Catherine Clutz, 8 Aug 1818; Michael Brown, bondsman; Roberts Nanny, wit.

Lentz, John & Sophia Hielick, 24 May 1841; Simeon Heilick, bondsman; Susan T. Giles, wit.

Lentz, John C. & Jane M. Gheen, 9 April 1866; George H. Gheen, bondsman; Obadiah Woodson, wit.

Lentz, Joseph & Rachael Beever, 1 Dec 1828; Jno. Lents, bondsman; Jno. H. Hardie, wit.

Lentz, Michael & Catharine Hornbaryer, 17 Jan 1800; Henry Hornbaryer, bondsman; Eli Gaither, wit.

Lentz, Peter & Elizabeth Beaver, 5 April 1820; Jacob Lentz, bondsman; Henry Allemong, wit.

Lentz, Peter & Polly Hornbarrier, 21 Feb 1824; Wm. Dickson, bondsman; Hy. Giles, wit.

Lentz, Peter & Polly Keisler, 8 Aug 1833; John M. Eller, bondsman; R. Cochran, J. P., wit.

Lentz, R. A. & Sarah Bullen, 23 Aug 1860; John Eagle, bondsman; John Wilkinson, wit.

Lentz, Robert A. & Mary May, 9 April 1857; David Barringer, bondsman; J. S. Myers, wit.

Lentz, Simeon & Mary Moyer, 21 Sept 1846; Eli Lents, bondsman; J. H. Hardie Jr., wit.

Lentz, Tobias & Lydia Hill, 18 Oct 1845; Henry W. Hill, bondsman.

Lentz, Tobias & Louiza Hartman, 21 Dec 1855; Abner Pace, bondsman; J. S. Myers, wit. married 21 Dec 1855 by H. W. Hill.

Lentz, William A. & Lunda M. Barringer, 26 Nov 1851; Joseph Barringer, bondsman; J. S. Myers, wit.

Lentz, Wilson A. & Mary Eddleman, 26 Oct 1846; Henry Kluts, bondsman; John H. Hardie Jr., wit.

Leonard, Peter & Betsy Sowers, 24 Dec 1815; Michael Leonard, bondsman; J. Willson, J. P., wit.

Leonard, Solomon & Malinda Airry, 23 May 1837; Daniel H. Workman, bondsman; Tobias S. Lemly, wit.

Leonard, Valentine & Lucy Leonard, 7 Dec 1861; Alfred Leonard, bondsman; Obadiah Woodson, wit. married 8 Dec 1861 by Jno. A. Bradshaw, J. P.

Leopard, Henry & Susanna Shee, 21 March 1822; Henry Giles, bondsman.

Lester, John & Elsy Biddleton, 25 July 1820; Saml. Lemly, bondsman.

Lester, Nathaniel B. & Margaret Cowan, 5 Feb 1848; John E. Poston, bondsman; J. H. Hardie, wit.

Letchco, Lark & Levina Rawl, 9 March 1808; Henry Coots, bondsman; Andrew Kerr, wit.

Lethco, William & Elizabeth Sawyers, 14 May 1842; Henry Moyer, bondsman; Jno. H. Hardie, wit.

Lewellin, John & Elizabeth A. Brown, 11 Nov 1844; Jno. J. Shaver, bondsman.

Lewey, Michael & Betsy Shepperd, 1 Oct 1815; Leonard Goss, bondsman; Geo. Dunn, wit.

Lewis, Charles & Elizabeth Fain, 25 May 1807; David Morton, bondsman; Jn. March Sr., wit.

Lewis, Daniel & Anne Turner, 4 May 1813; Samuel Marlin, bondsman; Geo. Dunn, wit.

Lewis, Elam G. & Teisey C. McCorkle, 10 Aug 1833; D. C. Foster, bondsman.

Lewis, Jacob & Sally Cowan, 22 Oct 1802; Samuel Cowan, bondsman; A. L. Osborn, wit.

Lewis, Joel & Rachael Stapleton, __ Jan 1795; Whitmell Ryall, bondsman.

Lewis, John & Margaret Coon, 24 April 1809; Henry Coon, bondsman; Jno Giles, wit.

Lewis, John & Ruthy Stinchcomb, 10 Jan 1832; Thos. Walker, bondsman; Thomas McNeely, J. P., wit.

Lewis, Noah & Elizabeth Linster, 20 Oct 1843; J. H. Hardie, bondsman.

Lewis, Noah & Joyce Swink, 22 April 1848; Otho Swink, bondsman; J. H. Hardie, wit.

Lewis, Richmon & Sally Benson, 31 Oct 1822; Henderson Benson, bondsman.

Lewis, Samuel & Jean McKay, 31 Oct 1785; Peter Lewis, bondsman; Spruce Macay, wit.

Lewis, William & Sarah Reid, 11 Aug 1778; James Lewis, bondsman; Spruce Macay, wit.

Lewy, Adam & Marian Cunningham, 16 Dec 1820; Noah Cunningham, bondsman; Hy. Giles, wit.

Leyerly, Aaron & Mary Steward, 22 March 1821; Samuel Hartwell, bondsman; E. Allemong, wit.

Liesser, John & Barbara Cobble, 7 Sept 1808; Peter Cobble, bondsman; A. L. Osborne, wit.

Lilly, E. W. & Julian Thomas, 19 Sept 1850; John F. Miller, bondsman; H. Kelly, J. P., wit.

Lilly, William H. & Camilla C. Tores, 11 Jan 1825; Joseph B. Ingram, bondsman; Hy. Giles, wit.

Lillycrop, William & Mahaley Jane Garmon, 10 May 1861; married 10 May 1861 by E. Mauney, J. P.

Limbaugh, Daniel & Sarah M. Hall, 26 Jan 1823; G. W. Grimes, bondsman; Hy. Giles, wit.

Linch, Stephen & Polly Loftin, 2 ____ 1803; Jno Brem, bondsman; A. L. Osborn, D. C., wit.

Lindsey, J. T. & A. E. Oates, 22 Feb 1866; W. H. Howerton, bondsman; Obadiah Woodson, wit.

Line, Joab & Jean Wiseman, 31 Oct 1791; Isaac Wiseman, bondsman; Chs. Caldwell, wit.

Line, William & Eleanor Wiseman, 13 Dec 1787; Isaac Wiseman, bondsman; Js. McEwen, wit.

Linebarre, William & Nancy Rousher, 22 Sept 1849; John L. Rusher, bondsman; James E. Kerr, wit.

Linebarrier, Cornelius & Sarah Glover, 21 March 1832; John Glover, bondsman; J. H. Hardie, wit.

Lineberger, John & Mary Ross, 20 Oct 1837; David Wise, bondsman; Hy. Giles, wit.

Lineberger, Nicholas & Katey Kyker, 10 Aug 1797; Philip Lemley, bondsman; Jno Rogers, wit.

Lineberger, Peter & Mary Airy, 8 Jan 1807; John Waller, bondsman; A. L. Osborn, D. C., wit.

Linebier, Holen & Nancy Stoner, 10 Sept 1858; Noah Canup, bondsman; James E. Kerr, wit.

Lingle, Alfred & Sarah Ann Coleman, 13 April 1860; Alexander Lamb, bondsman; John Wilkinson, wit.

Lingle, Anthony & Rebeca Cauble, 20 May 1803; Henry Dowland, bondsman; A. L. Osborn, D. C., wit.

Lingle, Anthony & Elizabeth Dolen, (no date, during Gov. Spaight's admn); Henry Doulin, bondsman; Mich. Troy, wit.

Lingle, Conrod & Christiana Sevetts, 21 Oct 1790; Casper Lingle, bondsman; C. Caldwell, D. C., wit.

Lingle, Jacob & Mary Gruss, 7 Aug 1788; Andres Gross, bondsman; Wm. Alexander, wit.

Lingle, Jacob & Elizabeth Sefford, 29 Dec 1830; John Sefford, bondsman; J. Perdue, wit.

Lingle, John & Caty Isahom, 28 July 1832; Henry Moose, bondsman.

Lingle, John & Eve Ann Peeler, 13 Aug 1853; J. E. Moore, bondsman; J. S. Myers, wit. married 18 Aug 1853 by Saml. Rothrock, Minister of the Gospel in the Ev. Luth. Church.

Lingle, John & Margarett Peeler, 13 March 1841; Solomon Peeler, bondsman; Susan T. Giles, wit.

Lingle, John & Margaret Ramsey, 22 Aug 1855; Thomas Rimor, bondsman; J. S. Myers, wit. married 23 Aug 1855 by John S. Heilig.

Lingle, Laurence & Betsey Lence, 17 Sept 1821; Joseph E. Todd, bondsman; Jno Giles, wit.

Lingle, Moses & Louize Trexler, 20 Feb 1847; Eli Lents, bondsman; J. H. Hardie, wit.

Lingle, Moses & Nancy C. Knox, 16 May 1853; David Fisher, bondsman; J. S. Myers, wit. married 17 May 1853 by P. H. Dalton.

Lingle, Moses & Jane C. Cowan, 4 Nov 1848; John Irwin, bondsman.

Lingle, Wilson A. & Martha J. Linch, 13 Dec 1858; William H. Smith, bondsman; John Wilkinson, wit. married 16 Dec 1858 by L. C. Groseclose.

Link, Aaron & Elizabeth Phifer, 5 Aug 1824; Jesse Pinkston, bondsman; Jno Giles, wit.

Link, Henry & Nancy Hinkle, 29 Oct 1812; Henry Sowers, bondsman; Jno Giles, C. C., wit.

Link, Jacob & Nancy Pinkston, 2 Jan 1793; James Gheen, bondsman; Jos. Chambers, wit.

Link, Jacob, aged 70 and Nancy Burge, aged 35, 20 Jan 1803; George Rary, bondsman; A. L. Osborn, D. C., wit.

Link, Jacob & Mary Rese or Rex, 6 Nov 1817; John Rainy, bondsman; Henry Giles, wit.

Link, James M. & Margaret R. Penninger, 20 March 1866; John W. Link, bondsman; Obadiah Woodson, wit.

Link, James R. & Nancy H. Bigham, 22 Dec 1860; Allison Scott, bondsman; John Wilkinson, wit. married 26 Dec 1860 by Daniel J. Dreher.

Link, John W. & Amey Emberson, 25 April 1844; John Harris, bondsman; Jno. H. Hardie Jr., wit.

Link, John W. & Elizabeth Casper, 7 Sept 1853; Henry Rary, bondsman; J. S. Myers, wit.

Link, Josiah & Jane Rex, 23 Feb 1831; Jacob H. Link, bondsman; Hy. Giles, wit.

Link, Oliver & Margaret Ann Green, 25 Feb 1858; married 25 Feb 1858 by Moses Powlass, J. P.

Link, William & Mary Hage, 4 March 1813; Jacob Hage, bondsman; Geo. Dunn, wit.

Link, William & Nancy Townsley, 4 Nov 1824; Wm. Hulin, bondsman;
Henry Allemong, wit.

Linn, David & Eliza Hartman, 23 June 1830; Jacob Brown, bondsman; M. A. Giles, wit.

Linn, David & Sophia R. Correl, 4 Feb 1840; John Linn, bondsman;
J. L. Beard, D. C., wit.

Linn, James R. & Elizabeth Bruner, 9 Oct 1829; Samuel Ribelin,
bondsman; Jno H. Hardie, wit.

Linn, Moses & Catharine M. Beaver, 24 July 1854; Simeon Beaver,
bondsman; James E. Kerr, wit.

Linn, Moses & Elizabeth Wermington, 4 Dec 1856; Green D. Redwine,
bondsman; D. W. Honeycut, wit. married 7 Dec 1856 by Saml.
Rothrock, Minister of the Gospel in the Ev. Luth. Church.

Linn, Samuel & Elizabeth Hiligh, 15 June 1818; George Heilig,
bondsman.

Linn, Robert J. & Joicey C. Redwine, 16 Nov 1855; J. J. McConnaughey, bondsman; John Wilkinson, wit. married 17 Nov 1858
by Saml. Rothrock, Minister of the Gospel in the Ev. Luth.
Church.

Linn, Thomas J. & Elizabeth Klutts, 26 April 1861; Alexander
Holshouser, bondsman; James E. Kerr, wit. married 26 April
1861 by L. C. Groseclose, Pastor of St. John's Ev. Luthan.
Church, Salisbury, N. C.

Linnster, Humphrey & Goodin Ford, 6 April 1816; John Foard,
bondsman; Geo. Dunn, wit.

Linster, Isaac & Hannah Kincade, 10 April 1804; Joseph Kincaid,
bondsman.

Linster, Isaac & Lishia Howard, 28 Jan 1822; John Howard,
bondsman; Hy. Giles, wit.

Linster, Robert & Mary Linster, 2 Aug 1796; Patrick Dougherty,
bondsman; J. Troy, wit.

Linster, William E. & Peggy Lewis, 14 Oct 1822; Richmond Lewis,
bondsman; M. A. Giles, wit.

Linton, Samuel & Roxanna O. Fraley, 25 March 1862; Moses B.
Murr, bondsman; Obadiah Woodson, wit. married 26 March 1862
by A. W. Mangum.

Linvel, Aron & Charity Hutchens, 23 May 1769; David Linvel,
John Hutchens, bondsmen; Charles McAnally, wit.

Linvil, John & Sarah Busby (no date, during Gov Martin's admn);
William Worthington, bondsman; Hugh Magoune, wit.

Lipard, John & Sarah Ann Peeler, 2 June 1851; Caleb Klutts,
bondsman; J. S. Myers, wit.

Lipe, Alexander & Jane Coleman, 15 Dec 1833; Samuel Hargrave,
bondsman; Jno. H. Hardie, wit.

Lipe, Aaron & Caty Overcash, 28 Sept 1827; Philip Overcash,
bondsman; J. H. Hardie, wit.

Lipe, Caleb J. & Huldah J. Houck, 1 June 1865; Wm. K. Albright, bondsman; Obadiah Woodson, wit.

Lipe, Elias & Anny Cossey, 29 Jan 1819; Robert Henry, bondsman; Jno Giles, wit.

Lipe, Alexander L. & Elizabeth L. Ketner, 2 Oct 1856; Felix E. Lipe, bondsman; J. S. Myers, wit. married 9 Oct 1856 by Saml. Rothrock, Minister of the Gospel in the Ev. Luth. Church.

Lipe, Elijah Irenius & Clarrissa E. Carriker, 26 Aug 1859; Joel J. Freeze, bondsman; John Wilkinson, eit.

Lipe, Jacob S. & Sarah Couger, 30 Aug 1859; Samuel J. Fetzer, bondsman.

Lipe, John K. & Esther Deaton, 20 Aug 1851; John C. Gillispie, bondsman; J. S. Myers, wit.

Lipe, Jonas & Polly Downes, 26 Aug 1826; Abraham Lipe, bondsman.

Lipe, Simon J. & Lydia S. Freeze, 18 Feb 1854; Alexander Lipe, bondsman; James E. Kerr, wit. married 9 March 1854 by C. L. Partee, J. P.

Lipe, William A. & Catharine E. Freeze, 13 Nov 1854; Alexander Lipe, bondsman; J. S. Myers, wit.

Lippard, Alison, L. J. & Sarah A. E. Holbrooks, 26 June 1862; Eli S. P. Lippard, bondsman; Obadiah Woodson, wit.

Lippard, C. W. & M. A. Dobbin, 1 Aug 1863; Jno. A. Hampton, bondsman; Obadiah Woodson, wit.

Lippard, Eli S. P. & Elizabeth L. Yost, 5 Sept 1855; George A. Rusher, bondsman; James E. Kerr, wit. married 12 Sept 1855 by J. A. Linn.

Lippard, Henry C. & Elizabeth M. Edwards, 13 Jan 1821; Saml. F. Love, bondsman.

Lippard, J. H. A. & Catherine D. Barger, 16 March 1861; Jacob A. Rendleman, bondsman; John Wilkinson, wit. married 20 March 1861 by L. C. Groseclose.

Lippard, John & Eliz. Sausamon, 12 May 1785; Jno Jose, bondsman.

Lippard, John & Sally Sefford, 16 March 1818; Henry Berger, bondsman; Roberts Nanny, wit.

Lippard, John & Sarah L. Beaver, 31 March 1862; A. H. Heilig, bondsman; Obadiah Woodson, wit.

Lippard, John H. A. & Louiza R. H. Greaber, 10 May 1852; George A. Rusher, bondsman; J. S. Myers, wit.

Lippard, Peter W. & Margaret Ann Bostian, 26 Aug 1851; John Lippard, bondsman; James E. Kerr, wit.

Lippard, William Alexander & Milly Josey, 6 March 1830; Daniel Lippard, bondsman; Jno. H. Hardie, wit.

Lippard, Henry & Christianner Berger, 4 March 1795; J. Troy, bondsman.

Lipperd, Henry & Priscilla Turner, 26 Feb 1827; Danl. H. Cress, bondsman; Jno. H. Hardie, wit.

Lippert, Christian & Elizabeth Sauserman, 6 March 1793; Martin Basinger, bondsman.

Lirely, Henry & Mary Fite, 12 Nov 1806; Georg Waller, bondsman.

Lister, John & Elizabeth Donlop, 16 Feb 1775; Thos. Cribs, bondsman.

Litaker, Jesse W. & Juliana Hall, 22 May 1845; John Litaker, bondsman; Jno H. Hardie Jr., wit.

Litaker, John & Mary Bostian, 10 Sept 1845; William R. Litaker, bondsman; John H. Hardie Jr., wit.

Litaker, Peter & Margaret C. Lyerly, 23 Jan 1845; John Litaker, bondsman; Jno. H. Hardie Jr., wit.

Litaker, Philip & Betsey Hilick, 15 Dec 1821; Philip Cruse, bondsman; Jno Giles, wit.

Litaker, William & Margaret Weaver, 19 July 1851; Wm. A. Gillon, bondsman; James E. Kerr, wit.

Litaker, William & Christiana Weaver, 8 Aug 1837; David Bostian, bondsman; R. Jones, wit.

Litaker, William R. & Emeline Stirewalt, 17 March 1856; George E. Bost, bondsman; J. S. Myers, wit.

Liteaker, Jacob & Elizab Cope, 19 March 1807; Michael Click, bondsman; Jn March Sr., wit.

Litherd, Abraham & Crade Lauson, 6 April 1797; Washton Lentz, bondsman; Jno. Rogers, wit.

Litten, James & Ann Thomson, 12 June 1769; Hendry Thompson, bondsman; Thomas Frohock, wit. consent from Henry Thompson, 11 June 1769.

Little, Daniel & Eliza Gullet, 19 March 1860; James Holt, bondsman; Wm. Locke, wit. married 19 March 1860 by Wm. H. Trott, J. P.

Little, John & Jean Hall, 24 Oct 1796; Moses Linster, bondsman; Jno Rogers, wit.

Little, John & Bellany Erwin, 1 Oct 1768; Tho Frohock, wit. consent from Wm. Erwen, 29 Sept 1768.

Little, Samuel & Elizabeth Boon, 14 Aug 1801; Hazel Black, bondsman.

Little, Wesley & Mary Killion, 17 Oct 1816; Drury Gillam, bondsman; Ezekiel Brown, Kres Little, wit.

Livengood, Daniel & Sarah Ijams, 23 April 1821; Jacob Livingood, bondsman; Zebulon Hunt, wit.

Livengood, George & Elizabeth Bumgarner, 20 June 1819; Matthias Hagee, bondsman; Sol. Davis, J. P., wit.

Livengood, Hartman & Elizabeth Attinger, 18 July 1794; Philip
Attinger, bondsman; J. Troy, D. C., wit.

Livengood, Michl. & Ef Hagey, _____ 1796; Christian Levingood,
bondsman; Jno Rogers, wit.

Livengood, Thomas & Eve Shewler, 13 April 1818; George Myers,
bondsman; S. Hunt, J. P., wit.

Livengood, Tobias & Margaret Adinger, 24 July 1818; John Livengood, bondsman; Z. Hunt, wit.

Livengood, Tobias & Sarah Knoy, 19 Aug 1820; John Livengood,
bondsman; Silas Peace, wit.

Livingston, William & Isbell Robins, 22 Sept 1767; Hugh Montgomery, bondsman; Thomas Frohock, wit.

Lock, Alexander & Rachel Clary (no date, during Gov. Martin's
admn.); Daniel Clary, bondsman.

Lock, Daniel & Margaret Hanna, 22 Jan 1816; William Locke,
bondsman; Jno Giles, C. C., wit.

Lock, John & Margaret Locke, 28 July 1779; Richard Trotter,
bondsman; Jo. Brevard, wit.

Lock, Matthew & Ann Lock, 20 Jan 1784; Mat. Locke, bondsman.

Lock, Richard & Jennet Robison, 24 March 1790; William Lock,
bondsman; Ad. Osborn, C. C., wit.

Lock, Richard & Martha McCulloch, 3 March 1785; William Lock,
bondsman.

Lock, William & Elisabeth Marshal, 20 Dec 1791; Mathew Lock,
bondsman; Chs. Caldwell, wit.

Locke, Alexander & Elizabeth Helard, 27 March 1816; Danl. Clary,
bondsman; Jno Giles, wit.

Locke, George A. & Sarah Anderson, 13 Sept 1845; Hardy H. Helfer,
bondsman; Jno H. Hardie, wit.

Locke, George W. & Margaret Locke, 20 Dec 1827; Alexander R.
Lourence, bondsman; J. H. Hardie, wit.

Locke, John & Ann Hanna, 21 Nov 1811; John Howard, bondsman;
Jno Giles, C. C., wit.

Locke, John & Mary Sloan, 12 Nov 1823; Hy. Giles, bondsman.

Locke, John F. & Margaret Locke, 22 May 1849; George L. Gibson,
bondsman; John H. Hardie Jr., wit.

Locke, M. A. & M. Adelade Graham, 1 Jan 1856; Thos. T. Locke,
bondsman; J. S. Myers, wit. married 2 Jan 1856 by Saml. B.
O. Wilson, V. D. M.

Locke, Matt & Nancy Brandon, 16 Nov 1791; John Locke, bondsman;
Chs. Caldwell, wit.

Locke, Matthew Sr. & Susan A. Fulton, 3 Feb 1824; Ezra Allemong,
bondsman.

Locke, Matthew B. & Margaret G. Gibson, 21 March 1830; Washington Byers, bondsman; Geo. Locke, wit.

Locke, Richard & Margaret Gheen, 2 Jan 1825; John F. Cowan, bondsman; Hy. Giles, wit.

Locke, Thomas & Nancy Elizabeth Smith, 10 Feb 1859; John M. Smith, bondsman; John Wilkinson, wit.

Locke, William & Jane A. Wheeler, 9 Nov 1843; Obadiah Woodson, bondsman.

Lockinhour, George & Katharine Costner, 27 Oct 1819; Samuel Reed, bondsman; Sol. Davis, J. P., wit.

Locklen, William & Agniss Stevenson, 9 Jan 1769; Saml Stevenson, bondsman; John Frohock, wit. Saml Stevenson "the Father of the Girl."

Loflin, John K. & Mary A. Josey, 18 Feb 1839; Whitson B. Taylor, bondsman; John Giles, wit.

Loftin, Henry of Montgomery County, & Anne Macay, 18 Feb 1796; Robert McKie, bondsman; J. Troy, wit.

Loftin, John & Sally Lambeth, 1 Aug 1822; James Tyer, bondsman; Ams. Wright, J. P., wit.

Logan, James & Mary Miller, 23 April 1776; John Miller, bondsman; Ad. Osborn, wit.

Logan, John & Margaret Dodson, 24 Aug 1830; Leonard Garver, bondsman.

Logan, William & Mary Bryan, 2 Oct 1798; David Enoch, bondsman; Ma. Troy, wit.

Loggins, J. N. & Laura C. Lyerly, 14 Jan 1865; M. Hughes, bondsman; Obadiah Woodson, wit.

Long, Fredrick & Charity Seylough, 11 Sept 1804; Jacob Long, bondsman; Jno Monroe, wit.

Long, George & Catharine Moyers, 3 Oct 1805; Peter Fine, bondsman; Jno Monroe, wit.

Long, J. H. & Fannie Caldwell, 8 March 1864; Charles D. Smith, bondsman; Obadiah Woodson, wit.

Long, Jacob & Elizabeth Clinart, 28 Oct 1804; John Motsinger, bondsman; Jno Monroe, wit.

Long, James F. & Laura Luckie, 18 April 1855; H. G. Jollie, A. S. Brown, bondsmen; James E. Kerr, wit. married 18 April 1855 by G. W. Farabee.

Long, John & Mary Craver, 16 Feb 1818; Phillip Copple, bondsman; Milo A. Giles, wit.

Long, John S. & Esther Barger, 22 March 1852; Elijah Rice, bondsman; J. S. Myers, wit.

Long, Joseph & Mary Sewell, 6 Jan 1793; Hugh Horah, bondsman.

Long, Joseph & Catharine Phillips, 13 June 1793; Joseph Sewell, bondsman; Jos Chambers, wit.

Long, Joseph & Mary Furrer, 29 Nov 1800; Wm. McClenehen, bondsman; J. Brem, D. C., wit.

Long, Mathias & Mary Beryer, 13 Nov 1812; George Long, bondsman; J. Willson, wit.

Long, Mathis & Barbara Miller, 27 Dec 1819; Armistead Owen, bondsman; Hy. Giles, wit.

Long, Richard W. & Mary Yarbrough, 30 Nov 1826; Geo. W. Brown, bondsman; Hy. Giles, wit.

Long, Thomas & Elizabeth Latham, 17 April 1816; Jacob Allen, bondsman; R. Powell, wit.

Long, William & Sarah Love, 22 April 1826; Leonard A. Henderson, bondsman; M. A. Giles, wit.

Long, William M. C. & Judith Oakes, 5 May 1829; Tho. J. Oakes, bondsman; Jno. H. Hardie, wit.

Longwith, George & Susanna Thomas, 21 Jan 1824; Lewis Thomas, bondsman; E. Brock, J. P., wit.

Lookinbee, David & Betsy Bryant, 9 Jan 1813; Daniel Warner, bondsman; Geo. Dunn, wit.

Lookinbee, John & Susanna Swesgood, 28 Jan 1813; Andrew Swicegood, bondsman; Geo. Dunn, wit.

Lopewaser, John & Mary Creson, 24 Jan 1797; Nichs. Creson, bondsman; Jno Rogers, wit.

Lopp, Jacob & Molly Waggoner, 1 Oct 1794; Henry Sleighter, bondsman.

Lopp, Jacob & Molly Yontz, 27 Dec 1821; Jacob Long, bondsman; Jno Giles, wit.

Lopp, Jacob & Mary Michael, 2 Feb 1822; John Lopp, bondsman.

Lopp, John & Mary Hedrick, 20 Nov 1816; Green Magee, bondsman; Jno Giles, wit.

Lopp, John Jr. & Cattharaine Hamm, 8 Aug 1790; Valantine Harman, bondsman; Jno Monroe, wit.

Lot, Mark & Mary Lefford, 28 Aug 1769; Will Lettford, bondsman; John Frohock, Jn. Brandon, wit. consent from John Ledford, father of Mary.

Louder, Daniel R. & Sophia Rebecca Ritchey, 25 Feb 1864; A. H. Heilig, bondsman; Obadiah Woodson, wit.

Lountz, John & Eliz. Overcash, 20 July 1797; Geo. Overcash, bondsman; Jno Rogers, wit.

Loupwasser, Adam & Catharine Lemly, 5 Jan 1802; Philip Lemley, bondsman; Jno Brem, wit.

Lourance, David & Agness Sherrell, 16 Jan 1768; John Lowrance, Danl. Little, bondsmen; Thomas Frohock, wit.

Loury, Richard & Isabella D. Young, 21 Feb 1831; James Owens, bondsman; Hy. Giles, wit.

Loury, Richard & Elizabeth Todd, 16 Feb 1837; Jas. Blackwell, bondsman; Tobias S. Lemly, wit.

Love, Julius M. & Elizabeth L. Kingsberry, 15 Aug 1843; Jos. F. Chambers, wit.

Love, Samuel & Lilley Mayes, 25 July 1782; James Mayes, bondsman; Tho. McCaule, wit.

Love, Samuel & Jane Sloan, 22 Jan 1784; Robert Sloan, bondsman; T. H. McCaule, wit.

Love, William C. & Betsey McCay, 20 March 1811; Jno. L. Henderson, bondsman; Jno Giles, C. C., wit.

Lovelace, Archibald & Nancey Holeman, 5 Feb 1827; David W. Holman, bondsman; L. R. Rose, J. P., wit.

Lovelace, Archibald & Jean Erwin, 7 Oct 1786; Evan Beall, bondsman; Jno Macay, wit.

Lovelace, Elias & Ann Roby, 31 Dec 1775; Daniel Bealle, bondsman; Ad. Osborn, wit.

Lovelace, Isaac & Susanna Wingler, 26 Feb 1811; Lewis Peck, bondsman; Geo. Dunn, wit.

Lovelace, James & Sarah MacDaniel, 3 Oct 1793; Isaac Hudson, bondsman; Elias Lovelace, Zadok Leach, wit.

Loven, James & Hannah Bratcher, 6 April 1795; David Buckner, bondsman; Isham Frohock, wit.

Lowder, John J. & Sarah L. Barringer, 21 June 1847; Clark Redwine, bondsman; Robert Murphy, wit.

Lowrance, Abraham & Anne Swann, 22 April 1786; Thomas Swann, bondsman; Jno Macay, wit.

Lowrance, Abraham & Catharine Frieze, 10 Aug 1815; John Freez, bondsman; Jno Giles, C. C., wit.

Lowrance, Alexander & Margaret Young, 24 March 1805; Joseph Young, bondsman; A. L. Osborn, D. C., wit.

Lowrance, Andrew & Hannah Adams, 4 Aug 1775; John Adams, bondsman; Ad. Osborn, wit.

Lowrance, Andrew J. & Mary C. Overcash, 23 Dec 1852; Jno A. Lowrance, bondsman; James E. Kerr, wit.

Lowrance, Daniel & Mary Cocks, 4 Aug 1809; Joseph Lowrance, bondsman; Jno Giles, C. C., wit.

Lowrance, David & Sarah Dobbins, 28 March 1804; William Cowan, bondsman; A. L. Osborn, D. C., wit.

Lowrance, Jacob & Rebecca Beard, 17 Nov 1783; John Baird, bondsman; Ad. Osborn, wit.

Lowrance, Joel & Ann Hughey, 17 Feb 1803; Saml. Hughey, bondsman; Hudson Hughes, wit.

Lowrance, John & Martha Lawrence, 28 Nov 1791; Joshua Lowrance, bondsman; Chs. Caldwell, wit.

Lowrance, John & Elizabeth Lourance, 20 Feb 1828; John N. Lowrance, bondsman; Jno H. Hardie, wit.

Lowrance, John M. & Mary Kincaid, 27 Oct 1859; John T. Stewart, bondsman; James E. Kerr, wit. married 8 Nov 1859 by Stephen Frontis.

Lowrance, John R. & Elizabeth Dickson, 14 Aug 1839; Obadiah Woodson, bondsman; John Giles, wit.

Lowrance, Joshua & Elisabeth Baxter, 9 Feb 1792; David Baxter, bondsman; Chs. Caldwell, wit.

Lowrance, Samuel M. & Nancy Bell, 25 Nov 1829; Richard Loury, bondsman; J. H. Hardie, wit.

Lowrance, William & Kaehaback Baker, 31 Dec 1803; Townsend Burroughs, bondsman.

Lowrence, Peter & Elizabeth Bridges, 10 April 1764; John Lowrance, bondsman.

Lowrey, John & Eleanor Lowry, 10 March 1780; Charles Lowry, bondsman; B. Booth Boote, wit.

Lowrey, Thomas & Sarah Richardson, _____ 178_; John Lowrey, bondsman; Jno Macay, wit.

Lowry, Charles & Sarah Lowry, 10 March 1780; John Lowrey, bondsman; B. Booth Boote, wit.

Lowry, Edmond & Elizabeth Wilkey, 2 Nov 1786; Thomas Lowrey, bondsman; Jno Macay, wit.

Lowry, George & Mary Arile, 3 Nov 1808; Morgan McMachan, bondsman; A. L. Osborne, wit.

Lowry, John & Mary Railsback, 24 Aug 1786; Henry Ralsback, bondsman; John Macay, wit.

Lowry, John & _____; 11 Aug 1798; Andrew Gray, bondsman; Ed. J. Osborn, D. C., wit.

Lowry, John & Sally Sainer, 12 April 1821; Thos. Hampton, bondsman.

Lowry, John & Margret Ward, 6 Jan 1824; Evan Ellis, bondsman; Joseph Adams, J. P., wit.

Lowry, Samuel & Susanna Gallaher, 27 Sept 1802; Saml. Lowrie, bondsman.

Lowry, William & Elisabeth Gillispie, 31 Dec 1789; Richard Gillispie, bondsman; Evan Alexander, wit.

Loyd, John & Elisabeth Harkle, 18 Jan 1783; Thomas Harkle, bondsman; William Crawford, wit.

Lucas, James & Elizabeth Hendricks, 12 March 1814; James Pickler, bondsman; Geo. Dunn, wit.

Lucas, John H. & Letitia Rainey, 16 Sept 1864; Burgess Cox, bondsman; Obadiah Woodson, wit.

Lucas, William & Goodin Hendricks, 5 Oct 1810; John Pickler, bondsman; Ezra Allemong, wit.

Luckey, George & Agniss Little, 14 Jan 1793; Thos Penery, William Pugh, bondsman; Basil Gaither, wit.

Luckey, John & Mary Morrison, 10 June 1818; Wm. Dicky, bondsman; Henry Allemong, wit.

Luckey, John & Susan Gibson, 7 Aug 1863; Robt. H. Smith, bondsman; Obadiah Woodson, wit.

Luckey, John & Esther Niblack, 7 April 1813; Johnston Niblock, bondsman; Geo. Dunn, wit.

Luckey, Richard & Margaret Gaffey, 13 Feb 1795; Ths. Dicky, bondsman; J. Troy, wit.

Luckey, Samuel & Thamar Husbands, 10 Jan 1821; John Davis, bondsman; R. Powell, wit.

Luckey, Samuel & Rebecca Neely, 12 Nov 1822; Meshack Pinkston, bondsman.

Luckey, Samuel & Polly Luckey, 28 Dec 1818; George J. Niblock, bondsman; Jno Giles, wit.

Luckey, W. A. & Mary Jane Kerr, 1 Aug 1865; James A. Hudson, bondsman; H. N. Woodson, wit.

Luckie, Robert & Elizabeth Anderson, 27 Nov 1792; Thos. Farmer, bondsman; Jos Chambers, wit.

Luckie, Samuel & Elizabeth Armstrong, 21 Feb 1793; John Rosebrough, bondsman; Jos. Chambers, wit.

Luckie, William & Mary Andrew, 22 March 1792; John Andrews, bondsman; Chs. Caldwell, wit.

Lucky, Eli & Sarah Robertson, 5 Dec 1828; Hiram Cook, bondsman; L. R. Rose, J. P., wit.

Lucus, Henry J. & Penina Crawford, 2 Feb 1843; Andrew J. Kincaid, bondsman; J. H. Hardie, wit.

Lucus, John & Sarah Eniss, 13 Aug 1846; Franklin Lucus, bondsman; J. H. Hardie, wit.

Lucus, John & Mary Dunn, 6 Feb 1861; William Dunn, bondsman; Wm. Locke, wit. married 6 Feb 1861 by M. Plumer, J. P.

Ludwick, Alfred F. & Margaret J. McCarn, 7 Jan 1858; Giles Bowers, bondsman; D. W. Honeycutt, wit. married 10 Jan 1858 by D. W. Honeycutt, J. P.

Ludwick, Alfred M. & Emeline Stoner, 23 Sept 1855; Edward Bame, bondsman; J. S. Myers, wit. married 23 Sept 1855 by Jos. A. Linn.

Ludwick, Daniel & Crissy Paine, 16 Oct 1840; John Stoner, bondsman.

Ludwick, Edmond R. & Elizer Braddy, 1 Nov 1855; Wm. Leonard, bondsman; Jac. C. Barnhardt, wit. married 1 Nov 1855 by Jac. C. Barnhardt, J. P.

Ludwick, Mathias & Milly Crotzer, 15 Nov 1825; Nicholas Ludwick, bondsman; Jno Giles, wit.

Ludwick, Paul & Christina Eller, 1 April 1834; Henry Harkey, bondsman; Jno Giles, wit.

Lueling, Jonathan & Jean Slavin, 20 Aug 1816; Samuel Penery, bondsman; R. Powell, wit.

Luff, Samuel & Mary A. Pape, 9 Oct 1865; William R. Garmon, bondsman; Obadiah Woodson, wit.

Luiss, Nathanial & Urith Roberts, 4 March 1783; John Kimbell Roberts, bondsman; Willm. Crawford, wit.

Lukinbill, John & Barbry Dottey, 9 Aug 1804; David Mikel, bondsman; Ph. Beck, wit.

Lumsden, J. D. & Elmira Brandon, 17 Aug 1840; Thos. T. Maxwell, bondsman; Susan T. Giles, wit.

Lund, John & Rachael Wiseman, 14 Sept 1778; Thos. Willis, bondsman; Ad. Osborn, wit.

Lundy, Thomas & Prudence Reavis, 27 Feb 1816; John Reavis Jr., bondsman; R. Powell, wit.

Lutewick, Mathias & Dianna Glover, 26 Feb 1827; Henry Lutewick, bondsman; J. H. Hardie, wit.

Luterwick, William & Mary Belton, 16 Aug 1828; John Wilds, bondsman; J. H. Hardie, wit.

Lutterloh, Charles & Eliza Comerford, 18 April 1813; Robt. Mitchell, bondsman; Geo. Dunn, wit.

Lyall, Thomas & Mary Byard, 17 April 1775; David Kerr, bondsman; Ad. Osborn, wit.

Lyarly, Charles & Barbara Kesler, 1 Dec 1826; Green Redwine, bondsman; J. H. Hardie, wit.

Lyerly--see also Leyerly, Lirely

Lyerly, Alexander & Sophia Hartman, 6 June 1849; Alexander Kesler, bondsman.

Lyerly, Alexander & Rosena Klutts, 24 March 1858; Daniel M. Holshouser, bondsman; James E. Kerr, wit. married 25 March 1858 by Saml. Rothrock, Minister of the Gospel in the Ev. Luth. Church.

Lyerly, Andrew & Polly Josey, 8 March 1817; Andrew Holshouser, bondsman; Roberts Nanny, wit.

Lyerly, Andrew & Margaret Kepley, 14 Nov 1820; Christian Goodman, bondsman.

Lyerly, Andrew & Clarisa Bostian, 15 March 1850; Henry Earnheart, bondsman; J. S. Myers, wit.

Lyerly, Christopher & Polly Trexler, 11 April 1818; Jacob Dillon, bondsman; Roberts Nanny, wit.

Lyerly, Charles & Sarah Holshouser, 15 Dec 1852; Adam Trexler, bondsman; J. S. Myers, wit.

Lyerly, Daniel & Peggy Barrier, 27 March 1821; Jacob Lyerly, bondsman; Jno Giles, wit.

Lyerly, George & Adaline E. Lyerly, 17 Feb 1858; married 18 Feb 1858 by L. C. Groseclose.

Lyerly, George H. & Elizabeth C. Brown, 15 April 1840; Henry A. Walton, bondsman; Susan T. Giles, wit.

Lyerly, George M. & Ann C. Graham, 11 Jan 1841; John C. Gillespie, bondsman; Susan T. Giles, wit.

Lyerly, Henry & Eliza Trexler, 23 Feb 1854; Jacob Lyerly, bondsman; J. S. Myers, wit. married 23 Feb 1854 by J. Thomason, J. P.

Lyerly, Isaac & Peggy Barber, 24 March 1819; Peter Lyerly, bondsman; Jno Giles, wit.

Lyerly, Jacob & Caty Barger, 4 March 1813; Casper Holshouss, bondsman; Geo. Dunn, wit.

Lyerly, Jacob & Elizabeth M. Barber, 31 Jan 1838; Abner Burke, bondsman; Jno. Giles, wit.

Lyerly, Jacob & Annie L. Fisher, 30 July 1849; H. A. Miller, bondsman; John H. Hardie Jr., wit.

Lyerly, Jacob & Nancy Rufty, 31 Jan 1856; J. G. Knox, bondsman; James E. Kerr, wit. married 31 Jan 1856 by M. A. Agner, J. P.

Lyerly, Jesse & Elizt. Barger, 19 April 1849; William C. Camel, bondsman; J. H. Hardie Jr., wit.

Lyerly, Joh & Polly G. Cowan, _____; Henry Robison, bondsman; S. Lemly Jr., wit.

Lyerly, John & Chrisey C. Klutts, 17 Jan 1855; Miles A. Kepley, bondsman; J. S. Myers, wit.

Lyerly, John S. & Eliza Hulin, 26 May 1854; Jesse Thomason, bondsman; J. S. Myers, wit. married 28 May 1854 by J. Thomason, J. P.

Lyerly, Jonathan & Mary Briggs, 2 July 1851; Julius A. Neely, bondsman; J. S. Myers, wit.

Lyerly, Joseph & Mary E. Briggs, 26 Oct 1853; M. C. Caldwell, bondsman; James E. Kerr, wit.

Lyerly, Maritin & Commella C. Fisher, 10 July 1855; Caleb Trexler, bondsman; J. S. Myers, wit. married 12 July 1855 by Thornton Butler, V. D. M.

Lyerly, Moses & Margred Trexler, 23 Oct 1837; Charles Miller, bondsman; Susan Giles, wit.

Lyerly, Oathy & Anny Hartman, 15 May 1845; Charles Earnhart, bondsman; John H. Hardie Jr., wit.

Lyerly, Otho & Margaret C. Barber, 17 Feb 1852; William Barber, bondsman; J. S. Myers, wit. married 19 Feb 1852 by James G. Jacocks, Rector of Christ Church Parish, Rowan County, N. C.

Lyerly, Otho & Sarah A. Hart, 21 Jan 1856; Wm. L. Barber, bondsman; J. S. Myers, wit. married 22 Jan 1856 by E. D. Junkin.

Lyerly, Peter & Margaret Cresson, 9 Aug 1816; Jno. Fraley, bondsman; Jno Giles, wit.

Lyerly, Samuel & Jane Briggs, 22 Jan 1851; Robt. L. McConnaughy, bondsman; J. S. Myers, wit.

Lyerly, William A. & Mary C. Grimes, 23 May 1842; Henry A. Jacobs, bondsman; J. H. Hardie, wit.

Lyerly, Zechariah & Rachael Boger, 12 Oct 1833; Isaac Lyerly, bondsman; Wm. Locke, wit.

Lyerly, Zechariah & Christena Klutts, 11 Jan 1853; Isaac Lyerly, bondsman.

Lynch, Andrew & Margaret Gellian, 7 May 1817; Henry Cowen, bondsman; Moses A. Locke, wit.

Lynch, Andrew J. & Hetty D. Bostain, 9 Dec 1854; James A. Bostian, bondsman; James E. Kerr, wit.

Lynche, John & Eliza E. Macnamara, 8 Sept 1842; Leander Killian, bondsman.

Lynn, Allin & Mary Biel, 7 Oct 1801; Benjamin Ellis, bondsman; Jno. Bean, D. C., wit.

Lynn, Henry & _____, 5 Dec 1796; James Smith, bondsman.

Lynn, Israel & Mary Smith, 5 Oct 1784; Andrew Smith, bondsman; Hu. Magoune, wit.

Lyon, Elijah & Ann Johnston, 15 April 1772; Geo. Dunn, Robert Tate, bondsmen; John Frohock, wit.

Lyon, John & Sarah Robinson, 11 Jan 1767; Adam Lash, bondsman; Thomas Frohock, wit.

Lyon, Nathan & Henny Smoot, 1 Jan 1819; Elijah Lyon, bondsman; Jno. Giles, C. C., wit.

McAdoo, William & Martha Black, 31 Oct 1788; James Houston, bondsman; M. Osborn, wit. consent 28 Oct 1788 from David Black.

McAlister, John L. & Mollie A. Jenkin, 16 Nov 1865; G. D. Snuggs, bondsman; Obadiah Woodson, wit.

McAlte, Zacharah & Susannah Letman, 9 Nov 1798; Thomas Gillaspie, bondsman.

Macan, Edward & Mille Cotton, 10 Oct 1791; Michael Heisler, bondsman; Chs. Caldwell, wit.

Macate, John & Margaret Dent, 8 Sept 1825; William Huline, bondsman; Jno Giles, wit.

McAtee, Abednego & Nancey Moore, 12 Nov 1796; Richd. Leach, bondsman; Jno Rogers, wit.

McAtee, Edmond & Betsy Jackson, 26 Nov 1814; Jno. Travis, bondsman; Geo. Dunn, wit.

McAtee, Hezekiah & Sarah Smith, 15 Nov 1796; Zach. McAtee, bondsman; Jno Rogers, wit.

Macatee, Nebednego & Kathrine Shanklin, 23 Oct 1792; J. George Laumann, bondsman; Jos. Chambers, wit.

Macay, Harmon & Delia Macay (colored), 24 Sept 1865; married 28 Sept 1865 by Zuke Haughton, D. C.

Macay, Thomas & Susanna Morr, 25 Jan 1802; George Morr, bondsman; Jno Brem, wit.

Macay, William S. & Isabella Loury, 18 Dec 1848; Saml. Reeves, bondsman.

McBride, Barzilla & Rachell Willson, 14 Sept 1815; William Wiseman, bondsman.

McBride, David & Sarah Jenkins (no date, during Gov. Martin's admn.); Samuel Jenkins, bondsman; Jno McNairy, wit.

McBride, John & Ann Beard, 15 Nov 1786; Pue Graham, bondsman; Jno Macay, Ad. Osborn, wit.

McBride, Leonard & Anna Riddle, 8 April 1824; Nicholas Miller, bondsman; E. Brock, J. P., wit.

McBride, Robert & Jean Ferguson; consent only from Andrew Ferguson.

McBride, William & Unis Wiseman; 21 Dec 1816; William Wiseman, bondsman; Jno Giles, wit.

McBroom, Alexander & Elizabeth Cowan, 12 March 1823; George Robison, bondsman.

McBroom, James & Jean Dobbins, 17 Jan 17__; Henry Dobbin, bondsman; Jno Kerr, wit.

McBroom, James H. & Elizabeth B. Thompson, 13 Feb 1839; Thomas Cowan, bondsman.

McBroome, John & Janett McBroome, 14 Jan 1769; Thomas McBroome, Benjamin Milner, bondsmen; Thos. Frohock, wit.

McCaleb, James & Anny Woodsides, 15 Aug 1826; Archd. M. Woodside, bondsman; Hy. Giles, wit.

McCracken or McCrackin, John & Elizabeth Dobbins, 17 Sept 1794; John Dobbin, bondsman; Isabella Troy, wit.

McCaheirn, Archibald & Elizabeth Campbell, 22 Dec 1798; Matthew Campbell, bondsman; Edwin J. Osborn, D. C., wit.

McCammon, Joseph & Dorcas Holmes, 9 May 1791; George Homes, bondsman.

McCan, John & Eve Lott (no date, but probably 1787-89); Samuel Lane, bondsman; Wm. Alexander, wit.

McCanless, David & Catey Wason, 15 Oct 1792; John Rees, bondsman; Basil Gaither, wit.

McCann, John H. & C. M. Mann, 22 July 1848; Jason Mann, bondsman; J. H. Hardie, wit.

McCannan, Horatio & Martha Smith, 10 March 1823; Nathaniel Cutrel, bondsman; E. Brock, J. P., wit.

McCannon, Neal & Ratchel Hutchens, 8 Nov 1801; Horatio Jones, bondsman; J. Hunt, wit.

McCarter, Alexander & Mary Gingles, 15 Dec 1784; Adla Gen, bondsman.

McCarter, William & Liddy Siddon, 19 Oct 1818; Anderson Hendrix, bondsman; Jn March Sr., wit.

McCarter, William & Ann Howard, 8 Dec 1822; John Bears, bondsman; L. R. Rose, J. P., wit.

McCaw, William B. & Elizabeth H. Slaughter, 10 Feb 1831; George W. Williams, bondsman.

McCay--see also McCoy

McCay, Alexander & Jennet McCay, 10 May 1780; Alexr. Gunn, bondsman; Jno. Kerr, wit.

McClamrah, Robert & Sarah Allen, 25 March 1818; J. Christopher Keller, bondsman; R. Powell, wit.

McClamroch, David & Delila Ijams, 23 May 1812; George McClamroch, bondsman; Geo. Dunn, wit.

McClanachan, Andrew & Sarah Cochran, 12 May 1772; Robert Linn, John Cochran, bondsmen; Thos Frohock, William Freeman, wit. consent from Samuel Cochran, father of Sarah, 12 May 1772; William Driskill, Andrew Cochran, wit.

McClannen, James & Mary Simmons, 25 Sept 1833; George W. Johnson, bondsman; C. Harbin, wit.

McCleen, Thomas & Nancy Guenny, 17 March 1809; Joseph Gibson, bondsman; Ad. Osborne, wit.

McClelland, Moses & Mary Ann Porter, 28 March 1861; George Valentine, bondsman; James E. Kerr, wit. married 28 March 1861 by D. W. Honeycutt, J. P.

McClelland, William & Rebecca McClelland, 10 April 1772; John Frohock, wit. consent from William McCleland, father of Rebecca, 5 April 1772.

McClotsky, Hamilton & Catherina McCollom, 12 Jan 1770; John Mitchell, bondsman; Thomas Frohock, wit. consent from John McCollum, 11 Jan 1770, Walt. Lindsay, John Gonnean(?), wit.

McCloud, Robert & Rachel McCoy, 9 Oct 1783; Robert McCoy, bondsman; Moses Wylie, wit.

McClure, Andrew & Mary Wilson, 13 June 1769; Thos. Blear, John Mcadow, bondsmen; Charles McAnaly, wit.

McClure, Francis & Mary Endsley, __ June 1769; John Endsley, George Coumins, bondsmen.

McCollum, James & Mary Harris, 14 April 1787; James Harris, bondsman; Max. Chambers, wit.

McCombs, Samuel of Mecklenburg County, & Alice Brandon, 15 Feb 1809; Alexander Gibney or McGibbuney, bondsman; Matt. Brandon, George Miller, wit.

McComic, H. S. & Sarah Rarey, 3 Oct 1860; D. F. Watson, bondsman; John Wilkinson, wit. married 3 Oct 1860 by D. W. Honeycutt, J. P.

McCommack, Edward L. & Martha A. Williford, 27 July 1855; Silas McLaughlin, bondsman; J. S. Myers, wit. married 30 July 1855 by John L. Hedrick, J. P.

McConaughey, Samson & Susan Cowan, 2 April 1789; William Cowan, bondsman; Wall Alexander, wit.

McConel, James & Elizabeth Butler, 5 April 1785; Robert Hillis, bondsman; H. Magoune, wit.

McConel, Philip & Sarah McClellan, 18 Feb 1763; John Fleming, Henry Horah, Thomas Evans, bondsmen.

McConnaughey, George & Ann Elizabeth Partee, 22 June 1826; Ezra Allemong, bondsman.

McConnaughey, James C. & Caroline Hall, 23 Nov 1827; Hy. Giles, bondsman.

McConnaughy, James & Anne Robeson, 12 May 1790; John Dobbin, bondsman; C. Caldwell, D. C., wit.

McConnaughy, Joseph & Mary Locke, 17 June 1820; George Locke, bondsman.

McConnell, Alexander & Catharine Boyd, 18 Feb 1782; John Boyd, bondsman; Ad. Osborn, wit.

McConnell, John & _____, 26 April 1762; John Graham, William Williams, bondsmen; Will Reed, Thos. Frohock, wit.

McCorkel, Francis & Elizabeth Brandon, 12 April 1780; Matt Brandon, bondsman; B. Booth Boote, wit.

McCorkle--see also McOrkle

McCorkle, Alexander G. & Jean Gillihan, 27 Nov 1804; Sam Miller, bondsman; A. L. Osborn, D. C., wit.

McCorkle, Francis & Sarah Work, 26 Aug 1768; John Work, bondsman; Thomas Frohock, wit.

McCorkle, Joel & Polly Fauster, 23 Sept 1801; Thomas L. Cowan, bondsman; Jno Brem, wit.

McCorkle, John F. & Jane C. Barr, 26 Oct 1830; Absolam K. Barr, bondsman; Jno H. Hardie, wit.

McCorkle, John F. & Elizabeth Brown, 28 Feb 1839; Andrew J. Brown, bondsman; Jno H. Hardie Jr., wit.

McCorkle, John R. & Mary E. Leazer, 3 May 1853; Thomas S. Atwell, bondsman; Jno McKnight, wit. married 4 May 1853 by Jno. E. McPherson, Min. of Gosp.

McCorkle, Joseph & Margaret Snoddy, 28 Feb 1775; William Snoddey, bondsman; Max. Chambers, wit.

McCorkle, Lewis & Nancy Cowan, 14 Sept 1815; Joseph Cowan, bondsman; Ls. Beard, wit.

McCorkle, M. B. & Lucy Ann Chaggin, 2 Jan 1858; Peter Fultz, bondsman; John Wilkinson, wit. married 3 Jan 1858 by Peter Williamson.

McCorkle, Robert & Betsey Blythe (no date, but probably 1787-1789); James Blythe, bondsman; William Alexander, wit.

M'Corkle, Samuel & Elizabeth Gillaspie, 29 June 1776; Adlai Osborn, bondsman.

M'Corkle, Samuel E. & Margaret E. Poston, 30 Jan 1844; Henry Hauck, bondsman; Jno. H. Hardie, wit.

McCoy, Daniel & Jennit McKay, 26 Sept 1781; Thos McKay, bondsman; Ad. Osborn, wit. consent from Donald McKay, sister of Jannet, 26 Sept 1781.

McCoy, Henry & Bettie M. Green, 14 July 1863; E. M. Featherstone, bondsman; Samuel B. Waters, wit.

McCoy, John & Jenet McCoy, 10 Sept 1783; John Nesbert, bondsman; Wm. Crawford, wit.

McCoy, Wiley & Julia Monroe (colored), 21 Sept 1865; married 21 Sept 1865 by Zuke Haughton.

McCracken, Ephraim & Elizabeth Graham, 25 Feb 1795; James Alexander, bondsman; J. Troy, D. C., wit.

McCracken, J. M. & Sue Ann F. Gatlen, 16 Oct 1854; Goodmon Spence, bondsman; D. W. Honeycutt, wit.

McCracken, Samuel & Jane Young, 13 Feb 1769; William Mortimore, Wm. Steel, bondsmen; Tho. Frohock, wit.

McCracken, Samuel & Anne Haithman, 27 Sept 1790; James Heathman, bondsman; C. Caldwell, D. C., wit.

McCrackin, John & Elizabeth Dobbins, 17 Sept 1794; John Dobbin, bondsman; Isabella Troy, wit.

McCrary, Boyd & Charity Mehaffy, 10 May 1819; Michl. Beard, bondsman; Henry Allemong, wit.

McCrary, Elisha & Sally Traler, 4 Aug 1813; Wilson McCrary, bondsman; Jno Giles, C. C., wit.

McCrary, Hugh & Mary Sluder, 6 Aug 1787; Reuben Pew, bondsman; Jno Macay, wit.

McCrary, Hugh & Charity Sluder, 11 April 1795; John Silver, bondsman; Thos Ashley, wit.

McCrary, William & Polley Wiseman, 3 April 1822; Richard Woolling, bondsman; An Swicegood, wit.

McCreary, Boyd & Annah Cooper, 28 March 1792; Samuel Lusk, bondsman; Jno Monro, wit.

McCree, Hugh L. & Sarah Donaldson, 5 Jan 1803; Joseph Donaldson, bondsman; Hudson Hughes, wit.

McCree, William & Mary White, 11 Feb 1776; Max. Chambers, bondsman; Ad. Osborn, wit. consent from Moses White.

McCuiston, John M. & Darcus McCuiston, 12 Jan 1768; James McCuiston, bondsman; Thomas Frohock, wit.

McCulloch, John & Elizabeth Locke, 21 Nov 1812; Francis Johnston, bondsman; Jno Giles, C. C., wit.

McCulloh, Alfred & Jinney Daniel, 5 March 1818; William Daniel, bondsman; Jno March Sr., wit.

McCulloh, Charles & _____; (no date, bondsman).

McCulloh, George & Elizabeth Bream, 26 Sept 1799; E. Jay Osborn, bondsman; John Hampton, wit.

McCulloh, Joseph & _____, 2 Jan 1760; Henry Horah, Jas. Cater, bondsmen; John Frohock, Thomas Frohock, wit.

McDaniel, Asbury & Martha A. Garner (Gardner), 27 Jan 1852; Washington Harwell, bondsman; J. S. Myers, wit. married 28 Jan 1852 by Jno. M. McConnaughey, J. P.

McDaniel, Charles & Elizabeth Dowell, _____; John Dowell, bondsman; Jno. Rogers, wit.

McDaniel, Ignatious & Polly Cornatzer, 10 Aug 1825; Aquilla Cheshier, bondsman; Thomas McNeely, wit.

McDaniel, John W. & Margaret McCarnes, 19 April 1866; A. M. Sullivan, bondsman; Obadiah Woodson, wit.

McDaniel, Nacey & Elizabeth Locker, 8 Feb 1802; Thomas Wood, bondsman; Jno. Brem, wit.

McDonald, Hany & Mary Sears, 14 April 1854; Thomas Seers, bondsman; J. S. Myers, wit.

McDonald, John & Nancy McDonald, 6 Jan 1787; Alexr. McKoy, bondsman; Jno Macay, wit.

McDonald, Joseph & Cidy Barlow, 24 Sept 1826; Alexandrew Chavous, bondsman; E. Brock, J. P., wit.

McDonell, William & Matilda Schools, 25 Aug 1830; Hy. Giles, bondsman.

McDowel, William & Elizabeth Templeton, 27 Feb 1772; Nathanael Tempelton (son of James), bondsman; Thomas Frohock, wit. consent from James Templeton, 26 Feb 1772, father of Elisabeth.

McEntire, M. L. & Emeline Doly, 27 Feb 1861; Jesse Klutts, bondsman; John Wilkinson, wit. married 27 Feb 1861 by L. C. Groseclose, Pastor of St. John's Ev. Luth. Church, Salisbury, N. C.

McEwen, David & Margaret Erwin, _____; Jno Kerr, bondsman.

McFalls, John & Martha Hill, 7 Aug 1783; James Curry, bondsman; Robt. Hall, wit.

McGauhy, John & Elizabeth Thompson, 19 Aug 1794; John Henderson, bondsman; J. Troy, D. C., wit.

McGee, Alvis & Christena Fraley, 27 Aug 1853; John Foster, bondsman; James E. Kerr, wit.

McGee, Pat Stuart--see Gee

McGill, Duncan & Mary Sleighter, 27 Feb 1823; Michael Swink, bondsman; Jno Giles, wit.

McGill, Neal & Barbara Walk, 4 Feb 1813; Applin Uslam, bondsman; Geo. Dunn, wit.

McGinn, Amzi & Harriet E. McCorkle, 1 Oct 1823; Saml. F. Love, bondsman; E. Allemong, wit.

McGoodwin, Daniel & Elizabeth Kerr, 1 May 1787; James Orr, bondsman; Ad. Osborn, wit.

McGuier, Daniel & Eleanor Berry, 30 Sept 1789; Josiah Elston, bondsman; Evan Alexander, wit.

McGuire, David & Famiel (?) Ham, 6 Aug 1810; John Ham Jr., bondsman; Jn March Sr., wit.

McGuire, John & Mary Brandon, 16 March 1767; George Brandon, Thomas McGuire, bondsmen; Thos Frohock, wit.

McGuire, Samuel & Minty Kelley, 3 June 1815; Christopher Keller, bondsman; R. Powell, wit.

McGuire, Thomas & Jane Rutledge, 1 May 1770; David Coldwell, William Bailiey, bondsmen; Thomas Frohock, wit.

McHargue, James & Elizabeth Beaty, 8 Aug 1771; John McHargue, bondsman; Ad. Osborn, wit.

McHargue, John & Margret McBroom, 8 Aug 1769; Robert Porter, bondsman; Thos Frohock, wit. consent from Elizabeth McBroom.

McHargue, William & Sarah McBroom, 3 Jan 1774; John McBroom, bondsman; Ad. Osborn, wit.

McHenry, Henry & Martha Morrison, 21 June 1794; David Morrison, bondsman; J. Troy, D. C., wit.

McHenry, Isaac & Eleanor Robinson, 17 Jan 1788; Hugh Robison, bondsman; Jas. McEwin, wit.

McHenry, John & _____, 1 Sept 1797; Geo. Robison, bondsman; Jno Rogers, wit.

McIllwreith, Robert & Jean Shields, 26 April 1776; William Shield, bondsman; Ad. Osborn, wit.

McIntosh, Angus & Jean McCoy, 22 Oct 1781; Alexandr. McCoy, bondsman; T. H. McCaule, wit.

McIntosh, Hector & Mary McCoy, 10 April 1782; William McLeod, bondsman; T. H. McCaule, wit.

McKarn, Edward & Peggy Hamelton, 24 July 1812; Aaron Hamilton, bondsman; Jno Giles, C. C., wit.

McKaughan, Hugh & Phebe Pope, 25 March 1804; George Pope, bondsman; James Pope, Joab Brooks, wit.

McKay--see also Macay, McCay, McCoy

McKay, Alexander & Jean Munro, 12 March 1779; Robert McKay, bondsman; Ad. Osborn, wit. consent from Alexr. Munroe and wife, Barbara, headed Third Creek, 8 March 1779; Thomas Mackay, wit.

McKay, George & Elizabeth Lister, 24 Oct 1820; Jacob Weant, bondsman.

McKay, Robert & Jennet McIntosh, 13 Dec 1788; Robert McKay, bondsman; Ad. Osborn, wit.

McKay, Thomas & Elizabeth McKay, 23 March 1780; Danl. McKay, bondsman; Jno. Kerr, wit. consent from Charles McKay and wife Barbara, 22 March 1780.

McKee, Alexander & Martha McCleland, 26 Aug 1790; Benjn. Brandon, bondsman; C. Caldwell, D. C., wit.

McKee, James & Agness McGuire, 19 Oct 1772; Benjamin Milner, bondsman; Ad. Osborn, wit.

McKee, John & Margret Miller, 2 March 1784; Ad. Osborn, C. C., wit. (original in John Abner Harris papers, Southern Historical Collection, Chapel Hill, N. C.)

McKee, Robert & Mary Parks, 29 Aug 1787; Thomas Smith, bondsman; Jno Macay, wit.

McKee, Theodore & Elener McGuyre, 22 Dec 1789; John Smith, bondsman.

McKee, William & Mary Welch, 3 Jan 1774; Peter McNamee, bondsman; Ad. Osborn, wit. consent from John Welch, 29 Dec 1774.

McKee, William & Mary McHenry, 4 May 1779; Archibald McHenry, bondsman; Ad. Osborn, wit.

McKeny, George & Margaret Robley, 4 Jan 1825; Robert Lyster, bondsman; W. Harris, wit.

McKenzie, Charles C. & Polly Savage, 9 Nov 1802; Francis Marshall, bondsman; A. L. Osborn, D. C., wit.

McKenzie, Charles H. & Ellen Summer, 14 Nov 1865; Joseph Horah, bondsman; Obadiah Woodson, wit.

McKenzie, Charles H. & Mary D. Wood, 18 July 1854; R. B. Patterson, bondsman; J. S. Myers, wit.

McKenzie, Kenny & Christian Gordon, 15 March 1780; William McKay, bondsman; B. Booth Boote, wit.

McKenzie, Montford L. & Margaret P. Hampton, 16 Dec 1833; Wm. Murphy, bondsman; Wm. Locke, wit.

McKerr, James & Mary C. Burke, 26 Jan 1855; John Irvin, bondsman; James E. Kerr, wit.

McKie, Robert & Sarah McCoy, 16 Feb 1790; John Smith, bondsman.

McKinley, Moses & Sarah C. Braley, 14 Jan 1823; Rowan C. Braly. bondsman.

McKinsey, Andrew & _____, 12 Jan 1785; John Murdoch, bondsman.

McKintosh, John & Barberow McCloud, 13 Feb 1788; William McCloud, bondsman; Margt. Osborn, wit.

McKleroy, Joseph P. & Salley Curry, 12 Nov 1819; William Beeman, bondsman; R. Powell, wit.

McKnight, Ezekiel & Mary Erwin, 5 May 1826; Jos. McKnight, bondsman.

McKnight, George & Patsey Powell, 18 Jan 1829; Gassaway Gaither, bondsman; L. R. Rose, J. P., wit.

McKnight, George G. & Jane H. Parks, 9 Feb 1849; Rufus A. Brandon, bondsman; J. H. Hardie, wit.

McKnight, George G. & Nancy E. Atwell, 16 Jan 1861; John Wilkinson, bondsman.

McKnight, Hugh & Margaret Cook, 26 Feb 1762; Joseph McGoun, bondsman; John Frohock, Will Reed, wit.

McKnight, Hugh F. & Mary Ann Reese, 23 Sept 1841; D. P. Cowan, bondsman; J. S. Myers, wit.

McKnight, James & Elinor McKoun, 24 Jan 1770; James McKoun, James Dobbin, bondsmen; Thomas Frohock, wit.

McKnight, James & Sarah McKee, 10 Dec 1766; John McKee, bondsman; John Frohock, wit.

McKnight, Joseph & Mary Gibson, 6 Jan 1821; Tho. Smith, bondsman; Henry Allemong, wit.

McKnight, Joseph & Mary Barber, 26 Dec 1842; John McKnight, bondsman; J. H. Hardie, wit.

McKnight, Thomas & Abigal Aston, 17 Oct 1772; James Aston, bondsman.

McKnite, George & Liddy Ellrod, 28 Sept 1822; Wm. Cheeks, bondsman; Tho. Hampton, wit.

McKouen, John & Elizabeth Killpatric, 24 Nov 1779; Michael Kilpatrick, bondsman; Ad. Osborn, wit.

McKoun, Joseph & _____, 28 Jan 1769; John Olyphant, Alexander Snell, bondsmen; Tho Frohock, wit.

McKoy, William & Ann Hall, 24 Sept 1823; Stewart Bosworth, bondsman; Hy. Giles, wit.

McLain, Andrew & Elizabeth Todd, 10 May 1775; John Todd, bondsman; David Flowers, wit.

McLane, John & Lydia Lourance, 11 April 1795; Joshua Lowrance, bondsman; Isham Frohock, wit.

McLaughlin, Fergus & Elizabeth Caruthers, 22 Oct 1827; Fergus Graham, bondsman.

McLaughlin, Hazlet E. & Sarah Donaldson, 8 April 1829; Samuel McLaughlin, bondsman.

McLaughlin, James & Anne Hart, 9 Aug 1786; John Bryant, bondsman; Jno Macay, wit.

McLaughlin, James & Martha Caruthers, 25 Dec 1827; Abner Adams, bondsman; Jno H. Hardie, wit.

McLaughlin, James H. & Harriet A. Corriher, 13 Sept 1852; Rufus A. Corriher, bondsman; James E. Kerr, wit.

McLaughlin, Samuel & Sarah H. Houston, 6 Sept 1858; F. M. Graham, bondsman; married 7 Sept 1858 by S. C. Alexander.

McLaughlin, Samuel Jr. & Anny Cooper, 20 Oct 1824; Fergus McLaughlin, bondsman.

McLaughlin, Samuel W. & Margaret C. Korriker, 7 Feb 1848; Rufus A. Corriker, bondsman; J. H. Hardie Jr., wit.

McLean, Alexander & Sarah Brevard, 22 May 1772; James Rankin, Richard Graham, bondsmen; William Freeman, wit. consent from Robt. Brevard, 21 May 1772, father of Sarah.

McLean, Daniel & Elizabeth Graham, 16 Nov 1808; Jones Graham, bondsman; A. L. Osborne, C. C., wit.

McLean, David & Cornelia K. Brown, 29 Feb 1864; James E. Kerr, bondsman; Obadiah Woodson, wit.

McLean, John & Agness McKay, 27 Jan 1783; Robert McKay, bondsman.

McLean, John & Margaret Erwin, 16 March 1819; Truth Woods, bondsman; Henry Allemong, wit.

McLean, John B. & Margaret Bostain, 8 Aug 1832; William Hoelbrooks, bondsman.

McLean, Robert G. & Mary S. Hedrick, 1 Feb 1862; Joseph Kelley, bondsman; Obadiah Woodson, wit. married 5 Feb 1862 by Stephen Frontis, Minister of the Gospel.

McLean, William & Sarah B. Graham, 26 April 1817; John Donaldson, bondsman; Jno Giles, Clk., wit.

McLean, William B. & Jane J. Cochran, 2 Oct 1849; John E. Jamison, bondsman; J. S. Myers, wit.

McMachan, David & Rachel Latham, 19 April 1817; John McMachan, bondsman; R. Powell, wit.

McMachan, George & Harriot Harbin, 1 Feb 1808; Samuel McMachan, bondsman; Jn March Sr., wit.

McMachan, John & Elizabeth Bryan, 29 March 1787; Hy. Horah, bondsman; Jno Macay, wit.

McMachan, Samuel & Susanah Ellis, 9 Oct 1809; George McMachan, bondsman; Jn March Sr., wit.

McMachan, William & Rebecca Foster, 20 Sept 1790; James Rees, bondsman; Basil Gaither, wit.

McMackin, David & Susanna Roblin, 13 May 1811; John Rogers, bondsman; Geo. Dunn, wit.

McMackin, James & Elizabeth Frick, 18 May 1818; David McMackin, bondsman; Roberts Nanny, wit.

McMackin, Michael & Patsey Rogers, 3 Jan 1795; James McMahan, bondsman.

McMekin, James & Barbary Myers, 31 Aug 1769; Henry Dowland, John Blankapicker, bondsmen; Thomas Frohock, wit. consent from Michel Mire, father of Barbary, dated 30 Aug 1769; Henry Dowland, Philip Hopkins, wit.

MacNamara, Robert & Eliza Ann Steele, 27 June 1814; Andrew Kerr, bondsman; Jno Giles, C. C., wit.

McNally, Samuel & Mary C. James, 11 Nov 1842; F. R. Roncehe, bondsman.

McNamee, Peter & Jane Richey, 3 June 1772; Geo. Magoune, Thomas Green, bondsmen; John Frohock, wit. consent from William Richey and wife Margrat, parents of Jane.

McNeary, John & Ann Hillis, 27 Feb 1780; Robert Cummins, bondsman; B. Booth Boote, wit.

McNeely, Adam & Lattice Kilpatrick, 17 Jan 1791; Willm Killpatrick, bondsman; C. Caldwell, D. C., wit.

McNeely, Archibald & Margaret Cowan, __ Dec 1795; Mich Troy, bondsman; J. Troy, wit.

McNeely, Barton & Emma Burns (colored), 27 Dec 1862; John Valentine, bondsman; Obadiah Woodson, wit.

McNeely, David & Ann Lorance, 18 July 1825; Alfred A. Lourance, bondsman.

McNeely, H. W. & Nancy E. Lype, 20 Dec 1865; W. A. Houck, bondsman; Horatio N. Woodson, wit.

McNeely, Issac & Rachel Eagle, 20 June 1805; David Baxter, bondsman; Andrew Kerr, wit.

McNeely, James & Elizabeth Kilpatric, 25 Feb 1793; William Kilpatrick, bondsman; Jos. Chambers, wit.

McNeely, James A. & Clarisa Lorance, 1 Nov 1826; John N. Lowrance, bondsman; J. H. Hardie, wit.

McNeely, James H. & Rebeca Wilson, 29 Sept 1840; Robt. F. Wilson, bondsman; Susan T. Giles, wit.

McNeely, John & Margret McNeely, 27 Feb 1787; David McNeely, bondsman.

McNeely, John & Polly Cowan, 22 July 1802; William S. Cowan, bondsman; Jno Brem, wit.

McNeely, John & Margaret PooJe, 18 Jan 1810; Saml. McNeely, bondsman; Jno Giles, C. C., wit.

McNeely, John & Jane Miller, 11 Feb 1840; Ebenezer McNeely, bondsman; Susan T. Giles, wit.

McNeely, John R. & Mary Shufford, 5 Jan 1826; David Kilpatrick, bondsman; Ezra Allemong, wit.

McNeely, John W. & Amelia Clodfelter, 26 Feb 1844; Caleb J. Webb, bondsman; Jno H. Hardie, wit.

McNeely, John W. & Mary McNeely, 24 Oct 1845; Ebenezer McNeely, bondsman; Jno. H. Hardie, wit.

McNeely, Joseph & Harriet E. Williford, 13 Nov 1839; Zachariah Blackwelder, bondsman; Hy. Giles, wit.

McNeely, Robert & Mary McNeely, 1 Jan 1784; Andrew McNeely, bondsman; Ad. Osborn, wit.

McNeely, Robert & Jean L. Cowan, 26 Dec 1832; Joel H. Jinkins, bondsman.

McNeely, Thomas & Margaret Gaither, 23 Feb 1820; Tho. L. Cowan, bondsman.

McNeely, William B. & Elizabeth McNeely, 1 Aug 1832; Abner Adams, bondsman.

McNeely, William G. & Ann Macay, 11 Dec 1860; C. A. Henderson, bondsman; Wm. Locke, wit. married 12 Dec 1860 by T. G. Haughton.

McNight, Richard & Ann Luckey, 27 July 1802; Gilbert Nowell, bondsman; Jno. Brem, wit.

McNinch, F. A. & Sarah V. Ramsay, 24 April 1866; R. A. Ramsay, bondsman; Obadiah Woodson, wit.

McOrkle, Alexander & Rebecca Brandon, 3 May 1791; John Patton, bondsman; C. Caldwell, D. C., wit.

McPheeters, Charles & Caty Anderson, 9 March 1815; Michael Baker, bondsman; Geo. Dunn, wit.

McPherson, Robert & Nelly McNeely, 7 April 1800; Isaac McNeely, bondsman; N. Chaffin, J. P., wit.

McQuown, Daniel & Margret Sloan, 25 Feb 1781; Archd. Kern, bondsman.

McQuown, William & Sarah Kerr, 24 Oct 1779; David Kerr, bondsman; Jo. Brevard, wit.

McRary, John D. & Maria F. Burris, 12 May 1846; Robt. Bradshaw, bondsman; John H. Hardie Jr., wit.

McRorie, John & Margaret S. McKenzie, 17 Sept 1835; Thales McDonald, bondsman; Abel Cowan, J. P., wit.

McWilliams, James & _____, consent from Mary Johnson for her daughter to marry James McWilliams, 23 Aug 1769, headed "Whetheroth Crick"; German Baxter, wit.

Mabry, Leonard & Mary Rounsavall, 5 Dec 1790; Benjamin Rounsavall, bondsman; H. Siffard, wit.

Macay, Angus & Jean Macay, 28 Jan 1776; George Mackay, bondsman; Ad. Osborn, wit.

Macay, Wilson & Peggy Hunt, 31 July 1792; Robert McKee, bondsman; S. Mitchell, wit.

Mace, Thomas & Jane James, 7 Feb 1793; Jesse Claywell, bondsman.

Mace, Thomas & Agness Brown, __ June 1795; Wm. Houston, bondsman; J. Troy, wit.

Mace, Thomas & Mary Bird, 2 Aug 1796; James Garmer, bondsman; Ad. Osborn, wit.

Mackey, Alexander & Barbara MaKay, 23 Nov 1778; George Mackay, bondsman; Ad. Osborn, wit.

Mackey, John & Elenor McCreary, 20 March 1795; Benjn. Hodgens, bondsman; J. Troy, D. C., wit.

Maddan, Elisha & Charlotte Robinson, 26 Sept 1803; Charles C. McKinzie, bondsman.

Maddan, Nathan & Rebeccah Hatley, 20 Oct 1815; John Holman, bondsman; R. Powell, wit.

Madden, Davison & Patsey Smith, 22 May 1830; Elisha Madden, bondsman; L. R. Rose, J. P., wit.

Madden, Jonathan & Elizabeth Beck, 31 Oct 1817; David Holman, bondsman; R. Powell, wit.

Maden, Laurance & Alander Clarck, 1 June 1781; William Alldredge, Johahuns Man, bondsmen.

Maeley, Owen & Eve Kinder (no date, but probably 1795-1798); Ad. Osborn, wit.

Maffet, William & Jaynet Tait, 24 Aug 1788; John Tevis, bondsman.

Maffit, John & Elizabeth Cox, 27 Sept 1766; William Williams, bondsman; Thoms. Frohock, wit.

Maffit, John & Sarah Whiteker, 13 April 1790; William Whiteker Jr., bondsman; Basil Gaither, wit.

Magee, Isaac B. & Nancy A. Griffin, 8 April 1861; Paschal Callicutt, bondsman; John Wilkinson, wit. married 8 April 1861 by Rev. Wm. Lambeth.

Mahaley, David & Elizabeth West, 13 May 1847; John S. Butner, bondsman; J. H. Hardie Jr., wit.

Mahaley, Franklin & Rebecca Bean, 1 April 1861; married 21 April 1861 by Henry Barringer, J. P.

Mahaley, Frederick & Elizabeth Agner, 4 Aug 1824; John Wise, bondsman; Hy. Giles, wit.

Mahaley, J. A. & Susana Swink, 16 Feb 1841; Adam A. Smithdeal, bondsman; Mary Harrison, wit.

Mahaley, Joseph & Mary Ann Gollan, 14 May 1853; Lewis Mahaley, bondsman; J. S. Myers, wit. married 15 May 1853 by W. A. Walton, J. P.

ROWAN MARRIACES 1753-1868

Mahaley, Joseph & Mrs. Julia Ann A. Owens, 29 Oct 1859; Daniel
Berble, bondsman; James E. Kerr, wit. married 30 Oct 1859
by J. K. Burke, J. P.

Mahan, Dennis & Agness Lamb, 27 Sept 1769; William Alexander,
Wm. Cathey, bondsmen; Thomas Frohock, wit. consent from
Maunns Lamb for his daughter Nancy to marry Dennis Mauhan,
25 Sept 1769; Timothy Brown, wit.

Mahan, John & Polly McFerson, 19 Sept 1801; Jacob Duke, bondsman; Jno Brem, wit.

Maley, Hugh & Nancy Owen, 1 Nov 1808; Peter Owens, bondsman;
A. L. Osborn, wit.

Maley, James & Fanny McGuire, 18 Dec 1817; Joshua Park, bondsman; Roberts Nanny, wit.

Maloney, James T. & Nancy Page, 5 March 1861; George W. McLean,
bondsman; married 7 March 1861 by D. W. Honeycutt, J. P.

Malt, William & Mary Marlin, 11 Oct 1819; Joshua Repult, bondsman; Hy. Giles, wit.

Malt, William & Elizabeth Brady, 12 May 1840; Wm. H. Fultz,
bondsman; J. L. Beard, wit.

Manewton, Francis & Lucy Brock (colored), 26 Sept 1865; married
26 Sept 1865 by J. Rumple, V. D. M.

Mangum, Adolphus W. & Laura Overman, 24 Feb 1864; Jas. H. Enniss,
bondsman; W. H. Bobbitt, wit.

Manlove, David & Isabella Piggott, 18 Oct 1822; Henry Grubb,
bondsman.

Mann, James A. & Sarah Ann Luffman, 24 Nov 1846; Madison Mann,
bondsman; J. H. Hardie Jr., wit.

Mann, Madison & Nancy A. Luffman, 17 Feb 1846; Alexander W. Buis,
bondsman; J. M. Turner, wit.

Mansier, John & Mary Blaster, 25 July 1816; Jacob Corier, bondsman; Henry Giles, wit.

Marbry, Isaac & Presay Moore, 24 Oct 1797; Edward Moore, bondsman; Jno Rogers, wit.

Marbry, William & Sarah A. Montgomery, 10 Oct 1855; W. C. Ludwick, bondsman; Jac. C. Barnhardt, James E. Kerr, Clk., wit.
married 10 Oct 1855 by Jac. C. Barnhardt, J. P.

Marbury, Isaac & Rebecca Biles, _____; Thos Giles, bondsman;
J. Troy, D. C., wit.

Marbury, Luke & Elizabeth Bullen, 28 Dec 1793; Phillip Bullen,
bondsman; Jos. Chambers, wit.

March, Abraham & Elizabeth Booe, 5 June 1816; Wm. Glascock,
bondsman; Jn March Sr., wit.

March, George & Mary Leneer, 6 July 1804; Hezekiah Smith,
bondsman; Jn. March, J. P.; Moses Nelson, wit.

March, Jacob & Margaret Hinkle, 26 Aug 1797; Peter Ruford, bondsman; Jno Rogers, wit.

March, Jacob & Fanny Booe, 19 Aug 1816; Thomas Bailey, bondsman; Jn March Sr., wit.

March, John & Elizabeth Peeler, 30 Aug 177_; Anthony Peeler, bondsman; Ad. Osborn, wit.

March, John & Caty Hinkle, 18 Feb 1802; Jno. Brem, bondsman.

March, John Jr. & Elizabeth Gather, 18 Jan 1810; Richmond Hughes, bondsman; Jn March Sr., wit.

March, Rudolph & Agnes Roberts, 27 Sept 1779; Ad. Osborn, C. C., wit.

Marche, George & Amelia Gardner, 27 Sept 1779; Rodolph Marche, bondsman; Jo Brevard, wit.

Markland, Nathaniel & Polley Orrell, 13 March 1823; Jilson Berryman, bondsman; Ml. Hanes, J. P., wit.

Markland, Nathaniel Jr. & Polly Dowel, 22 Jan 1824; Thomson Tucker, bondsman; Ml. Hanes, J. P., wit.

Markland, Thomas & Nancy Orrell, 13 March 1823; William Beeding, bondsman.

Markland, William & Phebee Monroe, 27 Aug 1816; Robt. Hampton, bondsman; Thos. Hampton, wit.

Marlen, John & Jane Culberson, 14 March 1789; Jam. Willson, bondsman; Will Alexander, wit.

Marlen, John & Mary Slavey, 6 Aug 1804; Daniel Clary, bondsman; Ad. Osborn, wit.

Marlin, Elijah & Eleanor McHenry, 10 Aug 1804; James Nevins, bondsman; A. L. Osborn, wit.

Marlin, Elijah & Melinda P. Johnston, 24 Nov 1818; John Marlin, bondsman; Jno Giles, wit.

Marlin, Jesse & Mary Turner, 18 April 1833; James Owens, bondsman; Hy. Giles, wit.

Marlin, John & Sophia Graham, 12 Jan 1845; Wm. T. Marlin, bondsman; Jno. H. Hardie Jr., wit.

Marlin, John & Margret Nevins, 13 May ____; Valentine Brown, bondsman; Wm. Crawford, wit.

Marlin, Samuel & Isabella Lowry, 18 April 1820; Gillespie Culbertson, bondsman.

Marlin, William T. & C. C. Craige, 16 Sept 1862; John C. Benson, bondsman; married 16 Sept 1862 by B. Scott Krider.

Marlin, William T. & Margaret L. Howard, 30 Dec 1847; M. S. Fraley, bondsman; J. H. Hardie, wit.

Marlow, Elijah & Patianc Whitecar, 14 July 1795; William Parke, bondsman; J. Troy, wit.

Marno, James & Nancy Woodhouse, 20 March 1813;· Alexander Watson, bondsman; Jno Giles, C. C., wit.

Marona, G. W. & Jinny E. Lyerla, 14 Jan 1865; M. Hughes, bondsman; Obadiah Woodson, wit.

Marr, Jeduthun & Margaret Haden, 30 Dec 1803; Wm. Bradbury, bondsman; A. L. Osborn, D. C., wit.

Marr, Joshua & Rebecca Payne, 15 May 1780; Joshua Payne, bondsman; B. Booth Boote, wit.

Marsh, Bramson J. & Elizabeth Page, 19 May 1846; Richard Surratt, bondsman; J. H. Hardie Jr., wit.

Marsh, David & Phoebe Scudder, 13 May 1795; Henry Scudder, bondsman; J. Troy, wit.

Marsh, E. H. & Martha C. Buis, 9 June 1855; Jno. A. Holt, bondsman; James E. Kerr, wit. married 12 June 1855 by Jos. L. Fisher, Pastor of M. E. Church So.

Marsh, Philip & Rebecca Low, 5 Aug 1794; Wm. Cole, bondsman; J. Troy, D. C., wit.

Marshal, David & Nancy Williams, 13 Aug 1812; Benjamin Ellis, bondsman; W. Eller, J. P., wit.

Marshal, George & Sarah McNeely, 22 Aug 1868; Thomas McNeely, bondsman; Thomas Frohock, wit.

Marshall, John & Polly Haiden, 2 Feb 1790; Edwd. Yarbrough, bondsman; C. Caldwell, D. C., wit.

Marshall, Thomas & Jean Williams, 19 Nov 1791; Zadock Easton, bondsman; Chs. Caldwell, wit.

Martin, B. F. & P. A. Gribble, 26 March 1861; D. W. Honeycutt, bondsman.

Martin, Benjamin & Christena Graves, 16 Sept 1826; Josiah D. Potts, bondsman; Thomas McNeely, J. P., wit.

Martin, Benjamin & Elizabeth Dedman, 15 May 1833; Isaac White, bondsman; L. R. Rose, J. P., wit.

Martin, Isaac & Esther Wilkeson, 20 Nov 1797; William Brannock, bondsman; Jno. Rogers, wit.

Martin, James & Nancy Woods, 6 April 1811; William Wood, bondsman; Jno. Giles, C. C., wit.

Martin, James & Elizabeth Goodman, 17 March 1857; Farly Ellis, bondsman; James E. Kerr, wit. married 17 March 1857 by W. H. Walton, J. P.

Martin, John & Lidy Gray, 3 Feb 1803; John B. Clarke, bondsman; Hudson Hughes, wit.

Martin, John & Silvee Clark, 3 Feb 1808; Ellick Daniel, bondsman; Jn March Sr., wit.

Martin, Joseph & Patsey Dickins, 20 July 1813; John Foster, bondsman; Jn. March Sr., wit.

Martin, Joshua & Elener Black, 20 Dec 1821; Jos. Snider, bondsman; A. R. Jones, wit.

Martin, Samuel & _____, 4 May 1779; John Snoddey, bondsman.

Martin, William & Elizabeth Campbell, 28 Feb 1843; Saml. Reeves,
bondsman.

Marton, Benjamin & Rebeckey Potts, 30 Jan 1816; Josiah Potts,
bondsman; Jno. March Sr., wit.

Mason, A. Judson & Sallie H. Kerr, 11 April 1861; M. D. L. Mc-
Leod, bondsman; John Wilkinson, wit. married 11 April 1861
by T. G. Haughton.

Mason, Edward & Polly Taggard, 23 Oct 1817; James Mason,
bondsman; Roberts Nanny, wit.

Mason, Frederick & Susanna Coldiron, 31 Dec 1791; Peter Hendrix,
bondsman; Chs. Caldwell, wit.

Mason, Henderson & Elizabeth Jones, 28 Aug 1827; John Prather,
bondsman; L. R. Rose, J. P., wit.

Mason, Thomas F. & Elizabeth Cook, 29 June 1833; John Brian,
bondsman; L. R. Rose, J. P., wit.

Massey, William & Elizabeth McCarter, 25 Jan 1831; Patterson
Chambers, bondsman; C. Harbin, J. P., wit.

Massy, Abraham & Rachael Sherrill, 30 June 1774; Danl. Little,
bondsman; Ad. Osborn, wit. consent from Use. Sherrill.

Massy, Jacob & Catharine Barrier, 9 April 1785; Abraham Pepper
(?), bondsman.

Masten, Mathias & Sarah Standley, 6 Nov 1794; Reuben Standley,
bondsman; Fridreck Miller, wit.

Master, George & Elizabeth Swan, 16 June 1789; Matthew Swann,
bondsman; M. A. Troy, wit.

Masters, Darius & Phebe Stanley, 8 Dec 1817; Philip Mock Jr.,
bondsman; Sol. Davis, wit.

Masters, David & Susanna Fink, 27 Jan 1817; Henry Barger, bondsman; Jno Giles, C. C., wit.

Masters, George & Katharine Swann, 8 May 1800; Mathew Swann,
bondsman; Ad. Osborn, wit.

Masters, George & Martha Forster, 4 Feb 1811; Joshua Woods,
bondsman; Geo. Dunn, wit.

Masters, Hillery & Mary Davies, 23 Dec 1779; Notley Masters,
bondsman; B. Booth Boote, wit.

Masters, Thomas & Ann Fleming, 29 Oct 1823; Hugh Gibson, bondsman; Hy. Giles, wit.

Matherly, Israel & Sarah Cheney, 4 Nov 1778; Joseph Matherly,
bondsman; Ad. Osborn, wit. consent from John Cheney, 24
Oct 1778.

Matherly, James & Martha Leatherman, 24 Dec 1816; Isaac Leatherman, bondsman; Mack Crump, wit.

Matherly, John & Peggy McCrary, 3 Jan 1815; Hugh McCrary, bondsman; Ezra Allemong, wit.

Matherly, Joseph & Elizabeth Patterson, 4 Nov 1778; Israel
Matherly, bondsman; Ad. Osborn, wit. consent from John
Patterson, 28 Oct 1778.

Matherly, Thomas & Elizabeth Jones, 13 May 1811; John Brewer,
bondsman; Saml. Jones, wit.

Matheson, Newton M. & Julia Wade, 27 May 1852; Noah W. Fry,
bondsman; J. S. Myers, wit.

Mathley, John & Rachael Patterson, 23 Dec 1777; John Patterson,
bondsman; Ad. Osborn, wit. consent from John Patterson.

Mathews, John & Susannah Stults, 1 Sept 1818; Wm. Chapman, bondsman; Thos Hampton, wit.

Matthews, Milus B. & Nancy Young, 12 Dec 1833; James B. Campbell,
bondsman; Jno Giles, wit.

Maxwell, Andrew & Sarah R. Hill, 21 Sept 1865; John R. Maxwell,
bondsman; Horatio N. Woodson, wit. married 21 Sept 1865 by
J. M. Coffin, J. P.

Maxwell, David & Rebecca Morrow, 29 Oct 1785; Joseph Maxwell,
bondsman; Max. Chambers, wit.

Maxwell, John & Louisa Little, 11 Aug 1847; Matthias Boger,
bondsman; Robert Murphy, wit.

Maxwell, Joseph & Rebecca Lions, 30 March 1792; Thomas Maxwell,
bondsman; Basil Gaither, wit.

Maxwell, Joseph & Mary Marr, 3 Aug 1797; John Brown, bondsman;
Jno Rogers, wit.

Maxwell, Samuel & Eliz. Work, 9 March 1768; Frances McBride,
bondsman; Thomas Frohock, wit.

Maxwell, Thomas T. & Rebecca Pool, 30 Nov 1842; Benj. Julian,
bondsman.

Maxwell, Thomas T. & Zelpha H. Graham, 3 July 1851; Wm. McHaynes,
bondsman.

May, Alexander & Sarah Clark, 15 March 1821; R. Powell, bondsman;
R. Powell, wit.

May, Alexander & Rosy Limbaugh, 2 July 1825; Thomas Bringle,
bondsman; Hy. Giles, wit.

May, Alexander & Lucinda Eller, 30 June 1851; Noah Peeler,
bondsman; J. S. Myers, wit.

May, Isaac & Nancy Bryan, 9 June 1789; James Messar, bondsman;
M. A. Troy, wit.

May, John & Mary Basinger, 14 June 1805; Jacob Lyerle, bondsman; Andrew Kerr, wit.

May, John & Ann Earnhart, 25 Oct 1835; Caleb Earnhart, bondsman; Hy. Giles, wit.

May, John E. & Elvira Goodman, 21 Aug 1851; Joel Jackson, bondsman; Archd. Honeycutt, J. P., wit.

May, Mark & Martha Belinda Beeman, 31 Aug 1833; Jonathan Cranfill, bondsman; Jno. Tomlinson, J. P., wit.

May, Martin & Rachel Clark, 8 May 1813; Wm. Holman, bondsman; R. Powell, wit.

May, Pleasant & Waney Airy, 16 Aug 1839; Alexander May, bondsman; John Giles, wit.

May, Pleasant & Eliza A. Michals, 2 May 1850; James Goodman, bondsman; J. S. Myers, wit.

Meaden, Andrew & Polly Madden, 13 Oct 1813; Jonathan Madden, bondsman; R. Powell, wit.

Meadows, Daniel & Sally Chambers, 8 Sept 1787; James Chambers, bondsman; Margt. Osborn, wit.

Mealy, John & Mary Linn, 20 March 1797; John Wilson, bondsman; Jno. Rogers, wit.

Meanos, Andrew & Mary Waggoner, 4 Feb 1840; John Waggoner, bondsman; Abel Cowan, J. P., wit.

Means, Joseph & Margaret Knatzer, 18 Nov 1794; Peter Brown, bondsman; J. Troy, D. C., wit.

Meanser, John & Chistena Corrier, 23 Feb 1805; John Sloop, bondsman; Moses A. Locke, wit.

Mearro, John & Rebecca Tate, 14 Sept 1774; Abel Armstrong, bondsman; Ad. Osborn, wit.

Mears, John Jr. & Elisebeth Tucker, 13 Aug 1823; Th. Mullikin, bondsman; M. Hanes, J. P., wit.

Mecarn, William & Mary Garn, 12 Nov 1812; Abraham Peppingar, bondsman; Geo. Dunn, wit.

Mecarton, James & Feurriday Snider, 30 March 1814; John Snider, bondsman; Jn March Sr., wit.

Medcaris, Malachi & Elizabeth Lane, 22 July 1798; Shadrach Lane, bondsman; Edwin J. Osborn, D. C., wit.

Mehaley, Franklin & Rebecca Bean, 1 April 1861; Charles W. Dry, bondsman; John Wilkinson, wit.

Mehaley, William & Hannah Miller, 18 Feb 1815; William Miller, bondsman; Geo. Dunn, wit.

Meinus, F. E. & S. O. Young, 13 Nov 1865; J. M. Cowan, bondsman; Obadiah Woodson, wit.

Meldar, James & Mary Hellard, 4 Nov 1799; Nathaniel Parson, bondsman; Edwin J. Osborn, D. C., wit.

Melford, John & Mary Flemming, 3 May 1783; Allison Fleming, bondsman.

Melton, Levi & Amanda Speck, 10 Aug 1865; Jack Hall, bondsman; Obadiah Woodson, wit.

Melton, Levi & Amanda Speck, 10 Aug 1865; Lewis H. Buis, bondsman; Obadiah Woodson, wit.

Melton, William & Nancy Hill, 14 Dec 1848; James Melton, bondsman; J. H. Hardie, wit.

Mendenhall, George D. & Eliza Cavender, 14 May 1835; Hubbard J. Peebles, bondsman; Joseph Hawes, J. P., wit.

Menies, John & Nancy Cress, 7 Dec 1848; J. H. Hardie, bondsman.

Menis, Henry & Nancy Turner, 28 June 1843; George Menis, bondsman; John H. Hardie, wit.

Menis, Jacob & Nancy Rex, 1 Dec 1851; Robt. L. McConnughy, bondsman; James E. Kerr, wit. married 2 Dec 1851 by Jno M. McConnaughey, J. P.

Menius, Andrew & Polly Cope, 2 Sept 1813; Jacob Liteaker, bondsman; Geo. Dunn, wit.

Menius, Frederick & Betsey Steller, 10 Sept 1821; Jacob Steller, bondsman.

Menius, George & Rachael Duke, 27 Nov 1827; Andrew Menius, bondsman; J. H. Hardie, wit.

Menius, George & Evaline Lamb, 9 June 1841; Daniel Menius, bondsman; Susan T. Giles, wit.

Menius, George M. & Mary A. Seaford, 24 July 1862; Samuel Elliott, bondsman; Obadiah Woodson, wit.

Menius, Jacob & Sarah Turner, 25 April 1837; Daniel Menius, bondsman; Tobias L. Lemly, wit.

Menius, John & Elizabeth Click, 3 Nov 1829; Andrew Menius, bondsman.

Menius, John Jr. & Aley Angeline Ketchey, 11 Dec 1860; Carmi J. Wagoner, bondsman; James E. Kerr, wit. married 13 Dec 1860 by Saml. Rothrock, Minister of the Gospel in the Ev. Luth. Church.

Menius, John C. & J. E. McLaughlin, 27 Jan 1858; James M. Menius, bondsman; John Wilkinson, wit. married 28 Jan 1858 by S. C. Alexander.

Menus, Daniel & Elizabeth Turner, 3 Aug 1835; George Menius, bondsman; J. H. Hardie, wit.

Menus, James M. & Mary E. McNeely, 20 Nov 1848; Jas. Albright, bondsman; J. H. Hardie Jr., wit.

Mercer, James & Margaret Rhodes Smith, 8 June 1779; Henry Fullenwider, bondsman; Henry Giffard, wit.

Merel, Andrew & Permilla Tatom, 4 June 1810; Abraham Jacobs, bondsman; Geo. Dunn, wit.

Merell, Abner & Ritter Jones, 22 Oct 1802; Thomas Gadbery, bondsman; A. L. Osborn, D. C., wit.

Merell, Jonathan & Polly Cooper, 24 May 1817; William Adams, bondsman; Milo A. Giles, wit.

Mererel, Benjamin & Lucy Derham, 8 Sept 1798; John Blalock, bondsman; Edwin J. Osborn, D. C., wit.

Merit, William & Margaret Freaser, 9 July 1788; Wm. Kazey, bondsman; Wm. Alexander, wit.

Meroney, John A. & Mary Hendrix, 22 July 1825; Joseph O. Welch, bondsman.

Meroney, Charles P. & Charity E. Burkhead, 1 Oct 1862; Michael A. Bringle, bondsman; Obadiah Woodson, wit. married 1 Oct 1862 by A. W. Mangum, M. G.

Meroney, P. P. & Lydia Allred, 25 July 1865; J. O. White, bondsman; Obadiah Woodson, wit. married 25 July 1865 by J. B. Laurens.

Meroney, P. P. & Delia Thomas, 20 July 1859; Moses B. Murr, bondsman; James E. Kerr, wit. married 20 July 1859 by H. F. Hudson.

Meroney, Philip F. & Saphronia Hughes, 8 Aug 1831; Jno. H. Hardie, bondsman.

Meroney, Thomas G. & Diana Hudson, 14 May 1833; Jonathan Nelson, bondsman; Thomas McNeely, J. P., wit.

Merrell, Benjamin & Penelope Merrill, 4 Feb 1778; William Merrell, Boyd M'Crerey, bondsmen; Jams. Robinson, wit.

Merrell, Benjamin & Elizabeth Garret, 3 March 1795; John Wiseman, bondsman; J. Troy, wit.

Merrell, John & Polly Chatman, 13 Sept 1814; Wm. Merrell, bondsman; Jno. Henderson, wit.

Merrell, John & Mary Wiseman, 21 Jan 1773; Garshom Hunt, bondsman; Max. Chambers, wit.

Merrell, Jonathan & Nancy Elliot, 25 Sept 1787; John Elliot, bondsman; Spruce Macay, wit.

Merrell, Timothy & Elizabeth Bradshaw, 30 Nov 1801; John Smt. Johnson, bondsman; Jno Brem, wit.

Merrell, William & Lucy Smith, 17 Oct 1814; George Willis Jr., bondsman; Moses A. Locke, wit.

Mesemore, Moses & Elizabeth Rainy, 14 Jan 1854; John A. Snider, bondsman; J. S. Myers, wit.

Mesimore, Charles & Mary L. Trexler, 7 Oct 1854; William H. Crawford, bondsman; J. S. Myers, wit. married 8 Oct 1854 by W. A. Walton, J. P.

Mesmore, John & Hannah Wooliver, 16 July 1813; Jacob Van Pool, bondsman; Ezra Allemong, wit.

Messemmer, George W. & Eliza M. May, 1 Aug 1861; Rufus P. Troutman, bondsman; M. L. Holmes, J. P., wit. married 18 Aug 1861 by E. Mauney, J. P.

Misser, Ase & Dianah Philips, 2 Aug 1803; Samuel Gentle, bondsman; Jn March, J. P., wit.

Metsler, John & Elizabeth Lewey, 21 Aug 1784; Henry Winkler, bondsman; H. McGoune, wit.

Mettauer, John Jr. & Malind Smoot, 28 April 1820; William Scott, bondsman; Jno Giles, wit.

Meyer, Piter & Mary Easton, 28 March 1768; Gideon Wright, bondsman; John Frohock, wit.

Meyerfeld, A. & Margaret L. Miller, 9 April 1864; L. D. Bencini, bondsman; Obadiah Woodson, wit.

Mice, Christopher & Nancy Parker, 9 May 1806; Ransom Dudley, bondsman.

Michael, Henry & Lidia Wood, 7 Feb 1809; Jesse Barber, bondsman; George Snider, wit.

Michael, Jacob & Beedy Ledford, 1 March 1813; Wilson McCrary, bondsman; Geo. Dunn, wit.

Michael, John & Sarah Scott, 8 May 1815; David Michel, bondsman; Geo. Dunn, wit.

Michael, John & Christianna Leonard, 7 Nov 1809; Jacob Shoaf, bondsman; Geo. Dunn, wit.

Michael, Peter & Eve Day, 30 Oct 1794; Sion Daniel, bondsman; Fridreck Miller, wit.

Michael, William & Mary Aplin, 28 Jan 1807; Jacob Michael, bondsman; J. Hanes, J. P., wit.

Michaely, Christian & Eve Smithdeal, 18 Aug 1817; George Smithteel, bondsman; Jno Giles, wit.

Michal, William H. & Isabella E. Ramsour, 16 Nov 1850; Jno. E. Boger, bondsman.

Michael, Jacob & Susana Coonce, 15 June 1818; Andrew Craver, bondsman; J. Willson, J. P., wit.

Michel, Frederick & Elizabeth Baker, 7 Aug 1786; Peter Baker, bondsman; Jno. Macay, wit.

Micinhimer, Reed & Jane F. Rufty, married 14 Sept 1854 by H. W. Hill, J. P.

Miers, George & Nancy Freeman, 11 March 1811; Vinson Wood, bondsman; Joseph Clarke, wit.

Miers, Henery & Katy Goss, 20 Aug 1804; Nathaniel Parker, bondsman; Moses A. Locke, wit.

Miers, Jacob & Hannah Smith, 20 Nov 1816; John Miers, bondsman; Roberts Nanny, wit.

Miers, Michael & Mary Nicholson, 12 June 1779; William Nicholson, bondsman; Ad. Osborn, wit.

Miers, Michael & Betsy Wilson, 27 Sept 1814; William Abbott, bondsman; Geo. Dunn, wit.

Miers, Michael & Polly Grimes, 16 Feb 1818; Mathias Grimes, bondsman; Roberts Nanny, wit.

Might, William & Sarah Isom, 20 Aug 1848; Benjam. Might, bondsman; J. H. Hardie Jr., wit.

Mikel, George & Caty Waggoner, 10 Feb 1816; Jno. Michael, bondsman; Jno Giles, C. C., wit.

Mikiel, David & Lucy Walser, 8 Oct 1794; Philip Wolser, bondsman; J. Troy, D. C., wit.

Mikle, Samuel & Margret Bryant, 22 March 1808; Daniel Warner, bondsman; Jn. March Sr., wit.

Milford, Thomas & Eleanor Jameson, 31 Jan 1780; Jno. Brown, bondsman; Ad. Osborn, wit.

Milleken, Zadock & Elizabeth Myers, 15 Dec 1810; Aquillar Chesier, bondsman; Jn March Sr., wit.

Miller, Aaron W. & Rachel L. Henly, married 7 April 1853 by Saml. Rothrock, Minister of the Gospel in the Ev. Luth. Church.

Miller, Abraham & Sophia Miller, 9 Jan 1810; John Cobble, bondsman; Ezra Allemong, wit.

Miller, Abraham & Celia Etcheson, 20 Aug 1825; Jacob W. Miller, bondsman; J. C. Weddington, wit.

Miller, Adam & Hannah Speets, 29 March 1791; Henry Swink, bondsman; C. Caldwell, D. C., wit.

Miller, Alexander M. & Christena Lents, 12 Oct 1835; David Lents, bondsman.

Miller, Alexander M. & Clotilda Ribelin, 22 April 1854; Charles A. G. Miller, bondsman; J. S. Myers, wit. married 27 April 1854 by Saml. Rothrock, Minister of the Gospel in the Ev. Luth. Church.

Miller, Alfred A. & Mary C. Hall, 14 May 1857; M. A. Bearnhardt, bondsman; J. S. Myers, wit. married 14 May 1857 by A. M. Nesbitt, J. P.

Miller, Allen & Mary Jane Miller (colored), 21 Sept 1865, by Rev. Wm. Lambeth.

Miller, Aron & Nancy Reed, 19 Nov 1833; Peter Cauble, bondsman; Wm. Locke, wit.

Miller, Aron Wiley & Rachel L. Henly, 4 April 1853; Jacob C. Miller, bondsman; J. S. Myers, wit.

Miller, Asa & Polly Mehaley, 16 March 1815; William Mehaley, bondsman; Geo. Dunn, wit.

Miller, Barton & Sophiah Rendleman, 13 Aug 1766; Christopher Rindleman, bondsman; Thoms. Frohock, wit.

Miller, Benjamin & Mary Hays, 16 Dec 1769; Joseph Hays, bondsman; John Frohock, wit.

Miller, Caleb & Mary Lopp, 23 Aug 1828; Peter Miller, bondsman.

Miller, Caleb A. & Sophronia J. Morgan, 8 Sept 1859; Henry C.
Waller, bondsman; Levi Trexler, wit. married 8 Sept 1859 by
Levi Trexler, J. P.

Miller, Calvin J. & Jane S. Ketchey, 11 Aug 1859; Geo. A. Miller,
bondsman; Levi Trexler, wit. married 11 Aug 1859 by L. C.
Groseclose, Pastor of St. John's Ch., Salisbury.

Miller, Charles & Sally Freeze, 11 Jan 1815; Benjamin Brown,
bondsman; Geo. Dunn, wit.

Miller, Charles M. & Catherine Redwin, _____; Caleb Earnhart,
bondsman; John Fulton, wit.

Miller, Charles R. & Sarah E. Sifford, 13 Sept 1858; Jesse W.
Miller, bondsman; James E. Kerr, wit. married 16 Sept 1858
by Saml. Rothrock, Minister of the Gospel in the Ev. Luth.
Church.

Miller, Christian & Mary Shoman, 27 July 1797; Jno Shoman,
bondsman; Jno Rogers, wit.

Miller, Chn. & _____, 2 Aug 1797; Fredk. Fonel, bondsman;
Jno Rogers, wit.

Miller, Conrad & Dorothy Goose, 22 Nov 1783; Jno Brandon,
bondsman.

Miller, Conrod & Susanna Lentz, 9 Jan 1826; Dawalt Lentz, bondsman; Hy. Giles, wit.

Miller, Daniel & Hannah L. Klutts, 6 June 1836; John Miller,
bondsman; Jno Giles, wit.

Miller, Daniel & Nancy J. Reid, 13 Jan 1851; Michael Miller,
bondsman; J. S. Myers, wit.

Miller, Daniel & Catharine Goodman, 11 Jan 1859; Saml Troutman,
bondsman; married 12 Jan 1859 by Saml. Rothrock, Minister of
the Gospel in the Ev. Luth. Church.

Miller, David & Elizabeth Scot, 15 July 1779; Joseph Ross,
bondsman; Jo. Brevard, wit.

Miller, David & Elizabeth Pitts, 26 Nov 1789; Christian Shroad,
bondsman.

Miller, David & Susanna Zevely, 1 May 1790; Peter Faust, bondsman; C. Caldwell, D. C., wit.

Miller, David & Catherine Krite, 17 April 1812; David Brown,
bondsman; Ezra Allemong, wit.

Miller, David & Elizabeth Butner, 30 April 1835; Solomon Brown,
bondsman; J. H. Hardie, wit.

Miller, David Alexander & Mary Boger, 12 June 1858; Milas J.
Walton, bondsman; John Wilkinson, wit. married 15 June 1858
by S. J. Peeler, J. P.

Miller, David L. & Isabella C. Brown, 27 Nov 1865; Uriah E.
Miller, bondsman; Horatio N. Woodson, wit.

Miller, Dawalt & Elizabeth Knup, 28 April 1823; Henry Lence,
bondsman; Geo. Locke, wit.

Miller, Dawalt & Sally Beaver, 27 Jan 1834; Peter Lentz, bondsman; Wm. Locke, wit.

Miller, Edmund & Abby Rendleman (colored), 2 Jan 1865; John
Heilig, bondsman; Obadiah Woodson, wit.

Miller, Elam F. & Lauria Hornbarrier, 10 May 1839; Alexander
Cauble, bondsman; Jno Giles, wit.

Miller, Elias & Fanny Winders, 10 Feb 1834; John Shaver, bondsman; Wm. Locke, wit.

Miller, Felly & Eve Fishel, 10 Aug 1795; Jacob Fisher, bondsman.

Miller, Frederick & Mary Haiden, 15 Dec 1801; David Miller,
bondsman; Jno Brem, wit.

Miller, Frederick & Salley Black, 30 Oct 1819; John Black,
bondsman; R. Powell, wit.

Miller, Fredrick & Margaret Brown, 10 May 1779; John Brown,
bondsman; Jo. Brevard, wit.

Miller, G. A. & Milly M. Trexler, 11 April 1863; Ira A. Little,
bondsman; Obadiah Woodson, wit.

Miller, G. W. & M. S. Ludwick, 23 June 1855; Eli Ludwick, bondsman; D. M. Honeycutt, wit. married 24 June 1855 by D. M.
Honeycutt, J. P.

Miller, George & Mary Bussel, 2 Aug 1779; Peter Butner, bondsman; Jo. Brevard, wit.

Miller, George & Peggy Brandon, 13 Aug 1795; Frederick Allemong,
bondsman; J. Troy, D. C., wit.

Miller, George & Peggy Smith, 20 Jan 1808; Philip Smith,
bondsman.

Miller, George & Rosanna Hunter, 15 Aug 1818; Jesse Etcheson,
bondsman; R. Powell, wit.

Miller, George & Anna Chambers, 13 June 1822; Chs. Fisher,
bondsman.

Miller, George & Elizabeth Cruse, 17 Oct 1842; Paul Miller,
bondsman; Jno. H. Hardie, wit.

Miller, George & Tirley S. Fite, 20 Feb 1856; Green Moury,
bondsman; Levi Trexler, wit. married 21 Feb 1856 by Levi
Trexler, J. P.

Miller, George A. & Louiza Lingle, 10 June 1856; James H. Heilig,
bondsman; J. S. Myers, wit. married 12 June 1856 by Saml.
Rothrock, Minister of the Gospel in the Ev. Luth. Church.

Miller, Henry & Susannah Miller, 16 Sept 1778; Thomas Philps,
bondsman; Ad. Osborn, wit.

Miller, Henry & Cathrine Lipps, 10 April 1787; Leonhardt _____,
bondsman; Jno Macay, wit.

Miller, Henry & Peggy Bruner, 11 Dec 1810; Harman Fisher,
bondsman; Jno Giles, wit.

Miller, Henry & Sally Cain, 21 Oct 1815; James Hudspeth, bondsman.

Miller, Henry & Christina Shuping, 9 Dec 1834; Jacob Shuping, bondsman; Jno. Giles, wit.

Miller, Henry & Elizabeth Hill, 7 Oct 1840; Green Miller, bondsman; Obh. M. Smith, J. P., wit.

Miller, Henry A. & Eve A. Seaford, 9 Dec 1850; Jesse W. Miller, bondsman; J. S. Myers, wit.

Miller, Henry D. & Mary S. Lentz, 13 Oct 1859; R. S. Miller, bondsman.

Miller, Henry M. & Malinda Buggs (Boggs), 5 July 1859; Eli Holshouser, bondsman; married 7 July 1859 by Saml. Rothrock, Minister of the Gospel in the Ev. Luth. Church.

Miller, J. W. & Susan J. Barringer, 2 Feb 1860; J. R. M. Barringer, bondsman; John Wilkinson, wit. married 2 Feb 1860 by W. H. Bobbitt.

Miller, Jacob & Elisabeth Coll, 14 Sept 1823; William Atchason, bondsman; M. Hanes, J. P., wit.

Miller, Jacob & Barbara Smith, 3 March 1785; Henry Giles, bondsman.

Miller, Jacob & Margaret Carter, 25 July 1796; William Knop, bondsman; J. Troy, wit.

Miller, Jacob & Polly Biles, 17 Nov 1799; Christian Coughanour, bondsman; Edwin J. Osborn, wit.

Miller, Jacob & Rachel Hendrick, 24 June 1818; George Miller, bondsman.

Miller, Jacob & Catharine Sefford, 22 Oct 1825; Martin Miller, bondsman; Jno Giles, wit.

Miller, Jacob & Anna Shaver, 19 Sept 1826; Jacob Brown, bondsman; J. H. Hardie, wit.

Miller, Jacob J. & Josey Parker, 16 Oct 1857; C. A. Morphis, bondsman; D. W. Honeycutt, wit. married 22 Oct 1857 by Saml. Rothrock, Minister of the Gospel in the Ev. Luth. Church.

Miller, Jacob O. & Eliza Parker, 5 July 1853; Green Moury, bondsman; Levi Trexler, wit. married 5 July 1853 by Levi Trexler, J. P.

Miller, James & Agnes Nevins, 7 Feb 1780; William Nevens, bondsman.

Miller, James & Barbara Foster, 3 Oct 1810; Joseph Cowan, bondsman; Jno. Giles, C. C., wit.

Miller, James & Polly Ricard, 2 Nov 1814; Henry Stirewalt, bondsman; Jno. Giles, C. C., wit.

Miller, James & Eliza Freeze, 6 April 1830; John D. Criswell, bondsman; Jno. H. Hardie, wit.

Miller, James & Margaret C. McNeely, 22 Dec 1854; James S. Lowrance, bondsman; J. S. Myers, wit.

Miller, Jesse & Margaret Holshouser, 20 Feb 1854; Milas A. Holshouser, bondsman; J. S. Myers, wit. married 23 Feb 1854 by Saml. Rothrock, Minister of the Gospel in the Ev. Luth. Church.

Miller, John & Mary Goss, 20 June 1783; Henry Giles, bondsman.

Miller, John & Mary Ritesman, 13 June 1791; Henry Miller, bondsman; Basil Gaither, wit.

Miller, John & Barbar Popst, 9 Feb 1796; John Williams, bondsman; J. Troy, wit.

Miller, John & Elizabeth Lintz, 1 July 1797; Fredrick Miller, bondsman; M. Stokes, wit.

Miller, John & Susanah Jefries, 2 Dec 1811; Enoch Eytcheson, bondsman; Jn March Sr., wit.

Miller, John & Barrey Doss, 10 Jan 1822; Daniel Rutledge, bondsman; John Cook, J. P., wit.

Miller, John & Sarah Harkey, 8 Aug 1831; Henry Harky, bondsman; Jno. H. Hardie, wit.

Miller, John & Anna Shuping, 20 Nov 1832; Jacob Shuping, bondsman; P. Click, wit.

Miller, John & Elizabeth A. Air, 10 Feb 1849; David Knup, bondsman.

Miller, John & Elizabeth Cifford, 13 Feb 1821; Martin Miller, bondsman; Hy. Giles, wit.

Miller, John & _____, _____; Conrat Klutz, bondsman; Jno Rogers, wit.

Miller, John & Mary McClannahan, 27 April 1781; David McClenachen, bondsman; Ad. Osborn, wit.

Miller, John A. & Aseneth S. Peeler, 30 Jan 1858; Jesse Miller, bondsman; James E. Kerr, wit.

Miller, John A. & Rosina S. Peeler, married 4 Feb 1858 by Saml. Rothrock, Minister of the Gospel in the Ev. Luth. Church.

Miller, John C. & Mrs. Mary Ann Redwine, 1 Nov 1859; Thomas McNeely, bondsman; married 1 Nov 1859 by Saml. Rothrock, Minister of the Gospel in the Ev. Luth. Church.

Miller, John H. & Carmilla C. Hilick, 25 Nov 1844; Caleb A. Heilig, bondsman; John H. Hardie Jr., wit.

Miller, John J. & Mary Ann Brown, 13 April 1846; Michael L. Brown, bondsman; John H. Hardie Jr., wit.

Miller, John M. & Flora Eller, 14 Aug 1834; Charles Lentz, bondsman; Jno Giles, wit.

Miller, Jonathan & Rody Wyatt, 21 March 1820; Christian Mehala, bondsman.

Miller, Joseph & Nicey Deavor, 25 May 1826; Stephen Shelton, bondsman; C. Harbin, J. P., wit.

Miller, Joseph & Mary Houldsouser, 10 Feb 1834; David Lentz, bondsman; Jno Giles, wit.

Miller, Joseph & Levina Smithdeal, 6 Oct 1852; Joseph Smithdeal, bondsman; J. S. Myers, wit.

Miller, Joshua & Mary D. Correll, 15 Sept 1849; David Freeze, bondsman; J. S. Myers, wit.

Miller, Joshua & Sarah C. McLaughlin, 30 June 1864; A. T. Graham, bondsman; Thomas McNeely, wit.

Miller, L. C. & Malinda Holshouser, 16 May 1854; A. L. Klutts, bondsman; Obadiah Woodson, wit.

Miller, Martin & Molly Beaver, 14 Sept 1812; Davault Lentz, bondsman; Ezra Allemong, wit.

Miller, Martin & Nelly Foutz, 7 Nov 1815; Dawalt Lentz, bondsman; Jno Giles, C. C., wit.

Miller, Martin & Milly Lyerly, 18 April 1827; John Miller, bondsman; J. H. Hardie, wit.

Miller, Michael & Nelly Turner, 20 Nov 1811; Thomas Miller, bondsman; Jno Giles, C. C., wit.

Miller, Michael & Amanda Owens, 6 Dec 1859; David C. Reid, bondsman; married 6 Dec 1859 by S. D. Peeler.

Miller, Michal & Susan Tickis, 8 Fob 1804; Jno. Getchy, bondsman; A. L. Osborn, D. C., wit.

Miller, Milees & Chaney Mowry, 29 Feb 1844; Green Mowrey, bondsman; Jno. H. Hardie Jr., wit.

Miller, Miles & Elizabeth Beaver, 11 March 1846; Jesse Thomason, bondsman.

Miller, Milf. G. & Mary Adaline Ketchey, 29 Feb 1848; Morgan Misenhamer, bondsman.

Miller, Milford G. & Anna Cauble, 18 July 1841; Mils Miller, bondsman; Susan T. Giles, wit.

Miller, Nicholas & Elizebeth Livengood, 5 Dec 1822; John Everhart, bondsman; An. Swicegood, wit.

Miller, Paul & Maria Miller, 11 July 1857; Chas. N. Price, bondsman; J. S. Myers, wit.

Miller, Peter & Sophia Bruner, 10 Nov 1823; Samuel Millery, bondsman; Hy. Giles, wit.

Miller, Peter & Polly Josey, 19 May 1831; Michael L. Brown, bondsman; D. J. J. W. Fulton, wit.

Miller, Peter & Polly Fraley, 1 April 1865; Jacob S. Myers, bondsman; Obadiah Woodson, wit.

Miller, Pleasant & Mary Miller, 10 Aug 1825; John Miller, bondsman; J. C. Weddington, wit.

Miller, Pleasant & Anna Crumpton, 20 Jan 1829; David Harbin, bondsman; C. Harbin, J. P., wit.

Miller, R. C. & Sarah C. Lentz, 24 Aug 1865; Clark Stoner, bondsman; Obadiah Woodson, wit. married 24 Aug 1865 by J. B. Laurens, Minister.

Miller, Roland & Sarah Ann Morgan, 19 Feb 1864; John F. Hodge, bondsman; Thomas McNeely, wit.

Miller, Rufus & Elizabeth C. Moyer, 22 June 1855; David Lentz, bondsman; J. S. Myers, wit.

Miller, Samuel & Elizabeth Walker, 25 April 1796; Thomas Cooper, bondsman.

Miller, Samuel & Martha Lowrance, 14 April 1818; John M'Neely, bondsman; Milo A. Giles, wit.

Miller, Samuel & Barbara Bruner, 13 Jan 1819; Edward Davis, bondsman; Roberts Nanny, wit.

Miller, Samuel & Nancy Parker, 17 Sept 1835; Jacob Miller, bondsman; Jno. Shaver, J. P., wit.

Miller, Samuel & Mary Graham, 27 Aug 1771; Fergus Graham, Samuel Cooper, bondsmen; John Frohock, wit.

Miller, Thomas & Anne N. Lorance, 18 March 1825; Alfred A. Lowrance, bondsman; W. Harris, wit.

Miller, Thomas & Nancy Criswell, 4 Dec 1802; Willie Coats, bondsman; A. L. Osborn, D. C., wit.

Miller, Vollentine & Eve Cresson, 12 Feb 1814; Jacob Weasner, bondsman; Joseph Clarke, wit.

Miller, Warren & Mary C. Rotan, 14 July 1824; Makinzey Willis, bondsman; Hy. Giles, wit.

Miller, William & Elizabeth L. McLaughlin, 14 Feb 1855; E. C. McLaughlin, bondsman; J. S. Myers, wit. married 20 Feb 1855 by J. Ingold, Minister of the Gospel.

Miller, William & Margaret Cauble, 29 Aug 1816; Jacob Cauble, bondsman; Jno Giles, C. C., wit.

Miller, William & Catharine Mowrie, 13 Aug 1825; Jno. Cauble, bondsman.

Miller, William & Matilda Eller, 29 Aug 1864; Paul Holshouser, bondsman; James E. Kerr, wit.

Miller, William & Margaret McNeily, 9 Oct 1792; James McNeely, bondsman; Jo Chambers, wit.

Miller, William C. & Mary Ann Albright, 9 Sept 1830; Jacob Shuping, bondsman; Jno. H. Hardie, wit.

Miller, William G. & Mary L. Freeze, 20 Feb 1844; David Arnhart, bondsman; J. H. Hardie, wit.

Miller, William W. & Margaret D. Pinkston, 19 Oct 1865; William Smithdeal, bondsman; Obadiah Woodson, wit.

Milligan, James & Eleanor Allen, 14 Feb 1775; Alexander Sloan, bondsman; Ad. Osborn, wit.

Millis, John Jr. & Sarah Bowers, 29 March 1821; Eli Burton,
bondsman; Silas Peace, wit.

Millis, Joseph & Crissilla Burton, 1 Nov 1820; Isaac Pope, bondsman; Z. Hunt, wit.

Mills, Andrew & Catharine S. Masters, 14 March 1831; James
Alexander, bondsman; Hy. Giles, wit.

Mills, Galbraeth & Elizabeth Brown, 7 Feb 1825; Benjamin Brown,
bondsman; W. Harris, wit.

Mills, Gilberth & Sarah M. Gougan, 17 Feb 1844; Thomas J.
Dotson, bondsman; J. H. Hardie, wit.

Mills, Henry M. & Mary Dickson, 3 Nov 1853; J. D. Ramsey,
bondsman; J. S. Myers, wit.

Mills, J. A. & C. T. Cook, 8 Jan 1853; A. C. Mclelland, bondsman; J. S. Myers, wit.

Mills, Jacob & Polley Chesheir, 25 Sept 1813; Walter Mills,
bondsman; Jn. March Sr., wit.

Mills, John & _____, 23 Aug 1797; Wm. Tippett, bondsman; Jno
Rogers, wit.

Mills, John B. & Rachael C. Moore, 15 June 1850; Jas. F. McNeely,
bondsman.

Mills, Nathan & Elizabeth Ovorman, 21 Dec 1803; Caleb Pegg,
bondsman; Willm. Welborn, wit.

Mills, Neil & Nancy Wotever, 7 May 1836; William Kiestler,
bondsman; Abel Cowan, wit.

Mills, Walter & Lovey Coker, 14 May 1812; George Coker, bondsman; R. Powell, wit.

Mills, William & Susanah Shammel, 20 Jan 1803; Nathan Russel,
bondsman; A. L. Osborn, D. C., wit.

Mills, Woodson D. & Milly Corl, 21 March 1855; Michael Corl,
bondsman; J. S. Myers, wit.

Millsaps, William & Ann Onail, 23 April 1770; William Frohock,
bondsman; Thomas Frohock, wit. consent from Arther O Nail,
24 April 1770, William Frohock, wit.

Mingis, Joseph H. & Sarah Cowan, 1 Jan 1842; Alfred M. Goodman,
bondsman; J. S. Johnston, wit.

Mingus, Joseph H. & Elizabeth A. Glasscock, 8 Feb 1855; Saml.
W. James, bondsman; J. S. Myers, wit. married 13 Feb 1855
by J. Thomason, J. P.

Minola, John B. & Penelope McCulloh, 19 Feb 1813; Francis Coupee,
bondsman; Geo. Dunn, wit.

Minor, Paschal R. & Mary Lentz, 3 May 1853; Jesse Waede, bondsman; J. S. Myers, wit. married 4 May 1853 by Levi Trexler,
J. P.

Minor, Pascal R. & Catharine A. Hill, 2 May 1857; James W. Sossaman, bondsman; J. S. Myers, wit. married 3 May 1857 by H. T. Hudson, Pastor M. E. Church, Chapel Hill, N. C.

Minzes, Joseph & Margaret Butrem, 23 Oct 1779; Nicholas White, bondsman; Jos. Brevard, wit.

Mires, Philip & Barbara Smith, 3 March 1784; Geo. Smith, bondsman; J. G. Laumann, wit.

Mirick, James & Eve Everhart, 31 Oct 1814; Fredrick Yountz, bondsman; Geo. Dunn, wit.

Misamer, Henry & Elizabeth Leonard, 3 May 1819; Frederick Mowery, bondsman; Henry Giles, wit.

Misamor, Belford & Eliza E. Mills, 3 Jan 1856; John Kirkpatric, bondsman; Levi Trexler, wit. married 3 Jan 1856 by Levi Trexler, J. P.

Misamor, George & Barbara Wiatt, 1 Jan 1848; Tilman Pearce, bondsman; J. H. Hardie, wit.

Misamor, Jacob A. & Edith Glover, 28 Feb 1843; John Linebarier, bondsman; J. H. Hardie, wit.

Misamor, Jacob A. & Sarah Rough, 26 Aug 1856; William W. Emery, bondsman; J. S. Myers, wit.

Mise, Benjamin & Rachael Richardson, 23 Dec 1772; John Richardson, bondsman; Ad. Osborn, wit.

Mise, Obadiah & Elizabeth White, 15 June 1820; Henry Mikel, bondsman; Jno Giles, wit.

Misemer, Matthew & Betsy Hornbarrier, 19 Nov 1823; Henry Hartmon, bondsman; Hy. Giles, wit.

Misemer, Matthew & Betsy Hornbarrier, 3 Dec 1823; Henry Lentz, bondsman.

Misenhamer, Morgan & Lucinda Casper, 14 Aug 1847; Moses Josey, bondsman; Robert Murphy, wit.

Misenheimer--see also Micinhimer

Misenheimer, Allison & Sophia L. Eagle, 8 Aug 1859; William Safrit, bondsman; James E. Kerr, wit. married 10 Aug 1859 by Saml. Rothrock, Minister of the Gospel in the Ev. Luth. Church.

Misenheimer, George W. & Susan C. Ketner, 1 Sept 1856; George M. Misenheimer, bondsman; James E. Kerr, wit. married 4 Sept 1856 by Saml. Rothrock, Minister of the Gospel in the Ev. Luth. Church.

Misenheimer, Reed & Jane F. Rufty, 14 Sept 1854; Jesse Wilhelm, bondsman; H. W. Hill, J. P., wit.

Misenheimer, William R. & Louiza E. Moose, 10 Dec 1845; Laurence Misenhimer, bondsman; Jno. H. Hardie, wit.

Misenheimmer, Jacob & Elizabeth Griss, 3 May 1779; John Misenhimer, bondsman; Ad. Osborn, wit.

283

Misenhimer, Archibald & Elizabeth Hartman, 24 May 1852; John U.
Vogler, bondsman; J. S. Myers, wit.

Misenhimer, Archibald & Polly Phillips, 25 Nov 1861; H. W. Hill,
bondsman; Obadiah Woodson, wit.

Misenhimer, Daniel J. & Eliza Lentz, 30 Oct 1849; Philip Lemley,
bondsman; J. S. Myers, wit.

Misenhimer, Jn. & Catereena Bushard, 24 June 1783; Nicholas
Bringel, bondsman.

Misenhimer, Lawrence & Christena L. Klutts, 1 Dec 1843; Nathan
L. Phillips, bondsman; J. H. Hardie, wit.

Misenhimer, Paul & Maria S. Brown, 3 May 1845; William Safrit,
bondsman; J. S. Myers, wit. married 8 May 1856 by Saml
Rothrock, Minister of the Gospel in the Ev. Luth. Church.

Mishammer, John & Rachel Pool, 20 Dec 1787; Jacob Pool, bondsman; J. McEwin, wit.

Mitchel, Andrew & Margret Snodey, 21 Feb 1775; Saml. Snoddey,
John Mitchell, bondsmen.

Mitchel, Elijah & Sarah Ireland, 15 Nov 1785; Samuel Mitchel,
bondsman.

Mitchel, Mathias & Isbell Frank, 12 Oct 1785; Jno Macay, wit.

Mitchel, William L. & Synthia Gence, 21 Aug 1833; Jno. J. Shaver,
bondsman; Wm. Locke, wit.

Mitchell, Adam & Elizabeth McMachen, 12 Sept 1769; Robert
Mitchell, bondsman; John Frohock, wit. consent from Jas.
MaMachen, father of Elizabeth, 4 Sept 1769.

Mitchell, Andrew & Mary Ham, 18 Nov 1815; John Cheshier, bondsman; R. Powell, wit.

Mitchell, Frederick & Rosanah Shogan, 2 March 1767; Michael
Bonaker, Henry Agner, bondsmen; Tho. Frohock, wit.

Mitchell, Lewis & Rachel McLean, (colored), 15 Jan 1866; Horatio
N. Woodson, bondsman; Obadiah Woodson, wit.

Mitchell, Lueco & Sarah J. Henderson, 24 Dec 1835; Robert M.
Bouchelle, bondsman.

Mize, William & Nancy Miner, 27 July 1822; Christian Hartmon,
bondsman; Andrew Swicegood, wit.

Mock, A. J. & Charlotte Cowan, 28 March 1855; A. M. Nesbitt,
bondsman; J. S. Myers, wit. married 28 March 1855 by Jesse
Rankin, Min. Presbyterian Ch.

Mock, George & Emilia Mire, 12 Nov 1815; Jesse Farebee, bondsman; Sol. Davis, J. P., wit.

Mock, Jacob & Euly Gill, 12 Nov 1801; John Knight, bondsman;
Jno. Monroe, wit.

Mock, Jacob & Sally Spauch, 17 Nov 1811; George Spach, bondsman;
W. Ellis, J. P., wit.

Mock, John & Catheran Graves, 4 Oct 1790; Peter Mock, bondsman; Basil Gaither, wit.

Mock, John & Lucinda Hall, 1 Oct 1830; Samuel Luckie, bondsman; Jno H. Hardie, wit.

Mock, Michael & Barbara Beaver, 1 Aug 1804; Devolt Beaver, bondsman; A. L. Osborn, wit.

Mock, Moses & Jane Williams, 14 March 1818; Adam Mock, bondsman; Thos. Hampton, wit.

Mock, Philip Jr. & Christiona Hoover, 15 Nov 1806; Ism. Wood, bondsman; Wm. Welbon, wit.

Monroe, Forrest & Precill Robley, 3 May 1820; Abner Hall, bondsman.

Monroe, Henry & Fanny Markling, 15 April 1812; John Davis, bondsman; Sol. Davis, wit.

Monroe, John & Sarah Daniel, 25 Jan 1806; John Bodenhamer, bondsman.

Monroe, Peter T. & Maria Craige, 24 Feb 1849; Thos. Chalmers McNeely, bondsman; Jno. H. Hardie Jr., wit.

Montford, Abraham & Polly Anthony, 11 Oct 1843; Erven Freeman, bondsman; John H. Hardie Jr., wit.

Montgomery, George & Rachel Bratton, 26 March 1815; Joshua Gefford, bondsman; Sol. Davis, wit.

Montgomery, James & Leah Earnhardt, 4 Aug 1851; Wm. Montgomery, bondsman; Archd. Honeycutt, J. P., wit. married 5 Aug 1851 by Saml. Rothrock, Minister of the Gospel in the Ev. Luth. Church.

Montgomery, James A. & Margaret Phifer, 7 Dec 1841; William T. Montgomery, bondsman; J. S. Johnston, wit.

Montgomery, James C. & Delilah Hill, 23 Feb 1825; James Sloan, bondsman.

Montgomery, John & Sarah Williams, 5 May 1785; Jno. Robley, bondsman.

Montgomery, John & Rachel Hayworth, 5 Oct 1807; Thomas Henderson, bondsman; Wm. Welborn, wit.

Montgomery, Nicholas & Jane Phifer, 11 Jan 1845; Robert W. Hughey, bondsman; Jno. H. Hardie, wit.

Montgomery, W. H. & B. C. Mowry, 4 May 1865; William Lambeth, bondsman; Obadiah Woodson, wit.

Moody, John A. & N. H. Hearen, 8 Jan 1854; J. P. Gowan, bondsman; D. W. Honeycutt, J. P., wit.

Moor, Eli & Jane Coal, 31 Jan 1804; William Davis, bondsman; William Piggatt, J. P., wit.

Moor, Jonah & Sarah Melstid, 14 May 1828; John A. Howell, bondsman; Wm. Hawkins, J. P., wit.

Moore, Alfred J. & Elizabeth Tough, 26 Sept 1822; Ezra Allemong, wit.

Moore, Arthur & Hannah Cox, 17 Feb 1789; Jon. Tunner, bondsman; Will Alexander, wit.

Moore, Audlen & Elizabeth Butner, 4 Sept 1786; Geo. Dunn, bondsman; Jno. Macay, wit.

Moore, Alex D. & Margaret C. Luckey, 15 Dec 1855; J. F. Bell Jr., bondsman; J. S. Myers, wit. married 18 Dec 1855 by Saml. B. O. Wilson, V. D. M.

Moore, Brison & Nancy Hudson, 26 Sept 1827; John Moore, bondsman; Thomas McNeely, J. P., wit.

Moore, Brison & Sarah Bracken, 5 May 1836; John B. Hawkins, bondsman; Wm. Hawkins, wit.

Moore, David & Sally Williamson, 24 March 1812; William Williamson, bondsman; Jno. Giles, C. C., wit.

Moore, Edward & Anna Biles, 4 Dec 1797; Jacob Stroop, bondsman; Jno. Rogers, wit.

Moore, Ezekiel & Neomy Thomson, 9 Jan 1787; Thomas Gilles, bondsman; R. Henderson, wit.

Moore, George & Mary Beck, 15 Dec 1798; William Moore, bondsman; Edwin J. Osborn, D. C., wit.

Moore, George & Elizabeth Humphras, 18 Dec 1827; Jonah Moor, bondsman; Wm. Hawkins, J. P., wit.

Moore, Henry & Mary Davis, 5 Dec 1853; James C. Roseman, bondsman; James E. Kerr, wit.

Moore, Jehue & Susannah Etcheson, 12 Dec 1827; Moses Hall, bondsman; Wm. Hawkins, J. P., wit.

Moore, John & Elenor Marbrey, 4 Oct 1786; William West, bondsman; Jno. Macay, D. C., wit.

Moore, John & Mary Kinley, 10 Nov 1795; Frances Gardner, bondsman; J. Troy, wit.

Moore, John & Mary Moore, 8 Aug 1857; James C. Roseman, bondsman; J. S. Myers, wit. married 20 Aug 1857 by Milo A. J. Roseman, J. P.

Moore, John & Lucinda A. Cowan, 8 Jan 1857; Sml. R. Harrison, bondsman; James E. Kerr, wit. married 13 Jan 1857 by Saml. B. O. Wilson, V. D. M.

Moore, John T. & Margaret E. Smith, 20 Oct 1857; Mathias Stike-leather, bondsman; married 28 Oct 1857 by Jno. M. McConnaughy, J. P.

Moore, Nathan & Margaret Jones, 6 Nov 1795; Wm. Smith Jr., bondsman; Fridreck Miller, wit.

Moore, P. H. & Mary E. Howard, 7 Jan 1865; T. G. Haughton, bondsman; M. W. Jarvis, wit.

Moore, Robert & Elizabeth Tays, 28 Nov 1775; Samuel Taes, bondsman; John Kerr, wit.

Moore, Robert & Elizabeth Ellis, 22 April 1818; William H. Horah, bondsman; Roberts Nanny, wit.

Moore, Robert & Thodocia Pinkston, 2 Oct 1839; Ebenezer Moore, bondsman.

Moore, Samuel & Ellener Clairy, 29 June 1791; Allen Rice, bondsman; C. Caldwell, wit.

Moore, Samuel & Margaret Rice, 3 Sept 1806; A. L. Osborn, bondsman.

Moore, Samuel & Sally Robinson, 25 June 1810; Solomon Hall, bondsman; Geo. Dunn, wit.

Moore, Samuel & Aley Dent, 22 Oct 1856; A. W. Owen, bondsman; J. S. Myers, wit. married 23 Oct 1856 by John C. Miller, Esq.

Moore, William & Martha Smith, 12 June 1810; Samuel Smith, bondsman; Jno. Henderson, wit.

Moore, William & Pattsy Summters, 31 July 1810; Samuel Hughey, bondsman; Geo. Dunn, wit.

Moore, William & Sarah Booe, 14 Jan 1836; James M. Ijams, bondsman; Wm. Hawkins, wit.

Moore, William & Margaret Patton, 4 Aug 1774; Danl. Little, bondsman; Ad. Osborn, wit. consent from Charity Patton, mother of Margaret, 28 July 1774.

Moores, Henry & Jane Ross, 5 May 1775; Benjamin Rounsavall, bondsman; David Flowers, wit.

Moose, John F. & Margaret C. Culverhouse, 2 Feb 1858; William H. Walton, bondsman; James E. Kerr, wit. married 2 Feb 1858 by L. C. Groseclose, Pastor of Ev. Luth. Church, Salisbury, N. C.

Moosginer, Jacob & Barbara Buzzard, _____; Lewis Beard, bondsman; Max. Chambers, wit.

Mordah, Robert & Jane Davison, 14 Nov 1769; John Oliphant, Joseph Davson, bondsmen; Francis Lock, wit.

Mordah, William & Agness Wasson, 14 Nov 1769; Joseph Wasson, Joseph Davison, bondsmen; John Oliphant, Robert Mardah, wit.

Mordott, John & Jane Morton, 6 Dec 1788; James Stewart, bondsman; Wm. Alexander, wit.

Moreland, Hazle & Hannah Willis, 8 Jan 1785.

Moreland, Vincon & Mary Clubb, 17 Jan 1789; Hazle Moreland, bondsman; W. Alexander, wit.

Morgan, Abram & Mary C. Park, 23 Aug 1862; James J. Wyatt, bondsman; Obadiah Woodson, wit.

Morgan, Anderson & Margaret Redwine, 24 June 1855; Jos. N. Bivins, bondsman; J. S. Myers, wit. married 24 June 1855 by Obadiah Woodson, J. P.

Morgan, Archibald M. & Martha A. Atwell, 27 Dec 1842; William
P. Rogers, bondsman; J. H. Hardie, wit.

Morgan, Charles & Joanna File, 16 Oct 1844; Jacob Morgan, bondsman; J. H. Hardie, wit.

Morgan, Daniel P. & Sarah M. Cruse, 5 Jan 1866; James N. Morgan,
bondsman; Obadiah Woodson, wit.

Morgan, David & Elizabeth Hofman, 9 Feb 1813; John Trexler,
bondsman; Jno. Henderson, wit.

Morgan, Green D. & Mary Smith, 4 Sept 1861; John Hall, bondsman;
Obadiah Woodson, D. Morgan, L. H. Buis, wit. married 4 Sept
1861 by D. W. Honeycutt, J. P.

Morgan, H. A. & Mary Melton, 17 March 1862; Joshua Smith,
bondsman; Obadiah Woodson, wit. married 17 March 1862 by
Jno. L. Shavers, J. P.

Morgan, Henry & Mary Hofner, 10 Jan 1821; Hugh Morgan, bondsman;
Hy. Giles, wit.

Morgan, Hughey & Polly Poole, 28 Sept 1816; Jacob Pool, bondsman; Milo A. Giles, wit.

Morgan, Jacob & Elizabeth Smith, 22 Oct 1800; Enoch Phillips,
bondsman; John Brem, wit.

Morgan, Jacob & Sarah A. Hodge, 7 July 1851; David Morgan,
bondsman; J. S. Myers, wit. married 10 July 1851 by Levi
Trexler, J. P.

Morgan, James & Sara Parks, 20 Aug 1804; Obed Hampton, bondsman;
Moses A. Locke, wit.

Morgan, James N. & Lovina Hill, 25 Sept 1855; Monrow Casper,
bondsman; H. W. Hill, wit. married 25 Sept 1855 by H. W.
Hill.

Morgan, John & Sally Hill, 31 Aug 1816; Moses A. Morgan, bondsman; Jno Giles, C. C., wit.

Morgan, John & Rachel E. Wiatt, 28 June 1855; William W. Wiatt,
bondsman; Levi Trexler, wit. married 28 June 1855 by Levi
Trexler, J. P.

Morgan, John G. & Julyan Eller, 14 Aug 1856; Henry Morgan,
bondsman; H. W. Hill, wit. married 14 Aug 1856 by H. W.
Hill, Esq.

Morgan, John N. & Sallie Graham, 29 Feb 1864; Jno J. Shaver,
bondsman; Obadiah Woodson, wit.

Morgan, Lindsey & Sarah Gales, 19 Aug 1857; Richard Hillard,
bondsman; J. S. Myers, wit. married 27 Aug 1857 by John
Rice, J. P.

Morgan, Milas P. & Milly Stoner, 16 Jan 1858; William Stoner,
bondsman; Levi Trexler, wit. married 17 Jan 1858 by Levi
Trexler, J. P.

Morgan, Nathan & Hannah Cline, 19 Feb 1798; Aron Latham, bondsman; E. J. Osborn, D. C., wit.

Morgan, Nathan & Margaret Freedle, 6 March 1823; George Eagle, bondsman.

Morgan, Nathan & Delila Wiatt, 18 Oct 1855; Jacob C. Miller, bondsman; Levi Trexler, wit. married 18 Oct 1855 by Levi Trexler, J. P.

Morgan, Nathaniel & Hannah Boon, 12 April 1779; Alexander Long, bondsman; Jno Kerr, wit.

Morgan, Robert & Rebecca Cox, 1 Oct 1792; David Barclay, bondsman; Jo. Chambers, wit.

Morgan, Solomon & Leuiza Wilhelm, 28 Aug 1858; Charles W. Stoner, bondsman; Levi Trexler, wit. married 28 Aug 1858 by Levi Trexler, J. P.

Morgan, Theophilus Jr. & Ruth Owens, 6 Aug 1784; Theophilus Morgan Sr., bondsman; Hugh Magoune, wit.

Morgan, Thomas & Mary Sapp, 8 Sept 1816; Hugh Robertson, bondsman; Sol. Davis, J. P., wit.

Morgan, Travis D. & Mary Morgan, 23 Feb 1862; Daniel P. Morgan, bondsman; Levi Trexler, wit. married 23 Feb 1862 by Levi Trexler, J. P.

Morgan, Wiley & Catharine Hodge, 29 Sept 1836; Anthony Peeler, bondsman; Jas. Shaver, J. P., wit.

Morgan, William W. & Melvina Holderbrand, 28 March 1852; Ezekiel Segraves, bondsman; J. S. Myers, wit.

Morgan, Wilson & Mary Trexler, 25 Feb 1850; Jacob Morgan, bondsman; James E. Kerr, wit.

Moris, Cornelius & Hannah Baker, 8 Jan 1784; William Holbrook, bondsman; Ad. Osborn, wit.

Morison, James & Elinor Snody, 21 Oct 1772; Saml. Snoddey, bondsman; Ad. Osborn, wit.

Morison, Noah P. & Maria Williford, 20 March 1847; Tobias Overcash, bondsman; J. H. Hardie, wit.

Morison, William & Elizabeth Mordoch, 4 Jan 1769; James Mordah, bondsman; John Frohock, wit. consent from James Mordock, 4 Jan 1769; father of Elizabeth.

Morisson, Andrew & Hetty Dickey, 7 Nov 1809; Robert Morrisone, bondsman; Geo. Dunn, wit.

Morr, George Michael & Easter Earnheart, 14 Jan 1789; Christian Shroad, bondsman; W. Alexander, wit.

Morris, Frederick & Margaret Paine, 29 Aug 1801; Colison Paine, bondsman; Jno. Brem, wit.

Morris, George W. & Dovey Foster, 5 June 1857; J. V. Barringer, bondsman; J. S. Myers, wit.

Morris, James R. & Mary L. Holshouser, 12 Nov 1849; John C. Hargrave, bondsman; J. S. Myers, wit.

Morris, John & Rachel Blackwelder, 23 July 1812; Michael Overcash, bondsman; Geo. Dunn, wit.

Morris, John & Martha Gheen, 14 Feb 1856; John U. Vogler, bondsman; J. S. Myers, wit. married 14 Feb 1856 by Obadiah
Woodson, J. P.

Morris, John A. & Mary Ann Leazer, 4 March 1843; John Gillon,
bondsman; Jno H. Hardie, wit.

Morrison, Andrew & Elizabeth Sloan, 26 March 1766; James Petterson, Walter Caruth, bondsmen; Thomas Frohock, wit.

Morrison, Andrew & Margarett Potts, 18 Feb 1768; Moses Potts,
bondsman; John Frohock, wit.

Morrison, Henry & Polly Johnston, 21 Sept 1816; Robert Johnston,
bondsman; Jno Giles, C., wit.

Morrison, James & Jemima Oxford, 18 Feb 1768; Hugh Montgomrey
bondsman; John Frohock, wit.

Morrison, James E. & Mary L. Krider, 2 Nov 1837; Matthew B.
Locke, bondsman; R. Jones, wit.

Morrison, John & Francis Wilson, 12 Jan 1784; Alexr. Wilson,
bondsman.

Morrison, John & Sarah Skilliton, 16 Oct 1809; Joseph Skilleton,
bondsman; Geo. Dunn, wit.

Morrison, Patrick & Ann Foster, 9 Aug 1768; Max. Chambers,
Robert Foster, bondsmen; John Frohock, wit.

Morrison, Rufus W. & Emmaline Gibson, 22 Dec 1850; James B.
Gibson, bondsman; Susan T. Giles, wit.

Morrison, Thomas & Martha Woods, 6 Dec 1769; Willm. Woods,
Wm. Steel, bondsmen; Thomas Frohock, wit. consent from
Martha Woods, mother of Martha, 5 Dec 1769.

Morrison, William & Martha Miller, 19 Feb 1767; Jas. Miller,
bondsman; Tho. Frohock, wit.

Morriss, Isaac & Shusanah Tacker, 11 May 1790; Seaborn Tucker,
bondsman; Jno. Monro, wit.

Morriss, Isaac & Susanna Workman, 25 Aug 1817; Amos Regan,
bondsman; Z. Hunt, J. P., wit.

Morriss, William & Margrerat Burnet, 3 Nov 1791; Thomas Sharpe,
bondsman; Jn. Monro, wit.

Morrow, Allen & Elizabeth Robinson, 22 Jan 1823; Jos. Robinson,
bondsman.

Morrow, Arthur & Mary Bean, 10 Sept 1811; Benjamin Bean, bondsman.

Morrow, Arthur & Jane Campbell, 22 Sept 1824; Reubin Ellis,
bondsman.

Morrow, Thomas & Nancy Price, 18 Oct 1815; Wm. Price, bondsman;
R. Powell, wit.

Morton, David & Mary Jamison, 22 April 1820; William Jamison, bondsman.

Moseley, Arthur & Licinda Cole, 13 Oct 1829; Alex. Gray, bondsman; L. R. Rose, J. P., wit.

Moss, Edward & Christinna Barringer, 23 Oct 1848; John J. Lowder, bondsman; J. H. Hardie, wit.

Moss, Green H. & Elizabeth Jacobs, 3 June 1818; Charles M. Jones, bondsman; Jno Giles, wit.

Moss, John & Susanna Fry, 9 June 1820; Phillip Agle, bondsman.

Moss, John & Sally West, 22 Aug 1821; Lewis Tyer, bondsman; Jno. Giles, wit.

Mossman, Robert & Ann Tod, 12 Oct 1786; Ho. Braly, bondsman; Mar. Osborn, wit.

Motsinger, Daniel & Milly Harman, 29 Sept 1815; Adam Weri, bondsman; Silas Peace, wit.

Motsinger, John & Susanah Long, 26 Nov 1791; Daniel Motzinger, bondsman; Jon Monro, wit.

Mott, Richbell & Mary Pearce, 24 Oct 1812; Mills Joyner, bondsman; Jn. March Sr., wit.

Mott, Richbell & Sarah Moore, 9 May 1827; Lemuel Kinyoun, bondsman; Wm. Hawkins, J. P., wit.

Motzinger, Filex & Elizabeth Longe, 27 Jan 1790; Thomas Long, bondsman; Jon. Monroe, wit.

Mountgomery, James & Mary Moore, 3 March 1762; Matt. Lang, Will Reed, bondsmen; Mary Hamilton, Thomas Frohock, wit.

Mourer, Peter & Elizabeth Keply, 12 Jan 1811; Obed Hamton, bondsman; Geo. Dunn, wit.

Mourey, Allison H. & Margaret M. Miller, 1 Jan 1852; Green Mourey, bondsman; J. S. Myers, wit.

Mourie, Frederick & Elizabeth Mowrie, 26 April 1825; Samuel Reaves, bondsman; Hy. Giles, wit.

Mourie, Peter & Mary Holdhouser, 14 March 1827; Daniel Josey, bondsman; Hy. Giles, wit.

Moury, A. J. & Rachel Z. Cozort, 7 April 1866; David F. Cozort, bondsman; Obadiah Woodson, wit.

Moury, Alexander & Levina Josey, 19 April 1854; Obadiah Woodson, bondsman; J. S. Myers, wit.

Moury, Allison H. & Mary A. C. Fite, 7 Aug 1854; Daniel Miller, bondsman; J. S. Myers, wit.

Mowery, Andrew & Martha C. McCombs, 10 May 1865; Arnold Friedheim, bondsman; married 14 May 1865 by E. E. Phillips, J. P.

Mowery, Henry & Sophia Ernhart, 5 June 1841; John Hartman, bondsman.

Mowery, George & Margaret Corl, 28 March 1858; George Basinger, bondsman; John Wilkinson, wit. married 28 March 1858 by J. M. Brown, J. P.

Mowery, Miles & Christina Boger, 1 Feb 1842; Nicholas Shuping, bondsman; J. S. Johnston, wit.

Mowery, Alexander & Hannah Rery, 6 Nov 1865; Obadiah Woodson, bondsman; Horatio N. Woodson, wit.

Mowrey, William G. & Barbara Gallimore, 11 Oct 1856; John C. Moore, bondsman; J. S. Myers, wit. married 12 Oct 1856 by H. L. Robards, J. P.

Mowrie, Jacob & Cary Agle, 16 April 1814; George House, bondsman; Geo. Dunn, wit.

Mowry, Alexander & Margret Hoffner, 4 Sept 1839; Henry Robinson, bondsman; John Giles, wit.

Mowry, Alfred W. & Mary Ann Rainey, 15 Sept 1842; Jno. B. Lord, bondsman; Thos. C. Cooke, wit.

Mowry, Charles & Nancy Frick, 5 Aug 1835; Jacob Casper, bondsman; J. H. Hardie, wit.

Mowry, Green & Barbara Miller, 8 July 1844; Miles Miller, bondsman; Jno. H. Hardie Jr., wit.

Mowry, John & Betsey Cobble, 12 Feb 1803; George Coldiron, bondsman; A. L. Osborn, D., wit.

Mowry, John & Barbara Messamer, 1 Aug 1803; Peter Cobble, bondsman; A. L. Osborn, D. C., wit.

Mowry, Noah & Sarah Beaver, 25 Aug 1845; Matthias Boger, bondsman; Jno. H. Hardie Jr., wit.

Mowry, Peter & Dolly Coleiron, 5 Nov 1796; Geo. Coleiron, bondsman.

Mowry, Peter R. & Lydia Hill, 19 Aug 1833; Hy. Giles, bondsman.

Mowry, Robert & Amy Bass (colored), 18 April 1866; Charles Myers, bondsman; Obadiah Woodson, wit.

Mowweryra, John & Eliza Eller, 20 Sept 1845; Jacob Mowery, bondsman; J. H. Hardie, wit.

Mowyer, William & Mary Ann Airey, 23 Oct 1838; Green Redwine, bondsman; Hy. Giles, wit.

Moyer, George & Milly Peacock, 24 May 1852; John Peeler, bondsman; J. S. Myers, wit. married 25 May 1852 by Saml. Rothrock, Minister of the Gospel in the Ev. Luth. Church.

Moyers, Jacob & Margreret Cereie, 25 Dec 1791; Michail Idol, bondsman; Jno Monro, wit.

Mucklewrath, Thomas & Mary Bridges, 17 Dec 1789; Joseph Robinson, bondsman.

Mull, Benedick & _____ 3 _____ 180_; John Martain Pless, bondsman; Jno Brem, D. C., wit.

Mull, Edward & Carolina Cauble, 9 Feb 1842; Jno. Waller, bondsman; Jno. H. Hardie, wit.

Mull, Henry & Rosa Fisher, 28 Nov 1829; Jno. Utzman, bondsman.

Mull, James & Mary Ann Fraly, 29 March 1831; John H. Hardie,
bondsman.

Mull, John & Hannah Cline, 19 Feb 1798; Thomas Mull, bondsman;
E. J. Osborn, D. C., wit.

Mull, John & Susannah Smith, 21 June 1798; Jeramiah Brown,
bondsman; M. A. Troy, wit.

Mull, Tobias & Susanah Brown, 30 Jan 1808; David Woodson, bondsman; A. L. Osborn, wit.

Mullikin, Humphrey & Nancy Howard, 6 Jan 1812; Reason Park,
bondsman; Jn. March Sr., wit.

Mullikin, Thomas & Casey Myers, 12 Dec 1812; Zadock Jarvis,
bondsman; Jn. March Sr., wit.

Mullins, Nathaniel & Peggy Wilson, 16 Oct 1807; Phill Smith,
bondsman.

Mumford, Giles E. & Mary B. Davis, 10 Sept 1855; J. S. Myers,
bondsman; James E. Kerr, wit. married 11 Sept 1855 by A.
Baker, Pastor of the P. Church, Salisbury.

Murchison, Daniel A. & Sally Hendricks, 15 Sept 1823; Jonathan
Soner, bondsman; Hy. Giles, wit.

Murdock, David & Rose Ann Freeman, 21 Feb 1859; J. J. Weisiger,
bondsman; James E. Kerr, wit. married 21 Feb 1859 by L. C.
Groseclose, Pastor of Ev. Luth. Church, Salisbury, N. C.

Murph, Jeffrey & Margaret C. Trott, 29 April 1852; Julius A.
Neely, bondsman; J. S. Myers, wit. married 29 April 1852
by H. L. Robards, J. P.

Murph, John & Jemima Baker, 25 Aug 1834; Jacob Freeze, bondsman;
Hy. Giles, wit.

Murphey, James & Margaret M. Swink, 19 Dec 1864; Victor Curt,
bondsman; Obadiah Woodson, wit.

Murphey, Joseph & Mary Green, 19 Dec 1819; Jesse Jones, bondsman.

Murphey, Zaphaniah & Jeane Graham, 18 Oct 1782; William Mephey,
bondsman; Ad. Osborn, wit.

Murphy, Andrew & Helen W. Long, 1 June 1852; Saml. Reeves,
bondsman; James E. Kerr, wit.

Murphy, James & Elizabeth C. Chunn, 20 Dec 1848; Julius D.
Ramsey, bondsman; J. H. Hardie, wit.

Murphy, John & Mary Berkeley, 19 Jan 1780; Arthur McCree,
bondsman; B. Booth Boote, wit.

Murphy, Robert & Mary R. Long, 27 April 1847; Jno. H. Hardie,
bondsman; John H. Hardie Jr., wit.

Murphy, William & Ellen J. Hampton, 9 Jan 1834; Wm. Locke,
bondsman; Wm. Locke, wit.

Murphy, William & Susan W. Chunn, 25 July 1845; J. S. McCubbins,
bondsman; J. H. Hardie, wit.

Murr, George M. & Julianna Trote, 14 Feb 1822; Richard B. Owen,
bondsman; Jno. Giles, wit.

Murr, Moses B. & Henrietta L. Brown, 20 Feb 1862; James W.
Sossamon, bondsman; Obadiah Woodson, wit. married 20 Feb
1862 by A. W. Mangum.

Murrell, George & Rebekah Holdcraft, 14 Sept 1802; Moses Wick,
bondsman; Wm. Welborn, wit.

Murton, Peter & E. Cagle, 14 May 1850; Henry Oliver, bondsman;
H. Riley, wit.

Myars, Conrod & Peggy Garves, 7 Nov 1810; William Park, bondsman; Jn. March Sr., wit.

Myars, David & Barbara Hughes, 21 Feb 1785; Michael Myars,
bondsman; H. Magoune, wit.

Myars, Jacob & Polly Winkler, 7 May 1816; Ephraim Daniel, bondsman; Jno Giles, C. C., wit.

Myer, George & Mary Houghtin, 13 Feb 1772; John Lop, Lodwing
Winkler, bondsmen; Thomas Frohock, wit.

Myer, Neete & Lucy Stanly (colored), 9 July 1865; married 10
July 1865 by Suck Horton (Zuck Haughton).

Myers, Abraham & Mary H. McRorie, 27 Aug 1859; William Myers,
bondsman; married 29 Aug 1859 by T. G. Haughton, Rector.

Myers, Andrew & Nancy Allen, 10 Feb 1812; George Myers, bondsman; J. Willson, J. P., wit.

Myers, E. & E. K. Lillington, 2 Sept 1856; A. Myers, bondsman.

Myers, George & Mary Cain, 4 March 1813; Joseph Gordon, bondsman; J. Willson, J. P., wit.

Myers, Jacob S. & Mary Cauble, 8 Feb 1838; John Shennan, J. P.,
bondsman; Jno Giles, wit.

Myers, Michal & Susanna Hepler, 18 Oct 1814; Philip Hepler,
bondsman; E. Morgan, J. P., wit.

Myers, Peter & Charity Ledinger, 16 Dec 1812; David Myers,
bondsman; J. Willson, J. P., wit.

Myers, Tobias & Mary Cauble, 24 Nov 1835; J. H. Hardie, bondsman.

Myers, William W. & Martha E. McRorie, 4 Feb 1865; A. J. Harris,
bondsman; Obadiah Woodson, wit.

Myres, Amos & Sarah Myers, 21 Nov 1819; Jacob Myers, bondsman;
David Mock, wit.

Nail, John & Clowe March, 27 March 1809; Jacob Hinkle, bondsman;
Jn. March Sr., wit.

Nail, Philip & Suse Adams, 18 Jan 1806; Daniel Booe, bondsman; Jn. March Sr., wit.

Nale, Philip & Margrit Nale, 2 Sept 1811; Henrey Nale, bondsman; Jn. March Sr., wit.

Nall, Nicholas & Mary Wyatt, 25 April 1787; J. Wyatt, bondsman; Jno. Macay, wit.

Nancarrier, James & Sarah A. Lilly, 26 Feb 1858; married 4 March 1858 by Ephraim Mauney, J. P.

Nash, W. A. & Jane Robeson, 24 Nov 1853; T. J. Holder, bondsman; married 24 Nov 1853 by A. Baker, Pastor of the Presbyterian Church, Salisbury.

Nash, William & Molly Sever, 17 May 1803; Wilhelm Houck, bondsman; Adlai L. Osborn, wit.

Nash, Wylie B. & Lydia Pool, 4 Oct 1849; M. C. Griffin, bondsman.

Naylor, Batson S. & Ann R. Chavous, 5 Oct 1835; Saml. W. Naylor, bondsman; Wm. Hawkins, wit.

Naylor, Samuel W. & Mahetable Rose, 19 Oct 1831; E. D. Austin, bondsman; Wm. Hawkins, wit.

Naylor, William A. & Elizabeth Harbin, 12 Nov 1835; Anderson Beauchamp, bondsman; Wm. Hawkins, wit.

Neagle, James R. C. & Albertine Utzman, 23 Oct 1827; Samuel E. Chapman, bondsman.

Neal, Henry & Molly Keller, 1 Sept 1798; Barnard Crider, bondsman; Edwin J. Osborn, D. C., wit.

Neal, William & Elizabeth Cole, 12 March 1825; Thos. J. Hawkins, bondsman; L. R. Rose, J. P., wit.

Neale, John & Margaret Booe, _____; John Seane, bondsman; Jas. Robinson, wit.

Neat, John & Asuneth Pelly, 25 Sept 1801; Geo. Knatzer, bondsman; Jno. Brem, wit.

Neel, Andrew M. & Jane C. Lorance, 7 March 1853; John F. Clotfelter, bondsman; J. S. Myers, wit. married 9 March 1853 by Jno. E. McPherson.

Neely, Alexander & Margaret Barber, 2 Oct 1822; Theophilus J. Allison, bondsman.

Neely, Alexander & Emma Shaver (colored), 17 Feb 1866; Robert Pearson, bondsman; Obadiah Woodson, wit.

Neely, Arthur & Isabella Welch, 5 Dec 1826; Abraham Vaneten, bondsman.

Neely, Arthur & Honor Austin, 5 Aug 1846; Geo. Campbell, bondsman.

Neely, Francis & Mary Holeman, 24 Dec 1793; Jesse Pearson, bondsman; Jo. Chambers, wit.

Neely, Houlman & Catherine Boroughs, 20 Sept 1819; Robert N. Fleming, bondsman; Roberts Nanny, wit.

Neely, Julius A. & Elizabeth A. Fraley, 16 June 1847; Montford S. Fraley, bondsman; J. H. Hardie Jr., wit.

Neely, Julius A. & Margaret Barger, 6 July 1853; Mumfort S. Fraley, bondsman; J. S. Myers, wit.

Neely, N. H. & Margaret C. Cowan, 26 April 1864; Jno. D. Brown, bondsman; Obadiah Woodson, wit.

Neely, Nathaniel H. & Isabella C. Cowan, 27 Oct 1847; Robt. W. Long, bondsman; J. H. Hardie, wit.

Neely, Richard & Sarah Campbell, 30 July 1824; John Davis, bondsman.

Neely, Washington & Providance Heathman, 13 Feb 1834; Hezekiah Turner, bondsman; Thomas McNeely, J. P., wit.

Neil, James & Ann Snoddy, 11 Aug 1759; William Neill, bondsman; John Frohock, wit.

Neil, William & Ann Allison, 24 Oct 1786; Jno. Allison, bondsman; Ad. Osborn by Jno Macay, wit.

Neill, James & Sarah Neal, 13 Aug 1788; William Neill, bondsman; Ad. Osborn, wit.

Neill, Robert & Margaret Clayton, 3 Oct 1785; George Clayton, bondsman; Max. Chambers, wit.

Ncill, William & Mary Fleming, 10 Feb 1772; James Neil, bondsman; Ad. Osborn, wit.

Neisler, Isaac & Patsey Smith, 5 Oct 1822; Hiram Smith, bondsman; Jno Giles, wit.

Nelson, Alexander & Mary Beaver, 5 Jan 1826; Joseph Rodgers, bondsman.

Nelson, Ebenezer & Frankey Burgis, 11 July 1800; William Burgis, bondsman; N. Chaffin, J. P., wit.

Nelson, Garret & Jean Glasscock, 19 Dec 1825; L. H. Austin, bondsman; L. R. Rose, J. P., wit.

Nelson, James & Margret Thompson, 14 Jan 1768; William Thompson, bondsman.

Nelson, James & Sary Nelson, 12 May 1823; Wm. Houston, bondsman; A. R. Jones, wit.

Nelson, Jonathan & Sarah Glasscock, 4 Feb 1822; John S. Carson, bondsman; Jno. Clement, wit.

Nelson, Jonathan & Nancey Burgess, 18 June 1824; David Jacobs, bondsman; L. R. Rose, J. P., wit.

Nelson, Moses & Kirrutah Parker, 3 Aug 1802; Joseph Hughes, bondsman; J. Hunt, wit.

Nelson, William & Elizabeth Parker, 9 Dec 1821; Turner S. Parker, bondsman; A. R. Jones, wit.

Nelson, William & Teny Bakel, 6 May 1823; Jacob Felker, bondsman; Jno Giles, wit.

Nesbet, John Y. & Lusilla M. Barr, 7 Oct 1834; Jas. A. King, bondsman; Jno H. Hardie, wit.

Nesbitt, Archibald M. & Ruth M. Boyden, 22 April 1858; N. N. Fleming, bondsman; James E. Kerr, wit. married 22 April 1858 by Jno. H. Parker, Min. of Prot. Epis. Church.

Nesbitt, John Maxwell & Jane McHenry, 16 Oct 1785; Archd. McHenry, bondsman; Max. Chambers, wit.

Nesbitt, William O. & Mrs. Barthena McClendon, 4 Sept 1858; William C. Miller, bondsman; James E. Kerr, wit. married 5 Sept 1858 by Milo A. J. Roseman, J. P.

Netter, George & Catharine Shafer, 24 Sept 1784; Geo. Hoover, bondsman; Hu. Magoune, wit.

Nevens, William & Jane Gilkey, 24 March 1772; Benjamin Hide, Robert Lowery, bondsmen; William Freeman, wit. consent from Rebeca Gilky, for Jean Gilky, 25 March 1772.

Nevins, James & Anne Robeson, 12 June 1805; William S. Cowan, bondsman; Andrew Kerr, wit.

Nevins, Robert & Ann Gillkey, 2 Feb 1774; John Carson, bondsman; Ad. Osborn, wit.

New, Benjamin & Ann E. Corl, 13 Feb 1841; Frady Safley, bondsman.

Newman, John & Margret Chambers, 12 Feb 1798; Edwd. Yarbrough, bondsman; E. J. Osborn, wit.

Newsom--see also Nusam

Newsom, Arthur & Ramy Loftin, 18 _____ 1805; Sterling Newsom, bondsman; A. L. Osborn, D. C., wit.

Newsom, Sterling & Nancy Moxly, 31 March 1803; Arthur Newsom, bondsman; Adlai L. Osborn, D. C., wit.

Newson, A. P. & Martha R. Rush, 1 April 1858; Peter A. Brown, bondsman; James E. Kerr, wit.

Newson, J. E. & M. E. Hampton, 20 Sept 1860; A. B. Wright, bondsman; John Wilkinson, wit. married 20 Sept 1860 by L. C. Groseclose, Pastor of St. John's Ev. Luth. Church, Salisbury, N. C.

Newton, Jacob & Cloah Burton, 13 Dec 1803; William Morriss, bondsman; William Piggatt, J. P., wit.

Niblack, George & Francis Morrison, 15 Feb 1793; William Luckie, bondsman; Jos. Chambers, wit.

Niblack, John & Elizabeth Miery, _____ 177_; John Miery, bondsman; Ad. Osborn, wit.

Niblack; John & Margaret Cowan, 20 Sept 1814; William Dickey, bondsman; Jno. Giles, C. C., wit.

Niblack, Wilson & Caty Luckey, 30 Jan 1820; Josiah Morrison, bondsman; Jno. Giles, wit.

Niblock, Alexander & Nancy A. Cowan, 2 March 1858; married 4 March 1858 by Saml. B. O. Wilson, V. D. M.

Niblock, George & Laura R. Cowan, 18 Dec 1858; James W. Shinn, bondsman; John Wilkinson, wit. married 22 Dec 1858 by Saml. B. O. Wilson.

Niblock, Levi & Molly R. Nooe, 27 Jan 1823; Henry Hughy, bondsman.

Niblock, Wilson & Elizabeth Embreson, 18 Dec 1840; John S. Carson, bondsman; Jno Giles, wit.

Nicholls, Thomas & Jemimah Moon, 5 March 1805; Samuel Smith, bondsman; Moses A. Locke, wit.

Nichols, George W. & Charlotte Murphy (colored), 17 Feb 1866; Samuel Reeves Sr., bondsman; Obadiah Woodson, wit.

Nichols, Jacob & Agness Lock, 17 May 1762; Francis Lock, George Lock, bondsmen; Will Reed, John Johnston, wit.

Nichols, James M. & Clementine Moyer, 29 Dec 1854; married 31 Dec 1854 by Jos. A. Linn.

Nichols, Joseph & Eliz. Conger, 16 Sept 1784; Thos. Morris, bondsman; Hugh Magoune, wit.

Nicholson, Daniel & Elizabeth Pegg, 11 May 1801; John Teague, bondsman; Em. Welborn, wit.

Nicholson, Gassaway & Nancey Elliott, 21 Nov 1796; Wm. Elliott, bondsman; Jno Rogers, wit.

Nicholson, John & Mary Fultz, 6 July 1811; Abner T. Caldwell, bondsman.

Nicholson, Joseph & Elizabeth Freedle, 26 Dec 1801; Gassaway Nicholson, bondsman.

Nicholson, Moses P. & Windsy Ann Barns, 15 Jan 1822; George Vogler, bondsman; M. A. Giles, wit.

Nicholson, Samuel & Lidia Dickhouse, 9 Aug 1768; Thomas Furner, bondsman; John Frohock, wit.

Nicholson, William & Susana Cosbey, 5 Dec 1796; Richard R. Barnes, bondsman; Humphry Marshal, wit.

Nicklous, William & Patsey Flemmons, 9 Oct 1819; Saml. Flemmons, bondsman; Saml Jones, J. P., wit.

Nickols, James & Martha Tolbert, 27 May 1855; D. M. Ludwick, bondsman; D. W. Honeycutt, wit. married 27 May 1855 by D. W. Honeycutt, J. P.

Nicles, James M. & Clementine Moyer, 29 Dec 1854; Wm. Marbry, bondsman.

Nighfong, Jacob & Betsey Lopp, 24 March 1813; David Waggoner, bondsman; Jno. Giles, C. C., wit.

Nilson, John & Levinia McCuistion, 19 June 1764; John Howard, George Magoune, bondsmen; John Frohock, wit. consent from James McCuiston, father of Levinia, 16 June 1764.

Nisbet, William & Mary Chambers, 16 Aug 1785; Max. Chambers, wit.

Noel, Joel & Rhody Howel, 14 July 1794; Whitmell Rylle, bondsman; J. Troy, D. C., wit.

Nolan, Joshua & Sarah Williams, 2 Feb 1779; Philip Williams,
bondsman; William R. Davie, wit.

Nolan, Rasha & Jean Fry, 25 Nov 1811; Jacob Mills, bondsman;
Jn. March Sr., wit.

Noland, Enoch & Lucey Traylor, 31 Dec 1821; Davalt Blaze,
bondsman.

Noland, James & Peggy Russel, 27 July 1801; James Noland, bondsman; Jno Brem, wit.

Noland, Jessee & Abigail Whitacre, 10 Nov 1795; Harman Glascock,
bondsman; J. Troy, D. C., wit.

Noland, John B. & Biddy Traylor, 27 July 1825; Jesse Tatum,
bondsman.

Noland, Led Stone & Mary Smallwood, 20 Feb 1801; Stephen Noland,
bondsman; J. Hunt, wit.

Noland, Stephen & Lyda Russel, 18 March 1803; Jesse Buckner,
bondsman; J. Hunt, wit.

Nolly, James B. & Mary Ann Hofman, 28 Dec 1850; Obadiah Woodson,
bondsman; J. S. Myers, wit.

Nolly, James B. & Eveline Gladson, 8 April 1854; Benjamin Julian,
bondsman; J. S. Myers, wit.

Nooe, Bennet & Sideny Sexton, 8 Jan 1817; Thomas H. Davis, bondsman; Milo A. Giles, wit.

Nooe, Thomas & _____, 17 May 1818; Benet Noeah, bondsman.

Nordyke, Israel & Mary Elmore, 18 Dec 1789; Fredk. Hargrave,
bondsman; Jn. Monro, wit.

Northcott, Benjamin F. & Martha A. Owens, 30 Jan 1855; Thomas
Jordan, bondsman; J. S. Myers, wit. married 31 Jan 1855 by
H. L. Robards, J. P.

Northern, Elijah & Ruthe Baer Humphrey, 10 July 1813; Ezekiah
Bean, bondsman; Wm. Bean, J. P., wit.

Northern, George & Patsy Newsom, 25 July 1810; Elijah Northern,
bondsman; Geo. Dunn, wit.

Northwood, James C. & Sallie E. Brown, 13 Feb 1865; Joseph
Kelly, bondsman; Obadiah Woodson, wit.

Norton, William N. A. & Dovey A. Milholen, 7 July 1865; N. P.
Watt, bondsman; Obadiah Woodson, wit. married 7 July 1865
by J. Rumple.

Nothing, Samon & _____, 28 Sept 1811; William Cowell, bondsman; J. Willson, wit.

Nowel, John & Patesey Tatom, 14 Jan 1____; Joseph Pickler,
bondsman; Edwin J. Osborn, wit.

Nowell, Gilbert & Nancy Benson, 29 Aug 1803; Laban Benson, bondsman; A. L. Osborn, D. C., wit.

Nunby, Littleberry & Elizabeth Wood, 18 Feb 1813; Thos. Jones Jr., bondsman; Jno Giles, wit.

Nunnally, Elisha & Betsy Cotes, 2 Aug 1804; Danl. Clary, bondsman; A. L. Osborn, D. C., wit.

Nunally, Levi & Nancy Butner, 3 Nov 1802; Elisha Nunally, bondsman; A. L. Osborn, D. C., wit.

Nusam, Devenport & Sarah Stevens, 2 Sept 1802; Harrison Nusam, bondsman; Js. McEwin, wit.

Nusam, Harrison & Mary Lowe, 2 Sept 1802; Devenport Nusam, bondsman; J. S. McEwin, wit.

Nuwsom, William & Peggy Gross, 29 Dec 1809; Devenport Nusom, bondsman; Jno Giles, C. C., wit.

Nussman, Adolph & Elizabeth Rantleman, 8 Aug 1774; Christopher Rintelman, bondsman; Ad. Osborn, C., wit.

Oakes, Benjamin F. & Elizabeth Moore, 11 Feb 1833; John Grimes, bondsman.

Oakes, Isaac N. & Minerva Fults, 17 July 1832; John W. Hilton, bondsman.

Oates, John & Mary Bralccy, 7 Feb 1799; Jas. Braly, bondsman; E. Jay Osborn, wit.

Oberkirsh, Michael & Peggy Blackwalder, 31 Jan 1809; Christn. Blackwelder, bondsman; A. L. Osborne, wit.

Oddie, H. E. & Sarah Klutts, 19 April 1862; William A. Walton, bondsman; Obadiah Woodson, wit.

Odell, Isaac & Charity Bodenhamer, 8 Aug 1789; John Bodenhamer, bondsman; Jn. Monroe, wit.

Odell, James & Ruth Erins, 15 Jan 1799; Isaac Odell, bondsman; Wm. Welborn, wit.

Odell, John & Susanna Moor, 8 May 1799; Solomon Davis, bondsman; Wm. Welborn, wit.

Odell, John & Elizabeth King, 27 Dec 1804; Isaac Odell, bondsman; Wm. Welborn, wit.

Odell, Thomas & Elizabeth Swallow, 6 Jan 1803; Solomon Davis, bondsman.

Ogden, Hatfield & Isabella Collins, 4 June 1846; J. S. Johnston, bondsman; J. M. Turner, wit.

Ogle, John & Sarah Dennis, 18 Jan 1773; Henry Sloan, bondsman; Max. Chambers, wit.

Okes, Jesse & Dorcas Gales, 28 Dec 1828; John Smith, bondsman; L. R. Rose, J. P., wit.

Oldfield, William & Barbar Ham, 2 Jan 1793; Reuben Standley, bondsman; Jno Monroe, wit.

Oliphant, John & Elizabeth Allison, 16 April 1770; Andrew Allison, bondsman; Thomas Frohock, wit.

Oliphant, Joseph D. & Charlott Belk, 17 Dec 1860; George S. Belk, bondsman; D. R. Bradshaw, wit. married 19 Dec 1860 by D. R. Bradshaw, J. P.

Oliphant, Robert & Rebecca Clayton, 7 Feb 1770; Francis Lock, George Clayton, bondsman; consent from John Oliphant and George Clayton, 7 Feb 1770.

Oliphant, Robert & Rebecca Douglas, 5 March 1783; George Clayton, bondsman; T. H. McCaule, wit.

Oliphant, William & _____; _____ 1768; John Oliphant, bondsman; Tho Frohock, wit.

Oliver, Pleasant & Mary Blackwood, 5 June 1812; Jesse Whitaker, bondsman; R. Powell, wit.

Olterman, Jacob & Rosey Fadenland, 22 Aug 1796; Jno Rogers, wit.

Omaria, Math & Cherine Fail, 24 Nov 1782; George Fail, bondsman; Willson McNairy, wit.

Oneal, Hugh & Margrate Trout, 22 Dec 1809; Jacob Koon, bondsman; Jn March Sr., wit.

Oneal, John & Margret Brackin, 27 March 1816; Thomas Oneal, bondsman; Jn March Sr., wit.

Oneal, Thomas & Elizabeth Harries, 18 July 1812; Benjamin Martin, bondsman; Jn March Sr., wit.

Oneil, Isaac P. & Mary Elizabeth Carper, 7 June 1858; Rial Riggs Jr., bondsman; James E. Kerr, wit. married 7 June 1858 by J. M. Brown, J. P.

Orns, George F. & Mary E. Owens, 5 Jan 1860; Thomas M. Crawford, bondsman; John Wilkinson, wit.

Orom, Henry & Jennett Bess, 23 Aug 1769; German Baxter, Geo. Felton, bondsmen; John Frohock, wit.

Orr, James & Mary Swink, 28 April 1849; Joseph Orr, bondsman; J. H. Hardie, wit.

Orr, William & Margaret Bershere, 6 June 1850; Jno. J. Shaver, bondsman; James Kerr, wit.

Orrel, Daniel Jr. & Susanna Tucker, 28 Dec 1818; Wm. Tucker, bondsman; Mack Crump, wit.

Orrel, Edgar & Ruthey Caton, 17 Jan 1810; Charles Caton, bondsman; Jn March Sr., wit.

Orrell, John & Nancey Chesier, 23 June 1814; Tenneson Cheshier, bondsman; Jn March Sr., wit.

Orrell, John & Betsey B. Buise, 6 Oct 1832; Saml. Rose, bondsman; L. R. Rose, J. P., wit.

Orrell, Robert & Candis Mustion, 5 May 1811; Pleasant Pruit, bondsman; W. Ellis, J. P., wit.

Orten, Andrew & Elizabeth Hall, 3 Nov 1829; Dyson Lovelace, bondsman; L. R. Rose, J. P., wit.

Orten, James & Sarah Vanderford, 3 Aug 1774; Charles Vanderford, bondsman; Ad. Osborn, wit.

Orten, James & Elizabeth Rensher, 21 Aug 1795; Hayes Dickey, bondsman.

Orten, James & _____, _____ 180_; Jno Niblack, bondsman.

Orten, John & Jane Bryan, 26 May 1770; Wm. Temple Cole, Robert Hughey, bondsmen; Thomas Frohock, wit. consent from John Bryan, 26 May 1770.

Orten, John V. & Rebecca Warson, 4 Oct 1814; John Brian, bondsman; R. Powell, wit.

Orten, Johnza & Rachel Campbell, 23 Feb 1805; James Orten, bondsman; Mack S. Crump, wit.

Orten, Joseph & Jannet Bryan, 2 Sept 1780; Samuel Bryan, bondsman; J. H. Giffard, wit.

Orten, Samuel & Rebecca Campbell, 7 May 1804; Joseph Orten, bondsman.

Orten, Thomas & Phebe Todd, 23 Jan 1779; Richard Auten, bondsman.

Osborn, Seth & Susanna James, 11 July 1797; Lewis Peck, bondsman; M. Stokes, wit.

Osburn, Benjamin & Mary Jones, 26 Aug 1818; Thomas Jones, bondsman; Zebulon Hunt, wit.

O'Sullivan, Daniel & Margaret Hess, 27 Aug 1864; Peter Bowling, bondsman; Obadiah Woodson, wit.

Otrich, William & Peggy Hartman, 25 Dec 1813; Joseph Basinger, bondsman; Geo. Dunn, wit.

Ottenwalder, Michael & Susan Smith, 9 Oct 1865; William R. Garmon, bondsman; Obadiah Woodson, wit.

Overcarsh, Jones W. & Mary C. Lipe, 1 Aug 1859; Abraham Overcarsh, bondsman; married 2 Aug 1859 by C. S. Partee, J. P.

Overcarsh, Leonard & Christena Yost, 20 April 1838; Charles Blackwelder, bondsman.

Overcarsh, Philip J. & Margaret J. Beaver, 20 May 1856; David Shollenberger, bondsman; J. S. Myers, wit.

Overcarsh, Reuben G. & Laura C. Rodgers, 12 July 1862; Henry W. Overcash, bondsman; Obadiah Woodson, wit. married 12 July 1862 by David Brown.

Overcarsh, Solomon & Soffire Bostian, 4 April 1840; William Overcarsh, bondsman; J. M. Turner, wit.

Overcarsh, Tobias & Cozby Yost, 9 March 1841; Aaron Yost, bondsman; Susan T. Giles, wit.

Overcash, Abraham & Margaret L. Shuping, 30 Oct 1854; Solomon W. Overcash, bondsman; J. S. Myers, wit.

Overcash, Alexander & Margaret E. Rodgers, 11 Feb 1851; William
A. Leazer, bondsman; J. S. Myers, wit.

Overcash, Allison & Sophia Overcash, 5 Dec 1865; Solomon Beaver,
bondsman; Obadiah Woodson, wit.

Overcash, Christopher & Jemimah Pahel, 16 Sept 1837; Leonard
Overcash, bondsman; Hy. Giles, wit.

Overcash, Daniel & Polly Masters, 31 May 1826; Jacob Overcash,
bondsman; Jno Giles, wit.

Overcash, Daniel E. & Nancy C. Corriher, 15 March 1856; Abraham
Goodnight, bondsman; James E. Kerr, wit.

Overcash, Francis C. & Penelope Freeze, 22 March 1856; Isarael
M. Overcash, bondsman; J. S. Myers, wit.

Overcash, G. M. & Flora E. Ketchey, 19 Dec 1865; J. M. Overcash,
bondsman; Obadiah Woodson, wit.

Overcash, Henry & Rachael Morris, 13 May 1821; Michael Overcash,
bondsman; Hy. Giles, wit.

Overcash, Henry & Polly Bostian, 1 April 1831; William A.
Bostian, bondsman; Jno. H. Hardie, wit.

Overcash, Henry & Cathrine Melinda Youst, 25 Nov 1833; John
Overcarsh, bondsman.

Overcash, Henry & Elizabeth Rose, 22 July 1854; William A.
Blackwelder, bondsman; J. S. Myers, wit. married 27 July
1854 by C. L. Partee, J. P.

Overcash, Henry W. & Mary Elizabeth Dawalt, 22 Jan 1862; Peter
Albright Jr., bondsman; Obadiah Woodson, wit. married 22
Jan 1862 by C. S. Partee, J. P.

Overcash, Ira E. & Martha Freeze, 24 May 1859; Simon J. Lipe,
bondsman; James E. Kerr, wit. married 16 June 1859 by C.
S. Partee, J. P.

Overcash, Israel M. & Sarah E. Overcash, 9 Nov 1854; Frances
C. Overcash, bondsman; J. S. Myers, wit.

Overcash, J. H. & Margaret E. Readling, 11 Oct 1864; Nathan
Allman, bondsman; Obadiah Woodson, wit.

Overcash, Jacob & Peggy Upright, 18 Feb 1823; Samuel Upright,
bondsman; M. A. Giles, wit.

Overcash, Jacob M. & Catharine Beaver, 24 Oct 1861; J. P.
Shields, bondsman; Obadiah Woodson, wit. married 24 Oct
1861 by D. A. Davis, J. P.

Overcash, James W. & Nancy J. E. Brawley, 21 Dec 1865; Thomas
S. Atwell, bondsman; Obadiah Woodson, wit.

Overcash, John & Betsy Beaver, 11 May 1823; Joseph Overcash,
bondsman; Hy. Giles, wit.

Overcash, John & Malchi Yost, 1 Feb 1831; Levi Rumple, bondsman;
J. H. Hardie, wit.

Overcash, John A. & Sarah Jane Rose, 6 March 1858; W. A. Rose, bondsman; James E. Kerr, wit. married 12 March 1858 by M. S. McKnight, J. P.

Overcash, John J. & Melkey D. Overcash, 20 March 1854; Abraham Overcarsh, bondsman; J. S. Myers, wit.

Overcash, Jones W. & Mary Ann Upright, 5 Jan 1849; Tobias Overcarsh, bondsman; J. H. Hardie, wit.

Overcash, Martin L. & Mary N. Deal, 15 May 1855; David Beaver, bondsman; J. S. Myers, wit. married 15 May 1855 by Jas. H. Enniss, J. P.

Overcash, Michael & Christena Ketner, 9 March 1819; Jacob Goodnight, bondsman; Roberts Nanny, wit.

Overcash, Nathan W. & Darcas A. Overcash, 17 Feb 1852; Cornelius A. Overcash, bondsman; J. S. Myers, wit.

Overcash, Noah & Mary Ann Kennerly, 29 Sept 1864; Solomon Beaver, bondsman; Obadiah Woodson, wit.

Overcash, Other C. & Mary Caroline Eagle, 2 June 1852; George A. Eagle, bondsman; James E. Kerr, wit.

Overcash, Philip & Polly Lipe, 30 April 1827; Aaron Lipe, bondsman; J. H. Hardie, wit.

Overcash, Solomon W. & Martha Ann Duke, 8 Dec 1855; Abraham Overcarsh, bondsman; James E. Kerr, wit.

Overcash, Solomon W. & Christina J. C. Ellis, 19 Aug 1858; Leonard F. Rodgers, bondsman; John Wilkinson, wit. married 25 Aug 1858 by T. L. Triplett.

Overcash, William J. & Sarah J. Bufle, 22 Aug 1853; H. M. Mills, bondsman.

Overcast, Caleb & Mary Yost, 10 Jan 1843; John Yost, bondsman; J. H. Hardie, wit.

Overcast, Daniel & Sarah Hartman, 14 June 1804; Geo. Hartman, bondsman; A. L. Osborn, D. C., wit.

Overcast, Francis & Mary Beaver, 22 Nov 1819; John Reynolds, bondsman; Hy. Giles, wit.

Overcast, Jacob & Cathron Lipe, 7 Dec 1818; Elias Leip, bondsman; Jno Giles, wit.

Overcast, Jacob & Anny Gibson, 4 May 1813; William Gibson, bondsman; Jno Giles, C. C., wit.

Overcast, Jacob & Katharine Albright, 17 Oct 1829; Aaron Lipe, bondsman.

Overcast, John & Easter Beaver, 10 June 1822; John Beaver, bondsman.

Overcast, Leonard & Catharine Slough, 26 Sept 1803; Jacob Overcast, bondsman; A. L. Osborn, D. C., wit.

Overcast, Levi A. & Sarah L. Overcash, 9 Nov 1847; Wm. T. H. Plaster, bondsman; J. H. Hardie, wit.

Owen, A. W. & Mary E. Cowan, 15 Dec 1856; Thos. L. White, bondsman.

Owen, Abraham & Betsy Beck, 9 Feb 1811; David Smith, bondsman; Geo. Dunn, wit.

Owen, Armistead & Sarah Miller, 21 Oct 1819; Silas Dunn, bondsman; Hy. Giles, wit.

Owen, Benjamin & Anna Cowan, 28 Jan 1825; Nathan Neely, bondsman; Jno Giles, wit.

Owen, Britian & Elizabeth Leach, 4 March 1822; John Monroe Jr., bondsman; Hy. Giles, wit.

Owen, David & Edy Wammie, 23 Dec 1815; William Owen, bondsman; Jno Giles, C. C., wit.

Owen, Efferd & Rebecca Owen, 23 Sept 1813; Hugh Maley, bondsman; Geo. Dunn, wit.

Owen, George & Nancy Peelor, 1 Jan 1814; Abraham Owen, bondsman; Geo. Dunn, wit.

Owen, James & Mary Patterson, 2 Sept 1840; Archibald Gillespie, bondsman.

Owen, James M. & Elizabeth Stilter, 3 July 1852; Daniel M. Lowders, bondsman; J. S. Myers, wit.

Owen, Jasper & Polly Aire, 16 Feb 1824; Jacob Stoner, bondsman.

Owen, Jiles S. & Laura Winders, 21 Feb 1866; John Y. Barbour, bondsman; Horatio N. Woodson, wit.

Owen, Joel & Edy Wiseman, 3 Jan 1818; William Owen, bondsman; Milo A. Giles, wit.

Owen, John R. & Ellender Seachrest, 23 Oct 1850; A. G. Allen, bondsman; J. S. Myers, wit.

Owens, Josiah & Lucy Nicholson, 3 Feb 1790; Michael Miers, bondsman; C. Caldwell, D. C., wit.

Owen, Martin & Betsey Owen, 27 July 1812; Samuel Owen, bondsman; Jno Giles, C. C., wit.

Owen, Peter F. & Mary L. Shuman, 16 Feb 1852; B. B. Roberts, bondsman; J. S. Myers, wit. married 3 March 1852 by J. M. Brown, J. P.

Owen, Samuel & Jane Winders, 17 Feb 1836; Hirma Rainey, bondsman.

Owen, William & Margaret Nash, 12 Aug 1788; Joseph Hanna, bondsman; Wm. Alexander, wit.

Owen, William & Sally Owen, 22 Aug 1817; Godfrey Winkler, bondsman; Henry Giles, wit.

Owen, William & Caty Yonce, 6 Aug 1819; Martin Owen, bondsman; Jno Giles, wit.

Owen, William & Susan Feizer, 8 Oct 1824; Peter Owen, bondsman; Henry Allemong, wit.

Owens, George F. & Mary E. Owens, 5 Jan 1860; Thomas M. Crawford, bondsman; John Wilkinson, wit.

Owens, Henry & Rainey Parker, 10 Jan 1835; Benja. Owens, bondsman; Hy. Giles, wit.

Owens, Henry C. & Elizabeth Ann Clodfelter, 29 Dec 1858; Peter P. Winders, bondsman; John Wilkinson, wit. married 29 Dec 1858 by W. R. Fraley, J. P.

Owens, J. F. & Mary Jane Chambers, 7 April 1866; William C. Hyde, bondsman; Obadiah Woodson, wit.

Owens, Jacky & Sally Wiseman, 17 Dec 1814; John Parke, bondsman; Jno Giles, wit.

Owens, Joseph & Mary G. Lowrance, 10 Sept 1846; George W. Brown, bondsman; John H. Hardie Jr., wit.

Owens, Joseph & Rebecca Dent, 29 Dec 1830; Robt. Newton Craige, bondsman.

Owens, Josiah & Mary Davis, 12 Sept 1821; Richard B. Owen, bondsman; Hy. Giles, wit.

Owens, Moses & Polly Harison, 3 Sept 1797; Gabriel Davis, bondsman.

Owens, Peter & Margarett Smith, 22 Aug 1809; Leonard Goss, bondsman; Jno Giles, wit.

Owens, Peter & Elizabeth Bullen, 24 Aug 1840; David Wise, bondsman; Susan T. Giles, wit.

Owens, Peter & Delia K. Brown, 21 Oct 1841; Saml. Reeves, bondsman; J. S. Johnston, wit.

Owens, Philip & Nancy Smith, 15 March 1833; Henry Owens, bondsman; J. H. Hardie, wit.

Owens, Thomas & Nelley Rarey, 15 Dec 1817; Humphry Owens, bondsman; Roberts Nanny, wit.

Owens, William & Sally Wilson, 20 Aug 1816; Joshua Park, bondsman; Jno Giles, C. C., wit.

Owens, William F. & Margaret L. Lee, 26 Jan 1850; Tho. B. Cowan, bondsman; J. S. Myers, wit.

Owin, Benjamin & Christeena Smith, 13 Feb 1790; Isaac Scudder, bondsman.

Owin, Norman & Edey Phelps, 9 March 1791; Edmond Howard, bondsman; C. Caldwell, C. C., wit.

Owings, Bezaleel & Edith Foster, 26 Oct 1789; Norman Oings, bondsman; Basil Gaither, wit.

Owings, James & Polley Patrick, 19 Dec 1812; Isaac Parker, bondsman; Jn March Sr., wit.

Owings, John & Afrey Foster, 12 April 1790; James Foster, bondsman; Basil Gaither, wit.

Owings, John & Racel Jobe, 11 Oct 1813; John Henline, bondsman;
Jn March Sr., wit.

Owings, Robard & Elizabeth Howard, 25 Aug 1817; Elijah Owings,
bondsman; Jn March Sr., wit.

Owings, Thomas & Rebeca Coker, 15 June 1818; George Coker,
bondsman; R. Powell, wit.

Owings, Thomas B. & Elenor Koon, 29 Aug 1824; John Hanelin,
bondsman; J. Hanes, J. P., wit.

Owins, Samuel & Mason Hilton, 4 April 1791; Thomas Hilton,
bondsman; C. Caldwell, D. C., wit.

Own, Humphrey & Elizha Smith, 13 June 1823; Hy. Giles, bondsman.

Ownsby, Thomas S. & Jane C. Overcash, 24 Jan 1849; W. T. H.
Plaster, bondsman; J. H. Hardie, wit.

Ozburn, Jesse & Elizabeth Gordon, 2 Nov 1819; Samuel Farrington,
bondsman; Sol. Davis, J. P., wit.

Ozburn, Stephen & Milley Haley, 19 April 1821; William Ozborn,
bondsman; J. Willson, J. P., wit.

Pack, Asariah & Levina Kester, 9 July 1857; John B. Foster,
bondsman; J. S. Myers, wit. married 9 July 1857 by Peter
Williamson.

Pack, James & Nancy Chaffin, 6 Jan 1804; Azariah Pack, bondsman; A. L. Osborn, D. C., wit.

Pack, John & Patsey Potts, 22 Dec 1801; Joseph Pack, bondsman;
Jno. Brem, wit.

Pack, John & Patsy Prewit, 26 Aug 1820; Wm. Coker, bondsman;
Geo. Coker, wit.

Pack, Joseph & Sarah Myers, 21 Dec 1813; William Pack, bondsman;
Jn. March Sr., wit.

Pack, Rezin & Agness Potts, __ Feb 1795; Peter Potts, bondsman.

Pack, William & Nancy Myers, 25 Jan 1804; Joseph Pack, bondsman;
A. L. Osborn, D. C., wit.

Pack, William & Susanna McCarter, 3 Nov 1824; William Tucker,
bondsman; Joseph Hanes, J. P., wit.

Pahel, John & Mary M. Sloop, 27 Jan 1842; Daniel W. Ramer,
bondsman; J. S. Johnston, wit.

Pahel, Levi & Juliann Yarbrough, 19 June 1845; John Pahel, bondsman; John H. Hardie Jr., wit.

Pahel, Solomon & Ann M. Overcash, 19 Oct 1846; Moses Beaver,
bondsman; John H. Hardie Jun., wit.

Pahele, Noah & Mary Ann Cotton, 21 Dec 1848; John Pahele, bondsman; J. H. Hardie Jr., wit.

Pain, Collison & Anna Brigs, 29 Aug 1801; Fredk. Morris, bondsman; Jno. Brem, wit.

Pain, Isaac & Jean Ragans, 21 Aug 1806; James Paine, bondsman.

Pain, John & Jeany Stoner, 10 May 1819; George Goodman, bondsman; Milo A. Giles, wit.

Pain, Laurence & Mary Scrivner, 2 Sept 1806; Jno. Pain, bondsman.

Pain, Nehemiah & Juday Richard, 20 Jan 1820; John Payn, bondsman; Sol. Davis, J. P., wit.

Paine, Christopher & Anna Moury, 30 Oct 1838; Jacob Holshouser, bondsman; John Giles, wit.

Paine, William & Mary Hollis, 19 March 1796; Jesse Hollis, bondsman.

Palmer, Edmund & Elizabeth Parks, 16 June 1816; Jesse Hodges, bondsman; Jno. Giles, wit.

Palmer, James & Hannah McKern, 15 Jan 1794; Abraham Pessinger, bondsman; Jo. Chambers, wit.

Palmer, John C. & Mary Ann Hampton, 16 Oct 1827; Lewis G. Slaughter, bondsman; J. H. Hardie, wit.

Palmer, Philip & Rachel Davis, 13 Oct 1796; James Palmer, bondsman; Jno. Rogers, wit.

Pame, Mathias & Sarah Madden, 3 March 1829; David Dayvalt, bondsman.

Pape, George A. E. & Martha A. Umsted, 10 Feb 1848; John Richards, bondsman; J. H. Hardie Jr., wit.

Pare, Philip & Jane N. Lancherri, 19 Dec 1864; Lucien Duval, bondsman; Obadiah Woodson, wit.

Park, Alexander & Sarah Been, 3 May 1849; Ebenezer Park, bondsman; H. F. Miller, wit.

Park, Calvin & Polley Messemore, 19 April 1849; Ebenezer Park, bondsman; H. F. Miller, wit.

Park, David & Polly Shepherd, 16 Jan 1827; John Shepherd, bondsman.

Park, Dempsey & Nancy Bean, 20 Jan 1824; John Park, bondsman.

Park, Ebenezer & Tabitha Mills, 6 Jan 1772; Matt. Troy, John Hankins, bondsmen.

Park, Ebenezer & Sally Pool, 17 March 1820; George Krider, bondsman; Milo A. Giles, wit.

Park, George A. & Hannah Hodge, 21 Dec 1829; Jonathan Miller, bondsman; Jno. H. Hardie, wit.

Park, Gilbert & Catharine Files, 6 Nov 1838; Phillip Lemly, bondsman; John Giles, wit.

Park, James & Anna Shemwell, 2 Dec 1799; David Ellis, bondsman; Edwin J. Osborn, D. C., wit.

Park, James & Betsy Shepperd, 5 March 1812; John Park, bondsman; Geo. Dunn, wit.

Park, Jesse & Susannah Reed, 19 July 1822; Noah Reed, bondsman; Jno Giles, wit.

Park, John & Elizabeth Owen, 27 Oct 1788; John Wiate, bondsman; W. Alexander, wit.

Park, John & Mary Peeler, 1 June 1793; Anthony Peeler, bondsman; Jos. Chambers, wit.

Park, John & Polly Bean, 30 Oct 1813; Thomas Todd, bondsman; Geo. Dunn, wit.

Park, Leonard R. & Mary Cox, 21 Nov 1839; Spruce M. Park, bondsman; John Giles, wit.

Park, Milas & Anny Wiatt, 17 April 1849; Ebenezer Park, bondsman; H. F. Miller, J. P., wit.

Park, Moses & _____, _____; John Douthet, bondsman; John Eccles, wit.

Park, Noah & Anna Reed, 8 Aug 1767; Moses Parke, Cornelus Smith, bondsmen; Thomas Frohock, wit.

Park, William A. & Nancy Park, 30 Dec 1853; William Westley Wiatt, bondsman; Willie Bean, J. P. married 20 Dec 1853 by Willie Bean, J. P.

Parke, George & Agness Nichols, 5 Feb 1762; Jacob Nichols, Henry Lively, bondsmen; Will Reed, Henry Horah, wit.

Parke, George & Betsy Winders, 14 Dec 1813; Henry C. Winders, bondsman; Geo. Dunn, wit.

Parke, Humphrey & Nancy Orr, 8 Oct 1811; Jesse Hodges, bondsman; Jno Giles, C. C., wit.

Parke, John & Jane Wiseman; 23 Nov 1816; Joshua Parks, bondsman; Jno Giles, C., wit.

Parke, Joseph & Rachel Wilson, 4 April 1789; Robert McKee, bondsman; Wall Alexander, wit.

Parke, Joseph & Nancey Childers, 12 Aug 1791; Joshua Whitaker, bondsman; Chas. Caldwell, D. C., wit.

Parke, Joseph & Ruth Douglas, 23 Jan 1796; John Douglass, bondsman; J. Troy, wit.

Parke, Timothy & Esther Shipton, 19 Feb 1773; Edwd. Con Debruhl, bondsman; consent from Eliz'h Shipton, 18 Feb 1773.

Parke, William & Polly Wiseman, 1 Dec 1810; Wm. W. Wiseman, bondsman; Jno. Giles, C. C., wit.

Parker, Alvan & Elizebeth Rice, 5 Oct 1816; Elisha A. J. Smoot, bondsman; Jn. March Sr., wit.

Parker, Benjamin C. & Mary C. Edmiston, 22 Oct 1844; John W. McLean, bondsman; Jno. H. Hardie, wit.

Parker, David C. & Clara Ann Miller, 6 Jan 1864; Thomas McNeely, bondsman; Obadiah Woodson, wit.

Parker, Drury & Rhoda Miller, 11 Feb 1836; Nathan Thomson,
bondsman; Jno. Shaver, J. P., wit.

Parker, Drury & Crissy Dry, 25 Jan 1864; Thomas M. Crawford,
bondsman; Obadiah Woodson, wit.

Parker, Emmanuel P. & Margaret M. Lentz, 29 Apr 1858; Aaron G.
Lentz, bondsman; John Wilkinson, wit.

Parker, Green & Catharine P. Bunn, 6 Dec 1854; married 7 Dec
1854 by Jos. A. Linn.

Parker, Henry S. & Lucy Craige, 8 Jan 1820; Roberts Nanny,
bondsman.

Parker, Henry S. & Nancy Pearce, 5 March 1824; Anthony Hatch,
bondsman.

Parker, Henry S. & Susan Pinkston, 26 May 1829; Woodson Monroe,
bondsman; Jno. H. Hardie, wit.

Parker, Howel & Sarah Dixmukes, 27 Dec 1842; E. D. Jinkins,
bondsman; _____ Sneed, wit.

Parker, Isaac & Mary Howard, 15 Oct 1808; Beal Gaither, bondsman;
Jn. March Sr., wit.

Parker, Isaac & Polly Parker, 5 Jan 1817; John Miller, bondsman;
Roberts Nanny, wit.

Parker, James B. & M. P. Clodfelter, 5 Dec 1864; Enos Dancy,
bondsman; Obadiah Woodson, wit.

Parker, John & Nelly Gerton, 1 May 1797; Risdon Fisher, bondsman; Jno. Rogers, wit.

Parker, John & Margaret Benson, 19 Sept 1812; William Benson,
bondsman; Saml. S. Savage, wit.

Parker, Jno. H. & Ann Lord, 25 Jan 1854; Obadiah Woodson, bondsman; James E. Kerr, wit.

Parker, Miles & Anny Murray, 12 Sept 1806; Joseph Brown, bondsman;
A. L. Osborn, wit.

Parker, Peter S. & Sally Hendren, 11 March 1809; W. L. Dufphey,
bondsman; A. L. Osborne, wit.

Parker, Reuben & Ruth Rutledge, 19 June 1795; Jeremiah Patrick,
bondsman; B. John Pinchback, Lydia Pinchback, wit.

Parker, Richard & Ruthey Adderton, 11 April 1839; Ivy Miller,
bondsman; Jno. Shaver, J. P., wit.

Parker, Richard & Mary S. Miller, 10 March 1866; Horatio N.
Woodson, bondsman; Obadiah Woodson, wit.

Parker, S. G. & Minerva Jacobs, 29 Aug 1846; Moses Brown,
bondsman.

Parker, Samuel & Catharine Kortzer, 19 Sept 1853; David Trexler,
bondsman; J. S. Myers, wit. married 20 Sept 1853 by Levi
Trexler, J. P.

Parker, Shelby G. & Dianitia Hughes, 11 Aug 1827; Jno. A. Meroney, bondsman; Thomas McNeely, J. P., wit.

Parker, Stephen & Judy Harrison, (colored), 9 Feb 1866; Boston Spillman, bondsman; Obadiah Woodson, wit.

Parker, Thomas & Mary Bostin, 9 July 1767; James Jones, bondsman; John Frohock, wit.

Parker, Thomas & Ann Olivan, 19 June 1801; Sentleger Beck, bondsman; Jno Brem, D. C., wit.

Parker, Turner S. & Betsey Daniel, 25 Jan 1822; Isaac D. Jones, bondsman; A. R. Jones, wit.

Parker, Uriah C. & Martha Golding, 9 Sept 1823; Preston Parker, bondsman.

Parker, William L. & Sophiah Miller, 10 Dec 1859; David Morgan, bondsman; Levi Trexler, wit.

Parkes, Charles & Betsy Minor, 1 Aug 1815; John Smith, bondsman; Geo. Dunn, wit.

Parkes, Joseph & Rachael McNeely, 3 Jan 1811; Hugh Reed, bondsman; Jno. Giles, C. C., wit.

Parks, Amos & Milly Brigs, 27 Aug 1800; Leonard Kaler, bondsman; John Brem, wit.

Parks, Ebenezer & Elizabeth Wyatt, 5 Nov 1791; Thomas Wyatt, bondsman; Chs. Caldwell, wit.

Parks, George & Anne Link, 28 April 1825; Alex Boyd, bondsman; W. Harris, wit.

Parks, James O. & Amanda Howard, 22 July 1858; Andrew Howard, bondsman; John Wilkinson, wit. married 25 July 1858 by J. M. Brown, J. P.

Parks, Jessee P. & Priscillar Boggs, 26 July 1853; William A. Parks, bondsman.

Parks, John & Caty Weavel, 26 Oct 1814; George Weavel, bondsman; Geo. Dunn, wit.

Parks, John P. & Mary Ann Smith, 29 Dec 1851; Samuel R. Harrison, bondsman; Obadiah Woodson, wit. married 29 Dec 1851 by H. L. Robards, J. P.

Parks, Joshua & Catharine Palmor, 10 March 1821; William Owen, bondsman; Hy. Giles, wit.

Parks, Noah & Mary Ann Bulen, 30 July 1850; Jacob O. Miller, bondsman; H. Riley, wit.

Parks, Wilson & Sarah Stuart, 26 Oct 1821; David Parks, bondsman.

Parmer, Moses & Betsey Hess, 2 Nov 1820; Tobias Hess, bondsman; Milo A. Giles, wit.

Parnell, Edward & Sophia Hess, 18 Aug 1819; Thos. W. Mitchell, bondsman; Henry Giles, wit.

Parnell, Franklin & Mary Eller, 29 Oct 1858; Alexander Sides, bondsman; John Wilkinson, wit. married 31 Oct 1858 by J. M. Brown, J. P.

Pascoe, James & Anna Griffin, 13 Sept 1850; David Sink, bondsman; Archd. Honeycutt, wit.

Pasenger, George & Suffy Hartman, 11 Aug 1784; Jno. Pasenger, bondsman; H. Magoune, wit.

Pasenger, James & Anna Parker, 21 June 1827; John Pasenger, bondsman; J. H. Hardie, wit.

Pasenger, John & Elizabeth Hessell, 6 Sept 1779; John Bullen, bondsman; Ad. Osborn, wit.

Pate, Edward & Milly Walton, 9 Dec 1808; P. Dickinson, bondsman; A. L. Osborn, D. C., wit.

Pateson, Canada & Sary Grace, 28 Nov 1803; William Patterson, bondsman; Ph. Beck, wit.

Patrick, James & Barthene Ollover, 14 Jan 1806; William Madden, bondsman; Jn. March Sr., wit.

Patrick, Jeremiah & Mary Ravies, 27 Dec 1811; John Myers, bondsman; Jn. March Sr., wit.

Patrick, William & Mary Jacobs, 25 Dec 1794; John Madan, bondsman; B. John Pinchback, Lydia Pinchback, wit.

Patrick, William & Elizabeth Hardin, 10 Nov 1816; Jonathan Madden, bondsman; R. Powell, wit.

Patten, John & Elisabeth McCartney, 23 Nov 1782; Nathaniel Park, bondsman; William Crawford, wit.

Patten, Joseph & Margaret Crawford, 14 July 1779; David Crawford, bondsman; Jo. Brevard, wit.

Patterson--see also Pateson

Patterson, Archibald & Ann Smith, 29 Oct 1803; Elisha Nunnally, bondsman; A. L. Osborn, D. C., wit.

Patterson, Canada & Jane Cunningham, 3 Sept 1802; Richd. Davis, bondsman; Js. McEwin, wit.

Patterson, Charles S. & Rosanna Smith, 13 April 1855; John Ketner, bondsman; J. S. Myers, wit. married 15 April 1855 by Saml. Rothrock, Minister of the Gospel in the Ev. Luth. Church.

Patterson, Elam A. & Christina E. Smith, 19 April 1858; John W. Smith, bondsman; James E. Kerr, wit. married 21 April 1858 by Rev. B. C. Hall.

Patterson, Elam A. & Barbara M. Ketner, 31 Jan 1851; John S. Patterson, bondsman; J. S. Myers, wit.

Patterson, George M. & Sarah E. Bostian, 16 Feb 1857; Saml. L. Ervin, bondsman; J. S. Myers, wit.

Patterson, James & Sarah Fleming, 18 May 1767; John Patterson, William Neill, bondsmen; Thos. Frohock, wit.

Patterson, James & Elizabeth Lowery, 6 Sept 1825; John N. Andrews, bondsman; Jno. Giles, wit.

Patterson, James M. & Caroline E. Bostian, 23 Feb 1850; Elam A. Patterson, bondsman; J. S. Myers, wit.

Patterson, Jno. & Charlotte Caudle, 26 Aug 1802; Saml. Johnson, bondsman; A. L. Osborn, D. C., wit.

Patterson, John & Mary Guffy, 17 March 1828; Thomas Bean, bondsman; Thomas McNeely, J. P., wit.

Patterson, John I. & Tirzah A. Woods, 20 Dec 1850; Philip A. Corell, bondsman; James E. Kerr, wit.

Patterson, John S. & Sarah C. Bostain, 12 Dec 1851; Henry A. Brantley, bondsman; James E. Kerr, wit.

Patterson, Robert A. & Sally Shulebarrier, 12 Oct 1820; Joseph D. Patterson, bondsman; Jno. H. Hardie, wit.

Patterson, Simpson G. & Mary J. Carrigan, 19 Feb 1859; James F. Carrigan, bondsman; James E. Kerr, wit. married 24 Feb 1859 by Bryant C. Hall, Pastor of Ev. Luth. Church.

Patterson, Thomas A. & Elizabeth Johnston, 14 Jan 1835; Benjamin F. Fraley, bondsman; Hy. Giles, wit.

Patterson, William & Susanna Brady, 8 April 1780; John Turner, bondsman; Jno. Kerr, wit.

Patterson, William & Nancy Willis, 2 Jan 1802; John Canaday, bondsman; Jno. Brem, wit.

Patteson, William & Lucey Mingum, 2 Oct 1779; Jonathan Harris, bondsman; Ad. Osborn, wit.

Patteson, William & Sarah Lethcom, 19 Aug 1798; James Willis, bondsman; Ma. Troy, wit.

Patton, Francis & Kath. McConnell, 18 Aug 1766; Richd. Brandon, Elijah Patton, bondsman; Thoms. Frohock, wit.

Patton, James M. & Phebe E. Cox, 16 Feb 1855; W. M. Jarrett, bondsman; J. S. Myers, D. C., wit. married 18 Feb by Rev. Wm. Lambeth.

Patton, John & Margarie A. McCorkle, 15 May 1827; J. H. Hardie, bondsman.

Payne, James & Tempe Taylor, 15 Aug 1805; Colleston Payne, bondsman.

Peacock, Davidson & Maria P. Eudie, 27 Sept 1864; John J. Eudin, bondsman; D. W. Honeycutt, wit.

Peacock, John & Amelia Klutts, 14 Aug 1837; James Earnheart, bondsman; Tobias S. Lemly, wit.

Peacock, John & Christina Holloway, 23 Feb 1821; Alex Stephens, bondsman; Jno. Giles, wit.

Peacock, William M. & Virginia W. Brown, 29 March 1853; Archd. H. Caldwell, bondsman; R. A. Caldwell, wit.

ROWAN MARRIAGES 1753-1868

Pealer, Abraham & Amey Pool, 27 Sept 1826; Green Redwine,
bondsman.

Pealer, Jacob & Mary Daniel, 25 Jan 1805; Edwd. Yarbrough,
bondsman; Moses A. Locke, wit.

Pealer, John & Nancy Hodge, 31 March 1836; Solomon Ritchey,
bondsman; Jno. Shaver, J. P., wit.

Pealer, Pleasant & Miss Redwine, 9 Sept 1806; Jno. Davis,
bondsman; A. L. Osborn, wit.

Pealor, Daniel & Sally Trexler, 26 Feb 1830; David Klutts,
bondsman.

Pearce, Jerry & Elisabeth Micinhimer, 26 Dec 1854; Adam Hartman,
bondsman; H. W. Hill, J. P., wit. married 26 Dec 1854 by
H. W. Hill, J. P.

Pearce, Reuben & Martha Williams, 12 April 1794; Robert Latham,
bondsman; M. Stokes, wit.

Pears, William & Hessey Messimer, 15 May 1819; Michael Rimer,
bondsman; Jno. Giles, wit.

Pearse, Adam & Elizabeth Hornbery, 29 Dec 1859; Wiley Earnhardt,
bondsman; E. Mauney, wit. married 29 Dec 1859 by E. Mauney,
J. P.

Pearson, Giles W. & Elizabeth Ellis, 9 March 1830; Richmond
Pearson, bondsman.

Pearson, Richard & Jean Smith, 11 June 1785; William Patton,
bondsman.

Pechtel, Solomon & Molly Overcash, 24 Jan 1852; John Pechtel,
bondsman; J. S. Myers, wit.

Peck--see also Pack

Peck, Fredreck & Mary Rickard, 7 March 1800; John Metzler,
bondsman; Matt. Troy, wit.

Peck, Henry & Anna Atkison, 14 March 1809; Jacob Peck, bondsman;
A. L. Osborne, wit.

Peck, Jacob & Molly Heplar, 21 Dec 1820; Thomas Heplar, bondsman; Silas Peace, wit.

Peck, Peter--see Beck

Peden, Thomas & Elizabeth White, 3 March 1772; John Morton, John
Morton Sr., bondsmen; Thomas Frohock, wit. consent of Moses
White, 2 March 1772.

Peeke, Beechum & Theodosia Owins, 29 Nov 1791; Jesse Rickman,
bondsman; Chs. Caldwell, wit.

Peeler, Adam & Elizabeth Mowery, 18 Sept 1857; Caleb Klutts,
bondsman; J. S. Myers, wit. married 20 Sept 1857 by E. E.
Phillips, J. P.

Peeler, Alexander & Sarah Ann E. Peeler, 22 Feb 1859; Paul Peeler,
bondsman; John Wilkinson, wit. married 23 Feb 1859 by Saml.
Rothrock, Minister of the Gospel in the Ev. Luth. Church.

Peeler, Alfred L. & Rose Ann Klutts, 24 April 1866; A. W. Klutts, bondsman; Obadiah Woodson, wit.

Peeler, Alfred M. & Elisa Lyerly, 18 Jan 1864; William Smithdeal, bondsman; Thomas McNeely, wit.

Peeler, Anthony & Vina Cook, 4 Dec 1804; Noah Park, bondsman; A. L. Osborn, D. C., wit.

Peeler, Anthony & Aimey Morgan, 21 Nov 1836; Caleb Peeler, bondsman; Hy. Giles, wit.

Peeler, Caleb E. & Mary E. Beaver, 12 March 1855; George W. Hartman, bondsman; J. S. Myers, wit. married 13 March 1855 by Obadiah Woodson, J. P.

Peeler, Charles & Elizabeth Miller, 18 Sept 1832; Samuel Peeler, bondsman; J. H. Hardie, wit.

Peeler, David D. & Camilla C. Trexler, 5 Sept 1849; Caleb Klutts, bondsman.

Peeler, David D. & Martha J. Cauble, 25 Oct 1855; Davault Klutts, bondsman; J. S. Myers, wit. married 25 Oct 1855 by W. H. Walton, J. P.

Peeler, George H. & Racheal Thomas, 3 March 1841; Moses Trexler, bondsman; Susan T. Giles, wit.

Peeler, Henry & Sophia Trexler, 6 April 1830; Peter Peler, bondsman; Jno. H. Hardie, wit.

Peeler, Henry & Anne Holshouser, 30 July 1849; David D. Peeler, bondsman; John H. Hardie Jr., wit.

Peeler, Henry M. & Sarah Arey, 26 Nov 1853; George H. Peeler, bondsman.

Peeler, Jacob M. & Sarah C. Heilig, 27 Feb 1860; J. W. Fisher, bondsman; John Wilkinson, wit. married 28 Feb 1860 by Thornton Butler, V. D. M.

Peeler, Jesse & Hannah Smith, 18 Feb 1814; Thomas Varner, bondsman; Ezra Allemong, wit.

Peeler, John & Elizabeth Miller, 16 March 1810; Peter Heldebrand, bondsman; Jno Giles, C. C., wit.

Peeler, John & Elizabeth Klutts, 6 March 1821; Michael Peeler, bondsman; Hy. Giles, wit.

Peeler, Joseph A. & Mary A. Klutts, 5 Nov 1855; Davault Klutts, bondsman; J. S. Myers, wit. married 6 Dec 1855 by W. A. Walton, J. P.

Peeler, Joseph A. & Mary J. Earnhardt or Eller, 11 Jan 1859; John A. Miller, bondsman; John Wilkinson, wit. married 18 Jan 1859 by S. J. Peeler, J. P.

Peeler, Lewis & Regina Fishern, 26 May 1805; Jacob Clutz, bondsman; A. L. Osborn, D. C., wit.

Peeler, Michael & Elizabeth Brown, 6 Jan 1821; Jacob Trexler, bondsman.

Peeler, Monroe & Emeline Holshouser, 30 May 1861; married 30
May 1861 by W. R. Fraley, J. P.

Peeler, Moses & Catharine Parks, 6 May 1841; Solomon Peeler,
bondsman; Susan T. Giles, wit.

Peeler, Moses & Mary L. Cauble, 16 May 1856; Thos. C. McNeely,
bondsman; J. S. Myers, wit.

Peeler, Moses M. & Margaret C. Heilig, 24 Oct 1860; C. E. Peeler,
bondsman; married 24 Oct 1860 by Thornton Butler, V. D. M.

Peeler, Noah & Linda Pool, 5 Nov 1840; Obediah Hampton, bondsman; Jno Giles, wit.

Peeler, Paul & Caty Fisher, 26 April 1830; Daniel Peeler, bondsman; Jno. H. Hardie, wit.

Peeler, Paul & Mary C. Hartman, 27 July 1859; Moses Peeler,
bondsman; John Wilkinson, wit. married 27 July 1859 by Saml.
Rothrock, Minister of the Gospel in the Ev. Luth. Church.

Peeler, Peter & Eve Boger, 2 April 1827; John Peeler, bondsman;
J. H. Hardie, wit.

Peeler, Peter & Sophia Sifford, 18 Aug 1827; Paul Barringer,
bondsman; J. H. Hardie wit.

Peeler, Solomon & America L. Smith, 14 July 1845; Jno. D. Brown,
bondsman; John H. Hardie Jr., wit.

Peeler, Solomon & Susanna Beaver, 7 Sept 1857; Otho Holshouser,
bondsman; James E. Kerr, wit. married 10 Sept 1857 by Saml.
Rothrock, Minister of the Gospel in the Ev. Luth. Church.

Peeler, Squire & Anny Shuping, 24 Oct 1825; Peter Cooper, bondsman; Hy. Giles, wit.

Peeler, Tobias & Mary L. Miller, 12 April 1859; William Overman,
bondsman.

Pegg, Isaac & Phibe Chamless, 10 May 1790; William Hunt, bondsman; Jno. Monro, wit.

Pegg, William & Sophiah Dial, 15 Nov 1789; Frederick Hargraves,
bondsman; Jno. Monro, wit.

Peirson, Thomas & Elisabeth Cain, _____; Jacob Hinkle, bondsman; Jn March Sr., wit.

Peler, Jesse & Joicey Woodson, 4 Jan 1817; Jacob Stoner, bondsman; Jno. Giles, Clk., wit.

Pell, Franklin M. & Susannah L. Sloop, 4 Sept 1848; George Sloop,
bondsman; J. H. Hardie, wit.

Pelley, James & Nancey Mils, 17 Feb 1810; John Berryman, bondsman; Jn March Sr., wit.

Pence, Henry & Eliza Litaker, 16 July 1829; Daniel Correll,
bondsman; J. H. Hardie, wit.

Pence, Henry H. & Margaret Towerl, 6 April 1847; John U. Vogler,
bondsman; J. H. Hardie Jr., wit.

Pence, John & Julian Ann Stockton, 7 Feb 1854; George H. Fesperman, bondsman; J. S. Myers, wit. married 7 Feb 1854 by Obadiah Woodson, J. P.

Pence, Valentine & Mary Ann Smith, 23 Aug 1833; George H. Brown, bondsman; R. Cochran, wit.

Pendleton, Richd. B. & Mary Wade, 22 March 1848; Chs. J. Alexander, bondsman; J. H. Hardie, wit.

Peninger, Moses & Maccy Barger, 8 Jan 1849; George H. Barger, bondsman.

Penix, Joshua & An Cathey, 15 July 1784; Samuel Wilson, bondsman.

Penney, Jon. & Anne Penny, 6 Feb 1811; Alexander Penny, bondsman; Geo. Dunn, wit.

Penninger, Mathias & Peggy Rendelman, 17 May 1815; William Rough, bondsman; Geo. Dunn, wit.

Penninger, William & _____, 10 Jan 1838; David Gardiner, bondsman; E. R. Buckhead, wit.

Penninger, William & Elizabeth Locke, 12 March 1822; Francis S. Locke, bondsman.

Penninger, William A. & Margaret R. Thomason, 22 Aug 1855; William A. Thomason, bondsman; J. S. Myers, wit. married 23 Aug 1855 by J. Thomason, J. P.

Pennington, G. B. & Emma B. Swink, 28 March 1863; John Monroe, bondsman; Obadiah Woodson, wit.

Pennington, Thomas & Lethe Bell, 29 March 1796; Wm. Pennington, bondsman; J. Troy, D. C., wit.

Penny, A. R. & Margaret Edmonson, 14 Jan 1834; Wm. Donaldson, bondsman; Wm. Locke, wit.

Penny, Alexander & Mary Gibson, 24 April 1788; George Gibson, bondsman; Js. McEwin, wit.

Penny, Alexander & Margaret Donaldson, 7 Jan 1828; Alex. B. Donaldson, bondsman; J. H. Hardie, wit.

Penny, Francis L. & Margaret Baker, 17 March 1835; Wm. Donaldson, bondsman; Jno. H. Hardie, wit.

Penny, John A. & Mary Jane Croner, 22 Sept 1857; Caleb M. Goodnight, bondsman; James E. Kerr, wit. married 22 Sept 1857 by C. L. Partee, J. P.

Penry, Daniel & Drake Hartwell, 23 Aug 1829; Moses Wood, bondsman; L. R. Rose, J. P., wit.

Penry, James & Kiziah D. Marlin, 23 Dec 1830; Samuel Penry, bondsman; Jno. H. Hardie, wit.

Penry, John & Susan Smith, 13 Dec 1827; A. Vaneten, bondsman; L. R. Rose, J. P., wit.

Peoples, Drury & Catherine Ryal, 11 March 1812; John Slagle, bondsman; Geo. Dunn, wit.

Peoples, John & Betsey Patterson, 15 Aug 1811; Thos. Willis,
bondsman; Jno. Giles, C. C., wit.

Perkins, Jonas & Martha Chambers (colored), 16 Sept 1865;
married 16 Sept 1865 by Zuck Haughton.

Perkins, Stephen & Nancy Anderson, 7 Aug 1767; William Perkins,
Henry Thompson Jr., bondsmen; Thomas Frohock, wit. consent
from Thomas Anderson, Mary Anderson and Isaac Perkins, 28
July 1767.

Perkle, Isaac & Rebecca Tanner, 2 Sept 1812; Peter Varnier,
bondsman; Jno Giles, C. C., wit.

Perle, Charles & Sarah Grant, 22 Sept 1779; Henry Winkler,
bondsman; Ad. Osborn, wit.

Perry, Richard & Elizabeth Hayse, 8 May 1767; Samuel Smith,
bondsman; Thos Frohock, wit.

Persons, James & Elizabeth Moselen, 15 Aug 1785; Jams. Houston,
bondsman; Ad. Osborn, wit.

Petchey, John Henry & Margret DeBruhel, _____; Ad. Osborn,
bondsman.

Petchey, John Henry & Ann Watt, 21 Aug 1788; John Watts,
bondsman; Ad. Osborn, wit.

Peteet, Thomas J. & Adaline Overcash, 20 April 1860; John
Pateet, bondsman; James E. Kerr, Clk., wit. married 21
April 1860 by C. S. Partee, J. P.

Peters, Louis & Jane Castle, 16 Jan 1865; Elam F. Miller,
bondsman; Obadiah Woodson, wit.

Petrea, Henry W. & Catharine A. E. Felker, 5 March 1866; William
D. Garver, bondsman; Horatio N. Woodson, wit.

Petree, Burton & Susanna S. Pahel, 24 Dec 1856; Joseph H. Bigham,
bondsman; J. S. Myers, wit. married 25 Dec 1856 by M. S.
McKenzie, J. P.

Pettiford, Eli & _____, 12 June 1802; Isaac Forgison, bondsman; Jno McClelland, wit.

Petty, Harbin & Phebe Moores, 10 Sept 1795; Joshua Moore,
bondsman; J. Troy, wit.

Pew, Reuben & Nancy Blanketpicler, 8 July 1784; Leonard Rickard,
bondsman; Max. Chambers, wit.

Phel, Andrew & Mary Ramer, 23 Dec 1824; Peter Sloop, bondsman;
Hy. Giles, wit.

Phelps, Hiram & Comfort Chaffin, 24 June 1822; Alexander Rea,
bondsman; Tho. Hampton, wit.

Phelps, William & Sarey Millar, 5 Jan 1816; Peter Barney Cassel,
bondsman; Jn March Sr., wit.

Phifer, Benjamin & Jane V. Cowan, 20 Dec 1826; Lewis W. Cowan,
bondsman; J. H. Hardie, wit.

Phifer, Caleb & Margaret Fullenwider, 3 May 1773; Henry Follen-
wodor, bondsman; Ad. Osborn, wit.

Phifer, George & Elizabeth Frank, 4 Dec 1786; Henry Furror,
bondsman; Jno. Macay, wit.

Phifer, Jacob W. & Martha J. Hughey, 15 Dec 1856; B. Niblock,
bondsman; J. S. Myers, wit. married 18 Dec 1856 by Saml.
B. O. Wilson, V. D. M.

Phifer, John & Jane Hughey, 5 June 1815; John Hughey, bondsman;
Geo. Dunn, wit.

Phifer, John C. & Mary A. Cowan, 21 Dec 1852; George E. Hughey,
bondsman; J. S. Myers, wit. married 25 Nov 1858 by Saml.
B. O. Wilson.

Phifer, Matthias M. & Sarah C. Cowan, 7 Oct 1849; George E.
Hughey, bondsman; J. S. Myers, wit.

Phifer, Paul & Nancy Webb, 13 Jan 1824; Benjamin Huie, bondsman.

Phifer, Silas & Matilda Cowan, 6 Dec 1823; Lewis H. Cowan,
bondsman.

Phifer, Thomas M. & Margaret E. Gillespie, 15 Feb 1861; W. W.
Hall, bondsman; John Wilkinson, wit. married 19 Feb 1861
by Walter W. Pharr, Minister of the Gospel.

Philips, Enoch E. & Susan Brown, 20 July 1835; Benjamin Fraley,
bondsman; Jno. H. Hardie, wit.

Philips, James & Markeret Johnston, 26 March 1803; Thomas G.
Deadman, bondsman; Jno March, John March Jr., wit.

Philips, Jonas & Phirlebe Gurley, 12 July 1778; John Phillps,
bondsman; Spruce Macay, wit.

Philips, Robert B. & Anny Mourie, 14 Aug 1815; John Mourie,
bondsman; Jno. Giles, C. C., wit.

Philips, Thomas & Martha Pits, 19 Dec 1816; Henry Pitts,
bondsman; Sol. Davis, J. P., wit.

Philips, Wade & Catharine Frize, 21 Sept 1832; James Scott,
bondsman.

Phillips, Barham & Litty Coles, 22 Aug 1818; John Robertson,
bondsman; Thos. Hampton, wit.

Phillips, Beddeo & Margret Wisemon, 13 Feb 1810; George March,
bondsman; Jn. March Sr., wit.

Phillips, Daniel & Elizabeth Keller, 25 July 1833; Uriah Keller,
bondsman; L. R. Rose, J. P., wit.

Phillips, Enoch & _____, 1 May 1801; Nathan Phillips, bondsman;
Jno Brem, wit.

Phillips,'F. G. & Polly Casper, 25 Sept 1847; Charles Earnhart,
bondsman; J. H. Hardie Jr., wit.

Phillips, Henry & Martha E. Morgan, 14 Dec 1865; Horatio N.
Woodson, bondsman.

Phillips, Jacob & Catherine Stirewalt, 17 Aug 1837; Georg G. Quilman, bondsman; Tobias S. Lemly, wit.

Phillips, Jesse & Lucy Smith, 2 Dec 1859; Lawson M. Rendlman, bondsman; John Wilkinson, wit.

Phillips, John & Margrate Henderson, 23 Sept 1806; David Phillips, bondsman; W. Welborn, wit.

Phillips, John A. & Mary Ann Wyatt, 9 June 1864; Moses Brown, bondsman; Obadiah Woodson, wit.

Phillips, Joshua & Sarah E. Stirewalt, 21 Feb 1855; Micheal Brown, bondsman; J. S. Myers, wit.

Phillips, Phillip & Mary Oneal, 7 Sept 1798; Barnard Crider, bondsman; Edwin J. Osborn, D. C., wit.

Phipps--see also Fips

Phipps, Esiah & Jane Doling, _____; John Crowell, bondsman; Robt. Troy, wit.

Phips, John & Margaret Miller, 7 May 1811; Christian Tar, bondsman; Jno Giles, C. C., wit.

Picket, Charles & Lucretia Williams, 11 March 1794; Adam Coppus, bondsman; Jo. Chambers, wit.

Picklehimer, John & Elizabeth Millar, 7 Jan 1793; Daniel Smith, bondsman; Jo. Chambers, wit.

Pickler, Garrett & Polly Barringer, 24 March 1828; Paul Barringer, bondsman; Jno. H. Hardie, wit.

Pickler, John & Catharine Beck, 24 Nov 1811; John Hodgens, bondsman; Jno Giles, C. C., wit.

Pickler, John & Ruthy Owens, 1 Jan 1825; Josiah Owen Jr., bondsman; Hy. Giles, wit.

Pickler, John & Nancy Johnson, 12 Sept 1826; Tho. L. Cowan, bondsman.

Pickler, Joseph Jr. & Charlotte Smoote, 16 Sept 1829; Nathaniel Carter, bondsman; Thomas McNeely, J. P., wit.

Picler, John & Barbara McMacken, 24 Feb 1796; Joseph Picler, bondsman.

Picler, Lewis & Eve Hartman, 25 March 1796; Nicholas Barringer, bondsman; J. Troy, wit.

Pierce, Jesse & Nancy Madden, 14 July 1818; John Pierce, bondsman; R. Powell, wit.

Pierce, Redmon & Lacey L. Parrish, 12 Dec 1822; Jno. Jarratt, bondsman; Ams. Wright, wit.

Pierson, John & Eva Mealy, 30 Oct 1803; Rd. Dickson, bondsman; A. L. Osborn, D. C., wit.

Piner, Benjamin & Polley Athan, 10 March 1825; Joseph Athan, bondsman; E. Brock, J. P., wit.

Pinex, Lawson G. & Elizabeth Cleary, 16 Sept 1832; Euin Clary, bondsman; Thomas McNeely, J. P., wit.

Pinkerton, James & Elizabeth Dancy, 6 Sept 1800; Robert Pinkerton, bondsman; J. Brem, wit.

Pinkerton, John & Caty Fox, 28 Dec 1796; David Pinkerton, bondsman; Jno. Rogers, wit.

Pinkerton, Robert & Mary Ray, 6 Sept 1800; James Whitaker, bondsman; John Brem, wit.

Pinkerton, William & Ruth Cunningham, 20 Jan 1795; David Pinkerton, bondsman; J. Troy, D. C., wit.

Pinkston, Aaron & Easter Lock, 12 Jan 1808; Jas. Wilson, bondsman; Jn March Sr., wit.

Pinkston, Aaron & Catharine Townsley, 25 July 1844; Jno. Utzman, bondsman; J. H. Hardie, wit.

Pinkston, Alexander & Elizabeth Trott, 16 March 1824; Jno. Leach, bondsman; Hy. Giles, wit.

Pinkston, Bazell & Keziah Pearis, 8 April 1769; Moses Pearis, Geo. Magoune, bondsmen; Thom. Frohock, wit.

Pinkston, Daniel & Elizabeth Thomason, 11 Nov 1784; Thomas Biles, bondsman; Max. Chambers, wit. consent from Gorge Thomason (sic), 11 Nov 1784.

Pinkston, David & Eliza Craige, 15 April 1840; Saml. Craige, bondsman; Susan T. Giles, wit.

Pinkston, Francis & Sarah Buise, 20 Dec 1826; Seth Morris, bondsman.

Pinkston, Francis & Elvira Woodson, 16 March 1846; J. H. Hardie, bondsman.

Pinkston, Francis & Susan Crittendon, 2 Feb 1851; Henry A. Jacobs, bondsman; James E. Kerr, wit.

Pinkston, Franklin & Jamima Sloan, 11 Jan 1854; George W. Jacobs, bondsman; J. S. Myers, wit.

Pinkston, George W. & Elizabeth W. Blackwell, 9 Jan 1850; Thomas T. Locke, bondsman; J. S. Myers, wit.

Pinkston, J. F. & Lucy Craige, 25 Nov 1845; H. W. Foard, bondsman; J. H. Hardie, wit.

Pinkston, John & Ann Donoho, 27 June 1788; Hugh Harrell, bondsman.

Pinkston, John L. & Elizabeth Hellard, 15 Sept 1847; John L. Sloan, bondsman; John H. Hardie Jr., wit.

Pinkston, Meshack & Rosanna Haden, 18 March 1823; Matthew Howard, bondsman; E. Allemong, wit.

Pinkston, Mesheck & Susanna Coughanour, 2 Dec 1793; Christian Coughanour, bondsman; Jos. Chambers, wit.

Pinkston, Meshack & Euphemia Brown, 7 July 1852; Joseph Henderson, bondsman; James E. Kerr, wit. married 7 July 1852 by J. M. Brown, J. P.

Pinkston, Micajah & Mary Howard, 10 June 1812; Jas. Sanders, bondsman; Geo. Dunn, wit.

Pinkston, Morris & Sally Wallace, 17 Jan 1817; Lewis Smith, bondsman; Roberts Nanny, wit.

Pinkston, Peter & Betsey Barns, 9 Dec 1815; Uriah Barns, bondsman; Jno. Giles, C. C., wit.

Pinkston, Peter & Louisa Matila Swink, 3 May 1825; Matthew Howard, bondsman; W. Harris, wit.

Pinkston, Richard & Rachael Gheen, 5 Nov 1810; Jas. Sanders, bondsman; Jno Giles, C. C., wit.

Pinkston, Richard & Savanah Lyerly, 29 June 1840; David G. Phillips, bondsman; Susan T. Giles, wit.

Pinkston, Thomas & Catharine Briggs, 30 Dec 1839; Geo. Utzman, bondsman; Jno. Giles, wit.

Pinkston, Thomas & Catharine Wilson, 4 Feb 1814; Jno. Utzman, bondsman; Geo. Dunn, wit.

Pinkston, Thomas & Elizabeth Parks, 23 Nov 1859; Mathew Plumer, bondsman; James E. Kerr, wit. married 24 Nov 1859 by M. Plumer, J. P.

Pinkston, Turner & Nelly Wood, 4 Feb 1797; Jno. Howard, bondsman; Jno. Rogers, wit.

Pinkston, William & Eudocia Biles, 10 Aug 1792; Mesheck Pinkstone, bondsman; Chs. Caldwell, wit.

Pinkston, William & Margaret Enlow, 3 Sept 1796; Wm. Pinkston, bondsman; Jno Rogers, wit.

Pinkston, William & Tabitha Biles, 23 April 1818; Benjamin P. Person, bondsman; Jno Giles, wit.

Pinkston, William & Peggy Coughenour, 8 Sept 1821; George Locke, bondsman; M. A. Giles, wit.

Pinkston, William H. & Fanny Rufty, 30 March 1854; Wilmon Cranford, bondsman; J. S. Myers, wit.

Pinnicks, William & Agnes Cathey, _____; Thos. Bailey, bondsman; James Robinson, wit.

Pinxton, William & Anne Phifer, 11 Nov 1802; Andrew Kincaid, bondsman; A. L. Osborn, D. C., wit.

Pipenger, Cornelius & Margart Hedrik, 10 Dec 1798; Barnaba Bowers, bondsman; Edwin J. Osborn, D. C., wit.

Pipher, Martin & Elizabeth Lock, _____ 177_; John Lock, Willm. Lock, bondsmen; Ad. Osborn, wit.

Pitman, George & Polly Trease, 30 Nov 1809; George Miller, bondsman.

Pitman, Jesse & Charlotte Skinner, 20 Dec 1796; Joseph P. Williams, bondsman; Jno Rogers, wit.

Pittman, Micajah & Lidy Morgan, 18 Sept 1771; Richard Quick, Wm. Temple Cole, bondsmen.

Pitts, Levi & Mary Salisbury, 12 March 1818; David Hendricks, bondsman; Sol. Davis, J. P., wit.

Place, Abram & Mary Clyne, 10 Feb 1791; Leonard Barbarick, bondsman; C. Caldwell, D. C., wit.

Plaster, Benjamin & Sarah Sewell, 10 Oct 1802; John Sewell, bondsman; Js. McEwin, wit.

Plaster, John & Susannah Barringer, 15 May 1803; Groves Sammons, bondsman; A. L. Osborn, D. C., wit.

Plaumer, John & Barbara Kessler, 4 April 1809; Peter Stoner, bondsman; A. L. Osborne, wit.

Pless, Aaron & Rachel A. Rendleman, (colored), 9 Jan 1866; George Bradshaw, bondsman; Obadiah Woodson, wit.

Pless, Henry J. & Mary E. S. Eagle, 26 Sept 1865; U. M. Pless, bondsman; Obadiah Woodson, wit.

Pless, Jacob & Louisa Barringer, 14 March 1835; John Barringer, bondsman; Jno. H. Hardie, wit.

Pless, Jacob & Sophia Ayle, 19 May 1845; Ambrose Eddleman, bondsman; Jno. H. Hardie, wit.

Pless, Joseph & Christine Rinehart, 21 Oct 1800; Jacob Rinehart, bondsman.

Pless, Philip & Catharin Betz, ___ Feb 1796; George Betz, bondsman; J. Troy, wit.

Pliler, John & Rebecca Smith, 2 Nov 1840; John Gillon, bondsman.

Plumer, Matthew & Nancy B. Pinkston, 11 Dec 1828; Jos. Blackwell, bondsman; J. H. Hardie, wit.

Plumer, Richard & Patsey Elliott, 24 Oct 1822; Robert Elliott, bondsman.

Plumer, Richard & Elizabeth Bowers, 26 Nov 1837; Noah Roberts, bondsman; Jno. Giles, wit.

Plummer, William & Margaret Robeson, 30 Dec 1789; Peter Wood, bondsman; Ed. Harris, wit.

Plummer, William J. Jr. & Bettie L. Shaver, 25 May 1864; N. R. Windsor, bondsman; Obadiah Woodson, wit.

Pogue, Elias J. & Barbara A. Rogers, 3 Jan 1858; Samuel A. Knerly, bondsman; John Wilkinson, wit.

Pool, Alexander & Ann L. Lentz, 25 May 1843; Henry Hill, bondsman; J. H. Hardie, wit.

Pool, Benjamin F. & Elizabeth West, 25 Jan 1858; Elisha Willis, bondsman; married 25 Jan 1858 by John D. Scheck.

Pool, David & Peggy Barger, 21 Dec 1813; William Henry Horah, bondsman; Geo. Dunn, wit.

Pool, Edward & Susannah Hartmon, 24 April 1839; Philip Lemly, bondsman; Hy. Giles, wit.

Pool, Henry & Margaret Brown, 29 Aug 1791; Hugh Morgan, bondsman.

Pool, Henry & Mary A. Smith, 18 April 1825; Oliver Glover, bondsman.

Pool, Jacob & Sarah Waller, 22 Oct 1828; Jacob Hartline, bondsman; J. H. Hardie, wit.

Pool, Jacob & Martha Cambell, 30 Nov 1839; Moses Hill, bondsman; John Giles, wit.

Pool, Jacob & Elizabeth Waller, 26 Nov 1847; Moses Earnheart, bondsman; J. H. Hardie Jr., wit.

Pool, John & Susannah Mowrie, 23 March 1838; Peter Cauble, bondsman.

Pool, Joseph & Mary J. Hardie, 1 Sept 1840; E. N. Parker, bondsman; J. L. Beard, wit.

Pool, Otho & Lucressa Lentz, 27 March 1848; Cornelius Kesler, bondsman.

Pool, Robert A. & Julia Ann Morrison, 9 June 1855; C. H. Gardner, bondsman; James E. Kerr, wit. married 9 June 1855 by Jas. H. Enniss, J. P.

Poole, Elihu N. & Hannah M. Freeze, 28 Dec 1840; William G. Miller, bondsman; J. L. Beard, wit.

Poole, Henry & Catharine Cauble, 13 April 1850 or 1851; John H. Waller Jun., bondsman; James E. Kerr, wit.

Poole, Joseph & Ann Cauble, 23 March 1812; John Pool, bondsman; Jno Giles, C. C., wit.

Poole, Peter & Mary Cross, 7 July 1789; John Jennens, bondsman; Will Alexander, wit.

Pope, Isaac & Mary Stueard, 28 Jan 1813; George Pope, bondsman; Aaron Kimbrough, George W. Pope, wit.

Poor, Enoch & Prudence Brevard, 8 April 1794; William Hamton, bondsman; Jos. Chambers, wit.

Porter, _____ & Jean Brown, 1 Dec 1769; (consent from Margret Brown, only).

Porter, Andrew & Rebekah Burner, 8 April 1790; Adam Burney, bondsman; C. Caldwell, D. C., wit.

Porter, David & Peggy Volentine, 29 Dec 1848; Jno Kelly, bondsman; J. H. Hardie, wit.

Porter, Francis H. & Isabella Kilpatric, 21 Sept 1811; William H. Horah, bondsman; Jno Giles, C. C., wit.

Porter, Henry & Mary Valentine, 1 March 1860; Harmon Proctor, bondsman; Wm. Locke, wit. married 1 March 1860 by L. C. Groseclose, Pastor St. John's Ev. Luth. Church, Salisbury, N. C.

Porter, Henry & Phebe Benson (colored), 17 Feb 1866; James E. Kerr, bondsman; Obadiah Woodson, wit.

Porter, James & Jenny Thomas, 29 April 1809; Chrs. Lippard, bondsman; Jno Giles, wit.

Porter, James & Alvina Pool, 6 March 1837; Peter Cauble, bondsman; John Giles, wit.

Porter, James P. & Levinia B. Seaford, 26 March 1866; A. M. Sullivan, bondsman; Obadiah Woodson, wit.

Porter, John A. & Melvina E. Glover, 18 Dec 1865; Michael Beaver, bondsman; Obadiah Woodson, wit.

Porter, Laurence & Betsey Parks, 3 July 1817; Robert Porter, bondsman; Jno. Giles, wit.

Porter, O. N. & M. E. Wilhelm, 7 Oct 1865; W. H. Crawford, bondsman; Obadiah Woodson, wit. married 12 Oct 1865 by H. Barringer, J. P.

Porter, Robert & Elizabeth McBroom, 29 Aug 1767; Alexr. Endsley, bondsman; John Frohock, wit.

Porter, Thomas & Mary Cole, 28 July 1810; Ransom Dudley, bondsman; Geo. Dunn, wit.

Portis, William & Polly Ward, 30 May 1821; John Pierson, bondsman; Jno. Giles, wit.

Poston, Benjamin & Rachael C. Knox, 6 Aug 1821; Thomas Foster, bondsman.

Poston, Edward & Mary Ann Christy, 25 Oct 1848; Thomas Christy, bondsman; J. S. Myers, wit.

Poston, John E. & Matilda M. Ramsey, 23 Oct 1849; Oni P. Houston, bondsman; James E. Kerr, wit.

Poston, John J. & Susannah Rice, 1 Aug 1817; John Foster, bondsman; Roberts Nanny, wit.

Poston, John Jorden & Polly Warner, 17 Jan 1812; Benjamin Abbott, bondsman; Geo. Dunn, wit.

Poston, Richard G. & Mary A. Harrison, 9 May 1854; Abner W. Owen, bondsman; J. S. Myers, D. C., wit. married 10 May 1854 by Saml. B. O. Wilson.

Poston, Robert & Sarah Cunningham, 3 April 1776; Will Vent, bondsman; Ad. Osborn, wit.

Potis, William & Betsey How, 24 March 1821; Wm. Dickson, bondsman; Milo A. Giles, wit.

Pots, Hamblin & Anney Daniel, 21 Dec 1813; Benjamin Martin, bondsman; Jn March Sr., wit.

Pots, Thomas & Fanney Nabit, 11 Aug 1815; Henrey Oneal, bondsman; Jn March Sr., wit.

Potts, Edwin & Elizabeth Hall, 19 Sept 1817; Jesse Hall, bondsman; Milo A. Giles, wit.

Potts, Giles & Sarah Volentine, 26 June 1859; George Volentine, bondsman; James E. Kerr, wit. married 25 June 1859 by Peter Williamson, J. P.

Potts, Jeremiah & Philendar Jentle, 6 Jan 1808; Humphrey Mullikin, bondsman; Jn March Sr., wit.

Potts, John K. & Mary L. Brown, 27 July 1852; A. F. Sharpe, bondsman; married 27 July 1852 by H. S. Robards, J. P.

Potts, Josiah D. & Sarah Graves, 19 Sept 1812; Joshua Briningar, bondsman; Jn March Sr., wit.

Potts, Peter & Mary Pack, 13 Dec 1794; Rezin Pack, bondsman; J. Troy, D. C., wit.

Potts, Stephen & Jane Edmunds, 16 Feb 1762; William Potts, bondsman; John Frohock, Will Reed, wit.

Potts, William & Ellender Robards, 30 Jan 1811; Azariah Pack, bondsman; Jn March Sr., wit.

Potts, William & Betsey Mullican, 20 Feb 1818; Lawrence Williams, bondsman; Jno Giles, wit.

Potts, William & Comfort Steward, 4 Nov 1828; Joseph Pack, bondsman; J. H. Hardie, wit.

Potts, William & Margret Purviance, 23 May 1787; Jno. Purviance, bondsman.

Poulson, George B. & Mary V. Hall, 8 Nov 1864; Julius D. McNeily, bondsman; J. W. Hall, wit.

Pouwles, Henry & Catharine L. Sifferd, 16 Feb 1858; Moses A. Bost, bondsman; John Wilkinson, wit. married 18 Feb 1858 by Saml. Rothrock, Minister of the Gospel in the Ev. Luth. Church.

Powe, William E. & Eliza A. S. Torrence, 31 Aug 1815; Hu. Torrence, bondsman.

Powe, Benjamin & Sarah Jenkins, 10 June 1819; Wm. M'Crary, bondsman; Sol. Davis, J. P., wit.

Powell, James & Susana Adams, 17 Oct 1797; Jno. Rogers, bondsman.

Powlas, Adam & Mary Dellow, 4 June 1785; Michl. Dellow, bondsman; Hu. Magoune, wit.

Powlas, Eli & Margaret A. Gillian, 13 May 1850; Moses Powlass, bondsman; J. S. Myers, wit.

Powlas, John & Amey Lentz, 11 July 1842; David Earnhart, bondsman; J. H. Hardie, wit.

Powlas, John & Mary C. Parks, 2 Feb 1859; Levi Klutts, bondsman; John Wilkinson, wit. married 4 Feb 1859 by Jas. A. Linn.

Powlass, Jesse & Sarah L. Gellean, 30 April 1851; Jonathan Lyerly, bondsman; J. S. Myers, wit. married 1 May 1851 by Wm. A. Hall.

Powlass, Jesse & Sarah E. Thompson, 23 March 1858; John Carson, bondsman; James E. Kerr, wit.

Powlass, Moses & Anne Trexler, 24 Aug 1849; Milas Gheen, bondsman; J. H. Hardie Jr., wit.

Powles, Adam & Margaret Hoffner, 11 June 1829; Andrew Earnheart, bondsman; Jno. H. Hardie, wit.

Powles, Henry & Caty Lentz, 6 April 1816; William Powles, bondsman; Geo. Dunn, wit.

Powles, Jacob & Mary Peeler, 24 June 1823; David Knup, bondsman; Jno Giles, wit.

Powles, Levi & Nancy M. Tucker, 21 Dec 1860; A. M. Webb, bondsman; John Wilkinson, wit. married 24 Dec 1860 by Rev. S. S. Barber.

Powles, William & Caty Kenupp, 5 March 1811; Edward Davis, bondsman; Geo. Dunn, wit.

Poyeus, John & Margret Biles, 2 April 1791; Thos. Dickey, bondsman; C. Caldwell, D. C., wit.

Poyner, Peter & Elizabeth Dulin, 17 Jan 1823; Bryan Ellis, bondsman; L. R. Rose, J. P., wit.

Prater, Thomas & Rachael Gaither, 20 March 1790; William Prater, bondsman; Ad. Osborn, wit.

Prather, John & Ann Cambell, 17 Sept 1827; Hiram H. Prather, bondsman; Thomas McNeely, J. P., wit.

Prather, Thomas & Vilinda Robey, 12 Jan 1783; William Williamson, bondsman; William Crawford, wit.

Prather, Thomas & Mary James, 27 Oct 1817; Leven Howard, bondsman; R. Powell, wit.

Pratt, William H. & Mary Nancy Eller, 17 Nov 1858; David Eller, bondsman; John Wilkinson, wit. married 18 Nov 1858 by H. S. Robards, J. P.

Prewett, Willis & Angeling Gallemore, 30 April 1849; George M. Weant, bondsman; Jno. H. Hardie Jr., wit.

Price, Charles N. & Jane E. Kesler, 23 Aug 1836; Hiram Rainery, bondsman; Hy. Giles, wit.

Price, John S. & Sally B. Hughs, 10 Oct 1815; John S. Hughes, bondsman; Geo. Dunn, wit.

Price, William & Darcus Campbell, 26 July 1814; Tho. L. Cowan, bondsman; Jno Giles, C. C., wit.

Pro. Christian & Patsey Downs, 14 Oct 1807; George Fry, bondsman; Lazarus Hege, J. P., wit.

Prock, Paul & Sarah Dehart, 29 May 1780; Elias Dehart, bondsman; Jno. Kerr, wit.

Proctor, Hermon & Anny Freeman, 22 Dec 1856; John Valentine, bondsman; J. S. Myers, wit. married 22 Dec 1856 by Jas. H. Enniss, J. P.

Propas, Jacob & Peggy Duke, 2 Nov 1815; Adam Roseman, bondsman; Jno Giles, C. C., wit.

Propst, Daniel & Betsey Roseman, 8 Oct 1818; Adam Rosemon, bondsman.

Propst, Jacob & Mary L. Roseman, 1 July 1854; James C. Roseman, bondsman; J. S. Myers, wit.

Propst, Jacob & Rebecca Shaver, 18 Oct 1856; Eli A. Propst, bondsman; J. S. Myers, wit.

Propst, Nelson & _____ Eddleman, 19 May 1840; Volantin Props, bondsman; Hy. Giles, wit.

Propst, Valentine & Harriet L. Pless, 14 Jan 1852; George H. Richey, bondsman; J. S. Myers, wit.

Propst, William Daniel & Mary E. Klutts, 13 Dec 1859; Valentine Propst, bondsman; James Kerr, wit. married 15 Dec 1859 by Saml. Rothrock, Minister of the Gospel in the Ev. Luth. Church.

Prow, John & Elizabeth Johnston, 2 Feb 1811; Jacob Douthit, bondsman; John Hanes, wit.

Pruitt--see also Prewett

Pruitt, Harrod B. & Lucey Smith, 19 Feb 1797; Obadiah Smith, bondsman; Jno Roger, wit.

Pruitt, Harrod B. & Elizabeth H. Baly, 28 Aug 1813; Jas. Gillaspie, bondsman; Jn March Sr., wit.

Pryor, Hiram W. & Lucy Brown, 24 Aug 1843; Littleton Brown, bondsman; Jno. H. Hardie, wit.

Pryor, Thomas & Elizabeth Calvorhouse, 23 Nov 1810; David Pryor, bondsman; Jno Giles, C. C., wit.

Pue, Reuben & Fanny Smith, 10 Dec 1785; Benjamin Smith, bondsman; Wm. W. Erwin, wit.

Pugh, Isaac & Mary Varner of Randolph County, 23 Nov 1819; Isaac Copple, bondsman; P. Copple, J. P., wit.

Purviance, Robert & Sally Miller, 26 April 1793; James Miller, bondsman; Ed. J. Osborn, D. C., wit.

Purvis, James & Eliza J. W. Baker, 4 Oct 1837; Wm. S. Johnson, bondsman.

Pyron, Thomas & Caty Crowell, 14 Nov 1809; Jacob Duke, bondsman; Geo. Dunn, wit.

Pyron, William & Nancy Crowell, 5 March 1812; Henry Hill, bondsman; Geo. Dunn, wit.

Queen, James & Margaret Wolfe, 9 Oct 1779; Wm. Brandon, bondsman; Jo. Brevard, wit.

Queen, John & Lucy Burton, 23 April 1825; James McGuire Jr., bondsman.

Quick, Benjamin & Eleanor Tucker, 3 Aug 1789; Henry Davis, bondsman; W. Alexander, wit.

Quillman, G. G. & Catharine Fesperman, 24 March 1864; W. L. Turner, bondsman; Obadiah Woodson, wit.

Quillman, George G. & L. D. Eller, 22 March 1866; John A. Bostian, bondsman; Obadiah Woodson, wit.

Quilman, George G. & Mackilisha M. Jacobs, 6 March 1842; Jehu Foster, bondsman; J. H. Hardie, wit.

Raiblin, Martin & Katharine Butner, 8 April 1794; Benjamin Walton, bondsman; Jo. Chambers, wit.

Raichard, John & Esther Sulivan, 15 Aug 1815; William Sullivan Jr., bondsman; William Conrod, David Mock, wit.

Railsback, David & Elizabeth Ellis, 13 Oct 1791; William Ellis, bondsman; Basil Gaither, wit.

Raimer, Aley & Anna Overcash, 6 Oct 1831; Henry Overcash, bondsman; P. Click, wit.

Rainey, Aaron & Mary Ann Julian, 28 Dec 1838; Hiram H. Rainey, bondsman; Hy. Giles, wit.

Rainey, Isaac & Elizabeth Gardner, 15 July 1852; E. E. Philips, bondsman; J. S. Myers, wit. married 15 July 1852 by Jas. P. Simpson.

Rainey, Isham & Rachel Stoner, 10 Nov 1842; John Shuman, J. P., bondsman.

Rainey, Milas & Caroline Mesimer, 28 March 1844; Henry Moyer, bondsman; Obadiah Woodson, wit.

Rainey, William & Barbra Jacobs, 28 Feb 1794; Jno. Howard, bondsman; M. Stokes, wit.

Rainey, William & Mary A. Miller, 15 June 1857; Wm. C. Brandon, bondsman; J. S. Myers, wit. married 18 June 1857 by M. L. McKenzie, J. P.

Rainy, Isham & Elizabeth Rymer, 25 Dec 1833; Hy. Giles, bondsman.

Rainy, William & Ann L. Coughenour, 1 Jan 1857; Moses A. Smith, bondsman; J. S. Myers, wit. married 1 Jan 1857 by R. G. Barrett.

Ralsback, Henry & Margaret Call, 16 Feb 1788; Henry Call, bondsman; Js. McEwen, wit.

Rampley, William & Mary Hughet, 11 May 1784; William Holbrook, bondsman; Hugh Magoune, wit.

Ramsay, Robert A. & Virginia M. C. Keistler, 20 April 1866; J. M. Shook, bondsman; Obadiah Woodson, wit.

Ramsey, Andrew & Mary Wilson, 26 Nov 1785; Jas. Willson, bondsman; Ad. Osborn, wit.

Ramsey, David & Margaret F. Graham, 2 Aug 1817; William P. Graham, bondsman; Jno. Giles, wit.

Ramsey, David & Margret Niblock, 30 May 1776; George Niblock, bondsman; Tho. Frohock, wit.

Ramsey, James & Margret Wallis, 5 Feb 1772; William Wallace, bondsman; Thomas Frohock, wit.

Ramsey, James W. & Mary McHenry, 30 Jan 1823; David McHenry, bondsman.

Ramsey, Julius D. & Ann W. Davis, 29 Oct 1851; Elijah Renshaw, bondsman; J. S. Myers, wit.

Ramsey, Robert & Mary M. Walton, 17 April 1834; David Ramsay, bondsman; John H. Hardie, wit.

Ramsey, Robert & Agness McCorkle, 18 Feb 1790; Jas. McCorkle, bondsman.

Ramsey, Thomas N. & Esther R. McNeely, 10 Jan 1852; James K. McNeely, bondsman; J. S. Myers, wit.

Randales, Charles & Nancey Willson, 6 April 1775; Alexander Neely, bondsman; Ad. Osborn, wit. consent from Jams. Willson, 7 April 1775.

Randall, Eli & Mary Brown (colored), 7 Feb 1866; David G. Julian, bondsman; Horatio N. Woodson, wit.

Randolph, W. C. & Louisa C. Vogler, 5 April 1848; J. M. Coffin, bondsman; J. H. Hardie Jr., wit.

Raney, Isam & Betsy Autridge, 28 Jan 1819; Jas. Dunn, bondsman; Jno. Giles, wit.

Rankin, James & Louisa Shuping, 20 May 1863; George W. Bostian, bondsman; Obadiah Woodson, wit.

Rankin, John D. & Mary M. S. Sechler, 18 Feb 1862; Rudolph S. W. Sechler, bondsman; Obadiah Woodson, wit. married 19 Feb 1862 by C. L. Partee, J. P.

Rankin, Levi & Malinda Knox (colored), 9 March 1866; Crawford Graham, bondsman; Obadiah Woodson, wit.

Rankin, Samuel D. & Mary E. Gillespie, 8 Nov 1843; James Cowan, bondsman; J. H. Hardie, wit.

Rantham, Levite & Ruella Robinson, 8 Dec 1792; Thomas Reed, bondsman; Jos. Chambers, wit.

Rape, Peter & Mary Shofner, 25 Sept 1779; Jno. Keagle, bondsman; Ad. Osborn, wit.

Rape, Solomon & Elizabeth Manlove, 12 Oct 1811; William Davis, bondsman; S. Davis, J. P., wit.

Raper, David & Sally Kimball, 8 April 1825; Calyer Kimball, bondsman.

Rarey, George & Magdelena Link, 8 July 1788; Jacob Link, bondsman (sein mark--his mark); Wm. Alexander, wit.

Rarey, George & Camilla Gheen, 9 Feb 1837; Burgess Cranford, bondsman; Jno. Giles, wit.

Rary, Giles & Lucinda M. Rice, 25 April 1844; Richard Steele, bondsman; J. H. Hardie, wit.

Rary, Jacob & Betsy Green, 18 May 1812; William Raney, bondsman.

Rary, Jacob & Sarah Thomas, 21 March 1850; William Howard, bondsman; J. S. Myers, wit.

Rary, James P. & Hannah Elliott, 17 Aug 1854; Upshaw D. Elliott, bondsman; J. S. Myers, wit.

Ratledge, Thomas & Lydia Holman, 14 July 1828; Daniel Casey, bondsman; Wm. Hankin, J. P., wit.

Ratts, Godfrey & Margaret Maley, 12 Dec 1809; John Shroat, bondsman; Jno. Giles, C. C., wit.

Ratts, Rinehart & Susanah Yearbrough, 12 Aug 1820; Richard Wilson, bondsman; An. Swicegood, wit.

Rattz, Godfrey & Elizabeth Gobble, 12 Jan 1799; Jacob Goble, bondsman; Edwin J. Osborn, wit.

Ray, Barea & Lyddy Travit, 10 Sept 1822; Thomas Wray, bondsman; A. R. Jones, wit.

Ray, Francis & Deborah Ervin, 4 Oct 1786; Wm. Ervin, bondsman; Mart. Osborn, wit.

Ray, James & Elizabeth Johnson, 29 Sept 1765; Wm. Nassery, Edward Parnel, bondsmen; Thomas Frohock, Whitmell Harrington, wit. consent from Gideon Johnson, 26 Sept 1765.

Ray, James T. & Margaret A. Correll, 4 April 1866; Joseph K. Burke, bondsman; Obadiah Woodson, wit.

Ray, James T. & Harriet A. Ervin, 3 Dec 1860; John T. Neal, bondsman; John Wilkinson, wit. married 4 Dec 1860 by T. W. Guthrie, Minister of the Gospel, M. E. Church, South.

Rea, Alexander & Sirer Douthit, 14 Oct 1819; Joel Chipman, bondsman; Saml Jones, J. P., wit.

Readling, Rufus M. & Margaret E. Rose, 25 March 1854; James S. Freeze, bondsman; J. S. Myers, wit.

Reary, John & Catherine Link, 8 Oct 1812; James Rix, bondsman; Geo. Dunn, wit.

Reaves, David & Patience Forlemon, 20 April 1809; Edward Reavis, bondsman; Jno March Sr., wit.

Reaves, James & Deborah Winright, 25 Oct 1803; Isaac Cowan, bondsman; Hudson Hughes, wit.

Reavis, David & Nancy Cain, 11 Nov 1815; John Reavis, Jr., bondsman; R. Powell, wit.

Reavis, Enoh & Tempy Reviss, 24 Aug 1829; Jeramiah Patrick, bondsman; Thomas McNeely, J. P., wit.

Reavis, Jesse & Alesey Cain, 8 Jan 1815; John Powell, bondsman; R. Powell, wit.

Reavis, John & Edy Beck, 28 Aug 1824; Ira W. Clark, bondsman; L. R. Rose, J. P., wit.

Recks, Nathaniel & Jane Rairey, 26 June 1827; Chs. L. Bowers, bondsman; J. H. Hardie, wit.

Rector, George & Polly Riddle, 31 July 1828; Solomon Elrod, bondsman; C. Harbin, J. P., wit.

Redley, William & Mary Ann Overcash, 13 Feb 1847; Michael Boston, bondsman; J. H. Hardie, wit.

Redman, Frederick & Margaret Setser, 22 Oct 1825; Jacob Shuping, bondsman; Hy. Giles, wit.

Redwine, Abraham & Polly Daniel, 18 June 1811; John Redwine, bondsman; Geo. Dunn, wit.

Redwine, Clark & Eve Ann Fulenwider, 7 June 1853; Calvin Cress, bondsman; J. S. Myers, wit. married 9 June 1852 by W. A. Walton, J. P.

Redwine, David & Fanny Daniel, 14 Dec 1822; Poindexter Daniel, bondsman.

Redwine, Green & Katharin Kimbrill, 10 April 1838; Abram Lentz, bondsman; E. R. Buckhead, wit.

Redwine, Jacob & Elisa Reed, 29 Oct 1835; Richard Parker, bondsman; Jno. Shaver, J. P., wit.

Redwine, Jesse & Polly Davis, 27 March 1821; Nathan Wallis, bondsman; Jno. Giles, wit.

Redwine, John & Rebecca Daniel, 24 May 1811; Abraham Redwine, bondsman; Jno. Giles, C. C., wit.

Redwine, Pleasant & Mary Ann Barringer, 10 Dec 1835; W. Stokes, bondsman.

Redwine, William & Mary Cox, 15 Aug 1820; Christian Bringle, bondsman.

Reed, Eldad & Aeshia Laning, 29 Aug 1793; Peter Reed, bondsman; Jos. Chambers, wit.

Reed, George & Cath. Chambers, 28 May 1767; Robert Chambers, bondsman; Thom. Frohock, wit.

Reed, George & Martha Green, 12 May 1785; H. Magoune, wit.

Reed, Henry & Agness Bell, 26 Dec 1766; William Bell, bondsman; Thos. Frohock, wit.

Reed, Hugh & Elizabeth Holmes, 7 Nov 1775; Richard Holmes, bondsman; Ad. Osborn, wit.

Reed, Hugh & Nancy Ball, 13 Aug 1814; John Bell, bondsman; Jno. Giles, C. C., wit.

Reed, Isaiah & Agness Luckey, 3 May 1779; Hugh Reed, bondsman; Ad. Osborn, wit.

Reed, James & Margret Baley, 2 Sept 1766; John Baily, bondsman; Thomas Frohock, D. C., wit.

Reed, James & Mary McMachan, 6 Dec 1774; William Douthit, bondsman; Ad. Osborn, wit. consent from James McMachan, 2 Dec 1774 headed "the fork of the adkin".

Reed, James & Cassina Gatha, 8 Nov 1782; Mat. Troy, bondsman.

Reed, James & Polly Davis, 26 March 1816; Alex. Shemwell, bondsman; Jno. Giles, C. C., wit.

Reed, Joel & Sarah Redwine, 2 Dec 1828; Thos. J. Reed, bondsman.

Reed, John & Levina Williams, 3 Nov 1772; Shedrick Williams, bondsman; Ad. Osborn, wit.

Reed, John & Mary McFeeters, 21 Nov 1783; Chas. McFeeters, bondsman; Wm. Crawford, wit.

Reed, John & Polly Parker, 24 Jan 1811; Jacob Smeather, bondsman; Henry Allemong, wit.

Reed, John & Rebecca Owen, 5 Jan 1814; Stephen Smith, bondsman; Geo. Dunn, wit.

Reed, James & Mary Luckey, 5 Nov 1774; John Hagin, bondsman; Ad. Osborn, wit.

Reed, Levi & Sally Helmstetler, 19 Nov 1817; William Felps, bondsman.

Reed, Noah & Ann Tomson, 19 March 1798; Jno. Ross, bondsman; Geo. Fisher, wit.

Reed, Noah & Nancy Shammell, 14 Jan 1823; Benjamin Carrel, bondsman; Hy. Giles, wit.

Reed, Samuel & Rebecah Johnston, 13 July 1808; Thomas Cox, bondsman; Jno March Sr., wit.

Reed, Thomas & Elizabeth Wilson, 23 April 1790; John Patten, bondsman; C. Caldwell, D. C., wit.

Reed, Thomas J. & Mary Miller, 2 Dec 1828; Joel Reed, bondsman.

Reed, William B. & Margaret C. Laurance, 11 May 1836; Archibald Gillespie, bondsman; Jno Giles, wit.

Reed, William E. C. & Susan Bevings, 28 Oct 1856; Abner Pace, bondsman; J. S. Myers, wit. married 28 Oct 1856 by Rev. Wm. Lambeth.

Rees, John & Elizabeth Beam, 14 Feb 1792; Gregory Doyal, bondsman; Chs. Caldwell, wit.

Rees, John & Easther Lyons, 25 April 1794; Joel Dicky, bondsman; Jo. Chambers, wit.

Reese, Fellty & Cristener Harmon, 6 April 1769; John Harmon, Fraedrick Shouse, bondsmen; Gideon Wright, wit.

Reeves, James & Christena Owens, 15 March 1834; Jacob Miller, bondsman; Hy. Giles, wit.

Reeves, Julius J. & Margaret Gillispie, 21 July 1830; George Gillespie, bondsman; Jno. H. Hardie, wit.

Reeves, Samuel & Catherine Coldiron, 20 Aug 1817; Frederick Miller, bondsman; Roberts Nanny, wit.

Reeves, Samuel & Mary Hughes, 8 Dec 1817; Silas Dunn, bondsman; Jno. Giles, wit.

Reeves, Thomas & Betsy Claver, 23 Oct 1813; Ralph Kesler, bondsman; Geo. Dunn, wit.

Reeves, Union & Elizabeth Stokes, 5 Jan 1859; Pleasant Stokes, bondsman; Levi Trexler, wit married 6 Jan 1859 by Aron Missek, J. P.

Regan, Charles & Gilly Greenwood, 13 Oct 1816; Moses Tomlinson, bondsman; Silas Peace, wit.

Regan, Filliam & Susannah Cesul, 24 Dec 1813; Thomas Cecil, bondsman; Sol. Davis, J. P., wit.

Regan, Joseph & Lucy Regens, 17 May 1838; Lawrence Porter, bondsman; L. A. Bringle, wit.

Reid, David & Ann Park, Hugh Park, bondsman; John Frohock, wit. consent from Hugh Park, 31 Aug 1769.

Reid, J. M. & Mary Earnheart, 5 Aug 1850; H. H. Coltharp, bondsman; Archd. Honeycutt, wit.

Reid, John & Sarah Sharpe, 27 Sept 1782; James Sharpe, bondsman; Ad. Osborn, wit.

Reilly, Henry & Mary Howard, 15 April 1858; Burgess Cranford, bondsman; John Wilkinson, wit. married 15 April 1858 by J. M. Brown, J. P.

Remington, Richard & Margret Largen, 13 Oct 1784; Jas. Swenford, bondsman.

Rencher, William & Nancy Leech, 11 May 1793; James Heathman, bondsman; Jos. Chambers, wit.

Rendleman, George & Eliza Roseman, 8 Oct 1834; George W. Brown, bondsman.

Rendleman, John & Nancy Brown, 11 Feb 1839; Joseph Cowan, bondsman; Hy. Giles, wit.

Renshaw, Andrew & Elisabeth Moon, 25 Feb 1812; John Brian, bondsman; Geo. Dunn, wit.

Renshaw, Francis & Rebekah Leach, 19 Aug 1816; John Renshaw, bondsman; R. Powell, wit.

Renshaw, Isaac & Jane Bryan, 4 Oct 1779; Abram Renshaw, bondsman; B. Booth Boote, wit.

Renshaw, James & Mildred Leach, 1 _____ 1809; Jacob Hinkle, bondsman; Jn. March Sr., wit.

Renshaw, John & Rebecca Dickey, 20 Sept 1805; Elisha Brown, bondsman; A. L. Osborn, D. C., wit.

Renshaw, John & Sarah Emberson, 12 June 1815; John Davis, bondsman; R. Powell, wit.

Renshaw, John & Mary Dunahoo, 3 Sept 1819; Thos. Renshaw,
bondsman; Hy. Giles, wit.

Renshaw, Robert & Polly Freeze, 19 Oct 1827; Wm. B. Willson,
bondsman; Jno. H. Hardie, wit.

Renshaw, Robert J. & Elizabeth A. Mason, 13 Jan 1834; Milas
Renshaw, bondsman; Thomas McNeely, J. P., wit.

Renshaw, Samuel & Peggy Trott, 3 Oct 1798; John Renshaw,
bondsman; Ma. Troy, wit.

Renshaw, Thomas & Prudey Rathage, 22 Feb 1823; William Smith Jr.,
bondsman; L. R. Rose, wit.

Renshaw, Thomas N. & Mary F. Huie, 7 Dec 1860; J. C. Irvin,
bondsman; John Wilkinson, wit. married 13 Dec 1860 by R. A.
Willis, Minister of the Gospel.

Renshaw, William & Mary Ann Luckey, 9 Oct 1786; Robert Buntain,
bondsman; Jno Macay, wit.

Renshaw, William & Mary Moore, 2 Feb 1796; James Orten, bondsman;
A. Balfour, wit.

Renshaw, William & Margaret Luckey, 20 Oct 1825; George E.
Cannon, bondsman; M. A. Giles, wit.

Rentleman, Jacob & Elizabeth Fullinwider, 20 Nov 1804; John
Linn, bondsman; Moses A. Locke, wit.

Repult, Jesse M. & Sarah Rice, 18 Aug 1847; David Heathman,
bondsman; J. H. Hardie Jr., wit.

Repult, John & Maryan Chambers, 2 June 1846; Tho. B. Cowan,
bondsman; J. M. Turner, wit.

Repult, John & Sarah C. Phifer, 13 June 1854; Thos. C. McNeely,
bondsman; J. S. Myers, wit.

Repult, Joshua & Ann Marland, 30 Sept 1811; John Clary, bondsman; Jno. Giles, C. C., wit.

Reudasil, John & Nancy Cook, 10 Dec 1832; Jonas Wisher,
bondsman.

Revells, John & Eliza Carter, 29 Aug 1855; Thomas C. Winders,
bondsman; J. S. Myers, wit.

Reves, Solomon & Sarah Maden, 9 April 1812; Richard W. Maddan,
bondsman; Jno. Giles, C. C., wit.

Revis, Joel P. & Susan A. Earnhardt, 6 Feb 1859; married 6 Feb
1859 by F. W. Scott, J. P., wit.

Rex, Alfred & Elizabeth Kennon, 25 Nov 1829; Richard Harrison,
bondsman; J. H. Hardie, wit.

Rex, George & Mary Emberson, 1 June 1830; Daniel Webb,
bondsman; Jno. H. Hardie, wit.

Rex, George & Amelia Dent, 18 June 1818; Aaron Pinkston,
bondsman; Jno. Giles, wit.

Rex, George W. & Mary E. Dobbin, 24 Jan 1850; Julius A. Neely, bondsman.

Rex, James & Sarah Plummer, 26 Jan 1815; Jacob Reary, bondsman; Geo. Dunn, wit.

Rex, John W. & Sarah Bowers, 20 Oct 1818; Jonathan Hulan, bondsman.

Rex, William & Caroline Frazier, 20 Nov 1844; Richard Burroughs, bondsman; John H. Hardie, wit.

Rex, William & Elizabeth Frazier, 30 April 1856; William Graham, bondsman; J. S. Myers, wit.

Reynolds, David N. & Nancey Tayloer, 27 Dec 1825; Samuel F. Reynolds, bondsman; Jac. Beddington, wit.

Reynolds, Henry & Anne Ward, 23 Dec 1793; Thomas Standly, bonds-man; John Pinchback, Lydia Pinchback, wit.

Reynolds, J. M. & Sarah E. Pearson, 17 Dec 1850; Myer Myers, bondsman.

Reynolds, Thomas & Elizabeth Williams, 30 Sept 1808; Christian Prow, bondsman.

Reynolds, William & Jane Huie, 21 Nov 1849; J. M. Brown, bondsman.

Rheudasil, Henry H. & Martha C. Evans, 4 Feb 1853; Wm. A. Luckey, bondsman; J. S. Myers, wit.

Rhymert, George & Elizabeth Beaver, 1 June 1824; Andrew Bostian Jr., bondsman; Hy. Giles, wit.

Rial, J. G. & _____, 14 June 1762; John Lewis Beard, bonds-man; John Frohock, C. C., wit.

Ribelein, Jesse & Elizabeth Trexler, 5 May 1846; Benjamin Braddy, bondsman.

Ribelin, Asa & Susan C. Walton, 23 April 1842; Alexander Brown, bondsman; Thm. Sneed, wit.

Ribelin, Isaac & Polly Agle, 10 Aug 1822; George Vogler, bondsman; Jno. Giles, wit.

Ribelin, Jacob & _____, _____ 1802; Daniel Agner, bondsman; Jno. McClelland, wit.

Ribelin, Jacob & Nancy Smith, 3 Feb 1825; Nathan Brown, bondsman; Hy. Giles, wit.

Ribelin, Jacob & Susana Shelton, 20 Oct 1827; Thomas M. Buford, bondsman; Thomas McNeely, J. P., wit.

Ribelin, Jesse & Catharine Goodman, 23 Jan 1858; Christopher Goodman, bondsman; Levi Trexler, wit. married 23 Jan 1858 by Levi Trexler, J. P.

Ribelin, Paul & Maria Eagle, 19 March 1851; Julius D. Ramsey, bondsman; James E. Kerr, wit.

Ribelin, Samuel & Margaret Holdshouser, 7 May 1831; Danl. H. Cress, bondsman; Hy. Giles, wit.

Ribelin, William & Mary Kiher, 29 Oct 1779; Martin Raiblin, bondsman; Jo Brevard, wit.

Rice, Allen & Peggy Cleary, 8 March 1791; Wm. Hamton, bondsman; C. Caldwell, D. C., wit.

Rice, Allen & Jane Bodenhamer, 23 Dec 1815; John Bodenhamer, bondsman; Sol. Davis, J. P., wit.

Rice, Cathew & Nancy Hellard, 11 Aug 1841; David Heathman, bondsman; Susan T. Giles, wit.

Rice, Coleman & Polly Wood, 12 April 1813; Philip Wray, bondsman; Geo. Dunn, wit.

Rice, Edmund & Jane Culbertson, 3 June 1834; Hezekiah Turner, bondsman; Thomas McNeely, J. P., wit.

Rice, Edmund & Elizabeth H. Robison, 30 Jan 1851; David Heathman, bondsman; James E. Kerr, wit. married 6 Feb 1851 by Wm. A. Hall.

Rice, Elijah & Sarah Barber, 20 Oct 1853; Peter Casper, bondsman; J. S. Myers, wit.

Rice, Enoch & Polly Sands, 13 April 1817; Walter Richards, bondsman; Jno Monroe, wit.

Rice, Francis & Mima Oliver, 12 Feb 1802; Daniel Clary, bondsman; Jno Brem, wit.

Rice, John & Elizabeth Heathman, 24 Feb 1855; John M. Heathman, bondsman; J. S. Myers, wit. married 25 Feb 1855 by Geo. B. Wetmore, Pastor of St. Andrews Church, Rowan.

Rice, John Y. & Elizabeth Bird, 5 Nov 1849; Amos R. Rice, bondsman; James E. Kerr, wit.

Rice, Phillip & Sarrey Tommison, 29 Jan 1806; Dnl. Clary, bondsman; Ad. Osborn, wit.

Rice, Samuel & Lucy Brooks, 30 July 1806; Wm. Hampton, bondsman; A. L. Osborn, wit.

Rice, Thomas & Betsey Wood, 27 Dec 1818; Ths. Reed, bondsman; Jno. Giles, wit.

Rice, Thomas S. & Mary R. Elliott, 9 Feb 1854; Geo. M. Lyerly, bondsman; J. S. Myers, wit.

Rice, William B. & Sally Marland, 2 May 1812; John Burke, bondsman.

Rich, J. W. & Mollie E. Brown, 19 Oct 1865; Wm. Smithdeal, bondsman; Obadiah Woodson, wit.

Rich, John & Nancey Uptegrove, 12 Feb 1808; Ezekeel Philips, bondsman; Jn. March Sr., wit.

Richard, Elias & Sarah Jones, 15 Jan 1817; Moses Merion, bondsman; Z. Hunt, J. P., wit.

Richards, Josiah & Laura Jane Milton, married 31 Dec 1855 by Ephraim Mauney, J. P.

Richardson, Edward & Mary Lock, 22 July 1786; Peter Faust, bondsman; Jno. Macay, wit.

Richardson, John & Seuse Beck, 7 May 1803; Jacob Beck, bondsman.

Richardson, John & Mary Dyson, 9 April 1822; Josiah Smoot, bondsman.

Richardson, Solomon & Becca Wassin, 24 Aug 1822; John Foard, bondsman; M. A. Giles, wit.

Richardson, William & Elizabeth Cline, 22 Oct 1860; U. D. Elliott, bondsman; James E. Kerr, wit. married 23 Oct 1860 by Wm. L. Marlin, J. P.

Richart, John D. & Margaret C. Smith, 4 Feb 1864; Richard A. Smith, bondsman; Obadiah Woodson, wit.

Richey, George H. & Eliza Safret, 4 Feb 1852; William Seafret, bondsman; J. S. Myers, wit.

Richey, George M. & Jane Hellard, married 20 Jan 1853 by J. Thomason, J. P.

Richwine, Martin & Rebecca C. Brown, 25 April 1854; Luke Blackmer, bondsman; J. S. Myers, wit. married 26 April 1854 by A. Baker, Pastor of the Presbyterian Ch., Salisbury.

Richey, George M. & Mary Sophia James, 4 March 1862; John C. Correll, bondsman; Obadiah Woodson, wit.

Richey, Jacob M. & Margaret D. Bostian, 12 Sept 1853; George H. Richey, bondsman; J. S. Myers, wit.

Richie, John & L. M. Holshouser, 15 Aug 1860; F. M. Y. McNeely, bondsman; Wm. Locke, wit.

Richison, Stephen & Elizabeth Jenkens, 1 May 1831; Wm. Richison, bondsman; Wm. Hawkins, wit.

Richy, George H. & Leah L. Propts, 19 July 1848; Valentine Propst, bondsman; J. H. Hardie, wit.

Richy, Henry & Peggy Fulk, 23 July 1824; Jos. Rodgers, bondsman.

Rickard, George & Nancy Boyd, 9 Nov 1813; John Burkhart, bondsman; Geo. Dunn, wit.

Rickard, Jasper & Mary Shules, 18 Aug 1787; Beacham Hilton, bondsman; Jno. Macay, wit.

Rickard, Leonard & Mary Shafer, 8 _____ 1785; John Tut, bondsman; Hugh Magoune, wit.

Rickard, Philip & Polly Friddle, 24 March 1829; Thomas F. Barr, bondsman; Jno. H. Hardie, wit.

Rickat, Jacob & Ann Locke, 25 Sept 1832; Abel Cowan, bondsman.

Rickets, Jonathan & Sareene Burns, 3 Feb 1813; James L. Smith, bondsman; Geo. Dunn, wit.

Rickhard, Will. & Luara Smith, 26 Nov 1859; Jno. A. Whitmon, bondsman; Wm. Locke, wit. married 27 Nov 1859 by M. Plumer, J. P.

Rickmon, Jesse & Mary Tranham, 10 Jan 1791; Samuel Owin, bondsman; C. Caldwell, D. C., wit.

Riddel, Stephen & Elizabeth Stockstill, 19 June 1772; Evan Ellis, bondsman; Basil Gaither, wit.

Riddle, Benjamin & Ellander Henline, 14 June 1813; John Henline, bondsman; Jn. March Sr., wit.

Riddle, Henry & Nancey Rinnick, 16 May 1817; Aquillar Cheshier, bondsman; Jn. March Sr., wit.

Riddle, John & Polly Mock, 28 Nov 1820; Solomon Elrod, bondsman; R. Powell, wit.

Riddle, R. & Martha L. Poteet, 11 May 1865; Jack Hall, bondsman; Obadiah Woodson, wit.

Riddle, William & Nancey Slater, 27 May 1817; Benjamin Riddle, bondsman; Jn March Sr., wit.

Ridenhour, Edward A. & Lydia H. Albright, 17 March 1865; L. S. Earnheart, bondsman; Obadiah Woodson, wit.

Ridenhour, Harris M. & Levina Miller, 18 Oct 1844; John J. Miller, bondsman; John H. Hardie Jr., wit.

Ridenhour, John & Betsy File, 5 April 1798; Henry Fesberman, bondsman.

Ridgway, Ausburn & Jane Phelps, 29 Sept 1803; David McBride, bondsman; J. Hunt, wit.

Ridings, James & Susannah Griggs, 12 May 1768; James Condon, West Cornelius, bondsmen; Thomas Frohock, wit. consent from Joseph Murphey, 10 May 1768.

Ridings, William & Milly Head, consent only from George Head, 15 March 1769; Wit: Tyree Glen, Joseph Murphey.

Ridley, Sedon S. & Peggy Wilds, 5 April 1813; Edward Old, bondsman; Geo. Dunn, wit.

Rigan, William & Maria Criddelbough, 25 Feb 1816; Joseph Idol, bondsman; Sol. Davis, J. P., wit.

Riggan, Jacob & Elizabeth Teague, 15 Jan 1818; Barnet Idol, bondsman; Sol. Davis, J. P., wit.

Riggs, Reuben & Mary Crawford, 2 March 1769; Edward Riggs, David Crawford, bondsmen; Gideon Wright, wit.

Rights, Christian Lewis & Elizabeth Hughes, 5 Sept 1842; Samuel W. James, bondsman; Thm. Sneed, wit.

Rights, Mathew & Elizabeth Hege, _____ 1819; John C. Blum, bondsman; Jno. Giles, wit.

Riley, Joshua & Chloe Russel, 5 Feb 1815; Henry Russel, bondsman; R. Powell, wit.

Riley, Joshua & Elizabeth Miller, 21 May 1826; James Ethesson, bondsman; John Giles, Clk., wit.

Riley, Peter & Rebecca Cox, 5 May 1817; William Cox, bondsman;
R. Harriss, J. P., wit.

Rimer, Henry & Sally Wendel, 20 Nov 1824; John Klutts, bondsman;
Hy. Giles, wit.

Rimer, Jacob W. & Mary A. Corl, 15 Nov 1855; David A. Rimer,
bondsman; J. S. Myers, wit.

Rimer, James Wiley & Lydia Ann Hill, 19 April 1859; Samuel
Monroe Rimer, bondsman; married 21 April 1859 by Saml.
Rothrock, Minister of the Gospel in the Ev. Luth. Church.

Rimer, John & Sophia Shulaberger, 1 March 1828; John W. Klutts,
bondsman; Jno. Giles, wit.

Rimer, John & Sally Holshouser, 3 Oct 1854; Thomas Rimer, bondsman; J. S. Myers, wit. married 5 Oct 1854 by Jos. A. Linn.

Rimer, Leonard & Eleanor Cauble, 30 March 1865; Danl. M. Sewell,
bondsman; Obadiah Woodson, wit.

Rimer, Mathias & Anne Earnhart, 12 Nov 1840; D. Wise, bondsman.

Rimer, Michael & Barbary Eller, 23 Aug 1832; J. S. Myers,
bondsman.

Rimer, Moses & Sarah M. Weant, 16 June 1842; C. A. Weant, bondsman; J. H. Hardie, wit.

Rimer, Nicholas & Mary Plyler, 25 March 1814; John Beaver,
bondsman; Jno. Giles, C. C., wit.

Rimer, Samuel M. & Sarah Jane Hill, 12 April 1859; Jacob W.
Rimer, bondsman; married 12 April 1859 by Saml. Rothrock,
Minister of the Gospel in the Ev. Luth. Church.

Rimer, Thomas & Fanny Hill, 24 March 1831; Guy Hill, bondsman;
B. Craige, wit.

Rimer, Thomas & Mary Rimer, 27 Sept 1836; John Shaver, bondsman.

Rimer, Volentine & Hannah Garner, 5 Aug 1811; John Garner,
bondsman; Jno. Giles, C. C., wit.

Rimerd, Peter & Polly Pearce, 30 May 1814; John Giles, C. C., wit.

Rinaman, Zachariah & Patience Smith, 2 May 1801; Walter Rinaman,
bondsman; Wm. Welborn, wit.

Rindley, William & Elizabeth Mils, 13 Jan 1811; Isaac Morgan,
bondsman; E. Morgan, J. P., wit.

Rinehart, John & Sally Boger, 30 Sept 1828; George Yost, bondsman; Jno. H. Hardie, wit.

Rintleman, John F. & Mary Wright, 8 Sept 1779; Jonas Young,
bondsman; Ad. Osborn, wit.

Rintleman, Martin & Mary Fur, 12 Aug 1783; Henry Fur, bondsman;
Jno. McNairy, wit.

Ritcherson, Stephen & Elizabeth Howel, 3 Feb 1796; John Doty,
bondsman; A. Balfour, wit.

Ritchey, Daniel M. & Tripheny Miller, 6 Jan 1855; Pleasant
Ritchey, bondsman; Levi Trexler, wit.

Ritchey, George & Betsey Phifer, 29 April 1817; Nicholas Rimer,
bondsman; Jno Giles, wit.

Ritchey, John & Eve Walsher, 4 July 1842; Dawald Lentz,
bondsman; Thm. Sneed, wit.

Ritchey, John & Sarah Rymer, 29 March 1850; Matthias Rimer,
bondsman; J. S. Myers, wit.

Ritchey, Noah & Franey Freeze, 26 Feb 1838; Jacob Fesperman,
bondsman; Hy Giles, wit.

Ritchey, Peter A. & Maria King, 4 Feb 1851; E. E. Philips,
bondsman.

Ritchie, George H. & Margaret S. James, married 11 March 1862
by F. H. Wood.

Ritchie, George M. & Martha J. Thomason, 18 Dec 1860; Franklin
W. Thomason, bondsman; Wm. Locke, wit. married 18 Dec 1861
by J. Thomason, J. P.

Ritchie, George M. & Jane Hellard, 20 Jan 1853; Peter A. Ritchie,
bondsman; J. S. Myers, wit.

Ritchie, Matthias & Nancy Mesimer, 16 June 1860; Anderson Morgan,
bondsman; John Wilkinson, wit. married 16 June 1860 by
Peter Williamson, J. P.

Ritchie, Peter A. & Elizabeth C. Shuping, 30 May 1865; S. J. M.
Brown, bondsman; Obadiah Woodson, wit.

Ritchy, John M. & Margaret Linn, 6 April 1840; John Fesperman,
bondsman; J. L. Beard, D. C., wit.

Ritchy, Noah & Sarah Freeze, 27 Jan 1846; Caleb Hampton, bondsman; J. H. Hardie Jr., wit.

Ritchy, Paul & Elizabeth Coleman, 12 March 1831; Aaron Coleman,
bondsman; Jno. H. Hardie, wit.

Ritinghur, Daniel & Betsey Buzzard, 26 Dec 1815; Michael Walker,
bondsman; Jno. Giles, C. C., wit.

Rivs, Ephraim & Sh. Chauman, 15 Oct 1798; Jas. Carrigen, bondsman; Edwin J. Osborn, D. C., wit.

Rix, John & Rachael Huskey, 5 Feb 1780; Lewis Beard, bondsman;
B. Booth Boote, wit.

Roach, James & Margret Trantham (no date, during Gov. Martin's
term); Willm. Crawford, bondsman; Wm. Crawford, wit.

Roads, Adam & Susey Fox, 30 Sept 1796; Marmaduke Nicholds,
bondsman; Jno. Rogers, wit.

Roan, Tunstall & Milley Bagby, 18 April 1766; Will Elliss,
bondsman; Thomas Frohock, wit.

Roark, William & Margrit Yose, 25 Nov 1768; John Wilson,
bondsman; Tho. Frohock, wit.

Robards, John R. & Sarah Smith, 27 Dec 1824; Jacob Ribelin, bondsman.

Robards, Larance & Susanah Foster, 1 May 1809; John Owings, bondsman; Jn. March Sr., wit.

Robeeson, Henry & Elizabeth Archaball, 19 Oct 1766; Willm. Archbald, bondsman; Thos. Frohock, wit.

Robensin, Jonathan & Elizabeth Freeman, 9 Oct 1821; Daniel Wood, bondsman; Hy. Giles, wit.

Roberts, Enoch & Polly Rousey, 25 Nov 1815; Larrance Owings, bondsman; Jno. Giles, wit.

Roberts, Humphry & Matty Cowan, 20 Jan 1811; William Howard, bondsman; Ezra Allemong, wit.

Roberts, John & Katharine Foster, 5 Jan 1777; James Foster, bondsman; Ad. Osborn, wit.

Roberts, John & Hellen Owins, 22 Feb 1779; Elijah Owings, bondsman; Ad. Osborn, wit.

Roberts, John & Sarah Gheen, 9 Nov 1795; Thomas Gheen, bondsman; J. Troy, wit.

Roberts, Joshua & Sarah Waddle, 5 Nov 1781; Wm. McKnight, bondsman; Ad. Osborn, wit.

Roberts, Shad. & Elenor Roberts, _____ 1785; Nathaniel Lewis, bondsman.

Roberts, Shadrach & Katharin Turner, 3 May 1773; Thomas Turner, John Turner, bondsmen; Ad. Osborn, wit.

Roberts, Shadrick & Christianna Swink, 6 Dec 1811; George Swink, bondsman; Geo. Dunn, wit.

Roberts, Thomas & Margaret White, 29 Nov 1779; Nicholas White, bondsman; B. Booth Boote, wit.

Roberts, Warren & Magdalin Ratz, 27 Aug 1804; Solomon Coats, bondsman; A. L. Osborn, D. C., wit.

Roberts, William & Anne Nerren, 18 Jan 1779; Benn. Nerren, bondsman; Wm. R. Davie, wit.

Roberts, William & Margaret Admire, _____ Sept 1793; John Stinchcomb, bondsman; Jos. Chambers, wit.

Roberts, William & Julia Frederica Lebeg, 14 March 1816; Lewis Jinkins, bondsman; R. Powell, wit.

Robertson, David & Mary Sheuls, 29 Nov 1808; Hugh Robertson, bondsman; S. Davis, J. P., wit.

Robeson, John & Sarah Cook, 12 Feb 1788; Mich. Troy, bondsman; Js. McEwen, wit.

Robey, Barton & Cloe Turner, 12 March 1821; William C. Summers, bondsman; Hy. Giles, wit.

Robins, Absalom & Sarah Spurgins, 12 Dec 1815; Christopher Robins, bondsman; Sol. Davis, J. P., wit.

Robins, Daniel & Phebe Teague, 5 Aug 1815; William Bodenhamer, bondsman; J. Manlove, wit.

Robins, Richard & Margret Anderson, 26 March 1765; Christopher Nation, bondsman; John Frohock, C. C., wit.

Robinson, David & Nancy Heler, 19 Feb 1813; Giles Johnson, bondsman; Geo. Dunn, wit.

Robinson, J. H. & E. Jane Carter, 11 Sept 1855; C. A. Morphis, bondsman; Jac. C. Barnhardt, wit. married 11 Sept 1855 by Jos. A. Linn.

Robinson, Joel & Jane Dailey, 16 Dec 1824; Wm. Heathman, bondsman; Hy. Giles, wit.

Robinson, Samuel & Rebecca McRorie (colored), 19 Aug 1865; married 20 Aug 1865 by Zuck Haughton.

Robinson, Thomas & Hannah Lewis, 15 May 1810; Samuel Thrift, bondsman; Geo. Dunn, wit.

Robison, Benjamin & Eals Lock, 19 Feb 1765; Peter Johnson, Robt. Pearis, Henry Horah, Wm. Temple Coles, bondsmen.

Robison, David & Isabella Anderson, 28 Nov 1780; Wm. Anderson, bondsman; Ad. Osborn, wit.

Robison, George & Jean McBroom, 10 Feb 1824; John Dobbin, bondsman.

Robison, George & Welthy Ann Blackwell, 1 Feb 1826; Joseph Blackwell, bondsman.

Robison, George & Mary Bell (no date, during Gov. Martin's term), Hugh Robison, bondsman.

Robison, George S. & Nancy Cowan, 18 Feb 1824; Jno. M. McConnaughey, bondsman.

Robison, Henry & Sarah Wilson, 9 June 1788; George Wilson, bondsman; W. Alexander, wit.

Robison, Henry & Margery Andrew, 9 Feb 1795; Richard Lock, bondsman; J. Troy, wit.

Robison, Henry & Nancy Culbertson, 28 March 1842; Wm. A. Luckey, bondsman; Jno. H. Hardie, wit.

Robison, Henry E. & Christena Shuping, 30 Nov 1846; Thomas S. Atwell, bondsman; John H. Hardie Jr., wit.

Robison, Hugh & Sarah Ann Brown, 2 Aug 1838; Henry Robison, bondsman; S. Lemly Jr., wit.

Robison, James H. & H. E. Freeze, 22 Sept 1859; Isaac Lyerly, bondsman; married 22 Sept 1859 by N. F. Hall, J. P.

Robison, James K. & Margaret Lyerly, 9 Dec 1857; James Gardner, bondsman; J. S. Myers, James E. Kerr, wit. married 10 Dec 1857 by W. R. Fraley, J. P.

Robison, John & Polly Powless, 14 Nov 1826; Henry Weaver, bondsman; Jno. H. Hardie, wit.

Robison, Jos. & Mary Taylor, 1 March 1784; Wm. Crawford, bondsman; Jno. McNairy, wit.

Robison, Moses & Mary Robinson, 7 Feb 1788; Richard Trotter, bondsman; Js. McEwen, wit.

Robison, Richard & Rebecka Easter, 9 Nov 1791; Jesse Brookshire, bondsman; Chs. Caldwell, wit.

Robison, Richard & Isabella McHenry, 17 Oct 1798; Wm. Robison, bondsman; Edwin J. Osborn, D., wit.

Robison, Richard & Polly R. Barkley, 23 Sept 1817; Richard Robison Jr., bondsman; Jno. Giles, wit.

Robison, Richard & Elizabeth Barkley, 25 Feb 1818; Thos. Todd, bondsman; Jno. Giles, wit.

Robison, Richard & _____, 26 Feb 1831; Abel Graham, bondsman; Jno. Giles, wit.

Robison, Samuel & Lucind Hall, 16 March 1820; John Cowan, bondsman.

Robison, Thoms. T. & Sarah A. Nash, 21 July 1858; James Gardner, bondsman; John Wilkinson, wit.

Robison, William & Elizabeth Robinson, 24 Aug 1803; James Nevins, bondsman; A. L. Osborn, D. C., wit.

Robison, Wm. & Agness Hogg, 8 July 1766; John Burnet, bondsman; Thomas Frohock, wit.

Robley, John & Elizabeth Ennis, 7 Jan 1791; J. George Laumann, bondsman; C. Caldwell, D. C., wit.

Robley, John & Betsy A. Nanny, 13 May 1824; Isaac Anderson Hall, bondsman; Hy. Giles, wit.

Roblin, Lewis & Barbara Helseley, 28 July 1800; David Burly, bondsman.

Robling, James & Mary Hill, 8 Nov 1823; John Barnes, bondsman; Hy. Giles, wit.

Robling, John & Elizabeth Traylor, 18 Oct 1818; Peter Robling, bondsman.

Robling, Lewis & Mary Barns, 25 Oct 1819; James Barnes, bondsman; Jno. Giles, wit.

Robling, Peter & Nancy Johnson, 27 Oct 1814; Isaac Simpson, bondsman; Jno. Smith, wit.

Robling, William & Polly Miller, 3 Oct 1819; Robin Wren, bondsman; Jno. Giles, wit.

Roby, Absalom & Polly Turner, 17 Aug 1822; William Turner, bondsman; L. R. Rose, J. P., wit.

Rodgers, J. C. & Margaret E. Rodgers, 6 Nov 1865; Tho. J. Foster, bondsman; Horation N. Woodson, wit.

Rodgers, James N. & Elizabeth Stirewalt, 13 April 1846; Jacob Stirewalt, bondsman; John H. Hardie, wit.

Rodgers, John & Wilhelmene Sloop, 23 Oct 1848; John Sloop, bondsman; J. H. Hardie, wit.

Rodgers, John C. & Jane L. Barr, 29 Sept 1851; R. R. Barr, bondsman; J. S. Myers, wit. married 30 Sept 1851 by John K. Graham, J. P.

Rodgers, Leonard F. & Martha H. Pogue, 20 Dec 1858; John C. Rodgers, bondsman; John Wilkinson, wit.

Rodgers, Lewis & Betsey Dowel, 10 Dec 1817; Reuben Burgess, bondsman; R. Powell, wit.

Rodgers, Martin & Caty Blackwelder, 24 Nov 1828; Sheppard Cole, bondsman; Jno. H. Hardie, wit.

Rodgers, Solomon C. & Margaret L. Barr, 24 Jan 1851; John C. Rodgers, bondsman; James E. Kerr, wit.

Rodgers, William & Rhody Skien, 12 Jan 1847; Burgess Wright, bondsman; J. H. Hardie Jr., wit.

Rodgers, William A. & Elmira Correll, 7 Feb 1842; McGuire Phillips, bondsman.

Rogers, Allin & Mary B. Shaver, 15 Oct 1801; Benjamin Davis, bondsman; Jno Brem, wit.

Rogers, Bennett & Drucilla Burgess, 20 Jan 1827; Moses Burgess, bondsman; L. R. Rose, J. P., wit.

Rogers, Drury & Ritte Bankston, 26 Feb 1800; Benjamin Rogers, bondsman; Edwin J. Osborn, D. C., wit.

Rogers, Elisha & Phebe Serrat, 20 Nov 1821; Frederick Goss, bondsman; Jno Giles, wit.

Rogers, George R. & Mary C. Rodgers, 4 Aug 1855; Jacob Stire-walt, bondsman; J. S. Myers, wit. married 8 Aug 1855 by C. S. Partee, J. P.

Rogers, Jeremiah & Laura V. Rose, 28 Sept 1865; Wm. Rogers, bondsman; Obadiah Woodson, wit. married 28 Sept 1865 by Rev. Wm. Lambeth.

Rogers, John & Zelpha Pitman, 12 March 1779; John Dunn, bonds-man; Ad. Osborn, wit.

Rogers, John W. & Margaret Albright, 14 Aug 1832; Joseph Rogers, bondsman.

Rogers, Joseph & Ann Graham, 24 Feb 1804; ____ Graham, bondsman; A. L. Osborn, D. C., wit.

Rogers, Robert & Jenny Mahon, 9 Jan 1811; Samuel Mahan, bonds-man; Geo. Dunn, wit.

Rogers, Robert & Nancy Dowel, 27 March 1806; Braxson Bryan, bondsman; Lewis Bryan, wit.

Rogers, Roland & Catharine Sevitz, 5 Oct 1803; Daniel Clary, bondsman; A. L. Osborn, D. C., wit.

Rogers, William & Polly Bostian, 19 Dec 1818; James Lamm, bondsman; Jno. Giles, wit.

Rogers, William & Christena G. Sechler, 28 Oct 1845; Henry
Sloop, bondsman; John H. Hardie Jr., wit.

Rogers, Zachariah & Sarah Chesher, 15 Aug 1820; Thos. Hatcher,
bondsman.

Roges, Asa M. & Jane Silliman, 26 July 1844; Thomas A. Rogers,
bondsman; J. H. Hardie, wit.

Roggers, John & Margret Smith, 5 Dec 1803; Joel Jinkins, bondsman; John March, wit.

Roland, Michael & Mary Howlett, 6 May 1857; John Shuman Sen.,
bondsman; James E. Kerr, wit. married 6 May 1857 by Jno. J.
Shaver.

Rominger, Jacob & Mary Wesner, 28 Jan 1823; John Folts, bondsman; W. S. Hanes, J. P., wit.

Rominger, Joseph & Susanah Crater, 26 March 1813; David Rominger,
bondsman; John Hanes, wit.

Rominger, Philip & Elisabeth Kreter, 16 Dec 1807; Thomas Yarrell,
bondsman; Lazarus Hege, J. P., wit.

Rosebrough, James & Elizabeth Luckey, 1 Feb 1776; John Luckie,
John Rosebrough, bondsman; Ad. Osborn, wit.

Rose, Allen & Elizabeth Eddlemon, 26 March 1835; Charles A.
Rose, bondsman.

Rose, Charles A. & Sarah Carriker, 20 Feb 1837; Daniel Carriker,
bondsman; Jno Giles, wit.

Rose, John A. & Mary Mehaley Walker, 25 Aug 1858; Jas. A.
Blackwelder, bondsman; married 9 Sept 1858 by Rev. B. C. Hall.

Rose, John F. & Martha Freeze, 15 April 1830; Danl. H. Cress,
bondsman; Jno. H. Hardie, wit.

Rosebrough, James & Julia Pittman, 14 Jan 1826; Samuel Davidson,
bondsman; Hy. Giles, wit.

Rosebrough, William & Daras Hall, 15 Nov 1769; Thomas Hall,
Samuel Long, bondsmen.

Rosebrough, William & Margret Sloan, 25 June 1787; Thomas Hall,
bondsman.

Roseman, Adam & Elizabeth Holshouser, 11 Dec 1820; Daniel
Propes, bondsman; Hy. Giles, wit.

Roseman, David & Eliza M. Roseman, 13 Dec 1841; Michael Bostian,
bondsman; Susan T. Giles, wit.

Roseman, George & Catharine Buzzard, 26 Sept 1800; Jacob
Coleman, bondsman.

Roseman, James C. & Christian Deal, 1 July 1841; David Roseman,
bondsman; Jno. Giles, wit.

Roseman, John W. & Mary M. Kesler, 4 March 1848; E. H. Roseman,
bondsman; J. S. Hardie, wit.

Roseman, Peter & Mary Duke, 16 Sept 1800; Jacob Duke, bondsman;
Jno. Brem, wit.

Ross, James & Charlotte Burnam, 15 April 1841; George Wise,
bondsman; Susan T. Giles, wit.

Ross, James & Peggy Youst, 13 Aug 1812; Jno. Ross, bondsman;
Jno. Giles, C. C., wit.

Ross, John & Rachel Hill, 13 April 1785; Andrew Smith, bondsman;
Hu. Magoune, wit.

Ross, John & Rabecah Ellis, 12 Aug 1811; Jas. Daniel, bondsman;
Geo. Dunn, wit.

Ross, John & Catherine Bullen, 30 Sept 1796; Isaac Moore,
bondsman; Jno. Rogers, wit.

Ross, Thomas & Catharine Youst, 19 Dec 1810; Christian Tarr,
bondsman; Jno. Giles, C. C., wit.

Ross, William & Elizabeth Paterson, 24 Aug 1795; John Patterson,
bondsman.

Rotan, James & Delia Walton, 27 June 1844; Alexander Swicegood,
bondsman; J. H. Hardie Jr., wit.

Rothrock, Jacob & Elizabeth Logan, 23 Jan 1806; Peter Rothrock,
bondsman; Jno. Monroe, wit.

Rothrock, Philip & Suzanah Hege, 31 Jan 1814; Vollentine Hege,
bondsman; Joseph Clarke, wit.

Rothrock, Samuel & Emilie Arey, 13 Sept 1837; Benjamin F.
Fraley, bondsman; Hy. Giles, wit.

Rouch, Daniel & Barbaray Wise, 29 Nov 1810; David Woodson,
bondsman; Jno. Giles, C. C., wit.

Rough, Amos & Sarah Casper, 14 July 1846; Robt. W. Long,
bondsman; Jno. H. Hardie, wit.

Rough, Charles & Elizabeth Frick, 17 July 1842; Jacob File,
bondsman; J. H. Hardie, wit.

Rough, Charles & Rosanna Stouck, 7 Feb 1848; George Eler,
bondsman.

Rough, Danel & Rachel Smith, 2 Dec 1815; William Rough, bondsman; Geo. Dunn, wit.

Rough, Daniel & Catharine Rickes, 16 Dec 1794; John Rough,
bondsman; J. Troy, D. C., wit.

Rough, John & Mary Kepley, 3 Aug 1820; Peter Kepley, bondsman;
Jno. Giles, wit.

Rough, Peter & Polly Wise, 7 Feb 1834; Charles Arnheart,
bondsman; Wm. Locke, wit.

Rough, Peter & Rachel Bost, 13 March 1843; Alexander Bost,
bondsman; J. H. Hardie, wit.

Rough, Peter & Tempy Phillips, 30 Sept 1852; Jos. Eller,
bondsman; J. S. Myers, wit.

Rough, William & Catharine Claver, 9 March 1811; Samuel Lemly, bondsman; Ezra Allemong, wit.

Roughy, Daniel & Polly Weaver, 28 Dec 1825; Henry Smith, bondsman; Jno. Giles, wit.

Rounsaval, Benjamin & Margaret Enochs, 3 Dec 1774; Jo. Rounsavall, bondsman; Ad. Osborn, wit.

Rounsavall, David & Elizabeth Leonard, 3 July 1790; William Moore, bondsman; C. Caldwell, D. C., wit.

Rounsavall, Josiah & Jane Moore, 14 Oct 1797; W. Moors, bondsman; Jno. Rogers, wit.

Rouse, Leonard & Eloner Gillispy, 10 Feb 1768; Benjamin Williams, Joseph Donoho, bondsmen; Tho. Frohock, wit.

Row, Jacob & Mary Slater, 13 April 1818; Jno. Giles, Clk, wit.

Rowe, Stephen A. & Crissy L. Klutts, 24 March 1866; Jesse Klutts, bondsman; Obadiah Woodson, wit.

Rowland, John M. & Sarah Ann Everhart, 5 June 1860; A. J. Phillips, bondsman; Thomas McNeely, wit. married 5 July 1860 by Peter Williamson, J. P.

Rowzee, Harriss & Juditha Parker, 10 April 1823; Lawrence Owings, bondsman; Hy. Giles, wit.

Rowzee, Madison & Emeling Brinagar, 14 March 1833; Enoch M. Leach, bondsman; Thomas McNeely, J. P., wit.

Rowzee, William & Pashins Jinkins, 16 Aug 1817; Benjamin March, bondsman; Jn March Sr., wit.

Royley, Daniel & Margrat Jones, 18 Oct 1810; Moses Estep, bondsman; Jn. March Sr., wit.

Rudasill--see also Reudasil, Rheudasil

Rudisill, Henry H. & Martha C. Evans, married 10 Feb 1853 by J. Thomason, J. P.

Rudasille, John & Sally Jacobs, 27 Oct 1810; John Jacobs, bondsman; Jno. Giles, C. C., wit.

Rudder, James & Dicey Durham, 28 Sept 1820; Humphrey Linster, bondsman; Jno Giles, wit.

Rudders, Freeman A. & Mary M. Holshouser, 18 Jan 1828; Saml. Reeves, bondsman; Jno. H. Hardie, wit.

Rudders, James & Dicey Dunham, 6 June 1821; John Leach, bondsman; Jno. Giles, wit.

Rudolph, Jacob & Rachel Low, 19 Feb 1802; John Thompson, bondsman; Jno. Brem, wit.

Ruff, James & Sarah Weant, 15 April 1854; Caleb Klutts, bondsman; J. S. Myers, wit.

Ruffin, Thomas R. & Mary McClelland, 9 June 1819; George Miller, bondsman; Jno. Giles, wit.

Ruffty, Wilie & Anna May, 29 May 1832; Samuel Cauble, bondsman; Jno. H. Hardie, wit.

Ruford, Peter & Catey Crouse, 21 Oct 1797; George Smith, bondsman; Jno. Rogers, wit.

Rufty, Edward & Elizabeth Brown, 15 May 1832; Chs. Wise, bondsman; Jno. H. Hardie, wit.

Rufty, George & Sophia Cobble, 16 April 1807; Peter Hartman, bondsman; A. L. Osborn, wit.

Rufty, John & Rosa Klutts, 13 Jan 1847; Othey Swink, bondsman.

Rufty, Peter & Karow Johannah Kenedey, 12 April 1865; E. B. Kennedy, bondsman; married 12 April 1865 by D. W. Honeycutt, J. P.

Rufty, William & Nancey Lyerly, 26 July 1860; Jacob M. Kepley, bondsman; Wm. Locke, wit. married 26 July 1860 by Moses Powlass, J. P.

Rumage, Henry & Jemima Rose, 25 Jan 1855; Alexr. Readling, bondsman; James E. Kerr, wit.

Rumbly, Thomas & Mary Brown, 15 Dec 1801; Thomas Brown, bondsman; Jno Brem, wit.

Rumple, Alexander & Katharine Smith, 11 March 1829; John Smith, bondsman; Jn. H. Hardie, wit.

Rumple, Jacob & Caty Rumple, 14 Nov 1812; Jacob Stirewalt, bondsman.

Rumple, John & Catharine Overcash, 26 Aug 1826; James Scott, bondsman; J. H. Hardie, wit.

Rumple, Joseph & Leah Carreher, 13 Nov 1830; John Scott, bondsman; Jno. H. Hardie, wit.

Rumple, Joseph & Rebecca Lorance, 16 Dec 1858; Caleb Hampton, bondsman; James E. Kerr, wit. married 30 Dec 1858 by Stephen Frontis.

Runelds, Abraham & Mary Leser, (no date); John Leser, bondsman; Jno. Rogers, wit.

Runyon, William & Katharine Low, 13 Dec 1793; Samuel Park, bondsman; Jos. Chambers, wit.

Rupard, John & Racheal Dickins, 17 Aug 1811; John Jones, bondsman; Jn. March Sr., wit.

Rusher, Alfred W. & Melissa C. Brown, 1 March 1860; Edward Rusher, bondsman; Wm. Locke, wit. married 1 March 1860 by Saml. Rothrock, Minister of the Gospel in the Ev. Luth. Church.

Rusher, Edward & Lucina Shoaf, 31 Oct 1857; J. L. Rusher, bondsman; J. S. Myers, James E. Kerr, wit. married 1 Nov 1857 by W. A. Walton, J. P.

Rusher, George & Polly Hartman, 19 July 1815; Henry Lefler, bondsman; Geo. Dunn, wit.

Rusher, George A. & Louisa M. Lippard, 30 July 1849; William
Linebarrier, bondsman; John H. Hardie Jr., wit.

Rusher, George A. & Selina Misenheimer, 28 July 1858; Michael
Holshouser, bondsman; James E. Kerr, wit.

Rusher, Jacob & Teny Verble, 6 Aug 1823; Jno. Beard Sr., bondsman; Hy. Giles, wit.

Rusher, John L. & Betty Misenheimer, 27 Oct 1857; Edward Rusher,
bondsman; James E. Kerr, wit. married 27 Oct 1857 by Saml.
Rothrock, Minister of the Gospel in the Ev. Luth. Church.

Rusher, Miles & Mary M. Hielig, 17 July 1856; James L. Brown,
bondsman; J. S. Myers, wit.

Russel, Alexander Ferguson & Jane Herron(?), 1 April 1812;
Samuel E. Irwin, bondsman; Jno Giles, C. C., wit.

Russel, Henry & Rebeccah Garner, 6 April 1816; Caleb Broch,
bondsman; R. Powell, wit.

Russel, Levi & Easter Buck, 17 Feb 1817; Martin Buck, bondsman;
Henry Giles, wit.

Russel, McKenzie & Martha Small, 9 May 1861; James E. Kerr, wit;
married 9 May 1861 by D. Barringer, J. P.

Russell, Curtis & Rebakh Jons, 18 March 1813; James Taylor,
bondsman; Wm. Bean, J. P., wit.

Russell, George & Agness McKlwrath, 27 Jan 1769; John Olyphant,
William McConnell, bondsmen; Thos. Frohock, wit consent
from Nancy McKlwrath, mother of Agness, 6 Jan 1769; John
Oliphant certifies that Agniss McKlewrath is above 21 years
of age.

Russell, James W. & Mary S. Ritchie, 8 Sept 1860; George
Basinger, bondsman; John Wilkinson, wit. married 9 Sept
1860 by L. J. Kirk, J. P.

Russell, Robert of Anson County & Mary Willson, 17 March 1762;
Henry Horah, John Cussens, bondsmen; Will Reed, John Burnet,
wit.

Russell, William & Elizabeth Hale, 25 Feb 1782; Charles McGorgor,
bondsman; Mat. Troy, wit.

Russell, W. H. & Catharine C. Swink, 8 Dec 1864; James W. Clark,
bondsman; Thomas McNeely, wit.

Rutherford, David & Elizabeth Williamson, 22 June 1802; Benj.
Howard, bondsman; Jno. Brem, wit.

Rutherford, Henry & Mary Johnston, 20 Jan 1787; Jno Macay, wit.,
consent from John Johnston, father of Mary.

Rutledge, Abel & Judea Corzine, 22 Oct 1811; John Hughey,
bondsman; Ezra Allemong, wit.

Rutledge, Joseph & Elizabeth Speer, 11 Aug 1772; Oliver Wallis,
bondsman; Ad. Osborn, wit. consent from Jacob Speer, 10
Aug 1772.

Ryal, William & Mary Speck, 3 Jan 1793; David Speck, bondsman; Jos. Chambers, wit.

Ryan, James C. & Sarah March, 22 Sept 1834; Mark D. Armfield, bondsman; Thomas McNeely, J. P., wit.

Rymer, Daniel & Eve Shulebarrier, 25 July 1835; Jno Rymer, bondsman; Jno. H. Hardie, wit.

Rymer, Jacob & Catharine Simmon, 4 July 1797; Peter Simmon, bondsman; M. Stokes, wit.

Rymer, John & Edy Hinson, 12 Sept 1833; Michael Rymer, bondsman; Wm. Locke, wit.

Sacyhower, Nicholas & Mary Mires, 19 April 1773; John Lewis Beard, bondsman.

Safret, Nelson & Anna A. Youst, 15 Feb 1839; John P. Youst, bondsman; John Giles, wit.

Safret, Peter & Catharine Bostian, 27 July 1821; Jacob Bostian, bondsman; Hy. Giles, wit.

Safriet, Eli & Mary Mitchell, married 19 Aug 1857 by John Yost, J. P.

Safrit, Eli & Mary Mitchell, 18 Aug 1857; John Yost, bondsman; J. S. Myers, wit.

Safrit, John & Rebeckah Kirk, 19 July 1859; John Yost, bondsman; Thomas McNeely, wit. married 19 July 1859 by John Yost, J. P.

Safrit, Moses & Christena L. Misenheimer, 29 Nov 1853; George H. Richey, bondsman; J. S. Myers, wit.

Safrit, Rufus A. & Jane M. Beaver, 22 Feb 1866; Crawford Beaver, bondsman; Obadiah Woodson, wit.

Safrit, William & Margaret B. Eagle, 9 Dec 1865; Allison Misenheimer, bondsman; Obadiah Woodson, wit.

Sain, Andrew & Lydia Etchison, 16 May 1821; James Etchison, bondsman; Ezra Allemong, wit.

Sain, Daniel & Mary Hainley, 9 Jan 1821; Jeremiah Welmon, bondsman; Hy. Giles, wit.

Sain, George & Lucey Cheshur, 13 March 1824; John Sain, bondsman; L. R. Rose, J. P., wit.

Sain, Jacob & Elizabeth Welmond, 18 Dec 1809; Thos. C. Mumford, bondsman; Jn March Sr., wit.

Sain, Jacob Jr. & Lydia Harbin, 7 Oct 1827; David Harbin, bondsman; C. Harbin, J. P., wit.

Sain, John & Priscilla Chesheuer, 10 Dec 1819; Jacob Sain, bondsman; R. Powell, wit.

Sain, John & Margarett Garwood, 14 April 1830; Joel H. Hinkins, bondsman; L. R. Rose, J. P., wit.

Sain, Willey & Margaret Clement, 20 Dec 1823; William Reynolds, bondsman; L. R. Rose, J. P., wit.

Sain, William & Jane Glascock, 24 Jan 1822; James Etchison, bondsman; Hy. Giles, wit.

Salisbury, John & Elizabeth Stuard, 12 March 1803; Moses Welborne, bondsman; Wm. Welborn, wit.

Saltz, Henry & Mary Brown, 17 May 1792; David Brown, bondsman; Chs. Caldwell, wit.

Sammon, James & Jencey Nixon, 29 June 1802; Groves Sammons, bondsman; Jno Brem, wit.

Sanar, George & Elizabeth Foust, 22 Dec 1818; Jonathan Chesher, bondsman; Jn March Sr., wit.

Sanar, George & Mary Brack, 5 Jan 1823; John Lowry, bondsman; Joseph Hanes, wit.

Sanders, Adam & Rebekah Haneline, 23 April 1834; William Sheek, bondsman; Thomas McNeely, J. P., wit.

Sanders, James & Hety Saine, 26 July 1814; George Saine, bondsman; Jno Giles, wit.

Sanders, Joe & Elizabeth Baker, 24 March 1804; Matt Howard, bondsman; A. L. Osborn, D. C., wit.

Sanders, Silas & Christeena Murr, 23 Jan 1813; Joseph Weant, bondsman; Geo. Dunn, wit.

Sanders, Sollineo & Polly Lunn, 24 July 1820; John Sheek, bondsman; Geo. Coker, wit.

Sandy, Thomas & Margat Williams, 31 July 1798; William Sandeys, bondsman; Geo. Fisher, wit.

Saner, Martin & Margaret Wellman, 2 March 1827; Daniel Armsworthy, bondsman; L. R. Rose, J. P., wit.

Saner, Peter Jr. & Anny Smith, 2 Feb 1813; Jacob Elrod Jnr., bondsman; John Hanes, wit.

Sapp, Brummal & Elizabeth Wire, 29 Nov 1814; Moses Evens, bondsman; Silas Peace, wit.

Sapp, Emanuel & Charity Gentle (no date, during admn. of Samuel Ashe); William Harper, bondsman; Ad. Osborn, wit.

Sappenfield, Christian & Christina Sowers, 15 Dec 1821; Jacob Sowers, bondsman; Jno. Giles, wit.

Sapenfield, George & Caty Myars, 5 Nov 1794; Valentine Leonard, bondsman; J. Troy, D. C., wit.

Satchfield, John W. & Susannah Blassingame, 13 June 1860; Obadiah Woodson, bondsman; John Wilkinson, wit. married 13 June 1860 by Obadiah Woodson, J. P.

Satterwhite, Horace B. & Sally Brown, 2 Dec 1809; Henry Chambers, bondsman; Jno. Giles, wit.

Saunders, George & Polly Hileman, 8 Feb 1813; Henry Allemong, bondsman; Moses A. Locke, wit.

Saunders, Isaac & Mary Harris, 4 Sept 1822; Isaac Harden, bondsman; L. R. Rose, J. P., wit.

Saunders, Jacob & Lidiah Lunsford, (no date, during admn. of Alexander Martin); Edward Dunkin, bondsman; Jno. McNairy, wit.

Sausaman, Daniel & Elizabeth Leopard, 31 Oct 1791; John Leopard, bondsman; Chs. Caldwell, wit.

Sawers, Joseph & Jeane Gardner, 16 May 1786; Henry Horah, bondsman; Jno Macay, wit.

Sawyers, James & Sophia Agner, 9 July 1840; Matthew Jones, bondsman; J. L. Beard, wit.

Sawyers, Thomas & Margaret Bullon, 19 Nov 1837; Henry Giles, bondsman.

Scales, N. E. & Minnie S. Lord, 22 May 1861; James E. Kerr, wit. married 22 May 1861 by T. G. Haughton.

Sceford, George & Scuffiah Bird, 4 Sept 1816; David Miller, bondsman; Milo A. Giles, wit.

Scherer, Rev. Simeon of Wythe Co., Va., & Mary Ann Davis, 24 July 1851; L. C. Groseclose, bondsman; married 24 July 1851 by J. H. Coffman.

Schlupp, Conrad & Mary Albright, 9 July 1778; Peter Albright, bondsman; Spruce Macay, wit.

Schonborg, F. L. & Catharine Hartman, 10 June 1863; H. M. Sossamon, bondsman; Obadiah Woodson, wit.

Scot, Andrew & Isable Bar, 11 Aug 1769; James Barr, Adam Mitchel, John McClintock, bondsmen; Alexander Breden, John Mitchell, wit.

Scott, Alexander & Elizabeth Woods, 11 Oct 1815; John Woods, bondsman; Geo. Dunn, wit.

Scott, J. W. & Martha L. Brown, 4 Sept 1849; H. L. Robards, bondsman; J. S. Myers, wit.

Scott, James & Lidia Martin, 26 Nov 1759; John Burnet, Jas. Carson, bondsmen; John Frohock, wit.

Scott, James & Mary Rumple, 13 April 1820; John Rumple, bondsman.

Scott, James C. & Sarah M. Suther, 15 Oct 1857; Martin Black-welder, bondsman; James E. Kerr, wit. married 15 Oct 1857 by J. J. Summerell, J. P.

Scott, Jno. & Eliza Locke, 29 Dec 1817; Abel Cowan, bondsman; Roberts Nanny, wit.

Scott, Thomas & Anna Maria Dobson, 27 Feb 1772; John Dobson, bondsman; Thomas Frohock, wit. consent from Joseph Dobson, father of Anna Maria, 22 Feb 1772; wit by John Dobson, Abram Scott.

Scott, Washington & Rebeckah Bailey, 6 Nov 1834; John Eli Foster, bondsman; Thomas McNeely, J. P., wit.

Scrivener, Benjamin & Mary Cox, 24 Dec 1779; Thomas Tate, bondsman; B. Booth Boote, wit.

Scrivnar, Thomas & Susanna Broils, 29 Sept 1779; Peter Todd, bondsman; Jo. Brevard, wit.

Scudder, Abner & Kitty Barkly, 19 Aug 1789; Saml. Roberts, bondsman; W. Alexander, wit.

Scudder, Henry & Catherine Crouel, 11 Aug 1795; Wm. Hamton, bondsman.

Scudder, Isaac & Martha Owen, 20 Jan 1789; Saml Roberts, bondsman; Will Alexander, wit.

Scudder, Isaiah & Sarah McCartney, 15 April 1785; Hugh Magoune, wit.

Scudder, Nathaniel & Agnus Blair, 1 Nov 1788; Andr. Smith, bondsman; Wm. Alexander, wit.

Scudder, William & Mary Todd, 22 Feb 1783; Thomas Adams, bondsman; Edm. Gamble, wit.

Seachrist, Daniel & Elizabeth Fouts, 30 March 1814; Christian Seachrist, Jacob Seachrist, bondsmen; Silas Peace, wit.

Seachrist, Jacob & Rachael Morkert, 10 Aug 1815; Daniel Seachrist, bondsman; David Mock, wit.

Seachrist, John & Mary Beck, 2 Jan 1822; Jacob Crouse, John Beck Sr., bondsmen; James Lowe Jr., wit.

Seaford, Eli & Margaret Holshouser, 27 Dec 1852; Jacob Kluttz, bondsman; J. S. Myers, wit.

Seaford, Henry & Lydia Glover, 19 June 1855; Daniel Klutts, bondsman; James E. Kerr, wit. married 19 June 1855 by E. E. Phillips, J. P.

Seaford, John & Betsy Klutts, 16 Dec 1822; Peter Josey, bondsman.

Seaford, Moses & _____, 8 Aug 1843; John Cress, bondsman; J. H. Hardie Jr., wit.

Seafort, Peter & Susan Coon, 22 Nov 1797; Leonard Cluttz, bondsman; Jno Rogers, wit.

Seafrit, William & Catherine Blackwelder, 9 Jan 1852; Nelson Safret, bondsman; J. S. Myers, wit.

Seagroves, Jacob & Susannah Tenison, 8 April 1824; Joel Woodel, bondsman; P. McNiell, wit.

Seamon, George & Nancy H. McLaughlin, 25 Nov 1857; John A. Christy, bondsman; James E. Kerr, wit. married 22 Dec 1857 by D. P. Bradshaw, J. P.

Sean, John & Elizth. Huff, _____; Jacob Faust, bondsman; Jams. Robinson, wit.

Seaner, Peter & Catharine Shaver, 14 Jan 1780; Conrad Brem, bondsman; B. Booth Boote, wit.

Searles, Thomas & Susanna Adamson, 6 March 1780; B. Booth Boote, wit.

Sears, Albert & Catherine Valentine, 21 July 1853; Henry Porter, bondsman; J. S. Myers, wit. married 21 July 1853 by J. M. Brown, J. P.

Sears, Albert J. W. & Elizabeth Kennedy, 28 Jan 1860; married 28 Jan 1860 by J. K. Burke, J. P.

Sears, Samuel & Atlas Mayner, 11 May 1852; John H. Scott, bondsman; Archd. Honeycutt, J. P., wit. married 13 May 1852 by Archd. Honeycutt, J. P.

Seats, Abner B. & Rosannah Skiles, 10 Oct 1837; David Gardiner, bondsman; R. Jones, wit.

Sechler, Abraham & Polly Freeze, 22 May 1817; Henry Sechler, bondsman; Roberts Nanny, wit.

Sechler, Gen. Andrew J. & Elizabeth Sechler, 6 Nov 1858; James F. Carrigan, bondsman; John Wilkinson, wit.

Sechler, Benjamin C. & Derinda C. Deal, 14 Sept 1865; W. D. Biggers, bondsman; Obadiah Woodson, wit.

Sechler, Enos & Mary Corriher, 13 April 1858; Moses A. Smith, bondsman; John Wilkinson, wit. married 22 April 1858 by Rev. B. C. Hall.

Sechler, Henry & Catharin Fink, 8 Feb 1813; James Woods, bondsman; Jno. Giles, wit.

Sechler, Henry Jr. & Betsy Correll, 10 June 1817; Henry Sechler, bondsman; Jno Giles, wit.

Sechler, Hezekiah A. & Manerva Anthony, 14 April 1846; David J. Correll, bondsman; J. M. Turner, wit.

Sechler, Hezekiah A. & Catherine L. Corriker, 17 Dec 1858; Richard A. Corriher, bondsman; John Wilkinson, wit.

Sechler, James P. & Mary J. Freeze, 18 Dec 1850; Henry E. Freeze, bondsman.

Sechler, Jesse & Elizabeth E. Bostian, 12 Jan 1857; Gen. A. J. Sechler, bondsman; James E. Kerr, wit.

Sechler, John & Teny Correll, 22 Jan 1819; Rudolph Seckler, bondsman; Roberts Nanny, wit.

Sechler, Joseph & Mary Ann Rebecca Corriher, 26 Aug 1861; Joel Corriher, bondsman; Obadiah Woodson, wit. married 29 Aug 1861 by J. S. Heilig, Min. of Gospel.

Sechler, Moses & Martha Moury, 23 March 1835; Henry Corriher, bondsman; Jno. H. Hardie, wit.

Sechler, Samuel & Rachael Dickson, 6 Aug 1829; James G. Bell, bondsman; John H. Hardie, wit.

Sechrest, Philip & Mary Sulivan, 10 June 1815; John Raikart, bondsman; David Mock, wit.

Sechrist, Thomas & Susanna Sink, 13 Sept 1814; Andrew Byrn, bondsman; David Mock, wit.

Sedan, Joseph & Mary Ann Frnah Speak, 20 Dec 1791; William White, bondsman; Chs. Caldwell, wit.

Sedwick, John & Sarah Baker, 11 Jan 1793; Jacob Henry, bondsman; Jos. Chambers, wit.

Seers, Thomas A. & Eliza Jacobs, 13 Oct 1853; Michael Swicegood, bondsman; J. S. Myers, wit.

Sefford, Daniel & Lydia Freeze, 4 Aug 1830; Daniel Stirawalt, bondsman; Jno. H. Hardie, wit.

Sefford, John & Katharine Smith, 26 Feb 1833; Jacob S. Myers, bondsman; J. H. Hardie, wit.

Sefford, Solomon & Mary Pealor, 22 March 1834; Paul A. Seaford, bondsman; Hy. Giles, wit.

Sefford, William & Elizabeth Lanson, 14 March 1787; Jno Macay, wit.

Segraves--see also Zegraves

Segraves, A. W. & Biddy T. Colly, 30 April 1862; James M. Colley, bondsman; Obadiah Woodson, wit.

Segraves, Ezekial & Lidia Mowry, 3 Oct 1844; Thomas Basinger, bondsman; John H. Hardie Jr., wit.

Segraves, Jas. M. & Cynthia A. Colly, 14 Feb 1866; S. B. Colley, bondsman; Obadiah Woodson, wit.

Sell, Thomas & Kezia Gray, 13 May 1819; David Robertson, bondsman; Sol. Davis, J. P., wit.

Sellers, James & Salley Snipes, 5 July 1815; request for bond only.

Sellers, Jeremiah & Jane McCulloch, 6 Jan 1780; John Erwin, bondsman; B. Booth Boote, wit.

Setzer, Jacob & Mary Anne Josey, 6 April 1840; Allison Stirewalt, bondsman; J. L. Beard, D. C., wit.

Setzer, John & Mary Goodman, 28 Sept 1790; Nicholas Fillhower, bondsman; C. Caldwell, D. C., wit.

Sewall, Samuel Jr. & Christian White, 1 Feb 1780; B. Booth Boote, wit.

Sewell, John & Mary Richmond, 5 Nov 1802; John Plaster, bondsman; Ad. Osborn, wit.

Sewell, Joseph & Esther Long, 25 Oct 1790; Nicholas Sewell, bondsman; C. Caldwell, D. C.

Shaffer, Jacob & Mary Link, 16 Sept 1794; Jacob Link, bondsman; J. Troy, D. C., wit.

Shamell, Henry & Susa Cox, 5 Jan 1818; Mark Cox, bondsman; Milo A. Giles, wit.

Shannon, Thomas & Anne Walter, 3 May 1776; Jno. Nokes, bondsman; Ad. Osborn, wit. consent from Robert Brevard, 4 May 1776.

Sharp, David & Maryan Brandon, 29 Aug 1819; Charles Lovelace, bondsman; R. Powell, wit.

Sharp, Walter & Elizabeth Hardin, 20 Jan 1775; Robert Hardin, bondsman; Jams. Robinson, wit.

Sharpe, Joseph & Jean Sloan, 8 Jan 1778; Archd. Sloan, bondsman; Ad. Osborn, wit.

Shaver, Abraham & Margaret Miller, 28 Aug 1822; Noah Reed, bondsman; Jno Giles, wit.

Shaver, Abraham & Christena Fouts, 24 Jan 1824; John Shaver, bondsman.

Shaver, Daniel & Lucy N. Weant, 13 July 1842; William B. Julian, bondsman; Jno. H. Hardie, wit.

Shaver, Daniel M. & Joyce Crowell, 15 Nov 1847; John Buchanan, bondsman; J. H. Hardie, wit.

Shaver, David & Catharine Berringer, 27 March 1795; Henry Rintleman, bondsman; Ad. Osborn, wit.

Shaver, Eli C. & Leah Peeler, 8 May 1848; Simeon D. Peeler, bondsman.

Shaver, John & Anna Blue, 19 May 1821; Isaac Earnhart, bondsman; Hy. Giles, wit.

Shaver, John & Rebecca Reed, 3 Jan 1826; Noah Reed, bondsman.

Shaver, John D. & Phebe Fraley, 1 Sept 1846; Abraham Shaver, bondsman; John H. Hardie Jun., wit.

Shaver, Jno. J. & Mary E. Lemly, 14 Jan 1840; Leander Killian, bondsman; Susan T. Giles, wit.

Shaver, Paul C. & Mary Jane Miller, 1 Sept 1859; William L. Parker, bondsman; Levi Trexler, wit. married 1 Sept 1859 by Levi Trexler, J. P.

Shaver, Philip & Sally Homes Dauze, 15 Oct 1801; David Craige, bondsman; Jno. Brem, wit.

Shaw, William G. & Lydia Huffman, 23 Sept 1827; Samuel Shaw, bondsman; C. Harbin, J. P., wit.

Sheapard, John & Sally Dobey, 2 Feb 1846; Miles Miller, bondsman; J. H. Hardie Jr., wit.

Sheats, Jacob & Mary Wood, 31 March 1807; John March Sr., bondsman; John March Jr., wit.

Shechen, Daniel & Jane Waller, 16 April 1857; W. Turner Fry, bondsman; J. S. Myers, wit. married by M. A. Agner, J. P., 16 April 1857.

Sheek, Adam & Jemiah Futz, 12 Sept 1823; James Ellis Jr., bondsman; L. R. Rose, J. P., wit.

Sheek, Christian & Caty Jones, 1 May 1811; William Sanders, bondsman; Jn. March Sr., wit.

Sheek, George & Peggy Call, 22 Nov 1809; Jacob Call, bondsman; Jn. March Sr., wit.

Sheek, Jacob & Sally Sain, 8 Oct 1817; Benjamin Taylor, bondsman; Milo A. Giles, wit.

Sheek, James W. & Levina Gheen, 20 Feb 1855; Hawkins Brooks, bondsman; J. S. Myers, wit.

Sheek, John & Winny Harrison, 14 Feb 1829; David Harbin, bondsman; C. Harbin, J. P., wit.

Sheerman, Henry & Barbra Spoonen, 11 Sept 1764; Daniel Hackett, George Hage, bondsmen; Thomas Frohock, wit.

Sheets, Andrew & Lourena Obriant, 19 Dec 1834; Allmon Taylor, bondsman; Thomas McNeely, J. P., wit.

Sheets, David & Nancy Orrel, 1 Dec 1807; Edger Orril, bondsman; John March Sr., wit.

Sheets, Jacob & Mary Philips, 11 Jan 1818; Mack Crump, bondsman; Daniel _____, wit.

Sheets, Jacob & Elizabeth Walker, 10 Jan 1835; Philip Call, bondsman; Thomas McNeely, J. P., wit.

Sheets, John & Rebecca Peck, 27 March 1804; John Pack, bondsman; A. L. Osborn, D. C., wit.

Sheffer, Richard & Elizabeth Seink, 21 May 1802; Geo. Swink, bondsman; Jno. Brem, D. C., wit.

Sheflea, George Philip & Easther Feslerman, 10 March 1829; Henry Baker, bondsman; J. H. Hardie, wit.

Shelhorse, John & Isabella Mitchell, 8 May 1788; Joseph Shinn, bondsman; Js. McEwin, wit.

Shell, Lemmon & Lucy Pinkston, 19 Nov 1849; J. S. Myers, bondsman.

Shellhorne, Jacop & Mary Peck, 31 July 1806; Jeams Zarvis, bondsman; Danl. Leathermon, J. P., wit.

Shelly, John & Susanna Hargrave, 29 Jan 1772; Danl. Little, George Patton, bondsmen; John Frohock, wit. consent headed "Guildford County: 28 Jan 1772 from John Shelly and Elisabeth, and Naomi Hargrave, parents of the couple".

Shelton, Woodlief & Sally Moore, 9 July 1811; James Graham, bondsman; Ezra Allemong, wit.

Shepherd, James A. & Ann L. Eller, 11 Nov 1846; James Caldwell, bondsman; Jno. H. Hardie Jr., wit.

Shepherd, John & Lurana Wall, 17 Dec 1829; Green Crowell, bondsman; J. H. Hardie, wit.

Shepherd, Silas & Margaret Cox, 3 Aug 1858; James O. Parks, bondsman; John Wilkinson, wit. married 4 Aug 1858 by W. R. Fraley, J. P.

Shepherd, William & Ann Fensen, 19 June 1790; Joseph Roland, bondsman; Basil Gaither, wit.

Shepperd, Roland & Barbary Hedrick, 4 May 1798; Gasper Hedrick, bondsman; Edwin J. Osborn, D. C., wit.

Shepperd, William & Susannah Reddell, 14 Sept 1814; Aquiller Reddell, bondsman; Silas Peace, wit.

Sherer, Loftin R. & Julia Ann Joicey Rose, 25 Oct 1858; J. J. McConnaughey, bondsman; John Wilkinson, wit.

Sherrell, Samuel Wilson & Elizabeth Thomas, 11 Jan 1782; James Thomas, bondsman.

Sherrill, Colbert R. & Elizabeth L. Wallace, 19 July 1841; Eli F. Sherrill, bondsman; Jno. Giles, wit.

Sherrill, Eli F. & Esther N. Wallace, 17 May 1841; Joseph M. Wallace, bondsman; Jno. Giles, wit.

Sherrill, Jacob & Margret Lowrance, 29 July 1767; Joshua Perkins, John Stog, bondsmen; John Frohock, wit. consent from Wm. Sherrill, father of Jacob; wit by Moses Sherill.

Sherrill, Jacob & Sarah Massy, 24 Oct 1771; Danl. Little, bondsman. consent from Nicholas Massy, 23 Oct 1771.

Sherrill, M. Osborne & Martha J. A. Rose, 23 July 1856; Henry A. Rumage, bondsman; J. S. Myers, wit.

Sherrill, Moses & Sarah Simpson, 29 Jan 1768; Will Simpson, bondsman; John Frohock, wit.

Shewler, Peter & Susanna Livengood, 17 April 1818; Daniel Myers, bondsman; Z. Hunt, J. P., wit.

Shields, Andrew & Elizabeth Lowry, 15 Dec 1775; Samuel Lowry, bondsman; Ad. Osborn, wit.

Shields, William & Jane Cowan, 27 Jan 1837; Christopher J. Cowan, bondsman; Jno. H. Hardie, wit.

Shiffer, Ezekiel & Elizabeth Bird, 6 April 1796; Whitmell Ryll, bondsman; J. Troy, wit.

Shilley, James & Mary Brothertin, 9 Sept 1788; William Brothertin, bondsman; W. Alexander, wit.

Shine, Bartholomew & Mary Swyers, 24 June 1769; Jas. Craige, Wm. McConnell Sr., bondsmen; Thoms. Frohock, wit.

Shinn, Alexander & Margaret Baker, 12 Feb 1861; Jas. M. Turner, bondsman; John Wilkinson, wit. married 14 Feb 1861 by M. A. Luckey, J. P.

Shinn, Calvin L. & Ellen Baker, 26 March 1858; T. J. Holder, bondsman; John Wilkinson, wit. married 1 April 1858 by Samuel B. O. Wilson.

Shinn, Samul & Margaret Josey, 17 May 1837; David Brown, bondsman.

Shinn, Warren L. & Sarah Cope, 18 June 1832; Benjamin Fraley, bondsman.

Shipton, Samuel & Anne Holleway, 14 Jan 1812; David Cross, bondsman; Geo. Dunn, wit.

Shive, John & Alvira McNeely, 1 June 1820; James McNeely, bondsman.

Shive, Joseph & Lea Shulibarger, 28 Dec 1824; John Smith, bondsman.

Shive, Martin & Ann H. McNeely, 2 Oct 1830; Wm. A. Weddington, bondsman.

Shoaf, Jacob & Susanna Hinkle, 3 Oct 1804; John Creaver, bondsman; Jno. Monroe, wit.

Shoat, Jacob & Elizabeth Barrier, 23 Oct 1772; Charles Barrier, bondsman; Ad. Osborn, wit.

Shoeman, George & Elizabeth Tarr, 15 June 1805; Richa. Tenpenny, bondsman; Andrew Kerr, wit.

Shoff, Christian & Christianne Shoff, 10 July 1792; Philip Lonard, bondsman.

Shofner, Henry & Clara Hart, 1 Aug 1780; Charles Hart, bondsman; H. Giffard, wit.

Shollenberaer, David & Mary Ann Bostian, 22 Sept 1843; Aaron Yost, bondsman; J. H. Hardie, wit.

Shoof, John & Franky Brinkly, 23 July 1812; Jacob Shoof, bondsman; J. Wilson, J. P., wit.

Short, John & Jane Cowan, 27 Jan 1808; Henry M. Broom, bondsman; A. L. Osborn, wit.

Short, Peter & Dinah Todd, 28 Sept 1780; Jas. Hacket, bondsman; Ad. Osborn, wit.

Short, William & Margaret Alison, 27 June 1816; John Cowan, bondsman; Henry Giles, wit.

Shorts, James & Elizabeth Moore, 11 July 1780; James Woods, bondsman; Jno. Kerr, wit.

Shouse, Henry & Elizabeth Jones, 5 March 1779; Thoms. Jones, bondsman; Wm. R. Davie, wit.

Shouse, Henery & Elizth. Bone, 20 Feb 1769; Adam Shouse, John Bone, bondsmen; Thos. Frohock, wit.

Showers, Charles & Martha Williams, 15 Feb 1780; Philip Williams, bondsman.

Shriver, William & Susan Bullen, 21 Nov 1838; S. Lemly, wit.

Shroat, John & Nancy McCrarey, 23 Nov 1811; Conrad Fite, bondsman; Jno. Giles, C. C., wit.

Shrode, Adam & Lucanny Smith, 2 June 1789; George Smith, bondsman; Will Alexander, wit.

Shrote, Henry & Elizebeth Rape, 18 Aug 1788; Wm. Alexander, wit.

Shuford, Daniel & Elizabeth Savage, 11 Jan 1800; Rd. Brandon, bondsman; R. Troy, wit.

Shuford, J. H. C. & S. E. R. Hughes, 6 July 1865; C. N. Price, bondsman; Obadiah Woodson, wit. married 6 April 1865 by W. B. Watts, Minister of the Gospel.

Shulenberrier, Frederick & Mary Slough, 1 Nov 1799; David Shullenberrier, bondsman; Edwin J. Osborn, wit.

Shuler--see also Shewler

Shuler, John & Mary Hagea, 12 Feb 1822; Peter Shuler, bondsman; Sol. Davis, wit.

Shulinbarger, David & Cuzby R. Overcash, 2 Sept 1854; married 6 July 1854 by J. S. Heilig.

Shullenberg, David & Cosby R. Overcash, 2 Sept 1854; Philip J. Overcash, bondsman; James E. Kerr, wit.

Shullobeer, Fredrick & Coe Stygerwalt, 2 Aug 1792; Peter Stygerwalt, bondsman; Chs. Caldwell, wit.

Shuman, Jacob & Teny Earnheart, 27 April 1815; Jacob Dillow, bondsman; Jno. Giles, wit.

Shuman, John & Rachl. Cobble, 24 Sept 1801; Adam Coble, bondsman; A. L. Osborn, D. C., wit.

Shuman, John & Polly Vervil, 19 July 1814; Peter Crider, bondsman; Henry Allemong, wit.

Shuman, John & Eliza C. Troxler, 24 Dec 1821; Isaac Earnhart, bondsman; Jno Giles, wit.

Shuman, John & Nancy Cauble, 2 March 1826; Henry Giles, bondsman.

Shuman, John Sr. & Elmira Williamson, 12 Oct 1844; Henry A. Smith, bondsman; John H. Hardie, wit.

Shuping, Absalom A. & Hetty Louisa Shuping, 24 Jan 1859; William A. Shuping, bondsman; John Wilkinson, wit. married 25 Jan 1859 by W. R. Fraley, J. P.

Shuping, Alpherd A. & Susannah Yost, 17 Dec 1861; Michael Shuping, bondsman; Obadiah Woodson, wit.

Shuping, Andrew & Katy Casper, 17 May 1797; Henry Casper, bondsman; Jno. Rogers, wit.

Shuping, Andrew & Polly L. Cruse, 23 Dec 1844; Nathan L. Phillips, bondsman.

Shuping, Andrew & Jane S. Walker, 27 Aug 1860; Samuel Spry, bondsman; James E. Kerr, wit.

Shuping, Caleb & Sarah Cope, 22 Dec 1845; Andrew Cleaver, bondsman; James M. Turner, wit.

Shuping, Jacob & Anne Casper, 20 March 1792; Adam Casper, bondsman; Chs. Caldwell, wit.

Shuping, Jacob & Catharine Setzer, 12 Feb 1822; Philip Litaker, bondsman; Jno. Giles, wit.

Shuping, Jacob & Mena Miller, 14 Dec 1827; John Litaker, bondsman; Jno. H. Hardie Jr., wit.

Shuping, Jacob & Margt. C. Smith, 20 Sept 1847; Alexander
Lamb, bondsman; J. H. Hardie, wit.

Shuping, John A. & Lucinda E. Winders, 26 Oct 1859; Jesse H.
Albright, bondsman; James E. Kerr, wit. married 27 Oct 1859
by W. R. Fraley, J. P.

Shuping, Michl. & Mariah Sifford, 23 July 1828; G. Michael P.
Hileigh, bondsman.

Shuping, Michael & Milly Freeze, 16 March 1830; Peter Barger,
bondsman.

Shuping, Michael & Mary Overcash, 28 Sept 1865; John R. Holshouser, bondsman; Obadiah Woodson, wit. married 28 Sept
1865 by Rev. Wm. Lambeth.

Shuping, Michael & Elizabeth Hartman, 5 June 1803; Nick. Shuping,
bondsman; A. L. Osborn, D. C., wit.

Shuping, Milas & Mary Cauble, 20 Dec 1852; Theophilus Josey,
bondsman; J. S. Myers, wit.

Shuping, Moses A. & Elizabeth Sifferd, 21 Sept 1854; Farly Ellis,
bondsman; J. S. Myers, wit. married 26 Sept 1854 by E. E.
Phillips, J. P.

Shuping, Wiley M. & Elizabeth C. Fisher, 4 Feb 1861; William M.
Gant, bondsman; Wm. Locke, wit.

Shuping, William A. & Hatty E. Wilhelm, 1 March 1852; Andrew
Shuping, bondsman; Obadiah Woodson, wit.

Shuping, William A. & Charlotte C. Myers, 5 May 1860; Michael
Klutts, bondsman; John Wilkinson, wit. married 6 May 1860
by W. R. Fraley, J. P.

Sichler, Solomon & Polly Shulibarger, 27 Aug 1824; Henry
Sichler, bondsman; Hy. Giles, wit.

Siddon, George & Jane Pack, 5 May 1809; John Pack, bondsman;
Jn. March Sr., wit.

Siddon, Joseph & Lucy Foster, 1 Nov 1816; John Myers, bondsman;
Jn March Sr., wit.

Sides, Christopher & Frances Castor, 27 May 1859; Cornelius
Sides, bondsman; John Wilkinson, wit. married 29 March 1859
by Milo A. J. Roseman, J. P.

Sides, Daniel A. & Nancy Ann Rowland, 21 July 1853; Charles
Sides, bondsman.

Sides, John & Esther Elizabeth Lowder, 20 Sept 1859; Green
Eller, bondsman; John Wilkinson, wit. married 21 Sept 1859
by M. Plummer, J. P.

Sides, Levi & Selena Shaver, 4 Sept 1854; Jacob A. Smith,
bondsman; J. S. Myers, wit.

Sides, Matthias & Sally Bost, 6 March 1843; Moses Peninger,
bondsman; Jno. H. Hardie, wit.

Sides, Nelson & Lydia Shulibarrier, 18 July 1837; Paul Klutts, bondsman; R. Jones, wit.

Sides, Ransom & Catharine E. Culp, 2 March 1850; Edwin J. Sell, bondsman; James E. Kerr, wit.

Sides, Simon C. & Chany Louisa Hopkins, 4 Aug 1857; John Sides, bondsman; James E. Kerr, wit. married 6 Aug 1857 by Thornton Butler, V. D. M.

Sifferd, Edmund & Mary A. E. Menius, 25 July 1861; James E. Kerr, wit. married 25 July 1861 by L. C. Groseclose, Pastor of St. John's Ev. Luth. Church, Salisbury, N. C.

Sifford, Samuel & Elizabeth Bost, 21 Feb 1831; John Seaford, bondsman; Hy. Giles, wit.

Sifford, Simeon & Catharine Bost, 18 Nov 1837; Solomon Sifford, bondsman; Susan T. Giles, wit.

Siford, Paul & Margaret Peeler, 19 April 1830; John Miller, bondsman; Jno. H. Hardie, wit.

Sigler, Jacob & _____, _____; F. Neely, bondsman; A. L. Osborn, D. C., wit.

Silliman, James & Elizabeth Miller, 26 March 1817; James McLaughlin, bondsman; Roberts Nanny, wit.

Silliman, John P. & Mary A. Linch, 24 June 1853; James Miller, bondsman; J. S. Myers, D. C., wit. married 30 June 1853 by Jno. E. McPherson.

Silliven, William & Peggy Jackson, 12 Nov 1811; Peter Bodenhamer Jr., bondsman; E. Morgan, J. P., wit.

Silvees, Hugh & Mary Davis, 15 Oct 1804; Mical Holshouser, bondsman; A. L. Osborn, D. C., wit.

Silver, Levi & Marian Lucas, 8 Dec 1794; Willm. Haddicks, bondsman; B. John Pinchback, Benjamin Tucker, wit.

Simes, John & Mary White, 1 Sept 1836; Andrew Cranfill, bondsman; Wm. Hawkins, J. P., wit.

Simmon, Peter & Eve Gethey, 11 May 1802; Christian Glentz, bondsman; John Brem, wit.

Simmon, Solomon & Mary L. Smith, 4 July 1842; George M. Shuford, bondsman; _____ Sneed, wit.

Simmons, John & Nancy Adams, 5 Sept 1809; George Travis, bondsman; Jno. Giles, C. C., wit.

Simmons, William & Pheby Ledford, 16 Oct 1787; John Buis, bondsman; Jno. Macay, wit.

Simms, Elijah & Phoeba Stilwell, 26 Dec 1795; David Stilwell, bondsman; J. Troy, wit.

Simon, Solomon & Molly Tuffy, 2 May 1825; James Buckner, bondsman; Hy. Giles, wit.

Simonton, Julius R. & Jane L. Knox, 29 April 1853; A. F. Sharpe, bondsman; James E. Kerr, wit. married 4 May 1853 by P. H. Dalton.

Simonton, Theophilus & Anne Fauls (no date, during admn. of Richard Caswell); Wm. Falls, bondsman; Margaret Osborn, wit.

Simpson, Benjamin & Anna Houldsouzer, 2 Oct 1818; John Simson, bondsman; Thos. L. Cowan, wit.

Simpson, Caleb & Elizabeth Maria Pool, 12 Nov 1845; Jacob Pool, bondsman; J. H. Hardie, wit.

Simpson, Isaac & Elizabeth Birely, 29 Aug 1816; Jesse Simpson, bondsman; Jno. Giles, wit.

Simpson, John & Elizabeth Hagler, 20 June 1854; Jacob Holshouser, bondsman; J. S. Myers, wit.

Simpson, Obadiah & Lucintha Noland, 7 Oct 1823; James Robling, bondsman.

Simpson, Rignall & Anny Burgett, 16 Dec 1794; William Adams, bondsman; J. Troy, D. C., wit.

Simpson, Samuel & Sarah Hooker, 29 Sept 1826; James Booth, bondsman; J. H. Hardie, wit.

Simpson, Will & Eliz. Hocking (Hawkins), 28 Jan 1768; Moses Sherrill, bondsman; John Frohock, C. C., wit. consent from John and Elizabeth Hocking, wit by Moses Sherill.

Simpson, William & Betsy Swisgood, 1 Aug 1813; Isaac Simpson, bondsman; Geo. Dunn, wit.

Simpson, William & Peany Miller, 25 Aug 1824; Daniel Cauble, bondsman; Hy. Giles, wit.

Simpson, William & Polly Holshouser, 9 May 1827; Peter Kepler, bondsman; J. H. Hardie, wit.

Simrel, James & Elizabeth Stephens, 22 June 1803; Daniel Hunt, bondsman; J. Hunt, wit.

Simril, James & Vilet Henderson, 11 Feb 1762; Hugh Barry, George Davison, bondsmen; Will Reed, Mary Hamilton, wit.

Simson, John & Rachel Wills, 1 Oct 1787; John Bussell, bondsman.

Simson, Ross & Elisabeth Adams, 3 Dec 1787; John Russell, bondsman; Js. McEwin, wit.

Singeltary, T. C. & Harriet E. Williams, 18 Oct 1864; Chas. H. Snead, bondsman; Obadiah Woodson, wit.

Sink, Andrew & Elizabeth Livengood, 14 March 1821; Thomas Livengood, bondsman; Sol. Davis, J. P., wit.

Sink, Andrew & Eliza Byerly, 11 Sept 1830; Philip L. Sink, bondsman; Jno. H. Hardie, wit.

Sink, Christian & Molly Myers, 8 Jan 1818; George Sink, bondsman; Silas Peace, wit.

Sink, Christian & Mary Lenard, 10 Nov 1807; Peter Sink, bondsman; Jno. Monroe, wit.

Sink, David & Molly Seachrist, 12 April 1815; Thomas Seachrist, bondsman; Silas Peace, wit.

Sink, Jacob & Mary Snider, 12 April 1821; Micheal Sink, bondsman; An. Swicegood, wit.

Sink, Peter & Magdalene Motsinger, 11 Jan 1808; Valentine Harman, bondsman; Wm. Welborn, wit.

Sinklear, Amos & Mary Poar, 24 Jan 1770; James Poar, bondsman; Thomas Frohock, wit. consent from John and Mary Poar, 23 Jan 1770; wit by James Poar.

Sinston, Joshua & Christian Burnhart, 5 Oct 1808; Frederick Disinger, bondsman; A. L. Osborne, wit.

Sithloff, George & Susanah Waggner, 3 Nov 1791; Fredrick Albright, bondsman; Jno Monro, wit.

Sitter, Conrad & Elizabeth Craglow, 12 March 1814; William Craglow, bondsman; Geo. Dunn, wit.

Sizemore, William & Catharine Adams, 3 Jan 1780; Elisha Adams, bondsman; B. Booth Boote, wit.

Skeen, Brantly & Rebecca Henly, 4 May 1847; William Burrage, bondsman; J. H. Hardie Jr., wit.

Skeen, Jesse & Sarah Ann Marbray, 6 July 1858; John S. Nichols, bondsman; Saml Rothrock, wit.

Skiles, Jacob & Jane P. Thompson, 6 May 1840; John Dobbins, bondsman; Susan T. Giles, wit.

Skiles, John D. & Naomy M. Graham, 4 Oct 1843; Alexander Graham, bondsman; John H. Hardie Jr., wit.

Skinner, Cortlin & Hannah Reed, 18 June 1793; Madad Reed, bondsman; Jos. Chambers, wit.

Skirving, Alexander & Susanna Harrison, 30 March 1791; Richard Graham, bondsman.

Slade, Jonah P. & Susannah Leizar, 20 Oct 1828; Hiram Smith, bondsman; M. A. Giles, wit.

Slade, Jonah P. & Matilda Brantly, 17 Aug 1830; Truth Woods, bondsman; Jno. Giles, wit.

Slagly, Abraham & Elisabeth Lee, 2 April 1850; William Griswill, bondsman; Ph. Beck, wit.

Slater, Fielding & Alice Smith, 5 Oct 1826; Henry Giles, bondsman.

Slegle, Fredrick Jr. & Catharine Waggoner, 31 Oct 1791; Fredrick Slegler Sr., bondsman; Chs. Caldwell, wit.

Sleighter, Henry & Barbary Bettz, 26 Dec 1799; Henry Giles, bondsman; Edwin J. Osborn, wit.

Sleighter, Henry & _____ Hanline, 31 Aug 1821; Jno Giles, bondsman.

Slinig, James & Margaret T. Leazer, 19 Feb 1840; Joseph M. Wallace, bondsman; Susan T. Giles, wit.

Sloan, Calib & Ann Sloan, 4 Oct 1816; George Betz, bondsman; Jno Giles, wit.

Sloan, J. F. & M. J. Allison, 27 Dec 1859; S. Y. Allison, bondsman; James E. Kerr, wit.

Sloan, James & Britiania Smoot, 29 Jan 1821; William F. Kelly, bondsman; Hy. Giles, wit.

Sloan, James & Elizabeth Biles, 5 May 1804; John Cuningham, bondsman; Hudson Hughes, wit.

Sloan, James C. & Susan H. Bowers, 21 Nov 1818; Richard A. McRee, bondsman; Jno. Giles, wit.

Sloan, John & Mary Green, 23 Dec 1765; Robert Johnston, bondsman; Thomas Frohock, wit.

Sloan, John Jr. & Jemima Smith, 24 Oct 1785; John Sloan Sr., bondsman; Max. Chambers, wit.

Sloan, John L. & Mary C. Cowan, 20 Dec 1848; Robt L. McConnaughy, R. B. Sloan, bondsmen; Jno. H. Hardie Jr., wit.

Sloan, John L. & Selena W. Crowell, 30 Aug 1858; C. G. Hix, bondsman; married 1 Sept 1858 by B. Scott Krider, A. M. M. G.

Sloan, Richard & Anne Caughmon, 17 April 1813; Jocl Sloan, Thomas Jones, bondsmen; Geo. Dunn, wit.

Sloan, Robert & Mary Logan, 29 May 1786; George Logan, bondsman; Ad. Osborn, wit.

Sloan, Robert & Martha Herris, 5 March 1788; Wm. Rosebrough, bondsman.

Sloan, Robert & Faitha Donnell, 16 Jan 1852; Calvin Cress, bondsman; James E. Kerr, wit. married 22 Jan 1852 by Jno. M. McConnaughy, J. P.

Sloan, Robert J. & S. J. Goodman, 25 Oct 1858; John G. Sloan, bondsman; John Wilkinson, wit. married 27 Oct 1858 by S. C. Alexander.

Sloan, Samuel & Sophia Penninger, 2 Aug 1827; Joseph Cowan, bondsman.

Sloan, Samuel A. & Sarah J. Cowan, 4 Sept 1860; D. S. Cowan, bondsman; James E. Kerr, wit. married 4 Sept 1860 by B. S. Krider.

Sloan, Thos. B. & Sarah E. McCorkle, 21 Dec 1857; J. J. McConnaughey, bondsman; James E. Kerr, wit. married 22 Dec 1857 by E. D. Junkin, Minister.

Sloan, William & Jane Stevenson, 13 May 1783; John Stevenson, bondsman; Robt. Nalle, wit.

Sloop, Abraham & Telilah Bostian, 27 Nov 1848; John Sloop, bondsman; J. H. Hardie, wit.

Sloop, Alexander & Judy Sechler, 25 April 1842; Christian
Sechler, bondsman; _____ Sneed, wit.

Sloop, D. A. & Bettie S. Ervin, 9 Nov 1865; W. W. Miller,
bondsman; Horatio N. Woodson, wit.

Sloop, Edward & Adeline C. Albright, 7 Dec 1848; William C.
Sloop, bondsman.

Sloop, Edward & Mary A. L. Ketchey, 14 May 1857; Thomas A.
Albright, bondsman; J. S. Myers, wit. married 14 May 1857
by J. J. Summerell, J. P.

Sloop, George W. & Barbara E. Baker, 21 March 1859; Absalom
Freeze, bondsman.

Sloop, Henry & Rosena Sechler, 10 Oct 1838; John Sloop Jr.,
bondsman; S. Lemly Jr., wit.

Sloop, Henry O. & Franey A. Correll, 9 Oct 1858; James Coburn,
bondsman; John Wilkinson, wit.

Sloop, Hiram A. & Delilah M. Creswell, 20 Dec 1847; Noah A.
Freeze, bondsman; J. H. Hardie, wit.

Sloop, J. G. & A. E. Corriher, 29 March 1866; David McLean,
bondsman; Obadiah Woodson, wit.

Sloop, Jacob & Betsey Cress, 27 Sept 1822; John Pachel, bondsman; Jno Giles, wit.

Sloop, Jacob & Leah Peahel, 13 March 1839; John Peahel, bondsman; John Giles, wit.

Sloop, Jacob & Mary T. Woods, 10 March 1846; Christian Sechler,
bondsman; J. H. Hardie, wit.

Sloop, Jacob Jr. & Catherine Correll, 8 May 1837; John Sloop Jr.,
bondsman; Tobias S. Lemly, wit.

Sloop, John & Anna Katherine Beaver, 20 Aug 1832; David Beaver,
bondsman.

Sloop, John & Christianna Correll, 13 Feb 1835; Henry Sloop,
bondsman; Jno. H. Hardie, wit.

Sloop, Monroe & Elizabeth Albright, 20 Dec 1852; Mumford S. M.
Sloop, bondsman; James E. Kerr, wit.

Sloop, Monroe & Catharine A. Albright, 31 March 1857; M. S.
McSloop, bondsman; J. S. Myers, wit. married 1 April 1857
by J. J. Summerell, J. P.

Sloop, Peter & Nancy Baker, 2 Oct 1841; Philip Litaker,
bondsman; J. S. Johnston, wit.

Sloop, William J. & Penelope E. Freeze, 9 Sept 1850; Caleb
Freeze, bondsman; J. S. Myers, wit.

Sluder, James & Betsy Meheley, 18 Nov 1810; John Wilson,
bondsman; Joseph Clarke, wit.

Sluider, Mark & Mary Morefield, 16 Oct 1789; Peachum Helton,
bondsman.

Smalley, Abner & Nancey Murray, 13 July 1774; Fredk. Krider, bondsman; Ad. Osborn, wit. consent 9 July 1774 by Jeremiah Murrey; wit. by Fredaric Crider.

Smallwood, William & Nelly Noland, 24 Nov 1801; James Noland Sr., bondsman; J. Hunt, wit.

Smalwood, Elijah & Sally McHorneyk, 28 April 1829; William Garener, bondsman; C. Harbin, J. P., wit.

Smart, Edward & Lisha Hendricks, 22 Sept 1825; John Hendricks Jr., bondsman; L. R. Rose, J. P., wit.

Smart, Edward & Susan Green, 18 April 1853; James B. Nolly, bondsman; J. S. Myers, wit.

Smart, John & Tabby Williams, 1 July 1815; Thomas Womax, bondsman; Jno Giles, C. C., wit.

Smather, Jacob & Kathrine Dew, 16 April 1795; Peter Brown, bondsman; J. Troy, wit.

Smether, William & M. Lentz, widow, 17 March 1809; George Betz, bondsman; A. D. Osborne, wit.

Smith, Adam & Elizabeth Richardson, 23 April 1830; Saml. Lemly, bondsman; Jno. H. Hardie, wit.

Smith, Alexander & Barb Freezor, _____; Peter Freezor, bondsman; James Lowe Jr., wit.

Smith, Alexander F. & Nancey Hartman, 2 Feb 1826; Henry Freezar, bondsman; Jno. Giles, wit.

Smith, Alfred & Susanna Goss, 21 Aug 1820; Obadiah M. Smith, bondsman.

Smith, Anderson & Priscilla Williams, 4 Sept 1763; Vinson Williams, Andrew Smith, bondsmen; John Frohock, wit. consent from Rebeckah Smith and James Smith, 2 Sept 1763; James Smith, brother of Anderson, and Rebeckah, mother of Anderson Smith.

Smith, Anderson & Mary H. Williford, 6 Sept 1860; William Williford, bondsman.

Smith, Andrew & Sarah McKee, 10 March 1789; Thomas Smith, bondsman; R. Martin, wit.

Smith, Arthur & Susanah Brown, 3 Jan 1815; William Aytchson, bondsman; Jn. March Sr., wit.

Smith, Arthur & Polley Ellis, 18 Oct 1815; Enoch Ellis, bondsman; Jno. March Sr., wit.

Smith, Benjamin & Elizabith Sibella, 12 Sept 1801; Nathan Smith, bondsman; Jno Brem, wit.

Smith, Benjamin & Nancy Thomason, 25 Nov 1819; Peter Hinkle, bondsman; Hy. Giles, wit.

Smith, C. O. & Mary A. E. Lyerly, 1 Nov 1865; Wm. A. Lyerla, bondsman; Obadiah Woodson, wit. married 1 Nov 1865 by Rev. Wm. Lambeth.

Smith, Caleb & Sarah Parker, 12 Jan 1802; Thomas Nixon, bondsman; Adlai Laurens Osborn, D. C., wit.

Smith, Casper & Jane Hadin, 29 Dec 1817; John McKee, bondsman;
Jno. Giles, wit.

Smith, Caleb & Sophia Freeze, 1 Jan 1850; J. S. Myers, Rufus
Linebough, bondsmen.

Smith Charles & Phoeby Cowan, 21 Aug 1793; Peter Lewis, bondsman; Jos. Chambers, wit.

Smith, Christopher & Nancy Harris, 23 Dec 1824; Aaron Stinson,
bondsman; E. Brock, J. P., wit.

Smith, Christopher & Sarah Barlow, 21 Dec 1834; Edward Hill,
bondsman; J. Tomlinson, J. P., wit.

Smith, Cornelius & Winney Adams, 13 Oct 1789; Joseph Haden,
bondsman; Ed. Harris, wit.

Smith, Cornelius & Jean Merrill, 4 June 1810; Russa Grace,
bondsman; Geo. Dunn, wit.

Smith, Cornelous & Rachel Lynn, 26 Aug 1768; Andrew Smith,
Edward McGuire, bondsmen; Thomas Frohock, wit.

Smith, Daniel & Katharine Miller, 14 Nov 1792; George Smith,
bondsman; Jos. Chambers, wit.

Smith, Daniel & Nancy Walton, 3 Jan 1833; George W. Smith,
bondsman.

Smith, Daniel W. & Julian M. Walton, 18 Aug 1852; Caleb Barger,
bondsman; J. S. Myers, wit.

Smith, David & Elizabeth Idol, 15 Jan 1803; Jonathan Manlove,
bondsman; Jno. Monroe, wit.

Smith, David & Sally Smith, 20 Feb 1821; William Haden Jr.,
bondsman.

Smith, David & Jona Wilkerson, 8 Oct 1829; David Johnson,
bondsman; Wm. Hawkins, wit.

Smith, Davie & Margaret Fezer, 22 June 1811; Richmond Hughes,
bondsman; Jno. Giles, C. C., wit.

Smith, Drew & Mary Jacobs, 20 Oct 1842; Jno. H. Hardie, bondsman.

Smith, Drurey & Margaret Pinkston, 14 March 1832; Jacob
Coughenour, bondsman; J. H. Hardie, wit.

Smith, E. Delafield of New York, son of Dr. Archelaus Green
Smith & Charlotte Eliphel Morgan, eldest daughter of Gilbert
Morgan, M. G., married 17 Sept 1851 by Gilbert Morgan.

Smith, Edm. & Lewsy Varner, 26 May 1810; Wilie Davis, bondsman;
Jas. Morgan, J. P., wit.

Smith, Eli & Catharine Bean, 16 Nov 1825; Dempsey Parks, bondsman; W. Harris, wit.

Smith, Elijah & Sally Jones, 3 Nov 1821; Obediah Butler,
bondsman.

ROWAN MARRIAGES 1753-1868

Smith, George & Phebe Ellis, 25 Oct 1786; J. G. Lauma_n, bondsman; R. Henderson, wit.

Smith, George & Elizabeth Ribely, 24 Oct 1792; Tobias Farror,
bondsman; Jos. Chambers, wit.

Smith, George & Rachael Miller, 14 Feb 1793; Daniel Smith,
bondsman; Jos. Chambers, wit.

Smith, George & Sarah McGuire, 5 Nov 1793; Fredrick Miller,
bondsman.

Smith, George & Peggy Cathey, 16 Dec 1804; Jno. Brem, bondsman;
A. L. Osborn, D. C., wit.

Smith, George & Sarah Holemes, 22 May 1812; Jno. Henry Freeling,
bondsman; Jno Giles, C. C., wit.

Smith, George & Margaret A. Bostian, 13 Dec 1852; Alexander
Bostian, bondsman; J. S. Myers, wit. married 16 Dec 1852 by
Saml Rothrock.

Smith, George D. & Keziah Pearson, 7 Aug 1827; Chs. L. Bowers,
bondsman; J. H. Hardie, wit.

Smith, George F. & May E. Roberson, 6 Aug 1846; Rc. Loury,
bondsman.

Smith, George M. & Deannah Cauble, 12 April 1832; Harres Allen
Brown, bondsman.

Smith, George M. & Mary Brown, 26 Oct 1844; John H. Verble,
bondsman; J. H. Hardie, wit.

Smith, George Road & Polly Smith, 2 April 1800; Henry Giles,
bondsman.

Smith, George W. & Matilda Walton, 6 Oct 1835; Henry A. Walton,
bondsman; Hy. Giles, wit.

Smith, George W. & Susan Beaver, 12 June 1837; Joseph Woods,
bondsman.

Smith, George W. & Anny Beaver, 31 Oct 1854; Willis Elles,
bondsman; J. S. Myers, wit.

Smith, George W. & Sarah E. Bostian, 10 Nov 1857; Willis Ellis,
bondsman; James E. Kerr, wit. married 10 Nov 1857 by D. R.
Bradshaw, J. P.

Smith, Henderson M. & Anny A. Harris, 14 Nov 1854; David Smith,
bondsman; J. S. Myers, wit.

Smith, Henry & Barbra Hison, 15 July 1767; John Hison, bondsman;
_____ Frohock, wit.

Smith, Henry & Mary Dillon, 20 Aug 1793; John Rauche, bondsman;
Jos. Chambers, wit.

Smith, Henry & Eve Cleevor, 20 Aug 1803; David Woodson, bondsman; A. L. Osborn, D. C., wit.

Smith, Henry & Anny Kinder, 13 May 1819; Michael Swink, bondsman; Jno. Giles, wit.

Smith, Henry A. & Sarah Ann Weant, 1 Aug 1843; Benjamin Julian, bondsman; J. H. Hardie, wit.

Smith, Hiram & Catharine Overcash, 7 June 1825; Isaac Neisler, bondsman; Hy. Giles, wit.

Smith, Israel & Eliza Jane Houston (colored), 25 Sept 1865; married by J. Rumple, V. D. M.

Smith, Jacob & Christina Shulenbarger, 4 Feb 1801; Philip Correll, bondsman; Jno Brem, wit.

Smith, Jacob & Hannah Martin, 12 Jan 1810; Samuel Creson, bondsman.

Smith, Jacob & Phebe Traylor, 10 April 1819; Adam Hedrick, bondsman; Jno. Giles, wit.

Smith, Jacob & Elizabeth Gents, 11 Nov 1823; John Smith, bondsman; Hy. Giles, wit.

Smith, Jacob A. & Leah L. Shaver, 7 July 1846; Daniel House, bondsman; J. S. Johnston, wit.

Smith, Jacob G. & Sarah Clingman, 3 Oct 1833; Michael Swink, bondsman; Jno. H. Hardie, wit.

Smith, Jacob G. & Lauretta Brown, 26 April 1842; Jno. H. Hardie, wit.

Smith, James & Hannah Hunt, 13 Jan 1779; Gosham Hunt, bondsman; Wm. R. Davie, wit.

Smith, James & Mary Marlin, 25 Feb 1780; Henry Nevins, bondsman; B. Booth Boote, wit.

Smith, James & Ellis Cole, 8 Oct 1792; Andw. Smith, bondsman.

Smith, James & Mary Sheets, 29 Jan 1794; Luis Little, bondsman; G. Enochs, wit.

Smith, James & Eve Feazer, 2 March 1802; Israel Lynn, bondsman; Jno. Brem, wit.

Smith, James & Patsy Anderson, 7 Feb 1804; Ransom Powell, bondsman; A. L. Osborn, D. C., wit.

Smith, James & Milly Owens, 23 Dec 1814; Peter Owen, bondsman; Jno. Giles, wit.

Smith, James & Patsey Yarboro, 2 Feb 1818; Duncan McGill, bondsman; Jno. Giles, wit.

Smith, James & Mary Brown, 19 Feb 1818; George Dunn, bondsman; Roberts Nanny, wit.

Smith, James & Hannah Owens, 5 Sept 1822; Henry Giles, bondsman.

Smith, James & Elizabeth Weeant, 21 June 1825; Henry Giles, bondsman.

Smith, James & Nancy Beck, 4 July 1834; Wiley Bird, bondsman; Susan T. Giles, wit.

Smith, James & Sophia Weant, 22 Aug 1848; Robert Cox, bondsman.

Smith, James A. & Sarah Myors, 14 Feb 1846; Abner W. Owen, bondsman; J. M. Turner, wit.

Smith, James D. & Catharine Krider, 31 Jan 1826; Jacob G. Smith, bondsman; Jno. Giles, wit.

Smith, James H. & Margt. G. Locke, 24 Sept 1842; A. A. Scroggs, bondsman; Jno. H. Hardie, wit.

Smith, James L. & Elizabeth Morton, 23 Dec 1812; Sihon Keeth, bondsman; Jno. Giles, C. C., wit.

Smith, Jeremiah & Lyda Teague, 19 Feb 1812; Isaac Teague, bondsman; Sol. Davis, wit.

Smith, Joel & Elizabeth Miller, 24 March 1828; Wm. H. Smith, bondsman; Jno. H. Hardie, wit.

Smith, John & Jeade Robey, 18 Jan 1788; Tobias Roby, bondsman; Dd. Caldwell, wit.

Smith, John & Hannah McGuire, 9 March 1790; John McKee, bondsman; Ed. Harris, wit.

Smith, John & Judah Bradford (no date, during Admn. of Gov. Dobbs, 1792-1795); Robert Bartley, bondsman; J. Troy, D. C., wit.

Smith, John & Polly Bryan, 14 April 1804; Peter Walton, bondsman; A. L. Osborn, D. C.,wit.

Smith, John & Rachel Sapp, 11 March 1812; William Davis, bondsman; Sol. Davis, wit.

Smith, John & Sally Owen 12 Dec 1812; Peter Owen, bondsman; Jno Giles, C. C., wit.

Smith, John & Polly Smith, 17 May 1817; Peter Smith, bondsman; Jno. Giles, wit.

Smith, John & Visey Ratlege, 15 July 1817; James Partrick, bondsman; R. Powell, wit.

Smith, Jno. & Anny Smith, 24 June 1820; Alfred Smith, bondsman.

Smith, John & Catharine Bellings, 28 Sept 1820; David Smith, bondsman; Jno. Giles, wit.

Smith, John & Sarah Jones, 20 Oct 1820; Jessee Childress, bondsman; R. Powell, wit.

Smith, John & Prudence Smith, 8 Dec 1823; Aaron Stinson, bondsman; E. Brock, J. P., wit.

Smith, John & Jean B. Ijams, 14 Feb 1825; Scarlet Glascock Jr., bondsman; L. R. Rose, J. P., wit.

Smith, John & Susanah Upright, 29 Jan 1827; Jacob Smith, bondsman; John H. Hardie, wit.

Smith, John & Mary Ann Leezer, 2 Nov 1830; William Leazar, bondsman; Jno. H. Hardie, wit.

Smith, John & Mary E. Weeb, 26 Aug 1840; George M. Lyerly, bondsman; Susan T. Giles, wit.

Smith, Jno. & Catharine Stirewalt, 5 May 1845; J. H. Hardie, wit.

Smith John & Mary E. J. Crothers, 26 Dec 1846; Obadiah Woodson, bondsman; John H. Hardie Jr., wit.

Smith, John Christian & Sophia Desh, 7 May 1792; John Mull, bondsman; Chas. Caldwell, wit.

Smith, John G. & Phebe Broadway, 6 May 1854; David Upright, bondsman; J. S. Myers, wit.

Smith, Jno. M. & Joyce Smith, 3 June 1847; H. Turner, bondsman.

Smith, John W. & Teena Ann Smith, 19 April 1858; Elam A. Patterson, bondsman; James E. Kerr, wit. married 27 April 1858 by Rev. B. C. Hall.

Smith, Jonathan & Elizabeth Daniel, 8 Oct 1804; Saml. Johnson, bondsman; A. L. Osborn, D. C., wit.

Smith, Joseph & Mary Kingery, 2 Dec 1774; Daniel Kingry, bondsman; Ad. Osborn, wit.

Smith, Joseph & Susanna Earls, 27 Feb 1788; John Buis, bondsman; Js. McEwin, wit.

Smith, Joseph & Sally Wisemon, 16 Nov 1821; James Wiseman, bondsman.

Smith, Joseph & Rempe Busey, 16 March 1825; John Holobaugh, bondsman; W. Harris, wit.

Smith, Joshua & Miney Jane Wilson, 31 May 1857; Bennet Russell, bondsman; James E. Kerr, wit. married 1 June 1857 by J. W. Brown, J. P.

Smith, Julius L. & Laura A. Wade, 12 June 1862; B. C. Trexler, bondsman; Obadiah Woodson, wit.

Smith, Jurard K. & Joicey C. S. Shuping, 24 Dec 1864; William A. Shuping, bondsman; Obadiah Woodson, wit.

Smith, Leander & Susanna Tucker, 23 June 1785; Daniel Hull, bondsman.

Smith Leonard & Susannah Holmes, 9 March 1805; Leonard Smith, bondsman.

Smith Leonard & Rebecca Workman, 9 Jan 1823; Turley Harriss, bondsman; Hy. Giles, wit.

Smith, Levi & Patsey Holden, 24 Feb 1809; Adam Little, bondsman.

Smith, Lewis & Sarah Esteb, 7 Sept 1791; Isaac Esteb, bondsman; Basil Gaither, wit.

Smith, Mathias & Peggy Josey, 18 Aug 1822; Daniel Josey, bondsman; Jno. Giles, wit.

Smith, Michael & Mary Moser, 3 Oct 1801; Richard Leach, bondsman; Jno. Brem, wit.

Smith, Michael H. & Sarah Ann Smith, 2 Sept 1828; James Mull, bondsman; J. H. Hardie, wit.

Smith, Michal & Ellen Dreneeks, 7 July 1789; Enoch Enochs, John
Beard, bondsman; Will Alexander, wit.

Smith, Moses A. & Ellen S. Correll, 20 May 1857; C. L. Shinn,
bondsman; J. S. Myers, wit. married 20 May 1857 by R. G.
Barrett, Pastor M. E. Church, Salisbury.

Smith, Nicholas & Jane Waters, 3 Dec 1848; Wm. A. Martin,
bondsman; Jac. C. Barnhardt, J. P., wit. married 4 Dec 1858
by E. Mauney, J. P.

Smith, Oliver & Mary Gee, 7 Feb 1825; William Marlow, bondsman;
John Cook, J. P., wit.

Smith, Perrey & Polley Etcherson, 21 Jan 1815; Aquillar Cheshier,
bondsman; Jno March Sr., wit.

Smith, Peter & Patsey Haden, 4 Feb 1818; Ezra Allemong, bondsman.

Smith, Peter M. & Polly Swink, 20 Aug 1812; George Rood Smith,
bondsman; Jno Giles, C. C., wit.

Smith, Philip & Rachael McGuire, 25 June 1796; Robert Bartley,
bondsman; J. Troy, wit.

Smith, Ralph & Mary Sample, 24 Sept 1767; James Potts, bondsman;
Thomas Frohock, wit.

Smith, Reuben & Courtney Lee, 30 Sept 1826; Roberson W. Grant,
bondsman; E. Brock, J. P., wit.

Smith, Richard & Nancey Sweeting, 2 Oct 1765; Hugh Montgomery,
Abner Nash, bondsman; Thomas Frohock, wit.

Smith, Richard & Elizebeth Harwood, 4 Nov 1816; Cornelius Howard,
bondsman; Jn. March Sr., wit.

Smith, Richard A. & Elizabeth Niceler, 9 April 1850; Joshua B.
Woods, bondsman; James E. Kerr, wit.

Smith, Robert L. & Mary Graham, 1 May 1848; Rufus A. Brandon,
bondsman; John H. Hardie Jr., wit.

Smith, Samuel & Dolly Gates, 12 May 1797; William Renshaw,
bondsman; Jno. Rogers, wit.

Smith, Samuel & Catherine Swink, 16 Oct 1826; Enoch Frost,
bondsman; Wm. Hawkins, J. P., wit.

Smith, Samuel J. & Sarah Ann E. Rymer, 5 Nov 1856; Peter Weaver,
bondsman; James E. Kerr, wit. married 6 Nov 1856 by Rev.
B. C. Hall.

Smith, Samuel S. & Nancy Niolas, 20 Oct 1808; John Webb, bondsman; A. L. Osborne, wit.

Smith, Stephen & Nancy Wiseman, 21 March 1813; Wilson MaCrary,
bondsman; Jno. Giles, C. C,, wit.

Smith, T. V. & Mary E. Overman, 20 Nov 1865; John S. Hampton,
bondsman; Obadiah Woodson, wit.

Smith, Thomas & Molly Mackie, 21 Jan 1775; Robert Mackie,
bondsman; Jams. Robinson, wit.

Smith, Thomas & Polly Boss, 10 Dec 1803; Abner Hill, bondsman;
A. L. Osborn, D. C., wit.

Smith, Thomas & Anne Gibson, 15 Aug 1811; Jno. Brandon, bondsman; Geo. Dunn, wit.

Smith, Thomas & Elizabeth Etcherson, 25 Dec 1813; William
Atchason, bondsman; Jn March Sr., wit.

Smith, Thomas H. & Polly Upright, 10 Jan 1853; David K. Woods,
bondsman; J. S. Myers, wit.

Smith, Thomas H. & Sally Upright, 13 Feb 1854; Anderson Broadway, bondsman; J. S. Myers, wit.

Smith, Thomas W. & Mary Bracken, 30 Jan 1820; William Bracken,
bondsman; R. Powell, wit.

Smith, Thomies & Salley Johnson, 27 July 1805; Aron Tucker,
bondsman; Jn. March Sr., wit.

Smith, Tobias & _____, 18 Aug 1796; Hu Horah, bondsman; Jno.
Rogers, wit.

Smith, Tully & Polly McCoy, 18 Sept 1823; Samuel Moore, bondsman;
L. R. Rose, J. P., wit.

Smith, Vinson & Anny Dolin, 21 Dec 1796; James Smith, bondsman;
Jno. Rogers, wit.

Smith, W. H. & Nancy Arey, 9 Sept 1858; A. M. Nesbitt, bondsman;
J. E. Honeycutt, wit. married 9 Sept 1852 by L. C. Groseclose.

Smith, Wellington & E. Elliott, 21 Nov 1838; Jno. J. Shaver,
bondsman; S. Lemly Jr., wit.

Smith, Wesley & Narcissa Burnes, 25 Oct 1851; Gastain Burns,
bondsman; J. S. Myers, wit.

Smith, William & Hannah Justis, 17 Nov 1772; William Ross,
James Ross, bondsmen; Ad. Osborn, wit. consent from Moses
Justus.

Smith, William & Catharine Moore, (no date, during admn. of
Abner Nash 1780-1); Jas. Hacket, bondsman; H. Gifferd, wit.

Smith, William & Marthah Gay (no date, during admn. of Alex.
Martin 1782-3, 1790-1792); Jas. Townsley, bondsman.

Smith, William & Jane Nevins, 3 Feb 1786; John Nevens, bondsman;
Wm. W. Erwin, wit.

Smith, William & Betsy Jones, 11 June 1797; Charles Hutson,
bondsman; Jno. Rogers, wit.

Smith, William & Elizabeth Neat, 29 May 1802; Geo. Knatzer,
bondsman; Jno. Brem, wit.

Smith, William & Sarah Rice, 16 Sept 1814; Richard Smith,
bondsman; Geo. Dunn, wit.

Smith, William & Eliza Steel, 13 Feb 1826; Giles Webb, bondsman;
Hy. Giles, wit.

Smith, William A. & Elizabeth Broadway, 25 Jan 1865; Richard A. Smith, bondsman; Obadiah Woodson, wit.

Smith, William C. & Marthy Hodge, 27 Aug 1835; Wiley Morgan, bondsman; Jno. Shauser, wit.

Smith, William H. & Nancy Smith, 4 Jan 1827; Henry Sloan, bondsman; J. H. Hardie, wit.

Smith, William J. & Sarah Smithdeal, 30 Dec 1852; Saml. Reeves, bondsman; J. S. Myers, wit.

Smithdeal, Adam A. & Rebecca Coughenour, 7 May 1844; Stephen G. Murr, bondsman; Obadiah Woodson, wit.

Smithdeal, George & Rebecca Smith, 16 Dec 1851; Saml. Reeves, bondsman; J. S. Myers, wit.

Smithdeal, John & Polly Cauble, 19 Dec 1821; James Cauble, bondsman; Jno. Giles, wit.

Smithdeal, John & Margt. Peeler, 8 Aug 1843; Adam A. Smithdeal, bondsman; J. H. Hardie, wit.

Smithdeal, John & Mary Morgan, 4 June 1864; Thomas McNeely, bondsman; Obadiah Woodson, wit.

Smithdeal, Joseph & Maria Owens, 29 March 1855; Adam A. Smithdeal, bondsman; J. S. Myers, wit. married 29 March 1855 by W. A. Walton, J. P.

Smithdeal, William & Laura K. Smith, 21 Dec 1865; William H. Smith, bondsman; Obadiah Woodson, wit.

Smitheel, George & Caty Hartman, 28 Aug 1817; Jacob Rusier, bondsman; Milo A. Giles, wit.

Smoot, Alexander & Temperance Neely, 28 Feb 1828; Abel McNeely, bondsman; Thomas McNeely, J. P., wit.

Smoot, Daniel J. & Polley Anderson, 27 Dec 1811; Garland Anderson, bondsman; Jn. March Sr., wit.

Smoot, Eliphelet & Jean Hannah, 24 Sept 1818; Daniel J. Smoot, bondsman; R. Powell, wit.

Smoot, Elisha A. J. & Jemima Rice, 19 March 1817; William Hawkins, bondsman; R. Powell, wit.

Smoot, John Jinneber & Marey Trout, 24 Sept 1808; Wilm. Smoot, bondsman; Jn. March Sr., wit.

Smoot, Thomas & Elezabeth Holeman, 5 Jan 1829; Abel McNeely, bondsman; L. R. Rose, J. P., wit.

Smoot, Vernon & Elizabeth Wilkerson, 21 Aug 1820; Duncan McGill, bondsman; Milo A. Giles, wit.

Smyth, David & Anne Poyner, 29 June 1818; Benjamin Poyner, bondsman; R. Powell, wit.

Smyth, James C. & Julia E. Long, 26 Feb 1857; C. S. Brown, bondsman; James E. Kerr, wit. married 26 Feb 1857 by Jno. H. Parker, Min. Prot. Epis. Church.

Snead, Charles H. & S. L. Williams, 3 Oct 1864; Junius A. Fox, bondsman; Obadiah Woodson, wit.

Snider, Adam & Cristena Lucable, 17 Oct 1811; Frederick Walser, bondsman; George Snider, Joseph Clarke, wit.

Snider, Andrew & Rebecca Parker, 7 April 1821; Lawrence Porter, bondsman; Hy. Giles, wit.

Snider, David & Barbara Workman, 7 Sept 1817; Jonathan Snider, bondsman; R. Harriss, J. P., wit.

Snider, Henry & Tilly Porter, 20 July 1813; Jacob Smeather, bondsman; Ezra Allemong, wit.

Snider, Jacob & Sarah Mikel, 22 Jan 1810; Samuel Mickel, bondsman; Joseph Clarke, wit.

Snider, John A. & Sarah H. Smith, 4 Sept 1855; Philip P. Meroney, bondsman; J. S. Myers, wit.

Snider, Matthias & Elizabeth Eckle, 15 Jan 1779; Jacob Eckle, bondsman; Wm. R. Davie, wit.

Snider, Paul & Mary Spaugh, 21 Nov 1818; John Opitz, bondsman; Thos Hampton, wit.

Snider, Philip & Salley Walser, 11 June 1821; William Walser, bondsman; Andrew Swicegood, wit.

Snider, Samuel & Ann Layton, 17 May 1865; Charles Mesimore, bondsman; Obadiah Woodson, wit.

Snoddy, William & Margret McNeely, 26 Sept 1782; Thos. Patton, bondsman; Ad. Osborn, wit.

Snow, Henrey & Anney Evins, 14 Dec 1803; Cornelious Howard, bondsman; John March Sr., wit.

Snow, Henry & Peggy Edwards, 30 Oct 1794; Stephen Ellis, bondsman; John Eccles, wit.

Snow, William & Elizabeth Jacks, 12 Oct 1788; Thos. Cooper, bondsman; Wm. Alexander, wit.

Snow, William & Milly Robison, 15 March 1775; Wm. Gilbert, bondsman; Ad. Osborn, wit.

Sochler, Christian & Margaret S. Anthony, 15 April 1847; Philip Freeze, bondsman; J. H. Hardie Jr., wit.

Sommers, Jesse & Rachel Gaither, 31 Dec 1793; Thomas Forcam, bondsman; B. John Pinchback, John Thomas Pinchback, wit.

Sossaman, Daniel & Mary Owens, 16 Feb 1844; M. C. Griffin, bondsman; J. H. Hardie, wit.

Sossaman, Henry & Barbara Fisher, 5 Aug 1786; Peter Faust, bondsman; Jno. Macay, wit.

Sossamon, Henry H. & Sally Fisher, 22 April 1822; Tobias Brown, bondsman.

Sossaman, Jacob & Sarah Reeves, __ March 1811; Jas. Gillaspie, bondsman; Jno. Giles, C. C., wit.

Sossaman, James W. & Elizabeth Hill, 4 Nov 1854; Jacob Correll, bondsman; J. S. Myers, wit.

Sossamon, Harvey M. & Nancy Wadsworth, 11 Aug 1847; Cyrus West, bondsman.

Sotherlin, Alvis & Charity Hitchcock, 27 Jan 1819; William Davis, bondsman; Sol. Davis, wit.

Sour, Michael & Barbara Sink, 6 Oct 1792; Volentine Sour, bondsman; Max. Chambers, wit.

Sour, Peter & Catharine Heckler, 29 May 1794; John Sour, bondsman; J. Troy, D. C., wit.

Sours, Valentine & Mary Derr, 14 Feb 1792; Peter Faust, bondsman; Chs. Caldwell, wit.

Soughers, Philip & Polly Leonard, 26 March 1816; Michael Craver Jr., bondsman; Joseph Clarke, wit.

Southers, Michael & Elizabeth Miller, 20 Aug 1822; Absolom Brewer, bondsman; M. A. Giles, wit.

Sowers, David & Sally Long, 12 Feb 1818; Henry Verble, bondsman; Milo A. Giles, wit.

Sowers, Felix & Martha Ann Bradshaw, 29 June 1843; Saml. W. James, bondsman; J. H. Hardie, wit.

Sowers, George & Catharine Kesler, 4 Nov 1821; John Kesler, bondsman; Jno. Giles, wit.

Sowers, Henry & Sally Link, 6 June 1812; George Swink, bondsman; Geo. Dunn, wit.

Sowers, John & Rebeca Sink, 4 Sept 1818; Henry Verble, bondsman; Roberts Nanny, wit.

Sowers, Michael & Christianna Long, 8 Oct 1815; David Sowers, bondsman; Silas Peace, wit.

Sowers, Peter & Anna Goodman; 23 Nov 1829; George Vogler, bondsman; J. H. Hardie, wit.

Sowers, Rufus A. & Hannah Beefle, 11 Aug 1853; William J. Overcash, bondsman; J. S. Myers, wit.

Spach, Christian & Faner Stephens, 16 Dec 1809; Aquillar Cheshier, bondsman; Jn. March Sr., wit.

Spach, Joseph & Elizabeth Miller, 30 March 1821; Fredrick Spach, bondsman; Sol. Davis, J. P., wit.

Spafford, Samuel & Susannah Boyd, 26 Sept 1803; James Wallen, bondsman; A. L. Osborne, wit.

Sparks, Cornelius & Susanah Stephens, 14 Dec 1812; Abraham March, bondsman; Jn March Sr., wit.

Sparks, Ephram & Sarah Douthit, 10 Aug 1811; James E. Brown, bondsman; Jn. March Sr., wit.

Sparks, Jonas & Mary Eakle, 5 Sept 1786; Peter Little, bondsman; Hu. Magoune, wit.

Sparks, Jonas & Anney Katon, 15 Oct 1796; John Hill, bondsman; Jno. Rogers, wit.

Sparks, Joseph & Febey Hinkle, 28 Jan 1811; Jesse Walker, bondsman; Jn. March Sr., wit.

Sparks, Joseph & Polley Call, 15 Dec 1814; Jesse Walker, bondsman; Jn March Sr., wit.

Sparks, Joseph & Polly Cole, 28 Aug 1823; Fielding Slater, bondsman; M. Hanes, J. P., wit.

Speak, Martin & Rebekah Blackwood, 8 Feb 1799; William Bruner, bondsman.

Spears, Josiah W. & Martha H. Earnhardt, 10 Feb 1859; Jesse Thomason, bondsman; married 10 Feb 1859 by J. Thomason, J. P.

Spears, Sidney W. & Margaret Shaver, 29 Jan 1835; Benjamin Fraley, bondsman; Jno Giles, wit.

Speck, George & Jareda Berry, 14 June 1796; Michael Avault, bondsman; J. Troy, wit.

Speck, Monroe & Carolina Bever, 27 Jan 1852; Monford S. Beaver, bondsman; James E. Kerr, wit. married 27 Jan 1852 by James H. Enniss, J. P.

Speck, William & Amanda Allen, 13 March 1854; Thomas Rimer, bondsman; J. S. Myers, wit.

Spence, Joseph & Ally Skean, 7 Aug 1821; Osborn Skeen, bondsman; Hy. Giles, wit.

Spencer, Goodmon & Elizabeth Gadlin, 21 May 1844; Jno Hartman, bondsman; John H. Hardie Jr., wit.

Spikes, Peter & Ann Forkinson, 16 Aug 1820; Peter Clemmons, bondsman; A. Swicegood, wit.

Spolman, Frederick & Salley Spurgin, 10 Dec 1795; Squier Ledford, bondsman; Fredrick Miller, wit.

Spoolman, Ephraim & Jean Stout, 29 Dec 1807; Jeremiah Kimbrough, bondsman; Wm. Welborn, wit.

Sport, Benjamin & Isbol Hendrix, 1 Jan 1815; Elijah Lyons, bondsman; R. Powell, wit.

Sport, Daniel & Mary Rogers, 19 Dec 1830; H. F. Willson, bondsman; L. R. Rose, J. P., wit.

Sport, James & Catherine Baxter, 21 April 1825; Eliphelet Smoot Sr., bondsman.

Sprague, Henry B. & Dorcas M. Happoldt, 9 Nov 1858; married 10 Nov 1858 by T. G. Haughton.

Springs, Adam Alexr. & Eliza March, 15 Oct 1833; Henry Giles, bondsman.

Spry, Asberry & Serena Yarbrough, 4 Nov 1851; Micajah Griffin, bondsman; J. S. Myers, wit. married __ Nov 1851 by T. Page Ricaud, Pastor M. E. C. South, N. C. Conf.

Spry, Benjamin & Hinson Chaffin, 24 Feb 1825; William Drake, bondsman; Joseph Hanes, J. P., wit.

Spry, Enoch & Mary Lingle, 1 Sept 1852; Chivans Spry, bondsman; J. S. Myers, wit. married 1 Sept 1852 by Jno. M. McConnaughey, J. P.

Spry, Enuck & Polley Phelps, 26 Nov 1816; John Spry, bondsman; Jn. March Sr., wit.

Spry, Frances & Sarah Jones, 29 Dec 1808; Samuel Branick, bondsman; Jn. March Sr., wit.

Spry, James & Elizebeth Wood, 15 Jan 1818; Daniel Wood, bondsman; Mack Crump, wit.

Spry, John & Elizabeth Jones, 29 April 1829; John Monday, bondsman; C. Harbin, J. P., wit.

Spry, Martin & Milly Ballard, 5 May 1826; Rubin Ballard, bondsman; M. Hanes, J. P., wit.

Spry, Samuel & Mary Ann Shuping, 4 Aug 1858; R. H. Smith, bondsman; James E. Kerr, wit.

Spry, William & Elizabeth Phelp, 4 Jan 1817; Abenton Phelp, bondsman; Wm. Piggott, J. P., wit.

Spurgen, Squier & Nancy Williams, 7 May 1822; Joseph Delk, bondsman; Ams. Wright, wit.

Spurgin, Ely & Rachel Nuscomb, 20 April 1806; Wm. Newcomb, bondsman; William Piggatt, J. P., wit.

Spurgin, Samuel & Mary Houk, 8 Aug 1806; John Spurgin, bondsman; Jno. Monroe, wit.

Spurgin, Zachaus & Mary Teague, 2 Dec 1813; Jeremiah Smith, bondsman; Sol. Davis, J. P., wit.

Stafford, James & Dobby G. Johnston, 18 Aug 1825; Rufus D. Johnston, bondsman; Hy. Giles, wit.

Stagner, Barney & Sarah Proter, 27 Aug 1783; John James, bondsman; Jno. McNairy, wit.

Stagner, Georg & Catharine Hendrix, 1 June 1805; James Hendrix, bondsman; A. L. Osborn, D. C., wit.

Stagner, George & Sarah Hillard, 16 March 1793; Stephen Pearson, bondsman; Jos. Chambers, wit.

Stallings, Thomas & Nancy Faugson, 24 Aug 1808; William Ward, bondsman; Jn. March Sr., wit.

Standly, Jehu & Sally Bedwell, 7 March 1805; James Bedwell, bondsman; J. Hunt, wit.

Standly, Joseph & Mary Moore, 9 Dec 1802; George Moore, bondsman; A. L. Osborn, D. C.,wit.

Stanfield, Thomas & Mary Wood, 11 Dec 1779; Edward Pointer, bondsman; B. Booth Boote, wit.

Stanly, John & Elizabeth Veach, 18 June 183_; Wm. Moor, bondsman; Wm. Hawkins, wit.

Stanly, Jonah & Mary Brandon, 20 March 1827; Bryson Moore, bondsman; Thomas McNeely, J. P., wit.

Stanly, Zachariah & Polly Curry, 26 March 1803; James Pierce, bondsman; J. Hunt, wit.

Stansill, John B. & Laura L. Bradshaw, 15 Dec 1860; T. F. Hall, bondsman; John Wilkinson, wit.

Star, John & Rachel Jobe, 24 March 1795; Thomas Job, bondsman; John Eccles, wit.

Starnes, Henry R. & Jane Earnhart, 6 Oct 1857; David Crotzer, bondsman; H. W. Hill, wit. married 6 Oct 1857 by H. W. Hill.

Starnes, John & Jane Thompson, 5 June 1821; Robert Lindsay, bondsman; Sol. Davis, J. P., wit.

Starns, Conrod & Margret Brown, 16 Sept 1778; George Brown, bondsman; Ad. Osborn, wit.

Starns, Daniel & Sophia Arnhart, 12 Jan 1814; John Trexler, bondsman; Geo. Dunn, wit.

Starns, David & Barbaria Starns, 28 Feb 1784; Joseph Starns, bondsman.

Starns, John & Jena Thompson, 5 June 1821; request for license by J. W. Moyer.

Starr, Matthew & Editha Bowden, 22 April 1834; James K. Smith, bondsman; J. Tomlinson, J. P., wit.

Starratt, James L. & _____, 5 May 1862; Jesse P. Wiseman, bondsman.

Steel, Franklin & Milly Felker, 24 Feb 1843; Davison Madden, bondsman; J. H. Hardie, wit.

Steel, James & Esther Dickey, 12 March 1788; Samuel Steel, bondsman; Jas. McEwin, wit.

Steel, John L. & Mary A. H. Williamson, 3 Jan 1845; Davison Madden, bondsman; J. H. Hardie, wit.

Steel, Ninian & Agnes Graham, 31 March 1768; Robrt Steel, William Knox, bondsmen; John Frohock, wit. consent from Richard Graham, 31 March 1768.

Steel, Ninian & Elizabeth Chambers, 12 March 1770; Henry Chambers, bondsman; Thomas Frohock, wit.

Steel, Ninian & Jane Locke, 29 July 1793; James Lock, bondsman; Jos. Chambers, wit.

Steele, Austin & Amey Porter, 25 Dec 1850; James Mitchell, bondsman; J. S. Myers, wit.

Steele, David & Nancy Brandon, 19 Jan 1819; William Foster, bondsman.

Steele, Henry & Susanna Andrews, 27 March 1800; John Andrews, bondsman; Matt. Troy, wit.

Steele, J. W. & Margaret Ann Irvin, 14 April 1860; W. A. Luckey, bondsman; John Wilkinson, wit. married 19 April 1860 by Saml. B. O. Wilson.

Steele, James A. & Minta W. Williamson, 7 Jan 1833; Robert Chunn, bondsman; Jno. H. Hardie, wit.

Steele, John & Easther M. McNeely, 13 Jan 1829; John S. Carson, bondsman; Jn. H. Hardie, wit.

Steele, John L. & Elizabeth Donaho, 21 March 1856; Silas L. Smith, bondsman; James E. Kerr, wit.

Steele, John W. & Rebecca C. Luckie, 30 July 1830; James Kerr, bondsman; J. S. Myers, wit.

Steele, M. H. & Emily K. Cowan, 26 Oct 1865; Joseph C. Irvin, bondsman; Obadiah Woodson, wit.

Steele, Matthew L. & Fanny Knox, 5 Aug 1825; Ezekiel Knox, bondsman; W. Harris, wit.

Steele, Ninian & Mary Robison, 11 March 1809; Henry Robison, bondsman; A. D. Osborne, wit.

Steele, Prince & Mary Valentine (colored), 16 Aug 1865; married by Zuck Haughton.

Steele, Richard & Pearmealy Lightell, 9 June 1847; Hezekiah Turner, bondsman.

Steele, William L. & Catharine Hughey, 1 March 1856; Jas. W. Shinn, bondsman; J. S. Myers, wit. married 4 March 1856 by Saml. B. O. Wilson, V. D. M.

Steelman, Mathias & Salley Estep, 15 Jan 1816; Abraham Creson, bondsman; R. Powell, wit.

Steelman, William & Catharina Cain, 1 July 1823; Hiram Cook, bondsman; John Cook, wit.

Steelmon, Joshua & Mary Holemon, 4 Nov 1811; George Steelmon, bondsman; Jn March Sr., wit.

Steller, Jacob & Sarah Litacar, 23 June 1825; Lewis Willhelm, bondsman; Hy. Giles, wit.

Stephens, John & Anny Thomas, 1 Nov 1800; Thomas Williams, bondsman; Jno. Brem, wit.

Stephens, William & Nancy March, 31 Oct 1795; James Ellis, bondsman; John Eccles, wit.

Stephens, William & Jensy Martin, 13 Feb 1815; John Marton, bondsman; Geo. Dunn, wit.

Stephenson, James & Jane Stephenson, 1 Sept 1781; Joseph Sharpe, bondsman; Jams. Robinson, D. C. C., wit.

Stephenson, John & Polly Welman, 14 Jan 1817; William Lane, bondsman; R. Powell, wit.

Stephenson, William & Polly Hess, 17 May 1815; John McDaniel, bondsman; Geo. Dunn, wit.

Sterns, Nicholas & Sophia Cress, 19 Dec 1791; Charles Starns, bondsman; Chs. Caldwell, wit.

Stevens, William & Elsee Hinkle, 8 Dec 1802; Rudolph Eastep, bondsman; A. L. Osborn, D. C., wit.

Stevenson, John & Jane McClalland, 6 Feb 1767; Will McClalland, bondsman; Tho Frohock, wit.

Stevenson, John & Elizabeth Cohran, 23 July 1811; Thos. McEwen, bondsman; Geo. Dunn, wit.

Stevenson, John W. & Mary C. Luckey, 16 Dec 1845; John T. Murdock, bondsman; J. H. Hardie, wit.

Stevenson, William & Prudence Hall, 22 Feb 1788; James Hall, bondsman; Js. McEwin, wit.

Stewart, Hugh T. & Catherine M. Barr, 26 July 1833; Jno. J. Blackwood, bondsman; Robt. Cochran, J. P., wit.

Stewart, J. J. & Clara L. Bruner, 2 April 1861; J. A. Ramsay, bondsman; James E. Kerr, wit. married 2 April 1861 by L. C. Groseclose, Pastor of St. John's Ev. Luth. Church, Salisbury, N. C.

Stewart, Jacob & Nancy Potts, 17 Dec 1823; Samuel Stewart, bondsman; Jno. Giles, wit.

Stewart, John & Margrett Potts, 12 March 1770; Moses Potts, bondsman; Thomas Frohock, wit.

Stewart, John & Mary Sawyers, 10 March 1818; Duncan Campbell, bondsman.

Stewart, John T. & Martha C. Neal, 7 Feb 1855; Jos. F. Chambers, bondsman; married 15 Feb 1865 by John E. Pressly, Minister.

Stewart, Joseph & Marey Tucker, 15 Dec 1768; William Knox, bondsman; Thos. Frohock, wit.

Stewart, Joseph & Joannah Potts, 29 May 1824; Paschal Rowzer, bondsman; Jno. Giles, wit.

Stewart, R. S. & Margaret A. Barr, 7 Feb 1841; Robt. F. Wilson, bondsman; J. H. Hardie, wit.

Stewart, William & Uranah Lasefield, 7 March 1768; Mark Armstrong, John Stewart, bondsmen; Thomas Frohock, wit.

Stewart, William & Francis Sullivan, 11 Oct 1821; Daniel Wood, bondsman; Hy. Giles, wit.

Stierwalt, David M. & Sallie M. Honeycutt, 24 April 1865; Adam Cline, bondsman; Obadiah Woodson, wit.

Stierwalt, Fredrick A. & Sena Yost, 17 Dec 1855; Edmound Trout-man, bondsman; J. S. Myers, wit. married 20 Dec 1855 by Thornton Butler, V. D. M.

Stikeleather, Joseph & Amanda C. Cook, 27 July 1839; Tobias Goodman, bondsman; J. S. Johnston, wit.

Stikeleather, Matthias & Rachel L. Lemly, 28 Nov 1857; James B.
Gibson, bondsman; James E. Kerr, wit. married 29 Nov 1857
by F. W. Scott, J. P.

Stikeleather, Nicholas & Jane Cooper, 31 July 1821; Andrew
Rickard, bondsman; Jno. Giles, wit.

Stiller, Henry & Elizabeth Willis, 2 Aug 1842; Francis G.
Phillips, bondsman; J. H. Hardie, wit.

Stiller, Julius M. & Rose C. Goodman, 7 Dec 1859; John L.
Ketchey, bondsman; Wm. Locke, wit. married 7 Dec 1859 by
D. Barringer, J. P.

Stiller, William & Martha Ann Laura Wilhelm, 24 Aug 1861; William
C. Brandon, bondsman; Obadiah Woodson, wit. married 29 Aug
1861 by W. A. Houck, J. P.

Stilwell, David & Sarah Maryman, 2 July 1792; Tunis Quick,
bondsman; S. Mitchell, wit.

Stine, Jacob & Molly Hillman, 9 Feb 1802; John Stine, bondsman;
Jno Brem, wit.

Stinson, George & Christena Miller, 18 March 1826; Jacob W.
Miller, bondsman; J. C. Weddington, wit.

Stinson, Joshua & Elizabeth Eastborne, 17 Nov 1798; Isaac Ellis,
bondsman; Edwin J. Osborn, D. C., wit.

Stinson, Theopolis M. & Jane McWilson, 21 Nov 1839; James P.
Stinson, bondsman; John Giles, wit.

Stipe, Christian & Esther Sparks, 9 Dec 1806; Charles F. Bagge,
bondsman; Lazarus Hege, J. P., wit.

Stirawalt, Daniel & Catharine Sifford, 27 Sept 1830; Volentine
Propts, bondsman; Jno. H. Hardie, wit.

Stirewalt, A. G. & Mary A. E. Phillips, 1 March 1862; Jacob
J. Pleuss, bondsman; James E. Kerr, wit.

Stirewalt, Adam & Judy C. Shulibarger, 3 Jan 1840; Mathew Plumer,
bondsman; Hy. Giles, wit.

Stirewalt, Caleb & Michel Newman, 4 Aug 1835; Henry Pless,
bondsman; Jno. Giles, wit.

Stirewalt, Charles M. & Jemima L. Blackwelder, 27 Jan 1857;
Caleb Stirewalt, bondsman; James E. Kerr, wit. married 29
Jan 1857 by Henry Miller, J. P.

Stirewalt, Frederick & Catharine Smith, 22 March 1825; George
Youst, bondsman; Hy. Giles, wit.

Stirewalt, Henrey & Christena Holtimer, 27 Sept 1824; Abraham
Holtaman, bondsman; Hy. Giles, wit.

Stirewalt, Henry & Betsey Recard, 23 Dec 1812; George Lipe,
bondsman; Jno Giles, C. C., wit.

Stirewalt, Jacob & Jean Johnston, 11 Sept 1809; Francis Johnson,
bondsman; Geo. Dunn, wit.

Stirewalt, Jacob & Mary K. Shaver, 27 July 1846; Jacob A. Smith, bondsman; J. S. Johnston, wit.

Stirewalt, Jacob & Margaret E. Rodgers, 27 Nov 1851; James Rodgers, bondsman; J. S. Myers, wit.

Stirewalt, John & Elizabeth Randleman, 22 Marvh 1794; Frederick Styerwalt, bondsman; Jo. Chambers, wit.

Stirewalt, Michael & Mary Hoffman, 20 Feb 1796; Frederick Stirewalt, bondsman; J. Troy, wit.

Stirewalt, Paul & Margaret Smith, 9 Nov 1836; Jacob Smith, bondsman.

Stirewalt, W. & Mary A. E. Jacobs, 21 March 1846; L. C. Rodgers, bondsman; J. H. Hardie, wit.

Stirewalt, William & Elmira Rogers, 15 July 1851; James Rogers, bondsman; James E. Kerr, wit.

Stiyerwalt, Adam & Barbara Buice, 21 Oct 1797; Michl. Styrwalt, bondsman; Jno. Rogers, wit.

Stockstal, Morriss & Sarah Williams, 4 March 1768; Shadrack Williams, bondsman; Jno Frohock, wit.

Stockstill, Masheck & Anne Call, 23 Nov 1790; Daniel Call, bondsman; Basil Gaither, wit.

Stoker, Allen & Mary Hampton, 16 April 1810; David Gardner, bondsman; Robt. Morgan, wit.

Stoker, James A. & Frances Griffin, 1 Dec 1852; A. M. Nesbitt, bondsman; J. S. Myers, wit. married 2 Dec 1852 by D. W. Honeycutt, J. P.

Stoker, John & Sarah A. Turner, 22 Feb 1853; D. C. Parks, bondsman; J. S. Myers, wit. married 22 Feb 1853 by Jas. G. Jacocks.

Stokes, John & Betsy Pearson, 8 May 1788; Spruce Macay, bondsman.

Stokes, Kinchen & Nancy Newsom, 13 Dec 1802; John Aderton, bondsman; A. L. Osborn, D. C., wit.

Stokes, Littleberry & Prucilla Henley, 4 May 1832; Alexander Henley, bondsman; J. H. Hardie, wit.

Stone, Abner & Mary Ball, 10 Jan 1818; James Veach, bondsman; Silas Peace, wit.

Stone, Joseph & Eve Sink, 1 Oct 1814; James Veach, bondsman; Jno. Giles, C. C., wit.

Stone, William & Ann Hodges, 11 Feb 1780; Darby Henley, bondsman; B. Booth Boote, wit.

Stoner, Alexr. & Rachael Stoner, 12 April 1833; Peter Stoner, bondsman; J. H. Hardie, wit.

Stoner, Alexander & Lovina Mull, 1 Sept 1840; Peter Stoner, bondsman; Susan T. Giles, wit.

Stoner, C. W. & Peny Morgan, 25 Dec 1856; D. J. Misenhimer, bondsman; H. W. Hill, J. P.; married 26 Dec 1856 by H. W. Hill.

Stoner, Charles & Leah Lutwick, 25 March 1833; Henry Harkey, bondsman.

Stoner, Charles W. & Elizabeth Bruner, 1 Jan 1851; Milas A. File, bondsman; James E. Kerr, wit.

Stoner, Daniel & Rachel A. Bruner, 16 Aug 1856; Henry Wilhelm, bondsman; James E. Kerr, wit. married 16 Aug 1856 by Levi Trexler, J. P.

Stoner, Henry & Barbara Earnheart, 1 May 1818; Henry Wilhelm, bondsman; Jno. Giles, wit.

Stoner, Jacob & Barbara Trexler, 2 March 1814; Clement Arnold, bondsman; Geo. Dunn, wit.

Stoner, Jacob & Rachael Mull, 21 Dec 1850; Edward Mull, bondsman; J. S. Myers, wit.

Stoner, Jonathan & Easter Lutewick, 26 April 1830; John Canup, bondsman; Jno. H. Hardie, wit.

Stoner, Levi & Elizth Chanly, 22 Feb 1845; Milas Ramey, bondsman; J. H. Hardie, wit.

Stoner, Peter & Peggy Eller, 26 May 1807; John Eller, bondsman; A. L. Osborn, D. C., wit.

Stoner, Peter & Mary Campbell, 3 Nov 1842; John Campbell, bondsman; J. H. Hardie, wit.

Stoner, Rily & Edy Eller, 27 Nov 1841; David Campbell, bondsman; J. S. Johnston, wit.

Stoner, Samuel & E. C. Richey, 14 April 1857; Daniel Miller, bondsman; H. W. Hill, wit. married 14 April 1857 by H. W. Hill.

Stoner, Samul & Peggy Wilhelm, 3 April 1830; Peter Stoner, bondsman; Jno. H. Hardie, wit.

Stoner, William & Roamy Morgan, 27 Jan 1857; Solomon Morgan, bondsman; Levi Trexler, wit. married 27 Jan 1857 by Levi Trexler, J. P.

Stonestreet, Elisha & Margaret West, 13 Sept 1809; John Baley, bondsman; John Hanes, wit.

Stonestreet, Benjamin & Nancy Smith, 18 Jan 1814; Joseph Snider, bondsman; John Hanes, wit.

Stonestreet, Willburn & Sarah Ann Ijames, 8 March 1832; Jacob Allen, bondsman; Wm. Hawkins, wit.

Storck, Charles & Christian Beard, 14 Feb 1790; Lewis Beard, bondsman.

Storey, Benjamin & Hester Meconel, 3 Sept 1787; H. Horah, bondsman; Fanny Macay, wit.

Story, Thomas & Mary Pitman, 15 June 1785; Nathaniel Parker, bondsman; Hu. Magoune, wit.

Stowe, Joel & Catharine Buck, 29 Oct 1847; Martin Buck, bondsman; Jno. Giles, wit.

Stowe, John & Martha Jones, married 13 Jan 1853 by D. W. Honeycutt, J. P.

Strange, Julius & Polly Miller, 2 May 1809; Robert Strange, bondsman; Jno. Giles, wit.

Strange, William & Frances McKee, 1 May 1779; Henrey Strange, bondsman; Archid. Kerr, wit.

Stricker, Daniel & Chloe Willhelmisson, 3 Jan 1788; Peter Crull, bondsman; Js. McEwen, wit.

Striker, Moses & Elizabeth Casper, 23 Aug 1836; Martin Youts, bondsman; John Giles, wit.

Stringer, John & Mary Turmour, 27 July 1802; Conrad Eller, bondsman; A. L. Osborn, D. C., wit.

Stroop, Jacob & Elisabeth Moor, 24 Sept 1799; Felder Bevin, bondsman; N. Chaffin, J. P., wit.

Stroud, Arthur & Nancy Evans, 14 April 1829; William Crittendon, bondsman; C. Harbin, J. P., wit.

Stuart, Benjamin & Elizabeth Winscut, 16 Aug 1769; Isiah Stuart, Mathew Bailey, bondsmen; John Frohock, wit. consent 19 August 1769 from Abraham Coron, stating that her father and mother is dead and she is of age, and her brothers and sisters all hve given consent.

Stuart, Isaac & Susannah Thornbery, 8 May 1770; William Mongumerey, Charles Russell, bondsmen; Thomas Frohock, wit. consent from Thomas Thornbery, wit by William Mongumery, Thomas Harbens(?).

Stuart, Issiah & Mary Cox, 1 Sept 1764; Samuel Stuart, bondsman; Thomas Frohock, wit. consent from Dinah Co(x̄), 30 Aug 1764.

Stroud, John & Elender Leach, 13 March 1830; Isam Gaither, bondsman; L. R. Rose, J. P., wit.

Stroud, Thomas & Lyllyann Critenton, 30 April 1819; Moses Granger, bondsman; R. Powell, wit.

Stuart, James & Sarah Howel, 6 Dec 1789; James McFeeters, bondsman; Ed. Harris, wit.

Stuart, John & Sarah Bostian, 24 Jan 1791; Conrad Brem, bondsman.

Stuart, John & Martha Gordon, 6 Dec 1803; Wm. Were, bondsman; Willm. Welborn, wit.

Stuart, Thomas & Marah Shoaf, 10 Aug 1816; Francis Barnycastle, bondsman; Thos. Hampton, wit.

Stub, Anthony & Rosena Kesler, 16 Jan 1845; Saml Fraley, bondsman.

Stubblefield, George & Keziah Harvey, 13 April 1773; George McKnight, bondsman; consent from Jno. Harvey, 13 April 1773, father of Kezia.

Styers, Samuel & Sarah Moore, 21 April 1842; Robt. Morris, bondsman; Jno. H. Hardie, wit. married 21 April 1842.

Subgraves, John & Elizabeth Morris, 24 May 1802; John Hyatt, bondsman; Wm. Welborn, wit.

Sumers, Bazel & Anna Ellis, 12 Feb 1788; Saml. Ellis, bondsman; Js. McEwin, wit.

Summe, Peter & Dorrothy Darky, 24 Oct 1794; John Summe, bondsman; Mat. Troy, wit.

Summit, Penkny & Barby B. Miller, 15 Feb 1851; Wilie Knup, bondsman; M. S. Holmes, wit.

Sumner, Moses & Nancy Henley, 30 Sept 1802; John Cornelison, bondsman; Js. McEwin, wit.

Sunner, John & Sucky Vernon, 17 Feb 1789; Arthur Mathis, bondsman; Will Alexander, wit.

Supenfield, Michael & Sarah Mires (no date, during admn. of Alex. Martin); H. Magoune, bondsman; Hugh Magoune, wit.

Sutherland, Daniel & Anne Renshaw, 25 Dec 1778; William R. Davie, bondsman; Ad. Osborn, wit. consent from Abram Renshaw.

Swain, William & Ann Robbins, 27 April 1765; Will Ledford, Jonath. Robins, bondsmen; William Frohock, wit.

Swan, Benjamin & Betsey Adams, 6 Jan 1820; John Black, bondsman; R. Powell, wit.

Swan, Charles & Polly B. Cowan, 22 April 1818; Hezekiah Swann, bondsman; Milo A. Giles, wit.

Swan, John & Catherine Bouden, 11 Oct 1827; Miles West, bondsman; L. R. Rose, J. P., wit.

Swan, Joseph & Keziah Porter, 26 Oct 1774; William Porter, bondsman; Ad. Osborn, wit.

Swan, Richard & Catherine Barber, 12 Aug 1812; John Williamson, bondsman; Geo. Dunn, wit.

Swann, Hezekiah & Susanna Marlin, 8 Feb 1814; Charles Swan, bondsman; Geo. Dunn, wit.

Swann, James H. & Irena Beaman, 16 Dec 1832; Anderson Cain, bondsman; Jas. Frost, J. P., wit.

Swann, John & Mary Elrod, 8 Feb 1813; James Humphries, bondsman; Geo. Dunn, wit.

Swann, Thomas S. & Sally Hillard, 22 Oct 1817; Charles Swann, bondsman; Roberts Nanny, wit.

Swann, William & Rosanna McCloud, 8 June 1793; Daniel Matheson, bondsman; Jos. Chambers, wit.

Swann, Zedekiah & Ann A. Wright, 23 March 1846; John Harris, bondsman; J. H. Hardie, wit.

Swartslander, Philip & Sarah Medly, 31 July 1828; Tully Smith, bondsman; C. Harbin, J. P., wit.

Sweet, Isaac & Anny Black, 9 Feb 1811; Andrew Griffin, bondsman; John Hanes, wit.

Sweet, Stephen & Martha Fraizer, 1 Jan 1815; Minter Mulliner, bondsman; David Mock, wit.

Swicegood, Andrew & Nancy Traylor, 21 Aug 1824; John Robling, bondsman; Hy. Giles, wit.

Swicegood, H. H. & F. E. Myers, 7 Feb 1861; George W. Myers, bondsman; James E. Kerr, wit. married 7 Feb 1861 by David Lentz, J. P.

Swicegood, Phillip & Barbary Doty, 28 Dec 1818; Michael Doty, bondsman; Jno. Giles, wit.

Swicegood, S. J. & Sarah D. Shaver, 29 Oct 1862; D. R. Newsom, bondsman; Obadiah Woodson, wit.

Swift, John & Elizabeth Welborn, 14 July 1791; James Welborn, bondsman; Jno Monro, wit.

Swinford, Elisha & Thankfull Dow, 26 Oct 1784; Kainser Rodger, bondsman.

Swinford, Joshua & Marey Doan, 8 April 1788; Isaciah Doan, bondsman; Dd. Caldwell, wit.

Swink, Barnhart & Suzanah Sappenfield, 28 Jan 1811; John Sappenfield, bondsman; Joseph Clarke, wit.

Swink, Daniel & Susanah Bullen, 25 June 1805; William West, bondsman; Andrew Kerr, wit.

Swink, George & Elizabeth Culp, 19 Jan 1796; Daniel Jacobs, bondsman; J. Troy, wit.

Swink, George & Elizabeth Ford, 3 Sept 1807; Jacob Weant, bondsman.

Swink, George & Maria L. Howlet, 3 Oct 1850; Radford Bailey, bondsman; J. S. Myers, wit.

Swink, George B. & Laura E. Eller, 18 Jan 1855; Benj. F. Weant, bondsman; J. S. Myers, wit. married 19 Jan 1855 by Obadiah Woodson, J. P.

Swink, George L. & Ellen Cozort, 27 Dec 1838; Jno. Coughenaur, bondsman; John Giles, wit.

Swink, George R. & Levina Kincaid, 11 Sept 1828; James Owens, bondsman; J. H. Hardie, wit.

Swink, George W. & Crissy Sophia Fesperman, 28 Sept 1861; William Swisher, bondsman; Obadiah Woodson, wit. married 29 Sept 1861 by Wm. T. Marlin, J. P.

Swink, Henry & Elizabeth Krider, 7 June 1803; Francis Coupee, bondsman; A. L. Osborn, D. C., wit.

Swink, Henry & Elizabeth Jacobs, 4 March 1823; David Jacobs, bondsman; Hy. Giles, wit.

Swink, Henry S. & Ann M. McClellan, 9 April 1852; James Rufus Swink, bondsman; J. S. Myers, wit.

Swink, Jacob & Catharine Agner, 16 Dec 1811; Daniel Swink, bondsman; Jno. Giles, wit.

Swink, James R. & Nancy Wade, 1 Jan 1846; N. W. Fry, bondsman; J. H. Hardie, wit.

Swink, James Rufus & Nancy Kinney, 17 Jan 1842; Charles A. Weant, bondsman; J. S. Johnston, wit.

Swink, John Henry & Polly Shrout, 1 Feb 1815; Peter H. Swink, bondsman; Jno. Giles, C. C., wit.

Swink, Johnson & Eliza Weant, 30 Dec 1829; George M. Weant, bondsman; Jno. H. Hardie, wit.

Swink, Johnson E. & Mary Ann Sanders, 21 May 1849; Wm. A. Swink, bondsman.

Swink, Joseph & Sophia Cauble, 11 Dec 1834; Leonard Krider, bondsman.

Swink, Leonard & Mary Smith, 21 Sept 1779; Christian Barbarick, bondsman; Ad. Osborn, wit.

Swink, Michael & Barbara Smith, 18 Sept 1786; Peter Faust, bondsman; Jno. Macay, wit.

Swink, Michael & Lotty Culenhouse, 29 July 1818; Jno. Giles, wit.

Swink, Michl. & Mary E. Sloan, 12 Aug 1829; Lewis Utezman, bondsman; Jno. H. Hardie, wit.

Swink, Michael H. & Mary Weant, 31 Jan 1818; John H. Swink, bondsman; Henry Giles, wit.

Swink, Otho & Catharine Cauble, 29 March 1849; Noah Lewis, bondsman; J. H. Hardie, wit.

Swink, Peter H. & Catharine Roadsmith, 14 Feb 1803; George Betz, bondsman; Ad. L. Osborn, D. C., wit.

Swink, Peter H. & Rebecca Shuman, 8 May 1851; Rufus W. Woodside, bondsman; J. S. Myers, wit.

Swink, Peter J. & Polly Pinkston, 11 Nov 1818; George Dunn Jr., bondsman; Roberts Nanny, wit.

Swink, Peter R. & Catharine Weant, 10 Sept 1836; Jacob Coughenour, bondsman; Jno. H. Hardie, wit.

Swink, Wiley & Polly Ford, 7 Aug 1830; Fredk. Mowry, bondsman; Jn. A. Giles, wit.

Swink, William A. & Sarah Sawyers, 6 May 1847; John L. Beard, bondsman; John H. Hardie Jr., wit.

Swinney, Anderson & Sarah Bailey, 18 April 1824; Peter Renigar, bondsman; John Cook, J. P., wit.

Swinney, William & Polley White, 6 Aug 1813; William Michael, bondsman; Jn. March Sr., wit.

Swisegood, Jno. & Betsey Delop, 16 Dec 1818; Jno. Haines, bondsman; J. Willson, J. P., wit.

Swisher, Jonas & Mary Jacobs, 14 Dec 1826; Mathiss Swisher, bondsman; John H. Hardie, wit.

Swisher, Mathias & Polly Clodfelter, 26 Dec 1822; Thomas Kincaid, bondsman; M. A. Giles, wit.

Swisher, Michael & Polly Pinkston, 4 March 1824; David Coughanour, bondsman; Hy. Giles, wit.

Swisher, Michael & Sophia Sawyers, 26 Nov 1851; Thomas D. Fraley, bondsman; J. S. Myers, wit. married 27 Nov 1851 by J. Thomason, J. P.

Tacker, Joshua & Susanah Kernut, 2 June 1803; John Tacker, bondsman; Jno. Hawkins, wit.

Tacket, Thomas & Milbrew Williams, 13 June 1829; William Tacket, bondsman; C. Harbin, J. P., wit.

Tagart, William & Edy Ham, 16 Oct 1818; Baker Johnson, bondsman; R. Powell, wit.

Tait, Alex. & Julia Ann Earnhart, 24 Nov 1857; James Elam, bondsman; James E. Kerr, wit. married 24 Nov 1857 by J. M. Brown, J. P.

Tait, Alexander & Elizabeth E. Gibson, 26 July 1854; William Brown, bondsman; James E. Kerr, wit.

Talley, Stephen & Polley Glascock, 24 March 1812; Charles Freeman, bondsman; Jn March Sr., wit.

Tally, Nicholas & Elizabeth Clampitt, 20 Feb 1817; Jesse Chipman, bondsman; Sol. Davis, J. P., wit.

Talor, Gust & Nancey Jones, 15 Dec 1808; William Howard, bondsman; Jn. March Sr., wit.

Talor, Pearce & Margrat Call, 5 Jan 1814; Hezekiah Smith, bondsman; Jn. March Sr., wit.

Tanihill, Zachariah & Rhoda Girs, 1 March 1813; John Girs, bondsman; R. Powell, wit.

Tanner, Taswell & Elizabeth Wade, 2 June 1855; Robert O. Cox, bondsman; J. S. Myers, wit. married 3 June 1855 by Obadiah Woodson, wit.

Tanners, James & Margret Hare, 14 March 1783; Davd. Hare, bondsman; Ad. Osborn, wit.

Tarrh, F. M. & Martha Jane Cranford, 8 June 1864; Calvin J. Miller, bondsman; Obadiah Woodson, wit.

Tarrh, G. C. & Maria M. Canady, 20 June 1838; C. T. Trott, bondsman; S. Lemly Jr., wit.

Tate, Alexander & Elizabeth E. Gibson, 26 July 1854; married 27 July 1854 by Jos. P. Pritchard.

Tate, Samuel & Martha M. Jones, 11 Feb 1860; E. Myers, bondsman; James E. Kerr, wit. married 12 Feb 1860 by T. G. Haughton, Rector of St. Luke's, Salisbury.

Taylor, George & Unity Wyatt, 27 Jan 1795.

Taylor, Henry & Mariah Doby, married 27 Dec 1853 by Levi Trexler, J. P.

Taylor, Lamb & Margaret Cornell, 28 April 1825; Wilie Gaither, bondsman; Jac. Weddington, wit.

Tate, John & Ann Shields, 30 March 1795; Wm. Lowry, bondsman; J. Troy, D. C., wit.

Tatum, Jesse & Leah Owens, 19 March 1810; Barnett Wiatt, bondsman; Jno Giles, C. C., wit.

Taylor, Allomon & Martha Howard, 19 Dec 1834; Andrew Sheets, bondsman; Thomas McNeely, J. P., wit.

Taylor, Benjamin & Margaret Gray, 5 May 1827; Bryan Ellis, bondsman; C. Harbin, J. P., wit.

Taylor, Charles & _____, _____ 179_; John Treadwell, bondsman.

Taylor, Edmond & Hetty Sain, 3 Oct 1816; Wm. Jarvis, bondsman; R. Powell, wit.

Taylor, Francis & Mary Murphey, 18 March 1779; John Taylor, bondsman; Wm. R. Davie, wit.

Taylor, Francis & Sarah Patterson, 24 Sept 1779; Thomas Jones, bondsman; Jo. Brevard, wit.

Taylor, Georg & Polly Lane, 12 April 1815; Isaac Causey, bondsman; Jn. March Sr., wit.

Taylor, H. C. & Catharine R. Klutts, 23 Oct 1865; H. B. Hess, bondsman; Obadiah Woodson, wit.

Taylor, Henry & Maria Doby, 27 Dec 1853; Jacob O. Miller, bondsman; Levi Trexler, wit.

Taylor, James & Eveline Hudges, 27 Jan 1836; Hiram Rainey, bondsman; Jno. Giles, wit.

Taylor, Josiah & Penelope Riddle, 28 Feb 1828; Benjamin Cornell, bondsman; C. Harbin, J. P., wit.

Taylor, Samuel & Eleanor Chambers, 2 Feb 1830; Francis M. Ross, bondsman; Jno. H. Hardie, wit.

Taylor, Samuel P. & Eliza Graves, 1 July 1855; John Snider, bondsman; J. S. Myers, wit. married 3 July 1858 by John C. Miller, J. P.

Taylor, Spence & Easther Etheridge, 11 Feb 1814; Willeby M. Hornely, bondsman; Jn March Sr., wit.

Taylor, Spence & Margaret Eaton, 2 Jan 1834; Beal Ijames, bondsman; E. D. Austin, wit.

Taylor, William & Elizabeth Blackwood, 2 Nov 1798; Benjamin Trott, bondsman; Edwin J. Osborn, wit.

Taylor, William & Elizabeth Crouse, 18 Feb 1802; John March, bondsman; Jno. Brem, wit.

Teague, Abraham & Emlia Brown, 6 Aug 1816; Jacob Teague, bondsman; Sol. Davis, J. P., wit.

Teague, Isaac & Susannah Shields, 28 May 1801; Ezekiel Teague, bondsman; Wm. Welborn, wit.

Teague, Isaac & Sarah Teague, 11 Oct 1812; Jacob Teague, bondsman; Sol. Davis, J. P., wit.

Teague, Jacob & Mary Bennit, 2 Nov 1815; Isaac Teague, bondsman; J. Manlove, wit.

Teague, John & Mary Thomas, 1 Oct 1811; William Davis, bondsman; S. Davis, J. P., wit.

Teague, Moses & Martha Evens, 20 July 1813; Benjamin Shield, bondsman; Sol. Davis, J. P., wit.

Teague, William & Phebee Clinard, 5 Feb 1819; Hugh Robartson, bondsman; Sol. Davis, J. P., wit.

Teal, Henry & Susan Wilhelm, 28 Jan 1822; John Wilhelm, bondsman; Hy. Giles, wit.

Teal, Jacob Jr. & Sally Keever, 3 April 1810; Jacob Teal Sr., bondsman; Geo. Dunn, wit.

Teas, Samuel & Mary Maffett, 25 Feb 1787; William Maffit, bondsman; Jno. Macay, wit.

Teeter, John H. & Sarah Sossaman, 26 Nov 1851; Wm. W. Emery, bondsman.

Temples, Edom & Polly Foutz, 18 Sept 1817; Isaac Leatherman, bondsman; Robt. Nanny, wit.

Temples, Nedam & Polly Fouts, 17 Feb 1816; William Felps, bondsman; Jn. March Sr., wit.

Templeton, David & Peggy Fisher, 11 Oct 1811; John Fisher, bondsman; Jno. Giles, C. C., wit.

Templeton, George & Elenor Greacy, 19 Aug 1775; John Calahan, bondsman; David Flowers, wit.

Templeton, Robert & Mary Black, 27 Aug 1768; George Davison, John Olyphant, bondsmen.

Templeton, Robert & Anny Wells, 9 Dec 1788; Thomas Templeton, bondsman.

Tenerson, James & Catharine Mock, 23 Nov 1832; James Smith, bondsman.

Tenneson, Joseph & Sibella Brandon, 5 Feb 1795; Cobb Webb, bondsman.

Tennisson, Isaac & Susanna Smith, 6 Feb 1834; Robert Ervin, bondsman; Wm. Locke, wit.

Tenpenny, Richard & Barbara Shuman, 2 Jan 1802; Jno Brem, wit.

Terrence, George & Margret McKnight, 14 Nov 1787; William Cooke, bondsman; Ad. Osborn, wit.

Tharp, Boaz & Airy Whiteker, 14 June 1802; Thos Pain, bondsman; J. Hunt, wit.

Tharp, Zadock & Leurany Parker, 18 Aug 1800; James Parker, bondsman; John Brem, wit.

Tharps, Thomas & Hannah Hitchcock, 29 March 1792; Stephenas Haworth, bondsman; Jno. Monroe, wit.

Thomas, Absolam & Sarah A. Wright, 4 July 1838; Jno. M. Wright, bondsman; Jno. M. Hardie, wit.

Thomas, Absolom & Charity Parks, 27 Jan 1837; John Josey, bondsman.

Thomas, Alexander & Hanna McDorman, 25 Oct 1803; Eleazer Smith, bondsman.

Thomas, Alexander & Nancy Hitchcock, 7 Oct 1816; Obadiah Chipman, bondsman; Sol. Davis, J. P., wit.

Thomas, Alexander & Mary Spoolmon, 7 Sept 1818; Adam Grimes, bondsman; Z. Hunt, wit.

Thomas, Elijah & Betsy Black, 18 Oct 1823; Ryla Etcheson, bondsman; L. R. Rose, J. P., wit.

Thomas, Henry & Jane McKnight, 14 Nov 1783; W. McKnight, bondsman; T. H. McCaule, wit.

Thomas, Henry & Sarah Holeman, 9 Jan 1832; Archibald Lovelace, bondsman; James Frost, J. P., wit.

Thomas, James & Eliza Ann Moyle, 12 May 1857; Thomas Shayle, bondsman; James E. Kerr, wit. married 12 May 1857 by W. M. Hereford.

Thomas, Jeremiah & Dorcus Morris, 14 April 1818; Nicholas Thomas, bondsman; Z. Hunt, J. P., wit.

Thomas, Joel & Christel L. Comer, 22 Dec 1836; John Heath Jr., bondsman; Tho. Cheshier, wit.

Thomas, John & Barbar Fight, 7 March 1803; Nicholas Moyer, bondsman; Adlai L. Osborn, D. C., wit.

Thomas, Joseph & Mary Morgan, 24 Feb 1823; Haynes Morgan, bondsman; Jno. Giles, wit.

Thomas, Levi & Susan Walton, 11 Aug 1845; Wm. A. Walton, bondsman; J. H. Hardie, wit.

Thomas, Levi & Sarah Ann Klutts, 5 Oct 1854; A. W. Buis, bondsman; James E. Kerr, wit.

Thomas, Lewis & Pinky Longwith, 11 Sept 1823; John West, bondsman; E. Brock, J. P., wit.

Thomas, Massy & Elizabeth Myers, 23 March 1802; Henry Miers, bondsman; Jno. Brem, wit.

Thomas, Ryal B. & Betsey Simpson, 27 Dec 1802; Frederick Allemong, bondsman; A. L. Osborn, D. C., wit.

Thomas, William & Lucy Monroe, 10 Oct 1808; Sam. Naltz, bondsman; A. L. Osborne, D., wit.

Thomason, Evan & _____, _____ 180_; Danl. Sharpe, bondsman.

Thomason, George W. & Lavina Jacobs, 6 Oct 1842; Jno. Jos. Bruner, bondsman; J. H. Hardie, wit.

Thomason, James & Margaret Marlin, 8 June 1830; Jesse Marlin, bondsman.

Thomason, Jesse & Mary Trott, 25 Nov 1840; William Trott, bondsman; Susan T. Giles, wit.

Thomason, Jesse & Hariette S. Fraley, 12 Dec 1848; Wilson Trott, bondsman; J. H. Hardie Jr., wit.

Thomason, Jesse & Julia A. Briggs, 27 Feb 1864; Wm. T. Marlin, bondsman; Obadiah Woodson, wit.

Thomason, John & Harriet E. Fraly, 28 June 1848; Richard Thomason, bondsman.

Thomason, Richard & Mary E. Krider, 22 Jan 1842; Jno. Craige, bondsman; J. S. Johnston, wit.

Thomason, William & Margaret Townsley, 7 June 1805; Stephen Biles, bondsman; Thos. L. Cowan, wit.

Thomason, William & Ann Trott, 11 Jan 1841; James Thomason, bondsman; Susan T. Giles, wit.

Thomason, Zachariah & Kuty Turner, 21 Aug 1826; Jno. Turner, bondsman.

Thomasson, Bias & Nelly Gheen, 8 Oct 1816; Malachi Bowers, bondsman; Robrts Nanny, wit.

Thompson, Abner & Catherine Robison, 15 April 1846; Thomas Dickson, bondsman; J. M. Turner, wit.

Thompson, Alfred & Betsy Link, 4 April 1815; Benjamin Pearson, bondsman; Geo. Dunn, wit.

Thompson, Azariah & Anney Buckner, 17 Oct 1815; Levi Buckner, bondsman; Jn. March Sr., wit.

Thompson, Benjamin T. & Nancy B. Pinkston, 15 Dec 1865; James F. Robinson, bondsman; Obadiah Woodson, wit.

Thompson, Brien & Bethana Torentine, 10 Jan 1835; Reason Thompson, bondsman; A. E. Foster, J. P., wit.

Thompson, C. J. (son of R. Thompson) & Eliza E. McClelland, aged 20 years (daughter of Rudolph McClelland), 5 April 1867; married __ April 1867 by S. A. Daniel.

Thompson, David L. & Jean Pinkston, 28 May 1812; Jas. Wilson, bondsman; Geo. Dunn, wit.

Thompson, Elisha & _____, 7 Aug 1767; Joseph Thompson, ____ Nichol, bondsmen; Thom Frohock, wit.

Thompson, Elisha & Elizebeth Talor, 25 April 1809; Edward Buckner, bondsman; Jn. March Sr., wit.

Thompson, J. H. & Sarah C. Tucker, 26 Aug 1851; William E. Barber, bondsman; James E. Kerr, wit.

Thompson, James & Caty Rex, 8 June 1815; Andrew Thompson, bondsman; W. M. Bean, J. P., wit.

Thompson, James C. & Margaret E. Hall, 31 Oct 1855; Geo. M. Lyerly, bondsman; James E. Kerr, wit. married 1 Nov 1855 by Moses Powlass, J. P.

Thompson, James L. & Malinda Ann Hembrey, 15 June 1844; H. C. Gillean, bondsman; J. H. Hardie, wit.

Thompson, James T. & Nancy Hillard, 8 June 1853; John S. Hyde, bondsman; James E. Kerr, wit. married 9 June 1853 by J. Thomason, J. P.

Thompson, James W. & Sarah C. Barber, 4 Sept 1860; William L. Carson, bondsman; James E. Kerr, wit. married 4 Sept 1860 by B. Scott Krider.

Thompson, John & Ann Hewing, 24 Sept 1767; George Davison, bondsman; _____ Frohock, wit.

Thompson, John & Mary Clark, 9 Nov 1774; James Clark, bondsman; Max. Chambers, wit.

Thompson, John & Sarah McLane, 21 Feb 1775; John Wells, bondsman; Max. Chambers, wit.

Thompson, John & Nancy Partrick, 11 Dec 1816; Humphrey Mullikin, bondsman; T. Hampton, wit.

Thompson, John & Margaret S. Nox, 30 Sept 1829; Robert Chunn, bondsman.

Thompson, Laurence & Eleanor Thomson, 8 April 1779; Lawrence Thompson, bondsman; Ad. Osborn, wit.

Thompson, Lemuel & Jane Shaver, 17 Aug 1863; W. H. Davis, bondsman; Obadiah Woodson, wit.

Thompson, Moses & Catharine Higdon, 29 Dec 1813; Thomas Todd, bondsman; Jno. Giles, C. C., wit.

Thompson, Moses & Anny Cook, 16 Feb 1818; Aquila Davenport, bondsman; Jno. Giles, wit.

Thompson, Moses & Peggy Irwin, 23 Dec 1822; Bennet A. Reeves, bondsman.

Thompson, Moses & Providence Davenport, 30 Aug 1825; Hy. Giles, bondsman; Hy. Giles, wit.

Thompson, Moses W. & Sarah S. Murph, 31 Oct 1848; Danl. J. Webb, bondsman; J. S. Myers, wit.

Thompson, Reasen & Hannah Robards, 1 Jan 1823; Laurince Owings, bondsman; Jno. Giles, wit.

Thompson, Rial & Mary Blue, 30 May 1825; Michael Wallen, bondsman; Hy. Giles, wit.

Thompson, Sandy & Elenor Clarke, 20 March 1797; David Montgomery, bondsman; Jno Rogers, wit.

Thompson, Thomas & Mary Stewart, 29 April 1768; James Stewart, bondsman; Thom. Frohock, wit.

Thompson, Thomas & Elizabeth Linvile, 2 May 1780; Sergeant Hughes, bondsman; B. Booth Boote, wit.

Thompson, Thomas & Elizabeth H. Cowan, 28 July 1830; Thomas C. Graham, bondsman; Jno. H. Hardie, wit.

Thompson, Thomas Locke & Nancy Elizabeth Smith, married 10 Feb 1859 by M. A. Luckey.

Thompson, William & Sarah Coles, 5 Nov 1777; Hugh Montgomery, bondsman; Jams. Robinson, wit.

Thompson, William & Betsy Cowan, 5 Feb 1805; Moses Graham, bondsman.

Thompson, William & Lucy Banks, 23 Dec 1810; Joel Banks, bondsman; Geo. Dunn, wit.

Thompson, William & Mimeth Floyd, 9 March 1811; Abraham Owen, bondsman; Geo. Dunn, wit.

Thompson, William & Ester Williams, 22 Feb 1812; John Zimerman, bondsman; D. Leatherman, wit.

Thompson, William A. & Harriet J. Lyerly, 28 May 1856; Wm. L. Barber, bondsman; J. S. Myers, wit.

Thompson, William H. & Lucinda A. Umsted, 26 March 1862; F. W. Scott, bondsman.

Thompson, Zedock & Elizabeth Mullikin, 2 Nov 1816; John Thompson, bondsman; J. Hampton, wit.

Thomson, Closs & _____, 17 Oct 1759; Daniel Boone, Thomas Jones, bondsman; John Frohock, wit.

Thomson, John & Martha Linster, 13 Sept 1780; John Lister, bondsman; Ad. Osborn, wit.

Thomson, Joseph & Anne Porter, 3 May 1775; John Lock, bondsman; Ad. Osborn, wit.

Thomson, Moses & Rebeca Hughs, 14 July 1767; Benjamin Hide, bondsman; Thos. Frohock, wit.

Thomson, William & Milly Hammett, 4 Aug 1786; Thomas Leaverley, bondsman; Ad. Osborn, wit.

Thomson, William & _____, _____ 180_; Moses Read(?), bondsman.

Thorn, John R. & Jane Trott, 4 April 1839; Richard Pinkston, bondsman; John Giles, wit.

Thornton, Theophilus & Sarah Miller, 10 Nov 1786; Jn. Proviance, bondsman; M. Macay, wit.

Thrift, Samuel M. & Sally F. Cowan, 24 April 1811; Will Wood, bondsman; Ezra Allemong, wit.

Tice, Charles & Sarah Gillum, 5 Aug 1819; William Roberts, bondsman; Sol. Davis, J. P., wit.

Tice, Henry & _____, ____ 180_; Daniel Moe, bondsman.

Tigart, Andrew & Rachel Irving, 14 April 1820; Baker Johnson, bondsman; R. Powell, wit.

Tigner, Isaac & Elizabeth Hornbarier, 28 May 1834; Daniel Hornbarier, bondsman; Hy. Giles, wit.

Tike, Francis & Mary Martin, 21 May 1851; David Martin, bondsman; James E. Kerr, wit.

Tinkle, John & Johannah Burridge, 16 Jan 1813 or 1816; David Butner, bondsman; Henry Allemong, wit.

Tippet, William & Rebecca Mills, 3 March 1796; Philemon Mayfield, bondsman; J. Troy, wit.

Tips, David & Sally Lingle, 14 Dec 1819; Jacob Lingle, bondsman; Jno. Giles, wit.

Todd, Benjamin & Margret Barkley, 24 Jan 1785; Thomas Todd, bondsman; William Crawford, wit.

Todd, John & Ann Brandon (no date, during admn of Gov. Martin 1782-5, 1789-92); Obadiah Doty, bondsman.

Todd, John B. & Sarah Dent, 13 Feb 1823; Abel Cowan, bondsman; Hy. Giles, wit.

Todd, John T. & Dorothy C. Reese, 30 Aug 1853; R. H. Todd, bondsman; James E. Kerr, wit. married 7 Sept 1853 by Stephen Frontis.

Todd, Joseph & Mary Berry, 3 May 1779; Lawrence Shanp, bondsman; Ad. Osborn, wit.

Todd, Joseph & Elizabeth Young, 18 Dec 1786; James Scrivner, bondsman; Jno. Macay, wit.

Todd, Joseph E. & Margaret Robison, 16 April 1818; Roberts Nanny, bondsman.

Todd, Joshua & Elizabeth Palmer, 3 March 1792; Matthew Wommack, bondsman; Chas. Caldwell, wit.

Todd, Thomas & Jean Simonton, 11 Dec 1771; David Nisbet, bondsman; Thomas Frohock, wit. consent from Robt. Simonton, father of Jean, 9 Dec 1771; wit. by Nenien Steell, William Simonton.

Todd, Thomas & Sarah Cox, 2 Nov 1779; John Gardner, bondsman.

Tood, Thomas & Elizabeth Blackwell, 13 July 1826; Joseph Cowan, bondsman.

Toff, Lawrence & Bettie L. Krimminger, 23 Jan 1865; A. W. Buis, bondsman; Obadiah Woodson, wit.

Tomlinson, James & Anna Jones, 25 Dec 1815; John Smith, bondsman; R. Powell, wit.

Tomlinson, John & Tabithey Summers, 30 July 1787; Benjamin Belt, bondsman; Jno. Macay, wit.

Tomlinson, John & Anna Murphey, 27 Dec 1819; Joseph Murphey, bondsman; Silas Peace, wit.

Tomlinson, Joseph & Susanah Smith, 13 Jan 1812; Jacob Mills, bondsman; Jno. March Sr., wit.

Tomlinson, Joseph & Elezebeth McMahan, 3 Aug 1824; Samuel Smith, bondsman; E. Brock, J. P., wit.

Tomlinson, Sothey & Sarah Vanninton, 5 Nov 1825; John Call, bondsman; Thomas McNeely, J. P., wit.

Tomlinson, William & Elizabeth Easton; 12 Dec 1816; Zachariah Jones, bondsman; R. Powell, wit.

Tompson, William & Polly Owens, 25 June 1800; Joshua Conger., bondsman; Jos. Pearson, wit.

Tomson, Joseph & Agnes Todd, 6 Aug 1805; Henry Robison, bondsman.

Tomson, Samuel & Seners Talor, 14 June 1808; Leven Benson, bondsman; John March, wit.

Torance, Hugh & Isabella Talls, 29 May 1783; Ja. Ker, bondsman; T. H. McCaule, wit.

Torrance, Robert & Goodwin Marshall, 7 July 1796; Jno. McClellan, bondsman; J. Troy, wit.

Torrence, A. P. & Mary A. Jamison, 17 Aug 1860; Jas. S. Johnston, bondsman; John Wilkinson, wit. married 4 Sept 1860 by Rev. William W. Pharr.

Torrence, Albert & Elizabeth Hackette, 25 Oct 1791; Chas. Harris, bondsman; Chs. Caldwell, wit.

Torrence, Alexr. & Laura T. Chambers, 17 April 1840; Wilson Knox, bondsman.

Torentine, James & Elizabeth Graves, 21 Dec 1826; John Hendrix, bondsman; Thomas McNeely, J. P., wit.

Torrentine, John W. & Mary Basinger, 5 May 1822; Daniel Helfer, bondsman; Thomas McNeely, J. P., wit.

Tothoro, Jacob & Sarey Whitaker, 9 Dec 1804; Thos. Whitaker, bondsman; John Irwin, J. P., wit.

Tounsley, James & Susannah Rough, 30 Oct 1819; Jon. Craige, bondsman; Jno. Giles, wit.

Tow, Anderson & Elizabeth Freemon, 15 Oct 1817; Jesse Tow, bondsman; Henry Giles, wit.

Tow, Anderson & Polley Freeman, 8 Jan 1818; Thomas Hall, bondsman; Thos Hampton, Robt Hampton, wit.

Tow, Jessy & Nancy Haw, 1 Feb 1815; George Miers, bondsman; Henry Giles, wit.

Tow, John F. & Polly Bowers, 10 April 1823; Peter Trexler, bondsman; Jno. Giles, wit.

Towel, John J. & Elizabeth Felker, 1 Aug 1853; Paul Safrit, bondsman; J. S. Myers, wit.

Towel, Robert B. & Elizabeth Innis, 19 Dec 1837; David Holo-bough, bondsman; Hy. Giles, wit.

Towell, William A. & Alice Clampett, 9 Oct 1858; Wiley Felker, bondsman; James E. Kerr, wit. married 9 Oct 1858 by Jas. H. Ennis, J. P.

Townsend, Genoa C. & Catharine L. Caruthers, 19 Aug 1833; James Allen, bondsman.

Townsley, Oliver & Sally Thomas, __ Oct 1792; Richard Dickson, bondsman; Max. Chambers, wit.

Townsley, Oliver & Sarah Thomas, 21 Nov 1795; Robert Gay, bondsman.

Townsley, Oliver & Margaret Green, 2 June 1825; William Hulin, bondsman; Hy. Giles, wit.

Townsley, Oliver J. & Polly Rairey, 24 Feb 1824; Peter Pinkston, bondsman; Hy. Giles, wit.

Townsley, William & Elitha Owens, 26 Aug 1847; Wm. Campbell, bondsman; J. H. Hardie Jr., wit.

Townsly, Jesse & Catharine Agner, 30 Oct 1822; Mathias Swisher, bondsman.

Trafinger, Philip B. & Barbara Albright, 20 Feb 1822; William Miller, bondsman; Hy. Giles, wit.

Trail, Abraham & Eliza Churchill Evans, 29 Jan 1818; Benjamin D. Jones, bondsman; E. Brown, wit.

Trantham, John & Elizabeth Cunningham, 3 Feb 1819; Charles Dunn, bondsman; Jno. Giles, wit.

Trantham, Joseph & Sarah Michaels, 15 Aug 1820; William Owen, bondsman.

Trantham, Rantham Levite & Ruella Robinson, 8 Dec 1792; Thomas Reed, bondsman; Jos. Chambers, wit.

Trantham, Martin & Mary Yontz, 13 Aug 1811; John Warner, bondsman; Joseph Clarke, William Douglas, wit.

Travis, Benjamin & Phebe Conger, 12 Dec 1791; Daniel Biles, bondsman; Chs. Caldwell, wit.

Travis, Jacob & Elizabeth Swink, _____ 180_; Danl. Clary, bondsman.

Travs, Jacob & Polly Miller, 28 Jan 1809; George Travis, bondsman; A. L. Osborn, wit.

Traylor, Joel & Teney Thingleton, 24 Feb 1821; Thos. P. Ives, bondsman; George Locke, wit.

Traylor, Thomas & Temperance Walk, 14 April 1820; Orton Bradshaw, bondsman.

Trease, Adam & Peggy Airey, 24 Dec 1818; William Brown, bondsman; Jno. Giles, wit.

Trees, George & Polly Caster, 18 May 1814; Peter Earnheart, bondsman; Jno. Giles, C. C., wit.

Trees, Henry & Elizabeth Cailer, 14 May 1805; Jacob Troutman, bondsman; A. L. Osborn, wit.

Trees, William & Susannah Lentz, 13 Aug 1802; Geo. Fisher, bondsman; A. L. Osborn, wit.

Trent, William H. & Margaret Locke, 14 June 1826; Hugh Meenan, bondsman; Hy. Giles, wit.

Trentham, Martin & Mealy Nicolinson, 6 April 1795; Michael Miers, bondsman; Isham Frohock, wit.

Trentham, Martin & Ritter Traylor, 27 Dec 1820; William Owen, bondsman; Hy. Giles, wit.

Trevellion, Richard & Patty Stots, 14 Jan 1768; Geo. Magoune, John Trevilion, bondsmen; Thomas Frohock, wit.

Trexler, Adam & Margarett Erwin, 20 Feb 1820; Richard Harrison, bondsman.

Trexler, Adam & Artamessa Pinkston, 18 June 1823; David Gheen, bondsman; Jno. Giles, wit.

Trexler, Adam & Tena Setzer, 3 Jan 1828; Andrew Setzer, bondsman; J. H. Hardie, wit.

Trexler, Adam & Rosanna Fesperman, 7 Jan 1846; Isaac Lyerly, bondsman; J. H. Hardie Jr., wit.

Trexler, Adam & Mary Ann Garner, 10 Feb 1848; J. Lyerly, bondsman; J. H. Hardie Jr., wit.

Trexler, Adam & Elizabeth Besherer, 15 June 1849; Henry A. Walton, bondsman.

Trexler, Adam & Catharine L. Weaver, 11 Jan 1855; Lafayett McEntire, bondsman; James E. Kerr, wit. married 11 Jan 1855 by Obadiah Woodson, J. P.

Trexler, Adam Jr. & Margaret Lyerly, 1 Jan 1844; Adam Trexler, bondsman; Obadiah Woodson, wit.

Trexler, Alexander & Amanda J. Craven, 20 Nov 1860; W. M. Jacobs, bondsman; Wm. Locke, wit. married 21 Nov 1860 by L. C. Groseclose.

Trexler, Caleb & Elizabeth L. Peeler, 2 Feb 1852; David D. Peeler, bondsman; J. S. Myers, wit.

Trexler, David & Sarah Eller, 20 Aug 1834; Hy. Giles, bondsman.

Trexler, David & Rachel Moyer, 7 June 1849; Samuel Reeves Jr., bondsman; John H. Hardie Jr., wit.

Trexler, David & Crisse C. Ribelin, 20 Jan 1852; Jesse Ribelin, bondsman; Levi Trexler, wit.

Trexler, George & Barbara Peelor, 2 Oct 1811; John Trexler, bondsman; Ezra Allemong, wit.

Trexler, George & Mary Ketchey, 1 July 1824; Michael Davis, bondsman; Geo. Locke, wit.

Trexler, Henry & Betsey Earnheart, 6 May 1813; Jacob Fulenwider, bondsman; Jno. Giles, C. C., wit.

Trexler, Jacob & Mary C. Fraley, 31 Aug 1846; Moses Trexler, bondsman.

Trexler, Jacob & Mary E. Kern, 20 Feb 1863; William C. Parks, bondsman; Obadiah Woodson, wit.

Trexler, James M. & Maria Smithdeal, 11 Nov 1865; Saml. Reeves, Sr., bondsman; Obadiah Woodson, wit.

Trexler, John & Elizabeth Morgan, 9 Feb 1813; David Morgan, bondsman; Jno. L. Henderson, wit.

Trexler, John & Peggy Holshouser, 26 July 1831; Henry Peeler, bondsman; Jno. H. Hardie, wit.

Trexler, John & Anna Lingle, 15 April 1852; Moses Trexler, bondsman; J. S. Myers, wit.

Trexler, John & Carolina Ribelin, 8 Aug 1861; David Trexler, bondsman; Obadiah Woodson, wit. married 8 Aug 1861 by S. J. Peeler, J. P.

Trexler, John W. & Barbara File, 7 May 1849; Arch. Misenhimer, bondsman; Jno. H. Hardie Jr., wit.

Trexler, Jonathan & Eliza Leach, 2 Feb 1843; Samuel Kincaid, bondsman; J. H. Hardie, wit.

Trexler, Joseph & Delilah Stoner, 12 Dec 1850; Robt. Bradshaw, bondsman; James E. Kerr, wit.

Trexler, Moses & Margaret Cauble, 22 Aug 1839; Henry A. Walton, bondsman.

Trexler, Moses & Elizabeth Miller, 20 June 1846; John Trexler, bondsman; John H. Hardie, wit.

Trexler, Moses & Eve C. Klutts, 20 Aug 1850; Henry A. Miller, bondsman; Obadiah Woodson, wit.

Trexler, Peter & Julia Ann Murry, 14 May 1829; Woodson Monroe, bondsman; Jno. H. Hardie, wit.

Trexler, Peter & Sarah C. Peeler, 31 July 1854; Lewis Agner, bondsman; J. S. Myers, wit.

Trexler, Peter & Rosa L. Lyerly, 6 Feb 1865; H. C. Cranford, bondsman.

Trexler, William H. & Emeline Russell, 6 Jan 1857; Thos. E. Brown, bondsman; James E. Kerr, wit. married 7 Jan 1857 by Th. S. McKenzie, J. P.

Trexler, William H. & Lucinda M. Brown, 6 March 1860; Jacob Trexler, bondsman; James E. Kerr, wit. married 6 March 1860 by S. J. Peeler, J. P.

Triplett, Thomas L. & Martha S. Hedrick, 28 Nov 1859; Abner W. Owen, bondsman; James E. Kerr, wit. married 1 Dec 1859 by N. F. Reid, Minister of the Gospel.

Trivitt, William & Lydia Latham, 29 March 1817; Moses Estep,
bondsman; R. Powell, wit.

Trolinger, Moses B. & Susan S. Chunn, 16 May 1860; John S. Hyde,
bondsman; John Wilkinson, wit. married 16 May 1860 by Rev.
B. Scott Krider.

Trott, Abraham & Elizabeth Harris, 11 Feb 1803; Daniel Clary,
bondsman; Adlai L. Osborn, D. C., wit.

Trott, Benjamin & Sarah Jenkins, 20 Feb 1800; Samuel Genkins,
bondsman; John Hampton, wit.

Trott, Henry & Elizabeth Todd, 12 Nov 1811; Benjm. Trott,
bondsman; Jno Giles, C. C., wit.

Trott, John H. & Ellenor Turner, 17 March 1842; Jno. H. Hardie,
bondsman.

Trott, S. S. & Elcy Wadsworth, 9 Jan 1864; Thomas McNeely,
bondsman; Obadiah Woodson, wit.

Trott, Sabert S. & Elizabeth Dent, 3 Jan 1839; Jacob Fraley,
bondsman; Hy. Giles, wit.

Trott, Stephen & Patsy Hulen, 7 Jan 1813; John Holobaugh,
bondsman; Ezra Allemong, wit.

Trott, Tho. & Elizabeth Gheen, 22 Sept 1814; John Kennedy,
bondsman; Jno Giles, C. C., wit.

Trott, William B. & Rachael C. Gheen, 11 July 1857; Jas. A.
Trott, bondsman; J. S. Myers, wit. married 12 July 1857 by
W. R. Fraley, J. P.

Trott, Willis H. & Sarah S. Thompson, 18 Jan 1855; John Lyerly,
bondsman; J. S. Myers, wit.

Trotter, Richard & Jinny Locke, 2 Dec 1789; Edward Harris,
bondsman.

Trout, Jacob & Elizabeth Lien, _____; George Miller, bondsman;
H. Giffard, wit.

Trout, John & Permelia Pierce, 23 Feb 1819; George Coon,
bondsman; R. Powell, wit.

Trout, John & Susanna Godeby, 29 Jan 1825; Burch Chesheir,
bondsman; L. R. Rose, wit.

Trout, Joseph & Anny Hendricks, 19 Jan 1825; John Trout,
bondsman; L. R. Rose, J. P., wit.

Trouteman, Monrow & Margaret E. Lentz, 23 Oct 1856; Jeremiah
Basinger, bondsman; J. S. Myers, wit.

Troutman, Adam & Mary Caule, 5 May 1796; Peter Caule, bondsman.

Troutman, Andrew & Catharine Aronheart, 22 Jan 1839; James
Troutman, bondsman; John Giles, wit.

Troutman, Andrew & Alley Sell, 23 July 1857; John Sell, bondsman; M. L. Holmes, wit. married 23 July 1857 by M. L.
Holmes, J. P.

Troutman, Daniel & Catharine Brady, 10 Dec 1835; David Brady, bondsman; J. S. Myers, wit. married 13 Dec 1855 by Saml. Rothrock, Minister of the Gospel in the Ev. Luth. Church.

Troutman, David & Caty Earnheart, 14 March 1831; John Troutman, bondsman; Jno. H. Hardie, wit.

Troutman, George & Sophia C. Yost, 24 April 1847; Jacob A. Yost, bondsman; J. H. Hardie, wit.

Troutman, George & Catharine Fespermon, 25 Jan 1825; Daniel Josey, bondsman; Hy. Giles, wit.

Troutman, Henry & Elizabeth Isahover, 7 May 1822; Peter Troutman, bondsman.

Troutman, Henry & Polly Fesperman, 6 Feb 1829; Geo. Troutman, bondsman; Jno. H. Hardie, wit.

Troutman, Henry & Rachel Casper, 30 Dec 1858; Jacob Isenhouer, bondsman; married 2 Jan 1859 by Saml. Rothrock, Minister of the Gospel in the Ev. Luth. Church.

Troutman, Jacob & Polly Harkey, 10 March 1818; Jacob Aronhart, bondsman; Milo A. Giles, wit.

Troutman, James & Catharine Earnheart, 27 Oct 1835; John Canup, bondsman.

Troutman, John & Polly Ketchey, 20 Dec 1830; John L. Randleman, bondsman; Jno. H. Hardie, wit.

Troutman, Laurence & Elizabeth Dolon, 9 Aug 1825; Jos. E. Todd, bondsman.

Troutman, Michael & Christian Sifford, 4 Sept 1801; George Genz, bondsman; Jno Brem, wit.

Troutman, Monroe & Amelia Troutman, 24 April 1847; Nicholas Lutewick, bondsman; J. H. Hardie, wit.

Troutman, Noah B. & Julia Ann Holshouser, 28 Sept 1859; J. A. Gulener(?), bondsman; James E. Kerr, wit. married 28 Sept 1859 by J. K. Burke, J. P.

Troutman, Rufus P. & Sarah Jackson, 26 Jan 1860; Richard Small, bondsman; E. Mauney, wit.

Troutman, Travis & Charlotte C. Troutman, 9 Sept 1861; Aron W. Miller, bondsman; Obadiah Woodson, wit.

Troutman, Travis & Elizabeth Casper, 22 March 1866; A. W. Miller, bondsman; Obadiah Woodson, wit.

Troutman, William & Sally Stirewalt, 11 Nov 1830; George Duke, bondsman; Jno. H. Hardin, wit.

Troy, John & Isabella Balfour, 21 June 1790; Chas. Harris, bondsman; Cs. Caldwell, D. C., wit.

Troy, Matthew & Rebecca M. Nesbit, 17 Aug 1809; Henry Chambers, bondsman; Jno. Giles, wit.

Tucker, Andrew & Bice Rumley, 25 Sept 1795; Reuben Allen, bondsman.

Tucker, Edward & Polly Felps, 1 March 1791; Henry Eranwood, bondsman.

Tucker, John & Keziah Breshears, 31 Aug 1772; Geo. Magoune, William Brashiers, bondsmen; Davis Woodson, Wm. Temple Coles Jr., wit.

Tucker, John & Ruthey Howard, 16 July 1811; Benjamin Clary, bondsman; Jn. March Sr., wit.

Tucker, John & Tempey Wilkeson, 16 Nov 1796; Benjamin Martin, bondsman; Jno. Rogers, wit.

Tucker, Thomson & Elizebeth Rogers, 29 May 1824; William Orell, bondsman.

Tucker, William & Polly Walcer, 13 April 1825; John Miers Jr., bondsman; L. R. Rose, J. P., wit.

Turnbull, John & Jane Rutledge, 5 March 1772; John Rutledge, bondsman; John Frohock, wit.

Turner, Dread & Polley Canter, 9 Dec 1823; John Jones, bondsman; E. Brock, J. P., wit.

Turner, Etheldred & Sele Lee, 9 Dec 1818; Charles Fox, bondsman; Jn. March Sr., wit.

Turner, James & Mary Rickart, 19 Dec 1853; Levi Ludwick, bondsman; D. W. Honeycutt, wit.

Turner, John & Jane Cooper, 29 April 1780; James Patterson, bondsman; B. Booth Boote, wit.

Turner, John & Mary Luckey, 7 Nov 1826; Nathan Neely, bondsman; J. H. Hardie, wit.

Turner, John W. & Jane T. Luckey, 18 Aug 1851; Thomas K. Turner, bondsman; J. S. Myers, wit. married 21 Aug 1851 by Wm. A. Hall.

Turner, Joseph & Ann Gray, 10 Feb 1828; James Heathman, bondsman; Jno. H. Hardie, wit.

Turner, Joshua & Rebekah Pinkston, 3 Aug 1775; John Pinkston, bondsman; David Flowers, wit.

Turner, Josiah & Elizabeth Baker, 19 May 1829; John Johnson, bondsman; J. H. Hardie, wit.

Turner, Paul & Hannah Dancey, 21 Aug 1826; John Turner, bondsman; Jno. Giles, wit.

Turner, Peter & Elizabeth Coble, 23 Jan 1830; John A. Hudson, bondsman; L. R. Rose, J. P., wit.

Turner, Samuel & Elizabeth Heathman, 22 May 1821; Abner Hall, bondsman; Hy. Giles, wit.

Turner, Thomas & Cathrine Paterson, 16 Aug 1784; James Paterson, bondsman; Hugh Magoune, wit.

Turner, Thomas & Polly Hunt, 1 Sept 1790; Richd. Holland, bondsman; C. Caldwell, D. C., wit.

ROWAN MARRIAGES 1753-1868

Turner, Wilson & Ann Barber, 14 Dec 1824; Bennet A. Reeves, bondsman; Hy. Giles, wit.

Turner, Zepheniah & Mary S. Cowan, 5 Sept 1837; David Heathman, bondsman.

Tush, Henry & Barbary Harman, 5 Feb 1822; Barnet Wier, bondsman; Sol. Davis, wit.

Tush, John & Milley Murrel, 31 March 1804; George Morrell, bondsman; Wm. Welborn, wit.

Tussey, Daniel & Nancy Miller, 23 Aug 1819; John Burkhart, bondsman; Hy. Giles, wit.

Tussey, John & Elizabeth Hunt (no date, during admn. of Gov. Martin 1782-1785; 1789-1792); Davis Hunt, bondsman.

Tutorow, Davis & Ruthey Bradley, 28 Oct 1811; David Bradley, bondsman; Jn. March Sr., wit.

Twiddell, Thomas & Polly Wayman, 5 March 1815; John Kenneday Jr., bondsman; Silas Peace, wit.

Twomey, Thomas & Margrat Lewies, 19 Sept 1811; Patrick Twomey, bondsman; Jn March Sr., wit.

Tworney, Isaac & Fanny Anderson, 16 Aug 1815; Thos L. Tworney, bondsman; Jn. March Sr., wit.

Tyer, James & Elizabeth Lambeth, 30 June 1811; Council Lambeth, bondsman; E. Morgan, wit.

Tyner, Geo. R. & Mary S. Correll, 31 Jan 1865; L. S. Davis, bondsman; Obadiah Woodson, wit.

Upright, David & Elizabeth Albright, 9 Jan 1816; Thomas Cowan, bondsman; Geo. Dunn, wit.

Upright, John & Nancy R. Poston, 23 Feb 1852; A. F. Poston, bondsman; James E. Kerr, wit.

Upright, Peter & Barbara Freed, 4 Jan 1813; Samuel Upright, bondsman; Geo. Dunn, wit.

Upright, S. S. & Thyrza Broadway, 2 March 1861; George Karriker, bondsman; John Wilkinson, wit.

Upright, Samuel S. & Catharine Sechler, 29 Sept 1844; Christan Sechler, bondsman; John Giles, wit.

Upright, William & Julia Ann C. Leazar, 25 May 1857; David K. Woods, bondsman; James E. Kerr, wit. married 4 June 1857 by D. R. Bradshaw, J. P.

Upton, James & Nancy Holmes, 17 Sept 1802; Jas. Blair, bondsman; J. McEwin, wit.

Vail, John & Abbigail Cowan, 16 July 1817; John Cowan, bondsman; Roberts Nanny, wit.

Valentine, Elijah & Dorcas Turner, 25 May 1832; Hy. Giles, bondsman.

Valentine, George & Marie Volentine, 31 July 1859; married 31 July 1859 by Peter Williamson, J. P.

Valentine, George & Drucilla Carter (free persons of color); married 12 June 1853 by Obadiah Woodson, J. P.

Valentine, Hutson & Sarah Ann Freeman, married 13 Nov 1854 by Jesse Rankin, Min. Pres. Ch.

Van Barrens, John & Susanna. Pfifer, 18 Aug 1808; Joseph Biles, bondsman; A. L. Osborne, wit.

Vance, Davis & Priscilla Brank, 21 Sept 1775; Joseph White, bondsman; Dd. Flowers, wit. consent of Robert Brank, 18 Sept 1775, father of Priscilla.

Vancleave, Benjamin & Ruth Monson, 14 July 1765; Wm. McConnell, Wm. Nassery, bondsmen; Thomas Frohock, wit.

Vandeveer, John & Amelia Speer, 9 Jan 1773; Aaron Speer, bondsman; Ad. Osborn, wit.

Vandever, Mathew & Sarah Doane, 4 March 1779; Hezekeah Doane, bondsman; Wm. R. Davie, wit.

Vaneaton, John & Liddy Lowry, 12 Dec 1820; Abram Neely, bondsman; Henry Allemong, wit.

Vareɔion, Abram & Avis Stapleton, 17 Dec 1789; James McDaniel, bondsman; Ed. Harris, wit.

Vanetton, Richard & Catherine March, 14 Jan 1826; John Call Jr., bondsman; L. R. Rose, J. P., wit.

Varas, Arron & Rebecah Woods, 7 Aug 1788; William Danielson, bondsman; Wm. Alexander, wit.

Varner, Christian A. & Mary Lewis, 4 Nov 1840; Mathew Plumer, bondsman; Jno. Giles, wit.

Varner, John & Rebecca Davis, 4 May 1784; Jno. Varmer, bondsman; Ad. Osborn, wit.

Varner, Mathew & Susannah Henley, 17 Aug 1787; Darby Henly, bondsman; Jno. Macay, wit.

Vaughan, Richard B. & Julia Ann Lynch, 6 May 1851; Richard S. Mayes, bondsman; J. S. Myers, wit.

Veach, John & Rachell Jones, 5 Oct 1803; John Tacker, bondsman; William Welborn, wit.

Veatch, Henson & Rebakah Snow, 1 May 1815; Abraham March, bondsman; Jn. March Sr., wit.

Veatch, John & Nelley Hunter, 4 May 1812; Thomas Foster, bondsman; Jn. March Sr., wit.

Veno, Francis & Susan A. Hartman, 28 Feb 1866; J. W. Earnhart, bondsman; Horatio N. Woodson, wit.

Vensel, Jacob & Peggy Freeze, 5 Feb 1805; Henry Frieze, bondsman; A. L. Osborn, D. C., wit.

Vent, William & Margaret Logan, 3 April 1776; Robert Poston, bondsman; Ad. Osborn, wit.

Verbal, Daniel & Mary Hartman, 14 Aug 1798; Peter Brown, bondsman; Edwin J. Osborn, C., wit.

Verbel, Henry & Aley Locke, 1 April 1817; Francis Gardner, bondsman.

Verble, Charles & Susannah Beam, 13 Dec 1821; Lewis Utzman, bondsman; Jno. Giles, wit.

Verble, Daniel & Anny Smithdeal, 6 March 1860; John H. Verble, bondsman; J. S. Myers, wit.

Verble, Henry & Susanna Tarr, 16 June 1812; Henry Crider, bondsman; Jno. Giles, wit.

Verble, Henry & Caty Cauble, 28 Oct 1817; John Tinkle, bondsman; Jno. Giles, wit.

Verble, Henry & Polly Hettinger, 11 March 1818; John Hartman, bondsman; Robts. Nanny, wit.

Verble, Jacob & Marey Tuckor, 12 June 1769; Danl. Little, George Tuckor, John Lewis Beard, bondsmer; Thomas Frohock, wit.

Verble, John & Betsey Dillow, 24 Dec 1817; Daniel Vervel, bondsman; Jno Giles, wit.

Verble, John H. & Nancy Smith, 8 Jan 1842; Adam A. Smithdeal, bondsman; J. H. Hardie, wit.

Vernon, Tinsley & Catharine Hicks, 5 June 1843; Thos. S. Poore, bondsman; J. H. Hardie, wit.

Vervil, John & Eve Rakis, 30 April 1796; Jacob Vervil, bondsman; J. Troy, wit.

Vestal, Joseph & Angeline Rary, 20 Nov 1854; Joseph Eller, bondsman; J. S. Myers, wit. married 21 Nov 1854 by Obadiah Woodson, J. P.

Vestal, Silas & Priscilla Ward, 19 Sept 1826; Neel Vestal, bondsman; E. Brock, wit.

Vicars, John & Ann Irwin, 16 Dec 1784; Alexr. Sneed, bondsman; T. H. McCaule, wit.

Vickers, Alex & Martha Hartley, 26 Nov 1795; Thos. Vickers, bondsman; J. Troy, wit.

Vickers, Will & Martha Gardiner, 5 Sept 1789; Thos. Vickers, bondsman; Evan Alexander, wit.

Vinagum, D. H. & Anna Bame, 10 Aug 1865; John M. Coffin, bondsman; Obadiah Woodson, wit.

Vincent, Abraham & Elizabeth Badget, 19 Oct 1792; David Badgett, bondsman; Jos. Chambers, wit.

Vincent, James B. & Mary C. Lilly, 9 Feb 1857; Wm. Jenkins, bondsman; E. Mauney, wit. married 9 Feb 1857 by E. Mauney, J. P.

Vogler, George & Henrietta W. Love, 1 June 1852; Saml. Reeves, bondsman; James E. Kerr, wit. married 8 June 1852 by Jas. P. Simpson, Pastor Methodist Church, Salisbury.

Vogler, George & Teeny Utzman, 3 Aug 1811; Jacob Crider, bondsman; Ezra Allemong, wit.

Volentine, George & Drucilla Carter, 11 June 1853; George Basinger, bondsman; James E. Kerr, wit.

Volentine, Hutson & Sarah Ann Freeman, 13 Nov 1854; David Potter, bondsman; James E. Kerr, wit.

Volentine, Hutson & Susan Bonaparte, married 30 Oct 1859 by Peter Williamson, J. P.

Volentine, William & Delia Reid, 18 May 1859; married by Peter Williamson, J. P.

Vormington, Samuel & Nancy C. Waller, 8 Oct 1851; Tobias Harkey, bondsman; J. S. Myers, wit.

Wacaster, Jacob & Margaret McCarn, 29 Aug 1793; George Henkle, bondsman; Jos. Chambers, wit.

Wacaster, Jacob & Gracy Pryan, 6 Nov 1814; Richard Harris, bondsman; R. Powell, wit.

Waddle, David & Polly Dickey, 2 Sept 1819; Jonathan Young, bondsman; Jno. Giles, wit.

Wade, Edward & Ann Miller, 26 Aug 1830; Hy. Giles, bondsman.

Wade, Jesse H. & Mary Barnett, 19 March 1852; Thomas A. Hartley, bondsman; James E. Kerr, wit. married 21 March 1852 by Obadiah Woodson, J. P.

Wade, John W. & Casey Cowan, 8 Jan 1825; Thomas Jones, bondsman; Washington Harris, wit.

Wade, Nathan & Amariliss Little, 20 June 1829; Mathias Cook, bondsman; L. R. Rose, J. P., wit.

Wadkins, Lewis & Jane Burlison, 19 June 1861; married by Peter Williamson, J. P.

Waggoner, Christian & Rachel Pool, 7 July 1824; Francis Johnson, bondsman; Milo A. Giles, wit.

Waggoner, Daniel & Elizabeth Harmon, 28 March 1767; John Kimbrough, Will Draper, bondsman; Thos Frohock, wit. consent of Georg Harmon, 20 March 1767 (consent written in German).

Waggoner, Daniel Jr. & Cristena Eler, 25 July 1811; William Thomasson, bondsman; Joseph Clarke, wit.

Waggoner, George & Alley Williams, 11 Jan 1804; Danl Waggoner, bondsman; A. L. Osborn, D. C., wit.

Waggoner, Michael & Susannah Willhelm, 2 March 1795; Nicholas Waggoner, bondsman; J. Troy, D. C., wit.

Wagner, H. M. & H. C. Thomason, 23 Nov 1865; John H. Cress, bondsman; Obadiah Woodson, wit.

Wagner, Simeon & Lelah Troutman, 12 Feb 1848; John Waggoner, bondsman; J. H. Hardie, wit.

Wagoner, Carmi J. & Margaret R. Wilhelm, 18 April 1861; Jacob B. Wilhelm, bondsman; James E. Kerr, wit. married 25 April 1861 by Wm. Λ. Houck, J. P.

Wagoner, Jacob & Cathrine Menius, 7 Sept 1809; John Correll, bondsman; Jno. Giles, wit.

Wagoner, Peter F. & Mary C. Clodfelter, 15 March 1852; Alfred M. Goodman, bondsman; James E. Kerr, wit.

Walk, David & Margaret Barret, 13 Nov 1819; Orston Bradshaw, bondsman; Jno. Giles, wit.

Walk, George & Elizibeth Billens, 30 March 1811; Philip Mok, bondsman; J. Willson, J. P., wit.

Walk, Jonathan & Sarah Frank, 28 Nov 1795; Saml Walk, bondsman; J. Troy, wit.

Walk, Joseph & Elizabeth Goss, 11 April 1803; John Creavor, bondsman; Jno Monroe, wit.

Walker, George & Peggy Cheshire, 9 Oct 1817; Tennison Chesheir, bondsman; Roberts Nanny, wit.

Walker, George & Lusinda Rachel, 23 March 1839; Alison Ridenhour, bondsman; Jno Hanes, J. P., wit.

Walker, Henry & Molly Fesperman, 10 July 1800; Henry Fesperman, bondsman; N. Chaffin, J. P., wit.

Walker, Howard & Mary Stephens, 10 May 1818; William Tumbelston, bondsman; Saml. Jones, wit.

Walker, Isaac & Ezelphia Ross, 6 Sept 1816; Simeon Walker, bondsman; Roberts Nanny, wit.

Walker, James & Kity Dimit, 17 Nov 1812; Benjamin Beatch, bondsman; Jno. Giles, C. C., wit.

Walker, James J. & Polly Biles, 4 July 1815; Hugh Ferguson, bondsman; Geo. Dunn, wit.

Walker, Jesse & Piety Bevel, 21 May 1816; Charles Phillips, bondsman; R. Powell, wit.

Walker, Jesse & Susanah Howard, 30 Aug 1816; Peter Potts, bondsman; Jno March Sr., wit.

Walker, John & Salley Yagley, 10 Feb 1798; Stephen Treadwell, bondsman; Geo. Fisher, wit.

Walker, John & Sally Call, 22 Oct 1809; William Howard, bondsman; Jn. March Sr., wit.

Walker, Richard & Mary Ann Swink, 8 Jan 1859; John Beard, bondsman; James E. Kerr, wit. married 9 Jan 1859 by W. R. Fraley, J. P.

Walker, Thomas & Sally Stinchicombe, 2 April 1814; John Tucker, bondsman; Jno. Giles, C. C., wit.

Walker, William & Agnus Aston, 17 July 1780; James Aston, bondsman.

Walker, William & Charity Wood, 25 April 1789; Leonard Watkins, bondsman; Wall Alexander, wit.

Walker, William & Polley Call, 23 May 1820; Isaac Call, bondsman; Saml. Jones, J. P., wit.

Wall, Absalom & Elizabeth Ellis, 8 Sept 1819; James Davis, bondsman; Roberts Nanny, wit.

Wall, Hiram & Betsey Ritchy, 7 March 1825; Adam Goodman, bondsman; W. Harris, wit.

Wall, Richmond & Belinda Rand, 3 Oct 1820; John Hembre, bondsman; Jno Giles, wit.

Wall, William & Sally Jordan, 17 Dec 1829; Green Crowell, bondsman.

Wallace, Alexander & Christina Fraley, 9 Dec 1840; Washington Henly, bondsman; Jno. H. Hardie, wit.

Wallace, J. R. & Mary C. Overcash, 6 Feb 1866; R. F. Fleming, bondsman; Obadiah Woodson, wit.

Wallace, Joseph & Barbary Blackwelder, 26 April 1815; Christian Blackwelder, bondsman; Jno. Giles, wit.

Wallace, William & E. Bost, 25 Sept 1838; John Goodnight, bondsman; S. Lemly Jr., wit.

Wallam, Phillip & Rose Blades, 17 Dec 1811; Isaac Blades, bondsman; Jno Giles, C. C., wit.

Wallan, Richard & Polly Singleton, 9 April 1813; James Walling, bondsman; Jno. Giles, C. C., wit.

Wallen, George & Eliza Broomhead, 14 Jan 1845; Wm. Swink, bondsman; Jno. H. Hardie, wit.

Waller, Burrel & Dolly Merritt, 3 Oct 1796; Benj. Waller, bondsman; Jno Rogers, wit.

Waller, Frederick & Crisey M. Cauble, 21 July 1849; Lewis Agner, bondsman.

Waller, George & Elizabeth Trexler, 13 July 1802; Fredk. Waller, bondsman; John Brem, D. C., wit.

Waller, George & Polly Brinkle, 11 Sept 1837; Joseph Eleam, bondsman; John Giles, wit.

Waller, George & Barbara Harkey, 11 Oct 1856; George Earnhart, bondsman; J. S. Myers, wit. married 12 Oct 1856 by David Barringer, J. P.

Waller, Henry C. & Polly S. Morgan, 3 July 1859; John Trexler, bondsman; Levi Trexler, wit. married 3 July 1859 by Levi Trexler, J. P.

Waller, Jacob & Margt. Casper, 15 May 1849; Moses Cauble, bondsman.

Waller, Jesse & Nancy Fouts, 3 March 1849; Israel Misenhimer, bondsman; John H. Hardie, wit.

Waller, John & Eliza Mull, 10 Nov 1849; George Redwine, bondsman; Susan T. Giles, wit.

Waller, John Jr. & Sarah Hodgens, 12 May 1858; George Earnhart, bondsman; John Wilkinson, wit. married 13 May 1858 by P. Trexler, J. P.

Waller, Lawrence & Anny Parkes, 26 Feb 1835; John Bringle, bondsman; J. H. Bringle, wit.

Waller, Lewis A. & Martha Jane Morris, 13 May 1861; married by Peter Williamson, J. P.

Waller, Michael & Betsey Messimir, 22 Sept 1818; Jno. Utzman, bondsman; Jno. Giles, wit.

Waller, Peter & Catharine Hess, 14 Feb 1834; John Bringle, bondsman; Wm. Locke, wit.

Waller, Peter & Elizabeth Mull, 13 Sept 1843; Jno. Waller, bondsman; J. H. Hardie, wit.

Waller, Peter & Eliza Blackwell, 10 April 1852; J. S. Myers, bondsman; married 11 April 1852 by W. A. Walton, J. P.

Wallies, Samuel & Sarah Hicks, 24 Jan 1809; Jacob Myers, bondsman; Jn. March Sr., wit.

Wallin, James & Betsy Lynn, 26 March 1814; J. Washington Smoote, bondsman; Geo. Dunn, wit.

Wallis, Isham & Edy Reed, 2 Dec 1822; David Butler, bondsman; Jno Giles, wit.

Wallis, Revel & Elibeth Cowan, 26 March 1807; John Cowan, bondsman.

Wallis, Samuel & Mary Lewis, 27 March 1780; James Handrih, bondsman; B. Booth Boote, wit.

Wallis, William & Jane Foster, 27 Oct 1812; John Hughston, bondsman; Jno. Giles, C. C., wit.

Wallis, William A. & Nancy H. Williford, 28 June 1855; Robert O. Cox, bondsman; J. S. Myers, wit. married 28 June 1855 by Wm. Lambeth.

Wallser, William & Solama Snider, 21 Feb 1820; Adam Snider, bondsman; Hy. Giles, wit.

Walser, Jacob & Margaret Slagel, 30 Dec 1793; Henry Earnest, bondsman; Jo. Chambers, wit.

Walser, John & Lucey Dotey, 17 March 1792; Moses Doty, bondsman.

Walser, Thomas & Rebecca Reed, 22 Feb 1820; Samuel Barnacastle, bondsman; Hy. Giles, wit.

Walten, Peter M. & Sarah Agner, 29 Aug 1856; J. S. Myers, bondsman.

Walter, Elias M. & Elizabeth M. Heilig, 16 July 1860; Miles Rusher, bondsman.

Walton, Albert T. & Nancy Cauble, 24 Dec 1856; Caleb Barger, bondsman; J. S. Myers, wit. married 24 Dec 1856 by Jacob Crim, Pastor Ev. L. Church.

Walton, Benjamin & Marthew Butner, 16 Jan 1794; William Butner, bondsman; Jo. Chambers, wit.

Walton, Benjamin & Sarah Walton, 28 June 1847; Jno. H. Hardie, bondsman; Robert Murphy, wit.

Walton, Benjamin F. & Catherine Kisler, 30 Oct 1855; W. A. Walton, bondsman; married 30 Oct 1855 by Saml. Rothrock, Minister of the Gospel in the Ev. Luth. Church.

Walton, Danel & Margaret Yost, 8 May 1792; George Smith, bondsman; Chs. Caldwell, wit.

Walton, G. S. & Catharine Byerly, 4 March 1847; Silas Keney, bondsman.

Walton, George A. & Sarah Klutts, 11 Sept 1849; Henry A. Walton, bondsman; J. S. Myers, wit.

Walton, George S. & Mary E. Walton, 16 Jan 1841; David W. Smith, bondsman.

Walton, Harmon & Betsey Bartley, 5 Sept 1815; Isaac Walton, bondsman; Jno. Giles, C. C., wit.

Walton, Henry A. & Ann Trexler, 18 March 1841; John D. Brown, bondsman; Susan T. Giles, wit.

Walton, Jacob & Susan Holebaugh, 29 June 1812; John Holobaugh, bondsman; Ezra Allemong, wit.

Walton, Jesse & Sophia Brown, 19 April 1815; Isaac Walton, bondsman; Geo. Dunn, wit.

Walton, Joseph & Catharine Kerns, 6 March 1821; John Cooper, bondsman; Hy. Giles, wit.

Walton, Lewis A. & Aley C. Boger, 15 March 1851; Geo. Smithdeal, bondsman; J. S. Myers, wit.

Walton, Milas J. & Sarah L. Boger, 24 Feb 1853; George W. Smith, bondsman; J. S. Myers, wit. married 24 Feb 1853 by W. A. Walton, J. P.

Walton, Peter & Susanna Hollebrook, 16 Feb 1814; John Smith, bondsman; Jno Giles, C. C., wit.

Walton, Peter & Susannah Adams, 18 Jan 1819; John Simmons, bondsman; Roberts Nanny, wit.

Walton, Richard & Peggy Adams, 23 Feb 1813; Peter Adams, bondsman; Jno. Giles, wit.

Walton, Richard B. & Joicy L. Eller, 17 Feb 1855; Nathan Johnston, bondsman; James E. Kerr, wit. married 18 Feb 1855 by D. W. Smith, J. P.

Walton, Thomas & Elizabeth Monroe, 11 Aug 1842; Wm. H. Fultz, bondsman.

Walton, Thomas R. & Harriet Hellard, 10 Nov 1847; Milas A. Agner, bondsman; Jno. H. Hardie, wit.

Walton, William & Marry Holebaugh, 20 Dec 1808; George Holebaugh, bondsman; A. L. Osborne, D. C., wit.

Walton, William & Catharine Grimes, 24 June 1837; Mumford B. Walton, bondsman.

Walton, William & Clarisa Luckey, 17 Feb 1832; Jno. A. Rosebrough, bondsman; J. H. Hardie, wit.

Wammack, Abraham & Susanna Parker, 14 Jan 1804; Allen Wammack, bondsman; A. L. Osborn, D. C., wit.

Wamox, Thomas & Narcissa Chapman, 29 March 1815; Wm. Dickson, bondsman; Geo. Dunn, wit.

Ward, Anthony & Lidia Vincent, 21 Sept 1810; Jacob Crider, bondsman; Jno Giles, C. C., wit.

Ward, David of Randolph County & Polly Tyre, 7 July 1814; Alexander Gray, bondsman; David Mock, wit.

Ward, Elijah & Elizabeth Austin, 6 March 1823; Caswell Harbin, bondsman; Enoch Brock, J. P., wit.

Ward, Francis A. & Sarah Miller, 26 Feb 1828; David Harbin, bondsman.

Ward, Franklin & Jane Maria Waller, 23 July 1859; John H. Greer, bondsman; James E. Kerr, wit. married 24 July 1859 by S. J. Peeler, J. P.

Ward, John & Martha Stevens, 8 Nov 1793; John Ford, bondsman; Jos. Chambers, wit.

Ward, Lewis & Elizabeth Stout, 15 Aug 1822; Simeon Morris, bondsman; R. Harriss, J. P., wit.

Ward, Wiley J. & Polley Smith, 16 Dec 1824; Levin Ward, bondsman; E. Brock, J. P., wit.

Warford, Abraham & Rebeka _____, _____; Thon Buffle, bondsman.

Warford, John & Mary Bartly, 11 Oct 1791; William Owin, bondsman; Chs. Caldwell, wit.

Warford, Joseph & Betsy Cress, 13 Aug 1813; Jacob Stoner, bondsman; Geo. Dunn, wit.

Warford, William & Hannah Cross, 26 Aug 1816; Robert Moore, bondsman; Jno Giles, C. C., wit.

Warlick, David & Cathrine Murr, 18 March 1818; Jno. Beard, bondsman; Milo A. Giles, wit.

Warner, Jacob F. & Christena Overcast, 8 Jan 1846; William C. Brandon, bondsman; J. M. Turner, wit.

Warner, Jacob Frederick & Christena Stiller, 27 March 1846; William C. Brandon, bondsman; J. M. Turner, wit.

Warner, John Jr. & Elizebeth Michael, 11 Dec 1817; Daniel Warner, bondsman; Mack Crump, wit.

Warner, Vinson & Sally Michael, 11 Oct 1821; John Warmer Jr., bondsman; Hy. Giles, wit.

Warrne, Peter M. & Margt. Shoaf, 26 April 1849; John L. Wright, bondsman.

Warsham, Alexander & Sarah Irwin, 30 March 1824; David F. Caldwell, bondsman; Hy. Giles, wit.

Warvel, Henry & Elizabeth Powlus, 2 Oct 1800; Jacob Fisher, bondsman; John Brem, wit.

Washington, Thomas & Elvira Waddell (colored), 9 Sept 1865, married by Rev. Wm. Lambeth.

Washington, William & Ann Collier (colored), 20 Sept 1865, married by Zuck Haughton, Parson.

Wason, Archibald & Nanny Cavin, 21 Sept 1769; Theophilus Morgan, bondsman; Thos Frohock, wit. consent from Archibald Wason, 20 Sept 1769.

Wason, Will & Jane Kiswell, 5 Feb 1795; Rot. Wason, bondsman.

Wasson, Archibald & Ann Lansdill, 27 Jan 1769; Wm. Steel, Max. Chambers, bondsmen; Tho. Frohock, wit.

Wasson, William & Elisabeth Lawrence, 4 Oct 1802; Edison Foster, bondsman; Js. McEwen, wit.

Waters, John & Jane Moyle, 12 Oct 1856; Richard Gribble, bondsman; Jac. C. Barnhardt, wit.

Watkins, David & Ruth Hendricks, 21 April 1789; Benjamin Story, bondsman; Wall. Alexander, wit.

Watkins, Henry T. & Margaret Miller, 17 Dec 1860; David Weil, bondsman; John Wilkinson, wit.

Watkins, John & Mary Jones, 28 Nov 1787; Vechel S. James, bondsman; Mich. Troy, wit.

Watkins, John Jr. & Susannah Hughes, 16 Jan 1800; Thomas Gaither, bondsman; Edwin J. Osborn, wit.

Watkins, William & Sylvia Wood, 13 Jan 1796; Zachariah Booth, bondsman; J. Troy, wit.

Watson, Ferrand & Mary M. Thompson, 8 April 1840; Jesse Thomason, bondsman; Susan T. Giles, wit.

Watson, Ferrand & Nancy Dent, 31 Jan 1848; Jno. H. Hardie, bondsman; J. H. Hardie, wit.

Watson, Ferrand & Nancy Dent, 17 Feb 1848; Jacob Lefler, bondsman; John H. Hardie Jr., wit.

Watson, Henry W. & Sarah A. Monroe, 25 Dec 1839; David Watson, bondsman; Jno. Giles, wit.

Watson, James & Mary Gray, 12 Nov 1845; Jno. H. Hardie, bondsman.

Watson, John W. & Sarah F. Trott, 29 Dec 1827; Wm. Hulin, bondsman; Jno. H. Hardie, wit.

Watson, Joseph B. & Abigail Ward, 26 Sept 1822; David Ward, bondsman; David Mock, wit.

Watson, Thomas C. & L. A. Cowan, 7 July 1863; Abel A. Cowan, bondsman; Obadiah Woodson, wit.

Watson, Wentworth & Elizabeth Gheen, 12 Aug 1805; Thomas Pinkston, bondsman; A. L. Osborn, D. C., wit.

Watson, William F. & Martha Jane Locke, 25 Feb 1858; William W. McKenzie, bondsman; James E. Kerr, wit. married 25 Feb 1858 by S. C. Alexander.

Watson, William G. & Amanda Lawrence, 9 Feb 1866; D. F. Watson, bondsman; Obadiah Woodson, wit.

Watts, Enoch & Nancy Leazar, 28 Sept 1858; Calvin S. McLean, bondsman; James E. Kerr, wit. married 30 Sept 1858 by T. L. Triplett.

Watts, James & Peggy Morrison, 10 April 1811; John Niblack, bondsman.

Watts, Joel H. & Mary Ann Cooper, 22 Oct 1855; J. W. Gibson, bondsman; John L. Hedrick, J. P., wit. married 23 Oct 1855 by John L. Hedrick, J. P.

Waugh, David W. & Jane Cook, 12 March 1825; Joseph Cowan, bondsman; W. Harris, wit.

Wayman, Edmund & Elizabeth Scott, 23 Oct 1822; Wm. Twoney, bondsman; Z. Hunt, wit.

Weand, Joseph & Betsey Murr, 19 Oct 1808; Thomas McCoy, bondsman; A. L. Osborne, wit.

Weant, Benj. F. & Polly West, 3 Aug 1850; Charles A. Weant, bondsman; J. S. Myers, wit.

Weant, Benjamin F. & Margaret E. Ketchie, 29 Mar 1856; C. W. Weant, bondsman; J. S. Myers, wit.

Weant, Charles A. & Rebecca West, 22 Feb 1845; David West, bondsman; J. H. Hardie, wit.

Weant, Charles A. & Mary Corl, 14 June 1854; William B. Coughenour, bondsman; J. S. Myers, wit.

Weant, Georg & Elizabeth Dickson, 19 Feb 1829; Jacob Coughenour, bondsman.

Weant, Jacob & Polly Smith, 17 Dec 1814; Jno. Craige, bondsman; Jno. Giles, C. C., wit.

Weant, John & Betsey Butner, 21 April 1810; Daniel Jacobs, bondsman; Jno. Giles, C. C., wit.

Weant, John & Martha Nowland, 18 Dec 1816; David Craig, bondsman; Jno. Giles, C. C., wit.

Weant, John H. & Delilah Crider, 20 Dec 1832; George M. Weant, bondsman; Jno. H. Hardie, wit.

Weant, William D. & Alecy Hulin, 16 Nov 1848; Wm. W. Jacobs,
bondsman; J. H. Hardie Jr., wit.

Weant, William D. & Martha Hulen, 11 Jan 1854; Tobias Honeycut,
bondsman; J. S. Myers, wit. married 12 Jan 1854 by Obadiah
Woodson, J. P.

Weant, William D. & Sarah L. Brown, 7 July 1863; William H.
Kester, bondsman; Obadiah Woodson, wit.

Weavel, Jacob & Mary Hagey, 5 April 1802; George Hagey, bondsman; Jno. Brem, wit.

Weaver, Adam & Nancy Proctor, 15 Oct 1793; Laurence Clinard,
bondsman; Jno Monroe, wit.

Weaver, Addom & Rutha Tarnel, 10 May 1806; Mager Daniels,
bondsman; D. Leatherman, J. P., wit.

Weaver, Daniel & Susannah Hartman, 30 March 1819; Michael
Bruner, bondsman; Jno. Giles, wit.

Weaver, George M. & Polly C. McCulloch, 14 May 1855; John M.
Weaver, bondsman; J. S. Myers, wit. married 17 May 1855
by Henry Miller, J. P.

Weaver, Henry & Anne Hill, 24 Feb 1816; Thomas Pinkston,
bondsman; Geo. Dunn, wit.

Weaver, Henry M. & Elizabeth Beaver, 9 Oct 1860; Levi A. Veaber,
bondsman; John Wilkinson, wit.

Weaver, Jacob & Lavina Hornbarrier, 11 Jan 1842; Tilman Pearce,
bondsman; J. H. Hardie, wit.

Weaver, John & Sally Lyerly, 25 Dec 1820; Jonathan Lyerly,
bondsman; Jno Giles, wit.

Weaver, Paul & Susannah Beaver, 7 Sept 1819; John Clutz,
bondsman; Milo A. Giles, wit.

Weaver, Peter & Susan J. Weaver, 17 May 1858; James A. Bostian,
bondsman; James E. Kerr, wit. married 20 May 1858 by Rev.
B. C. Hall.

Weaver, Solomon & Celia Hill, 5 July 1830; Isaac Burns, bondsman.

Weaver, William & Elizabeth Deaver, 24 Feb 1803; Edward Stuart,
bondsman; Jn March, J. P., Elijah Veatch, wit.

Weaver, William W. & Anna Klutts, 22 Nov 1845; George F. Smith,
bondsman; J. H. Hardie, wit.

Weaver, William W. & Mary J. Fesperman, 14 May 1854; Henry
Fesperman, bondsman; J. S. Myers, wit.

Weavor, Christian & Caty Leatherman, 14 Nov 1813; George Weavor,
bondsman; Joseph Clarke, wit.

Webb, Calip & Mary Wason, 19 Nov 1812; Daniel Webb Jr., bondsman; Jno Giles, C. C., wit.

Webb, Daniel & Jean Young, 17 Aug 1783; William Young, bondsman; Wm. Crawford, wit.

Webb, Daniel & Mary Ann Dent, 22 Feb 1831; Joseph Webb, bondsman; Jno. Giles, wit.

Webb, Daniel Jr. & Catharine Griffith, 6 Nov 1813; Charles Griffith, bondsman; Jno. Giles, C. C., wit.

Webb, David & Peggy Dobbins, 13 Dec 1819; Jas. Waddle, bondsman; Jno. Giles, wit.

Webb, John & Sally Phifer, 18 Nov 1817; Caleb Webb, bondsman; Jno. Giles, wit.

Webb, John P. & Mary C. Lyerly, 28 Nov 1865; Ira A. Little, bondsman; Obadiah Woodson, wit.

Weddington, Eli B. & Margaret Parmer, 16 May 1815; Evan Ellis, bondsman.

Weddington, James C. & Rebecca Ellis, 30 March 1819; Evan Ellis, bondsman; R. Powell, wit.

Weddington, John R. & Mary E. Atwell, 19 Nov 1853; C. F. Atwell, bondsman; J. S. Myers, wit.

Weesner, Christian & Susanah Daniel, 19 Oct 1819; Hugh Delapp, bondsman; Jno. Monroe, wit.

Weesner, John & Susannah Fagg, 4 Dec 1817; George Hanes, bondsman; T. Hampton, Saml. Jones, wit.

Wein, John W. & Charlotte E. Barr, 25 Aug 1860; Jas. Slater, bondsman; James E. Kerr, wit. married 29 Aug 1860 by J. K. Graham, J. P.

Welborn, Davis & Hannah Haworth, 31 Dec 1816; Jacob Raper, bondsman; Wm. Piggott, J. P., wit.

Welborn, John & Lyda Teague, 6 Dec 1802; Thoma Odell, bondsman; Wm. Welborn, wit.

Welborn, William & Rachel Pane, 7 Nov 1807; David Mock, bondsman; William Piggott, J. P., wit.

Welch, Isaac & Martha Smith, 3 Jan 1825; William Job, bondsman; E. Brock, J. P., wit.

Welch, John & Hyena Adams, 24 Dec 1802; John Willson, bondsman; Adlai L. Osborn, D. C., wit.

Welch, Joseph W. & Elen Locke, 14 Nov 1825; Richard Locke, bondsman; Jno. Giles, wit.

Welch, Thomas & Jane Thomson, 28 Oct 1772; Jno. Thomson, bondsman; Ad. Osborn, wit.

Wellman, Joseph & Mary Miles, 6 Aug 1793; Williams Hinkle, bondsman; Jos. Chambers, wit.

Wells, Barnard & Margrat Pool, consent from Edwd. Pool, 29 Nov 1769.

Wells, David & Christian White, 22 Dec 1786; Thomas White, bondsman; Jno Macay, wit.

Wells, James & Marey Graham, 15 April 1809; Joseph Clifford,
bondsman; Jn. March Sr., wit.

Wells, John & Mary Lyttle, 5 June 1801; Samuel Littel, bondsman; Jno Brem, wit.

Wells, John & Frances Grigory, 14 Oct 1815; Josiah Inglis,
bondsman; R. Powell, wit.

Wells, Newman & Rebecca Edwards, 18 Feb 1794; William Edwards,
bondsman; B. John Pinchback, John Thomas Pinchback, wit.

Wells, Silas & Alesey Skinner, 5 Nov 1813; Chas. Anderson Sr.,
bondsman; R. Powell, wit.

Wells, William & Jean Clifford, 18 Oct 1819; Daniel Horn,
bondsman; R. Powell, wit.

Welman, Samuel & Anne McMahon, 6 Dec 1791; David Johnson, bondsman; Chs. Caldwell, wit.

Welman, Thomas & Lucinda Nichols, 30 Oct 1789; Jeremiah Welman,
bondsman; Ed. Harris, wit.

Welman, Thomas & Polly Sains, 20 Aug 1814; Jeremiah Welmon Jr.,
bondsman; Jno Giles, wit.

Welmon, Jeremiah Jr. & Marey Sain, 16 Nov 1805; L. Moses,
bondsman; Jn. March Sr., wit.

Wence, John & Catharine Starns, 14 Jan 1791; Arche Blue, bondsman; C. Caldwell, D. C., wit.

Wensil, Henry A. & Milla Yost, 26 Jan 1859; John A. Cook,
bondsman.

Werner, William & Mary Mengleberg, 17 June 1816; Henry Sleighter,
bondsman; Jno. Giles, C. C., wit.

Werwell, Henry & Mary Kryder, 15 April 1792; Barney Kryder,
bondsman; Chas. Harris, wit.

West, Alexander & Hannah Willis, 3 Jan 1822; Charles Brown,
bondsman; Hy. Giles, wit.

West, Alford & Fanny Dannel, 1 Feb 1809; Phillip Brown, bondsman; A. L. Osborn, wit.

West, Austin & Elizebeth Brogdon, 5 Jan 1825; Samuel Baker,
bondsman; E. Brock, J. P., wit.

West, Cyrus & Caroline Griffin, 11 Aug 1847; Harvey M. Sossaman,
bondsman.

West, Cyrus & Margaret West, 22 Sept 1853; Obadiah Woodson,
bondsman; J. S. Myers, wit.

West, David & Amalea Varner, of Randolph Co., 23 Dec 1818;
William Varner, bondsman; P. Copple, J. P., wit.

West, Henson & Margaret Albright, 28 Feb 1817; Alex. Boyd,
bondsman; Milo A. Giles, wit.

West, Isaac & Mary Bevins, 4 Dec 1793; Jenkin West, bondsman;
Jos. Chambers, wit.

West, James H. & Dorcas C. Lourance, 26 Dec 1854; Harey B. Reese, bondsman; J. S. Myers, wit.

West, Jesse & Peggy Butner, 29 Dec 1819; Adam Brown, bondsman.

West, Jonathan & Polly Pierce, 14 Nov 1809; Wm. Hodge, bondsman; A. Hunt, wit.

West, Joseph S. & Margaret Felhom, 1 April 1844; A. C. McLelland, bondsman; J. H. Hardie, wit.

West, Miles & Easter Adams, 17 Jan 1815; Shadrick Etcheson, bondsman; Jn. March Sr., wit.

West, Miles & Susannah Swan, 22 Oct 1826; Enoch James, bondsman; E. Brock, J. P., wit.

West, Sterling & Christena Mengleberg, 15 March 1813; Jacob Travis, bondsman; Jno. Giles, C. C., wit.

West, Thomas & Mary Wrencher, 11 Jan 1804; Abm. Hall, bondsman; A. L. Osborn, D. C., wit.

West, William & Sally Blades, 23 Jan 1815; Henry Swink, bondsman; Geo. Dunn, wit.

West, William & Sally Sain, 2 Nov 1825; George Sain, bondsman; Thomas McNeely, J. P., wit.

West, William & Mary Swink, 23 Jan 1805; John Weand, bondsman; A. L. Osborn, D. C., wit.

Wever, Thomas & Rebecky Hendricks, 7 Sept 1816; Joshaway Hendricks, bondsman; Jn. March Sr., wit.

Weyatt, Asa & Elisebeth Graves, 2 Feb 1813; Jno. Phillips, bondsman; Jn. March Sr., wit.

Whalen, Andrew & Terrissa A. Pool, 30 April 1866; John L. Bogle, bondsman; H. N. Woodson, wit.

Whaley, Joseph & Esther Davis, 20 Dec 1781; Thos McKay, bondsman; Ad. Osborn, wit.

Whaley, Joseph & Lidia Justice, 5 Dec 1785; Hance Justice, bondsman; W. Cupples, wit.

Wheeler, Claudius B. & Ann J. Chaffin, 7 Dec 1835; Isaac Burns, bondsman.

Wheler, William & Lucy Ellis, 15 Feb 1791; Benjamin Abbott, bondsman; C. Caldwell, D. C., wit.

Whilhalm, Deniel & Polly Baker, 13 March 1828; John Wilhalm, bondsman; J. H. Hardie, wit.

Whitacre, John & Margaret Stocksdill, 22 Dec 1780; Thos Stocksdale, bondsman; Jno. Kerr, wit.

Whitacre, Mark & _____, 29 Jan 1767; Francis Taylor, Abner Baker, bondsmen.

Whitaker, Jesse & Lettice Charlotta, 25 Sept 1802; Barney Bowers, bondsman; A. L. Osborn, D. C., wit.

Whitaker, L. F. & Rowena Oates, 6 Jan 1866; W. B. Lindsey,
bondsman; W. H. Howerton, wit.

Whitaker, Mark & Catherine Boon, 1 March 1780; Thomas Jones,
bondsman; B. Booth Boote, wit.

Whitaker, Thomis & Pholey Coon, 30 Nov 1805; Philip Coon,
bondsman; John March Sr., wit.

Whitaker, William & Betsey Atchason, 4 Sept 1805; Thos. Chambers,
bondsman; Jn. Hunt, wit.

White, Andrew & Ezabella Gellah, 8 Aug 1788; John Mitchell,
bondsman; Wm. Alexander, Ad. Osborn, wit.

White, Aquila & Susanna Noland, 26 Jan 1765; Francis Taylor,
bondsman; John Frohock, wit. consent of William Noland,
25 Jan 1765.

White, Asa & Elibeth Oens, 19 March 1807; Lennard Rickard,
bondsman.

White, Henry & Heathy Barnecasle, 29 Aug 1810; Daniel Brinkley,
bondsman; W. Ellis, J. P., wit.

White, James & Mary Lawson, 13 April 1770; George Davison,
bondsman; Thomas Frohock, wit.

Whitek, James & Polley Barker, 2 June 1803; William Harwood,
bondsman; Ph. Beck, wit.

White, James & Frances March, 23 Aug 1831; R. L. Hargrove,
bondsman.

White, Jessee & Grace Harwood, 18 Nov 1802; John Harwood, bondsman; A. L. Osborn, D. C., wit.

White, John & Sarah Miller, 2 June 1806; Jacob Weasner, bondsman; Lazarus Hege, J. P., wit.

White, John R. M. & Harriet N. R. Lowrance, 18 Nov 1861; Wm. D.
White, bondsman; Obadiah Woodson, wit. married 20 Nov 1861
by Rev. W. B. Watts.

White, Joseph O. & Bettie U. Rowzee, 10 Dec 1862; J. H.
Renneker, bondsman; Obadiah Woodson, wit.

White, Lewis & Polly Hicks, 13 Nov 1813; Peter Eaton, bondsman;
R. Powell, wit.

White, Ovelton & Rachel Clifford, 10 Dec 1817; James C. Weddington, bondsman; R. Powell, wit.

White, Philo & Nancy R. Hampton, 9 May 1822; Ezra Allemong,
bondsman.

White, Thomas & Lucy Traylor, 10 Nov 1813; James Lowe Jr.,
bondsman; Geo. Dunn, wit.

White, Thomas & Nancy Wright, 23 Oct 1814; Absalom Morgan,
bondsman; E. Morgan, J. P., wit.

White, Walker & Sarah Bowden, 3 March 1822; Cilas Etcheson,
bondsman; Geo. Coker, wit.

White, William R. & Margaret Cowan, 18 July 1851; G. C. McHenry, bondsman; James E. Kerr, wit.

Whiteacre, Alexander & Mary McCartey, 13 Sept 1779; James Whitakker, bondsman; B. Booth Boote, wit.

Whiteacre, Peter & Lowrahoma Patchit, 8 Aug 1767; Thomas Stanfield, Eldad Reed, bondsmen; Thomas Frohock, wit.

Whiteaker, Jesse & Elizabeth Beal, 12 March 1813; Thomas Holmes, bondsman; R. Powell, wit.

Whiteaker, John & Mary Wilson, 2 Sept 1798; George Thomason, bondsman.

Whiteaker, Joshua & Mary Reed, 12 Sept 1764; Eldad Reed, Wm. Nassery, bondsmen; Thoms. Frohock, wit.

Whiteaker, Joshua & Mary Frits, 14 Jan 1783; Joshiah Davis, bondsman; William Crawford, wit.

Whiteaker, Richard & Margaret Hinkle, 16 Nov 1819; Arthur Smith, bondsman; R. Powell, wit.

Whiteaker, Thomas & Anney Blackwood, 9 Jan 1808; Beal Ijames, bondsman; Jn. March Sr., wit.

Whiteaker, William & Mary Kenneday, 29 Jan 1792; Peter Whiteaker, bondsman.

Whitehead, Edward & Sarah McCoy, 22 March 1790; William Willcockson, bondsman; Nichol. W. Gaither, William Michael, wit.

Whitlock, Thomas & Catharine Steelman, 2 April 1794; James Cain, bondsman; B. John Pinchback, Mary Pinchback, wit.

Whitlock, Thomas & Temperance Holeman, 22 May 1824; Hamilton Summers, bondsman; John Cook, wit.

Whitman, John A. & Sarah Ann Roberson, 8 Aug 1844; William Trott, bondsman; J. H. Hardie, wit.

Whitman, Peter & Rachel Owens, 23 June 1821; Moses Lyster, bondsman; Milo A. Giles, wit.

Whitman, Philip & Mary Swisher, 17 Jan 1818; Michael Swisher, bondsman; Roberts Nanny, wit.

Whitman, Philip & Polley Johnson, 11 July 1822; Thos. Gibbs, bondsman; Tho. Hampton, wit.

Whittaker, William & Miram Church, 4 _____ 1802; Jno. McClelland, bondsman; Jno. Brem, wit.

Wiatt, Barnet & Nelly Willice, 20 June 1808; Samuel Foster, bondsman; R. Pearson, Jr., wit.

Wiatt, Brantly & Juley Daniell, 5 April 1836; Matthew Skeen, bondsman.

Wiatt, James E. & Mary A. Bean, 27 July 1854; John Morgan, bondsman; H. W. Hill, J. P., wit. married 27 July 1854 by H. W. Hill, Esq.

Wier, David & Cathreena Burk, 7 Nov 1802; Jno. Spurgins, bondsman; Jno. Monroe, wit.

Wiatt, Rolin Henry & Mary L. Roseman, 15 May 1856; William W. Wiatt, bondsman; Levi Trexler, wit.

Wice, Henry A. & Christina Lefler, 15 April 1858; Robert F. Freeman, bondsman; John Wilkinson, wit. married 15 April 1858 by J. M. Brown, J. P.

Wice, Tobias & Mary Swink, 15 March 1837; Henry Moyer, bondsman.

Wier, Adam & Catharine Clodfelter, 2 April 1817; Samuel Farrington, bondsman; Ezl. Brown, A. Brown, wit.

Wier, Barney & Elizabeth Clodfelter, 3 May 1820; Baret Wier Jr., bondsman; Jno Monroe, wit.

Wiett, Thomas & Rachel Parks, 12 Jan 1793; Jordan Wiette, bondsman; Jos. Chambers, wit.

Wike, Jacob & Susanah Moir, 5 Oct 1783.

Wiles, George & Susan Canup, 10 April 1851; James Kirk, bondsman; J. S. Myers, wit.

Wiles, Harvey & Sarah J. Simpson, 8 Sept 1865; G. W. Marona, bondsman; Obadiah Woodson, wit. married 9 Sept 1865 by Reuben J. Holmes, J. P.

Wiles, John & Polly Bruner, 20 Oct 1824; George Kesler, bondsman; Hy. Allemong, wit.

Wiles, John & Catharine Bowers, 15 June 1840; George Hoffner, bondsman; Susan T. Giles, wit.

Wiley, John F. & Mary Ann Frick, 8 March 1859; Ferris Dulin, bondsman; John Wilkinson, wit. married 10 March 1859 by E. E. Phillips, J. P.

Wiley, S. H. & Miriam C. Murdoch, 3 July 1861; married 4 July 1861 by J. Rumple, V. D. M.

Wilhelm, Alexander & Mary Houston, 29 July 1843; James Graham, bondsman; J. H. Hardie, wit.

Wilhelm, Danniel & Elvira Tenison, 3 March 1835; George Baker, bondsman; Hy. Giles, wit.

Wilhelm, Fredrick & Polly Caster, 23 Oct 1817; Henry Fite, bondsman; Roberts Nanny, wit.

Wilhelm, George & Susanna Stiller, 29 Jan 1819; Jacob Steller, bondsman.

Wilhelm, George L. & Catharine Hartman, 21 Aug 1850; Green C. Kesler, bondsman; Obadiah Woodson, wit.

Wilhelm, Henry & Margarett Earnhart, 5 March 1818; George Kesler, bondsman; Moses A. Locke, wit.

Wilhelm, Henry & Betsey Dean, 4 Sept 1827; George Wilhelm, bondsman; J. H. Hardie, wit.

Wilhelm, Henry & Sophia Phile, 28 Jan 1838; Philip Lemly, bondsman; Hy. Giles, wit.

Wilhelm, Henry & Sophia Bruner, 21 June 1850; Robert Harris,
bondsman; James E. Kerr, wit.

Wilhelm, Jacob & Betsey Croner, 12 July 1827; D. Crawford Locke,
bondsman; J. H. Hardie, wit.

Wilhelm, James M. & Sarah Ann T. Turner, 29 Jan 1851; William
A. Shuping, bondsman; James E. Kerr, wit.

Wilhelm, John & Catherine Peeler, 18 Feb 1846; Henry W. Hill,
bondsman; J. M. Turner, wit.

Wilhelm, John & Nancy Bostian, 19 Nov 1849; William Wilhelm,
bondsman; J. S. Myers, wit.

Wilhelm, John A. & Elizabeth Ritchey, 12 Aug 1851; George H.
Richey, bondsman; J. S. Myers, wit.

Wilhelm, John C. & Sarah E. Ketchey, 22 Sept 1860; Jacob B.
Wilhelm, bondsman; John Wilkinson, wit. married 27 Sept
1860 by Saml. Rothrock, Minister of the Gospel in the Ev.
Luth. Church.

Wilhelm, Leuis & Sophia Boston, 4 Sept 1828; Michael Bostian,
bondsman; Jno. H. Hardie, wit.

Wilhelm, Lewis A. & Maria Phifer, 20 Dec 1853; Wm. Montgomery,
bondsman; J. S. Myers, wit.

Wilhelm, Moses & Peney Lytaker, 29 Jan 1838; David Bostian,
bondsman; Jno. Giles, wit.

Wilhelm, Mumford S. & Elizabeth Kimbrough, 2 Sept 1858; N. N.
Fleming, bondsman; James E. Kerr, wit. married 2 Sept 1858
by M. S. McKenzie, J. P.

Wilhelm, Peter & Susan Baker, 12 May 1822; Henry Wilhelm,
bondsman.

Wilhelm, Sammual & Mary Stiller, 23 June 1825; Lewis Wilhelm,
bondsman; Hy. Giles, wit.

Wilhelm, Samuel & Dorotha Thomas, 6 Dec 1823; John Thomas,
bondsman; Jno Giles, wit.

Wilhelm, William A. & Priscilla Kimmer, 22 Aug 1860; James B.
Wilhelm, bondsman; James E. Kerr, wit. married 23 Aug 1860
by Milo A. J. Roseman, J. P.

Wilhelm, William L. & Margaret Stiller, 15 Aug 1851; Fergus M.
Graham, bondsman; James E. Kerr, wit.

Wilhelm, William M. & Mary L. Thomas, 22 April 1856; Philip P.
Meroney, bondsman; J. S. Myers, wit.

Wilherlmn, George A. & Sarah Goodman, 22 April 1850; David
Trexler, bondsman; James E. Kerr, wit.

Wilkenson, David & Lucy A. M. Williford, 15 Sept 1840; Thos.
C. Cooke, bondsman.

Wilkerson, Daniel B. & Mary Hudson, 16 July 1842; Henry W. Hudson, bondsman; Jno. H. Hardie, wit.

Wilkerson, William A. & Rebecca E. Noe, 1 March 1866; Horatio N. Woodson, bondsman; Obadiah Woodson, wit.

Wilkesen, John & Mary Massey, 29 June 1787; Henry Beroth, bondsman; Jno. Macay, wit.

Wilkeson, Allen & Iona Call, 20 Dec 1823; Adam Little, bondsman; M. Hanes, J. P., wit.

Wilkins, Alexander & Ann Runande, 27 Dec 1802; Charles Beeman, bondsman; Hudson Hughes, wit.

Wilkinson, John & Frances Beryman, 7 March 1793; William Snow, bondsman; G. Enochs, wit.

Wilkinson, Samuel & Easther McBride, 5 May 1783; John Hiett, bondsman; John McNairy, wit.

Wilkinson, William & Lucy Reives, 25 July 1814; Thomas Robinson, bondsman; Jno. Giles, C. C., wit.

Wilkinson, William & Drucilla Hampton, 11 June 1825; Moses L. Brown, bondsman; Hy. Giles, wit.

Willcockson, George & Elizabeth Beam, 20 Oct 1767; George Boone, John Wilcockson, bondsmen; Thomas Frohock, wit.

Willcockson, George & Elizabeth Pinchback, 23 Feb 1789; William Hall, bondsman; Will Alexander, wit.

Willhelm, Lewis & Rebekah Bosten, (no date, during admn. of Alexander Martin); Peter Stiller, bondsman.

Williams, Absalom & Sarah Spurgin, 19 Nov 1817; Peter Peace, bondsman.

Williams, Alexander & Phebee Pickett, 22 Dec 1810; John Crover, bondsman; J. Willson, wit.

Williams, Benjamin & Sarah Gillispie, 26 March 1765; Jno. Oliphant, bondsman; Thomas Frohock, wit.

Williams, Benjamin & Polley Ellet, 27 Jan 1817; Cornelius Howard, bondsman; Jn March Sr., wit.

Williams, Dilly & Nancy Brooks, 2 June 1795; James Owens, bondsman; J. Troy, wit.

Williams, Edward & Liddy Wood, 23 Jan 1767; Edward Turner, Anderson Smith, bondsmen; Thomas Frohock, wit. consent of John and Mary Wood, parents of Liddy Wood.

Williams, Edward & Ann Dimmett, 20 Aug 1772; Anderson Smith, Edward Williams Jr., Phillip Williams, William Butler, bondsmen; Thomas Frohock, wit. consent of James Dimmett, 20 Aug 1772.

Williams Edward & Nancy Defreize, 1 Jan 1814; Warran Williams, bondsman; Jn. March Sr., wit.

Williams, Federick & Elizabeth Partrick, 28 Sept 1822; Isaac Parker, bondsman; L. R. Rose, J. P., wit.

Williams, Francis & Jean Phelps, 28 Oct 1778; John Giles, bondsman; Jno. Kerr, wit.

Williams, Francis & Ann Dismukes, 24 Jan 1826; Daniel E. Brock, bondsman; E. Brock, J. P., wit.

Williams, Henry & Nancy Allemong, 25 Aug 1811; Andrew Zimmerman, bondsman; Geo. Dunn, wit.

Williams, Henry & Mary Barnhill, 21 Dec 1819; Tho. L. Cowan, bondsman.

Williams, Henry R. & Polly Upchurch, 12 Oct 1830; Wm. Pinkston, bondsman; Jno. H. Hardie, wit.

Williams, Hudson & Patsey Parker, 10 Sept 1829; William R. Hughes, bondsman; Jno. H. Hardie, wit.

Williams, Jacob & Mary Clifford, 31 Dec 1834; Stephen L. Furches, bondsman; Jm Tomlinson, J. P., wit.

Williams, James & Tabathia Hedgepathe, 13 Nov 1787; Andrew Carson, bondsman; Dd. Caldwell, wit.

Williams, James & Polly Short, 27 Jan 1808; Jasper Star Jr., bondsman; John Hanes, J. P., wit.

Williams, James & Nancy Cooper, 25 Sept 1828; Godfrey Clement, bondsman; L. R. Rose, J. P., wit.

Williams, John & Marey Donnelson, 28 Jan 1788; James Donnelson, bondsman; Dd. Caldwell, wit.

Williams, John & Tabitha Banks, 4 April 1803; Christopher Bateman, bondsman; Adlai L. Osborn, D. C., wit.

Williams, John & Eliza Wyngate, 27 Nov 1810; Samuel Pryor, bondsman; Ezra Allemong, wit.

Williams, John & Buley Etcheson, 12 Jan 1818; Joel Ellis, bondsman; R. Powell, wit.

Williams, John & Anne Beal, 16 Feb 1819; Samuel Little, bondsman; Jno. March Sr., wit.

Williams, John & Elizabeth Bostian, 28 Aug 1821; Jacob Bostian, bondsman; Hy. Giles, wit.

Williams, John & Louisa Edleman, 4 Jan 1841; Hardy Kluttes, bondsman; J. L. Beard, D. C., wit.

Williams, John & Mary L. Bringle, 14 April 1866; D. L. Bringle, bondsman; Obadiah Woodson, wit.

Williams, John A. & Elizabeth Walk, 4 Dec 1820; Orsten Bradshaw, bondsman; Hy. Giles, wit.

Williams, Jonathan & Margaret Monroe, 19 March 1818; John Markland, bondsman; Ezl. Brown, wit.

Williams, Joseph & Hannah Dodridge, 13 April 1802; Thos. Hutson, bondsman; Jn. Jqnes, wit.

Williams, Joseph & Catharine Goodman, 14 Nov 1809; George Bean, bondsman; Jno Giles, C. C., wit.

Williams, Joseph & Dolly Jacobs, 24 June 1846; Paul Goodman, bondsman; John H. Hardie Jr., wit.

Williams, Milas or Miles & Elizabeth Jacobs, 18 Oct 1856; George H. Jacobs, bondsman; J. S. Myers, wit. married 19 Oct 1856 by Jacob Crim, Pastor of Ev. Luth. Church.

Williams, Phillip Jr. & Gerner Taylor, 17 Sept 1779; Phillip Williams Sr., bondsman; Ad. Osborn, wit.

Williams, Ralph & Agness Morgan, 3 April 1819; William Butler, bondsman; Jno. Giles, wit.

Williams, Richard & Nancy Smoot, 7 May 1825; Bennet Rogers, bondsman; Jno. Clement, J. P., wit.

Williams, Robert & Eastor Deadman, 13 Dec 1820; Joel Ellis, bondsman; John Cook, wit.

Williams, Robert H. & Maria Smith, 30 Sept 1859; Edmund Burke, bondsman; James E. Kerr, wit.

Williams, Samuel & Mary Williams, 27 Sept 1769; Danl. Little, Benj. Milner, bondsmen; Thomas Frohock, wit.

Williams, Samuel & Anna Macay Hoffman, 12 April 1822; David Billings, bondsman; George Locke, wit.

Williams, Slowmon & Margrat Carter, 27 June 1804; Barnid Copper, bondsman; Ph. Beck, wit.

Williams, Stephen & Johannah Flemmons, 17 Jan 1807; Benjamin Ellis, bondsman; John Hanes, J. P., wit.

Williams, Stephen & Elizabeth Ellis, 8 March 1813; William Hendricks, bondsman; Jn. March Sr., wit.

Williams, Steven & Nancy Flemmins, 18 June 1816; Michael Akel, bondsman; Joseph Clarke, wit.

Williams, Thomas & Elizabeth Butner, 24 Jan 1792; John Brown, bondsman; Chs. Caldwell, wit.

Williams, Thomas & Sarah Marlin, 5 Aug 1826; Wm. S. Morgan, bondsman.

Williams, William & Liddy Howard, 4 March 1768; Thomas Frohock, wit.

Williams, William & Jinsy Ellit, 23 Aug 1822; Cornelis Howard, bondsman; Geo. Coker, wit.

Williams, William & Christena Miller, 7 Dec 1825; Elijah Etcheson, bondsman; J. C. Weddington, wit.

Williams, William & Sarah Ward, 19 July 1805; Anthony Ward, bondsman.

Williams, William & Margaret Ford, 10 Jan 1824; Samuel Williams, bondsman.

Williamson, Jesse F. & Sarah F. Williamson, 31 Dec 1846; Thos H. Pierce, bondsman; John H. Hardie Jr., wit.

Williamson, John & Elmina L. Smith, 25 Nov 1841; Kinchen
Elliott, bondsman; J. S. Johnston, wit.

Williamson, Peter & Elizabeth Krider, 27 Nov 1848; A. S. Utzman,
bondsman.

Williamson, Thomas & Rachel Graham, 24 May 1804; Daniel Clary,
bondsman.

Williamson, Thomas A. & Mary A. Hall, 12 Jan 1842; K. Elliott,
bondsman; J. S. Johnston, wit.

Williamson, William & Nancy Cozort, 10 Dec 1828; David Rutherford, bondsman; J. H. Hardie, wit.

Williford, Edwin & Mary Overcast, 30 July 1821; Michael Overcash, bondsman; Hy. Giles, wit.

Williford, John A. & Lyndy M. Hair, 24 Feb 1863; Richd. Graham,
bondsman; Obadiah Woodson, wit.

Williford, John T. & Rachel C. C. Williford, 25 Feb 1845;
David Willkison, bondsman; Jno. H. Hardie Jr., wit.

Williford, William & Jane C. Smith, 12 Dec 1855; Rowan J.
Wilaford, bondsman; John L. Hedrick, wit. married 13 Dec
1855 by John L. Hedrick, J. P.

Willis, George & Polly Patterson, 26 Oct 1803; William Patterson, bondsman; A. L. Osborn, D. C., wit.

Willis, George & Detsey Hayes, 7 Nov 1818; John S. Long,
bondsman; Jno. Giles, wit.

Willis, James & Patsy Coats, 17 Dec 1804; L. Willis, bondsman;
A. L. Osborn, wit.

Willis, John & Elizabeth West, 4 Oct 1817; Orston Bradshaw,
bondsman.

Willis, Jonathon & Susanna Smith, 16 Oct 1817; John Adams,
bondsman; Henry Giles, wit.

Willis, Mackenzey & Jane Miller, 1 Jan 1826; Alexander West,
bondsman; Hy. Giles, wit.

Willis, Philip & Edy Coats, 28 Dec 1813; John Merrell, bondsman;
Jno. Giles, C. C., wit.

Willis, Thomas & Jane Willis, 3 Dec 1809; Wm. Willis, bondsman;
Jno. Giles, C. C., wit.

Willis, Thomas & Sally Simpson, 19 Sept 1815; William Coats,
bondsman; Jno. Giles, wit.

Willis, Thomas & Lydia Hall, 21 Dec 1833; Levi Brown, bondsman;
Wm. Locke, wit.

Willis, William & Cecily Coats, 27 Feb 1810; Abner Coats,
bondsman; Jno. Giles, C. C., wit.

Willis, William & Nancy Garret, 17 March 1809; Thos. Willis,
bondsman; A. L. Osborne, wit.

Willkie, L. D. & Emeline Allen, 4 Jan 1859; Jas. Blakly, bondsman; James E. Kerr, wit. married 4 Jan 1859 by Levi C. Groseclose.

Willson, Abraham & Rachel Johnston, 14 Sept 1802; Charles Hunt, bondsman.

Willson, Benjamin & Faney Callar, 25 Feb 1811; James Jonniscea, bondsman; Jn. March Sr., wit.

Willson, D. C. & Caroline Hall, 5 Jan 1841; Wm. Emerson, bondsman; Susan T. Giles, wit.

Willson, John & Marey Kinsey, 24 Feb 1769; James Archer, Wm. Temple Coles, bondsmen; Thos. Frohock, wit.

Willson, Joshua & Farabee Baker, 26 Aug 1805; Jacob Clinard, bondsman.

Willson, Matthew & Sarah Orten, 6 May 1772; Robert Tate, James Orten, bondsmen; John Frohock, wit. consent of James Orten, 6 May 1772.

Willson, Robert & Elizabeth Johnson, widow, 28 Dec 1767; Wm. Steel, bondsman; Thomas Frohock, wit.

Wilson, Alexander & Jean Brandon, 11 Feb 1788; John Brandon, bondsman; Dd. Caldwell, wit.

Wilson, Benjamin & Margrit Bowman, 30 Dec 1788; Moses Winsley, bondsman; Ad. Osborn, wit.

Wilson, Boon & Nancy Leatherman, 25 Nov 1812; Jno. Smith, bondsman; Geo. Dunn, wit.

Wilson, Boyd & Nancy Slater, 1 July 1789; William Dancey, bondsman; William Alexander, wit.

Wilson, George & Martha Culbertson, 4 Feb 1792; John White, bondsman; Chs. Caldwell, wit.

Wilson, George & Rachael Wiseman, 17 Feb 1813; John Merrell, bondsman; Jno. Giles, wit.

Wilson, George & Polly Gaither, 23 May 1835; Alexander Smoot, bondsman.

Wilson, Henry F. & Mary Leach, 18 Sept 1819; Francis Renshaw, bondsman; Hy. Giles, wit.

Wilson, Hiram & Nancy Smith, 12 Sept 1812; Wm. McCrary, bondsman; Exra Allemong, wit.

Wilson, Isaac & Margaret McCreary, 17 Sept 1795; Peter Whitaker, bondsman; J. Troy, wit.

Wilson, Isaac & Caty Heartley, 27 March 1819; Micheal Anderson, bondsman; Jno. Giles, wit.

Wilson, James & Hannah Bryant, 1 Sept 1783; Morgan Bryan, bondsman; Wm. Crawford, wit.

Wilson, James & Jean Caldwell, 6 May 1788; A. Caldwell, bondsman; Dd. Caldwell, wit.

Wilson, James & Elizabeth Smith, 27 June 1803; Sam Walk, bondsman; A. L. Osborn, D. C., wit.

Wilson, James & Elizebeth Dial, 8 Dec 1812; John Dial, bondsman;
J. March Sr., wit.

Wilson, James & Elizabeth Kerr, 23 Aug 1823; Isaac Burns,
bondsman.

Wilson, James M. & Margaret T. Smith, 20 May 1846; Rufus A.
Brandon, bondsman; J. M. Turner, wit.

Wilson, John & Sarah Boone, (no date, during admn. of Gov.
Martin 1782-5, 1789-92); Samuel Harper, bondsman; Max.
Chambers, wit.

Wilson, John & Nancy Hilton, 26 Aug 1806; Geo. March, bondsman;
John March Sr., wit.

Wilson, John & Jincy Robertson Orten, 19 April 1809; Jas. Orten,
bondsman; Jno. Giles, wit.

Wilson, John & Elisabeth Todd, 3 Nov 1819; Joshua Wilson,
bondsman.

Wilson, John & Marth Turner, (colored), 21 April 1866; George
Turner, bondsman; Obadiah Woodson, wit.

Wilson, Joseph L. & Jane E. Beeker, 5 March 1866; W. T. Shinn,
bondsman; Obadiah Woodson, wit.

Wilson, Lewis F. & Pegey Hall, 4 Oct 1787; Dd. Caldwell, bondsman.

Wilson, Richard & Elisabeth Ratts, 16 Feb 1820; Wm. Wilson,
bondsman; Jno. Giles, wit.

Wilson, Robert & Mary Warner, 29 Nov 1791; George Reed, bondsman; Chs. Caldwell, wit.

Wilson, Robert & Rachel Hughey, 9 Feb 1813; Thomas Wilson,
bondsman; Henry Allemong, wit.

Wilson, Robert & Mary Myers, 12 May 1814; James Wiseman, bondsman; Geo. Dunn, wit.

Wilson, Robert & Mary Clemmons, 21 Nov 1816; Godfrey Batts,
bondsman; Jno. Giles, C. C., wit.

Wilson, Sam & Margrett Jack, 6 April 1768; Jas. Jack, bondsman;
Tho Frohock, wit.

Wilson, Samuel & Lucy Headen, 22 Jan 1810; William Hargrave,
bondsman.

Wilson, Samuel & Margaret Robinson, 15 Nov 1817; Jno. W. Robison,
bondsman; Jno. Giles, wit.

Wilson, Thomas & Cath. Leuiston, 22 Jan 1767; Hugh Montgomery,
bondsman; Thom. Frohock, wit.

Wilson, Thomas & Mary Anderson, 3 Aug 1785; Richard Holmes,
bondsman; Max. Chambers, wit.

Wilson, William & Caroline Earnheart, 16 Dec 1857; James E.
Kerr, wit.

Wilson, William & Fanny Broox, 9 Dec 1816; Abraham Sharp, bondsman; Roberts Nanny, wit.

Wilson, William & Ann Trot, 1 March 1784; David Cowan, bondsman; Hu. Magoune, wit.

Wilson, William R. & Sarah A. F. Slater, 25 March 1852; John E. Boger, bondsman; J. S. Myers, wit. married 25 March 1852 by Jas. P. Simpson.

Winchel, Solomon & Mary Sheek, 17 March 1821; John Sheek, bondsman; Hy. Giles, wit.

Winders, A. C. & Elizabeth B. Kincaid, 12 July 1827; James Owens, bondsman; J. H. Hardie, wit.

Winders, P. P. & Mary Elizabeth Owens, 26 Nov 1859; Giles S. Owens, bondsman; John Wilkinson, wit. married 27 Nov 1859 by M. Plumer, J. P.

Winders, Thomas C. & Angeline S. Swisher, 18 Sept 1856; Thomas D. Fraley, bondsman; J. S. Myers, wit.

Windser, N. R. & Isabella M. Dickson, 27 Nov 1851; R. B. Patterson, bondsman; J. S. Myers, wit.

Windsor, Bennit & Sarah Holeman, 27 April 1823; Wm. Marlous, bondsman; Jno. Cook, J. P., wit.

Winecoff, David & Mary A. Baker, 1 May 1843; John Osborne Baker, bondsman; Jno. Giles, wit.

Winecoff, John & Anny Sloop, 20 July 1829; David Winecoff, bondsman; Hy. Giles, wit.

Winecoff, Levi A. & Susan M. Sloop, 6 Jan 1856; Henry Sloop, bondsman; J. S. Myers, wit.

Winford, Alexander & Elizabeth Harris, 1 Dec 1800; Risdon Fisher, bondsman; J. Brem, wit.

Winford, John & Nancey Smith, 11 Oct 1792; Isaac Smith, bondsman; G. Enochs, wit.

Wingfield, Thomas & Beersheba Williams, 23 Aug 1782; John Templeton, bondsman; T. H. McCaule, wit.

Winglar, Francis & Betsey Helsley, 21 April 1803; Peter Wingfler, bondsman; Adlai L. Osborn, D. C., wit.

Wingler, Peter & Susanna Helsly, 27 Dec 1811; Jacob Helsly, bondsman; Geo. Dunn, wit.

Wingler, Peter & Mary Hellsly, 6 March 1800; Michl. Hellsly, bondsman; Matt. Troy, wit.

Winingham, Wood & Polly Sanders, 6 Jan 1824; Isaac Hardin, bondsman; L. R. Rose, J. P., wit.

Winkler, Godfay & Elizebeth Ray, 11 Aug 1816; Jesse Simpson, bondsman; Henry Giles, wit.

Winningham, John & Hannah Morgan, 3 Dec 1815; Thomas Morgan, bondsman; Silas Peace, wit.

Winsent, John & Catherina Elrod, 14 Dec 1769; Adam Elrod, Hermon Butner, bondsmen; Thomas Frohock, wit.

Winsutt, Isaac & Rachel Inyart, 26 Jan 1765; John Enyart, bondsman; John Frohock, C. C., wit.

Wise, Charles & Sophia May, 15 May 1832; Edward Rufty, bondsman; Jno. H. Hardie, wit.

Wise, David & Elisabeth Myers, 26 July 1831; Jacob S. Myers, bondsman; Jno. H. Hardie, wit.

Wise, Edward & Catharine Blackwell, 22 May 1858; Benjamin Blackwel, bondsman; John Wilkinson, wit. married 23 May 1858 by S. J. Peeler, J. P.

Wise, George & Margaret Cox, 18 July 1854; Jacob Correll, bondsman; J. S. Myers, wit. married 18 July 1854 by D. A. Davis, J. P.

Wise, Henry & Louisa C. Brown, 19 Jan 1839; David Wise, bondsman; John Giles, wit.

Wise, Henry & Elizabeth Badget, 14 Nov 1848; Otho Swink, bondsman; Jno. H. Hardie Jr., wit.

Wise, Henry A. & Mary Gullett, 7 July 1864; Julius L. Smith, bondsman; Obadiah Woodson, wit.

Wise, Jacob & Barbara Waller, 2 Jan 1804; John Getchy, bondsman; A. L. Osborn, D. C., wit.

Wise, Jacob & Levina Paine, 10 Aug 1841; Henry Moyer, bondsman; Susan T. Giles, wit.

Wise, John Jr. & Christena M. S. Moyor, 23 Oct 1827; Jno. W. Moyer, bondsman; J. H. Hardie, wit.

Wise, Jordan & Betsy Butner, _____; David Trexler, bondsman.

Wise, Michael & Mary Rough, 18 Aug 1809; Jacob Rusher, bondsman; James Cowan, wit.

Wise, W. A. & S. A. Tarrh, 26 July 1865; W. A. Walton, bondsman; Obadiah Woodson, wit.

Wiseman, A. N. & Sarah A. Brown, 5 March 1862; J. W. Wadsworth, bondsman; Obadiah Woodson, wit. married 6 March 1862 by A. W. Mangum.

Wiseman, Isaac & Eleanor Murrell, 2 Feb 1808; Elijah Hunt, bondsman.

Wiseman, Jesse P. & Mary Hicks, 27 April 1841; Joseph J. Bruner, bondsman; Susan T. Giles, wit.

Wiseman, Jonathan & Margaret Daniel, 19 Dec 1800; Warran Roberts, bondsman; J. Brem, D. C., wit.

Wiseman, Samuel & Polly Harper, 7 March 1812; Boon Wilson, bondsman; Jno. Giles, C. C., wit.

Wiseman, William & Sarah McBride, 30 Jan 1807; Christopher Helmstetter, bondsman; A. L. Osborne, D. C., wit.

Wiseman, Wilson & Betsy Stoafwall, 12 Dec 1809; Wm. Parke, bondsman; Jno. Giles, C. C., wit.

Wisenhunt, George Michel & Eve Lamon, 31 Dec 1762; Valentine Botfell, Martin Botfell, bondsmen; John Frohock, wit.

With, Ambrose & Margret Rider, 27 May 1811; Canada Patterson, bondsman; Geo. Dunn, wit.

Witherow, George H. & Margaret Goss, 4 March 1819; Jno. Utzman, bondsman; Roberts Nanny, wit.

Witherspoon, Isaac A. & Ann McNeely, 11 Nov 1834; Noble N. Mills, bondsman; Abel Cowan, wit.

Withrow, Samuel & Jane Gray, __ Sept 1766; George Black, John Carson, bondsmen; Thomas Frohock, wit.

Wizenhunt, George Michel & Eve Lamon, 31 Dec 1762; Valentine Botfell, Martin Botfell, bondsmen; John Frohock, wit.

Wolser, Philip & Christianna Arrawood, 17 March 1795; David Mikel, bondsman; J. Troy, wit.

Womack, Archer & Sarah Brookshire, 14 Feb 1791; Peter Arthur Gibbons, bondsman; C. Caldwell, D. C., wit.

Womack, Daniel & Polly Owen, 31 July 1813; Joshua Park, bondsman; Geo. Dunn, wit.

Womack, Hezekiah & Peggy Owen, 19 Feb 1820; William Owen, bondsman; Jno. Giles, wit.

Womack, James & Polly Wiseman, 1 Dec 1810; Wm. W. Wiseman, bondsman; Jno. Giles, C. C., wit.

Wood, Archibald & Mary Cress, 23 Sept 1788; Archibald Womak, bondsman; Will Alexander, wit.

Wood, B. H. & Martha Jane Phillips, 5 Dec 1865; J. S. Hampton, bondsman; Obadiah Woodson, wit.

Wood, Burel & Peggy Burkett, 8 Aug 1796; Wm. Lee, bondsman.

Wood, D. B. & Margaret M. Cowan, 31 March 1849; Alex. M. Henderson, bondsman; J. H. Hardie, wit.

Wood, DAniel & Sally Ellit, 8 Jan 1811; Joseph Chaffin, bondsman.

Wood, Daniel & Lucy Harriwood, 29 Sept 1815; John Wood, bondsman; Henry Giles, wit.

Wood, Daniel & Jane M. Locke, 12 Dec 1846; Robt. Ellis, bondsman.

Wood, Danniel & Abagail Reed, 1 Dec 1813; Obadiah Biles, bondsman; Jn. March Sr., wit.

Wood, Edom & Ann E. Swink, 18 June 1850; Joel H. Jenkins, bondsman; J. S. Myers, wit.

Wood, Green & Mary A. Lilly, 30 Sept 1862; Abner Pace, bondsman; Obadiah Woodson, wit. married 30 Sept 1862 by A. W. Mangum, M. G.

Wood, Henry & Nancy Brackin, 6 April 1819; Jacob Cook, bondsman.

Wood, Isom & Susanna Dancy, 17 July 1788; John Dancy, bondsman; Wm. Alexander, wit.

Wood, James & Sarah Annsdale, 26 July 1803; Henry Lee, bondsman; A. L. Osborn, D. C., wit.

Wood, James & Anna Hamton, 10 June 1795; Henry Giles, bondsman.

Wood, James & Rhody Smith, 25 May 1793; Richrd. Leach, bondsman; Jos. Chambers, wit.

Wood, James & Lucinder Bates, 24 Dec 1818; George Howard, bondsman; Mack Crump, wit.

Wood, Jarratt & Polly Lacy, 20 Feb 1821; Pleasant Hall, bondsman; Milo A. Giles, wit.

Wood, Jerret & Polley Walser, 4 Jan 1821; Fredrick Gobbel, bondsman; An. Swicegood, wit.

Wood, John & Avis Beard, 24 Dec 1793; Zachariah Booth, bondsman; Jo. Chambers, wit.

Wood, John & Lydia Adcock, 28 July 1814; Benjamin Sherwood, bondsman; Jno. Giles, C. C., wit.

Wood, John & _____, _____; Joshua Howard, bondsman.

Wood, Joshua & Rachael Lykins, 16 March 1790; Danil Wood, bondsman.

Wood, Robert & Pegey Krider, 1 Nov 1809.

Wood, Thomas & Sarah Hampton, 28 Feb 1786; Menus Griggs, bondsman; J. McEwen, wit.

Wood, Thomas & Catharine Young, 20 Dec 1824; Hy. Giles, bondsman.

Wood, Thos. S. & Margaret C. Kerr, 13 May 1856; Jos. Henderson, bondsman; J. S. Myers, wit.

Wood, William & _____, 2 March 1805; John L. Hodgson, bondsman; John Irwin, wit.

Wood, William & Anne Likens, 12 March 1813; John Garrett, bondsman; Geo. Dunn, wit.

Wood, William & Mary Gobble, 9 June 1815; Nedam Bryant, bondsman; Jno. Giles, wit.

Wood, William & Sophia Barnes, 23 April 1831; Richard Beck, bondsman; Jno. H. Hardie, wit.

Wood, William B. & Margaret D. Knox, 22 March 1830; Hy. Giles, bondsman.

Woods, Abram & Peggy Woods, 7 March 1803; Wm. Erwin, bondsman; A. L. Osborn, D. C., wit.

Woods, Andrew & Elizabeth Woods, 23 March 1768; Samuel Woods, Francis Cross, bondsmen; Tho Frohock, wit. consent of Samuel Woods.

Woods, Benjamin & Mary Lowrance, 20 Oct 1768; Matthew Woods, William McCulloch, bondsmen; Tho. Frohock, wit. consent of John Lowrance.

Woods, David & Elizabeth Brandon, 4 Jan 1762; David Alexander, Henry Horah, bondsmen; Will Reed, John Johnston, wit.

Woods, David K. & Mary Masters, 21 Dec 1857; Samuel W. McLaughlin, bondsman; James E. Kerr, wit. married 24 Dec 1857 by D. R. Bradshaw, J. P.

Woods, John & Mary Anne Scott, (no date, during admn. of Richard Caswell, 1776-1780; 1785-1787); Robert Scott, bondsman; Ad. Osborn, wit.

Woods, John & Mary Clary, 1 Nov 1815; William Woods, bondsman; Jno. Giles, C. C., wit.

Woods, Joseph & Elisabeth Robinson, 8 Feb 1819; George Robison, bondsman; Roberts Nanny, wit.

Woods, Joseph C. S. & Adelaide A. C. Davis, 18 July 1863; Joel D. Brawley, bondsman; Obadiah Woodson, wit.

Woods, Joshua & Tenny McKnight, 8 Nov 1808; Hugh McKnight, bondsman; A. L. Osborne, C. C., wit.

Woods, Joshua B. & Mary A. Atwell, 6 Nov 1855; Wm. L. Atwell, bondsman; J. S. Myers, wit. married 15 Nov 1855 by Stephen Frontis.

Woods, Martin & Betsey Shuler, 23 Dec 1817; Adam Shuler, bondsman; Silas Peace, wit.

Woods, R. L. & Jane H. Corrier, 23 June 1859; S. J. Brown, bondsman; James E. Kerr, wit. married 30 June 1859 by John S. Heilig.

Woods, Robert & Jane Robison, 14 Aug 1824; Joseph Woods, bondsman; Hy. Giles, wit.

Woods, Samuel & Margret Holms, 29 Sept 1768; James Holmes, bondsman; Tho Frohock, wit. consent from John Holms, father of Margret, 29 Sept 1768.

Woods, William B. & Lydia Young, 1 May 1820; Abner Hall, bondsman.

Woodside, William & Celia Whaley, 23 Sept 1782; Joseph Whaley, bondsman; Ad. Osborn, wit.

Woodson, David & Margaret T. Johnson, 19 May 1842; Jno. H. Hardie, bondsman.

Woodson, Obadiah & Ann Maria Fraley, 15 Dec 1840; J. J. Bruner, bondsman.

Woodward, George B. & Sarah Jane Edmonston, 6 March 1860; G. W. McLean, bondsman; James E. Kerr, wit.

Woolever, Joseph & Nancy Pool, 18 Aug 1787; Fanny Macay, wit.

Wooliver, Joseph & Betsy Fennil, 25 May 1815; John Messimore, bondsman; Jno. Giles, C. C., wit.

Woolliver, Jacob & Barbay Hover, 2 Jan 1809; Joseph Wooliver, bondsman; Jno. Giles, C. C., wit.

Woolworth, Aaron & Mary Hampton, 15 Nov 1827; Saml. Jones, bondsman; J. H. Hardie, wit.

Wooten, William & Clary Gibson, 11 Feb 1813; Thos. Jones, bondsman; Jno. Giles, C. C., wit.

Wooton, William & Edy Madden, 11 March 1813; Solomon Reavis, bondsman; Ransom Powell, wit.

Workman, George & Sally Daniel, 15 Feb 1813; William Workman, bondsman; Geo. Dunn, wit.

Workman, Will & Catharine Garon, __ Feb 1795; Thos. Workman, bondsman.

Worldley, Williee & Matildy Henderson, 19 Jan 1825; Jas. Renshaw, bondsman; L. R. Rose, J. P., wit.

Wormington, David & Celia Earnheart, 9 Aug 1848; Jacob Fulenwider, bondsman; J. H. Hardie, wit.

Wormsley, Thomis & Patsey Morefield, 12 Jan 1809; Peter Mallet, bondsman; Jn. March Sr., wit.

Worner, Michal & Sarah Hill, 4 March 1822; Anderson Warner, bondsman; An. Swicegood, wit.

Worrick, Samuel & Laura Garham (colored), 1 Aug 1865; married 3 Aug 1865 by Rev. Wm. Lambeth.

Worsham, William & Elizabeth Erwin, 14 Sept 1824; John Erwin, bondsman; Hy. Giles, wit.

Worsham, William & Frances Ann Baley, 24 Aug 1818; Milas Washam, bondsman; Mack Crump, wit.

Wortman, Daniel & Margaret Knatzer, spinster, 13 Sept 1779; Bollzer Knatzer, bondsman; B. Booth Boote, wit.

Wotzman, Solomon & Harriet E. Pool, 29 March 1866; Henry C. Pool, bondsman; Saml Rothrock, wit.

Wray, Philip & Sally Jones, 12 April 1813; Coleman Rice, bondsman; Geo. Dunn, wit.

Wright, A. B. & Jane Bell, 20 Sept 1860; J. E. Newsom, bondsman; John Wilkinson, wit. married 20 Sept 1860 by L. C. Groseclose, Pastor of St. John's Ev. Luth Church, Salisbury.

Wright, Adam & Judana Bolabaugh, 4 Aug 1821; Thomas Tucker, bondsman; P. Copple, J. P., wit.

Wright, Benjamin & Sarah Trott, 16 March 1852; Upshaw Elliott, bondsman; J. S. Myers, wit. married 16 March 1852 by J. M. Brown, J. P.

Wright, Henry & Alie Man, 7 Nov 1771; Moses Winsley, bondsman; Thomas Frohock, wit.

Wright, Isaiah & Polly White, 17 March 1814; John Jarratt Jr., bondsman; E. Morgan, wit.

Wright, Isom & Lane Parrish, 21 Dec 1820; Ezekiel Parrish, bondsman; P. Copple, J. P., wit.

Wright, James A. & Mary D. Overcash, 9 Feb 1858; married 2 March 1858 by John S. Heilig.

Wright, James J. & Bethsheba Dickson, 26 Dec 1844; Jno. L. Pinkston, bondsman; Jno. H. Hardie, wit.

Wright, James J. & Francerine R. Wright, 14 Nov 1848; Benjamin Wright, bondsman; Jno. H. Hardie Jr., wit.

Wright, John & _____, __ _____180_; _____Kreiter (German signature), bondsman.

Wright, John & Sarah Richards, 27 July 1815; John Johnson, bondsman; Sol. Davis, J. P., wit.

Wright, John L. & Mary Shoaf, 7 June 1849; Thos. C. McNeely, bondsman; John H. Hardie Jr. ,wit.

Wright, John M. & Mary C. Powles, 11 Jan 1841; Jacob Rary, bondsman; Susan T. Giles, wit.

Wright, Jordan & Barbara Fox, 25 Feb 1819; Ezl. Brown, bondsman; C. Brown, wit.

Wright, Philburt & Mary Sear, 15 Aug 1793; William Bodenhamer, bondsman; Jno. Monroe, wit.

Wright, Richardson & Mary Haworth, 24 Aug 1805; William Leech, bondsman; William Piggatt, J. P., wit.

Wright, William & Sarah Kirk, 17 Feb 1809; Joseph Standley, bondsman; S. Davis, J. P. wit.

Wright, Williams M. & Adelade Smith, 19 April 1855; Henry Moore, bondsman; J. S. Myers, wit. married 19 April 1855 by J. M. Brown, J. P.

Wurmington, John & Mary Kanup, 10 May 1818; Sihon Keeth, bondsman; Milo A. Giles, wit.

Wurzback, Frederik & Margaret Hardman, 21 May 1788; John Hildebrand, bondsman; W. Alexander, wit.

Wyatt--see also Wiatt, Wiett

Wyatt, Henry R. & Mary L. Rosemon, 15 May 1856; married 16 May 1856 by Levi Trexler, J. P.

Wyatt, Noah C. & Nancy E. Reid, 10 March 1866; William L. Parker, bondsman; Obadiah Woodson, wit.

Wyatt, Richmond & Lucy Foster, 23 Feb 1822; Laurance Owings, bondsman; Hy. Giles, wit.

Wyatt, Sandy (Alexander) & Eliza Banks, 24 Oct 1829; Richmond Wyatt, bondsman; J. H. Hardiw, wit.

Wyatt, Thomas & Nancy Pierce, 12 March 1849; Michael File, bondsman; Jno. H. Hardie Jr., wit.

Wyatt, W. M. & Maria Wise, 29 Aug 1865; Charles F. Waggoner, bondsman; Obadiah Woodson, wit.

Wyatt, William & Susan Cope, 23 Aug 1823; Thos. Walker, bondsman; Hy. Giles, wit.

Wyatt, William W. & Mary Buchanan, 24 June 1858; Silas Wyatt, bondsman; Levi Trexler, wit. married 24 June 1858 by Levi Trexler, J. P.

Wyman, Henry & Caty Kern, 15 Nov 1784; Conrad Brem, bondsman; Jno. McNairy, wit.

Yarbrey, Ruben & Elizabeth Willis, 23 Feb 1815; William Julian, bondsman; Geo. Dunn, wit.

Yarbrough, Edward & Sarah Marshall, 8 April 1788; J. McEwin, bondsman.

Yarbrough, Edward & Mrs. Sarah E. Giles, 24 Dec 1836; Richard W. Long, bondsman; R. Jones, wit.

Yarbrough, Edward & Rebecca H. Long, 7 Jan 1823; Henry A. Chambers, bondsman; Hy. Giles, wit.

Yarbrough, Henry & Mary Cunningham, 13 Sept 1803; Henry Rats, bondsman; A. L. Osborn, wit.

Yarbrough, Henry & Bridgett Davis, 29 Aug 1785; Joseph Hannah, bondsman.

Yarbrough, Ruben & Malisa Vaughan, 22 Nov 1842; Alphaus Howard, bondsman.

Yarbrough, Thomas & Susanna Nicks, 17 Nov 1820; Joseph Hall, bondsman; Roberts Nanny, wit.

Yeoust, Aaron & Mary M. Shollonbarggor, 5 Aug 1839; Leonard Overcash, bondsman; John Giles, wit.

Yeost, George & Caty Stirewalt, 26 May 1813; Christian Reinhart, bondsman; Geo. Dunn, wit.

Yerwood, Thomas & Catharine Summay, 24 April 1779; Thomas Bryan, bondsman; Jno Kerr, wit.

Yonds--see Jonds

Yonts, William & Catharine Aplin, 21 Dec 1806; Henry Aplen, bondsman; Jno Monroe, wit.

York, John & Nancy Brawlay, 16 Oct 1826; Hy. Giles, bondsman.

Yost, Franklin M. & Sophia Beaver, 21 Aug 1855; Henry Beaver, bondsman; J. S. Myers, wit. married 21 Aug 1855 by Obadiah Woodson, J. P.

Yost, John & Sarah Safret, 2 Feb 1842; Nelsaf Safret, bondsman; J. S. Johnston, wit.

Yost, John & Lydia E. Freeze, 15 Oct 1846; Peter Freeze, bondsman; Jno. H. Hardie Jr., wit.

Yost, John & Caty Hilemon, 11 Feb 1804; Geo. Sifferd, bondsman; A. L. Osborn, wit.

Yost, Martin & Christina R. Brown, 4 Jan 1860; Henry W. Hill, bondsman; James E. Kerr, wit. married 5 Jan 1860 by Thornton Butler, V. D. M.

Yost, S. M. & Mary A. C. Bostian, 29 Sept 1865; E. S. P. Lippard, bondsman; Horatio N. Woodson, wit. married 4 Oct 1865 by W. Kimball, Pastor of St. Pauls, Rowan.

Youkly, William & Mary Barnat, 13 Oct 1772; John Kimbrough, Lewis Coffers, bondsmen; Ad. Osborn, C. C., wit. consent of John Barnat, 9 Oct 1772.

Younce, William & Elizebeth Aplen, 14 Feb 1813; Henry Aplen, bondsman; J. Willson, J. P., wit.

Young, Alexander & Sarah Davidson, 5 May 1783; Ja. Robinson, bondsman.

Young, Asa & Polley Mobley, 2 March 1819; Wm. Tucker, bondsman; Saml. Jones, J. P., wit.

Young, Burrell B. & Isabella M. Lingle, 27 Oct 1858; Wm. Locke, bondsman; married 2 Nov 1858 by L. C. Groseclose.

Young, Chancey H. & Catharine Crouse, 1 Feb 1865; M. O. Davis, bondsman; Obadiah Woodson, wit.

Young, James & Elizabeth Davidson, 14 Sept 1784(?); Alex. Young, bondsman; Ad. Osborn, wit.

Young, James & Anna Srock, 5 Aug 1801; Saml. Young, bondsman; Jno. Brem, wit.

Young, James & Saloma Roseman, 24 Aug 1835; Rich P. Harris, bondsman; Jno Giles, wit.

Young, John & Margaret Burress, 12 Jan 1797; Caleb Burroughes, bondsman; Jno Rogers, wit.

Young, John & Salley Broadway, 30 Dec 1820; Barny Young, bondsman; An. Swicegood, wit.

Young, John & Julia Ann Cooper (colored), 5 Aug 1865; married 6 Aug 1865 by J. B. Lowens(?), Minister.

Young, Jonathan & Nelly Dickey, 29 Feb 1820; Thomas Wood, bondsman; Jno Giles, wit.

Young, Jonathan & Hannah Brandon, 16 May 1827; William B. Wood, bondsman.

Young, Jonathan & Sarah B. Smith, 13 Nov 1834; Richard Loury, bondsman; Hy. Giles, wit.

Young, Joseph & Ann Armstrong, 2 Feb 1803; James Armstrong, bondsman; Hudson Hughes, wit.

Young, Joseph & Sarah Graham, 3 Oct 1786; Hugh Hall, bondsman; Jno Macay, D. C, wit.

Young, Mordecai & Ann Runnolds, 19 July 1787; Thomas Hutson, Joseph Stanley, bondsmen; Jno Macay, wit.

Young, Peter & Katharine Totorow, 29 Dec 1802; Jacob Tototow, bondsman; Adlai L. Osborn, D. C., wit.

Young, Samuel & Rebeckah Hall, 25 Oct 1784; John Hall, bondsman.

Young, Samuel & Anny Redwine, 13 Nov 1854; Elias Huie, bondsman; J. S. Myers, wit.

Young, Samuel J. & Jane L. Knox, 18 April 1853; Wm. L. Barber, bondsman; J. S. Myers, wit. married 20 April 1853 by Saml. B. O. Wilson.

Young, William & Ann Burris, 19 Sept 1797; Caleb Burroughes, bondsman; Jno Rogers, wit.

Young, William & Ann J. Cowan, 4 Feb 1824; Joseph T. Burris, bondsman; Jno Giles, wit.

Younts, Eli & Delia Agner, 27 Oct 1842; L. A. Bringle, bondsman; Jno H. Hardie, wit.

Yountz, Christian & Cathrine Wever, 24 Aug 1822; Lasres Applen, bondsman; Andrew Swicegood, wit.

Youst, Jacob & Sisena Miller, 10 Aug 1815; John Jordan, bondsman; Geo. Dunn, wit.

Youst, Jacob & Pegg Miller, 30 Dec 1822; Jacob Miller, bondsman; Ezra Allemong, wit.

Youst, John & Lodema Barrier, 15 Nov 1838; Martin Barger, bondsman; Saml. Lemly Jr., wit.

Youst, Paul & Caty Beairn, 8 Fcb 1815; George Yougest, bondsman; Jno Giles, C. C., wit.

Yowst, John P. & Margaret Schulibarrier, 22 Sept 1843; Aaron Yost, bondsman; Jno H. Hardie, wit.

Yutter, Conrod & Katharine Huffman, 20 June 1775; Michael Brown, bondsman; Ad. Osborn, wit.

Zachary, William & Sarah Huffman, 2 Nov 1808; Joseph Chambers, bondsman; A. L. Osborne, D. C., wit.

Zanony, John B. & Sophia Brinkle, 11 Oct 1813; John Kerr, bondsman; Geo. Dunn, wit.

Zerick, John & Rachel Dedman, 10 Jan 1792; Thomas Deadman, bondsman; Chs. Caldwell, wit.

Zegraves, Ezekial & Elizabeth Morgan, 25 Dec 1855; Nathan Morgan, bondsman; Levi Trexler, wit. married 25 Dec 1855 by _____.

Zevly, Hy. & Elenor Enochs, 3 April 1762; John Johnston, William Williams, bondsmen; Will Reed, John Brandon, wit. consent of Jno Enochs, 29 March 1762.

INDEX

Phelps (cont.)
Polley 380
Phenoy, Susanna 98
Phifer, Anne 322
Benjamin 202
Betsey 341
Catharine 87
Elizabeth 241
Jane 285
J. C. 87
Lydia A. 61
Margaret 285
Maria 424
Sally 418
Sarah C. 335
Susanna 407
Phile, Sophia 424
Philhour (Filhour),
Michael 28
Philips, Catharine 95
Dianah 274
E. E. 121, 215, 329,
341
Ezekeel 337
Henson 160
Jean 224
Mary 358
Mary Ann 97
Peggy 122
Phebe 188
Pheby 123
Rachel 91
Phillips, A. J. 34, 348
Catharine 247
Charles 410
Charlotte C. 111
David 320
David G. 322
Elizabeth 195
Enoch 191, 288
Francis G. 384
Jane 52
Jeane M. 52
Jno/John 20, 116, 420
McGuin 82a
McGuire 345
Margaret R. 147
Margaret Ruan 118
Martha Jane 433
Mary 121
Mary A. E. 384
Nathan 284, 319
Nathan L. 361
Peggy 54
Polly 284
Sarah 82a
Susanna 211
Tempy 347
Phillips (Fillips), ____
21
Phillps, John 319
Philps, Thomas 277
Phips, Catharine 176
Elizabeth 215
Pickett, Phebee 425
Pickler, James 249
John 250
Joseph 210, 299
Mary 178
Susannah 170
Picler, Joseph 320
Pidgeon, Charles 232
Piearce, Patience 8
Pierce, James 381
John 15, 320
Mariah 58
Nancy 437
Permelia 403

Pierce (cont.)
Polly 420
Thos/Thomas H. 52, 427
Wm. 46
Pierson, John 106, 325
Piggott, Isabella 266
Ruth 205
Pinchback, Elizabeth 425
John 56
Jno. T. 191(2)
John Thomas 191
Liddy 191
Martha 191
Sarah 191
Piner, Nancy 28
Pines, Margaret 187
Pinkerton, David 321(2)
Robert 321
Thomas 145
Pinkston, Aaron 150, 335
Artamessa 401
David 91
Dinah 198
Eliza 76
Elizabeth 76, 215
Euphemia E. 131
Jean 395
Jesse 241
John 76, 405
Jno. L. 437
Lucy 358
Margaret 23, 369
Margaret D. 281
Mary E. 50
Mathew 41
Matthew L. 160
Meshack 23, 53, 250
Mesheck 322
Nancy 241
Nancy B. 323, 395
Oney 91
Peter 400
Polly 390, 391
Rebekah 405
Richard 397
Susan 310
Thodocia 287
Thomas 24, 161, 416,
417
Turner 105
Wm. 322, 426
Pinkstone, Cathrine 77
Pinxton, Mary 150
Ruth 23
Pirkins, Moses 99
Pitchey, Julietta 33
Pitman, Betsy 131
Jesse 131
Mary 386
Zelpha 345
Pittman, Julia 346
Rebecca 4
Pits, Martha 319
Pitts, Elizabeth 276
Henry 319
Plaster, John 356
Wm. T. H. 304
W. T. H. 307
Pless, Harriet L. 328
Henry 384
John Martain 292
U. M. 323
Pleuss, Jacob J. 384
Plowman, John 75
Plumer, Mathew 322, 384,
407
Matthew 18
Richard 121

Plummer, Delila 85
Elizabeth 45
Margaret 18
Richard 121
Sarah 336
Plyer, Sarah 168
Plyler, Mary 340
Poar, James 365
John 365
Mary 365
Poarch, Martha 116
Pock, Margert 47
Pock(Prock?), Mary 47
Pogue, Martha H. 345
Pohl, Henry 54
Pointer, Edward 380
Polk, Jane G. 42
Pool, Alvina 325
Amey 314
Catharine 38
Edwd/Edward 115, 418
Elizabeth Maria 364
Hannah 235
Harriet E. 436
Henry C. 436
Jacob 284, 288, 364
John 170, 194, 324
Linda 316
Louisa 52
Lydia 295
Margaret 62
Margrat 418
Maria 236
Mary 225
Milly 188
Nancy 435
Nancy C. 59
Otho Z. 187
Poley 194
Rachel 284, 409
Rebecca 270
Sallie 24
Sally 113, 176, 308
Sophia 187
Terrissa A. 420
Poole, Hessy 119
Jacob 210
Margaret 263
Polly 288
Rebecca 154
Poor, Elizabeth 81
Moses 81
Poore, Thos. S. 408
Pope, Charles 74
George 260, 324
Isaac 121, 282
Mary 74
Phebe 260
Popst, Barbar 279
Porter, Amey 381
Anne 397
Betsy 25
Elizabeth 112
Henry 355
James 10, 115, 190
Jessee 228
Keziah 388
Lawrence 93, 334, 377
Londa 92
Margaret 158
Margarett 228
Mary Ann 255
Rebecca 82
Robert 259, 325
Susannah 115
Thomas 82
Tilly 377
Wm/William 115, 388

489

Templeton (cont.)
  Silas 53
  Thomas 393
Tenbenry, Daniel 132
Tenison, Susannah 354
Tenneson, Jenney 125
Tennison, Elizabeth 15
  Elvira 423
  Lucinda 148
Tenpenny, Elizabeth 224
  Richa. 360
Terrill, Bethena 78
Tevis, John 265
Thingleton, Teney 400
Thomas, Anna 102
  Anny 382
  Cathrine 162
  Delia 273
  Dorotha 424
  Eliza 219
  Elizabeth 359
  Ellendor 173
  Fanny 48
  Feby 9
  James 359
  Jenny 325
  Jeremiah 16
  John 95, 96, 115, 424
  Julian 240
  Levina 112
  Lewis 247
  Lucy 203
  Mary 393
  Mary L. 424
  Nicholas 234, 394
  Racheal 315
  Sally 400
  Sarah 331, 400
  Sethey 49
  Susanna 247
  Susannah 60
  William 102
Thomason, Anna 82a
  Burgess 35
  Elizabeth 223, 321
  Elizabeth H. 35
  Fanny 216
  Franklin W. 68, 381
  George 422
  Gorge 321
  H. C. 409
  J. 198
  James 395
  Jesse 105, 155, 226,
    252, 280, 379, 415
  John P. 237
  Margaret R. 317
  Martha J. 341
  Mary Ann 91
  Nancy E. 179, 368
  Richard 395
  Sarah M. 36
  William A. 317
  William 409
Thompson, Airey 13
  Alexd. 90
  Andrew 396
  Ann 152
  B. S. 66
  Charlotte 164
  Elizabeth 259
  Elizabeth B. 254
  Elizabeth M. 158
  Fredrick 8
  Hannah 46
  Hendry 244
  Henry 245
  Henry Jr. 318

Thompson (cont.)
  Jane 186, 381
  Jane P. 365
  Jena 381
  John 200, 348, 397
  Joseph 395
  Julia A. S. 181
  Lawrence 396
  Lucinda A. 155
  Margaret 78
  Margret 296
  Mary 66
  Mary C. 141
  Mary M. 415
  Morgant 83
  Moses 83
  Nancy 56
  Peggy 205
  Polly S. 83
  R. 395
  Rachel 24
  Reason 395
  Rebecca 223
  Sarah 211
  Sarah E. 327
  Sarah S. 403
  Thos. 43
  Thomas L. 122
  Wm/William 25, 201,
    296
Thomson, Ann 244
  Barbara 78
  Eleanor 396
  Jane 418
  Jno/John 78, 107, 418
  Nathan 310
  Neomy 286
Thorn, Elizabeth 216
  Mary Ann 164
Thornbery, Susannah 387
  Thomas 387
Thrift, Samuel 343
Tickis, Susan 280
Tillet, Sally 105
Tinkle, John 408
Tinnecks, Kelly 77
Tilmon, Sarah 121
Tippett, Wm. 282
Tisinger, Geo. W. 72
  Sarah 72
Tod, Ann 291
Todd, Agnes 399
  Ann 150
  Benjamin 183
  Dinah 360
  Elisabeth 430
  Elizabeth 248, 261,
    403
  Elizabeth A. 92
  Gasper 99
  James 235
  Jean 117
  John 136, 261
  John B. 79, 122
  John S. 90
  Joseph 183
  Jo/Jos/Joseph E. 88,
    155, 217, 241, 404
  Mary 354
  Mary E. 207
  Nancy 6
  Peter 85, 354
  Phebe 302
  Polly 106, 220
  Ratchel 235
  R. H. 398
  Tho/Thos/Thomas 82a,
    88, 111, 138, 159,

Todd (cont.)
  Tho/Thos/Thomas cont.
    176, 236, 309, 344,
    396, 398
Tolbert, Martha 298
Toll, Nicholas 190
Toll(in), Anna Margretta
    190
Tomlinson, John 2
  Moses 334
  Nancy 198
  William 14
  Zadock G. 148
Tommison, Sarrey 337
Tompson, Celery 210
  Rachael 231
Tomson, Ann 333
Torentine, Bethana 395
Tores, Camilla C. 240
Torrence, Adam 10
  Alexander 220
  Eliza A. S. 326
  Goodwin 42
  Hu. 326
  Susanna 45
Torrentine, Anne 137
  Sarah 82a
Tototow, Jacob 439
Totorow, Katharine 439
Tough, Elizabeth 286
Touson, Mary 2
Tow, Jesse 399
Towel, John J. 128
Towerl, Margaret 316
Towsend, James 77
Townsley, Catharine 321
  Jas/James 16, 224, 375
  Margaret 395
  Nancy 242
  Oliver 230
Tracksler, Molly 56
Traler, Sally 257
Tranham, Mary 339
Trantham, Margret 341
Trautman, Peter 192
Traves, Susanna 219
Travis, George 363, 400
  Jacob 420
  Jno/John 192, 254
Travit, Lyddy 331
Traylor, Biddy 299
  Caty 19
  Elizabeth 344
  Lucey 299
  Lucy 421
  Nancy 389
  Phebe 371
  Ritter 401
Treadwell, John 392
  Stephen 123, 410
Trease, Betsy 21
  Polly 322
Trevilion, John 401
Trexler, Adam 123, 182,
    202, 252, 401
  Allen 43, 113, 154
  Amanda 35
  Ann 413
  Anna 227
  Anne 327
  Barbara 386
  B. C. 373
  Caleb 252
  Camilla C. 315
  Catharine 31, 71, 101
  Catharine C. 194
  David 310, 402, 424,
    432

INDEX

Willson (cont.)
Henry F. 183
H. F. 379
Jacob 205
Jam/Jams/Jas. 267,
329, 330
James M. 224
John 418
Mary 149, 350
Nancey 330
Nancy 214
Rachell 254
Robert 209
W. B. 209
Wm. B. 102, 335
Wilson, Alexr. 228, 290
Betsey 30
Betsy 274
Boon 432
Boyd 48
Catharine 228, 322
Catharine C. 19
Elizabeth 124, 169,
189, 191, 333
Francis 290
George 343
Jas/James 44, 122,
144, 169, 191, 220,
321, 395
James B. 201
Jean 220
John 144, 271, 341,
367
John H. 17
Joshua 430
Katherine 168
Mary 38, 101, 143,
255, 329, 422
Miney Jane 373
Nancy 99
Peggy 293
Phebe 218
Polly 144
Rachel 232
Rebeca 263
Richard 331
Robt. F. 263, 383
Sally 306
Samuel 317
Sarah 173, 343
Thomas 168, 430
Wm/William 220, 430
Wm. R. 136
Winecoff, David 431
Winders, Betsy 309
Fanny 277
Fanny L. 150
Henry C. 309
Jane 305
Laura 305
Louisa E. 70
Lucinda E. 362
Lucy Ann 4
Peter P. 306
Sarah 150
Thomas C. 335
Windsor, N. R. 227, 323
Winford, Margret 2
Wingfler, Peter 431
Wingler, Peggy 98
Susanna 248
Winkler, Dotia 135
Godfrey 305
Heinrich 34
Henry 58, 91, 274,
318
Lodwing 294
Peter 3, 181

Winkler (cont.)
Polly 294
Winnford, Mary 101
Winright, Deborah 331
Winscut, Elizabeth 387
Winsley, Moses 10, 429
Winsly, Moses 436
Wire, Elizabeth 352
Wise, Barbaray 347
Benjamin 4
Caty 3
Chs. 349
D. 340
David 240, 306, 432
Elizabeth 113
George 10, 347
H. A. 74
John 3, 265
Malinda 131
Margaret 117
Maria 34, 437
Mary A. 115
Pauline C. 36
Polly 23, 347
William A. 36
Wiseman, Edy 305
Eleanor 240
Isaac 240(2)
James 373, 413
Jane 309
Jean 240
Jesse P. 381
John 273
Margaret 170
Mary 161, 273
Nancy 374
Polly 203, 257, 309,
433
Rachael 251, 429
Sally 306, 373
Unis 254
William 203, 254
Wm. W. 309, 433
Wisemon, Margret 319
Wisher, Jonas 335
Withrow, Rachel 34
Samuel 34
Wolfe, Margaret 328
Wolfscale, Mary 116
Wolfskill, Joseph 183
Margret 183
Wolser, Philip 275
Womac, Nancy 84
Womak, Archibald 433
Womax, Thomas 368
Wommack, Matthew 398
Wommock, William 48
Wood, Betsey 337
Charity 411
Chas/Charles 5, 63
Daniel 108, 135, 342,
380, 383
Danil 434
D. Burton 63
Elisabeth 180
Elizabeth 300
Elizebeth 380
Ism/Isam 98, 285
James 12
Jaret 181
Jarratt 168
John 43, 425, 433
Lewis H. 233
Liddy 425
Lidia 274
Margaret 102
Margaret L. 182
Margret 24

Wood (cont.)
Mary 64, 177, 357, 380,
425
Mary D. 260
Moses 317
Nancy 169
Nelly 322
Peter 132, 323
Polly 168, 337
Rachael 32
Rebecca 97
Rbt/Robt/Robert 35,
202, 219
Sally 230
Sarah 47
Sylvia 415
Thomas 258, 439
Vinson 200, 274
Will 397
William 268
Wm/William B. 162, 439
Woodel, Joel 354
Woodhouse, Nancy 268
Woods, Agnes 86
Ann 80
Citizen S. 63
David K. 234, 375, 406
Elizabeth 196, 234,
353, 434
Elizabeth D. 102
Harriet J. 11
Isom 232
James 86, 355, 360
John 353
Joseph 370, 435
Joshua 269
Joshua B. 374
Margaret 44
Margret 10
Martha 290(2)
Mary 151, 164
Mary T. 367
Matthew 235, 435
Nancy 268
Oliver C. 102
Peggy 434
Pinkey 109
Rachael 125
Rebecah 407
Ruth 73
Samuel 73, 434
Tirzah A. 313
Truth 262, 365
Willm/William 8, 146,
290, 435
Woodside, Ann E. 141
Archd. M. 254
Elisabeth 128
Rufus W. 390
Woodsides, Anny 254
Woodson, Anne E. 11
Ann M. 219
D. 3
David 15, 34, 45, 99,
176, 195, 216, 230,
293, 347, 370
Elvira 321
Horatio 85, 92, 425
Horation N. 11, 37,
96, 140, 154, 284,
310, 319
Horatio W. 82
Joicey 316
Judith 170
Obadiah 44, 50, 57,
90, 131, 208, 217,
236, 246, 249, 291,
292, 299, 310, 352,

Woodson (cont.)
Obadiah cont. 373, 419
Obediah 11, 26
Wooliver, Esther 195
Hannah 273
Joseph 436
Woollever, Jacob 195
Wooling, Richard 257
Woolworth, Julia A. E.
174
Work, Eliz. 270
John 256
Sarah 256
Workman, Anne 157
Barbara 377
Daniel H. 238
Rebecca 373
Susanna 290
Susannah 225
Thos. 436
William 436
Worry, Mary 129
Worthington, Richard 201
William 242
Wotever, Nancy 282
Wray, Philip 337
Thomas 331
Wren, Robin 344
Wrencher, Mary 420
Wright, A. B. 297
Ann A. 388
Benjamin 437
Burgess 345
Elizabeth 61
Elizabeth A. C. 31
Esau 224
Francerine R. 437
Gideon 274
James J. 31
J. G. 105
John L. 210
Jno. M. 394
Mary 340
Nancy 421
Richard 91
Sarah A. 394
Wyatt, Angeline 147
Delinda 56
Elizabeth 311
J. 295
James J. 287
Martha 56
Mary 295
Mary Ann 111, 320
Nancy 84
Richmond 93, 437
Rody 279
Sarah 56
Silas 438
Thomas 311
Unity 391
Wyett, William 84
Wyld, John 110
Wyngate, Eliza 426
Wysell, Catharine 145

Yagley, Salley 410
Yarberry, Sarah 188
Yarboro, Patsy 371
Yarborough, Betsey 140
Jinny 33
Yarbrough, Edwd/Edward
84, 268, 297, 314
Judah 42
Juliann 307
Mary 247
Nancy 25

Yarbrough (cont.)
Serena 379
Yarrel, Mary 197
Yarrell, Thomas 346
Yearbrough, Susanah 331
Yeost, Mary 215
Yockley, Elizabeth 31
Yokeley, Charity 79
Yokely, Mary 118
Yonce, Caty 305
Yontz, Mary 400
Molly 247
Yoose, Mary 232
Yose, Margrit 341
Yost, Aaron 302, 360, 440
Anna 28
Catherine R. 235
Christena 302
Christina R. 187
Cozby 302
Elizabeth 35
Elizabeth L. 243
George 340
Jacob A. 404
John 39, 304, 351(4)
Maggie S. 210
Malchi 303
Margaret 41, 413
Mary 304
Mary L. 50
Milla 419
Philip 76
Polly Eliza 41
Sena 383
Sophia C. 404
Susannah 361
Yougest, George 440
Younce, John 58
Mary 138
Young, Alex 439
Ann 174
Ann J. 206
Barny 439
Catharine 28, 434
Catherine 16
Caty 164
Eleanor M. 63
Eliza 223
Elizabeth 398
Elizabeth C. 159
H. 77
Hy 201, 207
Isabella 248
Jane 257
Jane E. 159
Jane L. 158, 229
Jean 72, 417
John D. 158
Jonas 340
Jonathan 409
Joseph 59, 125, 248
Lydia 435
Margaret 89, 248
Margret 125
Mary 58, 184
Nancy 270
Rachell 224
Saml/Samuel 88, 89,
125, 174, 439
Samuel F. 229
Sarah 89
Sarah B. 125
Sarah W. 135
S. O. 271
William 17, 72, 158,
417
Younts, Peter 9
Yountz, Fredrick 283

Youst, Anna A. 351
Catharine 347
Cathrine Melinda 303
George 384
John P. 351
Paul 27
Peggy 347
Youts, Martin 387

Zarvis, Jeams 358
Zebely, James 172
Zell, Edmond 96
Zeody, Henry 82
Zevelly, Margaret 24
Zevely, Susanna 276
Zimerman, John 397
Zimmerman, Andrew 426
Zink, Maria 180

_____,Daniel 232
_____,Elizabeth 167
_____,Elijah 77
_____,Eliza Ann 82a
_____, Jacob 83
_____, John 77
_____, Leonhardt 277
_____, Mary 127
_____,Rebeka 172, 414